ENCYCLOPEDIA OF
THE WORLD'S
COMMERCIAL and
PRIVATE AIRCRAFT

ENCYCLOPEDIA OF
THE WORLD'S
COMMERCIAL and
PRIVATE AIRCRAFT

CRESCENT BOOKS
New York

Produced by Stan Morse
Aerospace Publishing Ltd
10 Barley Mow Passage
London W4 4PH
England

First English edition published
1981 by The Hamlyn Publishing
Group Limited
London • New York • Sydney •
Toronto
Astronaut House, Hounslow Road,
Feltham, Middlesex, England

This edition is published by
Crescent Books.

Distributed by Crown Publishers, Inc.

h g f e d c

ISBN: 0-517-362856

Printed and bound in Italy

Credits
Authors: David Mondey
John Cook
Michael John Hooks
Chris Chant
Editor: Trisha Palmer
Design: Rod Teasdale
Artwork (large three-views):
Keith Fretwell
Typesetting: Modern Text
Typesetting
Colour reproduction: Process
Colour Scanning Ltd
Film work: Precise Litho Ltd
Monochrome reproduction:
Tenreck Ltd

Acknowledgements
The Publishers would like to thank
those airlines and aircraft
manufacturers who provided
photographs and information for
this book.

Contents

Aero Boero 95/115 Series

History and Notes

Aircraft production in the Argentine Republic is centred on Cordoba, the factories of both Aero Boero and Fabrica Militar de Aviones being situated there. The former company has concentrated on the single-engine high-wing monoplane formula, and has built a number of such machines.

The Aero Boero 95 flew in prototype form on 12 March 1959, and initial production models from 1961 had a 95-hp (71-kW) Continental C90 engine. All-metal construction was used, with fabric covering, and the Aero Boero 95 was a three-seater suitable for private flying or, in a modified form, for agricultural work. Other variants flown included the 95A de Lujo with a 100-hp (75-kw) Continental O-200-A engine; the 95A Fumigador with the same engine and equipped with crop dusting or spraying equipment which included a 55-Imp gallon (250-litre) capacity chemical tank; and the 95B, construction of which began in 1953, and which had an unspecified 150-hp (112-kW) engine. By mid-1965 Aero Boero was producing a second series

of ten 95s and was planning to offer licence production to Peru and Uruguay, but it is not known if this plan came to fruition.

Further development led to the Aero Boero 115, with a 115-hp (86-kW) Avco Lycoming O-235 engine and a number of cosmetic improvements to the airframe including wheel fairings. Reinforced plastics and aluminium alloy were introduced respectively for the engine cowling and flaps and ailerons, and this variant made its first flight in March 1969, receiving its Certificate of Airworthiness in May 1969, with production beginning two months later.

By early 1972, 45 of the 95/115 series had been built, and production ended in January 1973. The following month a modified version, the 115BS was flown. This featured a bigger wing span, swept fin and rudder, and greater fuel capacity, and about 25 were built before production ended.

Specification

Type: three-seat general-purpose monoplane

Powerplant: one 95-hp (71-kW) Continental C90-8F flat-four piston engine
Performance: maximum speed 124 mph (200 km/h); cruising speed 106 mph (170 km/h); service ceiling 17,060 ft (5200 m); range 559 miles (900 km)
Weights: empty 930 lb (422 kg); maximum take-off 1,543 lb (700 kg)

The Aero Boero 95 was the first of a series of Argentinian three-seat light-planes available in a number of models with engines ranging from 95 to 180 hp (71 to 134 kW).

Dimensions: span 34 ft 2¼ in (10.42 m); length 22 ft 7½ in (6.90 m); height 6 ft 10¾ in (2.10 m); wing area 176.1 sq ft (16.36 m²)

Aero Boero 180/150 Series

History and Notes

Though it used the same basic airframe as the 95/115 series, the Aero Boero 180 was a little larger and accommodated four people. Its 180-hp (134-kW) Avco Lycoming O-360-A1A engine gave improved performance and extended its ceiling to 23,000 ft (7010 m), a particularly useful feature in the mountainous areas of South America. However, this version was rapidly succeeded in production by a three-seater bearing the same designation and using the same engine; further descriptions of the 180 refer to this model.

First standard production aircraft were designated 180RV and deliveries began at the end of 1969; a number of variants were available, and those with the 180-hp (134-kW) Avco Lycoming engine included the 180RVR glider-tug and the 180Ag agricultural aircraft. For customers who wanted the economy of a smaller engine, the 150RV and 150Ag were available, powered by a 150-hp (112-

kW) Avco Lycoming O-320-A2B engine, but in other respects similar to the 180s.

Production of the 180/150 series is nearing the 100 mark, and an unorthodox development is the 180SP, basically a 180Ag with the addition of short-span (19 ft 8 in: 6,00 m) lower wings to make it a biplane. While retaining the 115 mph (185 km/h) maximum cruising speed of the 180Ag, the biplane can offer a stalling speed of only 35 mph (56 km/h) compared with the 180Ag's 55 mph (89 km/h), and greatly reduced take-off and landing runs. The agricultural tanks on the SP are carried in the lower wings, instead of beneath the fuselage, as is the case with the 180Ag. Both versions are, of course, operated as single-seaters in the agricultural role.

A high-altitude version of the 180, known as the Condor, was flown in June 1971. This was a two-seater with modified wing tips, and a turbocharger for the engine was optional. At least four were built.

Specification

Type: three-seat general purpose monoplane
Powerplant: one 180-hp (134-kW) Avco Lycoming O-360-A1A flat-four piston engine
Performance: maximum speed 152 mph (245 km/h) at sea level; cruising speed 131 mph (211 km/h) at sea level; service ceiling 21,982 ft (6700 m); range 733 miles (1180 km)

The Aero Boero 180 is the most powerful of this series of Argentinian lightplanes, and is available in standard, glider-towing and agricultural versions, the last in alternative biplane form.

Weights: empty 1,212 lb (550 kg); maximum take-off 1,861 lb (844 kg)
Dimensions: span 35 ft 2 in (10.72 m); length 23 ft 10¼ in (7.27 m); height 6 ft 10¾ in (2.10 m); wing area 177.3 sq ft (16.47 m²)

Aero Spacelines Guppy Series

History and Notes

Aero Spacelines, then based at Van Nuys, California, was quick to appreciate the potential of outsize cargo aircraft that would be able to airlift large booster rocket stages being employed in the American space programme, as well as for the transport of aircraft assemblies, oil drilling equipment, and other items too large to be carried by any then existing aircraft. Work started in 1961 on the conversion of a Boeing B-377 Stratocruiser to fulfil such a role: the fuselage was extended by 16 ft 8 in (5.08 m) aft of the wing, and a new 'bubble' structure was added over the top of the fuselage to allow the loading of items up to 19 ft 9 in (6.02 m) in diameter. The resulting B-377PG Pregnant Guppy was flown for the first time on 19 September 1962, and was used from the summer of 1963, under contract to NASA, for the transport of space programme hardware.

An even larger B-377SG Super Guppy followed: this featured not only an outsize fuselage, with a cargo compartment measuring 108

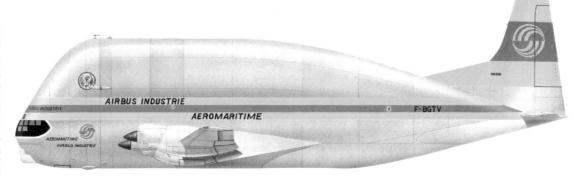

Aero Spacelines Guppy-201 of the Compagnie Aéromaritime d'Affretement.

ft 10 in (33.17 m) in overall length, 25 ft 0 in (7.62 m) in width, and 25 ft 6 in (7.77 m) in height, but also an increased wing span and four 7,000-eshp (5220-ekW) turboprop engines. This Super Guppy was also used in the American space programme, it being the only aircraft able to carry the third stage of a Saturn V launch vehicle, and the Lunar Module adapter.

To be seen in European skies are two Guppy-201s, acquired by Airbus Industrie for the transport of large Airbus assemblies from various construction points, these Guppy-201s being operated on the builder's behalf by a Union de Transports Aériens (UTA) subsidiary known as Aéromaritime. These are also conversions of Boeing B-377/C-97 airframes, with increased wing span

and Allison 501-D22C engines, the cargo compartment having a maximum length of 111 ft 6 in (33.99 m), with a height of 25 ft 6 in (7.77 m) and a width of 25 ft 1 in (7.65 m), and usable volume of 39,000 cu ft (1104.4 m³). To facilitate loading and unloading, the forward fuselage, including the flight deck, can be swung 110° to port, providing unrestricted access. The Guppy-201s have been

9

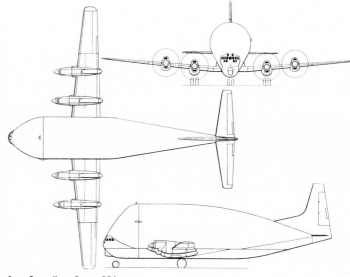

Aero Spacelines Guppy 201

Aéromaritime currently employs two Aero Spacelines Guppy-201s, and plans to build another two under licence.

in operation since 1972 and 1973, and Airbus Industrie have acquired two more to cater for the demand for Europe's wide-body Airbus.

The following specification applies to the Guppy-201.

Specification
Type: heavy transport
Powerplant: four 4,912-eshp (3663-ekW) Allison 501-D22C turboprops

Performance: maximum cruising speed 288 mph (463 km/h) at 20,000 ft (6100 m); economic cruising speed 253 mph (407 km/h) at 20,000 ft (6100 m); certificated service ceiling 25,000 ft (7620 m); range with maximum payload and 45-min reserves 505 miles (813 km)

Weights: empty 100,000 lb (45359 kg); maximum take-off 170,000 lb (77111 kg)
Dimensions: span 156 ft 3 in (47.63 m); length 143 ft 10 in (43.84 m); height 48 ft 6 in (14.78 m); wing area 1,964.6 sq ft (182.51 m²)
Operator: Aéromaritime

Aérospatiale (Nord) 262 and Frégate/Mohawk 298 Series

History and Notes

Max Holste, well-known French aircraft designer, evolved the design of a small transport for commuter services. Designated MH-250 with Pratt & Whitney radial piston engines, and MH-260 with Turboméca Bastan turboprops, the prototypes of these two variants flew first on 20 May 1959 and 29 July 1960 respectively. The nationalised company Nord-Aviation was to take part in production of an initial batch of MH-260s, but was to develop an improved version with pressurised accommodation. The first of these Nord 262s, as the modified type was designated, flew initially on 24 December 1962.

Of high-wing monoplane configuration, the Nord 262 featured wings,

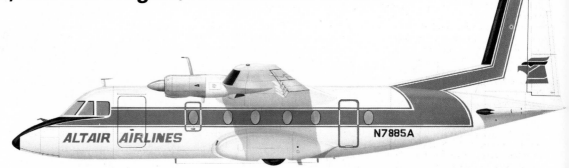

Aérospatiale N.262 of Altair Airlines, USA.

circular-section fail-safe fuselage and tail unit that were entirely conventional. The landing gear was of the retractable tricycle type, with a

single wheel on each unit, and the main gear retracting into fairings built on each side of the fuselage. The powerplant of the standard Nord

262A comprised two wing-mounted Turboméca Bastan VIC turboprops, each of 1,080 ehp (805 ekW). Standard accommodation was for 26 passengers, with a maximum of 29, and a movable forward bulkhead made it possible for users to have passenger or mixed freight/passenger configurations. The designation Nord 262B applied only to the first four production aircraft.

Following the merger of Nord- and Sud-Aviation to form Aérospatiale, this new company was to produce an improved N.262C with more powerful Bastan VII engines and new wingtips that increased wing span by 2 ft 3½ in (0.70 m). This was named Frégate, and a generally similar version for military use was known as the N.262D Frégate or Frégate D. One other variation was evolved, in the USA, where Mohawk Air Services planned the installation of 1,180-shp (880-kW) Pratt & Whitney Aircraft of Canada PT6A-45 turboprops to replace the Bastans in Allegheny's Nord 262As. The last of

Production of the Aérospatiale N.262 totalled a mere 110 examples, and of these only about 35 are still in service with airlines, the main operators being Ransome Airlines with 12 and Altair Airlines with seven. Both airlines operate commuter services based on Philadelphia, Pennsylvania and stretching mainly into the north-east USA.

these conversions, carried out by Frakes Aviation, was completed in 1978, the resulting aircraft being redesignated Mohawk 298. During this conversion, the opportunity was taken to update the aircraft by the introduction of improvements and new equipment. The details below apply to the Nord N.262A.

Specification
Type: commuter transport
Powerplant: two 1,080-ehp (805-ekW) Turboméca Bastan VIC turboprops
Performance: maximum speed 239 mph (385 km/h); cruising speed 233 mph (375 km/h); service

ceiling 23,500 ft (7160 m); range with 26 passengers, no reserves 865 miles (1392 km); range with maximum fuel, no reserves 1,325 miles (2132 km)
Weights: operating empty 15,498 lb (7030 kg); maximum take-off 23,369 lb (10600 kg)
Dimensions: span 71 ft 10¼ in (21.90 m); length 63 ft 3 in (19.28 m); height 20 ft 4 in (6.20 m); wing area 592.03 sq ft (55.00 m²)
Operators include: Air Algérie, Allegheny Commuter Consortium, Altair Airlines, Cimber Air A/S Denmark, Ransome Airlines, Swift Aire Lines, and Touraine Air Transport

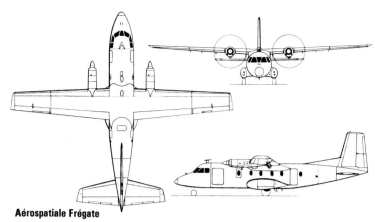

Aérospatiale Frégate

Aérospatiale SE 313B and SA 318C Alouette II

History and Notes
Of conventional configuration but sturdy design, the Aérospatiale Alouette II was one of the first true light multi-purpose helicopters and excelled in a variety of roles. This adaptability was facilitated by its reliable turboshaft engine, easy maintenance, and landing gear, which could be either of wheel or skid type, or floats, with provision for emergency flotation gear.

The Alouette II originated as the Sud-Est SE 3120 Alouette (Lark), a three-seat light helicopter designed mainly for agricultural purposes. The first SE 3120 prototype was flown on 31 July 1952, powered by a 200-hp (149-kW) Salmson 9NH radial engine, and a year later established a new international helicopter closed-circuit duration record of 13 hours 56 minutes. The basic airframe was then completely redesigned to take the 360-shp (269-kW) Turboméca Artouste I turboshaft, and the first of two prototypes, designated SE 3130, was flown on 12 March 1955, followed by three pre-production aircraft in 1956. The Alouette II was granted a French certificate of airworthiness on 2 May 1956, and was soon in demand on the international market. In 1957 Sud-Est merged with Sud-Aviation, at which time the designation of the Alouette II was altered to SE 313B, remaining unchanged after Sud's take-over by Aérospatiale.

From the beginning, the Alouette II proved a most successful design and was found particularly suitable for operations in higher altitudes. Thus, during the period 9-13 June 1958, an Artouste-powered Alouette II set up an international helicopter altitude record of 36,027 ft (10984 m) for all classes, and a height record of 31,440 ft (9583 m) in the 1000/1750kg category. By September 1960 no less than 598 Alouette IIs had been ordered by customers in 22 different countries and the type was being assembled by Republic in the USA and Saab in Sweden. It also became the first French aircraft of any kind, and the first helicopter in the world, to be granted an American certification.

A development of the Alouette II with a 400-shp (298-kW) Turboméca Turmo II engine, with the designation SE 3140, was announced in May 1957 but did not reach the production stage. Another derivative, powered by the more economical Astazou IIA turboshaft engine and featuring a new centrifugal clutch, was far more successful. The first prototype, designated SA 3180, was flown on 31 January 1960 and after thorough trials an extension of the Alouette II French certificate of airworthiness was granted on 18 February 1964.

Production, as the SA 318C, commenced in the same year, with first deliveries taking place in 1965. Of generally similar appearance and versatility, the SA 318C had a slightly higher level speed, longer range, and was capable of lifting heavier loads, but was less suitable for operations in higher altitudes. The success of the basic Alouette II design was reflected in the growing number of civil and military customers: by 1 June 1967 a total of 988 Alouette IIs (including those with Astazou engines) had been ordered (and 969 delivered); by 21 May 1970 the total had increased to 1,200 (923 with Artouste and 277 with Astazou engines); this total included 450 Alouette IIs delivered to the French air force, army and navy as well as private customers. By the spring of 1975, when the production of this helicopter was terminated, the number of Alouette IIs sold had reached 1,300, and it was used by 126 civil and military operators in 46 countries.

Specification
Type: (SE 313B Alouette II) light general-purpose helicopter
Powerplant: one 530-shp (395 kW) Turboméca Artouste II C-6 turboshaft, derated to 360 shp (269 kW)
Performance: (at maximum take-off weight) maximum speed at sea level 115 mph (185 km/h); maximum cruising speed at sea

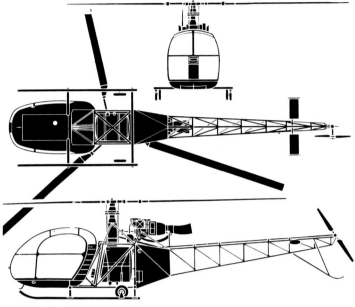

Aérospatiale SA 318C Alouette II Astazou

level 102 mph (165 km/h); rate of climb at sea level 925 ft (252 m) per minute; service ceiling 7,050 ft (2150 m); hovering ceiling in ground effect 5,400 ft (1650 m); hovering ceiling out of ground effect 3,000 ft (920 m); range with maximum fuel at sea level 350 miles (565 km); range with 1,200-lb

The Aérospatiale Alouette series has been the most successful helicopter of European origins yet to appear. Seen here is an SE 313B Alouette II of Aircraft Innsbruck Luftfahrt, an Austrian air-taxi line. Some 923 Alouette IIs were built, as well as about 350 SA 318C Alouette II Astazous. In the air-taxi role the Alouette II can carry up to four passengers.

(545-kg) payload at sea level 62 miles (100 km); range with 860-lb (390-kg) payload at sea level 186 miles (300 km); flight endurance with maximum fuel at sea level 4 hours 6 minutes
Weights: empty 1,973 lb (895 kg); maximum take-off 3,527 lb (1600 kg)
Dimensions: diameter of main rotor 33 ft 5⅝ in (10.20 m); diameter of tail rotor 5 ft 11 in (1.81 m); length (rotor blades folded) 31 ft 10 in (9.70 m); width (rotor blades folded) 6 ft 10 in

(2.08 m); height 9 ft 0 in (2.75 m); main rotor disc area 880 sq ft (81.7 m²)
Type: (SA 318 C Alouette II Astazou) light general-purpose helicopter
Powerplant: one 530-shp (derated to 360-shp) (395-/269-kW) Turboméca Astazou IIA turboshaft
Performance (at maximum military take-off weight): maximum speed at sea level 127 mph (205 km/h); maximum cruising speed at sea level 105 mph

(170 km/h); rate of climb at sea level 1,312 ft (400 m) per minute; service ceiling 10,800 ft (3300 m); hovering ceiling in ground effect 4,985 ft (1520 m); hovering ceiling out of ground effect 2,950 ft (900 m); range with maximum fuel at sea level 447 miles (720 km); range with 1,322-lb (600-kg) payload 62 miles (100 km); range with 1,058-lb (480-kg) payload 186 miles (300 km); maximum flight endurance at sea level 5 hours 18 minutes

Weights: empty 1,961 lb (890 kg); maximum take-off (civil version) 3,527 lb (1600 kg)
Dimensions: diameter of main rotor 33 ft 5⅝ in (10.20 m); diameter of tail rotor 6 ft 3 in (1.91 m); length of fuselage (tail rotor turning) 31 ft 11¾ in (9.75 m); width (rotor blades folded) 7 ft 6½ in (2.30 m); height 9 ft 0 in (2.75 m); main rotor disc area 880 sq ft (81.7 m²)

Aérospatiale SA 316B and SA 319B Alouette III

History and Notes
The Aérospatiale Alouette III is an enlarged and most successful development of the Alouette II, with increased cabin capacity, improved equipment, more powerful turbine engine and generally enhanced performance. The prototype, designated SE 3160, was first flown on 28 February 1959, followed by the first production series known as SA 316A. In June 1960 an Alouette III with seven people aboard demonstrated its extraordinary performance by making landings and take-offs at an altitude of 15,780 ft (4810 m) on Mont Blanc in the French Alps. Five months later the same Alouette III with two crew and a 550-lb (250-kg) payload made landings and take-offs at an altitude of 19,698 ft (6004 m) in the Himalayas—both hitherto unprecedented achievements for a helicopter. The SA 316A was built for domestic and export market and, in June 1962, became subject to a licence-production agreement with HAL in India. The first Indian-assembled Alouette III was flown on 11 June 1965.

Various experimental developments followed, including an all-weather variant which made its initial flight on 27 April 1964. The subsequent SA 316B, first flown on 27 June 1968, featured strengthened main and tail rotor transmissions and was generally slightly heavier, but could carry more payload. It became the principal production version, with first deliveries made in 1970, and was an immediate export success. The Alouette III prototypes and the first two production series were powered by Turboméca Artouste IIIB turboshaft engines, replaced by the Artouste IIID on the SA 316C, built in limited numbers only.

The Alouette III's cabin is more enclosed than that of the Alouette II, and can accommodate up to seven. All passenger seats are easily removable to provide an unobstructed cargo space. There is provision for an external sling for hauling loads up to 1,650 lb (750 kg) or, for the air/sea rescue role, a hoist of 380-lb (175-kg) capacity. Like most other light general purpose helicopters the Alouette III can also be used for casualty evacuation, carrying two stretcher cases and two seated persons behind the pilot.

Experiments with the thermally more efficient and more economical Astazou turboshaft engine led to the SA 319B, which is a direct development of the SA 316B. The first experimental SA 319B prototype was completed and flown in 1967, but full production did not start until 1973.

The Alouette III variants were even more successful on the international market than those of its predecessor, and by 1 April 1978 not less than 1,382 machines had been

sold (with 1,370 delivered) to 190 civil and military operators in 92 countries. In addition to licence-production by HAL at Bangalore in India (200) similar agreements were signed with ICA-Brasov in Romania (for 130) and Switzerland (for 60).

Specification
Type: Aérospatiale SA 316B Alouette III) general-purpose helicopter
Powerplant: one 870-shp (649-kW) Turboméca Artouste IIIB turboshaft, derated to 570 shp (425 kW)
Performance: (standard version, at maximum take-off weight) maximum speed at sea level 130 mph (210 km/h); maximum cruising speed at sea level 115 mph (185 km/h); maximum rate of climb at sea level 950 ft (260 m) per minute; service ceiling 10,500 ft (3200 m); hovering ceiling in ground effect 9,450 ft (2880 m); hovering ceiling out of ground effect 5,000 ft (1520 m); range with maximum fuel at sea level 298 miles (480 km); range at optimum altitude 335 miles (540 km).
Weights: empty 2,520 lb (1143 kg); maximum take-off 4,950 lb (2200 kg)
Dimensions: diameter of main rotor 36 ft 1¾ in (11.02 m); diameter of tail rotor 6 ft 3¼ in (1.91 m); length overall (rotor blades folded) 32 ft 10¾ in (10.03 m); width overall (rotor blades folded) 8 ft 6¼ in (2.60 m);

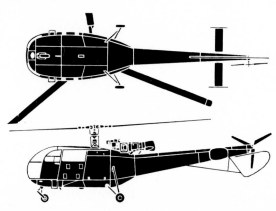

Aérospatiale SA 316C Alouette III

height 9 ft 10 in (3.00 m); main rotor disc area 1,026 sq ft (95.38 m²)
Type: (Aérospatiale SA 319B Alouette III Astazou) light general purpose helicopter
Powerplant: one 870-shp (649-kW) Turboméca Astazou XIV turboshaft, derated to 600 shp (448 kW)
Performance: (at maximum take-off weight) maximum speed at sea level 136 mph (220 km/h); maximum cruising speed at sea level 122 mph (197 km/h); maximum rate of climb at sea level 885 ft (270 m) per minute; hovering ceiling in ground effect 10,170 ft (3100 m); hovering ceiling out of ground effect 5,575 ft (1700 m);

range with six passengers (take-off at sea level) 375 miles (605 km)
Weights: empty 2527 lb (1146 kg); maximum take-off 4,960 lb (2250 kg)
Dimensions: diameter of main rotor 36 ft 1¾ in (11.02 m); diameter of tail rotor 6 ft 3¼ in (1.91 m); length (rotor blades folded) 32 ft 10¾ in (10.03 m); height 9 ft 10 in (3.00 m); main rotor disc area 1,026.5 sq ft (95.38 m²)

The Aerospatiale SA 319B Alouette III Astazou is no longer a particularly up-to-date design, but is still widely used, especially in roles where its excellent high-altitude performance is of benefit. Illustrated is an example of the French police, used for mountain patrol.

Aérospatiale/Westland SA 330 Puma

Aérospatiale/Westland SA.330J Puma of Bristow Helicopters Group, UK.

History and Notes

In the early 1960s Sud-Aviation began the design and development of a twin turbine-powered helicopter that would not only meet a French army requirement for an all-weather tactical and logistic transport, but which would be suitable also for use by other armed forces. The first of two prototypes made its maiden flight on 15 April 1965, and the Anglo-French helicopter agreement (concluded on 2 April 1968) gave Westland Helicopters in the UK joint production of these aircraft. Intended initially for service with the French army and the Royal Air Force, the latter required this helicopter for deployment as a tactical transport.

The fuselage of the SA 330 Puma, as this aircraft has been named, is a conventional all-metal semi-monocoque structure, with the powerplant mounted externally on top of the fuselage shell and forward of the main rotor assembly. The rotor is driven via a main gearbox, with twin free-wheeling spur gears to combine the outputs of the two turboshaft engines to a single main drive shaft. In the event of an engine failure the remaining engine continues to drive the rotor, and should both engines fail the auto-rotating main rotor continues to drive the auxiliary take-offs for the shaft-driven tail rotor, alternator, dual hydraulic pumps, and ventilation fan. The tail boom, which carries the flapping-hinge five-blade tail rotor on the starboard side and a horizontal stabiliser on the port side, is a monocoque continuation of the aft fuselage. Early main rotor blades were of light alloy construction, but those fitted since 1976 are composite units of glassfibre, carbon fibre and honeycomb construction, with anti-abrasion leading-edges of stainless steel. The landing gear is of the semi-retracting tricycle type, with twin wheels on each unit, all of which are partly exposed when retracted.

There have been a number of changes in powerplant: the first SA 330Bs for the French army and air force, and the SA 330Es for the Royal Air Force, were powered by Turmo III C4 turboshaft engines

with a take-off rating of 1,328 shp (990 kW); and the SA 330C/H military export versions, first flown in September 1968, had originally 1,400-shp (1044-kW) Turmo IVBs, but from the end of 1973 SA 330H aircraft were equipped with 1,575-shp (1174-kW) Turmo IVC engines which include anti-icing of the engine air intakes. The first SA 330F/G civil versions had Turmo IVA engines of 1,435 shp (1070 kW) as first flown on 26 September 1969 and delivered from the end of 1970; but like the SA 330H the SA 330G acquired Turmo IVC engines from the end of 1973; and this latter powerplant is installed also on the SA 330J (civil) and SA 330L (military) helicopters which were introduced in 1976.

Accommodation of the SA 330J provides for a standard crew of two on the flight deck, and the cabin can have 8, 9, or 12-seat VIP layouts, or can seat up to 20 passengers in a high-density configuration, with a toilet and baggage compartment at the rear of the cabin. Equipped with thermal de-icing of the main rotor blades, thermal anti-icing of the tail rotor blades, special intakes and weather radar, the SA 330J can be flown in all weather conditions, including known icing conditions, since receiving certification in this form on 25 April 1978. The following specification applies primarily to the SA 330J at maximum take-off weight.

Specification

Type: medium-size transport helicopter
Powerplant: two 1,575-shp (1174-

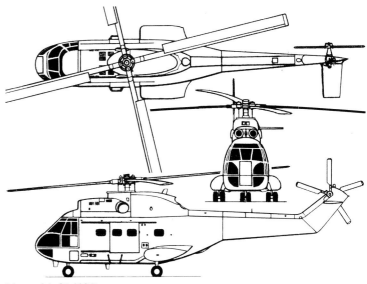

Aérospatiale SA 330 Puma

kW) Turboméca Turmo IVC turboshafts
Performance: maximum cruising speed 160 mph (258 km/h); service ceiling 15,750 ft (4800 m); maximum range, no fuel reserves 342 miles (550 km)
Weights: empty 8,303 lb (3766 kg); maximum take-off 16,314 lb (7400 kg)
Dimensions: diameter of main rotor 49 ft 2½ in (15.00 m); diameter of tail rotor 9 ft 11½ in (3.05 m); length overall with rotors turning 59 ft 6½ in (18.15 m);

height 16 ft 10½ in (5.14 m); main rotor disc area 1,905.3 sq ft (177.0 m³)

Operators include: Asahi Helicopter, Bristow Helicopters, and Schreiner Airways

For the support of offshore operations Asahi Helicopter deploys two Aérospatiale SA 300J medium-lift helicopters. The main civil version of the military Puma, the SA 330J is well suited to its task by reason of its IFR capability, anti-icing provision and possession of weather radar.

Aérospatiale/Westland SA 341/342 Gazelle

History and Notes
The SA 341 Gazelle all-purpose light-weight helicopter originated as Aérospatiale project X 300 to meet a French army requirement for a light observation helicopter. The designation was changed to SA 340 soon afterwards. The finished design showed close affinity to the SA 318C Alouette II, and eventually used the same Astazou II powerplant and transmission system. Unlike the Alouette II, however, the new helicopter features a fully enclosed fuselage structure and has two pilots side by side, with full dual controls. It also introduced two innovations: the *fenestron*, or shrouded tail rotor, and a rigid modified Bölkow-type main rotor. And it shows every sign of sharing its predecessor's sales success.

While still in the final design stages the SA 340 attracted British interest, leading to a joint development and production share-out agreement signed on 22 February 1967 and officially confirmed on 2 April 1968. The first prototype, designated SA 340.001, was flown on 7 April 1967, and the second on 12 April 1968. These were followed by four pre-production SA 341 Gazelles (first flown on 2 August 1968), of which the third was equipped to British army requirements, assembled in France, and then re-assembled by Westland in the UK as the prototype Gazelle AH.1. It was first flown on 28 April 1970.

On 14 May 1970 the first Aérospatiale-built SA 341 pre-production aircraft, in slightly modified form, established three new speed records for helicopters of its class, arousing even more foreign interest.

The first French production Gazelle, SA 341.1001, was cleared for its initial test flight on 6 August 1971; it had a longer cabin than its predecessors, an enlarged tail unit and an uprated Astazou IIIA engine. The initial Westland-assembled Gazelles followed early in 1972 (first flown on 31 January 1972).

Specification
Type: five-seat utility helicopter

Powerplant: one 590-shp (440-kW) Turboméca Astazou IIIA turboshaft
Performance (SA 341 at maximum take-off weight): maximum permissible speed at sea level 193 mph (310 km/h); maximum cruising speed at sea level 164 mph (264 km/h); economical cruising speed at sea level 144 mph (233 km/h); maximum rate of climb at sea level 1,770 ft (540 m) per minute; service ceiling 16,400 ft (5000 m); hovering ceiling in ground effect 9,350 ft (2850 m); hovering ceiling out of ground effect 6,560 ft (2000 m); range at sea level with maximum fuel 416 miles (670 km); range with pilot and 1,102 lb (500 kg) payload 223 miles (360 km)
Weights (SA 341G): empty 2002 lb (908 kg); maximum take-off 3,970 lb (1800 kg)
Dimensions: diameter of main rotor 34 ft 5½ in (10.50 m); diameter of tail rotor 2 ft 3⅜ in

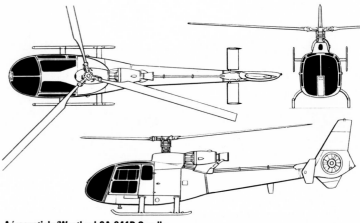

Aérospatiale/Westland SA 341D Gazelle

(0.695 m); length overall 39 ft 5⁄16 in (11.97 m); width (rotor blades folded) 6 ft 7 5⁄16 in (2.015 m); height 10 ft 2⅝ in (3.15 m); main rotor disc area 931 sq ft (86.5 m²)

The Gazelle utility helicopter was designed principally for military applications, though civil SA 341G and SA 342J variants have appeared.

Aérospatiale AS 350 Ecureuil

History and Notes
The Aérospatiale AS 350 Ecureuil six-seat general purpose helicopter was, like the SA 360 Dauphin, intended to supersede the long-established Alouette, but such is the excellence of this latter helicopter that it continues to be produced in SA 316B and SA 319B versions. As a result, the Ecureuil (Squirrel) must be regarded as an excellent complement to the Alouette family.

Benefitting from experience gained with the Alouettes, as well as from the SA 360, the design effort was concentrated in an attack on the two primary barriers to wider commercial use of the helicopter: operating costs and noise levels. It meant that a new rotor/rotor-drive/powerplant combination was needed to offer lower operating and maintenance costs, together with a reduction in rotor-induced noise. This has led to the development of a three-blade main rotor with an entirely new glassfibre hub which Aérospatiale has named the Starflex hub. Conventional main rotor blade hinges are replaced by maintenance-free ball-joints, and linked to glassfibre blades with stainless steel protection for the blade leading-edges.

A highly simplified transmission

unites the main and tail rotor with the turboshaft powerplant which, in the case of helicopters intended for other than North American markets, consists of a 641-shp (478-kW) Turboméca Arriel. This was a new single-shaft free-turbine turboshaft developed especially for applications such as the Ecureuil. AS 350s for sale in North America have the name Astar, and instead of the Arriel turboshaft have a 616-shp (459-kW) Avco Lycoming LTS101-600A.2 turboshaft developed in the USA at about the same time as the Arriel in France. First to fly on 27 June 1974 was an Astar version (F-WVKH), followed by an Arriel-powered Ecureuil (F-WVKI) on 14 February 1975.

The remainder of the structure follows what has come to be regarded as a fairly standard configuration for a light helicopter, comprising pod and boom construction, with a tail unit incorporating dorsal and ventral fins, and a horizontal stabiliser. Landing gear is of the steel-tube skid type, and emergency flotation gear is available. There is a wide range of optional avionics, together with equipment that includes a cabin air-conditioning system. The combined production of Astars and Ecureuils numbered

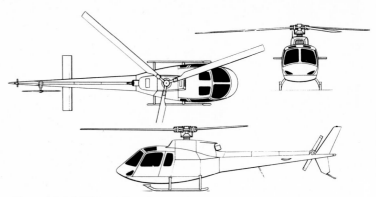

Aérospatiale AS 350 Ecureuil

about 600 exampoles in early 1981. The details below apply to the AS 250B Ecureuil.

Specification
Type: six-seat general-purpose helicopter
Powerplant: one 641-shp (478-kW) Turboméca Arriel turboshaft
Performance: maximum cruising speed 144 mph (232 km/h); service ceiling 16,000 ft (4875 m); range with maximum fuel at sea level, no reserves 441 miles (710 km)
Weights: empty 2,304 lb (1,045 kg); maximum normal take-off 4,299 lb

(1,950 kg)
Dimensions: main rotor diameter 35 ft 0¾ in (10.69 m); length, rotors turning 42 ft 8 in (13.00 m); height 10 ft 1¼ in (3.08 m); main rotor disc area 966.12 sq ft (89.75 m²)

Asahi Helicopter is the largest civil helicopter operator in the Far East, and has a fleet of 60 aircraft of nine types. Among these are two Aérospatiale AS 350B Ecureuils, here seen on the Shibaura roof-top heliport in Tokyo. The Ecureuils are used mainly for air-taxi work, a role in which their low internal and external noise levels are assets.

Aérospatiale SA 360 and SA 365 Dauphin

History and Notes
The Aérospatiale Dauphin is being developed in several versions, with single and twin engines, as a replacement for the Aérospatiale Alouette III. The first version to fly was the SA360, with a single Astazou XVI turboshaft, on 2 June, 1972. It was later re-engined with the Astazou XVIIIA and modifications were incorporated; in May 1973 this helicopter set up three speed records in its class. A second SA.360 prototype flew on 29 January 1973 and French airworthiness certification was awarded in December 1975. The first twin-engine Dauphin to fly was the SA 365 prototype, on 24 January, 1975, and by November 1980 some 175 of this effective twin-turbine helicopter had been ordered.

Specification
Type: twin-turbine general-purpose helicopter
Powerplant: two 650-shp (485-kW) Turboméca Arriel turboshafts
Performance: (at a weight of 6,614 lb (3000 kg) maximum speed 196 mph (315 km/h); cruising speed 158 mph (255 km/h); maximum rate of climb at sea level 2,460 ft (750 m) per minute; service ceiling 19,680 ft (6000 m); hovering ceiling in ground effect 11,000 ft (3350 m); hovering ceiling out of ground effect 8,530 ft (2600 m); maximum range (no reserves) 289 miles (465 km)
Weights: empty 3,946 lb (1790 kg); maximum take-off 7,495 lb (3400 kg)
Dimensions: main rotor diameter 38 ft 4 in (11.68 m); length 43 ft 7 in (13.29 m) height to top of rotor head 11 ft 6 in (3.50 m); main rotor disc area 1,154 sq ft (107.115 m²)

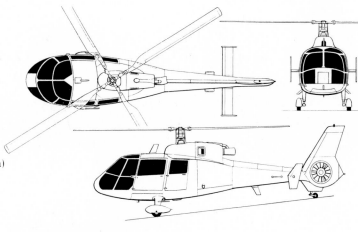

Aérospatiale SA 360 Dauphin

Aérospatiale SE 310 Caravelle

History and Notes
The first French turbojet-powered airliner, the Caravelle had also the distinction of being the world's first short/medium-range turbojet airliner, and was then unique in having its powerplant pod-mounted on the rear fuselage. A French ministry of civil aviation specification, of November 1951, called for the development in France of a turbine-powered airliner that could be marketed internationally, in competition with aircraft in this category already flown in Britain, and to be developed in the USA.

Design proposals were received from six national manufacturers, leading to selection of that from Sud-Est, from whom two prototypes were ordered by the Secretariat d'Etat à l'Air in January 1953: the name of Caravelle for the new airliner was chosen a few weeks later. Sud-Est, or Société Nationale de Constructions Aéronautiques du Sud-Est (SNCASE) to give its full title, was merged with Sud-Ouest (SNCASO) on 1 March 1957 to form Sud-Aviation. This latter company was merged subsequently with Nord-Aviation and SEREB to form, on 1 January 1970, the Société Nationale Industrielle Aérospatiale.

In its initial form the Caravelle, which had the Sud-Est designation SE 210, had been intended to acommodate 52 passengers, and the first of the two prototypes, both of which were powered by two Rolls-Royce Avon RA.26 turbojets each of 10,000-lb (4536-kg) thrust, flew for the first time on 27 May 1955. However, the initial production Caravelle I had a fuselage lengthened by 4 ft 7½ in (1.41 m), providing standard accommodation for 64 passengers in a mixed-class seating arrangement.

The Caravelle was of low-wing monoplane configuration, and of all-metal construction. The swept wing included such features as hydraulically powered ailerons, Fowler-type trailing-edge flaps, and airbrakes on both upper and lower wing surfaces forward of the flaps. The tail unit also had powered control surfaces, the tailplane being mounted on the fin to keep it clear of the efflux of the powerplant, located in pods on the sides of the rear fuselage. This pioneering use of rear-mounted turbojets was intended primarily to ensure that the wing remained 'clean' (free from the aerodynamic interference caused by engines, engine mountings and nacelles) to provide optimum performance of the wing, but second-

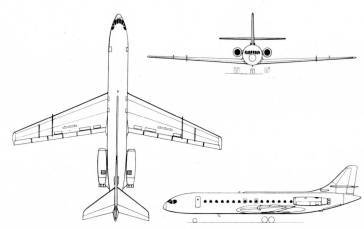

Aérospatiale Caravelle VI R

arily to reduce noise pollution of the cabin environment. In this latter respect those passengers seated furthest forward received the most benefit, and many that could later compare between the Caravelle, the Boeing 707 and the de Havilland Comet spoke glowingly of the Caravelle's 'quiet' cabin. Landing gear was of the hydraulically retractable tricycle type, with twin nosewheels, and a four-wheel bogie on each main

unit. The powerplant of the Caravelle I (19 built) consisted of two 10,500-lb (4763-kg) Avon RA.29 Mk 522 engines, but the Caravelle IA which followed (13 built) had RA.29/1 Mk 526 engines.

A total of 78 Caravelle IIIs followed, these differeing by the installation of 11,700-lb (5307-kg) thrust RA.29/3 Mk 527 engines. All but one of the Mk I and all 13 Mk IA Caravelles were subsequently converted to Mk III standard. Production of the Caravelle VI was to follow, the VI-N (53 built) and VI-R (56 built) differing in the following respect: the VI-N had two 12,200-lb (5534-kg) thrust RA. 29/6 Mk 531 turbojets, but the VI-VI-R had 12,600-lb (5715-kg) Mk 532R or Mk 533R engines which introduced thrust reversers to reduce the landing run. Other improvements incorporated in the VI-R included enlarged flight deck windows to improve fields of vision, more powerful brakes, and the provision of wing spoilers to serve as lift dumpers.

The next version to fly, on 3 March 1964, was the Super Caravelle (22 built), a considerably refined development of the basic Caravelle family, which introduced a number of aerodynamic improvements. These included a forward extension of the wing leading-edge, adjacent to the wing root, the introduction of double-slotted flaps and an extra 10° of flap travel, the provision of a bullet fairing at the intersection of the rudder and elevators, and an increase of 4 ft 7 in (1.40 m) in tailplane span. Other

Operating services within France, Air Inter (Lignes Aériennes Intérieures) uses, amongst other types, 16 Aérospatiale (Sud) Caravelle IIIs and seven Caravelle 12s. Seen here is one of the Caravelle IIIs with Avon turbojet engines.

Aérospatiale Caravelle

improvements included the installation of 14,000-lb (6350-kg) thrust Pratt & Whitney JT8D-7 turbofan engines; a fuselage 'stretch' of 3 ft 3½ in (1.00 m) to provide maximum tourist class accommodation for up to 104 passengers; introduction of an APU; updating of the electric and hydraulic systems; and provision of optional increased fuel capacity.

The Super Caravelle had been identified originally as the Caravelle 10B, and the model was followed by the 10R (20 built), the first of which flew on 18 January 1965. This was basically a Caravelle VI airframe, with JT8D-7 engines, cascade thrust-reversers designed by Sud-Aviation, and airframe modification to increase the capacity of the lower cargo holds. The company developed subsequently the Caravelle 11R, to meet a requirement for increased cargo capacity on medium-range routes. The Caravelle 11R was thus a mixed passenger/cargo version with typical accommodation for 50 tourist-class passengers and 2,331 cu ft (66.00 m³) of cargo. This was achieved by a 'stretch' of 33 ft 0³/₅ in (0.93 m) in the fuselage forward of the wing, the strengthening of the cabin floor and certain areas of the fuselage, the

Aérospatiale (Sud) SE 210 Caravelle 12 of Sterling Airways, Denmark.

provision of a 10 ft 10¾ in by 6 ft 0¼ in (3.32 m by 1.84 m) cargo door in the port side of the forward fuselage, and a movable bulkhead to separate cargo and passengers. Only six of this version were built, however, the first of them flying on 21 April 1967.

Last of the Caravelle production aircraft was the Mk 12, developed from the Super Caravelle, and having a fuselage which was lengthened an additional 10 ft 7 in (3.23 m) to provide accommodation for a maximum of 140 passengers. Other changes included structural reinforcement to cater for the higher gross weight, and introduction of Pratt & Whitney JT8D-9 turbofans. First flown on 29 October 1970, production of the Caravelle 12 totalled 12, bringing total production to 280

aircraft, including prototypes. At the height of their utilisation, Caravelles served with some 35 airlines. Many remain in service today, and a few are deployed by small armed forces in a transport capacity. The following specification applies to the Caravelle 12.

Specification
Type: short/medium-range transport
Powerplant: two 14,500-lb (6577-kg) thrust Pratt & Whitney JT8D-9 turbofans
Performance: maximum cruising speed, at AUW of 110,231 lb (50000 kg) 513 mph (825 km/h) at 25,000 ft (7620 m); range with maximum fuel, 24,780-lb (11240-kg) payload, no fuel reserves 2,510 miles (4040

km); range with maximum payload of 29,101 lb (13200 kg), no fuel reserves 2,153 miles (3465 km)
Weights: empty 65,036 lb (29500 kg); maximum take-off 127,868 lb (58000 kg)
Dimensions: span 112 ft 6 in (34.29 m); length 118 ft 10½ in (36.23 m); height 29 ft 7 in (9.02 m); wing area 1,579.1 sq ft (146.70 m²)
Operators include: Aerotal, Aerotour, Aerovias del Cesar, Air Afrique, Air Burundi, Air Charter International, Air France, Air Inter, Aviaco, China Airlines, CTA, Euralair, Europe Aero Service, Far Eastern Air Transport, Finnair, Indian Airlines, Midwest Air Charter, Minerve SA, SAETA, Servicios Aereos Nacionales, Sterling Airways, Syrian Arab Airlines, TAE, and Trans Europa

Aérospatiale SN 601 Corvette

History and Notes
First flown on 16 July 1970, the prototype SN 600 Corvette was Aérospatiale's late entry into the business-jet field. The Corvette had been anticipated, some seven years earlier, by the Dassault Falcon 20 which had succeeded in establishing itself before the Corvette flew, although the latter was designed more as a multi-purpose aircraft for the North American market.

The prototype was powered by two Pratt & Whitney Aircraft of Canada JT15D-1 turbofans, each rated at 2,200-lb (998-kg) thrust, but on production aircraft (SN 601) these were replaced by marginally more powerful JT15D-4s, each giving 2,300-lb (1043-kg) thrust. The first SN 601 flew on 20 December 1972, and two airframes were built for static testing. Three more Corvettes joined the test programme, in March and November 1973 and in January 1974; the programme then got into its stride and French certification was received on 28 May 1974, followed by FAA certification in September of that year.

Production SN 601s (Corvette 100s), featured a longer fuselage than the prototype with seats for up to 14 passengers and a crew of two; first customer to receive one was Air Alpes, in September 1974, in a 12-seat configuration, and other deliveries followed to operators in France, Belgium, the Netherlands, Sweden and Africa. The Corvette was found to be too small for commuter operations, which makes it all the more surprising that an 18-seat version, the Corvette 200, got no further than the design stage. Another proposed variant, the SN 602, was to have had 2,756-lb (1,250-kg) thrust SNECMA/Turboméca Larzac 03 turbofans, while looking even further ahead was a three-engined Corvette 300.

It came as no surprise when Aérospatiale announced, in 1977, that the programme was to be terminated with production of the 40th aircraft. By mid-1978, 36 had been sold or leased, with 10 of them in third-level service. Several were in use in the USA.

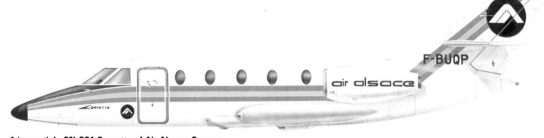

Aérospatiale SN 601 Corvette of Air Alsace, France.

Specification
Type: twin-turbofan multi-purpose monoplane
Powerplant: two 2,500-lb (1134-kg) thrust Pratt & Whitney Aircraft of Canada JT15D-4 turbofans
Performance: maximum speed 472 mph (760 km/h) at 29,530 ft (9000 m); cruising speed 352 mph (566 km/h) at 39,000 ft (11900 m); service ceiling 41,010 ft (12500 m); range with tip tanks 1,588 miles (2555 km)
Weights: empty 7,738 lb (3510 kg); maximum take-off 14,550 lb (6600 kg)
Dimensions: span 42 ft 2½ in (12.87 m); length 45 ft 4½ in 13.83 m); height 13 ft 10½ in (4.23 m); wing area 236.8 sq ft (22.0 m²)
Operators: Africair (Senegal), Air Algérie, Air Alpes, Air Alsace, Air Languedoc, Air Inter Gabon, Air National (USA), Bangui Government, Benin Government, Cogesat (France), JetStar Holland,

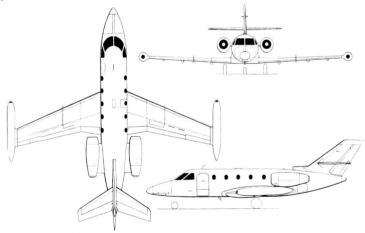

Aérospatiale SN 601 Corvette

Scan Fly (Sweden), SFACT (France), Sotramat (Belgium), Sterling Airways, TAT, Uni-Air

Despite its many attractions, the Aérospatiale Corvette was a commercial failure, only 40 being built.

Aérospatiale/British Aerospace Concorde

History and Notes

Until 14 October 1947 the attainment of supersonic flight by a manned aircraft had seemed to pose an insoluble problem; on that day, however, a USAF pilot, Captain Charles ('Chuck') Yeager, coaxed the Bell X-1 rocket-powered research aircraft through the 'buffeting' which had frustrated so many earlier attempts, into the smoothness of supersonic flight. The word supersonic is used to indicate flight at a speed in excess of that at which sound travels, and which in dry air at 32°F (0°C) is approximately 1,087 ft (331 m)/ second, or 741 mph (1,193 km/h). The actual speed of sound can vary quite considerably, according to the ambient air pressure and temperature, and a Mach number (named after Austrian physicist Ernst Mach) is used to express the speed of a body as a ratio of the speed of sound in the same ambient conditions. Thus Yeager's first record was achieved at a speed of 670 mph (1078 km/h) which, in the ambient conditions at the height of 42,000 ft

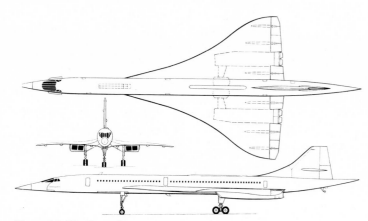

Aérospatiale/BAe Concorde of Air France.

(12800 m) at which the X-1 was flown, represented Mach 1.015, or slightly in excess of the speed of sound (Mach 1.0).

Supersonic flight was then very much the realm of specially designed research vehicles, but there was only minimal delay before the first military fighter/ interceptor aircraft able to attain safely speeds in excess of Mach 1 in a dive began to enter military service. By late 1953 the North American F-100 Super Sabre was entering service with the 479th Fighter Day Wing of the USAF's Tactical Air Command, and this was the world's first operational fighter capable of a speed in excess of Mach 1 in level flight. About two years later, on 20 August 1955, an F-100C established the first world speed

Aérospatiale/BAe Concorde

Aérospatiale/British Aerospace Concorde cutaway drawing key

1 Variable geometry drooping nose
2 Weather radar
3 Spring pot
4 Visor jack
5 'A'-frame
6 Visor uplock
7 Visor guide rails and carriage
8 Droop nose jacks
9 Droop nose guide rails
10 Droop nose hinge
11 Rudder pedals
12 Captain's seat
13 Instrument panel shroud
14 Forward pressure bulkhead
15 Retracting visor
16 Multi-layer windscreen
17 Windscreen fluid rain clearance and wipers
18 Second pilot's seat
19 Roof panel
20 Flight-deck air duct
21 3rd crew member's seat
22 Control relay jacks
23 1st supernumerary's seat
24 2nd supernumerary's folding seat (optional)
25 Radio and electronics racks (Channel 2)
26 Radio and electronics racks (Channel 1)
27 Plug-type forward passenger door
28 Slide/life-raft pack stowage
29 Cabin staff tip-up seat
30 Forward galley units (port and starboard)
31 Toilets (2)
32 Coats (crew and passengers)
33 Twelve 26-man life-rafts
34 VHF1 antenna
35 Overhead baggage racks (with doors)
36 Cabin furnishing (heat and sound insulated)
37 4-abreast one-class passenger accommodation
38 Seat rails
39 Metal-faced floor panels
40 Nosewheel well
41 Nosewheel main doors
42 Nosewheel leg
43 Shock absorber
44 Twin nosewheels
45 Torque links
46 Steering mechanism
47 Telescopic strut
48 Lateral bracing struts
49 Nosewheel actuating jacks
50 Underfloor air-conditioning ducts

51 Nosewheel door actuator
52 Nosewheel secondary (aft) doors
53 Fuselage frame (single flange)
54 Machined window panel
55 Underfloor forward baggage compartment (237 cu ft/ 6·72 m³)
56 Fuel lines
57 Lattice ribs
58 No 9 (port forward) trim tank
59 Single-web spar
60 No 10 (port forward) trim tank
61 Middle passenger doors (port and starboard)
62 Cabin staff tip-up seat
63 Toilets
64 Emergency radio stowage
65 Provision for VHF3
66 Overhead baggage racks (with doors)
67 Cabin aft section
68 Fuselage frame
69 Tank vent gallery
70 No 1 forward collector tank
71 Lattice ribs
72 Engine-feed pumps
73 Accumulator
74 No 5 fuel tank
75 Trim transfer gallery
76 Leading-edge machined ribs
77 Removable leading-edge sections, with:
78 Expansion joints between sections
79 Contents unit
80 Inlet control valve
81 Transfer pumps
82 Flight-deck air duct
83 No 8 fuselage tank
84 Vapour seal above tank
85 Pressure-floor curved membranes
86 Pre-stretched integrally machined wing skin panels
87 No 8 wing tank
88 No 4 forward collector tank
89 No 10 starboard forward trim tank
90 No 9 starboard forward trim tank

91 Quick-lock removable inspection panels
92 Spraymat leading-edge de-icing panels
93 Leading-edge anti-icing strip
94 Spar-box machined girder side pieces
95 No 7 fuel tank
96 No 7a fuel tank
97 Static dischargers
98 Elevon
99 Inter-elevon flexible joint
100 Combined secondary nozzles/reverser buckets
101 Nozzle-mounting spigots
102 Cabin air delivery/ distribution
103 Inspection panels
104 Cold-air unit
105 Fuel-cooled heat exchanger
106 Fuel/hydraulic oil heat exchanger
107 Fire-suppression bottles
108 Main spar frame
109 Accumulator
110 No 3 aft collector tank
111 Control linkage
112 "Z"-section spot-welded stringers
113 Riser to distribution duct
114 Anti-surge bulkheads
115 No 6 (underfloor) fuel tank
116 Machined pressurised keel box
117 Fuselage frame
118 Double-flange frame/floor join
119 Machined pressure-floor support beams
120 Port undercarriage well
121 Mainwheel door
122 Fuselage/wing attachments
123 Main spar frame
124 Mainwheel retraction link
125 Mainwheel actuating jack
126 Cross beam
127 Forked link
128 Drag strut
129 Mainwheel leg

130 Shock absorber
131 Pitch dampers
132 Four-wheel main undercarriage
133 Bogie beam
134 Torque links
135 Intake boundary layer splitter
136 Honeycomb intake nose section
137 Spraymat intake lip de-icing
138 Ramp motor and gearbox
139 Forward ramp
140 Aft ramp
141 Inlet flap
142 Spill door actuator
143 Intake duct
144 Tank vent gallery
145 Engine front support links
146 Engine-mounting transverse equalizers
147 Oil tank
148 Primary heat exchanger
149 Secondary heat exchanger
150 Heat-exchanger exhaust air
151 Rolls-Royce/SNECMA Olympus 593 Mk 610 turbojet
152 Outer wing fixing (340 high-tensile steel bolts)
153 Engine main mounting
154 Power control unit mounting
155 No 5a fuel tank
156 Tank vent
157 Transfer pump
158 Port outer elevon control unit fairing
159 Static dischargers
160 Honeycomb elevon structure
161 Flexible joint
162 Port middle elevon control hinge/fairing
163 Power control unit twin output
164 Control rod linkage
165 Nacelle aft support link

Aérospatiale/British Aerospace Concorde

record in excess of Mach 1 to be ratified by the Fédération Aéronautique Internationale.

Supersonic flight was, therefore, an accomplished fact, and very soon the first projects for larger aircraft in this category, to fulfil strategic bombing roles, were beginning to take shape. The realisation that the development of a large capacity airframe with a supersonic flight capability was within the bounds of possibility became of very considerable interest to those concerned with commercial aviation, particularly in relation to long ranges. This was not surprising, for speed of transit is the only real asset that airlines have to sell, and for the majority of air travellers there is no pleasure to be gained from many hours of confinement in an aircraft's cabin, however

The registration F-BVFA reveals this to be the fifth production Concorde, which first flew on 25 October 1975 and entered service on Air France's Paris-Dakar-Rio de Janeiro service on 21 January 1976.

166 Reverser-bucket actuating screw jack
167 Retractable silencer lobes ('spades')
168 Primary (inner) variable nozzle
169 Pneumatic nozzle actuators
170 Nozzle-mounting spigots
171 Port inner elevon control hinge/fairing
172 Control rod linkage
173 Location of ram-air turbine (RAT) in production aircraft
174 Accumulator
175 Vent and pressurisation system
176 Forged wing/fuselage main frames

177 Ground-supply air-conditioning connection
178 Control mixing unit
179 Control rod (elevon) linkage
180 Aft galley unit
181 Rear emergency doors (port and starboard)
182 Wingroot fillet
183 Air-conditioning manual discharge valve
184 Automatic discharge/relief valve

185 First-aid oxygen cylinders
186 Rear baggage compartment (door to starboard)
187 Rear pressure bulkhead
188 Fin support frames
189 No 11 aft trim tank
190 Machined centre posts
191 Shock absorber
192 Retractable tail bumper
193 Tail bumper door
194 Tank overflow and pressure relief lines
195 Tail cone bulkhead
196 Fuel jettison
197 Monergol-powered emergency power unit (pre-production aircraft only)
198 Tail cone
199 Rear navigation light
200 Rudder lower section
201 Servo control unit fairing (manual stand-by)
202 Fixed rubber stub

203 Multi-bolt fin-spar attachment
204 Fin construction
205 Fin spar
206 Air-conditioning ducting
207 HF antennæ
208 Finroot fairing
209 Leading-edge structure
210 Servo unit threshold bellcrank
211 Servo control unit fairing
212 VOR antenna
213 Rudder upper section
214 Static dischargers

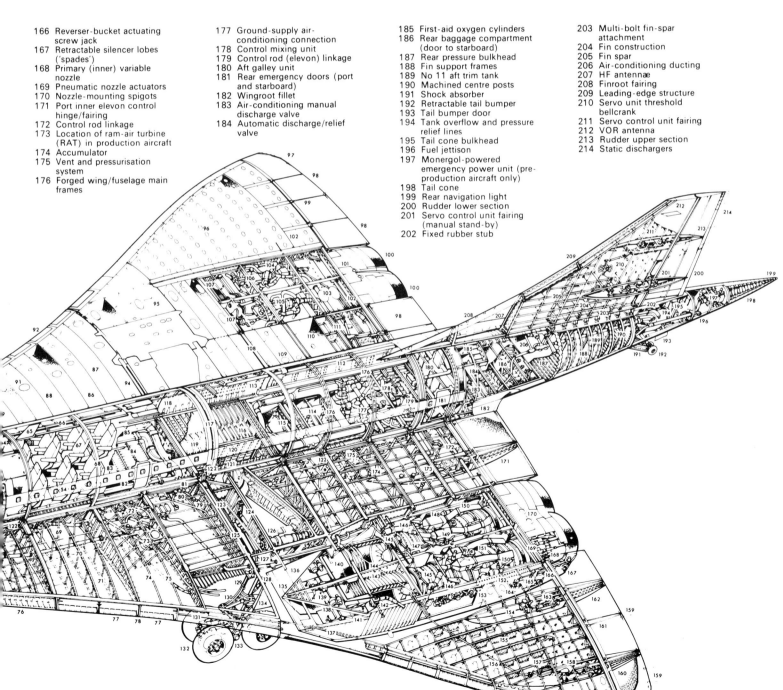

luxurious. Experience has shown that passengers will usually elect to travel by the fastest means over any particular route, and as a result the civil airliner has, for example, eliminated the ocean liner as a conventional means of business travel throughout the world. The realisation that long-range flight times could possibly be cut by half seemed a thrilling prospect, both to airline operators and to aircraft manufacturers.

In the late 1950s, therefore, Bristol Aircraft Ltd in the UK (which in 1960 became a wholly-owned subsidiary of, and was ultimately absorbed into, the British Aircraft Corporation, or BAC), and Sud-Aviation in France (which was merged with Nord-Aviation and SEREB in 1970 to form the Société Nationale Industrielle Aérospatiale) were each carrying out independent design studies for a practical supersonic transport. Both companies decided that the design and construction of such an aircraft was feasible, but

that the cost of its development would be completely beyond the capability of any individual company. Indeed, it soon became clear that development costs were likely to exceed a figure which could be faced by either the British or French government alone. There thus followed discussions which resulted in the signature of agreements on 29 November 1962 to bring about international collaboration for the realisation of what was seen then as a highly desirable and readily marketable commodity. The governments of the UK and France agreed to provide the cash to finance development, and the British Aircraft Corporation and Rolls-Royce finalised agreements with Sud-Aviation and the Société Nationale d'Etude et de Construction de Moteurs d'Aviation (SNECMA) for collaboration to design and manufacture a joint supersonic transport (SST), this eventually becoming named appropriately Concorde, symbolising the determination

of the two nations' manufacturing companies to produce a safe, reliable, world-beating aircraft.

It should be mentioned here that these moves to capture what was considered to be a lucrative market were followed closely by interested parties in the USA and the USSR. In the USA, the Federal Aviation Administration sponsored a design competition for the design and development of an SST with intercontinental range. Boeing's Model 2707 was selected as the winner, and the company was awarded a contract on 1 May 1967 for the construction of two prototypes. It was envisaged as a 350-passenger aircraft that would have a normal cruising speed of Mach 2.7 and range of 4,000 miles (6440 km) with 313 passengers. Good low-speed performance, for take-off, approach, and landing, would be ensured by the use of variable-geometry wings (swing wings). It was discovered, as design progressed, that there were structural and weight

problems resulting from the proposed swing-wings. This led to design finalisation on the Model 2707-300, with fixed gull-wings, and it was in this form that a go-ahead for construction was authorised by President Richard Nixon on 23 September 1969. However, the development of an American SST came to an end on 24 March 1971, when the US Senate voted against providing the necessary finance for the development and construction of this aircraft.

In the Soviet Union, design and development of an SST followed even more closely upon the moves in the UK and France, a model of the design proposals being exhibited at the Paris Air Show in 1965. This has resulted in development, manufacture, and entry into service of the Tupolev Tu-144.

Design and development of the Concorde needed the solution of many complex technological problems if the collaborating companies were to attain their aim of manufacturing

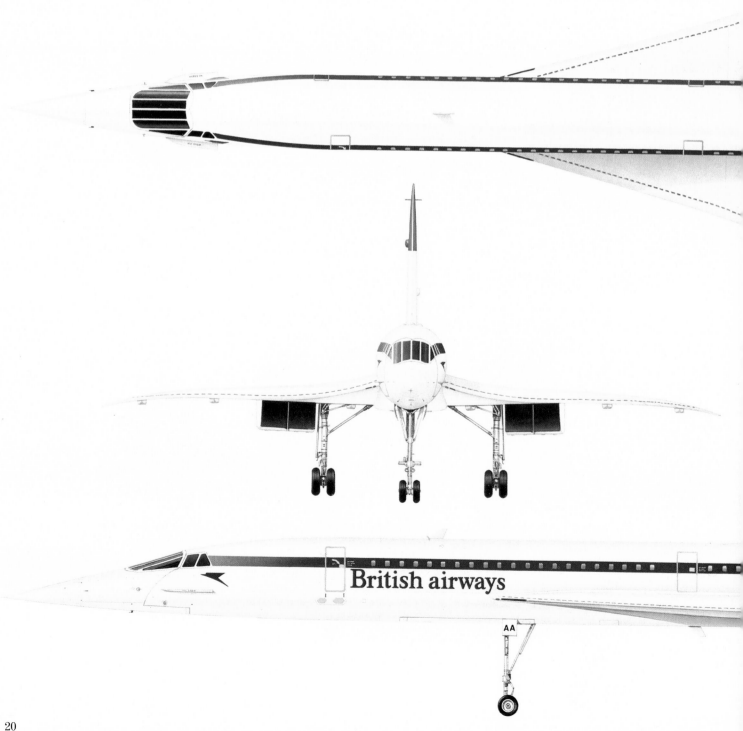

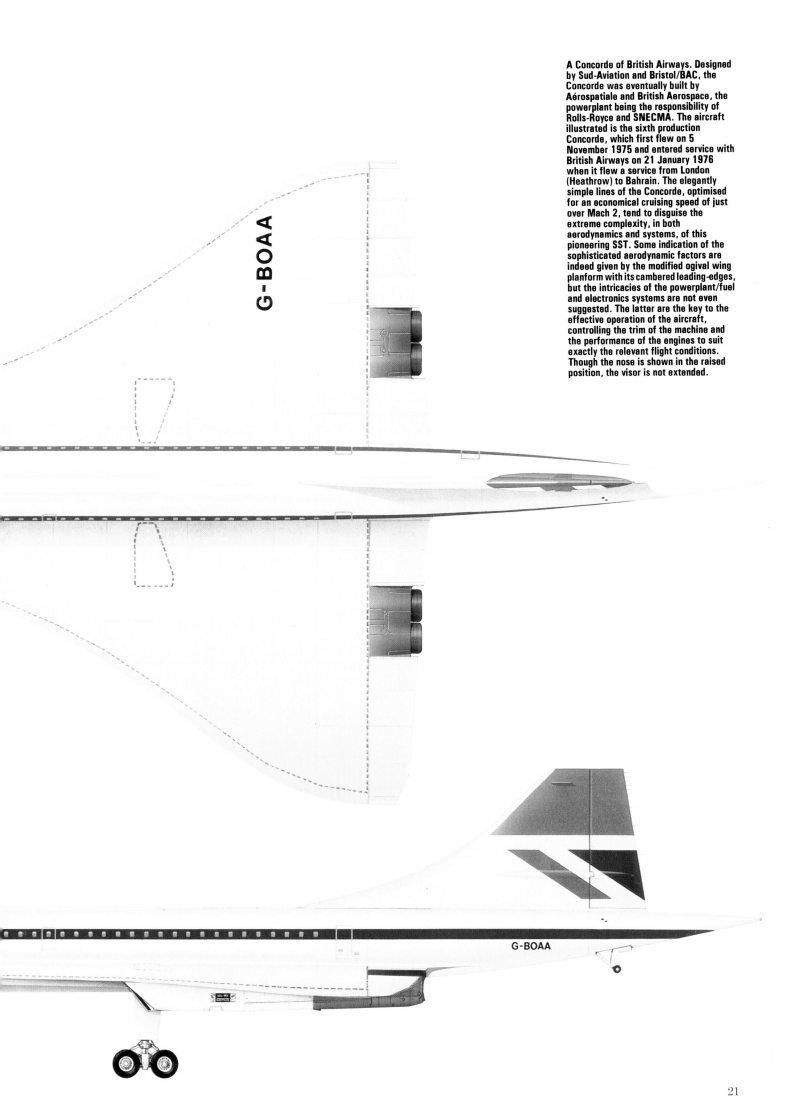

A Concorde of British Airways. Designed by Sud-Aviation and Bristol/BAC, the Concorde was eventually built by Aérospatiale and British Aerospace, the powerplant being the responsibility of Rolls-Royce and SNECMA. The aircraft illustrated is the sixth production Concorde, which first flew on 5 November 1975 and entered service with British Airways on 21 January 1976 when it flew a service from London (Heathrow) to Bahrain. The elegantly simple lines of the Concorde, optimised for an economical cruising speed of just over Mach 2, tend to disguise the extreme complexity, in both aerodynamics and systems, of this pioneering SST. Some indication of the sophisticated aerodynamic factors are indeed given by the modified ogival wing planform with its cambered leading-edges, but the intricacies of the powerplant/fuel and electronics systems are not even suggested. The latter are the key to the effective operation of the aircraft, controlling the trim of the machine and the performance of the engines to suit exactly the relevant flight conditions. Though the nose is shown in the raised position, the visor is not extended.

a safe and reliable SST. The first bridge to be crossed was a decision on maximum speed. If the intention was to cruise at a speed between Mach 2.5 and Mach 3.0 (the Americans had opted for Mach 2.7), then there were problems to be faced from kinetic heating resulting from air friction which, during extended periods of high-speed cruising flight, would raise the temperature of certain areas of the aircraft's structure to a figure where conventional light alloys would be unable to maintain their structural integrity. Such speeds can, and have been, very considerably exceeded by manned research vehicles, and the world has a number of operational military aircraft capable of Mach 3 or over. Their structures, however, contain considerable amounts of heat-resistant metals such as titanium and stainless steel, but their use on a fairly large scale for a Mach 2.5 to Mach 3.0 Concorde would have very considerably increased structural costs. Instead, it was decided to put a limit of Mach 2.2 on the speed of the airliner: at this figure there would be no kinetic heating problems, permitting the structure to be of conventional light alloy except for minimal use of heat-resistant alloys in hot-spot areas of the powerplant installation.

Design, development, and construction was shared between Aérospatiale and BAC, with the French partner responsible for wings and wing control surfaces; the rear cabin section; air conditioning, hydraulics, navigation and radio systems; and flying controls. BAC was responsible for the three forward fuselage sections; rear fuselage; vertical tail surfaces; engine nacelles and ducting; engine installation, fire warning and extinguishing systems; electrical, fuel, and oxygen systems; and noise and thermal insulation. Construction of the first two prototypes began in February 1965, Concorde 001 being built by Aérospatiale at Toulouse, and 002 by BAC at Filton, Bristol. The first flight of 001 (F-WTSS) was made on 2 March 1969, and that of the British-assembled 002 (G-BSST) on 9 April 1969.

As early flight testing of these two aircraft showed no fundamental problems, 001 was used for a sales and demonstration tour which began on 4 September 1971. More or less simultaneously, 002 was giving demonstration flights to interested airlines, politicians and the press, and it was not until 2 June 1972 that it, too, carried out a sales tour of the Middle and Far East, this including visits to Australia and Japan. Despite the inherent problems of Concorde, posed by the fact that it was an SST, and including such items as engine noise, sonic boom, fuel consumption and cost, there was considerable interest in the aircraft and its earth-shrinking potential for business and VIP travel. Soon more than 70 aircraft had been ordered, and the prospects for a resounding commercial success then seemed quite within the bounds of possibility. This was not just wishful thinking, for with such customers on the order book as Air Canada, Air France, American Airlines, BOAC, Eastern Air Lines, Japan Air Lines, Lufthansa, Pan American, Qantas, Sabena, TWA and United Airlines, it was reasonable to assume that successful deployment by these companies would result in the generation of new orders.

Concorde's appearance is well known, for colourful photographs and illustrations have appeared regularly in both aviation and general

press features which have extolled or denigrated this remarkable aeroplane. It is of cantilever low-wing configuration with a large-area delta wing, and a long, narrow fuselage with a maximum internal width of 8 ft 7½ in (2.63 m). The tail unit consists only of a vertical fin and rudder, for control in pitch and roll is provided by six elevons spaced across the trailing-edge of the delta wing. The landing gear is of the hydraulically retractable tricycle type, with twin wheels on the nose unit and a four-wheel bogie on each main unit. Standard accommodation provides for a crew of three on the flight deck, with provision for a fourth seat behind the pilot, and there is a variety of four-abreast seating layouts to suit the requirements of individual airlines. The maximum possible seating capacity allows for the carriage of up to 144 passengers. Powerplant consists of four Rolls-Royce/SNECMA Olympus 593 Mk 610 turbojet engines, this particular version of the Olympus being developed specially to power Concorde. By the time that certification was gained in September 1975, more than 50,000 hours of running time had been accumulated, and this had increased to over 54,000 hours when scheduled services began in 1976. These hours do not include those recorded by earlier versions of the the Olympus installed in the Avro (Hawker Siddeley) Vulcan and BAC TSR.2.

Concorde has some particularly interesting design features which are the result of its configuration and usage. For example, the delta wing planform requires that the aircraft is flown at a fairly steep angle of attack at low subsonic speeds, which means that its flight crew would have a much restricted view of the ground during take-off, initial climb, approach, and landing unless some special provision was made. This resulted in the design of a fuselage nose section which could be drooped to improve the forward view under the above conditions, and of a retractable visor, which is raised hydraulically, to fair in the windscreen during normal cruising flight.

Much of the Concorde's total fuel capacity of 26,350 Imperial gallons (119787 litres) is contained within

the wing, but a percentage is held in four fuselage tanks. The fuel is used for two other tasks in addition to the primary one of fuelling the engines: firstly, the large volume of fuel within the wing structure acts as a heat sink to reduce the wing temperature in prolonged supersonic flight; and secondly, fuel is transferred automatically throughout the network of storage tanks to maintain the aircraft's CG in cruising flight. In addition, a group of trim tanks maintains the correct relationship between the aircraft's CG and its aerodynamic centre of pressure, fuel being moved aft during acceleration, and forward as the aircraft returns to a subsonic flight regime.

Much of the efficiency and reliability of the powerplant results from the computer-controlled variable-area air intakes, which ensure the optimum air flow to each engine under all operating conditions. The Concorde's flight deck and cabin are air-conditioned and pressurised, and the advanced avionics include an automatic flight control system, and triplicated inertial navigation systems.

By the time that full passenger-carrying certification was awarded by the British and French authorities in late 1975, flight testing of prototype, pre-production, and the first production Concordes totalled 5,335 hours. SST scheduled services were inaugurated simultaneously by Air France and British Airways on 21 January 1976, but by then the escalating cost of these aircraft and the activity of anti-Concorde environmentalists had reduced the order book to the nine aircraft ordered by the above two airlines. There was, of course, a strong belief that the successful operation of these aircraft by Air France and British Airways would generate new orders, but this had not proved to be true by the beginning of 1981. A significant factor in this lack of sales has resulted from the large increases in the cost of fuel, which have more than offset the economies in operation resulting from experience gained during four years of airline use. Utilisation has been good, especially across the North Atlantic between London and New York, with average load factors as high as 86 per cent recorded during 1979.

A British Airways Concorde flew

from New York to London in 24 seconds under three hours on 16 December 1979, emphasising the significant high-speed no-fatigue role that SSTs offer to business executives. Five years of accident-free service by 21 January 1981 left little doubt of the integrity of these aircraft By 21 January 1980 British Airways' Concordes had carried just over a quarter of a million fare-paying passengers (two-thirds of them between London and New York), and so the airline acquired a sixth aircraft in 1980 to increase service frequency on the London-New York route.

Concorde has probably generated more pride, and more noise and environmental pollution hate, than any other civil airliner yet built. To whichever of these groups an individual belongs, there are few who will not agree that Concorde, one of the first fruits of international collaboration, has proved a supreme technological success.

Specification

Type: supersonic commercial transport
Powerplant: four Rolls-Royce/SNECMA Olympus 593 Mk 610 turbojet engines, each rated at 38,050-lb (17259-kg) thrust with 17 per cent afterburning
Performance: cruising speed for optimum range Mach 2.04 at 51,300 ft (15635 m), equivalent to 1,354 mph (2179 km/h); service ceiling 60,000 ft (18290 m); range with maximum range 4,090 miles (6582 km) with FAR fuel reserves and payload of 19,500 lb (8845 kg); range with maximum payload at Mach 2.02 cruise 3,870 miles (6228 km) with FAR fuel reserves
Weights: operating empty 173,500 lb (78698 kg); maximum take-off 408,000 lb (185066 kg)
Dimensions: span 83 ft 10 in (25.55 m); length 203 ft 9 in (62.10 m); height 37 ft 5 in (11.40 m); wing area 3,856 sq ft (358.22 m²)
Operators: Air France, British Airways

G-BOAA, the sixth production Concorde, entered service in 1976 with British Airways, which operates six of the type compared with Air France's four. Note the dropped nose and extended landing gear, including the small tail-bumper.

Agusta A 109A

History and Notes

The basic A 109A is notable as the first Agusta-designed helicopter to be built in large series, and is the end product of a special market analysis initiated in 1965. Initially envisaged for commercial use only, the A 109 was designed around a single 690-shp (515-kW) Turboméca Astazou XII engine, but mainly for additional safety considerations redesigned in 1967 to take two 370-shp (276-kW) Allison 250-C14 turboshafts. The projected A 109B military utility model was abandoned in 1969 in favour of the eight-seat A 109C Hirundo (Swallow) civil version, the first of three prototypes flying on 4 August 1971. Protracted trials, minor alterations and other factors caused unforeseen delays and the first A 109 pre-production aircraft was not completed until April 1975. Delivery of production machines, designated A 109A, commenced in 1976.

In addition to its designed role as a light passenger transport, the A 109A can be adapted for freight carrying, as an air ambulance, or for search-and-rescue tasks. It proved a great commercial success and by early 1978 the A 109A was subject to some 250 orders and options. Standard accommodation is for a crew of two, plus six passengers and baggage, or two litters and two attendants, or a useful freight load.

Specification
Type: light general-purpose helicopter
Powerplant: two Allison 250-C20B turboshaft engines, each developing 420 shp (313 kW) for take-off, 385 shp (287 kW) continuous power, derated to 346 shp (258 kW) for twin-engine operation
Performance: (at 5,400 lb/2450 kg AUW) maximum permissible level speed 193 mph (311 km/h); maximum cruising speed at maximum continuous power 165 mph (266 km/h); optimum cruising speed at sea level 143 mph

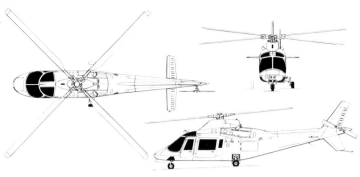

Agusta A 109C

(231 km/h); maximum rate of climb at sea level 1,620 ft (493 m) per minute; service ceiling 16,300 ft (4968 m); hovering ceiling in ground effect 9,800 ft (2987 m); hovering ceiling out of ground effect 6,700 ft (2042 m); maximum range at sea level 351 miles (565 km); maximum endurance at sea level 3 hours 18 minutes

Weights: empty 3,120 lb (1415 kg); maximum take-off 5,402 lb (2450 kg)
Dimensions: diameter of main rotor 36 ft 1 in (11.0 m); diameter of tail rotor 6 ft 8 in (2.03 m); length of fuselage 35 ft 1¾ in (10.71 m); height 10 ft 10 in (3.30 m); main rotor disc area 1,022.6 sq ft (95.0 m²)

Ahrens AR 404

History and Notes

The prototype Ahrens AR 404 four-engine utility transport first flew at Oxnard, California, on 1 December 1976, less than two years from the start of its design. Plans were made for production to begin in Puerto Rico, with the local government funding the certification process and the production of an initial batch of 18 aircraft. The first such production aircraft to be built entirely in Puerto Rico flew on 26 October 1979, and this joined the prototype in the programme to gain certification under the FAR25 regulations. Such certification is expected in January 1982.

Ahrens production plans, assuming satisfactory certification, cover between 12 and 16 aircraft for delivery in 1982, followed by some 24 to 30 aircraft in 1983. More than 100 letters of intent to purchase have been received by the company, and provisional delivery positions have been advised. More than half of the scheduled production is for operators in North America, the remainder being for an anticipated worldwide

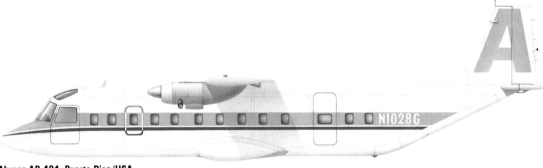

Ahrens AR 404, Puerto Rico/USA.

distribution.

Two-crew operation is planned for the flight deck, and a maximum of 30 passengers will be accommodated in 2+1 configuration with a central aisle. Baggage will be carried in a 160-cu ft (4.53-m³) rear-loaded container. In the freight role the AR 404 will be able to carry four standard D-3 containers. A split cargo door is fitted in the rear fuselage, one section serving as a loading-ramp. This is operable in flight to permit air-dropping of supplies or parachutists.

Specification
Type: 30-seat passenger/utility transport
Powerplant: four 420-shp 313-kW Allison 250-B17B turboprops
Performance: maximum speed 219 mph (352 km/h) at 5,000 ft (1525 m); cruising speed 195 mph (314 km/h) at 5,000 ft (1525 m); service ceiling 18,040 ft (5500 m); range 1,388 miles (2234 km)

Weights: empty 9,500 lb (4309 kg); maximum take-off 17,500 lb (7938 kg)
Dimensions: span 66 ft 0 in (20.12 m); length 52 ft 9 in (16.08 m); height 18 ft 6 in (5.64 m); wing area 422 sq ft (39.20 m²)

The Ahrens AR 404, US-designed but Puerto Rico-financed, is a simple yet versatile passenger/freight carrier, and should enjoy considerable success if the present price quotation can be met.

AIDC XC-2

History and Notes
The Aero Industry Development Center was established in Nanking in 1946, and moved to Taiwan in 1948. It is the only aircraft manufacturing plant in Nationalist China, and has built a number of light aircraft for training (modified Pazmany PL-1s), Bell UH-1H helicopters and Northrop F-5E fighters under licence, and a turboprop modification of the North American T-28 trainer.

Work on the AIDC's first indigenous design, the XC-2 transport,

began in January 1973 and the prototype flew on 26 February 1979. Intended for civil and military use, the XC-2 can operate from unprepared strips and has a quick-change capability, the interior four-abreast seating making way for an all-cargo (8,500 lb: 3856 kg), or mixed passenger/cargo layout. A rear-fuselage ramp can be opened in flight to permit airdropping, while the passenger version can be fitted with a toilet, galley and baggage compartment. The cabin can be

pressurised if required, and provision is made for a flight deck crew of three. No details of production plans had been released in early 1981.

Specification
Type: twin turboprop 38-seat transport
Powerplant: two 1,451-hp (1 082-kW) Avco Lycoming T53-L-701A turboprops
Performance: maximum speed 244 mph (393 km/h) at sea level; cruising speed 230 mph (370 km/h)

at 10,000 ft (3050 m); service ceiling 26,300 ft (8015 m); range 1,032 miles (1661 km)
Weights: empty 15,500 lb (7031 kg); maximum take-off 27,500 lb (12474 kg)
Dimensions: span 81 ft 8½ in (24.90 m); length 65 ft 11¼ in (20.10 m); height 25 ft 3¾ in (7.72 m); wing area 704 sq ft (65.40 m²)

Airbus Industrie A300

History and Notes
At very much the same time that Boeing, in the USA, was finalising the design of what was to emerge as the world's first wide-body commercial transport, the Model 747 initially flown in early 1969, discussions had started in Europe to consider the design and manufacture of a short/medium-range large capacity European transport aircraft. As first envisaged, the requirements were rather different from those of the operators to whom Boeing hoped to sell the Model 747, this latter aircraft being intended for ranges of approximately 6,000 miles (9,650 km) with almost 400 passengers.

European moves towards such an aircraft began with the establishment in the UK of a working party to study a short-range transport with low operating cost. The party's purview had been somewhat diverted from the initial wide-scale view, however, by BEA's requirement for a successor to the Vickers Vanguard. In France the Breguet, Nord-Aviation and Sud-Aviation companies were following somewhat similar studies, and in 1965 the Paris Air Show served as a catalyst to unite initially France and West German manufacturers in discussions. This led to the *Studiengruppe Airbus*, set up in West Germany by the nation's major aircraft manufacturers.

The 200-seat transport which had seemed ideal by BEA was used as a theoretical basis for discussion by a symposium of eight airlines which met in London in late 1965. It did not take long for them to agree that this seating capacity was too modest having regard to the need to limit operating costs per seat-mile to the lowest possible figure, and the anticipated large-scale growth of air traffic made large-capacity aircraft essential if the work load of air traffic controllers was to be contained within reasonable bounds. In Europe's crowded airspace the movement of one 300-seat transport, however revolutionary, seemed infinitely desirable to three separate movements of 100-seaters.

During 1965-6 there were various alignments of European manufacturers making design proposals for this new transport. Hawker Siddeley, Breguet and Nord had come up with five proposals, but their first HBN-100 with two new-technology turbofan engines and seating capacity of 200-300, according to fuselage length, aroused considerable interest. Sud-Aviation came up with a very similar design, in conjunction with Dassault offering the 241/269-seat Galion. It was these two very similar proposals which were considered in depth both by airlines and governments, for there was no doubt at even this very early stage that development costs would necessitate the international co-operation of both governments and manufacturers. With this latter

Airbus Industrie A300B4 of Thai Airways International.

point in mind, West Germany was invited to join a consortium for design, development and manufacture of a European 'airbus' which, it had by then been agreed, was to be based upon the HBN-100 design proposal. Arbeitsgemeinschaft Airbus was the initial title of the German industrial representative on the consortium, this becoming Deutsche Airbus GmbH on 4 September 1967. Hawker Siddeley was selected as the British partner and Sud-Aviation, rather than Nord-Aviation, because of the close links which had already been formed between these two companies by the Concorde project. Initial grouping of engine manufacturers to produce the powerplant for the 'airbus' brought together MAN Turbo, Rolls-Royce and SNECMA.

The original powerplants considered as alternatives by the HBN group consisted of the Pratt & Whitney JT9D or Rolls-Royce RB.178-51 advanced technology turbofans. Since, in 1966, these were the only suitable engines in prospect, they were selected also for the Sud/Dassault Galion proposal. However, the RB.178 was not developed, Rolls-Royce proposing instead the RB.207, a more powerful, developed version of the RB.178 three-spool turbine. Events taking place in the USA in mid-1966 were to bring yet another change, for American Airlines circulated a requirement to US manufacturers for a wide-body short/medium-haul domestic transport, which led to the design, development, and production of the Lockheed L-1011 TriStar and McDonnell Douglas DC-10. Both required engines of some 40,000-lb (18144-kg) thrust: General Electric's CF6 was selected for the DC-10, and Rolls-Royce's RB.211 proposal for the TriStar. With firm orders for the TriStar and at that time very little interest in the European Airbus, Rolls-Royce concentrated on development of the RB.211, and so the RB.207 also failed to materialise.

On 28 May 1969, France and West Germany decided to go ahead with development of the European Airbus, thus having the general designation A300, and construction of the first A300B1 began in September 1969. The lack of orders and enthusiasm for this project, despite the forward-looking approach of the British,

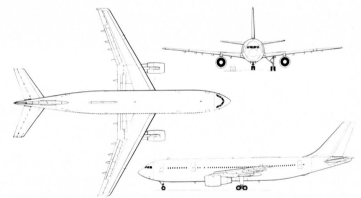

Airbus Industrie A300B4

French and German manufacturers, was responsible for the British government failing to become a member of the consortium. Hawker Siddeley financed separately a part of the development costs so that the company could participate in what it regarded as an important project. The Netherlands, represented by Fokker-VFW, and Spain by Construcciones Aeronauticas SA (CASA), were later to join this manufacturing group.

In December 1970 Airbus Industrie was established to manage the development, manufacture, marketing, and support of the A300. Aérospatiale, of which Sud-Aviation had become a part, was responsible for manufacture of the entire fuselage nose (including the flight deck), the lower centre fuselage, engine pylons, and also for the final assembly. Deutsche Airbus was concerned with the major proportion of the fuselage structure (including the forward fuselage between the flight deck and wing box), the upper centre fuselage, the rear fuselage, and the vertical tail surfaces. Hawker Siddeley Aviation, now British Aerospace, designed the advanced wing and works in collaboration with Fokker-VFW, now Fokker, which builds the wing's moving surfaces. CASA, in Spain, is responsible for the horizontal tail surfaces, fuselage main doors, and the landing gear doors.

The General Electric CF6 turbofan which McDonnell Douglas had chosen to power the DC-10 was selected for the A300. But whereas the DC-10

was a three-engine installation, the requirements of the European transport could be met by two of these large turbofans, mounted in underwing pods. This was a forward-looking aspect of the detail design, for the choice of an underwing pod-mounted installation means that virtually any turbine engine in the 50,000-lb (22680-kg) thrust class can be introduced to meet the requirements of individual operators. Thus, SAS were operating in the spring of 1980 two A300s (out of 4 plus 8 options on order) with Pratt & Whitney JT9D-59A turbofans of 53,000-lb (24040-kg) thrust, and Garuda Indonesian Airways and Iberia have both specified Pratt & Whitney engines for their outstanding orders. CF6 engines are installed in engine nacelles virtually identical to those of the McDonnell Douglas DC-10-30 and the nacelles are, in fact, supplied by that manufacturer. The General Electric CF6 engines, however, are assembled under licence by SNECMA in France, and both SNECMA and MTU in Germany build a percentage of the engine components under licence.

From the time that France and West Germany decided to go ahead with the construction of the first development aircraft in 1969, there has been only one major change in the airframe design, namely an increase of 3 in (0.08 m) in fuselage diameter, to make the freight holds compatible with those of US transports, and permit the interchange of US-adopted standard freight con-

tainers. In other respects the changes were limited to refinements, so that final detail design could end and manufacture begin.

An advanced feature of the A300 is the wing designed by Hawker Siddeley. This has moderate sweep-back of 28°, but the special wing section provides good distribution of lift across the entire wing chord. This has allowed the construction of a thicker, structurally more efficient wing, which not only enhances low-speed performance, but offers also greater fuel capacity. It incorporates leading-edge slats, Fowler type double-slotted trailing-edge flaps, all-speed ailerons (inboard) and low-speed ailerons (outboard), plus spoilers forward of the flaps on the wing upper surfaces, three acting as lift dumpers and four as airbrakes on each wing. The all-speed ailerons droop when the flaps are operated, and the Fowler flaps increase wing chord by 25% when fully extended. All flying controls are power-actuated via triplicated hydraulic systems, without a manual reversion system. Thus all three hydraulic circuits give priority to ailerons, elevators, and rudder; additionally, each of the three circuits fulfil secondary tasks, some of which have duplicated cover. In the event of failure of both engines, and consequently of the engine-driven hydraulic pump, a ram-air turbine-driven hydraulic pump is able to provide adequate standby power for essential flying control function. The retractable tricycle type landing gear has twin wheels on the nose unit, and four-wheel main units, each

Despite the hopes of Airbus Industrie for a wide breakthrough into the North American market for the A300, the only order so far received has been from Eastern Air Lines, which has two A300B2 and 12 A300B4 airliners.

comprising two tandem-mounted two-wheel bogies. Accommodation varies according to role and the requirements of individual airlines, but A300B2/B4 aircraft provide for a crew of three on the flight deck, with seating layouts for from 220 to a maximum of 336 passengers.

Construction of the first A300B1 began in September 1969 and this aircraft (initially F-WUAB) made its first flight on 28 October 1972, the second similar aircraft (F-WUAC) flying on 5 February 1973. The first two A300B2 aircraft, representing

the basic production version, flew on 28 June 1973 (F-WUAD) and 20 November 1973 (F-WUAA), and these four aircraft flew a combined total of almost 1,600 hours before French and German certification was gained on 15 March 1974. FAA certification, which included automatic approach and landing in Category 2 weather conditions, was received on 30 May 1974. Category 3A certification for automatic approach and landing was awarded on 30 September 1974.

The first A300B2s entered service

In the early 1980s Iberia was iln the process of acquiring the Airbus Industrie A300B4 wide-body airliner, with orders for four and options for another four.

with Air France on 30 May 1974, operating on the company's Paris-London route and making an immediate favourable impact on passengers. Comfortable and quiet internally, they also pleased near-airport dwellers, for the new-generation engines were significantly quieter than those of the majority of air transports. Continuing operations

proved that the claims of the 'marketing boys' had not been exaggerated, for the A300s were economical and reliable and, to complete the overall respect that these aircraft were earning, the ground crews found them easy to operate and maintain. Despite this excellent showing of a new airliner, orders were slow to materialise. There must have been moments during the mid-1970s when Airbus Industrie's management spent sleepless nights as they questioned whether Britain's failure to join the consortium, as a result of misgivings about sales prospects, had perhaps been justified. To highlight the situation, only one A300 was sold during 1976, and total sales at the end of 1977 covered 53 firm orders and 41 options. Once again it seemed that a European airliner, despite its excellence, had little chance of breaking into a market dominated by the US aircraft industry.

1979 saw a change of fortune, the big break coming on 6 April 1978 when Eastern Air Lines bought four A300B4s which it had been operating on an evaluation basis for six months, and then followed this with an order for 34 more aircraft (25 firm, 9 options). In fact, during 1978 a total of 70 firm orders were gained (plus 27 options), more than doubling the order book, and bringing new confidence to the consortium.

Also in 1978, it was decided to proceed with development and production of the short-fuselage A310, intended for short/medium-haul operations. Linked with this was the decision by the British government to become a risk-sharing partner of the group. Thus, in 1980, Aérospatiale and Deutsche Airbus each had a 37.9% interest. British Aerospace 20%, and CASA 4.2%. The initial A300B2 and A300B4 versions vary in having different fuel capacities and gross weights, and the longer-range B4 introduced wing-root leading-edge Krueger flaps to improve take-off performance. Development has been modest and, allied to some 10% increase in engine thrust, has been aimed at higher gross weight operation without penalising field performance. A convertible freighter version with the designation A300C4 has been developed: this has a large cargo door opening into the main cabin on the port side, a reinforced cabin floor, and a smoke detection system in the main cabin. Operable in all cargo, mixed cargo/passenger, or all passenger configurations, the first of these A300C4s was delivered to Hapag-Lloyd Fluggesellschaft in early 1980.

In the early summer of 1980 a total of 275 A300s had been ordered (194 firm orders, 81 options), of which 93 had been delivered. These figures do not include orders and options for the A310. Airbus Industrie has every reason, therefore, to be optimistic for the future, for even with allowance for the planned growth of airlines failing to reach the estimates projected for the 1990s, there seems little doubt that this economical, reliable airliner cannot fail to gain a fair share of the market. The following details apply to the A300B4-200.

Specification
Type: large-capacity short/medium-range commercial transport
Powerplant: two 52,500-lb (23814-kg) thrust General Electric CF6-50C1 advanced technology turbofans
Performance: maximum cruising speed 566 mph (911 km/h) at 25,000 ft (7620 m); long-range cruising speed 526 mph (847 km/h) at 31,000 ft (9450 m); range with 269 passengers and baggage 3,166 miles (5095 km); range with maximum fuel 3,685 miles (5930 km)
Weights: empty 176,000 lb (7983 kg); maximum take-off 363,760 lb (165000 kg)
Dimensions: span 147 ft 1¼ in (44.84 m); length 175 ft 11 in (53.62 m); height 54 ft 2¾ in (16.53 m); wing area 2,798.7 sq ft (260.0 m²)
Operators: Air Afrique, Air France, Air Inter, Alitalia, Cruzeiro, Eastern Air Lines Egyptair, Garuda, Hapag-Lloyd, Iberia, Indian Airlines, Iran Air, Korean Air Lines, Laker Airways, Lufthansa, Malaysian Airline System, Olympic Airways, Pakistan International, Philippine Airlines, SAS, Singapore Airlines, South African Airways, Thai International, Toa Domestic Airways, Trans-Australia Airlines, Trans European, Tunis Air, and others

Airbus A300B-2 cutaway drawing key

1. Weather radar scanner in upward-hinged radome
2. Dual control columns and rudder pedals
3. Flight deck for three crew members (plus optional observer seat)
4. Forward galley
5. Forward toilet
6. Water tank
7. Forward passenger-entry doors with attached escape-chutes (each side)
8. Folding seats for cabin crew
9. Galley service trolley
10. Control cables carried through under-floor beams
11. VHF blade antenna
12. Nose gear retraction jack
13. Nose gear drag strut
14. Overboard waste drain
15. Nose gear doors
16. Forward-retracting twin nosewheels
17. Main passenger-entry doors with attached escape-chutes (each side)
18. Power-operated forward cargo hold door
19. Escape-chute pack on starboard door
20. Cabin air-conditioning ducts
21. Type A2 cargo containers in forward hold
22. Eight-abreast passenger seating
23. Wing torsion-box carry-through structure
24. Air-conditioning equipment bay under torsion-box
25. Pressure-floor longitudinal beams
26. Starboard undercarriage door
27. Central walkway in undercarriage bay
28. Undercarriage bay aft pressure bulkhead
29. Emergency exit doors (each side)
30. Type A2 cargo containers in rear hold
31. VHF and ADF antennae in external fairing
32. Power-operated rear cargo door
33. Rearmost hold for non-containerized cargo
34. Manual plug-door for rearmost hold
35. Seven-abreast seating in aft passenger cabin
36. Overhead hat-racks
37. Air-conditioning valve gear and air outlet
38. Rear passenger-entry doors (each side)
39. Water tank
40. Optional seats at rear of cabin, or galley unit
41. Rear toilets (two each side)
42. Toilet collector tank
43. Water service panel
44. Overboard waste drain
45. Rear pressure dome
46. HF surface antenna
47. Fairing over fin-spar anchorages
48. Compressed air duct from APU
49. Tail bumper
50. Removable tailplane leading-edge
51. Tailplane pivot on reinforced fuselage frame
52. Tailplane inter-spar torsion-box, carried through fuselage
53. Tailplane hinge (Teflon swivel-bearing)

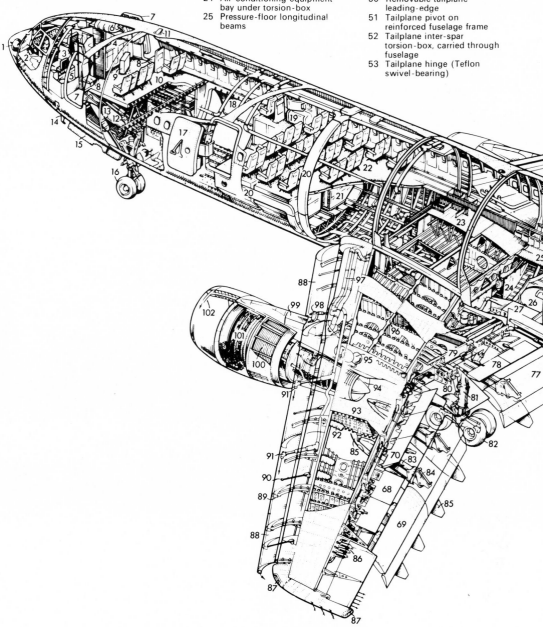

Airbus Industrie A300

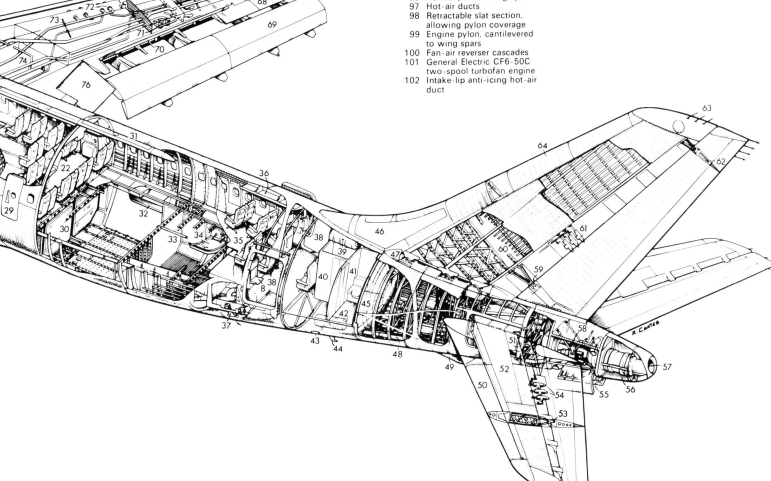

54 Triple elevator-actuating jacks
55 APU access doors (open)
56 Detachable tail cone
57 APU exhaust outlet
58 Garrett TSCP 700-5 auxiliary power unit
59 Rudder hinges (Teflon swivel bearings)
60 Multi-spar fin torsion-box
61 Triple rudder-actuating jacks
62 Rudder-section at topmost hinge
63 Static discharge wicks (at tips of all surfaces)
64 Detachable fin leading-edge
65 Low-speed aileron
66 Flush air intake for fuel-vent system
67 Outer integral fuel tank
68 Two-piece airflow spoilers
69 Outboard two-piece tabbed Fowler flaps (extended)
70 Three-piece air-brakes (open)
71 Fuel pumps (two per tank)
72 Refuelling points
73 Fuel contents indicators
74 Inner integral fuel tank
75 Fuel pipe circuitry
76 All-speed aileron (depressed)
77 Inboard tabbed Fowler flap section (extended)
78 Inboard two-piece lift-dumpers
79 Undercarriage load-bearing beam structure
80 Triple actuating jacks for all-speed aileron
81 Inwards-retracting main gear leg
82 Four-wheel main gear bogie
83 Flap track beam
84 Flap carriage
85 Flap track fairing
86 Triple actuating jacks for low-speed aileron
87 Navigation lamps

88 Three-piece full-span leading-edge slats (extended)
89 Slat tracks
90 Slat actuating jacks
91 Slat anti-icing hot-air ducts
92 Sealed cans in fuel tank, receiving retracted slat-tracks
93 Full-span inter-spar torsion-box structure, with integral fuel tanks
94 Engine jet efflux nozzle
95 Engine fire extinguisher bottles
96 Auxiliary inner wing spar
97 Hot-air ducts
98 Retractable slat section, allowing pylon coverage
99 Engine pylon, cantilevered to wing spars
100 Fan-air reverser cascades
101 General Electric CF6-50C two-spool turbofan engine
102 Intake-lip anti-icing hot-air duct

Trans-Australia Airlines is the national internal operator, and will have four Airbus Industrie A300B4 wide-body transports in service by the mid-1980s. The airline also maintains the aircraft of the Royal Flying Doctor Service.

27

Lufthansa

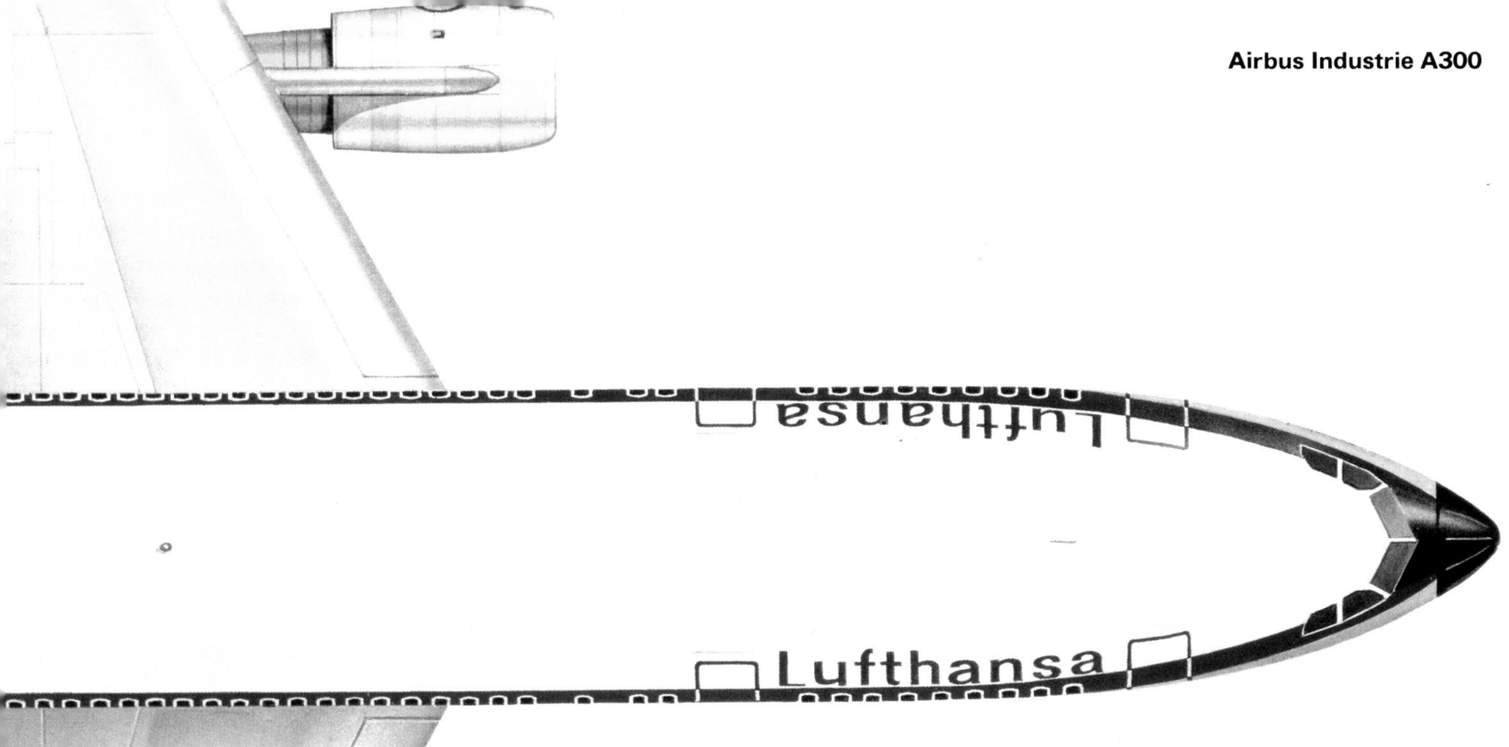

An Airbus Industrie A300B2 of Deutsche Lufthansa, West Germany's national airline. The only European competitor in the wide-bodied airliner field, the A300 enjoyed a spate of orders in 1978-9, and although this has since slowed down the future for the A300 and its A310 derivative looks promising. The largest single fleet of A300s comprises the 23 (with another 12 options) operated by Air France. Lufthansa is the second largest operator, with five **A300B2s** and six **A300B4s** in service, plus orders for 25 A310s and options for a further 25. There are two sub-models each of the **A300B2** and **A300B4**, all identical in exterior dimensions and very similar in outside appearance; however, the A300B4 models are intended for operations over longer ranges, and so have increased fuel capacities and higher gross weights. The A300B4-200 also has a strengthened structure and landing gear, plus larger tyres.

D-AIBC

Airbus A300

Airbus Industrie A310

History and Notes

From the early days of the 'European airbus' programme, one of the major difficulties facing the design team was a lack of clear guidance, from both European and world airlines, as to their specific requirements for a large capacity short-haul airliner. This resulted in proposals for a whole family of variants, numbering 11 at one period, the tenth (A300B10) much influenced by the requirements of British Airways for a smaller capacity, very economic aircraft. However, Britain's flag carrier was to show little interest in the Airbus proposal, but in the years that followed a number of European operators expressed growing enthusiasm for a version of about 200-seat capacity, especially if such an aircraft could offer fuel economy similar to that demonstrated by the A300B2/B4 already in service. Motivated by the growing interest, and by a more precise understanding of the requirement, the design and layout of the smaller-capacity variant, now identified as the A310, was finalised, and a decision made in July 1978 to proceed with its development.

The manufacturing process is able to take advantage of much commonality of components between the A300 and A310, for the latter is basically a shorter fuselage variant of the former. Lower-thrust versions of the CF6 or JT9D engines are standard, and the Rolls-Royce RB. 211-524B4 is available also if specified by any particular customer. Other changes include new engine pylons, modifications to the landing gear and tail unit, and new wings designed by the Hatfield/ Chester Division of British Aerospace. Although structurally similar to the wings of the A300, those for the A310 differ aerodynamically and provide a lift coefficient of 3.1 compared with 2.8 for the earlier design. This advance comes in part from continuing research by British Aerospace, but at the time when there was considerable uncertainty as to whether this company would become an active partner in the consortium, VFW initiated the design of a wing for the A310. The finalised design, therefore, benefits from the work of two design teams. Claimed to be aerodynamically more efficient throughout the entire flight regime than the earlier wing, this factor (coupled with optimum utilisation of the available cabin space) should enable the A310 to demonstrate an exceptional 'fuel per seat' factor when it begins to enter service in early 1983.

Variants which have been planned include the basic short-range A310-100, medium-range A310-200, A310C-200 convertible, A310F-200 freighter and A310-300 higher-weight versions. Some 129 had been ordered by the early summer of 1980 (63 firm orders and 66 options), with either General Electric or Pratt & Whitney engines specified for them. A flight crew of three will be standard, and accommodation will vary from a typical 214 mixed-class layout (18 first-class seats six-abreast) to a high-density one-class configuration for a maximum of 255 passengers. The following details apply to the A310-100.

Specification

Type: large-capacity short/medium-range commercial transport
Powerplant: two 46,500-lb (21092-kg) thrust General Electric CF6-45B2A advanced technology turbofans ·

Performance: (estimated) maximum operating speed 414 mph (667 km/h); range with 234 passengers, allowances for ground manoeuvring, 288-mile (463-km) diversion and 30-min hold, 2,110 miles (3395 km)
Weights: empty 166,204 lb (75389 kg); maximum take-off 266,760 lb (121000 kg)

Dimensions: span 144 ft 0¼ in (43.90 m); length 154 ft 10¾ in (47.21 m); height 51 ft 10½ in (15.81 m); wing area 2,367.0 sq ft (219.89 m²)
Orders: Air Afrique, Air France, Austrian Airlines, British Caledonian Airways, KLM, Lufthansa, Martinair, Sabena, Swissair

Airbus Industrie A310 cutaway drawing key

1 Radome
2 Radar scanner
3 Pressure bulkhead
4 Radar scanner mounting
5 Windscreen panels
6 Windscreen wipers
7 Instrument panel shroud
8 Control column
9 Rudder pedals
10 Cockpit floor level
11 ILS aerial
12 Access ladder to lower deck equipment bays
13 Pitot tubes
14 Captain's seat
15 First officer's seat
16 Overhead systems control panel
17 Engineer's control panel
18 Circuit breaker panel
19 Flight engineer's seat
20 Cockpit air conditioning duct
21 Observer's seat
22 Cockpit bulkhead
23 Wardrobe/locker
24 Nose undercarriage wheel well
25 Retraction jack
26 Twin nosewheels
27 Steering jacks
28 Nosewheel doors
29 Forward toilet
30 Galley
31 Starboard entry door
32 Cabin attendant's folding seat
33 Curtained cabin divider
34 Cabin attendant's seat
35 Port main entry door
36 Door latch
37 Door surround structure
38 Radio and electronics racks
39 Fuselage frame and stringer construction
40 Floor beam construction
41 Forward freight hold
42 Freight hold door
43 VHF communications aerial
44 Starboard engine nacelle
45 Curtained cabin divider
46 First class passenger compartment, 20 seats
47 Overhead baggage lockers
48 Air conditioning ducting
49 Baggage pallets
50 Pressurised fresh water tanks
51 Slat drive gearbox

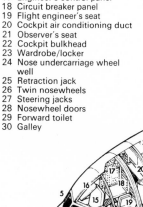

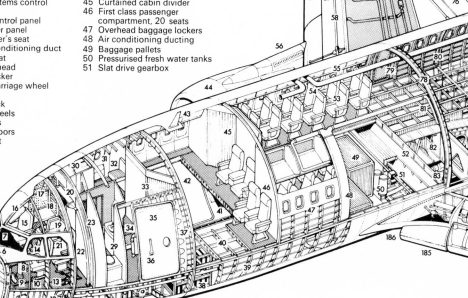

Airbus Industrie A310

The Airbus Industrie A310 is in essence a reduced-scale version of the A300, but the opportunity has been taken to develop a new wing with superior low-speed and cruise characteristics.

Airbus Industrie A310 of British Caledonian Airways.

52 Wing centre section spar
53 Tourist class seating, 197 seats
54 Air distribution ducting
55 Overhead stowage bins
56 Starboard nacelle pylon
57 Slat screw jacks
58 Screw jack drive shaft
59 Refuelling connections
60 Fuel system piping
61 Starboard wing integral fuel tanks
62 Leading edge slats
63 Slat fence
64 Leading edge de-icing
65 Starboard navigation lights
66 Wing tip fairing
67 Static discharge wicks
68 Fixed portion of trailing edge
69 Starboard spoilers
70 Flap drive mechanism
71 Airbrakes
72 Fuel jettison pipe
73 Outer double slotted Fowler flap
74 Starboard all-speed aileron
75 Inboard double slotted flap
76 Lift dumper/airbrake
77 Flap drive shaft
78 Wing attachment fuselage main frames
79 Starboard overwing emergency exit
80 Fuselage centre section construction
81 Centre section floor beams

82 Wing carry-through structure
83 Ventral air conditioning pack
84 Port overwing emergency exit door
85 Pressure floor above wheel well bay
86 Starboard main undercarriage retracted position
87 Undercarriage door jack
88 Equipment bay walkway
89 Undercarriage bay bulkhead
90 Flap drive motor
91 Hydraulic reservoir
92 Eight-abreast tourist class seating
93 DF loop aerial fairing
94 Cabin wall trim panels
95 Fuselage frame and stringer construction
96 Rear freight hold door
97 Baggage pallets
98 Freight hold rear bulkhead
99 Cabin floor panels
100 Seat attachment rails
101 Seven-abreast rear cabin seating
102 Central overhead stowage bins
103 Curtained rear cabin divider
104 Aft galley unit
105 Fin root fillet
106 HF notch aerial

107 Starboard tailplane
108 Starboard elevator
109 Fin leading edge
110 Fin construction
111 Fin tip fairing
112 Static discharge wicks
113 Rudder construction
114 Triplex rudder hydraulic jacks
115 APU intake duct
116 Garrett GTCP331 auxiliary power unit

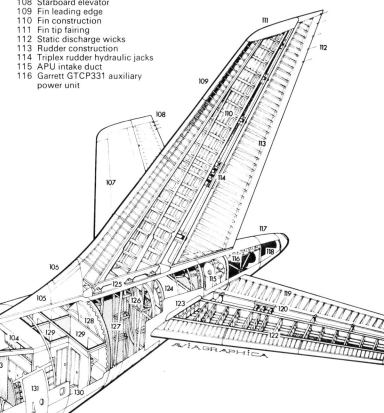

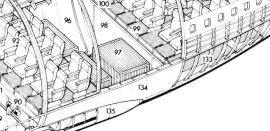

117 Tailcone fairing
118 APU exhaust duct
119 Port elevator construction
120 Elevator triplex hydraulic jacks
121 Static discharge wicks
122 Port tailplane construction
123 Moving tailplane sealing fairing
124 Tailplane centre section
125 Fin attachment joints
126 Tailplane trim screw jack
127 Fin support structure
128 Rear pressure bulkhead
129 Rear toilet compartments
130 Cabin attendant's folding seat
131 Rear entry door

132 Cabin window panel
133 Bulk cargo hold
134 Fuselage skin plating
135 Wing trailing edge fillet
136 Port inboard flap
137 Lift dumper/airbrake
138 Undercarriage side struts
139 Main undercarriage pivot fixing
140 Inboard flap drive mechanism
141 Flap track fairing
142 Aileron triplex hydraulic jacks
143 Port all-speed aileron
144 Port airbrakes
145 Flap down position
146 Flap guide rails
147 Flap track fairings
148 Fuel jettison pipe
149 Port roll spoilers
150 Fixed portion of trailing edge
151 Static discharge wicks
152 Wing tip fairing
153 Port navigation lights

154 Wing rear spar
155 Front spar
156 Port leading edge slats
157 Leading edge de-icing
158 Slat fence
159 Screw jacks
160 Slat guide rails
161 Wing rib construction
162 Port outer wing fuel tank
163 Telescopic de-icing air duct
164 Wing stringer construction
165 Wing skin joint strap
166 Main undercarriage leg strut
167 Retraction jack
168 Port main undercarriage four-wheel bogie
169 Nacelle pylon attachment joint
170 Engine pylon
171 Exhaust nozzle
172 Fan air duct exhaust
173 Reverser cascade, closed
174 Bleed air piping
175 General Electric CF6-45B2A/B turbofan
176 Engine fan blades
177 Intake duct
178 Intake de-icing air pipes
179 Detachable engine cowlings
180 Bleed air system pre-cooler
181 Inboard leading edge slat
182 Bleed air delivery pipes
183 Inner wing integral fuel tank
184 Three-spar inboard wing construction
185 Wing root Krueger flap
186 Leading-edge wing root fillet

Antonov An-2

History and Notes

With an interest in gliding that dated from his schooldays, Oleg Antonov was to become an established designer of gliders and sailplanes. During World War II he was concerned primarily with development and production of aircraft, but worked also as a designer within the Yakovlev organisation. Postwar he formed his own bureau to design and develop a new 'do anything—go anywhere' aeroplane, resulting in the An-2, identified briefly as the SKh-1 (*Selskokhozyaistvennyi*-1, or agricultural-economic-1) before the Antonov designation was applied. It is a most appropriate designation, if for no other reason than the fact that the letters An begin the word anachronism, which is how an observer in the 1980s must regard this large biplane. First flown in prototype form on 31 August 1947, it still continues in production, although not by Antonov in the USSR since the late 1960s.

A single-bay sesquiplane, with a single streamline interplane strut on each side and dual flying- and landing-wire bracing, the An-2 is almost entirely of all-metal construction. The exceptions are the wings, aft of the front spar, and tailplane, which are fabric-covered. The large-capacity fuselage is a semi-monocoque structure, providing a comfortable heated and ventilated crew compartment to accommodate two. The tailplane is strut braced, and the robust wide-track tailwheel type landing gear can be provided with low-pressure tyres, floats or skis, to cater for all surfaces.

Exceptional operating characteristics are provided by the wings: the upper wing includes electrically actuated automatic leading-edge slots, trailing-edge slotted flaps, and ailerons which can be used conventionally for roll control, but can also be drooped collectively up to 20° to complement the flaps. The lower wing has only full-span slotted trailing-edge flaps. Powerplant of the prototype consisted of a 760-hp (567-kW) Shvetsov ASh-21 radial engine, but later production aircraft from Antonov had a 1,000-hp (746-kW) Shvetsov ASh-62IR engine.

Russian-built versions have included the An-2P basic general-purpose aircraft, An-2S agricultural version of the same aircraft, An-2M specially-developed agricultural version, An-2V floatplane, and an An-2L water-bomber, able to uplift a volume of water in its floats. Production in Poland by WSK-PZL Mielec began in 1960, and is continuing. Designations of Polish-built versions include the An-2P passenger transport, An-2PK five-seat executive transport, An-2P-Photo equipped for photogrammetry, An-2PR for a tele-

vision relay role, An-2R agricultural, An-2S ambulance, An-2T equivalent to Soviet An-2P, An-2TD paratroop transport, An-2TP cargo/passenger transport, An-2M equivalent to Soviet An-2V, and an An-2 Geofiz geophysical survey aircraft. The An-2 has also been built under licence in China as the Type 5 Transport Aeroplane, and combined production from the three above sources is estimated at 15,000, of which about 60% have been built in Poland.

An-2s are still used extensively, and also in a variety of roles not included among the above designations. They have served widely in a passenger transport capacity (carrying up to 12 adults and 2 children) with Aeroflot and airlines of countries aligned with the East, but very few now remain in scheduled service: those of Interflug are possibly the last to be listed in such a role, but there is no doubt that many of these reliable aircraft are still used for passenger carrying, among other routine tasks.

Antonov An-2 of Cubana (Empresa Consolidata Cubana de Aviación), Cuba.

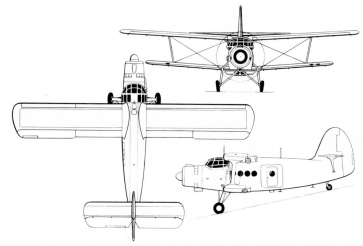

Antonov An-2

Specification

Type: general-purpose biplane
Powerplant (Polish An-2P): one 1,000-hp (746-kW) Shvetsov ASh-62IR radial piston engine
Performance: maximum speed 160 mph (258 km/h) at 5,740 ft (1750 m); economic cruising speed 115 mph (185 km/h); service ceiling 14,425 ft (4400 m); range 560 miles (901 km) with 1,102-lb (500-kg) payload at optimum altitude
Weights: empty 7,605 lb (3450 kg);

maximum take-off 12,125 lb (5500 kg)
Dimensions: span, upper 59 ft 7¾ in (18.18 m), lower 46 ft 8½ in (14.24 m); length 41 ft 9½ in (12.74 m); height 13 ft 1½ in (4.00 m);

wing area, upper 469.32 sq ft (43.60 m²), lower 301.4 sq ft (28.0 m²)
Operators include: Aeroflot, Interflug, and many airlines and air forces aligned with the Soviet Union

The Antonov An-2 is a magnificent anachronism: a large single-engined biplane. The type is still in production in Poland and plays a significant part in a number of roles—AN-2P passenger carrier, AN-2S or R agricultural version, An-2M improved model, An-2V or M floatplane, An-2L water bomber and several others.

Antonov An-12

History and Notes

In 1955 the Antonov bureau began the design of a four-turboprop pressurised civil airliner which was duly designated An-10 and named Ukraina. In its initial version, first flown in March 1957, there was accommodation for 84 passengers, but the lengthened fuselage An-10A which followed had standard seating for 100 passengers, or up to 130 in a high-density seating arrangement. Of high-wing monoplane configuration, the An-10 was of all-metal construction, had hydraulically actuated double-slotted Fowler type trailing-edge flaps, a tail unit which

included two large ventral fins, and a hydraulically actuated tricycle type landing gear with a twin-wheel steerable nose unit and a four-wheel bogie on each main unit. The powerplant comprised four Ivchenko turboprop engines, each driving four-blade reversible-pitch propellers. There followed an extended development period, and the An-10 did not enter operation with Aeroflot until 1959, the first scheduled service being flown on 22 July. The type was withdrawn from airline use in 1972.

Developed simultaneously with the An-10, the An-12 was a generally similar transport for military service

with the Soviet air force. Major difference was the provision of a completely new rear fuselage which was more sharply upswept to incorporate under-fuselage loading doors which, when opened, allowed for the direct onloading of vehicles. Also included was a gunner's position in the extreme tail position, the gunner being seated just below the trailing-edge of the rudder. The An-12 became a standard freight and paratroop transport in Soviet air force use, some 500-600 remaining in service in 1980 for this purpose, plus a small number equipped especially as airborne early warning and/or elec-

tronics countermeasures aircraft. An-12s have been supplied also for service with the air forces of countries such as Algeria, Bangladesh, Egypt, India, Indonesia, Iraq, Poland, Sudan, Syria and Yugoslavia.

In 1965 a civil version of the An-12 was demonstrated at the Paris Air Show. This had a differing arrangement of underfuselage doors which folded to permit the use of a detachable ramp for loading and unloading. Between the main aft cargo hold and the flight deck, a pressurised area was provided, this allowing for the accommodation of 14 passengers. These mixed passenger/cargo An-

Antonov An-12

12s began to enter service with Aeroflot in February 1966, and these have the tail gun position of the military freighter deleted and enclosed by a smooth fairing. Since that time civil An-12s have been supplied for similar mixed passenger/cargo services with several airlines.

Specification
Type: mixed passenger/cargo transport
Powerplant: four 4,000-ehp (2983-kW) Ivchenko AI-20K turboprops
Performance: maximum cruising speed 373 mph (600 km/h); normal cruising speed 342 mph (550 km/h) at 25,000 ft (7620 m); service ceiling 33,465 ft (10200 m); range 2,113 miles (3400 km) with 22,046-lb (10000-kg) payload and 1 hour fuel reserves
Weights: normal take-off 119,050 lb (54000 kg); maximum take-off 134,482 lb (61000 kg)
Dimensions: span 124 ft 8 in (38.00 m); length 108 ft 7¼ in (33.10 m); height 34 ft 6½ in (10.53 m); wing area 1,310 sq ft (121.70 m²)
Operators include: Aeroflot, Air Guinée, Balkan Bulgarian Airlines, CAAC, Egyptair, Iraqi Airways, and LOT Polish Airlines

Aeroflot still has in service some 200 Antonov An-12 freighters, but the only other European civil operator of the type is Balkan Bulgarian Airlines, which has a single example. Air Guinée has three, and Iraqi Airways has disposed of six.

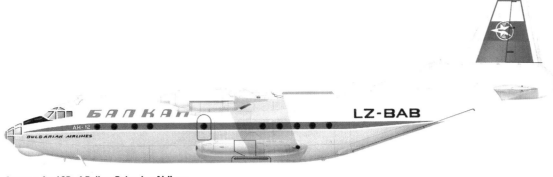

Antonov An-12B of Balkan Bulgarian Airlines.

Antonov An-14/-28 Series

History and Notes
The Antonov An-14 'Clod' was designed in 1957 as a STOL (short-take-off-and-landing) freighter and feederliner, with handling characteristics which would enable it to be flown by inexperienced pilots. With its high-aspect-ratio braced wing and twin tailfins, it shows signs of inspiration from the French Hurel-Dubois transports of the early 1950s, the experimental designs which also led to the British Shorts Skyvan and 330.

The development of the An-14 was protracted, and it was not until 1965 that the type entered service. Production versions feature a very different tail design from the prototype, and the planform of the wing and the arrangement of the high-lift devices are also modified. The nose was slightly lengthened, and clamshell doors were fitted to the rear fuselage.

If the evolution of the An-14 has been slow, that of its turboprop development, the An-28, has been even less hurried. It was announced in 1967 that a turboprop version of the type was under development, and the first prototype, designated An-14M, flew at Kiev in September 1969. Powered by two 810-shp (604-kW) TVD-850 turboprops, the new version was stretched to accommodate up to 15 passengers, and weighed 12,500 lb (5600 kg) fully loaded. A production prototype of the aircraft was demonstrated in 1974, at which time the change in designation to An-28 was announced. The Soviet press continues to report the progress of the An-28 and Aeroflot was to have introduced it as a feederliner in 1980. Production is by PZL in Poland.

All variants of the An-14 and An-28 share the same pod-and-boom fuselage layout, permitting easy loading of cargo in the freight role. The high wing carries full-span double-slotted flaps and slats, ailerons being built into the outer flap sections.

Specification
Type: (An-14) light STOL transport
Powerplant: two 300-hp (224-kW) Ivchenko AI-14RF radial piston engines
Performance: cruising speed 105-120 mph (170-180 km/h) at 6,560 ft (2000 m); maximum range with six passengers or 1,200-lb (570-kg) payload 400 miles (650 km); service ceiling 16,400 ft (5000 m); take-off run 330-360 ft (100-110 m); landing run 360 ft (110 m)
Weights: empty 5,700 lb (2600 kg); normal take-off 7,600 lb (3450 kg); maximum take-off 8,000 lb (3630 kg)
Dimensions: span 72 ft 3 in (22.0 m); length 37 ft 3½ in (11.36 m); height 15 ft 2½ in (4.63 m); wing area 422.8 sq ft (39.72 m²)
Type: (An-28) light STOL transport
Powerplant: two 960-shp (715-kW)

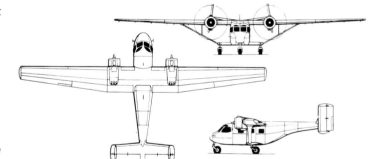

Antonov An-14 'Clod'

PZL-built Glushenkov TVD-10V turboprops
Performance: maximum cruising speed 217 mph (350 km/h); economical cruising speed 186 mph (300 km/h); range with 20 passengers 317 miles (510 km)
Weights: empty 7,716 lb (3500 kg); maximum take-off 13,448 lb (6100 kg)

Dimensions: span 72 ft 4½ in (22.06 m); length 42 ft 7 in (12.98 m); height 15 ft 1 in (4.6 m); wing area 433.5 sq ft (40.28 m²)

The Antonov An-28 started life as a turboprop version of the An-14, but has been widely modified before entering production in Poland. Aeroflot will use the type for its extensive network.

Antonov An-22

History and Notes

The Soviet Union has always been faced with the difficult problem of transporting cargo across its vast territories: this results not only from the very long distances involved, but also from a wide variety of terrain, and the need to provide a service of this nature into areas where little or no surface routes exist. Air transport has provided a solution to this problem, and explains why there has been considerable development and production of cargo and cargo/passenger aircraft in the USSR.

Antonov's bureau was given the task in early 1962 of originating the design of an aircraft which would be able to carry heavy or large loads over long ranges and which would, in addition, be able to operate from and into a variety of unprepared fields. The resulting An-22 prototype was flown for the first time on 27 February 1965, and was first seen by the Western aerospace industry when exhibited at the Paris Air Show some four months later. Almost certainly this aircraft was the prototype, and it was then suggested that in addition to being available as a bulk cargo transporter, it was also to be made available in civil airliner form, with upper and lower deck cabins to accommodate a total of 724 passengers. Two years later, again at the Paris Show, came the news that this latter proposal had been abandoned.

Antonov's design to meet the demanding requirements has resulted in a very large all-metal aircraft of high-wing monoplane configuration, the wing including wide-span double-slotted trailing-edge flaps. The large-capacity fuselage includes an upswept rear section with a large loading-ramp door for direct onloading of vehicles, and to provide stability

Antonov An-22 of Aeroflot, USSR.

during such operations, retractable jacks can be extended at a point adjacent to the loading ramp hinges. Twin fins extend above and below the tailplane, with the rudders likewise in two halves. The landing gear is of the retractable tricycle type, but is designed to permit off-runway operation: the steerable nose unit carries twin wheels, but each main unit consists of three twin-wheel levered-suspension units in tandem, so that on the ground the An-22 is supported on no fewer than 14 wheels. Tyre pressures of these wheels are adjustable in flight, or on the ground, to provide optimum performance for any particular airfield surface. It is reported that operation into and from water-sodden grass fields is possible.

Powerplant of production An-22s comprises four Kuznetsov turboprop engines, each of which drives a pair of contra-rotating four-blade propellers. Accommodation is provided for a crew of five or six, and in common with many Soviet transport aircraft, there is a small cabin area at the forward end of the fuselage, aft of the flight deck, with seating for 28 or 29 passengers. Travelling gantries and winches are provided in the main cabin area to facilitate the handling of cargo.

An-22s have established many payload-to-height and speed-with-payload records and, so far as is known, is still the only Soviet aircraft

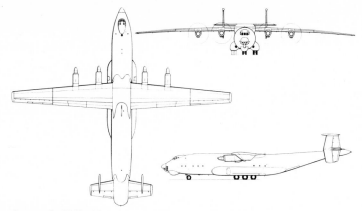

Antonov An-22 'Cock'

able to airlift the army's T-62 tank. Serving both with Aeroflot and the Soviet air force, the numbers remaining in service in 1980 were estimated at 20-30 and 40-50 respectively.

Specification

Type: long-range heavy transport
Powerplant: four 15,000-shp (11186-kW) Kuznetsov NK-12MA turboprops
Performance: maximum speed 460 mph (740 km/h); cruising speed 348-398 mph (560-640 km/h); range 3,107 miles (5000 km) with maximum payload; range 6,804 miles (10950 km) with maximum

fuel and 99,208-lb (45000-kg) payload
Weights: empty equipped 251,327 lb (114000 kg); maximum take-off 551,156 lb (250000 kg)
Dimensions: span 211 ft 3½ in (64.40 m); length 189 ft 7½ in (57.80 m); height 41 ft 1¼ in (12.53 m); wing area 3,713.7 sq ft (345 m²)
Operators: Aeroflot, and Soviet air force

In its time the largest aircraft in the world, the Antonov An-22 heavy freighter is still a prodigious aircraft used in small numbers by Aeroflot for the movement of exceptionally heavy or bulky loads into inhospitable regions.

Antonov An-24/-26/-30/-32 Series

History and Notes

With the requirement for a turbine-engined short-range civil transport to replace the piston-engined Ilyushin Il-14 in Aeroflot service, the Antonov bureau initiated in late 1957 the design of a 32/40-seat aircraft which could be employed over short/medium-range routes. Its design had to include the ability to operate from small unpaved airfields, and also required that flight characteristics and powerplant should be such that it could be used between points with considerable variations in altitude and/or temperature. It was not until just over two years later, in April 1960, that the first of two prototypes had flown; the period between the beginning of the design and completion of the first prototype had been extended somewhat by a capacity change to 44-seat accommodation.

Typically 'Antonov' in its high-wing configuration, the An-24 is fitted with a wing having wide-span Fowler type trailing-edge flaps, these being double-slotted outboard of the engine nacelles, and single-slotted inboard. The tail unit is conventional, with the addition of a fairly large ventral fin on production aircraft, and the fuselage is a semi-monocoque structure introducing bonded/welded construction. The hydraulically retractable tricycle type landing gear has twin wheels on each unit, a steerable and fully castoring nose unit, and includes the means of adjusting tyre pressures in flight, or on the ground, to permit operation from a variety of different surfaces. The powerplant comprises two Ivchenko AI-24A turboprop engines, each driving a constant-speed fully-feathering propeller.

Production aircraft began to enter service with Aeroflot in 1962 for crew training and proving flights, but it was not until September 1963 that the first 50-seat An-24Vs were used on the routes between Moscow, Voronezh and Saratov. Subsequent versions have included the An-24V Srs II, available with standard 50-passenger accommodation, but also with alternative mixed passenger/freight, convertible cargo/passenger, all-freight, or executive interiors; the An-24RV, similar to the foregoing, but with a 1,985-lb (900-kg) thrust auxiliary turbojet installed in the starboard engine nacelle and used for remote field engine starting, and operable also to improve take-off or airborne performance; the An-24T, equipped as a specialised freighter with the standard rear cabin passenger door deleted and replaced by an upward-opening ventral freight door, with twin ventral fins outboard of the freight door to replace the single ventral fin, and with cargo hoist and conveyor installed; and the An-24RT, as the An-24T but with auxiliary turbojet installed. Also evaluated was an An-24P, equipped to airdrop parachute-equipped firefighters to provide fast reaction to newly-reported forest fires.

Closely related versions of the An-24 include the An-26, which began to enter service during 1970, and is distinguished by more powerful 2,820-ehp (2103-ekW) Ivchenko AI-24T engines and a redesigned rear fuselage. The An-26 introduced a large downward-hinged rear ramp/door, which can be slid forward below the cabin floor to facilitate airdropping of freight or the direct loading of cargo at truckbed height.

The An-30 is basically a special aerial survey version of the An-26, using a similar powerplant, an ex-

Antonov An-24RV of Tarom (Transporturile Aeriene Romane).

tensively glazed nose and raised flight deck, and with four camera apertures; it was first flown in 1974. Final version is the An-32, with an airframe generally similar to that of the An-26, but introducing larger ventral fins and a full-span slotted tailplane. The major difference is the provision of 5,180-ehp (3863-ekW) Ivchenko AI-20M turboprop engines to give improved high-altitude/high-temperature performance. A single prototype of this version was completed and flown in 1979, and arrangements had been made in early 1980 for limited licence production in India, the plans subsequently being dropped and then resurrected in 1981.

Extensively used by Aeroflot, An-24s have served also with at least 14 airlines and many armed services. An-26s and An-30s are also used by Aeroflot in small numbers, and both are known to serve with some air forces. The specification applies to the An-24.

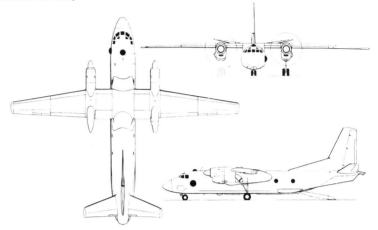

Antonov An-24V 'Coke'

Specification

Type: short-range transport
Powerplant: two 2,550-ehp (1902-ekW) Ivchenko AI-24A turboprops
Performance: (An-24V) cruising speed 280 mph (450 km/h); service ceiling 27,560 ft (8400 m); range with maximum payload 342 miles (550 km); range with maximum fuel 1,491 miles (2440 km)
Weights: (An-24V) empty 29,321 lb (13300 kg); maximum take-off 49,297 lb (21000 kg)
Dimensions: span 95 ft 9½ in (29.20 m); length 77 ft 2½ in (23.53 m); height 27 ft 3½ in (8.32 m); wing area 807.1 sq ft (74.98 m²)
Operators include: Aeroflot, Air Guinée, Air Mali, Air Mongol, Balkan Bulgarian Airlines, CAAC, Cubana, Egyptair, Hang Khong Viet-Nam, Interflug, Iraqi Airways, Lao Aviation, Lebanese Air Transport, Lina Congo, LOT Polish Airlines, and Tarom, plus a number of armed forces

The Antonov An-24 and its derivatives play an important part in Russian internal air services, on which some 700 of the family are deployed.

Antonov An-72

History and Notes

The prototype of Antonov's new An-72 twin-turbofan STOL freighter, the first jet aircraft produced by the Antonov bureau, is reported to have flown in December 1977 and was revealed to the West shortly afterwards. Its service status is uncertain; the prototype was shown in Aeroflot markings, but the type has obvious military applications.

Photographs of the An-72 released in early 1979 do not allow the accurate estimation of dimensions, but the general characteristics of the aircraft can be gauged by the size of the engines and the type's close resemblance to the Boeing YC-14 military transport. The Antonov bureau has elected to adopt the Boeing-developed concept of 'upper-surface-blowing', in which the exhaust from high-bypass-ratio turbofans is directed across specially designed trailing-edge flaps which divert the jet thrust downwards by the so-called Coanda effect. This principle demands the location of the engines above and ahead of the wing, close inboard to minimize the engine-out asymmetric problem. A T-tail is in consequence necessary, to lift the tailplane out of the wash from the engines.

The An-72 is considerably smaller than the US transport, being powered by two Lotarev D-36 three-shaft turbofans of 14,500-lb (6500-kg) thrust each, the first high-bypass-ratio engines to be developed in the Soviet Union. Comparison with the YC-14 suggests that the maximum-take-off weight would be in the region of 76,168 lb (34550 kg). Cruise speed is about Mach 0.7, but beyond this it is difficult to determine performance with any accuracy. The much larger Boeing YC-14 was designed to use 2,000-ft (600-m) strips.

The wing of the An-72 is fitted with full-span slats and double-slotted trailing-edge flaps on its outer sections, with the special USB flaps inboard. The main landing gear comprises four independent single-wheel units, retracting into bulges on the fuselage side. The fuselage is pressurised and is fitted with a rear loading door and integral ramp for the accommodation of small vehicles. Two ventral fins are fitted to the rear fuselage on either side of the ramp; they may be designed to reduce turbulence around the tail for parachute dropping.

It has been suggested that the An-72 may be a flying scale model of a larger military freighter, intended to prove the upper-surface-blowing concept, and that the aircraft may have flown before its 'official' first flight in 1977. The main problem in the design of an upper-surface-blowing STOL aircraft is ensuring stability and control in the event of an engine failure in partially jet-borne flight, and this demands high-authority sophisticated autopilots. Unless these problems can be solved, the An-72 is unlikely to enter service.

Specification unavailable

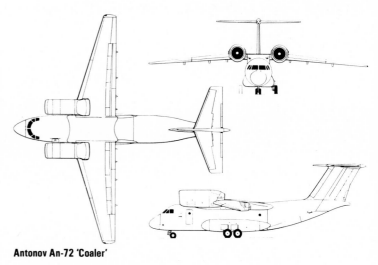

The production prospects of the Antonov An-72 advanced STOL transport are still uncertain, despite the presence of Aeroflot insignia on one of the prototype aircraft.

Antonov An-72 'Coaler'

Arctic Aircraft S1B2 Arctic Tern

History and Notes

The Interstate S1B Cadet was one of a number of high-wing two-seat light aircraft ordered for observation and liaison work early in World War II; others included the Piper Cub, and designs by Aeronca, Taylorcraft and Stinson. The Cadet went to war under the US Army designation L-6, and some 250 were built. A fair number survived to pass into civilian hands, but these have dwindled to a mere handful.

The design, however, has been resurrected, and the Arctic Aircraft Company at Anchorage, Alaska, has built a small batch under the name Arctic Tern. While the original Cadet used a 102-hp (76-kW) Franklin engine, the Tern has a 150-hp (112-kW) Avco Lycoming O-320, and improved construction techniques plus modern materials have resulted in an empty weight 40 lb (18 kg) less than the original design of 1940. Floats or skis, essential for all-season operations in Alaska, are optional fittings, as is a belly-mounted auxiliary fuel tank. The Tern's rear seat is removable to give additional space for cargo and the front seat can be folded for ease of loading; the cabin is soundproofed and carpeted.

Specification
Type: two-seat general utility monoplane
Powerplant: one 150-hp (112-kW) Avco Lycoming O-320 flat-four piston engine
Performance: maximum speed 175 mph (282 km/h); cruising speed 117 mph (188 km/h) at sea level; service ceiling 19,000 ft (5790 m); range 652 miles (1049 km)
Weights: empty 1,073 lb (487 kg); maximum take-off 1,900 lb (862 kg)
Dimensions: span 36 ft 0 in (10.97 m); length 24 ft 0 in (7.32 m); height 7 ft 0 in (2.13 m); wing area 186 sq ft (17.28 m²)

The Arctic Aircraft S1B2 Arctic Tern is an interesting example of the rejuvenation of an old design (in this case dating from 1940) with a new engine, detail refinements and versatile landing gear. Freight can be carried in the fuselage or in an underfuselage pack.

Armstrong Whitworth AW.650 Argosy

History and Notes

A British specification, issued in 1955 by the Air Ministry and calling for a medium-range freighter for military and civil applications, was the first step towards the AW.650 Argosy. In that year Armstrong Whitworth began work on a design project with twin booms and two turboprops, but by 1956 the chances of getting military orders dictated that emphasis should be placed on a civil version.

In September the company decided to proceed with a revised design as a private venture. Designated AW.650, the new aircraft had a twin-boom, four-turboprop layout and was initially named Freightliner, but this was changed to Argosy in July 1958. The designation became HS.650, reflecting Armstrong Whitworth's membership of the Hawker Siddeley Group.

The first Argosy flew at Bitteswell on 8 January 1959, less than two years after the drawings had been issued, and before the end of 1959 a further five had flown. The first four aircraft participated in the certification programme and a restricted certificate of airworthiness was issued in May 1959, full British and US certification being achieved in December 1960. The fourth aircraft was the first to appear in public—at the 1959 Paris Air Show, while the following year this and the fifth Argosy appeared at the Farnborough Show.

European demonstration tours in October 1959, as a combined passenger/freighter priced at £460,000 attracted interest but no orders. Riddle Airlines of Miami had been the first customer, ordering four (later increased to seven) Argosies in February 1959 to be used on bulky freight-carrying contracts for the US Air Force. On expiration of this contract, the seven Argosies were operated in the US by Capitol Airlines and Zantop Air Transport.

British European Airways took delivery of the first of three Argosy 102s in 1961 and operated its initial freight services in December of that year, replacing Douglas DC-3s and Avro Yorks. Ten Argosy Series 100 aircraft were built and all except one, the third aircraft, eventually found their way to USA. Operated by the companies mentioned above, at least four found their way back to the UK to operate with Sagittair, and later ABC, from East Midlands Airport. A batch of 56 AW.660 aircraft, based on the civil Argosy 100, was built for the RAF, which designated the type as Argosy C.Mk1.

The final Argosy variant was the Series 222, first of which flew in March 1964. An enlarged freight hold and wider doors permitted the carriage of six 108-in (2,74-m) cargo pallets, the standard size then in use on international jets. A redesigned

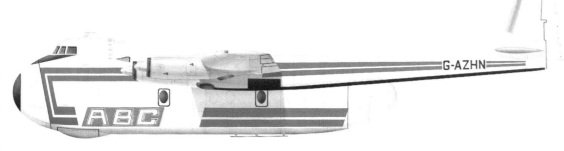

Armstrong Whitworth AW.650 Argosy 100 of Air-Bridge Carriers, UK.

wing saved 400 lb (181 kg) in weight and range was increased. With these improvements, BEA agreed to trade in its Series 102s in part exchange for five 222s; these were delivered between January 1965 and June 1966, and freight services were increased in frequency. Loss of one aircraft at Milan, in July 1965, caused BEA to buy the last of seven production aircraft (the first remained with the manufacturers until being withdrawn from use in November 1965), but when another Argosy was burnt out on the ground, in December 1967, no further replacement was made.

BEA's Argosy operations always lost money, and the corporation flew its last service with the type in April 1970. All four were subsequently sold to Transair at Winnipeg; later, two of these went to Australian freight operator IPEC, while the other two were sold to Safe Air in New Zealand. A few of the RAF aircraft eventually found their way to civil operators who were already using the Argosy, but one went to Philippine Air Lines. The specification applies to the Argosy Srs 100.

Specification

Type: four-engine transport aircraft

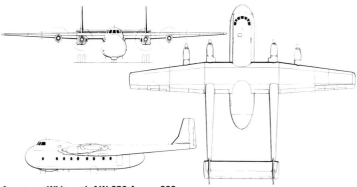

Armstrong Whitworth AW.650 Argosy 222

Powerplant: four 2,020-shp (1506-kW) Rolls-Royce Dart 526 turboprops
Performance: average cruising speed 280 mph (451 km/h); service ceiling 20,000 ft (6100 m); range 2,000 miles (3219 km)
Weights: empty 46,000 lb (20865 kg); maximum take-off 88,000 lb (39916 kg)
Dimensions: span 115 ft 0 in (35.05 m); length 86 ft 9 in (26.44 m); height 27 ft 0 in (8.23 m); wing area 1,458 sq ft (135.45 m²)
Operators: (civil): ABC (UK), BBA

Air Cargo (Australia), British European Airways, Capitol (USA), IPEC (Australia), Philippine Airlines, Riddle (USA), Rolls-Royce, Safe Air (New Zealand), Sagittair (UK), Transair (Canada), Zantop (USA)

The Hawker Siddeley (AW) Argosy freighter was in many respects ahead of its time, and was built only in small numbers. One of the major current users is an Australian company, IPEC Aviation, which uses its one Series 100 and two Series 200 Argosies for a freight service.

Auster (Beagle) D Series

History and Notes

The D Series aircraft were the final civil Auster variants in a long line which had developed from the prewar Taylorcraft. How the line would eventually have ended is hard to foretell, but the Auster Ds resulted from a Portuguese Air Force specification for a 2-3 seat liaison/training aircraft powered by an Avco Lycoming engine. Auster offered three basic types: the D.4/108 two-seater with an engine of 108 hp (81 kW), the D5/160 three-seater (160 hp:119 kW), and the D.6/180 four-seater (180 hp:134 kW), but there were variants

of these.

In November 1959 an agreement was signed whereby 20 complete aircraft (five D.4/180s and 15 D.5/160s) would be supplied to Portugal, and a further 150 would be assembled by the government factory (O.G.M.A.) in Lisbon from parts supplied by Auster. In addition to the Portuguese Air Force, deliveries went to aero clubs in that country and Angola.

UK production ended in 1961, after a few aircraft had been built for home and overseas customers. Apart from aircraft built for Portugal, three D.6/180s and one D.6/160 were joined

by two D.5/180s, a D.4/108, and 14 D.5/180s which were named Husky. Of the last, one went to Ghana, two to Tanzania, four to Burma, one to Austria and the remaining six were British registered. Five of the Portuguese Austers were assembled as D.5/180s and used for agricultural work.

When Auster was absorbed by the new Beagle company late in 1960, the aircraft adopted the company title of Beagle-Auster from 1962. The specification applies to the D.5/180 Husky.

Specification

Type: three-seat light monoplane
Powerplant: one 180-hp (134-kW) Avco Lycoming O-360-A2A flat-four piston engine
Performance: maximum speed 125 mph (201 km/h) at sea level; cruising speed 109 mph (175 km/h); service ceiling 14,500 ft (4420 m); range 580 miles (933 km)
Weights: empty 1,420 lb (644 kg); maximum take-off 2,400 lb (1089 kg)
Dimensions: span 36 ft 0 in (10.97 m); length 23 ft 2 in (7.06 m); height 8 ft 8 in (2.64 m); wing area 184 sq ft (17.09 m²)

Aviamilano P.19 Scricciolo

History and Notes

A side-by-side two-seater, the Avia-milano P.19 Scricciolo (Wren) was designed by Professor Ing. Ermenegildo Preti to meet the requirements of the Italian Aero Club. The prototype flew for the first time on 13 December 1959, and after receiving type approval in the following April, was delivered to the Milan Aero Club for evaluation.

An initial series of 25 aircraft was laid down at Aviamilano's factory at Bresso, Milan, and these had all been delivered by mid-1963 when work began on a similar batch. Three versions of the Scricciolo were offered. The first production batch, designated P.19, had a 100-hp (75-kW) Continental O-200-A engine with a two-blade fixed-pitch wooden propeller. Some were fitted with fixed tricycle landing gear in place of the normal tailwheel layout, and in this form were designated P.19trs. The prototype was completed in 1965,

but several of the earlier aircraft were retrofitted with the tricycle gear. Requirements for a glider tug led, in 1964, to the introduction of the P.19R with a 150-hp (112-kW) Lycoming O-320-A1A engine, which could use either a fixed-pitch or constant-speed propeller.

All versions of the Scricciolo had a welded steel-tube fuselage with fabric covering, while the wings and tail were of wooden construction, the wings with a glass-fibre reinforced plastic leading-edge.

Specification
Type: two-seat light monoplane
Powerplant: one 100-hp (75-kW) Continental O-200-A flat-four piston engine
Performance: maximum speed 130 mph (210 km/h) at sea level; cruising speed 115 mph (185 km/h); service ceiling 10,170 ft (3100 m); range 400 miles (644 km)
Weights: empty 1,157 lb (525 kg);

maximum take-off 1,731 lb (785 kg)
Dimensions: span 33 ft 7¼ in (10.24 m); length 23 ft 0¾ in (7.03 m); height 6 ft 7½ in (2.02 m); wing area 150.7 sq ft (14.0 m²)

The Aviamilano P.19 Scricciolo was designed for low-cost pleasure flying, and features a simple basic structure, angular flying surfaces which are easy to produce, and good fields of vision.

Aviation Traders ATL.98 Carvair

History and Notes

In the immediate years following the end of World War II, the Bristol Aeroplane Company produced Britain's first postwar civil transport, the Bristol Type 170. Most of those built (214 in all) were of the Series I Freighter version, able to accommodate in the Mk 32 configuration three motor cars in the forward hold and up to 20 passengers in the aft cabin. It was the Bristol Type 170 which, on 13 July 1948, was used to inaugurate with Silver City Airways the once famous cross-Channel car/passenger air ferry between Lympne and Le Touquet.

The need to supplement, and eventually replace, the Mk 32 Freighter in this led Aviation Traders Ltd to develop the ATL.98, which became named Carvair (a contraction of Car-via-air). Increased range and capacity were required, and Aviation Traders concluded that conversion of an existing aircraft would prove more economic than the development of a completely new design. Chosen for this role was the Douglas DC-4, robust and reliable, comparatively cheap to acquire from larger airlines that were updating their fleets, and with a considerable spares backing. The conversion, planned with technical assistance from Douglas Aircraft, consisted basically of a new and longer forward fuselage, with the flight deck high above the new front hold, which had a sideways-hinged nose door through which vehicles could be loaded. Standard layout could accommodate five cars forward and 22 passengers in the rear cabin, but an alternative all-passenger layout could carry a maximum of 65 passengers. In addition to the fuselage conversion, a new vertical tail of increased height and area was provided.

First flown on 21 June 1961, the Carvair entered service with British United Air Ferries in March 1962. Some 21 conversions were completed, serving initially with Aer Lingus, Aviaco, Ansett-ANA, British United Air Ferries, and Interocean Airways. They subsequently changed hands several times, and only a small number remain in service in 1980.

The bulbous nose of the ATL.98 almost conceals the type's DC-4 ancestry. The Carvair is no longer operated by British Air Ferries, although Falcon Airways has three ATL.98s and Nationwide Air two.

Specification
Type: air ferry transport
Powerplant: four 1,450-hp (1081-kW) Pratt & Whitney R-2000-7M2 Twin Wasp radial piston engines
Performance: maximum speed 250 mph (402 km/h); maximum cruising speed 213 mph (343 km/h); economic cruising speed 207 mph (333 km/h) at 10,000 ft (3050 m); service ceiling 18,700 ft (5700 m); range with maximum payload 2,300 miles (3700 km)
Weights: empty 41,885 lb (18999 kg); maximum take-off 73,800 lb (33475 kg)
Dimensions: span 117 ft 6 in (35.81 m); length 102 ft 7 in (31.27 m); height 29 ft 10 in (9.09 m); wing area 1,462 sq ft (135.82 m²)
Operators: Falcon Airways, Nationwide Air, and SFAIR-Secmafer SA

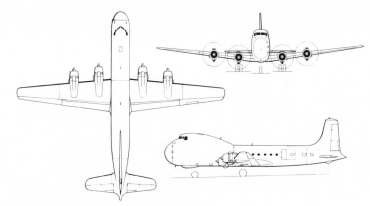

Aviation Traders ATL.98 Carvair

Beagle A.109 Airedale

History and Notes
In 1957, Auster displayed the fuselage of its C.6 Atlantic four-seat executive tourer at the Farnborough Air Show. This came to nothing, but in April 1961, when Auster had become Beagle Aircraft, the remarkably similar Airedale made its first flight, the difference in appearance being mainly in the stylish swept fin of the later aircraft. Unfortunately the Airedale, being based on earlier Auster models, inherited their faults as well as virtues; with heavier all-up weight, an enormous external exhaust system, multi-struts and fabric covering, it was no match for the contemporary Cessna 172s and 175s, to name only two of its rivals.

From the time of the prototype's first flight, in April 1961, to delivery of the final aircraft in August 1964, only 43 Airedales were built. Of these, 36 were registered in the UK, while seven were direct exports: one each to New Zealand, Portugal, the Netherlands and Denmark, and three to Australia. A number of the British-registered aircraft eventually found their way to other countries, including Eire, Switzerland, Pakistan, Sicily, Canada, Sweden and West Germany.

The Airedale's standard powerplant was the 180-hp (134-kW) Avco Lycoming O-360-A1A but, at the time of the prototype's first flight, aircraft which had US engines or major items of equipment could not participate in the then annual SBAC Display at Farnborough in September. Apparently this was considered by Beagle to be of such importance that the prototype was re-engined with a 175-hp (130-kW) British-built Rolls-Royce Continental GO-300 (a fine distinction!) to enable it to fly at Farnborough, and in this form it was designated A.111—the sole example.

A few Airedales have survived, mostly in the hands of Auster enthusiasts.

Specification
Type: four-seat light monoplane
Powerplant: one 180-hp (134-kW)

Avco Lycoming O-360-A1A flat-four piston engine
Performance: maximum speed 148 mph (238 km/h) at sea level; cruising speed 141 mph (227 km/h) at 5,000 ft (1525 m); service ceiling 14,900 ft (4540 m); range 650 miles (1046 km)
Weights: empty 1,630 lb (739 kg); maximum take-off 2,650 lb (1202 kg)

Based quite closely on the Auster design philosophy, the Beagle A.109 Airedale introduced refinements such as a tricycle landing gear and swept vertical tail surfaces, but had a high structure weight.

Dimensions: span 36 ft 4 in (11.07 m); length 26 ft 4 in (8.03 m); height 10 ft 0 in (3.05 m); wing area 185 sq ft (17.19 m²)

Beagle B.121 Pup

History and Notes
Britain's pre-eminence in light aircraft design before World War II was unquestioned, and it was to be expected that an attempt to regain a foothold in this lucrative market would be made once the industry had readjusted to peacetime conditions. Miles made a brave try but eventually foundered, and it was with great hopes that Beagle launched the all-metal B.121 Pup, the two-seat prototype of which flew from the company's Shoreham factory on 8 April 1967, with a 100-hp (75-kW) Rolls-Royce Continental O-200-A engine.

The new aircraft proved to be a delight to fly and the next two examples, flown in October 1967 and January 1968, were prototypes for the Pup Series 2 with an enlarged rudder and four seats. In this form the engine was changed to a 150-hp (112-kW) Avco Lycoming O-320-A2B, while the Series 3 had a 160-hp (119-kW) Avco Lycoming O-360-A. The Series 1, 2 and 3 were more usually known as Pup 100, 150 and 160 respectively.

Following the Pup's first public appearance at the 1967 Paris Air Show, Beagle launched a sales drive and the orders began to come in. The first operator, not surprisingly, was the Shoreham School of Flying, which received the first of four Pups on 12 April 1968, but operated them for less than 18 months before re-equipping. It was said at the time that Beagle were so busy building complete aircraft they did not pay sufficient heed to the requirement for an efficient after-sales service, and spares were hard to get. But deliveries were mounting, to customers in the UK, Germany, Eire, Austria, Finland, Sweden, Denmark, the Netherlands, Luxembourg, Switzerland, Iraq, Australia, Malaysia, South Africa, Iran and USA.

Requirements for a military trainer version led to the re-engining of the prototype with a 200-hp (149-kW) Avco Lycoming engine in April 1969, and the definitive version, the B.125 Bulldog, flew the following month.

Speed of production can be gauged by the fact that the 100th Pup was handed over on 23 September 1969, only 17 months after the first production aircraft had flown. But Beagle were by this time in difficulties, and when the government withdrew its financial support the company was put into receivership, the 152nd and

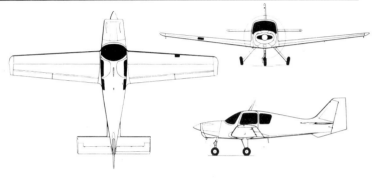

BAe (Scottish Aviation/Beagle) Pup 100

last Pup flying on 12 January 1970.

It is ironic that 121 Pups had been delivered and a further 276 were on order when Beagle collapsed. It was said that production costs were outstripping sales values, since the Pup was not really suitable for mass production. When Beagle closed and further development of the Bulldog was taken over by Scottish Aviation at Prestwick, considerable redesign was needed to make production easier and more economical. More than 320 Bulldogs were built for military customers. The specification applies to the Pup 150.

Specification
Type: four-seat light monoplane
Powerplant: one 150-hp (112-kW) Avco Lycoming O-320-A2B flat-four piston engine
Performance maximum speed 138 mph (222 km/h) at sea level; cruising speed 131 mph (211 km/h) at 7,500 ft (2285 m); service ceiling 14,700 ft (4480 m); range 633 miles (1019 km)
Weights: empty 1,090 lb (494 kg); maximum take-off 1,925 lb (873 kg)
Dimensions: span 31 ft 0 in (9.45 m); length 23 ft 2 in (7.06 m); height 7 ft 6 in (2.29 m); wing area 119.5 sq ft (11.10 m²)

Beagle B.206

History and Notes
Beagle's first completely original design was the attractive B.206, flown at Shoreham on 15 August 1961 as the B.206X, in which form it had five seats and was powered by two 260-hp (194-kW) Continental engines. Of all-metal construction, the new aircraft made its public debut at the Farnborough Air Show in the following month. Having second thoughts on the size, Beagle enlarged the design to a seven-seater, increased the span by 8 ft 0 in (2.44 m) and fitted geared Continental engines. This flew as the B.206Y on 12 August 1962.

First orders were, in fact, for a military version, designated Basset CC.Mk 1, of which 20 were delivered to the RAF from May 1965; two pre-production B.206Zs were supplied to Boscombe Down for evaluation.

The first production civil B.206 Srs 1, built at the former Auster factory at Rearsby, flew on 17 July 1964, while the first delivery was made to Rolls-Royce on 13 May 1965. Eleven Srs 1s were built for UK customers, mostly companies; two were later converted to Srs 2 standard, with supercharged engines and detail changes.

Total production of Srs 2s amounted to 47 aircraft, of which 28 were for UK customers and 19 for export. The latter included deliveries to Spain, Argentina, South Africa, Sudan, Zambia, USA, Nigeria, Brazil and the Royal Flying Doctor Service in Sydney, Australia.

Other B.206s were found to be suitable for instrument flying training. Three aircraft, known as Series 3s, had a deeper rear fuselage and accommodation for 10 people but this version was not developed further.

Production of the B.206 ended in 1969; 85 had been built, the majority for civil use, and when the Basset was declared surplus to RAF requirements in the late 1970s a number came on to the civil market. The specification applies to the Srs 2.

Specification
Type: five/eight-seat monoplane
Powerplant: two 340-hp (254-kW) Rolls-Royce Continental GTSIO-520-C flat-six piston engines
Performance: maximum speed 258 mph (415 km/h) at 16,000 ft (4875 m); cruising speed 218 mph (351 km/h) at 8,000 ft (2440 m) and 7,000-lb (3175-kg) AUW; service ceiling 27,100 ft (8260 m); range 1,600 miles (2575 km)

A Beagle B.121 Pup formates on a twin-engined B.206 from the same manufacturer. Both aircraft were extremely promising designs, but the Beagle company did not have production capacity to match demand.

Weights: empty 4,800 lb (2177 kg); maximum take-off 7,499 lb (3401 kg)
Dimensions: span 45 ft 9½ in (13.96 m); length 33 ft 8 in (10.26 m); height 11 ft 4 in (3.45 m); wing area 214 sq ft (19.88 m²)

Beech Model 18 and Derivatives

History and Notes

Little more than four years after the company's foundation in 1932, Beech Aircraft began the design of a twin-engine light transport to which it allocated the designation Model 18. First flown as a prototype on 20 January 1937, well over 9,000 of these aircraft were to be built before production of the H18 finally ended in the early 1970s. More than half of this number were produced for military use during World War II, but both civil and ex-service aircraft have entered operation in large numbers with third-level airline and air taxi operators.

The Beech 18 is a conventional low-wing monoplane, primarily of light alloy construction, with twin endplate fins and rudders, the majority having an electrically retractable tailwheel type landing gear. However, tricycle type landing gear could be installed optionally on the Super H18 from September 1963. A flight deck seating a crew of two is standard on later versions, and the usual accommodation is for seven to nine passengers.

In addition to the standard versions of the Model 18, there have been a number of conversions introduced by other American manufacturers to provide improved capability or greater capacity. These have included the Dumod Corporation's nine-passenger Dumod I, and lengthened-fuselage 15-passenger Dumod Liner; Pacific Airmotive's 10-passenger Tradewind; and Volpar Inc.'s Super Turbo 18 (a standard Beech 18 with tricycle landing gear and turboprop engines), and lengthened-fuselage 15-passenger Turboliner, also powered by turboprops. Still carrying out Beech 18 conversions in 1980, Hamilton Aviation had developed a 17-passenger turboprop-powered West-wind IISTD, a standard size turbo-prop-powered passenger/cargo West-wind III, and a larger capacity lengthened-fuselage utility Westwind IV with a variety of optional turbo-prop powerplants.

The details which follow apply to the final production Beech H18.

Specification

Type: light transport
Powerplant: two 450-hp (336-kW) Pratt & Whitney R-985AN-14B radial piston engines
Performance: maximum speed 236 mph (380 km/h) at 4,500 ft (1370 m); maximum cruising speed 220 mph (354 km/h) at 10,000 ft (3050 m); economic cruising speed 185 mph (298 km/h) at 10,000 ft (3050

The Beech 18 was built over a prolonged period to the tune of over 9,000 examples. Many are still in use, some still with radial engines.

Beech 18 of Air Cortez, USA.

m); service ceiling 21,400 ft (6520 m) at average cruise weight; maximum range with 45-min reserves 1,530 miles (2462 km)
Weights: empty 5,845 lb (2651 kg); maximum take-off 9,900 lb (4491 kg)
Dimensions: span 49 ft 8 in (15.14 m); length 35 ft 2½ in (10.73 m); height 9 ft 4 in (2.84 m); wing area 360.7 sq ft (33.54 m²)
Operators: in current service with a very large number of third-level airline and charter companies throughout the world, especially in North and South America

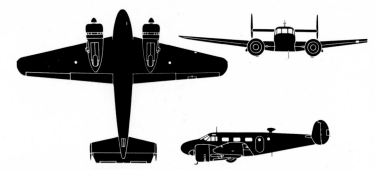

Beech Model 18 (C-45)

Beech Airliner 99

History and Notes

Steady demand for the Beech Model 18 during the first decade following World War II led Beech to design a six/nine-seat business aircraft that would be superior to it, particularly in terms of airfield performance and range. The resulting Queen Air 65, first flown as a prototype on 28 August 1958, led to a family of Queen Airs of which almost 1,000 were built before production ended in the late 1970s.

The growing importance of commuter airlines in the USA prompted Beech to embark on the design and construction of an aircraft to capture a share of this market. In 1965,

therefore, Beech became involved in what was then the largest aircraft to emanate from this company, the Model 99 Airliner, which was developed from the design of the Queen Airs. It was of the same general configuration, a low-wing monoplane of all-metal construction, with a conventional cantilever tail unit. Landing gear was of the tricycle type, with twin wheels on each main unit, and with the electrically actuated retraction which is a typical feature of Beech design. It had, of course, a lengthened fuselage to provide increased seating capacity, and an optional forward-hinged cargo door was available, installed forward of

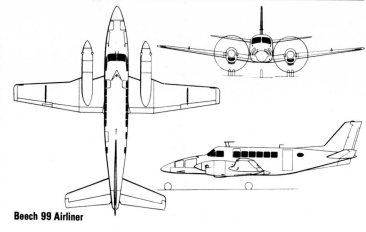

Beech 99 Airliner

Beech Airliner 99

Beech 99 Airliner of Mississippi Valley Airlines.

the standard airstair door on the port side of the cabin, to permit the easy loading of bulky cargo. A movable bulkhead, to separate freight and passengers, was also available for airlines wishing to operate combined cargo/passenger services.

The higher gross weight called for more powerful engines than those installed in the Queen Airs, and with economic operation being of importance for commuter airlines, turboprop powerplants were selected, initially 550-ehp (410-ekW) Pratt & Whitney Aircraft of Canada PT6A-20s. Accommodation was provided for a crew of two on a flight deck which could be separated from the cabin if desired by optional curtains or bulkhead. The main cabin could accommodate 15 passengers, in single seats on each side of a central aisle, and these were removable easily for all or part-cargo operations. Full blind-flying instrumentation was standard, and avionics could vary to suit customer requirements. Propeller anti-icing was standard, but pneumatic de-icing boots for wing and tail unit leading-edges were optional.

Initial deliveries of production aircraft went to Commuter Airlines Inc., beginning on 2 May 1968, and by the time production was terminated, in late 1977, a total of 164 aircraft had been supplied to 64 operators, most of them in the USA.

On 7 May 1979, Beech announced its intention to re-enter the commuter airliner market with an updated version of the Model 99, the aircraft to be used for the certification programme being an earlier construction aircraft purchased from the Allegheny Commuter Consortium. Completely refurbished and with PT6A-34 engines flat-rated at 783 ehp (9584 ekW), a development and certification flying programme was in progress during the summer of 1980, with initial production deliveries of the Commuter C99 scheduled during 1981 or 1982.

The details which follow apply to B99 late production versions of the original Beech 99 Airliner.

Specification
Type: light cargo, executive or passenger transport
Powerplant: two 680-ehp (507-ekW) Pratt & Whitney Aircraft of Canada PT6A-28 turboprops
Performance: maximum cruising speed 285 mph (459 km/h) at 12,000 ft (3660 m) and AUW of 9,500 lb (4309 kg); service ceiling 26,300 ft (8015 m); range with maximum fuel, at maximum range power and with 45-min reserves 1,173 miles (1887 km) at 16,000 ft (4875 m)
Weights: empty 5,777 lb (2620 kg); maximum take-off 10,900 lb (4944 kg)
Dimensions: span 45 ft 10½ in (13.98 m); length 44 ft 6¾ in (13.58 m); height 14 ft 4½ in (4.38 m); wing area 279.7 sq ft (25.98 m²)
Operators: US airlines which became equipped extensively with, and still operate, Beech 99s include Air Speed Inc., Henson Aviation, Mississippi Valley Airlines, Pennsylvania Commuter Airlines, Pocono Airlines, Rio Airways, Royale Airlines, and Skystream Airlines Inc.

The Beech Commuter C99 is essentially an updated version of the Airliner B99 with more powerful Pratt & Whitney Aircraft of Canada turboprops.

Beech Baron

History and Notes
Developed from the Beech 95 Travel Air, the Baron flew at the end of February 1960 and differed from its predecessor in several ways. Two 260-hp (194-kW) Continental IO-470 engines replaced the Travel Air's 180-hp (134-kW) Avco Lycomings, and a swept fin was introduced along with other refinements to the airframe. Deliveries began in November 1960, and further development of the design continued. While the original model was a four/five-seater, it was considered that there was sufficient demand for a five/six-seater, and the Model B55 with 260-hp (194-kW) Continental IO-470-L engines was introduced in 1963. The later C55, a full six-seater, had 285-hp (213-kW) Continental IO-520-Cs. By the end of 1965, 1,080 Barons had been built, and in February of that year the Baron won a US Army competition for an instrument trainer, Beech receiving an order for 55 aircraft designated T-42A.

Turbocharging was introduced on a new Model 56TC, deliveries of which began in September 1967. Air-conditioning was an optional extra, Beech claiming this to be the first production light twin to offer such a facility. The Model 56TC had two 380-hp (283-kW) Avco TIO-541-E1B4 engines and a maximum take-off weight 690 lb (313 kg) heavier than that of the contemporary D55. At sea level its rate of climb was 2,020 ft (615 m) per minute, 350 ft (107 m) per minute better than the lighter aircraft, while a 290 mph (467 km/h) cruise at 25,000 ft (7620 m) was considerably superior to the D55's 242 mph 389 km/h) at sea level; and in fact the latter's ceiling was 20,900 ft (6,370 m), so the advantage of turbocharging was very obvious. Production of the Model 56TC ended in December 1971, when 93 had been built.

The Baron D55 gave way to the E55 on the production line with minor cosmetic changes, but in 1969 the range was extended by the introduction of a larger model, the Model 58. First flown in June, the Model 58 was certificated in Novem-

Beech Baron 95-55

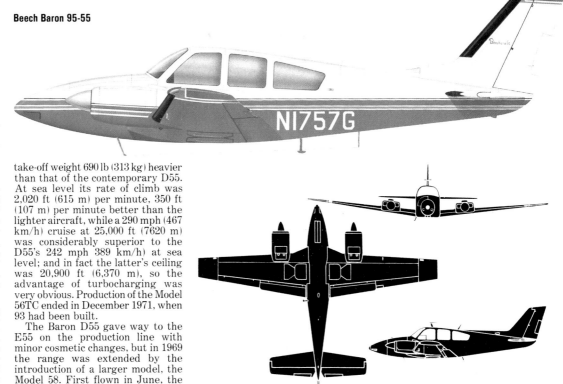

Beech Baron 55

Beech Baron

The Beech Baron series was introduced in 1960, and since then the type has undergone extensive modernisation. Illustrated is a Baron 95-E55 with larger tailplane and greater baggage volume.

ber 1969 and deliveries began during the following month. The Baron 58 featured a 10-in (25.40-cm) forward fuselage extension, which made room for double passenger/cargo doors, and increased the available internal space by permitting the instrument panel and two front seats to be moved forward; the wheelbase was also extended, and engines were 285-hp (213-kW) Continental IO-520 Cs as fitted in the E55.

By the end of 1971 deliveries of all Baron variants had topped the 2,600 mark, including 181 Model 58s, while nine years later, by early 1981, deliveries had exceeded 5,000. In 1981. Beech was still offering all four Barons—the B55, E55, 58 and 58P.

Before then, however, Beech decided to pressurise the Baron, and the result was the Model 58P, flown in August 1973, certificated in May 1974 and flown in production form the same year. Deliveries began late in 1975, powered by two 310-hp (231-kW) Continental TSIO-520-L turbocharged engines. As on the Model 55s, the standard seating was for four, with optional kits for a fifth and sixth seat. From 1979, the Continental TSIO-520-WB engines of 325 hp (242 kW) were used.

Mention should be made of a development initiated in France by SFERMA in 1960, when they re-engined a Travel Air with 440-shp (328-kW) Turboméca Astazou turbo-

props. This led to Baron airframes being supplied to SFERMA for conversion, which included the fitting of a taller fin and a dihedral tailplane. In this form the aircraft was known as the Marquis and a small number were built. Another turbine conversion, carried out by American Jet Industries in 1971, used 400-shp (298-kW) Allison 250-B17 turboprops. The specification applies to the B55.

Specification
Type: four/five-seat cabin monoplane
Powerplant: two 260-hp (194-kW) Continental IO-470-L flat-six piston engines
Performance: maximum speed 231 mph (372 km/h) at sea level; cruising speed 216 mph (348 km/h) at 6,000 ft (1830 m); service ceiling 19,300 ft (5880 m); range 1,141 miles (1836 km) at 12,000 ft (3660 m)
Weights: empty 3,233 lb (1466 kg); maximum take-off 5,100 lb (2313 kg)
Dimensions: span 37 ft 10 in (11.53 m); length 28 ft 0 in (8.53 m); height 9 ft 7 in (2.92 m); wing area 199.2 sq ft (18.51 m²)

Beech Bonanza 35

History and Notes
When the prototype Model 35 Bonanza flew on 22 December 1945, there could have been few who visualised production continuing for 36 years and construction exceeding 10,000 examples. At the time of the Bonanza's introduction, its V-tail attracted considerable comment, and even today is a unique feature on production general aviation aircraft although versions with a conventional fin and rudder, originally marketed as the Debonair, are also available.

The postwar light aircraft boom in the USA helped the Bonanza's launch at a price just below $8,000, and 1,209 were delivered in the first full year of production. A four-seat all-metal aircraft, the Model 35 ws certificated in the normal and utility categories and the first models were powered by a 165-hp (123-kW) Continental engine; gross weight was 2,550 lb (1157 kg). Valuable publicity was obtained when William P. Odom established a lightplane non-stop world's endurance record between 7-8 March 1949, flying a Bonanza from Honolulu to Teterboro, New Jersey, a distance of 4,957.240 miles (7977,90 km) at a take-off weight of 3,858 lb (1750 kg).

Each year Beech made improvements, giving an alphabetical prefix letter starting at A35 in 1949 and reaching V35 by 1966 (the letters I, L, O, Q, R and T were not used). Space does not permit full details, but typical improvements included an enlarged tail unit and metal propeller (C35), stronger wing and additional cabin window (F35), fuel-injection engine (J35), lengthening of cabin to increase capacity to six seats (S35), and optional turbocharging (V35TC).

Engine power increased every few years from the 185 hp (138 kW) of the A35 to the 205 hp (153 kW) of the C35, the 250 hp (186 kW) of the J35, the 260 hp (194 kW) of the N35, and the 285 hp (213 kW) of the S35 onwards. There were others within the above ranges, but Beech remained loyal to Continental engines.

An unusual feature, which has survived from the original Model 35 to the current V35B model, is the dual control with a single wheel which can be swung over to either occupant.

By any standards a design of remarkable longevity, the Beech Bonanza V-tail lightplane is still available in the form of the V35B.

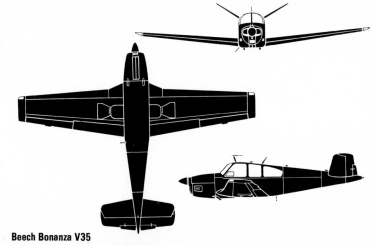

Beech Bonanza V35

A number of odd conversions were made to Bonanzas: the Model 40, of which a single example was built, had two Franklin engines geared to one propeller; while the Bay Super V conversion used two Avco Lycoming engines, a real 'Twin Bonanza' much more so than the Beech 50 which carried this name.

A version with a conventional tail was introduced in 1959 as the Debonair, and more than 3,000 were built in addition to the 10,000 Bonanzas. In 1967 the Debonair lost its name, and all subsequent Model 33, 35 and 36s were known as Bonanzas. The current models are the V-tail V35 B four/five-seater; the F33A which is a conventional-tail version of the V35B; the F33C, an aerobatic and utility version of the F33A; and the A36. This last aircraft, introduced in 1968, is a six-seat utility conventional-tail version of the V35B, with a 10-in (0.25-m) fuselage extension and large double doors for the carriage of bulky cargo. The price of the A36 at the time of writing is $113,000. A turbocharged version, the A36Tc, was introduced in 1979, with a 300-hp (224-kW) Continental TSIO-520-UB engine. The specification applies to the Bonanza V35B.

Specification
Type: four/five-seat cabin monoplane
Powerplant: One 285-hp (213-kW) Continental IO-520-BB flat-six piston engine
Performance: maximum speed 209 mph (336 km/h) at sea level; cruising speed 198 mph (319 km/h) at 6,000 ft (1830 m); service ceiling 17,800 ft (5445 m); range 1,023 miles (1646 km) at 8,000 ft (2440 m)
Weights: empty 2,117 lb (960 kg); maximum take-off 3,400 lb (1542 kg)
Dimensions: span 33 ft 6 in (10.21 m); length 26 ft 5 in (8.05 m); height 7 ft 7 in (2.31 m); wing area 181 sq ft (16.81 m²)

Beech Debonair 33

History and Notes
In 1959 the Beech 35 Bonanza had been in production for 14 years, but as its V-tail was still regarded as something of a novelty, Beech introduced the Debonair, to all intents and purposes a Bonanza with a conventional tail unit. The first Debonair was flown on 14 September 1959, and deliveries began the following year. In initial production form the Debonair had accommodation for four and a 225-hp (168-kW) Continental IO-470-J engine, while contemporary Bonanzas had the 250-hp (186-kW) IO-470-C enabling a fifth person to be carried; thus the Debonair could be considered as a cheaper or utility version of the Model 35 Bonanza. Production of the Debonair continued alongside the Bonanza, and by the end of 1966 almost 1,200 had been built. Most went to private owners in the USA and overseas, but an important customer was Lufthansa, which bought 31 for pilot training. Two models were available at that time: the C33 with a 225-hp (168-kW) Continental IO-470-K engine, and the C33A with 285-hp (213-kW) Continental IO-520-B engine.

From 1967 the name Debonair disappeared and the aircraft became known as the Model E33 Bonanza. In June 1968 there appeared an aerobatic version, the E33B with additional structural members in the rear fuselage and reinforcement of the ailerons and tail surfaces. This

model was otherwise similar to the E33, while the aerobatic E33C, deliveries of which began in August 1968, was similarly related to the E33A with a 285-hp (213-kW) Continental engine. They were followed later by the F33A and F33C.

Availability of aerobatic models led to several orders from overseas, and among customers were Pacific Southwest Airlines, who bought 12 F33As for crew training, Iran Air Force (16), Mexican Navy (15), Spanish Air Force (74) and the Netherlands Government Flying School (16). Total production of Model 33s by the beginning of 1981 exceeded 2,500. The specification applies to the Debonair C33.

Specification
Type: four-seat cabin monoplane
Powerplant: one 225-hp (168-kW) Continental IO-470-K flat-six piston engine
Performance: maximum speed 195 mph (314 km/h) at sea level; cruising speed 185 mph (298 km/h) at 7,000 ft (2135 m); service ceiling 17,800 ft (5425 m); range 1,170 miles (1883 km)
Weights: empty 1,780 lb (807 kg); maximum take-off 3,050 lb (1383 kg)
Dimensions: span 32 ft 10 in (10.01 m); length 25 ft 6 in (7.77 m); height 8 ft 3 in (2.51 m); wing area 177.6 sq ft (16.50 m²)

The Debonair series was developed by Beech as a conventionally-tailed version of the Bonanza, but the name did not last, and Debonairs are now known under the designation Bonanza 33.

Beech Duchess 76

History and Notes
The Beech entry into the four-seat light twin market was rather protracted. A prototype designed PD 289 had flown in September 1974, but it was not until 24 May 1977 that the first production Duchess appeared. By this time stylists had dictated that the 'in thing' was a T-tail (witness the King Air 200) and the Duchess was no exception, sharing this appendage with the rival Piper Seminole. Curiously, this phase lasted for only a short time on Piper's single-engined aircraft, and the Lance and Arrow soon reverted to a low-set tailplane.

Orders for 200 Duchesses had been placed by the end of 1977, for service with Beech Aero Centers, where the new aircraft was to be used primarily for flight training. Following certification, production was quickly got under way with first deliveries being made in May 1978, by which time Beech held more than 350 orders; at launch date a price of $81,950 was quoted. A number of overseas orders have also been received, and by the beginning of 1981 Beech had delivered about 300 Duchesses.

All Duchesses have counter-rotating propellers, and a variety of factory-installed options are available,

providing almost everything—from air temperature gauges, outside to visors, sun. An extensive range of optional avionics is also available.

Specification
Type: four-seat cabin monoplane
Powerplant: two 180-hp (134-kW) Avco Lycoming O-360-A1G6D flat-four piston engines
Performance: cruising speed 182 mph (293 km/h) at 10,000 ft (3050 m); service ceiling 19,650 ft (5900 m); range 898 miles (1445 km)
Weights: empty 2,460 lb (1116 kg); maximum take-off 3,900 lb (1769 kg)
Dimensions: span 38 ft 0 in (11.58 m); length 29 ft 0½ in (8.85 m); height 9 ft 6 in (2.90 m); wing area 181 sq ft (16.81 m²)

Unusual for a Beech design, the Duchess 76 has a T-tail, and was introduced in 1977 as a light four-seat twin to compete with Cessna and Piper twins. The prototype first flew with 160-hp (119-kW) engines, but these were replaced by 180-hp (134-kW) units on production Duchesses. Counter-rotating propellers are standard.

Beech Duke 60

History and Notes

Beechcraft's first entry into the field of pressurised general aviation aircraft was with the Model 60 Duke, flown on 29 December 1966, and certificated on 1 February 1968. With 380-hp (283-kW) turbocharged engines giving a maximum speed of more than 280 mph (451 km/h) and its pressurised cabin, the Duke was an expensive aircraft and, by American standards, has been built in comparatively small numbers. By January 1970, 116 had been delivered, rising to 208 by January 1973, 403 by January 1977 and close to 600 by January 1981.

Only two new models have been introduced in the 13 years of production to date: the A60 in 1971 and the B60 in 1974. The former had a 50 lb (23 kg) increase in gross weight, while the B60 had a slightly larger cabin and could carry more fuel.

Pressurisation maintains the cabin pressure altitude to an equivalent of 10,000 ft (3050 m) at 24,800 ft (7560 m), and standard accommodation is for four people in individual seats. Various options are available, including fifth and sixth seats. Comprehensive avionics, including colour weather radar, are available, and the current price for a Duke is around $380,000. The specification applies to the Duke B60.

Specification

Type: four six-seat cabin monoplane
Powerplant: two 380-hp (283-kW) Avco Lycoming TIO-541-E1C4 flat-six piston engines
Performance: maximum speed 283 mph (455 km/h) at 23,000 ft (7010 m); maximum cruising speed 275 mph (443 km/h) at 25,000 ft (7620 m); service ceiling 30,000 ft (9145 m); maximum range 1,344 miles (2163 km) at 25,000 ft (7620 m)
Weights: empty 4,406 lb (1998 kg); maximum take-off 6,775 lb (3073 kg)
Dimensions: span 39 ft 3¼ in (11.97 m); length 33 ft 10 in (10.31 m); height 12 ft 4 in (3.76 m); wing area 212.9 sq ft (19.78 m²)

The Beech Duke B60 is an altogether more advanced twin than the Duchess, offering cabin pressurisation and good high-altitude performance.

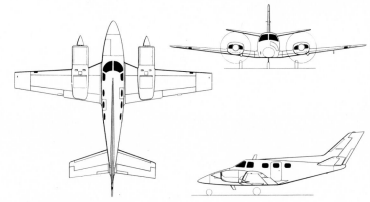

Beech Duke B60

Beech Musketeer/Sierra/Sport/Sundowner Series

History and Notes

From 1945 Beech progressively developed their Bonanza as a luxury touring aircraft. However, the company's range lacked a low-cost four-seater to compete with the successful Cessna and Piper offerings. This deficiency was remedied when the Model 23 Musketeer made its first flight on 23 October 1961. The flight test programme was completed rapidly, and FAA certification followed in February 1962, with initial deliveries in the autumn of the same year. The first improvement in the Musketeer series came in 1964, when the A23 was introduced. This featured a fuel-injection 165-hp (123-kW) Continental engine in place of the 160-hp (119-kW) Avco Lycoming unit that had powered the early Model 23 aircraft.

While the Musketeer lacked the external elegance of the Bonanza, it was nevertheless a sturdy if somewhat heavy machine. As a result the Musketeer was outperformed through almost the entire flight envelope by the lighter Piper Cherokee, which was powered by a 160-hp (119-kW) Avco Lycoming. Despite this factor, Beechcraft quality was still considered to be worth acquiring, and by March 1965 more than 700 had been delivered, another 1,000 or so being added by the end of 1967. The basic aircraft had been updated in 1965 as the Musketeer III, and three versions were introduced in 1967. These were the Custom III, re-engined with a 180-hp (134-kW) Avco Lycoming; the Sport III trainer with a 150-hp (112-kW) Avco Lycoming and an optional aerobatic kit; and, most powerful in the range, the Super III with a 200-hp (149-kW) Avco Lycoming. Production of this last variant ended in late 1971.

In 1969 there appeared the first Musketeer fitted with a retractable landing gear. This was identified as the Super R, but in December 1971 Beech introduced a new marketing programme involving three models. Gone was the name Musketeer, to be replaced by three Avco Lycoming-powered models: the Sundowner C23, a basic four-seater powered by a 180-hp (134-kW) engine and with fixed landing gear; the Sport B19, a two-seat trainer powered by a 150-hp (112-kW) engine, with fixed landing gear and an optional aerobatic kit; and the Sierra A24, a four/six-seater powered by a 200-hp (149-kW) engine and with a retractable landing gear. A large range of optional avionics and equipment was offered with the series.

No sooner had the general aviation scene become accustomed to the new names than Beech made further revisions to reflect the engine power: the A24 became the Sierra 200, the C23 became the Sundowner 180, and the B19 became the Sport 150. Production of the Sport ended in September 1978, after 903 of the type had been delivered. Beech concentrating its efforts on the surviving pair of the series, the Sundowner 180 and the Sierra 200. Well over 5,000 examples of the Musketeer range had been delivered by the beginning of 1981. Most of these had gone to civilian customers, but 20 went to the Mexican government and 25 to the Canadian Armed Forces for training purposes. other trainers went to Algeria (3), Indonesia (21), and the University of Illinois Institute of Aviation (21). The specification applies to the Sierra 200.

Specification

Type: four/six-seat cabin monoplane
Powerplant: one 200-hp (149-kW) Avco Lycoming IO-360-A1B6 flat-four piston engine
Performance: maximum speed 163 mph (262 km/h) at sea level; cruising speed 158 mph (254 km/h); service ceiling 16,400 ft (5000 m); range 790 miles (1271 km) at 10,000 ft (3050 m)
Weights: empty 1,693 lb (768 kg); maximum take-off 2,750 lb (1247 kg)
Dimensions: span 32 ft 9 in (9.98 m); length 25 ft 9 in (7.85 m); height 8 ft 1 in (2.46 m); wing area 146 sq ft (13.56 m²)

The Beech Sundowner is one of three lightplanes derived from the former Musketeer series.

Beech Queen Air 70/80/88 Series

History and Notes

Flown for the first time on 22 June 1961, the Queen Air 80 was a more powerful version of the Queen Air 65, itself flown in August 1968. The Model 80 was certificated on 20 February 1962 and, in appearance, differed from its predecessor in having a swept fin and rudder. The Model 65's 340-hp (254-kW) Avco Lycoming engines were replaced in the Model 80 by supercharged 380-hp (283-kW) engines by the same manufacturer, and the gross weight went up by 260 lb (118 kg). Development continued, and the A80 (with a further increase in gross weight and fuel capacity) was announced in January 1964, becoming certificated two months later. Other features were increased wing span and a redesigned nose compartment. Production rate was about 12 a month, and 218 had been delivered by March 1965.

A further improved B80 followed during 1965, and an offshoot from the family was the Queen Air 88, a pressurised version of which around 50 were built over the next few years. Combining features of two versions, the Queen Air 70 was introduced in 1968, powered by the engines of the Queen Air 65 and incorporating the B80's extended wing. Yet another variant was the Queen Airliner B80, an 11-seat commuter airliner with the wings, fuselage, tail unit and landing gear of the Model 70; 42 Model 70s had been built when production ended in 1971.

Detail improvements were incorporated in the B80 in 1971, and by the end of that year Beech had built 446 of these variants. Production continued at a reduced rate, with another 61 added in the next six years, but deliveries gradually dried up, with the last two B80s going to customers in 1977. The specification applies to the Queen Air A80.

Specification

Type: utility, business and commuter transport

Powerplant: two 380-hp (283-kW) Lycoming IGSO-540-A1A flat-six piston engines
Performance: maximum speed 252 mph (406 km/h) at 11,500 ft (3505 m); cruising speed 230 mph (370 km/h) at 15,000 ft (4570 m); service ceiling 29,000 ft (8840 m); range 1,565 miles 2519 km)
Weights: empty 4,900 lb (2223 kg); maximum take-off 8,500 lb (3855 kg)
Dimensions: span 50 ft 3 in (15.32 m); length 35 ft 3 in (10.74 m); height 14 ft 8 in (4.47 m); wing area 293.9 sq ft (27.30 m²)

The Beech Queen Air B80 is a nine-seat business aircraft, and is also available as the Queen Airliner B80 with seating for nine passengers.

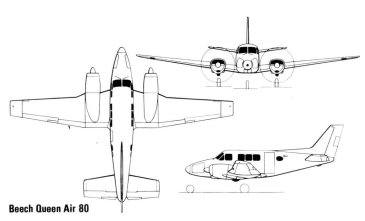

Beech Queen Air 80

Beech Skipper 77

History and Notes

Beech flew the prototype Model 77 as the PD 285, with low-set tailplane, on 6 February 1975, but it was not until September 1978 that the production prototype flew. This comparatively long gestation period enabled Piper to announce their rival Tomahawk in October 1977, and begin customer deliveries early the following year. It was not until April 1979 that the Model 77 Skipper began to come off the production lines, by which time the design had been modified to incorporate a T-tail.

By the beginning of 1981 about 12 a month were being built and around 200 had been delivered; by comparison Piper had delivered 1,000 Tomahawks in the first year of production, 220 in 1980, and established a rate of 20 a month by early 1981.

The Skipper was designed as a primary trainer for Beech Aero Centers, with low initial and operating costs, while simplicity of maintenance was emphasised. Its wing had a high-lift aerofoil developed by NASA, and an unusual feature was

the use of torque tubes, in place of cables and pulleys, to activate the flaps and ailerons. Powerplant consists of a 115-hp (86-kW) Avco Lycoming O-235-L2C.

Specification

Type: two-seat primary training monoplane
Powerplant: one 115-hp (86-kW) Avco Lycoming O-235-L2C flat-four piston engine
Performance: cruising speed 121 mph (195 km/h) at 4,500 ft (1370 m); service ceiling 12,900 ft (3930 m); range 475 miles (764 km)

at 8,500 ft (2590 m)
Weights: empty 1,100 lb (499 kg); maximum take-off 1,675 lb (760 kg)
Dimensions: span 30 ft 0 in (9.14m); length 24 ft 0 in (7.32 m); height 7 ft 11 in (2.41 m); wing area 129.8 sq ft (12.06 m²)

Designed as a training aircraft, the Beech Skipper offers docile handling characteristics combined with good fields of vision and a wide-track tricycle landing gear for ground safety.

Beech Super King Air/King Air Series

History and Notes

Among the many successful designs of the Beech Aircraft Corporation, pride of place must be given to the now-extensive King Air family. This began with the twin-engined pressurised Model 90 King Air, first announced in August 1963, that was considered to be the true monarch of its product line. Possibly regarded by the company as more than a little speculative when the production prototype made its first flight on 20 January 1964, it was the first Beech aircraft to introduce turbine power, in the form of two 500-shp (373-kW) United Aircraft of Canada PT6A-6 turboprop engines. It continues in production in 1981 as the King Air C90, powered by 550-ehp (410-ekW) PT6A-21 engines that are now identified with Pratt & Whitney Aircraft of Canada as their manufacturer.

The King Air name now embraces a range of aircraft with maximum accommodations that vary from 8 to 13 passengers, and with powerplants between 550 and 850 shp (410 and 634 kW), and a total of almost 3,000 of the combined versions had been delivered by early 1981. The Model 90 is the basic aircraft, which was followed by the King Air 100, first announced in May 1969. This had reduced wing span, and a lengthened fuselage to accommodate a maximum of 13 passengers. The current version is designated King Air A100, and this is powered by two 680-ehp (507-ekW) PT6A-28 turboprops. Five supplied to the US Army, under the designation U-21F, were the first turboprop-powered aircraft used by that service.

The King Air E90, announced in May 1972, combined the airframe of the original version with the more powerful engines of the King Air 100. A generally similar version, combining features of the C90 and E90, but powered by 750-ehp (560-ekW) PT6A-34Bs flat rated to 550 ehp (410-ekW), entered service with the US Navy as advanced pilot training aircraft from 1977, under the designation T-44A.

FAA certification of the Super King Air 200 was gained in December 1973, this version enhancing the King Air 100 by introducing wings of increased span, a T-tail, and 950-shp (634-kW) PT6A-41 turboprops. Military versions of the Super King Air 200 include C-12s for the US Army and Air Force, RU-21J special mission aircraft for the US Army, UC-12Bs for the US Navy and Marine Corps, and a Maritime Patrol 200T which, so far, has been supplied only to Japan's Maritime Safety Agency.

March 1975 saw the first flight of the King Air B100, almost identical to the A100 except for the introduction of 715-shp (533-kW) Garrett TPE331-6-252B turboprops which provided improved performance. Last of the family to be developed to date is the Super King Air F90 which combines the C90 fuselage, the reduced wing span of the 100s, the T-tail of the 200, and introduces low-noise PT6A-135 turboprops with slow-turning four-blade propellers. The details that follow apply to this last version.

Specification

Type: seven/ten-seat business transport
Powerplant: two 750-shp (559-kW) Pratt & Whitney Aircraft of Canada PT6A-135 turboprops
Performance: maximum cruising speed 307 mph (494 km/h) at 12,000 ft (3660 m); service ceiling 29,800 ft (9085 m); maximum range at maximum cruising speed 1,657 miles (2667 km) at 26,000 ft (7925 m); maximum range at economic cruising speed 1,814 miles (2919 km) at 26,000 ft (7925 km)
Weights: empty 6,640 lb (3012 kg); maximum take-off 10,950 lb (4967 kg)
Dimensions: span 45 ft 10¾ in (13.99 m); length 39 ft 9½ in (12.13 m); height 15 ft 1¼ in (4.60 m); wing area 279.7 sq ft (25.98 m²)

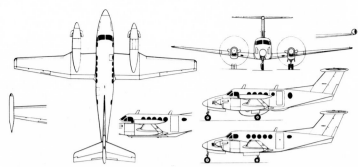

Beech Super King Air 200 (upper side view: Model 200T Maritime Monitor; scrap view: photo-survey version and optional tip-tank installation)

Beech Super King Air 200 cutaway drawing key

1 Nose cone
2 Weather radar
3 Radar transmitter
4 Landing and taxying lamps
5 Nose undercarriage leg strut
6 Nosewheel
7 Nosewheel doors
8 Air louvres
9 Air conditioning plant
10 Nose compartment construction
11 Electrical equipment bay
12 Radio and electronics bay
13 Access door
14 Brake hydraulic reservoir
15 Front pressure bulkhead
16 Rudder pedals
17 Ventral aerials
18 Cockpit floor level
19 Pilot's seat
20 Control column handwheel
21 Instrument panel
22 Opening side window panel
23 Co-pilot's seat
24 Instrument panel shroud
25 Windscreen wipers
26 Electrically heated windscreen panels
27 Starboard engine nacelle cowlings
28 Exhaust stubs
29 Engine intake
30 Propeller spinner
31 Blade root de-icing boots
32 Three-bladed variable pitch reversible propeller

Beech Super King Air/King Air Series

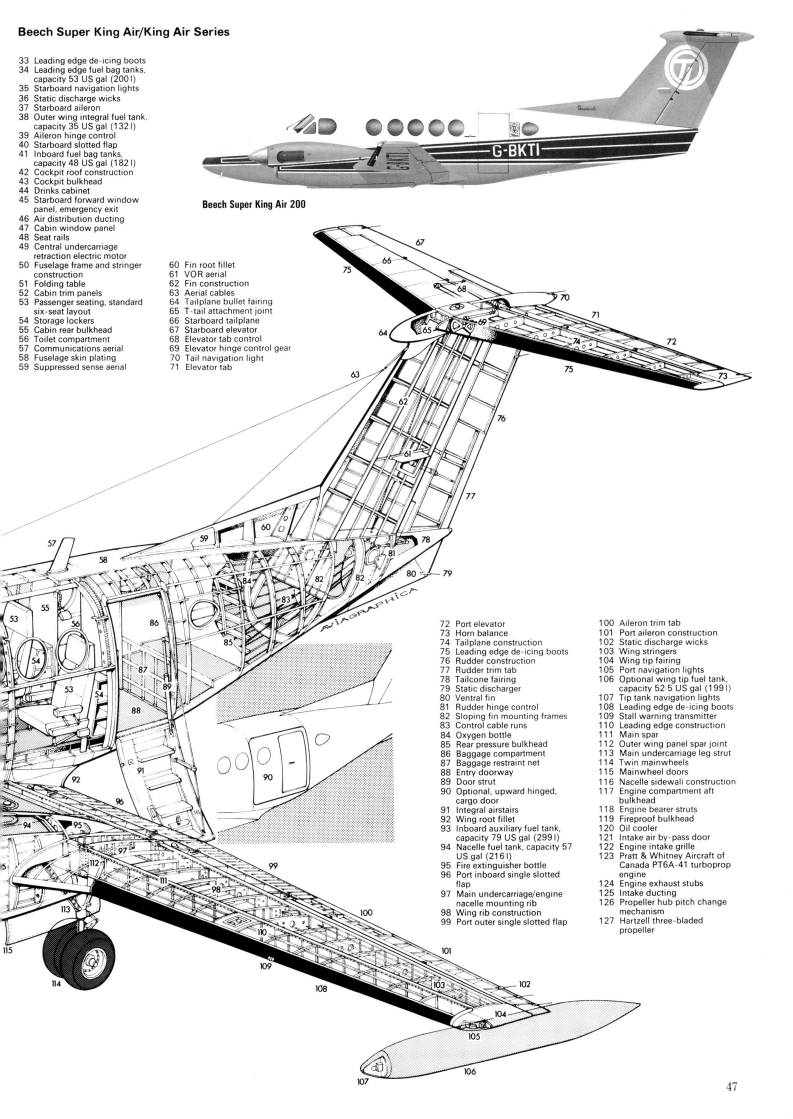

33 Leading edge de-icing boots
34 Leading edge fuel bag tanks, capacity 53 US gal (200 l)
35 Starboard navigation lights
36 Static discharge wicks
37 Starboard aileron
38 Outer wing integral fuel tank, capacity 35 US gal (132 l)
39 Aileron hinge control
40 Starboard slotted flap
41 Inboard fuel bag tanks, capacity 48 US gal (182 l)
42 Cockpit roof construction
43 Cockpit bulkhead
44 Drinks cabinet
45 Starboard forward window panel, emergency exit
46 Air distribution ducting
47 Cabin window panel
48 Seat rails
49 Central undercarriage retraction electric motor
50 Fuselage frame and stringer construction
51 Folding table
52 Cabin trim panels
53 Passenger seating, standard six-seat layout
54 Storage lockers
55 Cabin rear bulkhead
56 Toilet compartment
57 Communications aerial
58 Fuselage skin plating
59 Suppressed sense aerial

60 Fin root fillet
61 VOR aerial
62 Fin construction
63 Aerial cables
64 Tailplane bullet fairing
65 T-tail attachment joint
66 Starboard tailplane
67 Starboard elevator
68 Elevator tab control
69 Elevator hinge control gear
70 Tail navigation light
71 Elevator tab

Beech Super King Air 200

72 Port elevator
73 Horn balance
74 Tailplane construction
75 Leading edge de-icing boots
76 Rudder construction
77 Rudder trim tab
78 Tailcone fairing
79 Static discharger
80 Ventral fin
81 Rudder hinge control
82 Sloping fin mounting frames
83 Control cable runs
84 Oxygen bottle
85 Rear pressure bulkhead
86 Baggage compartment
87 Baggage restraint net
88 Entry doorway
89 Door strut
90 Optional, upward hinged, cargo door
91 Integral airstairs
92 Wing root fillet
93 Inboard auxiliary fuel tank, capacity 79 US gal (299 l)
94 Nacelle fuel tank, capacity 57 US gal (216 l)
95 Fire extinguisher bottle
96 Port inboard single slotted flap
97 Main undercarriage/engine nacelle mounting rib
98 Wing rib construction
99 Port outer single slotted flap

100 Aileron trim tab
101 Port aileron construction
102 Static discharge wicks
103 Wing stringers
104 Wing tip fairing
105 Port navigation lights
106 Optional wing tip fuel tank, capacity 52·5 US gal (199 l)
107 Tip tank navigation lights
108 Leading edge de-icing boots
109 Stall warning transmitter
110 Leading edge construction
111 Main spar
112 Outer wing panel spar joint
113 Main undercarriage leg strut
114 Twin mainwheels
115 Mainwheel doors
116 Nacelle sidewall construction
117 Engine compartment aft bulkhead
118 Engine bearer struts
119 Fireproof bulkhead
120 Oil cooler
121 Intake air by-pass door
122 Engine intake grille
123 Pratt & Whitney Aircraft of Canada PT6A-41 turboprop engine
124 Engine exhaust stubs
125 Intake ducting
126 Propeller hub pitch change mechanism
127 Hartzell three-bladed propeller

47

Bell Model 205/Agusta-Bell AB 205 Series

History and Notes

The undoubted success of the Bell UH-1A/B Iroquois gave convincing proof that there was little wrong with the basic design of this utility helicopter.

In early 1960 Bell proposed an improved version of the Model 204 design with a longer fuselage, plus additional cabin space resulting from relocation of the fuel cells, thus providing accommodation for a pilot and 14 troops, or space for six stretchers, or up to 4,000 lb (1814 kg) of freight. In July 1960, therefore, the US Army awarded Bell a contract for the supply of seven of these new helicopters for service test, these

having the US Army designation YUH-1D and being identified by Bell as their Model 205. The first of these flew on 16 August 1961, and following successful flight trials was ordered into production for the US Army.

Bell also produce a commercial version of the UH-1H under the designation Model 205A-1. It is powered by a 1,400-shp (1044-kW) Lycoming T5313B turboshaft, derated to 1,250-shp (932-kW). Normal fuel capacity of the Model 205A-1 is 215 US gallons (814 litres), optional fuel capacity 395 US gallons (1495 litres). Because it is intended for a wide range of users, special attention has been given to interior design to

permit quick conversation for air freight, ambulance, executive, flying crane and search roles. Maximum accommodation is for a pilot and 14 passengers.

Agusta in Italy also build the Model 205 under licence with the designation AB 205A-1, this being virtually the same as the Bell production model. Customers have included the Italian armed forces, as well as those of several other countries.

The specification applies to the Agusta-Bell AB 205A-1.

Specification
Type: utility helicopter
Powerplant: one 1,400-shp

(1044-kW) Lycoming T5313B turboshaft, derated to 1,250 shp (932 kW) for take-off
Performance: maximum speed 138 mph (222 km/h); initial climb rate 2,030 ft (619 m) per minute; service ceiling 14,700 ft (4480 m); range 331 miles (532 km)
Weights: empty 5,195 lb (2356 kg); maximum take-off 10,500 lb (4763 kg) with external load
Dimensions: main rotor diameter 48 ft 0 in (14.53 m); fuselage length 41 ft 11 in (12.78 m); height 14 ft 8 in (4.48 m); main rotor disc area 1,810 sq ft (168.1 m²)

Bell Model 206 JetRanger/Model 206L LongRanger/Agusta-Bell AB 206 Jet Ranger Series

History and Notes

The Bell Models 204, 205 and 206 were all developed to meet the requirements of the US armed forces, but whereas the civil versions of the Models 204 and 205 may be considered subsidiary to the military variants, the success of the civil Model 206 developments has at least equalled that of the military versions. The origins of the type lie with a US Army requirement, issued in 1960, for a Light Observation Helicopter (LOH). Bell's Model 206 was designed to meet the requirement, and the prototype first flew on 8 December 1962. However, the LOH competition was won by the Hughes OH-6, and it was only after a scandal about the Hughes delivery rate and unit price that the Model 206 was ordered into US Army production as the OH-58 Kiowa, the first such helicopter being delivered in May 1969.

After their initial loss of the LOH competition, Bell were able to console themselves with a steadily mounting order book for the civil Model 206. The first version to enter service was the Model 206A JetRanger, powered by the 317-shp (236-kW) Allison 250-C18A turboshaft, the civil version of the T63-A-700 used in Bell's OH-4 prototypes for the LOH competition. Production of the Model 206A JetRanger ended in 1972 after the delivery of the 660th example.

In 1970 Bell had developed the more versatile Model 206B JetRanger II. This was similar to its predecessor, but powered by the 400-shp (298-kW) Allison 250-C20 turboshaft in response to customer requirements for a JetRanger version with better 'hot and high' performance than the Model 206A. Bell's success in this matter is proved by the fact that although the Model 206B was only 5 mph (8 km/h) faster than the Model 206A at sea level, at 10,000 ft (3050 m) the speed differential had increased to 29 mph (47 km/h). Hovering weight and hovering ceiling were also significantly improved. Bell and Allison co-operated to develop a kit whereby Model 206As could be upgraded to Model 206B standard, and in 1976 Bell co-operated with the Collins Radio Group to produce an IFR package for the Model 206B.

Production of the Model 206B ended in the summer of 1977, after the delivery of more than 4,400 examples, some 1,550 of them for civil operators. The cessation of Model 206B production was the result of a further improved version, the Model 206B JetRanger III. This was announced by Bell on 7 February 1977, with deliveries beginning in the summer of that year. Although similar in most respects to the

JetRanger II, the Model 206B JetRanger had a more powerful engine, the 420-shp (313-kW) Allison 250-C20B; a larger and more efficient tail rotor; and a number of other detail improvements. Bell and Allison again co-operated to produce a kit enabling operators of earlier JetRanger models to upgrade their helicopters to JetRanger III standard. The effect of the improvements was again to increase the JetRanger III's 'hot and high' performance.

The other basic variation on the theme was the Bell Model 206L LongRanger, announced on 25 September 1973 as a medium-lift version of the basic Model 206. The new type, which first flew on 11 September 1974, and was based on the Model 206B JetRanger II. However, the fuselage was 'stretched' by 25 in (0.635 m) to provide accommodation for five passengers in addition to the two crew (compared with the Jet-Ranger II's three passengers); the 420-hp (313-kW) Allison 250-C20B drove a revised rotor with low-vibration elastomeric bearings; and the fuselage was suspended from the engine-mounting beam in Bell's new patented Noda-Matic fashion, attachment to these points of no relative motion greatly reducing cabin vibration levels.

The fuselage stretch gave the Long-Ranger a cabin volume of 83 cu ft (2.35 m³) compared with the Jet-Ranger's 49 cu ft (1.39 m³), and loading of bulky items was facilitated by a double door in the port side of the fuselage. Production Long-Rangers were first delivered in

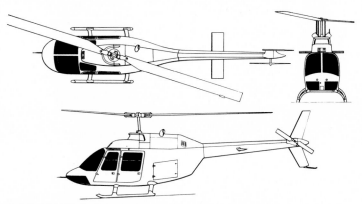
Bell Model 206A Jet-Ranger

October 1975. In 1978 Bell received FAA certification for an improved Model 206L-1 LongRanger II in May 1978. This has detail modifications but, more importantly, a 500-shp (373-kW) Allison 250-C28B turboshaft and uprated transmission, conferring useful increments in performance, especially in 'hot and high' conditions.

Production of all JetRanger and Long Ranger versions has been undertaken by Agusta in Italy under licence from Bell. The Italian versions are in all important respects similar to their American counterparts, but are slightly heavier, with a consequent lowering of performance. The specification applies to the Model 206B JetRanger III.

Specification
Type: general-purpose light helicopter

Powerplant: one 420-shp (313-kW) Allison 250-C20B turboshaft
Performance: maximum speed 140 mph (225 km/h) at sea level; maximum and economical cruising speeds 133 mph (214 km/h) at sea level; hovering ceiling in ground effect 12,700 ft (3870 m); range with maximum fuel 360 miles (579 km)
Weights: empty 1,455 lb (660 kg); maximum take-off 3,200 lb (1451 kg)
Dimensions: main rotor diameter 33 ft 4 in (10.16 m); fuselage length 31 ft 2 in (9.50 m); height 9 ft 6½ in (2.91 m); main rotor disc area 873 sq ft (81.1 m²)

The Bell Model 206 utility helicopter, as indicated by the use of this example in the crop-spraying role. The spraybars are attached to the fuselage sides, fed from a tank under the fuselage.

Bell Model 212 Twin Two-Twelve

History and Notes

On 1 May 1968 Bell Helicopter Company announced that following negotiations with the Canadian government and Pratt & Whitney Aircraft of Canada, it had been agreed to proceed with the development of a new helicopter based upon the airframe of the Bell Model 205/UH-1H Iroquois, of which the first of 10 for the Canadian Armed Forces (CAF) had been delivered on 6 March 1968 under the designation CUH-1H. Powerplant of the UH/CUH-1H consisted of a 1,400-shp (1044-kW) Avco Lycoming T53-L-13 turboshaft engine. The CAF considered that the incorporation of twin turboshaft engines would provide a number of benefits, and this led to development of the initial military Bell Model 212 and the Pratt & Whitney Aircraft of Canada (PWAC) PT6T powerplant for it. This programme was initiated as a joint venture, financed by Bell, the Canadian government and PWAC.

The revolutionary feature of this new helicopter was its powerplant, the PT6T Twin Pac designed and developed by PWAC, and consisting of two turboshaft engines mounted side by side and driving, via a combining gearbox, a single output shaft. This had an output in its initial production form of 2.83 shp per pound of dry weight (4.66 kW/kg), compared with 2.55 shp/lb (4.19 kW/kg) for the already-developed Lycoming T53 turboshaft. There was another very considerable advantage: as installed in the Model 212 the PT6T-3 is limited to an output of 1,290 shp (843 kW); in the event of a failure of one of the two turbines, sensing torquemeters in the combining gearbox signal the remaining turbine to develop full power, and the system thus provides true engine-out capability for a weight penalty of

only 86 lb (39 kg).

Initial deliveries of military Model 212s were made to the USAF in 1970, under the designation UH-1N, and the first CUH-1H for the CAF (later redesignated CH-135) was handed over on 3 May 1971. The airframe is generally similar to that of the UH-1H Iroquois, with an all-metal fuselage structure, skid landing gear, and rotor systems comprising a two-blade all-metal semi-rigid main rotor, and a two-blade all-metal tail rotor.

A 14-passenger commercial version known as the Twin Two-Twelve was developed more or less simultaneously, differing from the military model primarily in its cabin furnishing and avionics equipment. The Twin Two-Twelve gained FAA Transport Type Category A certification on 30 June 1971, and the type has since gained certification for IFR operation, requiring a new avionics package, new instrument panel, and stabilisation

controls for such use. In June 1977 it became the first helicopter to be certificated by the FAA for single-pilot IFR operation with fixed floats.

The enhanced safety offered by the Twin Pac powerplant has resulted in many sales to operators who provide support to offshore gas/oil prospecting and production companies, as well as to air taxi organisations.

Specification

Type: commercial transport helicopter
Powerplant: one Pratt & Whitney Aircraft of Canada PT6T-3 Turbo Twin Pac coupled turboshaft, flat rated to 1,290 shp (962 kW) for take-off and 1,130 shp (843 kW) for continuous operation
Performance: maximum cruising speed 143 mph (230 km/h) at sea level; service ceiling 14,200 ft (4330 m); range with standard fuel at sea level, no reserves 261 miles (420 km)

The Bell 212 Twin Two-Twelve utility helicopter is the numerical mainstay of the Bristow Helicopters Group, which has 31 of the type for a variety of roles including gas- and oil-field support.

Weights: empty 6,143 lb (2786 kg); maximum take-off 11,200 lb (5080 kg)
Dimensions: main rotor diameter 48 ft 2¼ in (14.69 m); length overall, rotors turning 57 ft 3¼ in (17.46 m); height 14 ft 10¼ in (4.53 m); main rotor disc area 1,809 sq ft (168.06 m²)
Operators include: Abu Dhabi Helicopters, Aerotecnia, Bristow Helicopters, British Helicopters, Far Eastern Air Transport Corporation, Gulf Helicopters, Helicopter Rentals, Helikopter Service A/S, Lider Taxi Aereo, Maersk Air, Offshore Helicopter A/S, Okanagan Helicopters, and Sea Airmotive

Bell Model 214ST

History and Notes

In late 1970 Bell Helicopters completed the construction of a prototype aircraft to which the identification Model 214 Huey Plus was allocated. It was, in effect, an improved version of the well-tried and proven UH-1H Iroquois, using the same airframe, but provided with increased power, some advanced features, and structural strengthening for operation at higher gross weights. From this helicopter Bell developed a Model 214A 16-seat utility version with a 2,930-shp (2185-kW) Avco Lycoming LTC4B-8D turboshaft engine and, following its demonstration in Iran, the company received an order for 287 of these aircraft, to be acquired by Iran through the US government. Soon after this the government of Iran began negotiations with European and US helicopter manufacturers, with the intention of establishing an indigenous aircraft industry, and concluded an agreement with Bell Helicopters in 1975. This envisaged that the Iranian government and Bell would jointly create facilities in Iran for this purpose, with the Bell 214A as its initial project, to be followed by a new Model 214ST developed especially for operation in Iran. The revolution of early 1979, and subsequent changed national policies in Iran, brought to an end these plans, but Bell decided to continue with independent development of the Model 214ST as a commercial transport with multi-mission capability.

A prototype Model 214ST was first flown in February 1977, and

was followed by the construction of three pre-production aircraft, beginning in 1978, the first of the latter flying in the summer of that year. These aircraft were all used in the development programme, with a target for certification by the British CAA and United States FAA by late 1980.

Features of the 214ST airframe include the large-capacity all-metal fuselage, which includes in its structure a roll-over protection ring, and accommodation for a pilot and co-pilot, plus 16 or 17 passengers according to customer specification. The rotor system includes an advanced

technology two-blade main rotor fabricated from glassfibre, its leading-edges protected by a titanium abrasion strip and the blade tips each having a replaceable stainless steel cap. The rotor hub incorporates elastomeric bearings which require no lubrication, and the rotor system is mounted on a Bell-developed nodal suspension beam from which the fuselage is suspended. This latter feature is based on the fact that a beam subjected to vertical vibrations will flex in wave form, with nodal points of no relative motion equidistant from the centre of the induced wave form. Bell suspends the heli-

The Model 214ST is the largest helicopter produced by Bell, with accommodation for 19 passengers suiting it for the city-centre commuter or oilfield support roles.

copter fuselage from the nodal points of such a beam, resulting in a reduction of more than 70 per cent in rotor-induced vibration.

The other major change, by comparison with the Model 214A, is the replacement of the single Lycoming turboshaft engine by two General Electric turboshafts which, driving the rotor through a combining gearbox, give true single-engine flight capability. Multi-mission roles are

49

catered for by the provision of easily-removable passenger seating to offer 316 cu ft (8.95 m³) cargo capacity, full IFR avionics and instrumention, emergency flotation gear, an external cargo suspension system, and an internal rescue hoist.

Specification

Type: commercial transport helicopter
Powerplant: two 1,625-shp (1212-kW) General Electric CT7-2 turboshafts
Performance: maximum cruising speed 164 mph (264 km/h) at sea level; maximum cruising speed 161 mph (259 km/h) at 4,000 ft (1220 m); range, VFR, standard fuel, no reserves 519 miles (835 km)
Weights: maximum take-off 15,500 lb (7031 kg) with internal load, 16,500 lb (7484 kg) with external load
Dimensions: main rotor diameter 52 ft 0 in (15.85 m); length overall, rotors turning 62 ft 2¼ in (18.95 m); height 15 ft 10½ in (4.84 m); main rotor disc area 2,124 sq ft (197.32 m²)
Operators: deliveries are scheduled to begin in 1982

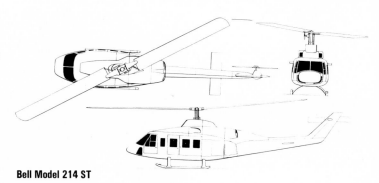

Bell Model 214 ST

Bell Model 222

History and Notes

Bell Helicopters first announced in April 1974 the company's intention to develop a new commercial helicopter which would be the first light twin-turbine commercial helicopter to be built in the USA. This was no blind decision for, shrewdly, a mock up of the company's design proposal had been exhibited at the annual convention of the Helicopter Association of America at the beginning of the year, giving potential customers an opportunity of making constructive suggestions for product improvement. The resulting interest was sufficient to warrant a decision to proceed with the construction of five prototypes, and the first of these flew on 13 August 1976.

Allocated the company designation Model 222, these prototypes were used to complete the development and certification programme as quickly as possible, with FAA certification in VFR configuration being gained on 20 December 1979. The Model 222 benefits from new-technology features developed at an earlier date for both civil and military helicopters, and includes the nodal suspension system described for the Model 214ST, a no-lubricant elasto-

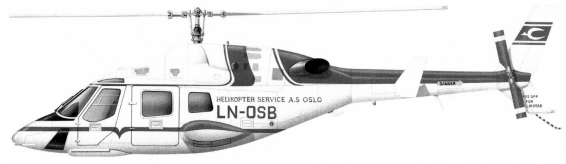

Bell Model 222 of Helikopter Service A.S., Norway.

meric bearing main rotor hub, and glassfibre/stainless steel main rotor blades.

The airframe structure is primarily of light alloy, the fuselage having a short-span cantilever sponson mounted on each side. Of aerofoil section, these provide some lift in forward flight and thus supplement the main rotor; in addition, they provide a housing for the main units of the tricycle type landing gear when retracted. The design includes more tail unit than seen on most helicopters, with both upper and lower sweptback fins and, mounted further forward on the aft fuselage, a tailplane with endplate fins. Maxi-

mum high-density seating capacity is for 10 occupants, comprising one or two crew, and nine or eight passengers respectively, but production aircraft are available in three versions. These comprise the basic Model 222 with a standard seating configuration for a pilot and seven passengers. Optionally there is the Model 222 Executive, fully equipped for IFR flight with a crew of one or two, and luxury accommodation for six or five passengers respectively; and the Model 222 Offshore, equipped for IFR operation with a crew of two, and with an emergency flotation system and auxiliary fuel tanks as standard.

The vital twin-turbine powerplant selected for the Model 222 consists of two Avco Lycoming LTS 101-650C-2 turboshafts, their dry weight of only 241 lb (110 kg) each providing a maximum power/weight ratio of 2.80 shp/lb (4.58 kW/kg) at maximum rating. It is interesting to note that the weight of the LTS 101 turboshaft is less than that of the APUs (auxiliary power units) which provide emergency electric and hydraulic power

The Bell 222 was the first commercial twin-engined light helicopter in the USA. It is of typical Bell design, but with a retractable landing gear. The interior can be modified to suit different roles.

in such aircraft as the British Aerospace Trident and BAC VC10.

Initial deliveries of VFR certificated Model 222s were made to Petroleum Helicopters and Schiavone Construction in January 1980.

Specification
Type: light commercial helicopter
Powerplant: two Avco Lycoming LTS 101-650C-2 turboshafts, each with a take-off rating of 675 shp (503 kW) and maximum continuous rating of 590 shp (440 kW)
Performance: maximum cruising speed 165 mph (265 km/h) at sea level; economic cruising speed 150 mph (241 km/h) at 8,000 ft (2440 m); service ceiling 20,000 ft (6100 m); range with maximum fuel and 20-min reserves 400 miles (644 km)
Weights: empty 4,550 lb (2064 kg); maximum take-off 7,650 lb (3470 kg)
Dimensions: main rotor diameter 39 ft 9 in (12.12 m); length of fuselage 36 ft 0¼ in (10.98 m); height 11 ft 6 in (3.51 m); main rotor disc area 1,241 sq ft (115.29 m²)
Operators: Petroleum Helicopters, Schiavone Construction and others

Bell Model 222

Bellanca Aries T-250

History and Notes
The Bellanca Aircraft Corporation is a subsidiary of Anderson, Greenwood & Company, and it is this latter company which has been responsible for the design and development of a new light aircraft under the designation T-250. It has had a remarkably long gestation period, for it was some nine years after work began that the design received FAA certification, in July 1976. At that time it was proposed that Bellanca should produce a first batch of 15 to 20, with deliveries during 1978; annual production was planned at 50.

Extensive demonstrations were undertaken with the prototype in 1977, but economic reasons forced Bellanca to suspend production of its light aircraft range early in 1980, and work on the T-250, by now named Aries, was continued on a reduced scale. The first production Aries was delivered in April 1980,

but the planned construction rate at that time had slumped to only one per month. Production aircraft were five-seaters, but the fifth seat could be folded to make a 250-lb (113-kg) baggage space at the end of the cabin.

The Aries was Bellanca's first all-metal aircraft and was ahead of its time in one respect so far as light aircraft were concerned — it had an all-flying T-tail.

By mid-1980 only two Aries had been delivered, while a third was almost complete, but plans for continuing production were not known in early 1981.

Specification
Type: four/five-seat cabin monoplane
Powerplant: One 250-hp (186-kW) Avco Lycoming O-540-A4D5 flat-six piston engine

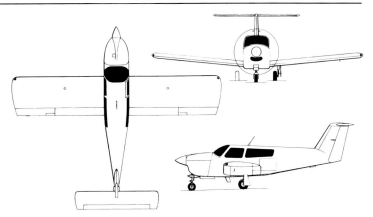

Bellanca Aries T-250

Performance: maximum speed 215 mph (346 km/h) at sea level; cruising speed 208 mph (335 km/h); service ceiling 18,100 ft (5515 m); range 1,170 miles (1883 km) with 4 occupants

Weights: empty 1,850 lb (839 kg); maximum take-off 3,150 lb (1429 kg)
Dimensions: span 31 ft 4 in (9.55 m); length 26 ft 2 in (7.98 m); height 8 ft 7 in (2.62 m) wing area 170 sq ft (15.79 m²)

Bellanca Citabria/Scout/Decathlon Series

History and Notes
When the Champion Model 7ECA Citabria made its first flight on 1 May 1964, it marked the first real change in appearance of the Champion family. A new, squared-off fin and rudder, plus smart wheel spats, gave the aeroplane an entirely new and more modern appearance, and in turn the basic Citabria design spawned a number of variants of its own. FAA certification was received on 5 August 1964, and the first production aircraft flew 13 days later. Initial aircraft could have either a 108-hp (81-kW) Avco Lycoming O-235-C1 engine or a 100-hp (75-kW) Continental O-200-A, and production was at the rate of seven aircraft a week.

Further models were the 7GCAA with a 150-hp (112-kW) Avco Lycoming O-320-AB, first flown in prototype

form on 30 May 1965, construction having taken just 30 days, with the first production model following on 20 July; the 7GCBC, which was similar but had increased span and offered the 108-hp (81-kW) Avco Lycoming as an option; and the 7KCAB with the 160-hp (119-kW) Avco Lycoming IO-320-A2B engine. It was with this last model, claimed to be the only aerobatic aircraft at that time certificated with a special fuel system for prolonged inverted flying, that the name became apparent, since Citabria spelled backwards is airobatic.

Following the merger in 1970 with the Bellanca Sales Company, when the name became Bellanca Aircraft Corporation, two new models were announced, the 7GCBC Scout and 8KCAB Decathlon. The Scout, a utility version of the Citabria, had an

increased span and metal flaps, a 150-hp (112-kW) Avco Lycoming O-320-A2B engine and the ability to carry a glassfibre underfuselage tank with a 90-US gallon (341-litre) capacity for crop dusting; it could also have a glider towhook installed.

The Decathlon which, except for a strengthened airframe, was generally similar to the 150-hp (112-kW) version of the Citabria, received its FAA certification on 16 October 1970, in the normal and aerobatic categories, and was designed for loads of +6g and -5g. A first tentative hand-built batch of 14 was rapidly sold out, the initial delivery taking place on 24 February 1971, and Bellanca placed the type in full-scale production.

Production of the three models continued until the beginning of 1980, when financial difficulties forced the suspension of further work. By that

time 5,186 Citabrias, 329 Scouts and 552 Decathlons had been built. The specification applies to the Bellanca 7GCAA Citabria.

Specification
Type: two-seat light monoplane
Powerplant: one 150-hp (112-kW) Avco Lycoming O-320-A2B flat-four piston engine
Performance: maximum speed 130 mph (209 km/h) at sea level; maximum cruising speed 125 mph (201 km/h) at 8,000 ft (2440 m); service ceiling 17,000 ft (5180 m); range 537 miles (864 km)
Weights: empty 1,037 lb (470 kg); maximum take-off 1,650 lb (748 kg)
Dimensions: span 33 ft 5 in (10.19 m); length 22 ft 8 in (6.91 m); height 6 ft 7¾ in (2.03 m); wing area 165 sq ft (15.33 m²)

Bellanca Viking Series

History and Notes
The present Bellanca Viking is descended, through a number of differently named companies, from the original prewar Model 14-9 Junior, via the early postwar Model 14-13-3 Cruisair and Model 14-19 Cruisemaster with a 230-hp (172-kW) Continental engine.

Bellanca Aircraft Corporation sold full rights and all tools and jigs for the Model 14-19 to Northern Aircraft Inc., which became the Downer Aircraft Company Inc. in January 1959. More than 100 Cruisemasters were built before production changed over to the Downer Bellanca 260, a modified version of the earlier aircraft with tricycle landing gear and a 260-hp (194-kW) Continental engine. The prototype flew on 6 November

1958, and the first production model on 20 February 1959. Further changes in company structure resulted in Inter-Air (International Aircraft Manufacturing Inc.) of Minnesota taking over manufacture, by which time the designation had changed to Model 14-19-3A in the early 1960s and the present shape of the Viking with its distinctive swept fin and rudder appeared.

By 1967, Inter-Air had become the Bellanca Sales Company (a subsidiary of Miller Flying Service) and had further developed the aircraft into the Bellanca 260C Model 14-19-3C, and at this time the Viking 300 made its appearance, with a 300-hp (224-kW) Continental engine married to the 260C airframe. Production of the

two aircraft continued at the rate of around 20 a month.

In 1970 the Bellanca Sales Company acquired the Champion Aircraft Corporation and the name was yet again changed, this time to Bellanca Aircraft Corporation. Early in 1980, financial problems caused the company to cease production; at that time 1,670 Vikings of various models had been built and the three versions offered in 1980 were the Model 17-30A Super Viking 300A with the 300-hp (224-kW) Continental IO-520-K engine; the Model 17-31A Super Viking 300A with the 300-hp (224-kW) Avco Lycoming IO-540-K1L5; and the Model 17-31ATC Turbo Viking 300 A with the same Avco Lycoming engine plus two Rajay

turbochargers. The specification applies to the Bellanca Viking 300A.

Specification
Type: four-seat light monoplane
Powerplant: one 300-hp (224-kW) Continental IO-520-K flat-six piston engine
Performance: maximum speed 226 mph (364 km/h); maximum cruising speed 188 mph (303 km/h); service ceiling 17,000 ft (5180 m); range 849 miles (1366 km)
Weights: empty 2,217 lb (1006 kg); maximum take-off 3,325 lb (1508 kg)
Dimensions: span 34 ft 2 in (10.41 m); length 26 ft 4 in (8.03 m); height 7 ft 4 in (2.24 m); wing area 161.5 sq ft (15.00 m²)

Boeing Model 707

History and Notes

Even before World War II had ended, there were those connected with the UK's aircraft industry who were actively using their brains to evolve a way in which the nation might break into the anticipated very large postwar market for transport aircraft. The early dominance of the civil transport scene gained by such aircraft as the Boeing 247 and Douglas DC-3 in the immediate prewar years had given the USA a significant lead. The fortunes of war, which resulted in Britain concentrating on the design and development of short-range military aircraft, with the USA responsible for long-range military transport/bombing aircraft, provided still wider experience for the US industry. This experience in the development of large capacity, long-range landplanes would, it was feared, almost certainly ensure their complete domination of the postwar market for long-range civil airliners.

The UK, however, held one ace: a very considerable lead in the development and construction of aircraft turbine powerplants, and it needed but little foresight to appreciate that these engines could revolutionise air travel for business and pleasure. By combining the gas turbine with an advanced airframe, the UK might well gain a lead in this class of aviation which the US manufacturers would find difficult to match. This explains why, as early as 1944, de Havilland's R.E. Bishop and his design team had started to crystallise their ideas into a positive design proposal. The story of the de Havilland Comet, of which the prototype (G-ALVG) flew for the first time on 27 July 1949, is well known. Its capability was revolutionary by comparison with the piston-engined airliners which it replaced, or with which it was in competition. Sir Miles Thomas,

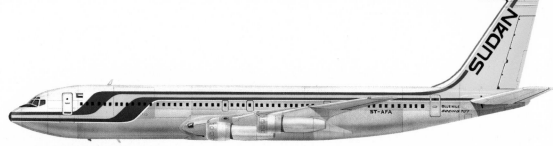

Boeing 707-320C of Sudan Airways.

who was BOAC's chairman when the Comet entered revenue service on 2 May 1952, emphasised that it represented the beginning of a new era in international travel, effectively halving the size of the world. Within two years, however, structural failure of the Comet's pressurised cabin brought the hopes and dreams of the British aviation industry to an end.

In the USA, The Boeing Company was the first to appreciate the potential of the gas turbine engine to power a new generation of civil transport aircraft, and to take positive action to design and construct such a machine. The process had begun when the company initiated studies for a turbojet- or turboprop-powered version of the military C-97 Stratofreighter, a heavy cargo/transport aircraft derived from the B-29 Superfortress. Little or no interest came in response to Boeing's proposals, and in August 1952 the company took the bold step of gambling some $16 million to build the prototype of a completely new turbojet-powered civil transport. To maintain a degree of secrecy for this project it was allocated the designation 367-80, known as 'Dash-80' to Boeing employees, although higher echelons of the company knew that it would be marketed as the Model 707.

Boeing were sufficiently realistic to appreciate from the very beginning

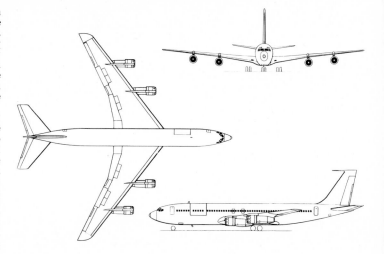

Boeing 707-320C

that their large private-venture investment, even in 1952 dollars, was nowhere near the amount that would be needed if large-scale production of a civil airliner was to become a reality. Shrewdly, they developed the initial design to serve as a high-speed military transport, or flight refuelling tanker, banking upon gaining a military contract which would underwrite the tooling

costs and provide finance for the development of a first-class civil airliner.

The 367-80 prototype, which was rolled out on 14 May 1954, had

The greatness of the Boeing 707 is confirmed by the number still in service, including this Model 707-320, one of seven operated by Avianca (Aerovias Nacionales de Colombia).

Boeing Model 707

clearly derived from the civil piston-engined Model 377 Stratocruiser and the military KC-97, but aerodynamically had a close relationship to the B-47 Stratojet which had entered service with the USAF in 1950. It retained the distinctive wing of the jet bomber, swept back 35°, and the mounting of the inboard powerplant of the B-47, with two turbojets paired in side-by-side nacelles and carried on a cantilever underwing pylon, had received serious consideration for the 'Dash-80'. However, it was appreciated that under certain circumstances the failure of one unit of the pair could result in the need to shut down the remaining operative engine, seriously compromising reserve power, and it was decided instead, as a safety measure, to install the engines in individual pylon-mounted pods which have become a characteristic feature of the Model 707/720 and later 747.

Flown for the first time on 15 July 1954, the 'Dash-80' prototype was powered by four 9,500-lb (4309-kg) thrust Pratt & Whitney JT3P turbojets, and as originally flown was primarily a military demonstrator. At an early stage in its flight test programme the 'Dash-80' acquired a Boeing-designed flight refuelling boom, which had been developed to simplify the rapid transfer of fuel from tanker to receiver. With this combination of a high-performance large-capacity aircraft with flight refuelling capability, Boeing was able to demonstrate effectively to the USAF the potential of such a tanker for refuelling in-service and future bomber, fighter, reconnaissance, and transport aircraft at or near their operational altitudes, and at speeds which would not present any real problems for either of the aircraft involved. In less than three months from the first flight of the prototype,

on 5 October 1954, Boeing received an initial contract for 29 KC-135A tanker/transports, and there must have been jubilation in the board room when it was realised that the gamble had paid off: in the long term the company was to build more than 800 military versions of the civil Model 707 under basic C-135 and C-137 designations.

With military interest secured,

the 'Dash-80' was equipped as a civil demonstrator offering, initially to US airlines, a turbojet aircraft that would soon make obsolete the existing piston-engine airliners operating US domestic transcontinental routes. The first contract came from pioneering Pan American, which on 13 October 1955 ordered six examples of the first production version, which had the designation Model 707-120.

The Boeing 707 is by any standards a classic among airliners. Seen here is one of the Model 707-320B Intercontinentals operated by Olympic Airways alongside four Model 707-320C Convertibles.

When operated as a pure freighter, the Boeing 707 has its windows blanked out. Illustrated is such a 707-320C of German Cargo Services, a Lufthansa subsidiary operating to Africa and the Far East.

Just three months prior to that date, the USAF had given Boeing clearance to build civil developments of the 'Dash-80' simultaneously with the manufacture of military C/KC-135s, and no time was lost in establishing a production line for civil aircraft. Pan American's first -120 flew initially on 20 December 1957, was delivered to the airline in the following August, and on 26 October 1958—despite being intended primarily for continental services—was used to inaugurate Pan Am's New York-London transatlantic jet airliner service. This move was, however, a flag-waving rather than a practical operation, and Pan Am's -120s soon reverted to the domestic routes for which they had been intended. It was not until this airline received its first true long-range versions of the 707, namely the 707-320 Intercontinental, that sustained scheduled transatlantic flights began on 10 October 1959.

Production of the Model 707 had virtually come to an end in the autumn of 1980, by which time 808 had been ordered and 784 delivered in a manufacturing programme of 25 years. In that time there have been a number of civil versions, these including the 707-020, which was the original designation of the intermediate-range Model 720, the 707-120, 707-120B (turbofan-powered), and 707-220 domestic models; and 707-320, 707-320B (turbofan-powered), 707-320C cargo or mixed cargo/passenger, and 707-420 (Rolls-Royce Conway-powered) Intercontinental long-range versions. A long-range variant with CFM International CFM56 turbofan engines was proposed in 1979 under the designation 707-700, but in early 1980 it had been decided not to proceed with the development of this aircraft.

Final version in production was the 707-320C Convertible, a multi-purpose aircraft which in a typical layout accommodates 14 first-class and 133 coach-class passengers; it is, however, certificated to carry a maximum of 219 passengers in a high-density seating arrangement. Alternatively it can be operated in mixed passenger/cargo, or all-cargo roles, and in the latter configuration can accept up to 13 Type A containers in the main upper-deck cargo space, in addition to the 1,700 cu ft (48.14 m³) of bulk cargo capacity on the lower, standard cargo deck. Throughout the 25 years that the 707 was in production, there had been continuing development to enhance performance, economy of operation, load-carrying capability, and range. Significant in the improvement of all four of these parameters had been the development of the wing structure, that of the -320C incorporating on each wing an inboard and outboard aileron, one fillet type and two Fowler type trailing-edge flaps, four spoilers forward of the trailing-edge flaps, and full-span leading-edge flaps. All ailerons and spoilers are used to provide lateral control at low speeds, but only the inboard ailerons and spoilers are used in cruising flight.

The landing gear, of the hydraulically retractable tricycle type, has a twin-wheel nose unit, and each main unit comprises a four-wheel bogie. The landing gear can be extended in flight to operate in conjunction with the spoilers to provide a high rate of descent for specific operational needs. Not surprisingly, for an aircraft that has a history which is contemporaneous with the development of the gas turbine engine, the 707 has had a variety of powerplants installed. The 9,500-lb (4309-kg) thrust JT3Ps,

which had powered the 'Dash-80' initially, were replaced by 13,500-lb (6123-kg) thrust JT3C-6s in the initial production version. Pratt & Whitney JT3D-1 or JT3D-3 turbofans of 17,000-lb (7711-kg) or 18,000-lb (8165-kg) thrust respectively were available for the 707-120B, and the highest powered turbojets for the first long-range 707-320 were JT4A-11s of 17,500-lb (7938-kg) thrust. The Rolls-Royce Conway Mk 508 turbofans which BOAC specified for installation in the 707-420 were of similar thrust. The late production 707-320Cs have Pratt & Whitney JT3D-7 turbofans, and the net result of this progression of engine powers is that the intercontinental 707-320C in all-cargo configuration has a maximum take-off weight almost 34 per cent greater than the domestic 707-220 of 1959. If one bears in mind that the -220's JT4A-3 engines developed 15,800-lb (7167-kg) thrust, a few quick jabs at a calculator will confirm the mental arithmetic which says that percentage engine thrust has not increased in the same proportion, and emphasise the benefits of the aerodynamic improvements.

Some of the improvements had derived from evaluation by BOAC of their first four 707-420s, as a result of which they requested the development of modifications to enhance control and stability. Thus, the vertical tail was increased in height, and additional fin area was provided beneath the fuselage tail cone, these

Seven Boeing 707-320B/Cs are used by Cathay Pacific Airways from its base in Hong Kong for operations throughout the Far East and into the Middle East and Australia's main cities.

changes being incorporated subsequently in most of the -320Cs, as well as in many of the earlier production versions.

The story of Boeing's remarkable Model 707 would be incomplete without a final mention of the 'Dash-80', a prototype *par excellence* which, in almost 18 years of service, must have become one of the most exten-

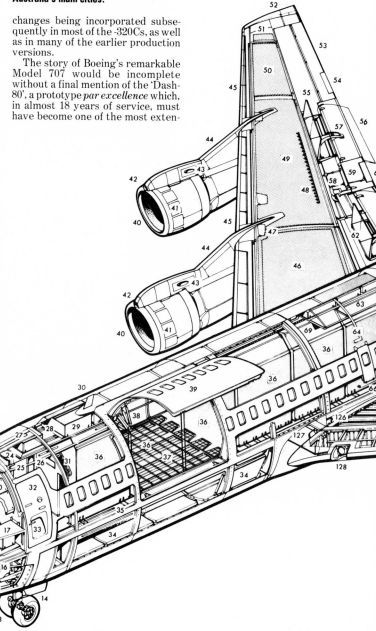

Boeing Model 707

sively modified aircraft in aviation history. In addition to changes which related to the continuing development programme of the Model 707, the 'Dash-80' was to be the subject of many major aerodynamic and structural changes, to test new ideas and advanced features of later Boeing jet transports. These included new wing planforms, aerofoil surfaces, powerplants, and an entirely new wing leading-edge and trailing-edge flaps. It was even flown with a fifth engine in an aft-mounted pod, to evaluate the proposed installation planned for the Model 727. Happily, it did not suffer final ignominious destruction at the hands of scrapyard breakers for, on 25 April 1972, Boeing

announced that the 'Dash-80' was being presented to the Smithsonian Institution. The following details apply specifically to the 707-320C Convertible.

Specification

Type: four-turbofan commercial transport
Powerplant: four 19,000-lb (8618-kg) thrust Pratt & Whitney JT3D-7 turbofans
Performance: maximum level speed 627 mph (1009 km/h); maximum cruising speed 605 mph (979 km/h); economic cruising speed 550 mph (885 km/h); service ceiling 39,000 ft (11890 m); range with maximum fuel and 147

passengers, international fuel reserves, 5,755 miles (9262 km)
Weights: operating empty, passenger, 146,400 lb (66406 kg), cargo 141,100 lb (64002 kg); maximum take-off 333,600 lb (151318 kg)
Dimensions: span 145 ft 9 in (44.42 m); length 152 ft 11 in (46.61 m); height 42 ft 5 in (12.93 m); wing area 3,050 sq ft (283.35 m²)
Operators include: Aer Lingus, Air France, Air India, Airlift International, Alia Royal Jordanian Airlines, American Airlines, Aerolineas Argentinas, Avianca, Braniff International, British Airways, British Caledonian Airways, CAAC, Cameroon

Airlines, China Airlines, Continental Airlines, Egyptair, El Al Israel Airlines, Ethiopian Airlines, Flying Tiger Line, Iran Air, Iraqi Airways, Korean Air Lines, Kuwait Airways, LAN-Chile, Libyan Arab Airlines, Lufthansa, Middle East Airlines, Nigeria Airways, Northwest Airlines, Olympic Airways, Pakistan International Airlines, Pan American World Airways, Qantas Airways, Sabena Belgian World Airlines, Saudia, Seaboard World Airlines, South African Airways, Sudan Airways, TAP-Air Portugal, Tarom, Trans World Airlines, Varig, and Western Air Lines

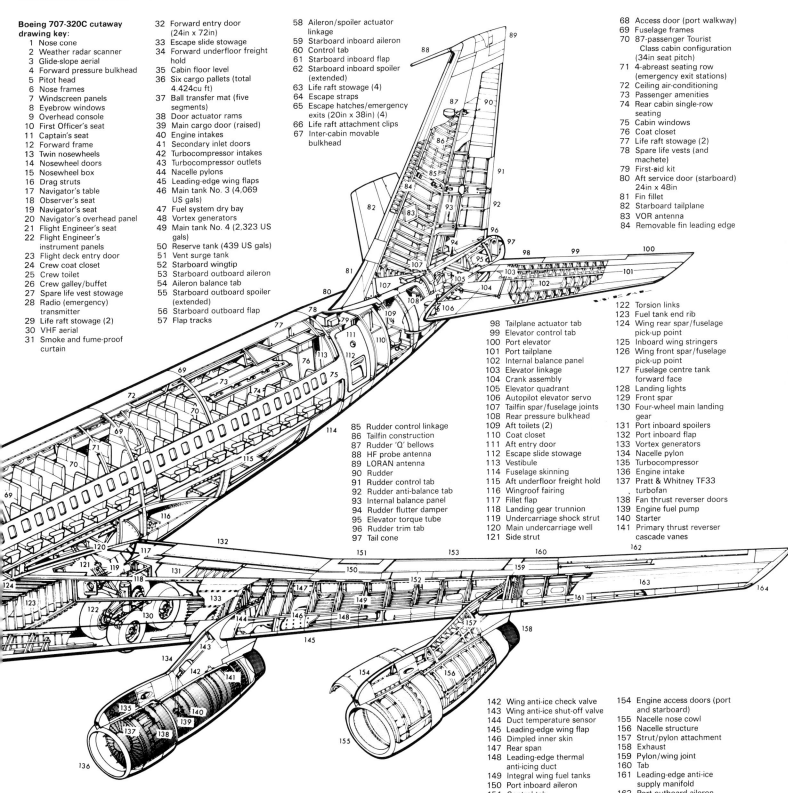

Boeing 707-320C cutaway drawing key:
1 Nose cone
2 Weather radar scanner
3 Glide-slope aerial
4 Forward pressure bulkhead
5 Pitot head
6 Nose frames
7 Windscreen panels
8 Eyebrow windows
9 Overhead console
10 First Officer's seat
11 Captain's seat
12 Forward frame
13 Twin nosewheels
14 Nosewheel doors
15 Nosewheel box
16 Drag struts
17 Navigator's table
18 Observer's seat
19 Navigator's seat
20 Navigator's overhead panel
21 Flight Engineer's seat
22 Flight Engineer's instrument panels
23 Flight deck entry door
24 Crew coat closet
25 Crew toilet
26 Crew galley/buffet
27 Spare life vest stowage
28 Radio (emergency) transmitter
29 Life raft stowage (2)
30 VHF aerial
31 Smoke and fume-proof curtain

32 Forward entry door (24in x 72in)
33 Escape slide stowage
34 Forward underfloor freight hold
35 Cabin floor level
36 Six cargo pallets (total 4.424cu ft)
37 Ball transfer mat (five segments)
38 Door actuator rams
39 Main cargo door (raised)
40 Engine intakes
41 Secondary inlet doors
42 Turbocompressor intakes
43 Turbocompressor outlets
44 Nacelle pylons
45 Leading-edge wing flaps
46 Main tank No. 3 (4,069 US gals)
47 Fuel system dry bay
48 Vortex generators
49 Main tank No. 4 (2,323 US gals)
50 Reserve tank (439 US gals)
51 Vent surge tank
52 Starboard wingtip
53 Starboard outboard aileron
54 Aileron balance tab
55 Starboard outboard spoiler (extended)
56 Starboard outboard flap
57 Flap tracks

58 Aileron/spoiler actuator linkage
59 Starboard inboard aileron
60 Control tab
61 Starboard inboard flap
62 Starboard inboard spoiler (extended)
63 Life raft stowage (4)
64 Escape straps
65 Escape hatches/emergency exits (20in x 38in) (4)
66 Life raft attachment clips
67 Inter-cabin movable bulkhead

68 Access door (port walkway)
69 Fuselage frames
70 87-passenger Tourist Class cabin configuration (34in seat pitch)
71 4-abreast seating row (emergency exit stations)
72 Ceiling air-conditioning
73 Passenger amenities
74 Rear cabin single-row seating
75 Cabin windows
76 Coat closet
77 Life raft stowage (2)
78 Spare life vests (and machete)
79 First-aid kit
80 Aft service door (starboard) 24in x 48in
81 Fin fillet
82 Starboard tailplane
83 VOR antenna
84 Removable fin leading edge

85 Rudder control linkage
86 Tailfin construction
87 Rudder 'Q' bellows
88 HF probe antenna
89 LORAN antenna
90 Rudder
91 Rudder control tab
92 Rudder anti-balance tab
93 Internal balance panel
94 Rudder flutter damper
95 Elevator torque tube
96 Rudder trim tab
97 Tail cone

98 Tailplane actuator tab
99 Elevator control tab
100 Port elevator
101 Port tailplane
102 Internal balance panel
103 Elevator linkage
104 Crank assembly
105 Elevator quadrant
106 Autopilot elevator servo
107 Tailfin spar/fuselage joints
108 Rear pressure bulkhead
109 Aft toilets (2)
110 Coat closet
111 Aft entry door
112 Escape slide stowage
113 Vestibule
114 Fuselage skinning
115 Aft underfloor freight hold
116 Wingroof fairing
117 Fillet flap
118 Landing gear trunnion
119 Undercarriage shock strut
120 Main undercarriage well
121 Side strut

122 Torsion links
123 Fuel tank end rib
124 Wing rear spar/fuselage pick-up point
125 Inboard wing stringers
126 Wing front spar/fuselage pick-up point
127 Fuselage centre tank forward face
128 Landing lights
129 Front spar
130 Four-wheel main landing gear
131 Port inboard spoilers
132 Port inboard flap
133 Vortex generators
134 Nacelle pylon
135 Turbocompressor
136 Engine intake
137 Pratt & Whitney TF33 turbofan
138 Fan thrust reverser doors
139 Engine fuel pump
140 Starter
141 Primary thrust reverser cascade vanes

142 Wing anti-ice check valve
143 Wing anti-ice shut-off valve
144 Duct temperature sensor
145 Leading-edge wing flap
146 Dimpled inner skin
147 Rear span
148 Leading-edge thermal anti-icing duct
149 Integral wing fuel tanks
150 Port inboard aileron
151 Control tab
152 Port outboard spoilers
153 Port outboard flap

154 Engine access doors (port and starboard)
155 Nacelle nose cowl
156 Nacelle structure
157 Strut/pylon attachment
158 Exhaust
159 Pylon/wing joint
160 Tab
161 Leading-edge anti-ice supply manifold
162 Port outboard aileron
163 Wing skinning
164 Port wingtip

Boeing Model 720

History and Notes

The early success of the Boeing 707 led the company to proceed with the development of an intermediate-range version under the initial designation of 707-020. Externally very similar in appearance to the 707-120, it retained the same wing and tailplane span, and needed the discriminating eye of a teenage enthusiast to note the modified wing profile with increased sweepback and changes to the trailing-edge at the wing roots. In fact, appearances were deceptive, for in terms of structure and weight the design was entirely new, resulting in the allocation of the designation Model 720 to add emphasis to the point that it was not merely a re-engined 707.

Most significant of the aerodynamic changes introduced on this new aircraft resulted from refinements to the wing leading-edge, which in turn increased the angle of sweepback and decreased the thickness/chord ratio. The leading-edge included also four additional segments of flaps, this being the first of the family with full-span leading-edge flaps, modifications that were later introduced to the Model 707 family on the -120B variant. The changes provided improved take-off performance and cruising speed. The length of the fuselage was reduced by 7 ft 9 in (2.36 m) by comparison with that of

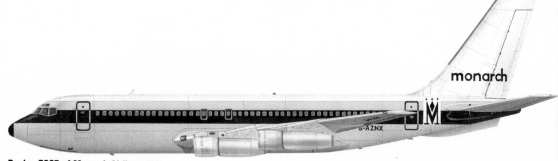

Boeing 720B of Monarch Airlines (UK).

the 707-120/-220, and reduction of the standard fuel load made it possible to lighten the structure. Typical accommodation was for 38 first-class and 74 tourist-class passengers, with facilities that included three galleys and three toilets.

The basic Model 720, powered by four 12,500-lb (5670-kg) thrust Pratt & Whitney JT3C-7 turbojet engines, flew for the first time on 23 November 1959, and entered service initially with United Airlines on 5 July 1960. It was followed by the improved Model 720B which introduced Pratt & Whitney JT3D turbofan engines, initially JT3D-1s of 17,000-lb (7711-kg) thrust. These not only made it possible to operate from still shorter runways, but their greater efficiency allowed for some increase in range despite a higher payload. First flown

on 6 October 1960, this version entered service with American Airlines on 12 March 1961. There was, however, only a limited demand for the smaller-capacity 720/720Bs, and production ended in 1969 after a total of 154 had been built and delivered.

Specification

Type: intermediate-range commercial transport
Powerplant (720B): four 18,000-lb (8165-kg) thrust Pratt & Whitney JT3D-3 turbofans
Performance: maximum level speed 627 mph (1009 km/h); maximum cruising speed 611 mph (983 km/h) at 25,000 ft (7620 m); economic cruising speed 557 mph (896 km/h) at 40,000 ft (12190 m); service ceiling 42,000 ft (12800 m);

range with maximum payload and no reserves 4,155 miles (6687 km)
Weights: operating empty 112,883 lb (51203 kg); maximum take-off 234,000 lb (106141 kg)
Dimensions: span 130 ft 10 in (39.88 m); length 136 ft 9 in (41.68 m); height 41 ft 6½ in (12.66 m); wing area 2,521 sq ft (234.20 m²)
Operators include: Aeroamerica, Aerocondor, Air Malta, Air Zimbabwe-Rhodesia, Avianca, Belize Airways, Conair, El Al Israel Airlines, Ethiopian Airlines, Maesk Air, Middle East Airlines, Olympic Airways, Pakistan Airlines

The Boeing 720 is the smaller brother of the Model 707. One of the major users of the type is Air Malta, which has five of these medium-range airliners, each able to carry up to 167 passengers.

Boeing Model 727

History and Notes

Even before the Boeing 707 was ready for service, the company had realised the desirability of complementing this aircraft with a new short/medium-range airliner, and in February 1956 began to study the market and its requirements. There were a number of important factors, some imposed by contemporary conditions, that played a significant part in the final design. For example, it was an era of rapid growth in air travel, when potential passengers

were multiplying at a higher rate than aircraft seats to carry them: a short-term solution was to increase the seating density of existing airliners, or to lengthen the fuselage of suitable machines to provide greater accommodation. This could be done comparatively fast; airport runways to cater for such conversions, however, could only be lengthened and strengthened on a worldwide basis over a much longer period of time.

This gave a design starting point, for the new aircraft would need good

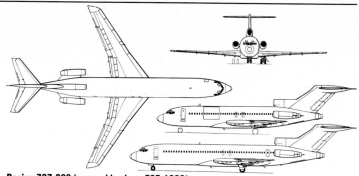

Boeing 727-200 (upper side view: 727-100C)

A Boeing 727-200 of Alaska Airlines, which uses the type largely for services within Alaska and to Seattle. The company has four such aircraft, as well as four of the shorter-fuselage Model 727-100s.

Boeing 727-200 of US Air (formerly Allegheny Airlines).

take-off and landing characteristics for the average runway length that was then general. Operation over 'short-haul' routes required an effective solution to a nasty problem: the provision of the highest possible cruising speed at the lowest possible altitude, whilst holding seat/mile costs at a minimum figure. Short stage lengths entail also a higher proportion of landings in relation to flight hours, not only affecting the design of landing gear, but of servicing access to the airliner to cater for the increased number of 'turn-rounds', which are non-revenue periods. And with the capability of operating into and out of smaller airports, often nearer to city centres, the question of engine noise emission might prove a critical factor in determining final acceptance or rejection.

It is not surprising, therefore, that Boeing's Preliminary Design Group spent some three years in examining almost 70 different design proposals, before finalising the broad definition of the airliner which was considered most suitable for this particular spectrum of the air transport scene at that time. Estimates suggested a potential market for 300 or more aircraft, and this factor also had some influence on design, emphasising the economic desirability of using as many Model 707 and 720 components and systems as possible.

It was assumed that engines of suitable power would be available, irrespective of whether a two-, three- or four-engine layout was selected, but engine position was not easy to define. The need to develop an efficient wing would be simplified if it did not have to serve also as a mounting for the powerplant, and this encouraged the investigation of rear-engine configurations. Several two- and four-engine wing-mounted arrangements were considered, as were rear-

mounted podded engines similar to those selected for the Sud-Aviation Caravelle (two) and BAC VC10 (four). Even when three engines appeared to be the most desirable solution, configurations which were evaluated included one beneath each wing and one at the tail; two beneath one wing and one under the other; and three mounted within the aft fuselage. The last evolved into the arrangement which was finally selected: one in the tail of the fuselage, with its air intake forward of the fin, and a pod-mounted engine on each side of the aft fuselage. At an early stage the intention was to use an Allison version of the Rolls-Royce Spey to power this new design, but the Pratt & Whitney JT8D was selected at a later date, all three engines being fitted with thrust-reversers to help with short-field landing problems.

Of the utmost importance to the success of this project was the design of an advanced wing that would provide the necessary broad range of performance. This was required not only to cater for short-field operation at comparatively low speeds, but at the other end of a wide speed range to permit economic high cruising speeds at the desirable lower altitudes of short-haul operations. In fact, the company appreciated that success or failure of the whole project could well be determined by the wing design; and since an advanced, high-lift wing could be a valuable asset in its own right, the design team began detail design and development long before a decision was made to proceed with the new airliner, by then identified as the Boeing 727.

As finalised, each 727 wing incorporates special aerofoil sections of Boeing design, and includes four slats on the outer two-thirds, and three Krueger flaps on the inner third of the leading-edge; inboard (high speed) and outboard (low speed) ailerons; seven spoilers on the upper surface, the five (outboard) being flight spoilers that operate in conjunction with the ailerons, and the remaining two being ground spoilers (lift dumpers), the spoilers also being usable as air brakes; and triple-slotted trailing-edge flaps. There is also a leading-edge fence at roughly the half-span point of each wing. At the period of its design this represented a fairly complex wing, and certainly one of the most advanced that had been projected for use on a civil airliner, resulting in extensive wind tunnel testing. The Model 707 'Dash-80' prototype became involved in the programme, not only completing almost a year of test flying to evaluate the triple-slotted flaps, but also posing as a five-engine aircraft, with a pod-mounted rear-engine on the port side of the fuselage. In the long term it was very worthwhile, resulting in the development of a wing with the wide speed range and high lift that had been considered essential, and there is little doubt that this structure has contributed significantly to the success of the Model 727.

A decision to use the fuselage upper lobe of the Model 707 for this new project also offered considerable economy in tooling, and the new lower fuselage was reduced in height (and consequently capacity) by comparison with the 707 because of the

smaller cargo/baggage space required for short-haul operations This new structure incorporated two features that gave the 727 an operational capability that was to help to make it attractive to operators working over very short stage lengths: a hydraulically actuated ventral airstair, and an auxiliary power unit (APU) to provide compressed air and electrical power, thus making this aircraft capable of independent operation at small airports (or to speed turn-around). With engine self-start capability (from the APU), and able to put down or pick up passengers without the need for any airport ground service vehicles, airbus cross-country services were entirely practical. A forward port passenger door was available for use with conventional airport equipment.

Despite the long gestation period of the 727 project, a decision to proceed with manufacture and certification was dependent upon sufficient airline interest to ensure that it was not a speculative gamble. United Airlines had shown a great deal of enthusiasm from an early date, and the requirements of this operator had considerable influence on the final configuration of the 727. Eastern Air Lines was also a potential customer, and with these two companies expected to order 40 aircraft each, Boeing's management authorised a construction go-ahead in August 1960. It was not until four months later, on 5 December, that the above airlines finalised their orders: 40 for Eastern, and 20 plus 20 options for United.

The first 727, a production aircraft in United insignia, made its maiden

A Boeing 727-200 of Trans World Airlines. The Model 727 is the world's best-selling airliner, with orders for more than 1,800 examples. Trans World Airlines, which has a major US network in addition to its international services, is one of the 727's main users: among the airline's fleet are numbered 27 Model 727-100s, eight Model 727-100Cs, and 46 Model 727-200s/Advanced 200s, with 10 on order.

flight on 9 February 1963, some months behind schedule, and was followed by a Boeing demonstrator aircraft on 12 March and two more production aircraft very shortly after this. These four aircraft completed the FAA certification programme by the end of the year, making good the time that had been lost, and enabling the initial deliveries to Eastern and United to be made on the contract dates.

Airline services with the Boeing 727 were initiated by Eastern Air Lines on 1 February 1964, and with United Airlines only five days later. Both companies were to discover very quickly that teething problems were minimal and, of even greater importance in the long term, that the Boeing 727's economics were better than anticipated: United found the 727s cheaper to operate than its twin-engine Caravelles, even on the shortest stage lengths. However, at that time the initial 727-100 was very much tailored to the operational requirements of these two airlines, and this point was emphasised by the fact that the order book for this aircraft totalled 127 in the early spring of 1962, and was unchanged by the end of the year. Clearly, if the hoped-for 300 or more sales were to be made, the airliner must prove attractive to a wider range of operators. This resulted in the certification of versions with higher gross weights and various fuel options, thus making them more flexible to operate. By the summer of 1964 total orders had crept slowly past the 200 mark, but there was still no clear indication that the 727 was likely to exceed by very much, if at all, the early sales estimates.

In an attempt to widen the market, Boeing announced in the summer of 1964 the 727-100C, a convertible cargo/passenger version with strengthened flooring, and the large cargo door (port, forward) and cargo handling system of the 707-320C. By comparison with the basic 727-100, with standard accommodation for 94 passengers in mixed-class, or 131 in high-density seating, the 727-100C could be all-cargo or seat a maximum standard of 94 mixed-class passengers: a movable bulkhead could provide a number of variations between the two. Shortly afterwards the 727-100QC (quick change) was announced, this having passenger seats, galleys, and toilets palletised to permit a change from all-passenger to all-cargo configuration in less than an hour. The first 727-100C entered service with Northwest Airlines (now Northwest Orient) on 23 April 1966, and the first 727-100QC with United in May 1966.

By late 1964 it had become clear to Boeing's management that there was a growing demand for a higher-capacity short-range transport, and the decision to develop a 'stretched' version of the 727, announced in August 1965, was to prove the turning point in the marketing of this aircraft. Designated 727-200, the new version had no significant differences from the earlier 727-100, except for the insertion of two 10-ft (3.05-m) fuselage plugs, one forward and one aft of the main landing gear wheel-well. Fuel tankage, gross weight and powerplant remained unchanged, leaving the individual airline to decide whether it needed maximum fuel and range with a smaller passenger load, or a maximum of up to 189 passengers with reduced fuel and range.

First airline to order this new version, shortly after the initial

The initial short-fuselage Boeing 727-100 sold well (571 including -100C/QC models). Of this number Transbrasil S/A Linhas Aereas has six -100s and 10 -100Cs, supplemented by two Model 727-200s with the fuselage stretch of 20 ft (6.1 m).

Boeing Advanced 727-200 cutaway drawing key

1 Radome
2 Radar dish
3 Radar scanner mounting
4 Pressure bulkhead
5 Windscreen panels
6 Instrument panel shroud
7 Back of instrument panel
8 Rudder pedals
9 Radar transmitter and receiver
10 Pitot tube
11 Cockpit floor control ducting
12 Control column
13 Pilot's seat
14 Cockpit eyebrow windows
15 Co-pilot's seat
16 Engineer's control panel
17 Flight engineer's seat
18 Cockpit door
19 Observer's seat
20 Nosewheel bay
21 Nosewheel doors
22 Twin nosewheels
23 Retractable airstairs (optional)

24 Handrail
25 Escape chute pack
26 Front entry door
27 Front toilet
28 Galley
29 Starboard galley service door
30 Cabin bulkhead
31 Closet
32 Window frame panel
33 Radio and electronics bay
34 First class passenger cabin, 18 seats in mixed layout
35 Cabin roof construction
36 Seat rails
37 Cabin floor beams
38 Cargo door
39 Anti-collision light
40 Air conditioning supply ducting
41 Forward cargo hold
42 Cargo hold floor
43 Baggage pallet container
44 Tourist class passenger cabin, 119 seats in mixed layout

45 Communications antenna
46 Fuselage frame and stringer construction
47 Cabin window frame panels
48 Air conditioning system intake
49 Air conditioning plant
50 Overhead air ducting
51 Main fuselage frames
52 Escape hatches, port and starboard
53 Wing centre section No 2 fuel tank
54 Centre section stringer construction
55 Cabin floor construction
56 Starboard wing No 3 fuel tank
57 Inboard Krueger flaps
58 Krueger flap hydraulic jack
59 Leading edge fence
60 Outboard leading edge slat segments
61 Slat hydraulic jacks
62 Fuel vent surge tank

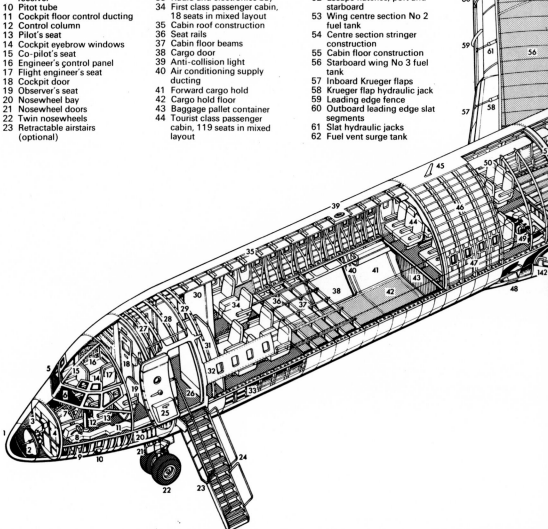

Boeing Model 727

63 Navigation lights
64 Starboard wing tip
65 Fuel jettison pipe
66 Static dischargers
67 Outboard, low speed, aileron
68 Aileron balance tab
69 Outboard spoilers
70 Outboard slotted flap
71 Flap screw jack mechanism
72 Inboard, high speed, aileron
73 Trim tab
74 Inboard spoilers
75 Inboard slotted flap
76 Fuselage centre section construction
77 Pressurised floor over starboard main undercarriage bay
78 Auxiliary power unit (APU)
79 Port main undercarriage bay
80 Tourist class, six-abreast, passenger seating
81 Overhead hand baggage stowage bins
82 Cabin trim panels
83 Rear cargo door
84 Aft cargo compartment floor
85 Passenger overhead service panels
86 Starboard service door/rear emergency exit
87 Aft galleys
88 Closet
89 Toilets, port and starboard
90 Cabin rear entry door
91 Starboard engine cowling
92 Centre engine intake
93 Noise attentuating intake lining

94 Intake S-duct
95 Duct de-icing
96 Fin root fairing construction
97 Fin construction
98 VOR aerial
99 Elevator control cables
100 Tailplane trim jack
101 Starboard tailplane
102 Elevator horn balance
103 Static dischargers
104 Starboard elevator
105 Elevator tab
106 Fin bullet fairing
107 VHF aerial boom
108 Elevator control jack
109 Port elevator
110 Tailplane construction
111 Port tailplane
112 Rudder upper section
113 Rudder control jacks
114 Rudder lower section
115 Lower section trim jack
116 Centre engine mounting pylon
117 Centre engine exhaust pipe
118 Thrust reverser
119 Centre engine
120 Rear fuselage construction
121 Side engine thrust reverser
122 Engine pylon fairing
123 Rear pressure bulkhead
124 Bleed air system pipes
125 Pratt & Whitney JT8D-9A turbofan engine
126 Detachable cowlings
127 Rear entry ventral airstairs
128 Engine air intake
129 Port rear service door/emergency exit

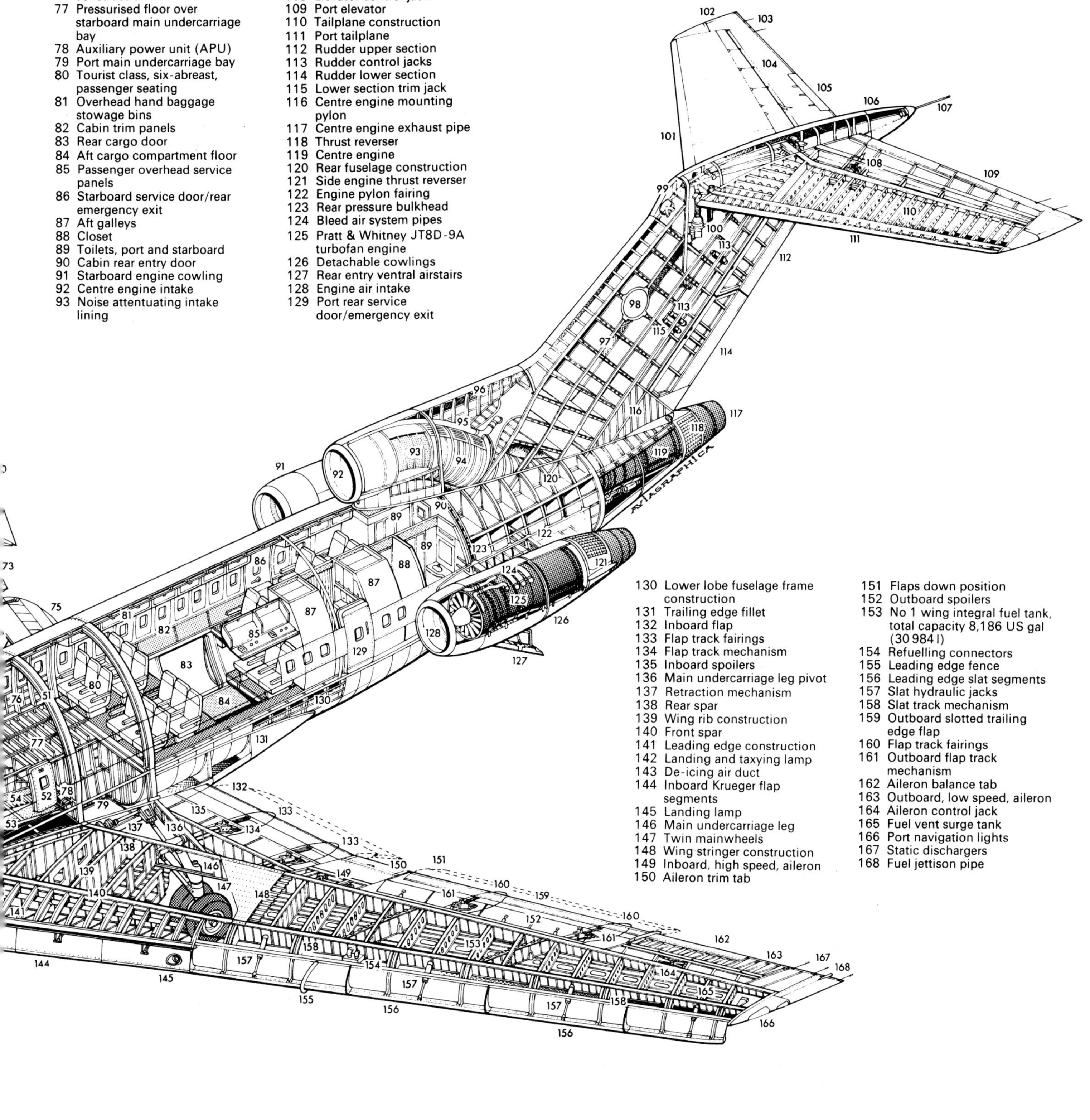

130 Lower lobe fuselage frame construction
131 Trailing edge fillet
132 Inboard flap
133 Flap track fairings
134 Flap track mechanism
135 Inboard spoilers
136 Main undercarriage leg pivot
137 Retraction mechanism
138 Rear spar
139 Wing rib construction
140 Front spar
141 Leading edge construction
142 Landing and taxying lamp
143 De-icing air duct
144 Inboard Krueger flap segments
145 Landing lamp
146 Main undercarriage leg
147 Twin mainwheels
148 Wing stringer construction
149 Inboard, high speed, aileron
150 Aileron trim tab

151 Flaps down position
152 Outboard spoilers
153 No 1 wing integral fuel tank, total capacity 8,186 US gal (30 984 l)
154 Refuelling connectors
155 Leading edge fence
156 Leading edge slat segments
157 Slat hydraulic jacks
158 Slat track mechanism
159 Outboard slotted trailing edge flap
160 Flap track fairings
161 Outboard flap track mechanism
162 Aileron balance tab
163 Outboard, low speed, aileron
164 Aileron control jack
165 Fuel vent surge tank
166 Port navigation lights
167 Static dischargers
168 Fuel jettison pipe

Boeing Model 727

One of the world's most successful operators, Delta Air Lines of Atlanta, Georgia, operates a fleet of some 114 Boeing 727-200s, with a further 12 on order. Eastern Air Lines is the only larger user of Boeing 727s.

announcement, was Northeast Airlines (now merged with Delta), and following certification of the 727-200 on 29 November 1967, it was this operator which flew the first revenue service on 14 December 1967. By then 727 orders had climbed to more than 500, of which almost 130 were for the -200, and thus orders for the 727-100 versions were approaching the 400 mark. They were, however, to increase to only a little over 500 before production of this version ended in late 1973. This emphasises the wisdom of the Boeing company in developing a stretched version, for 727 sales totalled more than 1,800 in mid-1980, of which almost 1,300 were 727-200s and Advanced 727-200s.

When the 727-200 was first launched, it will be remembered that seats could be traded against fuel, according to the stage lengths over which the airliner was operating. Boeing had appreciated that a maximum passenger load gave somewhat limited range, but had assumed that engine development would improve this situation. In this supposition the company was correct, for the 727-200 of 1967 had JT8D-7 or -9 engines of 14,500-lb (6577-kg) thrust, whereas powerplants with thrust ratings of up to 16,400 lb (7439 kg) were available for aircraft being ordered in 1980. Not only has engine thrust increased, but most of the later engines also offer greater fuel economy, permitting operations at increased gross weight or over longer range. This led to the company first announcing, on 12 May 1971, the introduction of a higher gross weight version, known as the Advanced 727-200. In addition to having a maximum brake release weight of 190,500 lb (86409 kg), it has also a redesigned interior, increased fuel capacity, and certification for Category IIIA automatic

landings. Following certification on 14 June 1972, the first revenue flight was made during the following month.

Features that are standard or optional for the Advanced 727-200 include modified nacelles which reduce engine noise emission; thicker wing skins; improved brakes and larger tyres to cater for the higher gross weight; improved air conditioning; and various fuel capacity options, with extra tanks in forward and aft cargo holds, to provide a maximum of 10,570 US gallons (40010 litres). To cope with the all-important feature of fuel economy, a performance data computer system is now standard, this ensuring that the powerplant is operated at optimum efficiency, irrespective of load, range, and variations in ambient conditions. A powerplant option, which improves significantly the take-off and initial climb performance in hot/high conditions, is available with 16,400-lb

(7439-kg) thrust JT8D-17R engines. Known as automatic performance reserve (APR), this equipment senses any significant loss in thrust by an engine during these two critical periods of flight operation, and increases automatically the thrust of the other two engines to 17,400 lb (7893 kg).

By the use of such advanced technology, coupled with steady improvement and refinement of the aircraft's structure, Boeing has ensured that this remarkable aeroplane has taken, and retained, a lead in the sales of large commercial turbine powered airliners. The company's decision in 1978 to develop the Model 757 a new short/medium-range advanced technology aircraft based on the Model 727 fuselage, may well mean that orders will go to this new aircraft rather than the 727. Even if this is the case, the performance and efficiency of the total of approxi-

mately 1,500 of these aircraft which were in service in mid-1980, would suggest that enthusiasts at airports will still be logging the registrations and details of these machines for many years to come.

Specification

Type: short/medium range three-turbofan commercial transport
Powerplant (standard): three 14,500-lb (6577-kg) thrust Pratt & Whitney JT8D-9A turbofans
Performance (727-200 at brake release weight of 184,800 lb: 83824 kg): maximum level speed 632 mph (1017 km/h) at 21,600 ft (6585 m); maximum cruising speed 592 mph (953 km/h) at 22,000 ft (6705 m); economic cruising speed 570 km/h (917 km/h) at 30,000 ft (9145 m); range at long-range cruising speed, 8,090 US gallons (30624 litres) fuel, ATA domestic reserves 2,303 miles (3706 km)
Weights (727-200): operating empty, typical 100,000 lb (45359 kg); maximum take-off 209,500 lb (95028 kg)
Dimensions: span 108 ft 0 in (32.92 m); length 153 ft 2 in (46.69 m); height 34 ft 0 in (10.36 m); wing area 1,700 sq ft (157.93 m²)
Operators: there are approximately 140 operators, but major users include Air Canada, Air France, Alaska Airlines, Alitalia, All Nippon Airways, American Airlines, Ansett Airlines, Avianca, Braniff International, Condor Flugdienst, Continental Airlines, Delta Air Lines, Eastern Air Lines, Hughes Airwest, Iberia, Iran Air, Libyan Arab Airlines, Lufthansa, Mexicana, National Airlines, Northwest Orient Airlines, Pacific Southwest Airlines, Pan American World Airways, Royal Air Maroc, Singapore Airlines, South African Airways, Sterling Airways, Trans-Australia Airlines, Transbrasil SA, Trans World Airlines, Tunis Air, United Airlines, and Western Airlines

Of Wien Air Alaska's fleet of Boeing 727-200s, one is a -200C convertible passenger/freight model, distinguishable by its large cargo door in the port side of the forward fuselage. Note the lowered ventral airstair door under the tail.

The mainstay of Iberia's short/medium-haul operations is a fleet of 37 Boeing 727-200s, each able to carry up to 189 passengers over a range of 2,465 miles (3965 km) at a long-range cruising speed of 592 mph (953 km/h).

Boeing Model 737

History and Notes

To complete the 'family' of airliners that had been initiated by the long-range Model 707, and short/medium-range Model 727, Boeing announced on 19 February 1965 the intention to build a complementary short-range twin-turbofan transport under the designation Model 737. A period of concentrated market research and design activity had preceded the company's decision, in November 1964, to develop this new aircraft, but no public announcement was made pending the receipt of an initial firm order. It was to come from Lufthansa, the first foreign airline to be first on the order book for a new airliner of US origin, this operator signing a contract for 21 737s which was announced simultaneously with the Boeing production decision.

The 'family' likeness of the 737 to its larger sisters was plain to see, due largely to retention of what was basically a 727 fuselage and a tail unit which was of similar configuration to that of the 707. In fact, there was some 60 per cent commonality of structure and systems between the 727 and 737 but the latter, nevertheless, was a very different aircraft. As originally conceived, accommodation for 60 to 85 passengers was envisaged, but the negotiations leading to finalisation of Lufthansa's contract showed that this operator required seating capacity for 100 passengers, and the fuselage length was sized accordingly. The ventral airstair of the Model 727 was not retained, and passenger doors and airstairs were provided at the forward and aft ends of the cabin, both on the port side. With an internal cabin length of just over 62 feet (19.90 m), and retention of the 727's maximum internal width, the accommodation appeared to be most spacious, and this undoubtedly contributed to the appeal of this transport.

The wing, like that of the 727, was required to provide good lift and low-speed handling characteristics for short-field operations, coupled with economic high-speed performance at the comparatively low altitudes of short-range commuter

Boeing 737-200 of Air Florida, USA.

services. It incorporated, therefore, much of the technology developed for the 727, including on each wing three leading-edge slats outboard of the engine nacelle, and Krueger leading-edge flaps inboard of the nacelle; a powered aileron, operating in conjunction with flight spoilers in the outer wing panel, these latter surfaces serving also as airbrakes; spoilers inboard of the engine nacelle to serve as lift-dumpers; and triple-slotted trailing-edge flaps.

The other major area of change concerned the powerplant, for the company's engineering studies had determined that only two engines would be required for the new aircraft. This virtually dictated a wing-mounted powerplant arrangement, avoiding any potential aerodynamic problems that might arise with a rear-engine/T-tail configuration. First choice was the Pratt & Whitney JT8D-1 turbofan of 14,000-lb (6350-kg) thrust, but by the time that the negotiations with Lufthansa had been completed the JT8D-7 turbofan had been substituted. Flat-rated to develop the same thrust at higher ambient temperatures than the JT8D-1, the -7 became the basic standard powerplant for the 737-100, with JT8D-9s of 14,500-lb (6577-kg) thrust optional.

The first 737-100, a company demonstrator aircraft, made its maiden flight on 9 April 1967, and the first of Lufthansa's aircraft flew during the following month. FAA certification was gained on 15 December 1967, and Lufthansa inaugurated its first services with the type on 10

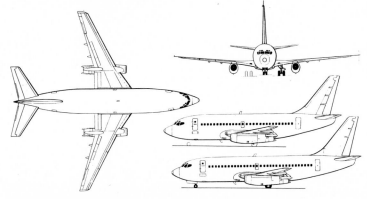

Boeing 737-200 (upper side view: 737-100)

February 1968.

Less than two months after Boeing's announcement of the intention to develop and market the 737, the company disclosed that a larger-capacity variant was also to be developed almost simultaneously. Identified as the 737-200, this was to become the standard model, the first of the type flying on 8 August 1967, gaining certification on 21 December, and entering revenue service with United Airlines on 29 April 1968. This version was evolved to satisfy the requirements of operators who needed greater seating capacity on 'local service' routes. The rapid growth in air travel, and consequently in seating capacity requirements, meant that there was virtually no demand for the 100/103-seat 737-100, which went out of production after a mere 30 had been built.

The 737-200 differed from the initial version in having a fuselage lengthened by 6 ft (1.83 m) and providing standard accommodation for 115 passengers. A maximum of 130 seats could be installed in a high-density arrangement, this being achieved without any reduction in other cabin facilities. Basic powerplant comprised the JT8D-9s which had been optional for the 737-100, and higher thrust versions of the JT8D engine were to become available at a later date. Within about a year from certification of the 737-200, convertible (737-200C) and quick-change (737-200QC) versions were made available to provide more flexibility in operation, and during a two-year period covering 1969-71 the company sought to enhance the sales potential of this aircraft by incorporating a number of improvements. These were developed to increase range, by the reduction of aerodynamic drag, and also to improve short-field performance. Changes within the first category introduced engine pods lengthened by 3 ft 9 in (1.14 m); refinement of the wing vortex generators, and leading-edge flaps and slats; the installation of more efficient thrust-reversers; and changes to the trailing-edge flaps to permit more effective settings for both take-off and landing.

The comparatively short take-off and landing distances required by the 737 meant that these aircraft were able to operate into airfields with unpaved or gravel runways. This required that the aircraft and its engines should be protected against impact and ingestion damage respectively, and Boeing developed suitable protection in kit form. This proved sufficiently effective for the company to gain FAA certification for 737s so equipped to operate from and to airports with gravel or unpaved runways. This kit includes vortex dissipators to prevent ingestion into the engines of damaging

The Boeing 737-200C convertible freight/passenger model of Royal Brunei Airlines, which also operates two Model 737-200s on its services to Singapore, Thailand, the Philippines and Hong Kong.

Air Europe is a British company which specialises in charter work and the air component of package holidays. The line's fleet consists of five Boeing 737-200s, with another two on order. This smallest of Boeing airliners possesses exceptional fuel economy, despite odd features such as landing gear main legs that retract into the lower fuselage but are not covered by doors to reduce drag.

foreign material, and the protection of antennae, beacons, hydraulic lines, landing gear, and the underside of the fuselage from impact damage.

In May 1971 new versions were announced under the overall designation Advanced 737-200, and included -200C and -200QC variants. All incorporated the improvements which had been introduced during the previous two years, plus minor aerodynamic refinement, automatic brakes, and a different anti-skid system. In the autumn of 1971 and in 1973, JT8D-15 and JT8D-17 turbofans respectively became available as optional equipment, the former rated at 15,500-lb (7031-kg) and the latter at 16,000-lb (7257-kg) thrust. Later improvements have included the introduction of a redesigned interior which gives the cabin a 'cleaner' and more spacious appearance; and acoustic treatment which reduces engine noise emission to the minimum attainable by contemporary technology. All current versions have a maximum take-off weight of 115,500 lb (52390 kg) when equipped with JT8D-9A engines, but installation of the optional higher rated engines provides a maximum take-off weight of 117,000 lb (53070 kg).

Although sales figures for the 737 have remained far below those of the 727, the demand has averaged in excess of 50 aircraft per year since the time that its availability was first announced. In mid-1980 orders and options totalled 836, of which 685 had been delivered, and there seems every reason to believe that a steady requirement for this excellent aircraft will continue throughout this decade. Included in 737 production are 19 aircraft which serve with the US Air Force as T-43A navigation trainers, and a small number have also been supplied to governments and business corporations for use a luxury executive transports. The following details apply to the basic Advanced 737-200.

In the first half of 1981 Boeing took the decision to proceed with the development of the Model 737-300. Designed specifically for the smaller trunk and larger regional airlines in the USA, the Model 737-300 will be an extensively refined aircraft, with a stretched fuselage and new engines. The main refinements planned are aerodynamic and structural: a lengthened nosewheel leg, strengthened wings, modified aerofoils for the leading-edge slats, revised tracks for the trailing-edge flaps, wingtip anti-flutter booms and a dorsal extension to the fin. The fuselage stretch will total 7 ft (2.13 m), with a plug of 2 ft (0.61 m) in front of the wings and one of 5 ft (1.52 m) behind them; the effect of this stretch, combined with an internal rearrangement, will be to increase economy-class seating from 113 to 128 passengers. However, the real key to the Model 737-300's success will be the new engines, initially the 20,000-lb (9072-kg) thrust General Electric CFM56-3, though the Rolls-Royce/Japanese RJ-500 will be a later option. These engines will possess markedly superior noise-emission characteristics than current engines, and their fuel economy will reduce operational seat-mile costs by nearly 20%. The first production Model 737-300 will probably be delivered in 1985.

Specification

Type: short-range transport
Powerplant: two 14,500-lb (6577-kg) thrust Pratt & Whitney JT8D-9A turbofans

Aloha Airlines operate an inter-island service in Hawaii using 11 Boeing 737-200s. The 737-200 is admirably suited for such operations over short ranges, for which it was specifically designed.

Performance: maximum level speed 586 mph (943 km/h) at 23,500 ft (7165 m); maximum cruising speed 576 mph (927 km/h) at 22,600 ft (6890 m); economic cruising speed 495 mph (797 km/h) at 30,000 ft (9145 m); range with 115 passengers and reserve fuel at cruising altitude of 33,000 ft (10060 m) 2,188 miles (3521 km)
Weights: empty 60,550 lb (27465 kg); maximum take-off 115,500 lb (52390 kg)
Dimensions: span 93 ft 0 in (28.35 m); length 100 ft 0 in (30.48 m); height 37 ft 0 in (11.28 m); wing area 980 sq ft (91.04 m²)
Operators: there are approximately 75 operators, but major users include Aer Lingus, Aerolineas Argentinas, Air Algérie, Air New Zealand, All Nippon Airways, Aloha Airlines, Braathens SAFE, Britannia Airways, British Airways, CP Air, Cruzeiro, Eastern Provincial Airways, Egyptair, Far Eastern Air Transport, Frontier Airlines, Gulf Air, Indian Airlines, Malaysian Airline System, Nordair, Olympic Airways, Pacific Western Airlines, Piedmont Airlines, Sabena, Saudia, South African Airways, Southwest Airlines, Transavia Holland, United Airlines, Varig, Vasp, Western Airlines, and Wien Air Alaska

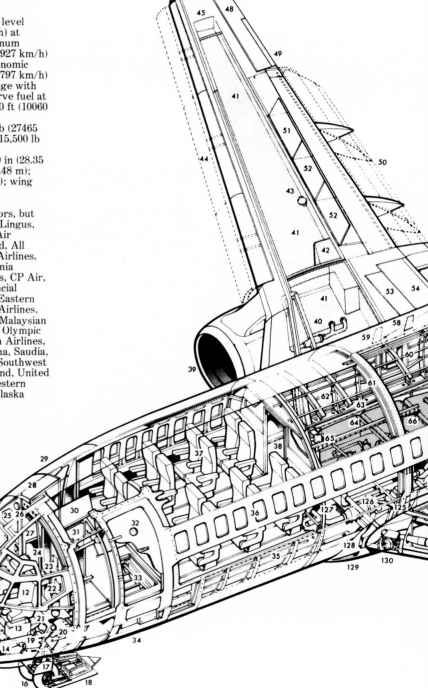

Boeing 737-200 cutaway drawing key

1 Hinged nose cone
2 Search radar
3 Glide-slope aerial
4 Forward pressure bulkhead
5 Instrument panel shroud
6 Windscreen sections
7 Sliding side windows
8 Eyebrow windows
9 First officer's seat
10 Overhead panel
11 Centre console
12 Captain's seat
13 Flight kit stowage
14 Circuit breaker panel
15 Nose gear deflector housing
16 Twin nosewheels
17 Nosewheel doors
18 Nose gear gravel deflector
19 Steering cylinders
20 Lock
21 Drag strut
22 Fixed side windows
23 Second observer's seat (optional)
24 First observer's seat (stowable)
25 Wall circuit breaker panel
26 Dome light
27 Flight deck door
28 Forward galley
29 Service door (starboard) 30 in by 65 in (76 by 165 cm)
30 Coat closet
31 Forward toilet
32 Forward entry door (port), 34 in by 72 in (86 by 183 cm)
33 Airstairs stowage (deployed through hatch)
34 Electrical/electronics bay
35 Underfloor forward freight hold
36 Cabin windows
37 Fourteen-seat first-class cabin configuration (38-in/96,5-cm seat pitch)
38 Inter-class bulkhead
39 Engine air intakes
40 Air-conditioning pre-cooler
41 Integral wing fuel tank (tank No 2)
42 Dry bay
43 Overwing filler

44 Leading-edge slats (extended)
45 Vent surge tank
46 Starboard navigation light (flashing)
47 Starboard navigation light (white)
48 Starboard aileron
49 Aileron balance tab
50 Triple-slotted flaps (extended)
51 Ground spoiler/lift dumper (outer)
52 Wing spoilers (two segments)
53 Ground spoiler/lift dumper (inner)
54 Triple-slotted flap (inner section)
55 Tailpipe shroud
56 Aft wing/nacelle fairing
57 Thrust reverser doors (closed)
58 VHF communications antenna
59 HF communications antenna (optional)
60 Starboard escape hatch frame surround
61 Forged alloy fuselage main frames (three off)
62 Rolled alloy intermediate frames
63 Floor level (air-conditioning outflow)
64 Centre-section fuel bladder cells (three off)
65 Fuel pump
66 Centre-section floor beams
67 Port escape hatch frame

68 Hydraulics service bay (starboard mainwheel well)
69 Pressure-bearing floor structure
70 Insulation blankets
71 Overhead air distribution duct
72 Flat cabin ceiling sections
73 Passenger conditioned air ducts and outlets
74 Overhead in-flight luggage stowage bins
75 Aerial
76 Tourist-class 88-seat cabin configuration (34-in/86-cm seat pitch)
77 Aft bulkhead
78 Aft service door (starboard) 30 in by 65 in (76 by 165 cm)
79 Aft galley
80 Fin forward spar/pressure bulkhead attachment
81 Crash-locator beacon
82 Starboard tailplane
83 Starboard elevator
84 Fin front spar
85 Fin structure
86 Fin skinning
87 VOR/ILS antennae
88 Rudder balance

89 Static dischargers
90 Rudder
91 Fibreglass honeycomb construction
92 Rudder stand-by actuator
93 Rudder dual-tandem actuator
94 Elevator actuator torque-tube
95 Tail cone
96 APU exhaust outlet
97 Port elevator tab
98 Port elevator
99 Port horizontal tailplane (variable incidence)

100 Tailplane ribs
101 APU exhaust pipe
102 APU package
103 Forged-beam tailplane centre-section
104 Fin rear spar terminal fittings
105 Variable-incidence screw-jack fitment
106 Air-conditioning
107 Collapsible airstairs (attached to door)
108 Aft pressure dome bulkhead
109 Aft galley
110 Aft toilet

111 Aft entry door (port) (lowered, deploying airstairs)
112 Door surround frame
113 Fuselage skinning
114 Aft underfloor freight hold
115 Wing root fillet
116 Mainwheel well
117 Forged undercarriage mounting
118 Triple-slotted flaps
119 Undercarriage side strut
120 Fuselage frame attachment
121 Wingroot/fuselage fairing
122 Air-conditioning conduits
123 Coolant air fan
124 Primary heat exchanger
125 Fuselage/front spar attachment
126 Water separator
127 Crew air (port)/passenger cabin air (starboard) ducts

128 Ram air intake
129 Intake scoop
130 Taxi/landing lights
131 Leading-edge Krüger flap (inboard section)
132 Pre-cooler air
133 Inboard wing ribs
134 Undercarriage drag strut
135 Twin mainwheels
136 Engine pylon nacelle strut
137 Vortex dissipator
138 Inlet centre body/starter
139 Fan
140 Pratt & Whitney JT8D-9 turbofan
141 Oil tank
142 High-pressure section
143 Forward wing box-spar
144 Outer wing ribs
145 Aft wing/nacelle fairing
146 Thrust-reverser doors (extended)
147 Thrust-reverser actuator fairing
148 Flap tracks
149 Wing integral fuel tank (tank No 1)
150 Leading-edge slats
151 Krüger flap anti-icing pipes (telescopic)
152 Flap hydraulic rams
153 Retractable taxi/landing lights
154 Aft wing-box spar
155 Port aileron balance tab
156 Vent surge tank
157 Fuel vent outlet
158 Port aileron
159 Port navigation light (white)
160 Port navigation light (flashing)

Boeing Model 747

History and notes

In 1963 the US Air Force began to study and define its requirements for a heavy logistics transport aircraft that would supplement the Lockheed C-141 StarLifters that were about to enter service. Identified originally as the CX-4 (Cargo, Experimental), this requirement envisaged an aircraft with a gross weight of 600,000 lb (272155 kg), but this was increased in the following year when other factors had been taken into consideration. In its final stages the requirement called for an aircraft with the capability to airlift a payload of 125,000 lb (56699 kg) over a range of 8,000 miles (12875 km), and the ability to operate from the same length of paved or semi-prepared runway as the C-141, and to land on 4,000 ft (1220 m) semi-prepared runways in combat areas. Known as the CX-HLS (Cargo, Experimental-Heavy Logistics System) at that stage, the aircraft became the object of a design competition that was initiated in May 1964, as a result of which the Boeing, Douglas and Lockheed companies were each awarded contracts to develop further their designs. Lockheed was declared winner of the competiton on 30 September 1965, following evaluation of the final proposals, so the company was nominated as prime contractor for the USAF's new transport, which entered service under the designation C-5A Galaxy.

Boeing had put considerable efforts into the CX-HLS design studies and, not surprisingly, was keenly disappointed to lose this military contract. Perhaps it had been envisaged that, as with the 707, a military contract would prove a sound stepping stone to a civil variant, an idea

Boeing 747 of Avianca (Aerovias Nacionales de Colombia).

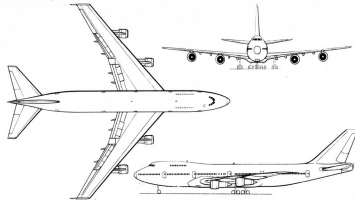

Boeing 747-200B

already in the background of the design team's thoughts, but which had not then been objectively studied in any detail. Market research conducted by Boeing had shown that a large-capacity airliner would become of considerable interest to operators during the early 1970s, and even before the destination of the military contract was announced in the autumn of 1965, the company had set a small design group working to outline the details of a civil transport.

With the C-5 contract awarded to Lockheed, Boeing was able to concentrate on the design of what was identified from the outset as the Model 747, continuing the 7X7 family of civil designations which had originated with the 707. Initial studies covered aircraft up to a gross weight of about 600,000 lb (272155 kg) that could accommodate as many as 430 passengers, but the high-wing layout which had been considered ideal for a military transport was changed initially to a mid-wing configuration and a two-deck 'double-bubble' fuselage with each deck some 15 ft (4.57 m) wide featured in the initial proposals that were considered by a number of airlines. The double-deck proposal failed to appeal to those operators which studied the Boeing

preliminary design, so the project was reappraised. This led, in early 1966, to what was basically a 'big brother' of the 707, featuring the same low-wing configuration, four wing-mounted podded engines, a somewhat similar conventional tail unit, and tricycle landing gear. The fuselage was of almost circular cross-section, the flight deck high on the forward fuselage within the now easily-recognisable 'hump' fairing, allowing the main passenger cabin to extend beneath it into the nose of

the aircraft.

The most staggering feature of this fuselage was its size, providing a cabin 20 ft 1½ in (6.13 m) wide and 185 ft 0 in (56.39 m) long, looking in mock-up form not unlike the imagined interior of some 21st century spacecraft, with an internal volume that

The Boeing 747-200B is the heavyweight passenger version of the series, with a choice of seven engine models for different gross weights. Swissair will eventually operate up to seven.

Boeing Model 747

appeared almost limitless. Nine-abreast seating with two aisles dispelled immediately the claustrophobia-inducing tubular interiors of many earlier airliners, and aft of the flight deck was an upper deck lounge with seating for up to 16 first-class passengers.

Early plans provided accommodation for 368 mixed-class passengers in a typical layout, with a basic gross weight of 625,000 lb (283495 kg), and to ensure that the Model 747 could operate from existing runways, the aircraft required landing gear that would support and distribute this 279-ton (283.5-tonne) load effectively without causing damage to the runway. The resulting main units, four in total, each had a four-wheel bogie, and the nose unit featured twin wheels. No firm conclusion had then been reached on the powerplant: General Electric, Pratt & Whitney and Rolls-Royce turbofan engines were all being considered.

It was with the design in this general form that Boeing began to seek prospective customers. Pan American was considered to be the most likely first buyer, but until there was positive airline interest it was not possible for the company to make a commitment to build the 747; with a price tag of more than £6 million ($16.8 million) each in 1966, it was too big a gamble for 'private venture' construction and development. Boeing's intuition proved to be correct, and on 13 April 1966 it was announced simultaneously that the company had designed and was to manufacture this new Model 747 long-range transport, and that Pan American had ordered no fewer than 25 of the giant aircraft, together with spares, in a contract valued at $525 million. However, it was not

until additional orders had been received from Japan Air Lines and Lufthansa that, on 25 July 1966, the decision was made to begin construction.

Pan Am's appraisal of Boeing's design had resulted in some changes being made, these increasing wing span, modifying landing gear layout, and raising the maximum take-off weight to 680,000 lb (308443 kg). Not surprisingly, the first press reports that followed Boeing's announcement were well laced with adjectives which implied magnitude: everything was on a giant scale, and very soon it was called a jumbo-sized aeroplane, leading to the name 'jumbo jet' which is perhaps better known to large numbers of the world's population than the official Model 747.

No prototype of the 747 was built. The original aircraft, intended as Boeing's demonstrator, was rolled out on 30 September, 1968 at Paine Field, Everett, where the company had established a completely new factory to house the 747 production line. The first flight was completed successfully on 9 February 1969, and with the participation of four production aircraft as they became available, these five 747s completed the certification programme just prior to the year's end, FAA approval being granted on 30 December. On 22 January 1970 Pan American inaugurated its first service with the type, introducing it on the New York-London route.

The period between the beginning of construction and certification had not been without its problems. Boeing's major difficulty had been to restrict weight growth in order to maintain the gross weight at the originally projected figure of 680,000 lb (308443 kg), but despite the most

strenuous efforts there was a steady increase of structural weight, and growing system complexity added to the total. This meant that in order to maintain the payload/range performance which had been specified, it was necessary to increase maximum take-off weight and this, in the case of the initial 747-100, rose to a figure of 710,000 lb (322051 kg).

The other major problem, one which was closely related to weight, concerned the powerplant. Pan American had opted for Pratt & Whitney engines, and the JT9D was an entirely new project which had been proposed for this aircraft at an initial thrust of 41,000 lb (18597 kg). The engine not only suffered its own development problems, but as the gross weight of the airframe increased it became essential that the engines should develop greater thrust. This accelerated evolution of the new turbofan engine created great difficulties for Pratt & Whitney, and although a JT9D-3 rated at 43,500-lb (19731-kg) thrust was readied for the production aircraft to be delivered for airline service, it it suffered innumerable teething troubles. Only when similarly rated but modified JT9D-3A engines were introduced into service later in 1970 were the problems overcome.

The 747-100, which first entered service with Pan Am, had a maximum fuel capacity of 47,210 US gallons (178709 litres), sufficient to enable a two-seat lightplane such as the Cessna 150, for example, to fly a distance in excess of 1.1 million miles (1.8 million km). The surprising thing is that the 747-100 could carry 385 passengers over a range of 5,677 miles (9136 km) and land with FAR specified reserves, which gave this turbofan-powered airliner about the

same efficiency, but a cruising speed some six times greater than that of the lightplane. Such excellent figures come from good aerodynamic design, and the 747 benefits from the features developed for the 707 wing, although its wing section differs to provide a slightly higher cruising speed. The leading-edge of each wing incorporates 10 variable-camber flaps outboard and three-section Krueger flaps inboard, while the trailing-edge has inboard (high-speed) and outboard (low-speed) ailerons, and triple-slotted flaps. Forward of these trailing-edge surfaces are four flight spoilers (outboard) and two ground spoilers, or lift dumpers (inboard).

The tricycle landing gear as planned originally was to have had all four main units (two beneath the fuselage and one beneath the inboard section of each wing) mounted in line abreast, but this was changed before production so that the under-fuselage units (retracting forward) were forward of the under-wing units (retracting inward). All of the 16 main wheels have disc brakes and individually controlled anti-skid units. All flight controls are powered, and an advanced automatic flight control system eases the pilots' workload, not only during long periods of cruising flight, but also in making automatic landings under suitable conditions. In fact, so well planned is the flight deck and equipment of the 747 that these large airliners are handled without difficulty by a flight crew of three, comprising usually all pilots or two pilots and a flight engineer. Navigation to great ac-

69

The bulk of the Boeing 747-200B, of which CP Air of Canada has four, is well displayed over inhospitable territory by the airline's striking livery. In practice the Model 747's maximum capacity of 500 passengers is almost never used.

curacy is catered for by standard avionics systems, plus (originally duplicated, but now triplicated) inertial navigation systems.

By the time that the first 747s were entering service with Pan Am, Boeing had accumulated some 190 orders from 28 airlines. This looks like big money, but Boeing's investment was even bigger money, and at one point in the mid-1970s the company must have felt some qualms about the entire project. Airlines were then suffering a recession, and it seemed unlikely that marketing forecasts would ever be met. This situation has changed, however, and in mid-1980 orders for 747s of all types totalled 558.

So far, however, only the basic

747-100 has been mentioned, though it was the company's intention from the outset to build a 'family' of 747s. The first to be planned was a developed version with increased payload and range, but as this involved higher gross weight its development was dependent upon the provision of higher-powered turbofans, and this became delayed somewhat by the early problems with the JT9D engines. The availability of 45,500-lb (20638-kg) thrust JT9D-7 engines in 1969 made possible the 747B (now 747-200B) with a maximum take-off weight of 775,000 lb (351534 kg). This version flew for the first time on 11 October 1970, was certificated just over two months later, on 23 December, and entered service first with KLM in early 1971. Since that time progressive engine developments, and the introduction of alternative optional powerplants, has allowed the certification of 747-200Bs at much higher gross weights. Thus with suitable strengthening,

maximum take-off weights of 820,000 lb (371946 kg) have been approved with General Electric CF6-50E/E1/E2, Pratt & Whitney JT9D-70A and Rolls-Royce RB.211-524B2 or -524C2 engines of 52,500-lb (23814-kg), 53,000-lb (24040-kg), 50,100-lb (22725-kg), and 51,600-lb (23405-kg) thrust respectively.

Other specialised variants of the 747-200 include the 747-200F freighter, which introduced a nose loading-door that opens forward and upward to allow clear access to the main deck for the loading of long or large loads. The variant includes a special loading system that makes it possible for only two men to handle and stow a load of up to 250,000 lb (113398 kg) in half an hour, and an additional large cargo door can be installed optionally in the side of the fuselage to permit simultaneous nose and side loading. First flown on 30 November 1971 and certificated on 7 March 1972, this initial -200F was delivered to Lufthansa only two

days later. At a take-off weight of 820,000 lb (371946 kg), this aircraft can deliver a 200,000 lb (90718 kg) payload over a range of 4,600 miles (7403 km).

Next version to appear was the 747-200C convertible, available with the same engine and gross weight options as the -200B, but equipped to operate in all-passenger, all-cargo, or combination seating/cargo arrangements. The first was flown on 23 March 1973, certificated just over three weeks later, and delivered to World Airways on 27 April 1973. A 747-200B Combi, introducing a large cargo door on the port side of the fuselage, aft of the wing, was rolled out in October 1974. This version allows for an all-passenger layout, or the carriage of passengers and up to 12 pallets or containers, with a movable bulkhead to separate them. The first of the Combis was delivered to Air Canada in March 1975. A similar Combi version of the 747-100 had appeared earlier, one of Sabena's aircraft being so modified and re-delivered in early 1974. One other special version was developed to meet the requirements of Japan Air Lines, an initial contract for four of these aircraft being announced on 30 October 1972. Known as the 747SR, this is a short-range version of the 747-100 which incorporates structural changes and strengthening to render it suitable for operations which involve a high incidence of take-off and landing cycles. In addition, accommodation is provided for a maximum of 516 passengers, the main cabin having a 10-abreast high-density arrangement and the upper deck being provided with 32 seats. The first 747SR was flown on 4 September 1973 and delivered to JAL just over three weeks later, and this operator had seven of these aircraft in service in early 1980, with two more scheduled for delivery. All

The Boeing 747-200F is a specialised freighter version of the 'jumbo' jet, able to carry a payload of up to 254,640 lb (115500 kg). Cargolux of Luxembourg has two of the type.

The Flying Tiger Line is a specialist US freight airline, and includes among its aircraft some nine Boeing 747s. The Model 747-200F can carry up to 29,640-cu ft (18.12-m³) containers, plus 30 173-cu ft (4.90-m³) lower-lobe containers and 800 cu ft (22.65 m³) of bulk freight; in terms of payload-range, the -200F can deliver a load of 200,000 lb (90720 kg) over a range of 4,490 miles (7225 km).

BRANIFF INTERNATIONAL

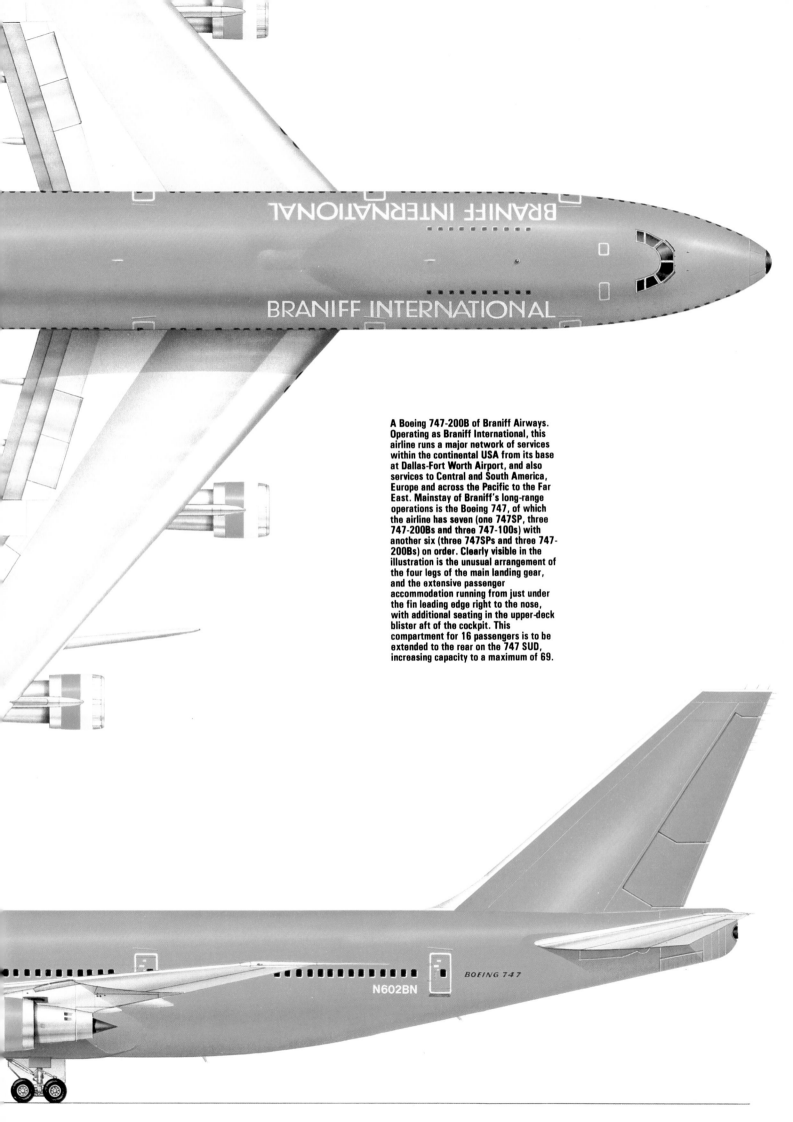

A Boeing 747-200B of Braniff Airways.
Operating as Braniff International, this
airline runs a major network of services
within the continental USA from its base
at Dallas-Fort Worth Airport, and also
services to Central and South America,
Europe and across the Pacific to the Far
East. Mainstay of Braniff's long-range
operations is the Boeing 747, of which
the airline has seven (one 747SP, three
747-200Bs and three 747-100s) with
another six (three 747SPs and three 747-
200Bs) on order. Clearly visible in the
illustration is the unusual arrangement of
the four legs of the main landing gear,
and the extensive passenger
accommodation running from just under
the fin leading edge right to the nose,
with additional seating in the upper-deck
blister aft of the cockpit. This
compartment for 16 passengers is to be
extended to the rear on the 747 SUD,
increasing capacity to a maximum of 69.

Nippon Airways also had seven 747SRs in service in mid-1980 and has order options on four additional aircraft.

Late delivery versions of the 747SR derive from the 747-100B which became available from September 1977. This improvement on the basic 747-100 has strengthened fuselage, landing gear and wing structure, and is available with a variety of optional General Electric, Pratt & Whitney and Rolls-Royce engines at maximum take-off weights up to 753,000 lb (341555 kg). The most recent variant to be announced by Boeing in mid-1980 has the provisional designation 747SUD (stretched upper deck). This provides for the accommodation of a maximum of 69 passengers on the upper deck by extending the bulged portion of the upper forward fuselage by 23 ft 4 in (7.11 m) to the rear. Additional windows and a new emergency exit are to be provided in this structure, and the existing circular staircase at the forward end is to be deleted and replaced by a straight staircase at the aft end of the new accommodation deck. Swissair have ordered four of these aircraft for delivery during 1983-4. This structural modification is applicable to -100B, -100B(SR), -200B, and -200B Combi aircraft.

The introduction into service of the Boeing 747 caused few serious problems for their operators, for the company had done its utmost to ensure that it was fundamentally a large-size 727 that could be flown by a similar flight crew of three, and maintained easily by ground crews with experience of the other members of the Boeing 7X7 family. The advent of these wide-body jets, with their large seating capacity, was welcomed by air traffic controllers for, potentially, two 747 flights could replace from five to 10 services by smaller aircraft. It was the airport operators that, initially, were caught on the hop. Unused to the arrival of an aircraft that could accommodate up to 500 passengers (but rarely did), the passenger handling facilities were completely swamped when two or three 747s arrived almost simultaneously to disgorge between 700 and 1,000 passengers. These conditions applied, of course, at the time of their early use, since when airports have become accustomed to handling the Airbus, Boeing, Lockheed, and McDonnell Douglas wide-body jets which today carry such a major portion of the world's air travellers. The worldwide fleet of 747s was alone carrying on average almost 4 million passengers each month in early 1980, some 11 years after its first flight, a period during which the aircraft has demonstrated a remarkable safety record.

It seems inevitable that with the anticipated growth in air travel there may appear a 'stretched' version, accommodating perhaps 600-700 passengers, before production of this remarkable, first 'jumbo-jet' comes to an end. Another possibility is a new wing with less sweep and more refined aerodynamics to reduce costs in cruising flight. However, its current history is not complete without mention of the E-4 military versions which are in the stage of delivery and development for the US Air Force. These are considered as survivable airborne command posts which can command and control the nation's entire air effort, including airlift, air superiority, interdiction, reconnaissance, strike, and support missions. An even stranger use of the 747 results from the National

A Boeing 747-100 of Trans World Airlines, which operates 11 such aircraft as the mainstay of its high-capacity long-haul operations. Training is carried out on a Singer-Link simulator.

Boeing 747-200 cutaway drawing key

1 Radome
2 Radar dish
3 Pressure bulkhead
4 Radar scanner mounting
5 First class cabin, typically 32 seats
6 Windscreen
7 Instrument panel shroud
8 Rudder pedals
9 Control column
10 Flight-deck floor construction
11 First-class bar unit
12 Window panel
13 Nose undercarriage bay
14 Nosewheel door
15 Steering mechanism
16 Twin nosewheels
17 Radio and electronics racks
18 Captain's seat
19 Co-pilot's seat
20 Flight engineer's panel
21 Observer's seats
22 Upper deck door, port and starboard
23 Circular staircase between decks
24 Cockpit air conditioning duct
25 First-class galley
26 First-class toilets
27 Plug-type forward cabin door, No 1
28 First-class seats
29 Cabin dividing bulkhead
30 Anti-collision light
31 Cabin roof construction
32 Upper deck toilet
33 Upper deck seating, up to 32 passengers
34 Window panel
35 Air conditioning supply ducts
36 Forward fuselage construction

37 Baggage pallet containers
38 Forward under-floor freight compartment
39 Communications aerial
40 Upper deck galley
41 Meal trolley elevator
42 Lower deck forward galley
43 No 2 passenger door, port and starboard
44 Air conditioning system intake
45 Wing-root fairing
46 Air conditioning plant
47 Wing spar bulkhead
48 Fresh water tanks

49 Forward economy-class cabin, typically 141 seats
50 Wing centre section fuel tank, capacity 17,000 US gal (64 345 l)
51 Centre section stringer construction
52 Cabin floor construction
53 Fuselage frame and stringer construction
54 Main fuselage frame

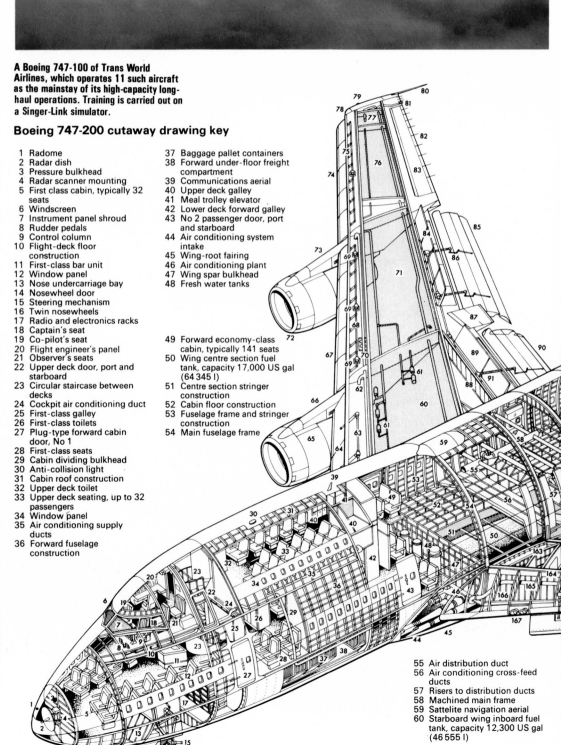

55 Air distribution duct
56 Air conditioning cross-feed ducts
57 Risers to distribution ducts
58 Machined main frame
59 Sattelite navigation aerial
60 Starboard wing inboard fuel tank, capacity 12,300 US gal (46 555 l)

Boeing Model 747

Aeronautics and Space Administration's (NASA's) requirement for a ferry aircraft able to carry 'piggy-back' fashion the Space Shuttle Orbiter. A 747-100, which NASA acquired from American Airlines for modification into this role, recorded on 18 February 1977 the first flight with the Space Shuttle Orbiter *Enterprise* mounted above its fuselage. So, not only has the 747 introduced a completely new dimension to everyday air travel, but it may also have played a significant role in the development of routine manned spaceflight.

The following details apply to the basic 747-200B passenger version.

Specification

Type: long-range heavy transport
Powerplant (805,000 lb:365142 kg gross weight version): four 50,000-lb (22680-kg) thrust Pratt & Whitney JT9D-7FW turbofans
Performance: maximum speed 602 mph (969 km/h) at 30,000 ft (9145 m); cruising ceiling 45,000 ft (13715 m); range with 442 passengers and baggage at maximum take-off weight 5,980 miles (9624 km)

Weights: operating empty 377,000 lb (171004 kg); maximum take-off 805,000 lb (365142 kg)
Dimensions: span 195 ft 8 in (59.64 m); length 231 ft 4 in (70.51 m); height 63 ft 5 in (19.33 m); wing area 5,500 sq ft (510.95 m²)
Operators: there are approximately 56 operators, those with three or more aircraft including Air Canada, Air France, Air India, Air Portugal, Aerolineas Argentinas, Alitalia, All Nippon Airways, American Airlines, Braniff, British Airways, Cathay Pacific Airways, China Air Lines, CP Air, El Al, Flying Tiger, Garuda Indonesian Airways, Iberia, Iran Air, Japan Air Lines, KLM, Korean Airlines, Kuwait Airways, Lufthansa, Northwest Orient Airlines, Pan American World Airways, Philippine Air Lines, Qantas Airways, Scandinavian Airlines System, Seaboard World Airlines, Singapore Airlines, South African Airways, Trans World Airlines, United Airlines, and Wardair Canada

61 Fuel pumps
62 Engine bleed-air supply
63 Krueger flap operating jacks
64 Inboard Krueger flap
65 Starboard inner engine
66 Starboard inner engine pylon
67 Leading edge Krueger flap segments
68 Krueger flap drive mechanism
69 Krueger flap motors
70 Re-fuelling panel
71 Starboard wing outboard fuel tank, capacity 4,420 US gal (16 730 l)
72 Starboard outer engine
73 Starboard outer engine pylon
74 Outboard Krueger flap segments
75 Krueger flap drive mechanism
76 Extended range fuel tank, capacity 800 US gal (3 028 l) each wing
77 Surge tank
78 Starboard wing tip
79 Navigation light
80 VHF aerial boom
81 Fuel vent
82 Static dischargers
83 Outboard, low-speed, aileron
84 Outboard spoilers
85 Outboard slotted flaps
86 Flap drive mechanism

87 Inboard, high-speed, aileron
88 Trailing edge beam
89 Inboard spoilers
90 Inboard slotted flap
91 Flap drive mechanism
92 Centre fuselage construction
93 Starboard undercarriage bay housing
94 No 3 passenger door
95 Wing-mounted main undercarriage bay

96 Flap drive motors
97 Undercarriage beam
98 Fuselage-mounted main undercarriage bay
99 Main undercarriage jack
100 Floor panels
101 Seat rails
102 Cabin window trim panels
103 Centre cabin economy-class seating, typically 82 passengers
104 Nine-abreast seating
105 Air distribution ducts
106 No 4 passenger door, port and starboard
107 Centre cabin galley
108 Overhead baggage racks (with doors)
109 Main air supply duct
110 Rear cabin galley

111 Rear cabin seating, typically 114 passengers
112 Economy-class seating
113 Overhead baggage racks
114 Cabin roof panels
115 Control cable runs
116 Rear fuselage construction
117 Rear cabin seats
118 Rear cabin toilets
119 Wardrobes
120 Rear pressure dome bulkhead
121 Fin root fairing
122 Starboard tailplane
123 Static dischargers
124 Starboard elevator
125 Fin leading edge construction
126 Fin spar construction
127 Fin-tip fairing
128 VOR aerial
129 Static dischargers
130 Upper rudder segment
131 Lower rudder segment
132 Rudder jacks
133 Tailcone fairing
134 APU exhaust
135 Auxiliary power unit (APU)

136 Port elevator inner segment
137 Port elevator outer segment
138 Static dischargers
139 Tailplane construction
140 Elevator jacks
141 Tailplane sealing plate
142 Aft fuselage frames
143 Fin attachment
144 Tailplane centre section
145 Moving tailplane jack
146 APU air duct

147 No 5 passenger door, port and starboard
148 Rear fuselage window panel
149 Rear under-floor freight hold
150 Freight and baggage pallet container
151 Fuselage frame and stringer construction
152 Trailing edge fillet
153 Fuselage-mounted undercarriage pivot
154 Trailing edge beam
155 Port inboard slotted flap
156 Flap tracks
157 Flap track fairings
158 Inboard spoilers
159 Flap drive shaft
160 Flap down position
161 Fuselage-mounted main undercarriage bogie
162 Wing spar and rib construction
163 Wing root attachment plate
164 Front spar
165 Engine bleed air supply pipe
166 Leading edge ribs
167 Landing lamps
168 Inboard Krueger flap
169 Krueger flap motor and drive
170 Wing-mounted main undercarriage leg
171 Four-wheel main undercarriage bogie
172 Main undercarriage side brace
173 Wing-mounted undercarriage jack
174 Wing skins
175 Wing stringer construction
176 Inboard engine mounting beam
177 Pylon attachment strut
178 Port inner pylon construction
179 Heat exchanger
180 Engine intake

181 Rolls-Royce RB.211-524B engine
182 Engine driven gearbox
183 Outer fan ducting
184 Core engine exhaust
185 Integral fuel tankage
186 Inboard, high-speed, aileron
187 Aileron jack
188 Outboard slotted flap
189 Flap track fairing
190 Flap down position
191 Outboard spoilers
192 Flap tracks
193 Flap track mounting beams
194 Wing spar and rib construction
195 Leading edge construction
196 Krueger flap segments
197 Krueger flap mechanism
198 Outboard engine mounting beam
199 Port outer engine pylon
200 Heat exchanger air duct
201 Port outer engine cowlings
202 Thrust reverser cascades
203 Thrust reverser cowling door, open
204 Door operating jacks

205 Outboard Krueger flap segments
206 Krueger flap mechanism
207 Outer wing construction
208 Aileron jacks
209 Outboard, low-speed, aileron
210 Static dischargers
211 Fuel vent
212 Wing-tip fairing
213 Navigation light
214 VHF aerial boom

AVIAGRAPHICA

Boeing Model 747SP

History and Notes

Boeing first announced on 3 September 1973 the company's decision to proceed with the development of a special performance, lighter-weight version of its wide-body airliner under the designation Model 747SP. Intended for operation over lower-density routes, or on services requiring above average non-stop long-range flights, the Model 747SP has a structure sufficiently different from that of the 747-100 from which it was developed to warrant its inclusion here as a separate aircraft.

The major structural change by comparison with the standard 747 is a reduction of 46 ft 7 in (14.20 m) in fuselage length, reducing the maximum high-density seating capacity to 400 passengers, but with basic mixed-class accommodation for 316. This requirement made possible a substantial reduction in gross weight and, consequently, weight saving became possible in other areas. Thus wing structural materials and those of the landing gear were reduced in weight, and the triple-slotted trailing-edge flaps were replaced by single-slotted variable pivot type flaps. The reduction in fuselage length meant, however, that the fixed and controllable tail surfaces had a shorter moment arm, necessitating an area increase for the vertical and horizontal tail surfaces, and the provision of a double-hinged rudder.

Following the receipt of an initial order from Pan American for 10 aircraft, construction of the first 747SP began in April 1974, the first flight being made on 4 July 1975. FAA certification was granted on 4 February 1976 and the first delivery to Pan American took place in the following month. During May 1976 one of Pan Am's 747SPs, commanded by Captain Walter H. Mullikin, established a round-the-world speed record of 502.84 mph (809.24 km/h), and in late 1977 the same pilot

Boeing 747SP of China Airlines (Taiwan).

circumnavigated the world via the North and South poles in a 747SP at an average speed of 487.35 mph (784.31 km/h). Proof of the long-range capability of the new aircraft came as early as 23-4 March 1976, when the first 747SP for South African Airways was flown non-stop from Paine Field, Washington to Cape Town. Taking off at a gross weight of 713,300 lb (323547 kg), and with 50 passengers on board, the aircraft landed with sufficient fuel for a further 2 hour 27 minutes of flight, having flown a world record non-stop distance for a commercial aircraft of 10,290 miles (16560 km).

The 747SP entered service initially with Pratt & Whitney JT9D-7A or -7F engines, but is now available optionally also with General Electric CF6-45A/B or Rolls-Royce RB.211-524B turbofans. The fuel system is basically similar to that of the 747-100B, but differs by having capacity for an additional 1,570 US gallons (5943 litres) of fuel.

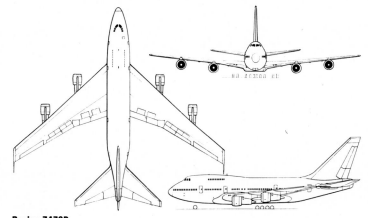

Boeing 747SP

Specification

Type: long-range commercial transport
Powerplant: (typically) four 48,570-lb (22031-kg) thrust Pratt & Whitney JT9D-7AF turbofans
Performance: maximum level speed at AUW of 500,000 lb (226796 kg) 609 mph (980 km/h) at 30,000 ft (9145 m); service ceiling 45,100 ft (13746 m); range with 321 passengers and baggage at 690,000 lb (312979 kg) 6,736 miles (10841 km)
Weights: operating empty 322,000 lb (146057 kg); maximum take-off 696,000 lb (315700 kg)
Dimensions: span 195 ft 8 in (59.64 m); length 184 ft 9 in (56.31 m); height 65 ft 5 in (19.94 m); wing area 5,500 sq ft (510.95 m²)
Operators include: Braniff International, CAAC, China Air Lines, Iran Air, Korean Air Lines, Pan American World Airways, Qantas, Saudia, South African Airways, Syrianair, and Trans World

The Australian operator Qantas Airways has ordered two of the short-fuselage Boeing 747SP model, designed to carry fewer passengers over longer ranges.

Boeing Model 757

History and Notes

Increased capacity versions of the highly successful Boeing 727 have been studied over the years, but despite several proposals none succeeded in attracting sufficient orders to warrant a production go-ahead. In the early months of 1978, however, the company announced that it proposed to develop a new family of advanced technology aircraft. Retaining the 7X7 designation formula, these three new designs carried the identifications 757, 767 and 777, the first of the three differing by retaining the same fuselage cross-section as the Model 727, whereas the 767 and 777 (assuming that this latter aircraft enters production) will have a fuse-cross-section this is virtually midway between that of the Models 727 and 747.

A short/medium-range airliner, with a typical capacity of 178 mixed-class or 196 tourist-class passengers, the Model 757 is intended to provide its operators with new standards of fuel efficiency, a vital area in the economics of the immediate future of airliner operations. A maximum of 223 passengers can be accommodated in a high-density seating arrangement. Boeing claim that when it enters service in early 1983, the 757 will be the world's most economical turbofan-powered airliner in the short/medium-range category, the result of combining a new advanced technology wing, high by-pass ratio turbofan engines, and avionics equipment that will enable the aircraft to be operated at optimum efficiency.

The production programme of the Model 767 was some five months in advance of that of the 757 in the summer of 1980, principally because the go-ahead for its construction was given some eight months before that of the 757. Initial orders for this latter aircraft were announced on 31 August 1978, comprising 19 and 21 respectively for British Airways and Eastern Air Lines, and after contract finalisation in early 1979, the company announced a production go-ahead on 23 March 1979. The five-month gap between the programmes is essential

Boeing 757 of Eastern Air Lines.

for Boeing's management and control of the almost simultaneous development of two new major aircraft, but the 757 has enjoyed the benefits of work already completed on its widebody sister, for there is a considerable degree of commonality between the two aircraft. However, some 53 per cent by value of the 757 is being manufactured by outside companies, and major sub-contractors include Avco Aerostructures (wing centre section and fuselage keel), Fairchild Industries (cabin centre-section), Rockwell International (forward and aft cabin sections) and Vought Corporation (fuselage tail cone, tailplane and fin).

Powerplant is to comprise two Rolls-Royce RB.211-535C or General Electric CF6-32C1 turbofan engines, both in the 37,000-lb (16783-kg) thrust class. The engines will be mounted in underwing pods, but the two launching airlines have opted for Rolls-Royce engines, and this is the first time that Boeing has introduced a new airliner with a non-American powerplant. The new-technology wing will have less sweepback than that of the 727, and the 757's fuselage is 19 ft 7 in (5.97 m) longer. Landing gear is of tricycle type, each main unit having a four-wheel bogie, with twin wheels on the nose gear. The 757 will be operated by a flight crew of two, or three optionally, and the advanced avionics available to them will include an inertial reference system incorporating laser gyroscopes, a flight management computer system, and a digital air data computer. These will integrate to

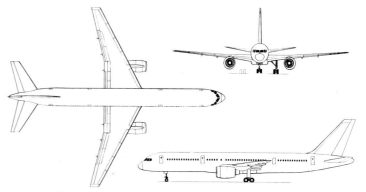

Boeing 757-200

provide optimum fuel efficiency when linked to automatic flight control and thrust management systems. This new generation avionics control will be capable of handling an entire flight from shortly after take-off, including the landing if desirable, the flight crew functioning as systems managers.

The first flight of a Model 757 is planned in February 1982, and orders and options for 96 aircraft had been received from four airlines by the summer of 1980. The following weight and performance estimates apply to a mixed-class version intended for medium-range operations with either of the alternative powerplants.

Specification

Type: short/medium-range commercial transport
Powerplant: two General Electric CF6-32C1 or Rolls-Royce RB.211- 535C turbofan engines, each developing approximately 37,400-lb (16964-kg) thrust
Performance: maximum cruising speed 494 mph (915 km/h) at 29,000 ft (8839 m); approach speed 154 mph (248 km/h); cruise altitude 37,500 ft (11430 m); design range 3,050 miles (4908 km)
Weights: operating empty 131,020 lb (59430 kg); maximum take-off 230,000 lb (104326 kg)
Dimensions: span 124 ft 6 in (37.95 m); length 154 ft 8 in (47.14 m); height 44 ft 7 in (13.59 m); wing area 1,994 sq ft (185.24 m²)
Orders include: Aloha Airlines, British Airways, Eastern Air Lines, and Transbrasil SA

The new Boeing 757 narrow-bodied airliner is currently being offered with Rolls-Royce RB.211 or General Electric CF6 turbofans.

Boeing Model 767

History and Notes

Announced simultaneously with the Model 757, the Boeing Model 767 introduces a completely new fuselage structure which is 4 ft 1 in (1.24 m) wider, providing seven- or eight-abreast seating with two aisles. Planned layouts cater for 211 mixed-class passengers, comprising 18 first-class in six-abreast accommodation, with the remaining 193 tourist-class seated seven-abreast; or 230 tourist-class in all seven-abreast seating; or a high-density eight-abreast configuration for a maximum of 289 passengers. The go-ahead for the 767 programme, however, was announced as early as 14 July 1978, following receipt of an order for 30 of these aircraft from United Airlines: just over two years later orders and options for this aircraft totalled 288 from 13 operators.

Computer Aided Design (CAD) has been used to speed the preparation of drawings for much of the principal structure, their high accuracy being of great benefit when, as in this case, a large amount of the construction is being carried out by other companies. These include Aeritalia, Canadair, Grumman and Vought, plus a Japanese consortium, known as the Civil Transport Development Corporation, that comprises Fuji, Kawasaki and Mitsubishi. Together, these companies are manufacturing assemblies and components which, in terms of value, represent some 45 per cent of the total cost.

Wing design differs somewhat from that of the 757, and features increased sweepback, and greater span and wing chord, to provide an approximate 53 per cent increase in wing area. The tail unit and landing gear are similar in configuration, and the Model 767 shares with the 757 twin turbofan engines pod-mounted beneath the wings. These, however, are of greater thrust in the 767, with alternative Pratt & Whitney JT9D-7R4D and General Electric CF6-80A powerplants, each of 48,000-lb (21772-kg) thrust, being specified by those airlines which had placed orders by the summer of 1980. It is intended that the Rolls-Royce RB.211 will also be available optionally to customer's requirements.

Boeing planned initially to offer two versions: a 767-100 with a shorter fuselage and accommodation for approximately 180 passengers, plus the standard 767-200 described above. It has since been decided not to build the shorter fuselage -100, and instead the 767-200 is to be available at alternative gross weights. Thus the version which was ordered initially by United Airlines for US domestic service will have a maximum take-off weight of 282,000 lb (127913 kg). That with a gross weight of 310,000 lb (140614 kg), is expected to carry 211 or 230 passengers over ranges of 3,675 miles (5914 km) and 3,545 miles (5705 km) respectively, making them suitable for non-stop transcontinental services, and also on many international routes.

With an optional flight crew of two or three, provided with the same avionics equipment as described for the 757, this new airliner is expected to demonstrate seat-mile costs some 32 per cent below that of current wide-body tri-jets when it enters service in the autumn of 1982. The new fuselage offers also significant air freight capacity, with a cargo hold able to accept up to 22 LD-2 containers, or LD-3/-4/-8 containers to similar volume. With the inclusion of an optional forward cargo door measuring 5 ft 9 in by 11 ft 2 in

(1.75 m by 3.40 m), Type 2 pallets can be loaded.

First flight of a Model 767 is scheduled for September 1981. The performance and weight estimates which follow apply to the basic mixed-class version with 211 passengers.

Specification

Type: medium-range commercial transport
Powerplant: two Pratt & Whitney JT9D-7R4 or General Electric CF6-80A turbofans, each developing approximately 48,000-lb (21772-kg) thrust
Performance: maximum cruising speed 506 mph (937 km/h) at 30,000 ft (9145 m); approach speed 154 mph (248 km/h); cruise altitude 39,000 ft (11885 m); design

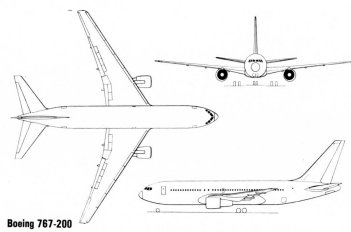

Boeing 767-200

Boeing 767-200 cutaway drawing key

1 Radome
2 Radar scanner dish
3 VOR localiser aerial
4 Front pressure bulkhead
5 ILS glideslope aerials
6 Windscreen wipers
7 Windscreen panels
8 Instrument panel shroud
9 Rudder pedals
10 Nose undercarriage wheel bay
11 Cockpit air conditioning duct
12 Captain's seat
13 Opening cockpit side window
14 Centre console
15 First officer's seat
16 Cockpit roof systems control panels
17 Flight engineer's station
18 Observer's seat
19 Pitot tubes
20 Angle of attack probe
21 Nose undercarriage steering jacks
22 Twin nosewheels
23 Nosewheel doors
24 Waste system vacuum tank
25 Forward toilet compartment
26 Crew wardrobe
27 Forward galley
28 Starboard overhead sliding door
29 Entry lobby
30 Cabin divider
31 Port entry door
32 Door control handle
33 Escape chute stowage
34 Underfloor electronics racks
35 Electronics cooling air
36 Skin heat exchanger
37 Fuselage frame and stringer construction
38 Cabin window panel
39 Six-abreast first class seating compartment (18 seats)
40 Overhead stowage bins
41 Curtained cabin divider
42 Sidewall trim panels
43 Negative pressure relief valves
44 Forward freight door
45 Forward underfloor freight hold
46 LD-2 cargo containers, 12 in forward hold
47 Centre electronics rack
48 Anti-collision light
49 Cabin roof frames
50 VHF aerial
51 Seven-abreast tourist class seating (193 seats)
52 Conditioned air riser
53 Air conditioning distribution manifolds
54 Wing spar centre section carry-through
55 Floor beam construction
56 Overhead air conditioning ducting
57 Front spar/fuselage main frame
58 Starboard emergency exit window
59 Starboard wing integral fuel tank; total system capacity 15,500 US gal (58 895 l)
60 Thrust reverser cascade door, open
61 Starboard engine nacelle
62 Nacelle pylon
63 Fixed portion of leading edge
64 Leading edge slat segments, open
65 Slat drive shaft
66 Rotary actuators
67 Fuel system piping
68 Fuel venting channels

Boeing Model 767

range 3,200 miles (5150 km)
Weights: operating empty 180,450 lb (81851 kg); maximum take-off 300,000 lb (136078 kg)
Dimensions: span 156 ft 4 in (47.65 m); length 159 ft 2 in (48.51 m); height 52 ft 0 in (15.85 m); wing area 3,050 sq ft (283.35 m²)
Orders include: Air Canada, All Nippon Airways, American Airlines, Ansett Airlines, Braathens SAFE, Britannia Airways, China Airlines, CP Air, Delta Air Lines, Pacific Western Airlines, Trans World Airlines, United Airlines, and Western Air Lines

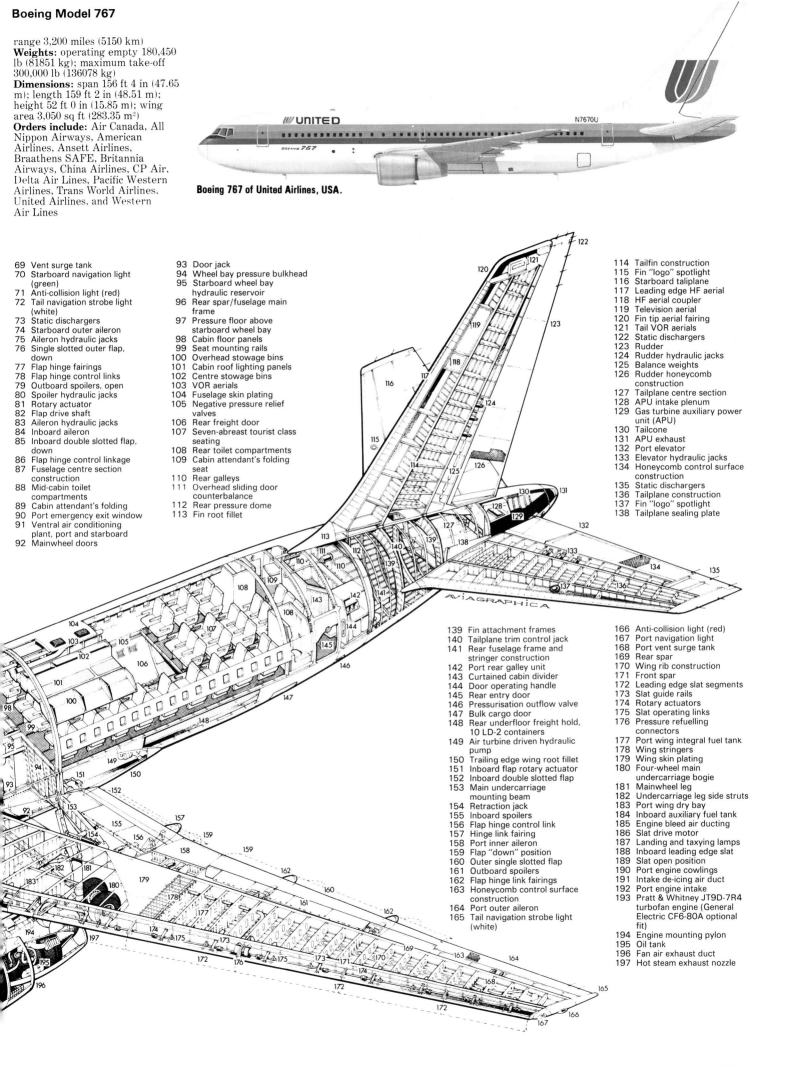

Boeing 767 of United Airlines, USA.

69 Vent surge tank
70 Starboard navigation light (green)
71 Anti-collision light (red)
72 Tail navigation strobe light (white)
73 Static dischargers
74 Starboard outer aileron
75 Aileron hydraulic jacks
76 Single slotted outer flap, down
77 Flap hinge fairings
78 Flap hinge control links
79 Outboard spoilers, open
80 Spoiler hydraulic jacks
81 Rotary actuator
82 Flap drive shaft
83 Aileron hydraulic jacks
84 Inboard aileron
85 Inboard double slotted flap, down
86 Flap hinge control linkage
87 Fuselage centre section construction
88 Mid-cabin toilet compartments
89 Cabin attendant's folding
90 Port emergency exit window
91 Ventral air conditioning plant, port and starboard
92 Mainwheel doors

93 Door jack
94 Wheel bay pressure bulkhead
95 Starboard wheel bay hydraulic reservoir
96 Rear spar/fuselage main frame
97 Pressure floor above starboard wheel bay
98 Cabin floor panels
99 Seat mounting rails
100 Overhead stowage bins
101 Cabin roof lighting panels
102 Centre stowage bins
103 VOR aerials
104 Fuselage skin plating
105 Negative pressure relief valves
106 Rear freight door
107 Seven-abreast tourist class seating
108 Rear toilet compartments
109 Cabin attendant's folding seat
110 Rear galleys
111 Overhead sliding door counterbalance
112 Rear pressure dome
113 Fin root fillet

114 Tailfin construction
115 Fin "logo" spotlight
116 Starboard taliplane
117 Leading edge HF aerial
118 HF aerial coupler
119 Television aerial
120 Fin tip aerial fairing
121 Tail VOR aerials
122 Static dischargers
123 Rudder
124 Rudder hydraulic jacks
125 Balance weights
126 Rudder honeycomb construction
127 Tailplane centre section
128 APU intake plenum
129 Gas turbine auxiliary power unit (APU)
130 Tailcone
131 APU exhaust
132 Port elevator
133 Elevator hydraulic jacks
134 Honeycomb control surface construction
135 Static dischargers
136 Tailplane construction
137 Fin "logo" spotlight
138 Tailplane sealing plate

139 Fin attachment frames
140 Tailplane trim control jack
141 Rear fuselage frame and stringer construction
142 Port rear galley unit
143 Curtained cabin divider
144 Door operating handle
145 Rear entry door
146 Pressurisation outflow valve
147 Bulk cargo door
148 Rear underfloor freight hold, 10 LD-2 containers
149 Air turbine driven hydraulic pump
150 Trailing edge wing root fillet
151 Inboard flap rotary actuator
152 Inboard double slotted flap
153 Main undercarriage mounting beam
154 Retraction jack
155 Inboard spoilers
156 Flap hinge control link
157 Hinge link fairing
158 Port inner aileron
159 Flap "down" position
160 Outer single slotted flap
161 Outboard spoilers
162 Flap hinge link fairings
163 Honeycomb control surface construction
164 Port outer aileron
165 Tail navigation strobe light (white)

166 Anti-collision light (red)
167 Port navigation light
168 Port vent surge tank
169 Rear spar
170 Wing rib construction
171 Front spar
172 Leading edge slat segments
173 Slat guide rails
174 Rotary actuators
175 Slat operating links
176 Pressure refuelling connectors
177 Port wing integral fuel tank
178 Wing stringers
179 Wing skin plating
180 Four-wheel main undercarriage bogie
181 Mainwheel leg
182 Undercarriage leg side struts
183 Port wing dry bay
184 Inboard auxiliary fuel tank
185 Engine bleed air ducting
186 Slat drive motor
187 Landing and taxying lamps
188 Inboard leading edge slat
189 Slat open position
190 Port engine cowlings
191 Intake de-icing air duct
192 Port engine intake
193 Pratt & Whitney JT9D-7R4 turbofan engine (General Electric CF6-80A optional fit)
194 Engine mounting pylon
195 Oil tank
196 Fan air exhaust duct
197 Hot steam exhaust nozzle

Boeing Vertol 234 Commercial Chinook

History and Notes

As long ago as 1956, Boeing Vertol began the development of an all-weather medium transport helicopter for the US Army, and this entered service as the CH-47. The type has been built in large numbers and in several versions, and with a total of more than 1.6 million flight hours logged by the US Army's Chinooks since their entry into service, it has demonstrated a remarkable safety record, many of these hours being accrued during bitter combat conditions in Vietnam. On one occasion a Chinook carried no fewer than 147 refugees to safety in a single flight, and by the end of 1972 CH-47s operating in south-east Asia had airlifted to repair bases some 11,500 disabled aircraft (valued at more than $3 billion), often rescued from no-man's land situations.

In the late summer of 1978, Boeing Vertol announced the development of a civil counterpart to the military Chinook, intended for commercial service. Two basic versions were planned, the long-range Model 234LR to serve in all-passenger, passenger/freight 'combi', or all-cargo civil roles; and the utility version (234UT) for more specialised tasks such as resources exploration and development, logging, and general utility heavy construction work.

The 234LR programme was launched in November 1978, following the finalisation of a contract with British Airways Helicopters (BAH) for the supply of three of these aircraft, required primarily by BAH to carry passengers and priority cargo from points in Scotland to and from North Sea platforms operated by the Esso and Shell petroleum companies.

To facilitate such operations, emphasis has been placed on the interior design so that it can be converted comparatively easily by the operator from all-passenger to 'combi' or all-cargo use. In full passenger configuration these Chinooks had the largest capacity of any commercial helicopter available in 1981, with four-abreast seating for a maximum of 44 passengers, who enjoy a standard of interior design and comfort similar to that which is found in The Boeing Company's airliners, with roomy, comfortable seats; individual service units; complete lavatory facilities; overhead baggage compartments; ample windows, and pleasant lighting conditions; a food or beverage galley; and a stereo system. Access for

Boeing Vertol 234 Commercial Chinook of British Airways.

passengers is via a door at the forward end of the cabin on the port side, and the undersurface of the upswept rear fuselage is formed by a hydraulically operated cargo-loading ramp.

In a typical 'combi' layout, 18 passengers are accommodated in the forward area of the cabin, with 16,000 lb (7258 kg) of freight at the rear. In an all-cargo configuration up to 20,000 lb (9072 kg) can be carried internally, or a maximum of 28,000 lb (12701 kg) externally, suspended from a cargo hook or hooks.

To lift and carry such loads, the Chinook has two three-blade main rotors, one fore and one aft, which rotate in opposite directions to cancel out the effects of rotor torque. The rotors are driven by two Avco Lycoming AL 5512 turboshaft engines, via a combining gearbox and interconnecting shafts which enable both rotors to be driven in emergency by either engine. To provide the essential range, large external fuel tanks are accommodated within the fairings which extend along both sides of the lower fuselage. These fairings serve a dual purpose, for they also provide a flotation capability that can ensure survival of the aircraft if forced down onto a sea surface with storm waves not exceeding 30 ft (9.15 m) in height. Overwater operation throughout the year demands a high standard of all-weather capability, and this is ensured by the provision of weather radar, duplicated full blind-flying instrumentation, and a dual four-axis automatic flight control system. Comprehensive de-icing provisions are embodied, though these are optional for service in less critical areas, and the glassfibre rotor blades incorporate an aluminium screen in their construction to provide adequate protection against lightning strikes. Safety equipment includes

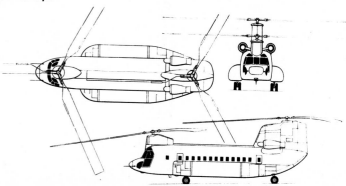

Boeing Vertol 234 Commercial Chinook

two liferafts, each of which is capable of accommodating up to 36 persons.

The first Model 234LR made its initial flight on 19 August 1980, completing successfully the hover and low-speed manoeuvres which had been planned. Two additional 234LRs were expected to become available before the end of 1980 to speed the CAA and FAA certification programmes, and the first of these new helicopters entered service with BAH during 1981.

The first Model 234UT version was ordered by Asahi Helicopters in the spring of 1981. The 234UT will have optional tankage in the sponsons, and though able to accommodate passengers in the fuselage, is seen mainly as a freighter. Hold volume is 1,619 cu ft (45.8 m³), and at a maximum weight of 51,000 lb (23182 kg) payload is 28,000 lb (12701 kg) carried for 58 miles (93 km).

Specification

Type: commercial transport helicopter
Powerplant: two 4,075-shp (3039-kW) Avco Lycoming AL 5512 turboshafts, each of which has a 30-minute contingency rating of 4,353 shp (3246 kW)
Performance: maximum level speed 167 mph (269 km/h); economic cruising speed 158 mph (254 km/h); service ceiling 15,000 ft (4570 m); maximum range with 44 passengers and 45-min reserves 627 miles (1009 km)
Weights: empty 24,449 lb (11090 kg); maximum take-off, internal load 47,000 lb (21319 kg); maximum take-off, external load, 51,000 lb (23133 kg)
Dimensions: rotor diameter (each) 60 ft 0 in (18.29 m); length overall, rotors turning 99 ft 0 in (30.18 m); height 18 ft 7.8 in (5.68 m); rotor disc area (total) 5,655 sq ft (525.34 m²)

British Airways Helicopters accepted the first of its three Boeing Vertol 234 helicopters in December 1980 for North Sea operations starting in mid-1981.

Bölkow Bö 207

History and Notes
The name of Dr.-Ing. Hanns Klemm was well known before World War II as the designer of a successful series of sporting aircraft in Germany. During the war a three-seat light cabin monoplane was designed, but priorities were elsewhere. After the end of the war, aircraft manufacture in Germany was banned, but this stricture was lifted in the early 1950s and in 1955 the prototype Klemm Kl 107 was completed.

Of wooden construction, and with non-retractable tailwheel landing gear, the Kl 107 was powered by a 95-hp (71-kW) Continental C90 engine. However, production versions, designated Kl 107B, had a 150-hp (112-kW) Avco Lycoming and the first of these flew in September 1956. Production rights were acquired by Bölkow, and the final model was the Kl 107C; total Kl 107 production amounted to 150 aircraft.

Further development of the basic design by Bölkow led to a larger version, originally the Kl 107D but redesignated as the F207, later Bö 207. This was a considerable redesign within the same basic layout, having a larger fuselage with accommodation for four people, increased wing and tail areas, and a larger engine (the 180-hp:134-kW Avco Lycoming O-360). The prototype Bö 207 flew on 10 October 1960 and an initial batch of 150 was planned by the end of 1962, with the first production aircraft flying in August 1961. In the event, production ceased in mid-1966 after 92 had been built.

A trainer version, the Bö 207T, was certificated for aerobatics, and several were used by the Swissair training school; the standard Bö 207 was also capable of glider-towing.

Specification
Type: four-seat cabin monoplane
Powerplant: one 180-hp (134-kW) Avco Lycoming O-360-A1A flat-four piston engine
Performance: maximum speed 158 mph (255 km/h) at sea level; cruising speed 146 mph (235 km/h); service ceiling 14,105 ft (4300 m); range 777 miles (1250 km)
Weights: empty 1,576 lb (715 kg); maximum take-off 2,646 lb (1200 kg)
Dimensions: span 35 ft 5½ in (10.81 m); length 27 ft 2¾ in (8.30 m); height 7 ft 4½ in (2.25 m); wing area 165.77 sq ft (15.40 m²)

Bristol Freighter

History and Notes
One of the earliest post-World War II projects of the Bristol Aeroplane Company was the Type 170 short-range utility transport. This had developed during the closing stages of the war, and its shape was determined largely by the British Army's needs, which included the ability to airlift the standard three-ton truck. The design was finalised with a high-wing monoplane configuration, clam-shell nose doors, flight deck above the cargo hold/cabin, fixed landing gear, and two wing-mounted Bristol Hercules sleeve-valve engines. Two civil prototypes were financed by the Ministry of Supply as the need for military transports appeared to be nearing an end. But there was a condition to the MoS funding: the company was required to cover tooling costs and also to build two additional prototypes.

As a result, the opportunity was taken to construct the company examples as passenger/cargo variants. Thus, the MoS aircraft became known as the Mk I Freighters, retaining nose loading doors; the company prototypes were Mk II Wayfarers, with a solid nose, side entrance/loading door, and with an optional reinforced freight floor. The Freighters were true cargo carriers, while the Wayfarers were available in several configurations, including a maximum of 32 passengers, with a galley and toilet.

First to fly was the Freighter prototype G-AGPV on 2 December 1945, followed by a Wayfarer (G-AGVB) in the 32-seat configuration on 30 April 1946. The first prototype was to be used for service trials at Boscombe Down, as a result of which the wing span was increased by 10 ft

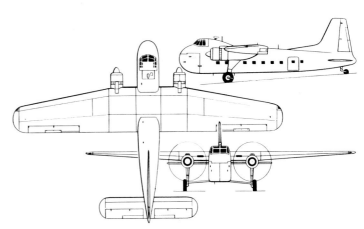

Bristol 170 Freighter of Safe Air, New Zealand.

(3.05 m) to allow an increase in gross weight. This, in turn, required the installation of more powerful engines, and resulted in the version designated Mk 21. The best known variant was the Mk 32, with a fuselage lengthened by 5 ft 0 in (1.52 m): it was developed for Silver City Airways to provide increased passenger/car capacity for service on their Channel air bridge. Silver City's 'Superfreighters' could accommodate two or three cars and up to 23 passengers. Acquired later were 'Super-Wayfarers', that could carry a maximum of 60 passengers. In 1962, Air Charter and Silver City Airways were merged to form British United Air Ferries, then operating a combined fleet of 24 Type 170s, increasing to 41 by 1970. When production ended in early 1958, a total of 214 of all variants had been built. The following details apply to Mk 31 and 32 aircraft.

Specification
Type: twin-engined utilılty transport
Powerplant: two 1,980-hp

Bristol 170 Freighter Mk 31

(1476-kW) Bristol Hercules 734 radial piston engines
Performance: maximum level speed 225 mph (362 km/h); cruising speed 163 mph (262 km/h); service ceiling 24,500 ft (7470 m); range 820 miles (1320 km)

Weights (Mk 32): empty 29,550 lb (13404 kg); maximum take-off 44,000 lb (19958 kg)
Dimensions: span 108 ft 0 in (32.92 m); length 73 ft 4 in (22.35 m); height, Mk 31 21 ft 8 in (6.60 m), Mk 32 25 ft 0 in (7.62 m); wing area 1,487 sq ft (138.14 m²)

Bristol Britannia

History and Notes
To meet early post-World War II requirements of the British Overseas Airways Corporation (BOAC) for a Medium Range Empire (MRE) civil transport, Bristol Aircraft, together with four other British manufacturers, submitted a total of eight designs to the specification which had been advised. Most nearly meeting the requirement was Bristol's Type 175, a pressurised low-wing monoplane with tricycle type landing gear, to be powered by four Bristol Centaurus sleeve-valve piston engines, and providing accommodation for 32 to 36 passengers. The Centaurus engines were, however, more powerful than required by the planned payload, and it was decided to amend the design to accommodate 40 to 44 passengers, this being increased again at a later stage to seat 42 to 48. It was anticipated that BOAC would order this version, but it was in fact

Bristol Britannia 253C of Gemini Air Transport (Ghana).

the UK's Ministry of Supply which ordered three prototypes on 5 July 1948.

More design changes were to follow, and when the first prototype (G-ALBO) made its maiden flight on 16 August 1952, it was of the same general configuration as the initial production Series 100 aircraft which could accommodate a maximum of 90 tourist-class passengers. Power-plant of this prototype comprised four Bristol Proteus turboprop engines, each of 2,800 ehp (2088 ekW), but the Series 100 production aircraft had the more developed Proteus 705 of 3,780 eph (2819 ekW). Fifteen of this version were to be built for BOAC, these being designated Britannia 102, and they first entered service on 1 February 1957 on BOAC's South African routes, operations to Australia

following in March. None of these original production aircraft remain in airline service.

A larger-capacity version was to follow under the designation Britannia 300, the prototype Britannia 301 (G-ANCA) making its first flight on 31 July 1956. This variant had been evolved not only to provide increased capacity, its fuselage being lengthened by 10 ft 3 in (3.12 m) to accommodate up to 133 tourist-class passengers, but also to have non-stop transatlantic capability. Although seven were ordered by BOAC they did not serve with this airline, being delivered instead to Aeronaves de Mexico (two Britannia 302s), Transcontinental SA (two 305s), Air Charter (two 307s), and Ghana Airways (one 309).

BOAC had transferred its order to series 300LR (long-range) aircraft with increased fuel tankage, and initially with 4,120-ehp (3072-ekW) Proteus 755 turboprops, this designation being changed subsequently to Series 310. The prototype Britannia 311 (G-AOVA) flew first on 31 December 1956, and BOAC's first Britannia 312 was delivered on 10 September 1957 and used for proving flights over the North Atlantic. This led to the inauguration of BOAC's London-New York service with Britannia 312s, the first scheduled transatlantic passenger service to be flown by turbine-powered airliners, with G-AOVC making the first revenue flight on 19 December 1957. Final development produced the Series 320 Britannia, which differed from its predecessors primarily in having 4,450-ehp (3318-ekW) Proteus 765 turboprops. Only two of these were built and leased to Canadian Pacific Air Lines (now CP Air).

It had seemed in the early days of Britannia production that this airliner might capture a significant bag of orders, but it was left behind in the wake of the new Boeing 707 and never recovered. Production of civil airliners totalled 60, and in addition a further 23 (3 Britannia 252s and 20 253s) were completed by Short Brothers and Harland at Belfast for service with the RAF's Transport Command as Britannia C. Mk 1s. Basically similar to the Series 310, they incorporated a large cargo freight door. The 22 remaining in service in 1975 were then retired, and were acquired by small airlines in Africa, Europe and the Middle East.

The last of the Britannias to be delivered from Filton, at the end of November 1960, was the original prototype (G-ALBO) which, by then, had an unusual powerplant mixture. This comprised Proteus 705s in the two inboard positions, and one Proteus

A few Bristol Britannia long-range airliners remain in service, mainly as freighters. One operator is Redcoat Air Cargo, which has a single Model 253C.

755 and one 5,500-ehp (4104-ekW) Bristol Orion turboprop in the starboard and port outer nacelles respectively: it ended its days at RAF St Athan, serving as an instructional airframe.

This, however, was not quite the end of the Britannia story, for a manufacturing licence had been granted to Canadair Ltd in 1954. This company built initially 33 CL-28 Argus maritime reconnaissance aircraft, derived from the Britannia, for service with the Royal Canadian Air Force. It was followed by the construction of a transport version designated CL-44, for both military and civil use. The details which follow apply to Britannia Seriers 310 aircraft.

Specification
Type: commercial transport
Powerplant: four 4,120-ehp (3072-ekW) Bristol Proteus 755 turboprops
Performance: maximum speed 397 mph (639 km/h); cruising speed 357 mph (575 km/h); service ceiling 24,000 ft (7315 m); range with

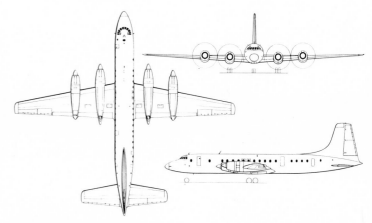

Bristol Britannia 310

maximum payload 4,268 miles (6869 km)
Weights: empty 82,537 lb (37438 kg); maximum take-off 185,000 lb (83915 kg)
Dimensions: span 142 ft 3 in (43.36 m); length 124 ft 3 in (37.87 m);

height 37 ft 6 in (11.43 m); wing area 2,075 sq ft (192.77 m²)
Operators include: Aer Turas Teoranta, Afrek, Cubana, Gaylan Air Cargo, Gemini Air Transport (Geminair), Invicta International Airlines, and Redcoat Air Cargo

British Aerospace (Avro/HS) 748

History and Notes
Starting life as an Avro (A.V.Roe & Company) project in 1958, the Type 748 resulted from the company's intention to re-enter the civil aircraft market. This followed upon an expressed belief of 1957 that ballistic missiles were then at such an advanced stage that it would be unnecessary to develop any new manned aircraft for service with the RAF. Avro's design team, under the leadership of J.R.Ewans, investigated a number of different configurations for a 20-seat short/medium-range feeder aircraft, a project allocated the indentification Avro 748. However, subsequent market research was to show there was little commercial interest in an airliner of this capacity, so the design was scaled up to make it a potential replacement for the enduring and ubiquitous Douglas DC-3.

At the beginning of 1959 the Hawker Siddeley Group, of which

BAe 748 of Bahamasair.

Avro had been a component since 1936, decided to proceed with construction of the Avro 748 in this latter form. Four prototypes were built as a private venture, two for static testing, and the first flight prototype (G-APZV) was flown at Woodford Aerodrome, Cheshire, on

24 June 1960. In this original form it was a conventional all-metal low-wing aircraft with pressurised accommodation for up to 44 passengers. Powerplant consisted of two Rolls-Royce Dart turboprop engines, these being mounted high over the wing leading-edge to provide adequate

clearance for large-diameter propellers. The forward-retracting twin-wheel main landing gear units were housed in somewhat ugly fairings forward of the wing leading-edge, and this powerplant/landing gear installation, which has since remained unaltered, provides a recognition

British Aerospace (Avro/HS) 748

feature that is unmistakable.

The first production Series 1 aircraft was flown for the first time on 31 August 1961, this having Dart 514 engines each of 1,740 ehp (1298 ekW), and accommodation for a maximum of 48 passengers as certified in early December 1961. The second flight prototype, first flown on 10 April 1961, subsequently had Dart 531 engines of 1,910 ehp (1424 ekW) installed to serve as the prototype of the Series 2 aircraft which, with structural strengthening, was initially certificated for a maximum of 52 passengers. Since that time Series 2, or Series 2A aircraft with still more powerful engines, have been developed, and these two versions accounted for the major proportion of the 350 aircraft which had been ordered by September 1980.

Known as the HS 748 since 1 July 1963, the latest version, introduced in early 1979, is the Series 2B. This has Dart 536-2 engines, increased wing span, modified tail surfaces, and a number of aerodynamic improvements. It is available optionally with a large rear freight door in the port side of the after fuselage, this providing a maximum aperture of 8 ft 9 in by 5 ft 7¾ in (2.67 m by 1.72 m), and with a strengthened floor. Models known as the Andover CC.Mk 1 and CC.Mk 2 have been supplied to the RAF, two specially-equipped aircraft being used in The Queen's Flight, and HS 748 military transports serve also with several foreign air forces. A maritime patrol version known as the Coastguarder was also developed, and in addition approximately 90 have been built under licence, for both civil and military use, by Hindustan Aeronautics Ltd in India. The details that follow apply to the HS 748 Series 2B.

Specification
Type: short/medium-range passenger or freight transport
Powerplant: two 2,280-ehp (1700-ekW) Rolls-Royce Dart RDa.7 Mk 536-2 turboprops
Performance: cruising speed 281 mph (452 km/h); service ceiling 25,000 ft (7620 m); range with maximum payload and fuel reserves 812 miles (1307 km); range with maximum fuel, reserves, and 7,787-lb (3532-kg) payload 1,549 miles (2493 km)
Weights: empty operating 25,671 lb (11644 kg); maximum take-off 51,000 lb (23133 kg)
Dimensions: span 102 ft 5½ in (31.23 m); length 67 ft 0 in (20.42 m); height 24 ft 10 in (7.57 m); wing area 828.87 sq ft (77.00 m²)
Operators include: Air Botswana, Air Cape, Air Illinois, Air Liberia, Air Malawi, Air Pacific, Air Senegal, Austin Airways, Bahamasair, Bouraq Indonesia

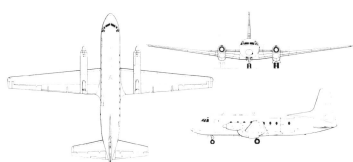

BAe (HS) 748 Series 2A

Airlines, Bradley Air Services, British Airways, Dan-Air Services, Eastern Provincial Airways, Fred Olsens Flyveselskap, Ghana Airways, Guyana Airways, Indian Airlines, LAV, LIAT, Merpati Nusantara Airlines, Mountain West Airlines, Mount Cook Airlines, Northern Wings, Northward Airlines, Philippine Air Lines, Polynesian Airlines, Royal Nepal Airline Corporation, SATA, Satena, South African Airways, Thai Airways Company, Transkei Airways, Trinidad & Tobago Air Services, and Zambia Airways

British Aerospace (HP/Scottish Aviation) Jetstream

History and Notes
The name Handley Page, once an integral part of the British aviation industry, disappeared from the active scene into aviation history in early 1970, following celebration of the company's Diamond Jubilee on 17 June 1969. The straw which finally broke the camel's back was the Handley Page H.P.137 project for a twin-turboprop executive/feederliner transport, within the 12 to 20-seat capacity as originally envisaged. When, in January 1966, the company decided to begin the construction of four prototypes, the launching costs were estimated at £3 million, but by the time that the certification programme was well advanced, in August 1969, these had already exceeded £13 million, and on 8 August the company went into voluntary liquidation.

Following attempts to continue production with financial backing from the USA as Handley Page Aircraft Ltd, and later as a newly formed Jetstream Aircraft Ltd, it was finally Scottish Aviation Ltd which continued manufacture of the aircraft. Even this company was to lose its identity, becoming the Scottish Division of the British Aerospace Aircraft Group on 1 January 1978.

The definitive civil version was the Jetstream Series 200, developed initially by Handley Page as a con-

BAe (Scottish Aviation) Jetstream of Apollo Airways, USA.

ventional low-wing monoplane of all-metal fail-safe structure. The landing gear was of the hydraulically retractable tricycle type, and the pressurised cabin accommodated a crew of two on the flight deck, and a maximum of 18 passengers. The powerplant of civil Jetstream 200s comprised two Turboméca Astazou XVI turboprop engines. Earlier versions completed by Handley Page and supplied to International Jetstream Corporation in America were powered by 840-ehp (626-kW) Astazou IV engines, but many were converted subsequently by Riley Aircraft of Carlsbad, California to Riley Jetstream configuration with Astazou XVI engines. One, named *Life of Riley*, had two 783-ehp (584-ekW) Pratt & Whitney

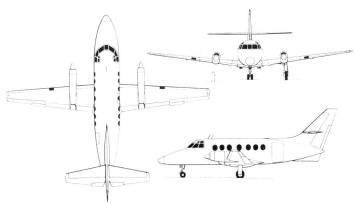

BAe (Scottish Aviation) Jetstream 31

British Aerospace (HP/Scottish Aviation) Jetstream

Aircraft of Canada PT6A-34 turbo-props installed by Jack Riley's company.

There may yet be further chapters of the Jetstream story to write, for on 5 December 1978, British Aerospace announced its intention to develop a new version of this aircraft. Designated Jetstream 31, and powered by two 900-shp (671-kW) Garrett AiResearch TPE331-10 turboprop engines, the prototype of this advanced version was flying in the summer of 1980. The following details apply to the Jetstream Series 200.

Specification
Type: executive/commuter transport
Powerplant: two 969-ehp (723-ekW) Turboméca Astazou XVID turboprops
Performance: maximum cruising speed 282 mph (454 km/h) at 10,000 ft (3050 m); economic cruising speed 269 mph (433 km/h) at 15,000 ft (4575 m); service ceiling 25,000 ft (7620 m); range with maximum fuel, with reserves

for 45-min hold plus 5 per cent of total fuel 1,380 miles (2221 km)
Weights: empty 7,683 lb (3485 kg); maximum take-off 12,566 lb (5700 kg)

Dimensions: span 52 ft 0 in (15.85 m); length 47 ft 1½ in (14.36 m); height 17 ft 5½ in (5.32 m); wing area 270 sq ft (25.08 m²)
Operators include: Air Illinois

A fine aircraft with many virtues, the BAe Jetstream has been produced with or converted to a number of turboprops. The type may enjoy a new lease of life with advanced Garrett TPE331 engines.

British Aerospace (HS) 125

History and Notes
Development of the aircraft known now as the British Aerospace HS 125 began in 1961, when a de Havilland design team under the leadership of J. Goodwin began work on the D.H.125. Intended to serve as a business transport aircraft, with accommodation for a crew of two and six to eight passengers, it was a forward-looking design and was known for a short period as the Jet Dragon. Of low-wing monoplane configuration and basically of all-metal construction, the design included a fail-safe pressurised fuselage, T-tail, retractable tricycle landing gear with twin wheels on each unit, and two Bristol Siddeley turbojet engines, one mounted in a pod on each side of the aft fuselage.

Two prototypes were built, the first (G-ARYA) making its maiden flight on 13 August 1962. Powered by Bristol Siddeley Viper 20 turbojets of 3,000-lb (1361-kg) thrust, these prototypes were both flown extensively to gain early certification, being joined in this programme by the first production aircraft, which differed in having Viper 520 turbojets of the same thrust, and with wing span and length increased by 3 ft 0 in (0.91 m) and 3 ft 11 in (1.19 m) respectively.

Only eight Series 1 production aircraft were built before the introduction of Viper 521 and 522 engines of 3,100-lb (1406-kg) thrust, which resulted in the Series 1A/1B aircraft operating at a higher gross weight. De Havilland believed that the D.H.125 would have good sales potential in North America, appointing distributors and using the eighth aircraft for a long demonstration tour. This faith was justified, for by the end of 1980 when total sales were approaching 650, exports accounted for about 80 per cent of this figure, by far the majority of the aircraft being operated on the North American continent.

By the time of that tour, de Havilland had been absorbed into the Hawker Siddeley group, and it was

The British Aerospace (HS) 125 Series 700 is a much improved variant with drag-reducing external modifications and low-consumption Garrett AiResearch TFE731 turbofans, increasing range.

BAe (HS) 125 of Qantas Airways, Australia.

this company that continued production and development of this aircraft under the designation HS 125. Series 2 accounted for 20 navigation trainers serving with the RAF as Dominie T.Mk 1s, and this service later acquired CC.Mk 1 and Mk 2 communications HS 125s from later series. Series 3 and Series 400 aircraft differed primarily by having more powerful variants of the Viper 522, but a major change was introduced on the Series 600 which had a fuselage lengthened by 3 ft 1 in (0.94 m) to provide accommodation for a maximum of 14 passengers in a high density layout.

Current production version in 1981 is the Series 700, first introduced in 1976, which benefits from the installation of Garrett turbofan engines that, by comparison with the Viper

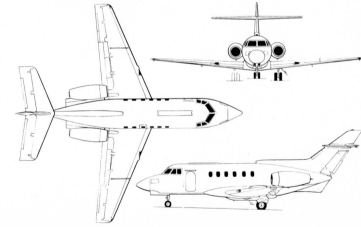

BAe (HS) 125 Series 700

The BAe 125 Series 700 is chiefly distinguishable from its predecessors by its larger-diameter turbofans, but other useful recognition features are the elimination of projecting aerials and a larger ventral fin.

British Aerospace (HS) 125

turbojets, are more efficient users of fuel. It also has many detail improvements to provide optimum performance and comfort, and this attractive civil/military transport seems likely to continue in production for some time. The following details apply to the Series 700.

Specification
Type: twin-turbofan light transport
Powerplant: two 3,700-lb (1678-kg) thrust Garrett TFE731-3-1H turbofans
Performance: maximum cruising speed 502 mph (808 km/h) at 27,500 ft (8380 m); economic cruising speed 449 mph (723 km/h) between 37,000 and 41,000 ft (11280 and 12495 m); service ceiling 41,000 ft (12495 m); range with maximum fuel and payload with allowances and 45-min reserves 2,785 miles (4482 km)
Weights: empty 12,845 lb (5826 kg); maximum take-off 25,500 lb (11567 kg)
Dimensions: span 47 ft 0 in (14.33 m); length 50 ft 8½ in (15.46 m); height 17 ft 7 in (5.36 m); wing area 353.0 sq ft (32.79 m²)

The BAe 125 Series 700 has an updated interior finish, and this should help the type keep its place as one of the best sellers in the US 'bizjet' market.

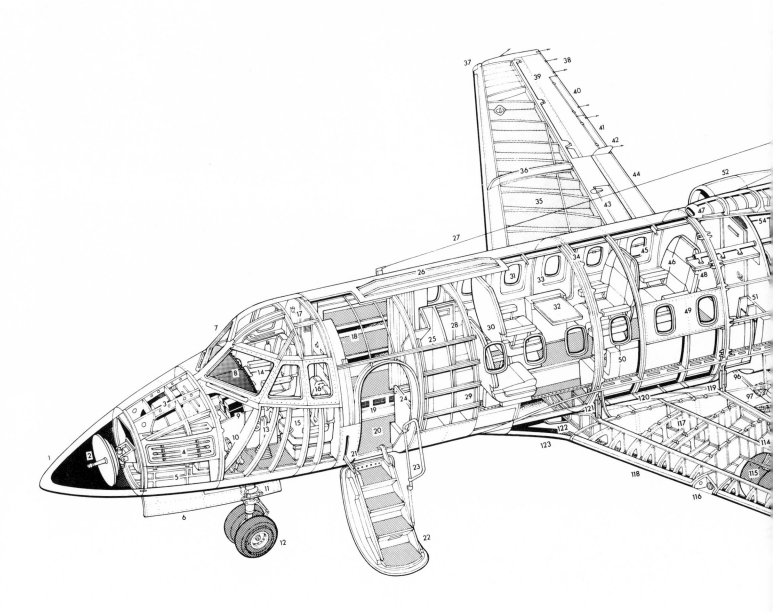

86

Hawker Siddeley HS.125-700 cutaway drawing key

1 Radome
2 Radar scanner
3 Nose equipment bay
4 VOR localiser aerial
5 Nose undercarriage bay
6 Nosewheel doors
7 Windscreen
8 Instrument panel shroud
9 Back of instrument panel
10 Rudder pedals
11 Nosewheel steering jack
12 Twin nosewheels
13 Control column
14 Second pilot's seat
15 First pilot's seat
16 Safety harness
17 Electrical distribution panel
18 Baggage compartment
19 Avionics racks
20 Vestibule
21 External doorhandle
22 Entry steps
23 Handrail
24 Galley
25 Galley storage locker
26 ADF aerial
27 HF aerial

28 Wardrobe
29 Fuselage stringer
   construction
30 Rearward facing passenger
   seats
31 Cabin windows
32 Folding table
33 Emergency exit window
34 Fuselage main frame
35 Starboard wing fuel tank
36 Wing fence
37 Starboard navigation light
38 Static dischargers
39 Starboard aileron
40 Trim tab
41 Geared tab
42 Aileron fence
43 Airbrake
44 Starboard flap
45 Window blind
46 Rear cabin seats
47 Ram air intake
48 Passenger service unit
49 Cabin window panel
50 Three seat settee
51 Magazine rack
52 Starboard engine cowling

53 Intake duct to heat
   exchangers
54 Water tank
55 Air conditioning supply
56 Wash basin
57 Toilet compartment
58 Pressure bulkhead frame
59 Dorsal fuel tank
60 Heat exchanger
61 Air conditioning plant
62 Auxiliary power unit
63 APU intake
64 Rear equipment
   compartment
65 Fin spar attachment
66 Fin root fairing
67 Fin construction
68 Control cable ducting
69 Aerial attachment
70 Starboard tailplane
71 Starboard elevator
72 Static dischargers
73 Elevator tab
74 Overfin
75 Anti collision light
76 VHF aerial
77 Fin bullet fairing

78 Tail navigation light
79 Port elevator
80 Tailplane construction
81 Leading edge de-icing
82 Elevator hinge control
83 Rudder construction
84 Rudder tab
85 Tailcone
86 Ventral fin
87 Rudder hinge control
88 Oxygen bottles
89 Batteries
90 Engine pylon fairing
91 Fire extinguisher
92 Garrett AiResearch TFE-731
   turbofan
93 Detachable cowling
94 Engine intake
95 Ventral fuel tank
96 Main undercarriage well
97 Flap hinge control
98 Undercarriage leg pivot
   fixing
99 Flap screwjack
100 Double slatted flap
   construction
101 Airbrake jack

102 Port airbrake
103 Aileron fence
104 Aileron hinge control
105 Geared tab
106 Trim tab
107 Aileron construction
108 Static dischargers
109 Aileron horn balance
110 Fuel filler cap
111 Integral wing fuel tank
112 Wing fence
113 Leading edge construction
114 Main undercarriage leg
115 Twin mainwheels
116 Landing and taxi lamp
117 Wing construction
118 Leading edge de-icing
119 Rear spar attachment links
120 Centre wing box
   construction
121 Front spar attachment links
122 Ventral strake
123 Wing root fillet

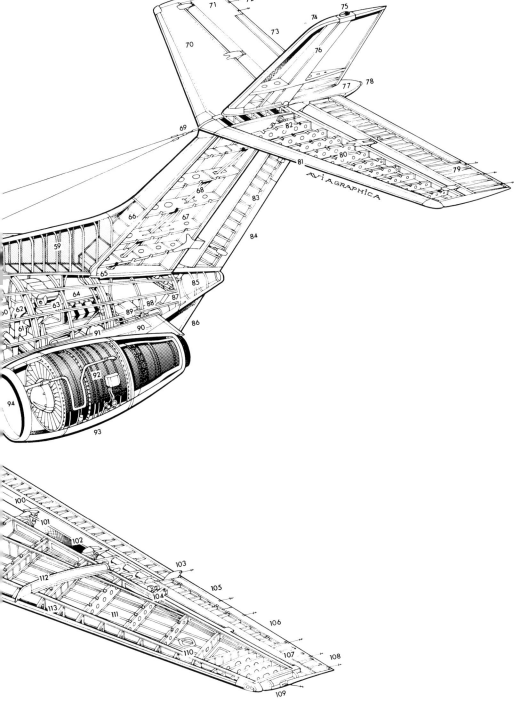

British Aerospace One-Eleven

History and Notes

Starting its history in 1956, the BAe One-Eleven originates from a 32-seat turbojet-powered transport which was designed as a project by Hunting Aircraft. Then identified as the H.107, the projected aeroplane was to have been powered by two rear-mounted Bristol Orpheus 12B turbojets, but following wind tunnel evaluation the design was amended to incorporate turbofan engines that were then in the development stage. This led to a delay of four years, by which time Hunting Aircraft had been acquired by the British Aircraft Corporation. It was then decided to resurrect the H.107 for further market research and development by the combined design teams of Hunting and Vickers at Weybridge. There was little commercial enthusiasm for the BAC.107 in its final Hunting configuration, with accommodation for 59 passengers, but there was sufficient interest for a version with a maximum of approximately 80 seats to warrant the construction of a prototype and static test airframes.

Designated BAC.111 (and later to be called One-Eleven), the airliner incorporated a circular-section all-metal pressurised fuselage, low-set swept monoplane wings incorporating Fowler type trailing-edge flaps, and airbrakes/spoilers on the wing upper surface, forward of the flaps. The T-tail included a variable-incidence tailplane, and the landing

gear, of the hydraulically retractable tricycle type, had twin wheels on each unit. Accommodation was provided for a maximum of 79 passengers in five-abreast high-density seating, and in addition to a conventionally placed passenger door at the forward end of the cabin on the port side, the BAC.111 had also a ventral airstair below the tail unit, giving access to or from the aft end of the cabin. Powerplant of the prototype (G-ASHG) Series 200, which was intended as the basic production version, consisted of two 10,410-lb (4722-kg) thrust Rolls-Royce Spey Mk 506 turbofans, and the aeroplane flew for the first time on 20 August 1963 at Hurn, Hampshire. Two months later, on 22 October, this aircraft was lost during the flight development programme, together with a highly experienced crew of seven that included test pilot M.J. Lithgow. Investigation showed the cause to be a deep stall, resulting from the T-tail and rear-mounted engine configuration. Remedial action included the installation of powered elevators, a stick-pusher, and modification of the wing leading-edges.

These changes were adequate to prevent the aircraft from assuming an inadvertent and dangerous angle of attack, a condition peculiar to this configuration: the wing loses lift and the horizontal tail surfaces are unable to restore longitudinal stability. Although responsible for extending

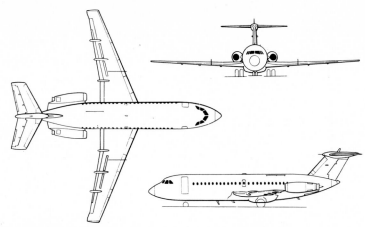

BAe (BAC) One-Eleven Series 500 of Cyprus Airways.

BAe (BAC) One-Eleven Series 475

The British Aerospace One-Eleven Series 475 is well-suited to 'hot and high' operations from secondary airfields, as indicated by such an aircraft operated by the Compania de Aviacion Faucett in Peru. The airline has two One-Elevens, one of which is seen taking off from Tingo Maria in the foothills of the Andes.

A BAe One-Eleven Series 500 short-haul
airliner is seen on a test flight before
delivery to British Airways, which has 28
One-Elevens, including 21 Series 500s.

considerably the test and development programme of the One-Eleven (the full Certificate of Airworthiness was not awarded until 5 April 1965), this detailed investigation of the cause and remedy of the deep-stall phenomenon was to prove of considerable value to aircraft designers and manufacturers worldwide.

Long before certification, in May 1963, the British Aircraft Corporation (BAC) announced that it intended to develop two other versions in addition to the basic Series 200. These were to include an increased payload/range Series 300, with 11,400-lb (5171-kg) thrust Spey Mk 511 turbofans, and a generally similar Series 400 that would incorporate modifications to meet US requirements. As well as introducing more powerful engines, the Series 300 had increased fuel capacity, and strengthened wings and landing gear to cater for an 8,500-lb (3856-kg) increase in gross weight.

Interest in the One-Eleven was growing, following the initial order of 10 Series 200 aircraft from British United Airways (BUA), and market potential within the USA was demonstrated by an early order for six aircraft from Braniff International. When this was followed by orders from other US carriers, including American Airlines, the prospect for fairly large US sales seemed very good. However, by the time that FAA Type Approval was awarded, on 16 April 1965, there was a growing number of aircraft competing within the same payload/range category, and total sales to US carriers failed to reach the figures that had at one time seemed possible. Initial One-Eleven services were flown by British United, from Gatwick to Genoa, on 9 April 1965; in the USA, Braniff's first Corpus Christi—Minneapolis revenue flight was made on 25 April. In January 1966, BUA inaugurated London - Scotland and London - Northern Ireland One-Eleven domestic routes. Production of the three initial versions of the One-Eleven was to total 134: 56 Series 200, nine Series 300, and 69 Series 400.

The steadily increasing number of air travellers meant that, within most categories of aircraft, carriers were looking for greater accommodation/payload capacity. 'Stretched', or increased capacity, versions of the One-Eleven had been under consideration by BAC at much the same time as the original Series 200/300/400 aircraft were announced. However, it was not until British European Airways (BEA) began to show interest in an enlarged One-Eleven that design of what was to become the Series 500 was finalised.

With a fuselage lengthened by 8 ft 4 in (2.54 m) forward of the wing, and 5 ft 2 in (1.57 m) aft of the wing, the Series 500 can accommodate a maximum of 119 passengers. More powerful engines were introduced, the wing span increased by 5 ft 0 in (1.52 m), and the structure of both the landing gear and wings strengthened to make possible a significant increase in gross weight. This was originally 91,000 lb (41277 kg) for take-off, but has since been raised to a maximum of 104,500 lb (47400 kg). The prototype for the Series 500 was produced by conversion of the Series 400 development aircraft (G-ASYD), and this flew for the first time in its new configuration on 30 June 1967. ARB certification of a production example was gained on 15 August 1968, and BEA's first revenue flight was flown three months later, on 17 November.

Final variant of the One-Eleven to appear to date is the Series 475, intended for operation from and into smaller airports, or in higher temperature/altitude environments. This retains the standard fuselage/accommodation of the Series 400, and combines the powerplant and wings of the Series 500, plus a modified landing gear to permit operation from lower-grade surfaces.

Total sales for One-Elevens had reached a figure of 230 in the autumn of 1980, and in addition British Aerospace has concluded licence arrangements under which these aircraft are to be built in Romania, both for domestic and export markets. Three complete One-Elevens are being supplied, plus components for an additional 21 aircraft for assembly during the period 1980-5, to be followed by production in Romania of complete aircraft and engines from 1986.

In addition to Series 475 and 500 aircraft which are available from BAe in standard configuration, two other special variants are available. These comprise executive or freighter configurations, and approximately 40 examples of the former are in service worldwide. The freighter conversion includes installation of a 10 ft 0 in by 6 ft 1 in (3.05 m by 1.85 m) hydraulically actuated cargo door in the port forward fuselage, and a quick-conversion freight handling system. New-technology options for new aircraft, and in some cases suitable for retrospective installation, include a fully certificated Category II automatic landing system, automatic throttle control, and engine 'hush-kits'.

Philippine Airlines operate eight types of aircraft, the most important short-haul type being the British Aerospace (BAC) One-Eleven Series 500, of which the airline has 12. The maximum passenger capacity of each is 119.

British Aerospace One-Eleven 670 cutaway drawing key

1 Radome
2 Weather radar scanner
3 Radar scanner mounting
4 Pressure bulkhead
5 Windscreen panels
6 Windscreen wipers
7 Instrument panel shroud
8 Rudder pedals
9 Nose equipment bay
10 Cockpit floor level
11 Control column
12 Pilot's seat
13 Co-pilot's seat
14 Cockpit roof construction
15 Supernumerary crew seat
16 Cockpit bulkhead
17 Radio rack
18 Starboard galley
19 Cockpit door
20 Port galley
21 Forward entry door

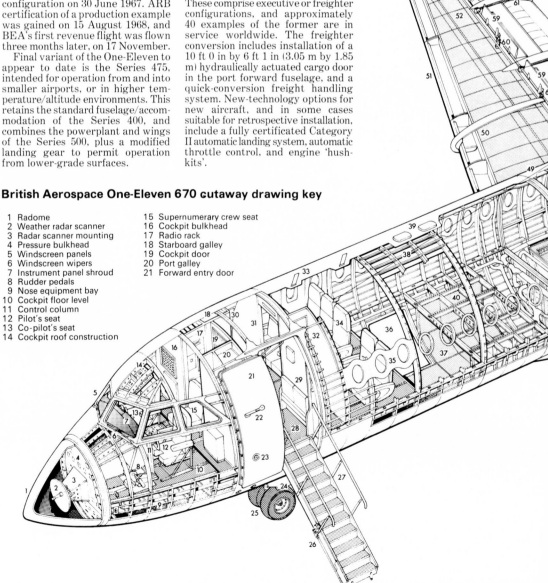

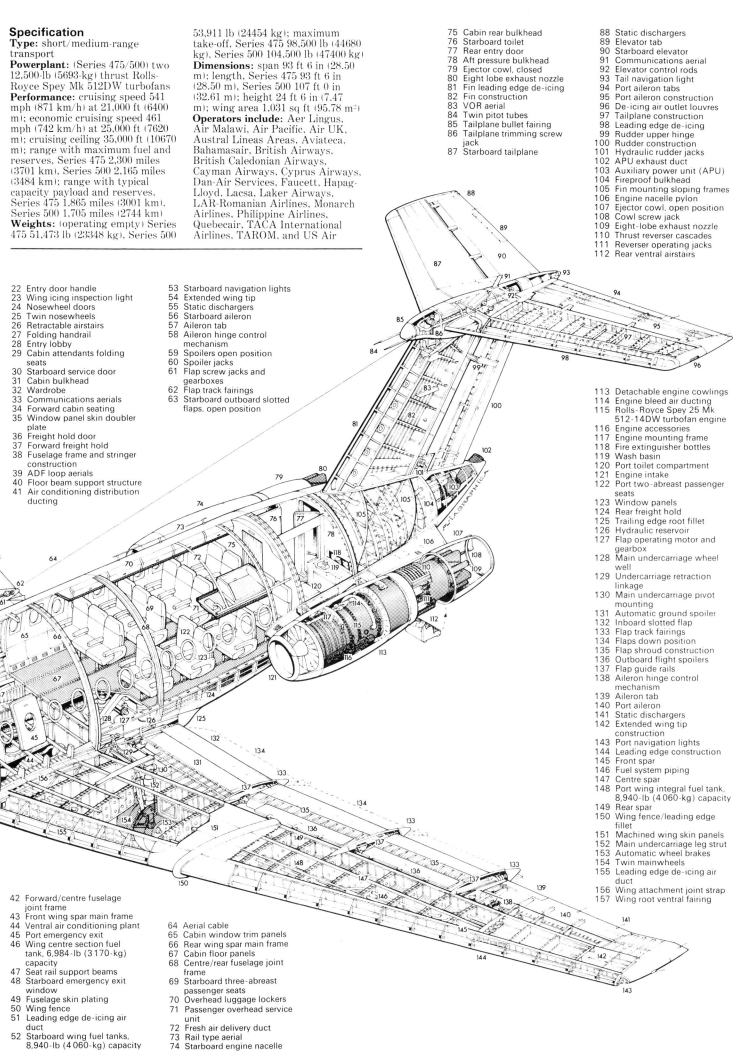

Specification

Type: short/medium-range transport

Powerplant: (Series 475/500) two 12,500-lb (5693-kg) thrust Rolls-Royce Spey Mk 512DW turbofans

Performance: cruising speed 541 mph (871 km/h) at 21,000 ft (6400 m); economic cruising speed 461 mph (742 km/h) at 25,000 ft (7620 m); cruising ceiling 35,000 ft (10670 m); range with maximum fuel and reserves, Series 475 2,300 miles (3701 km), Series 500 2,165 miles (3484 km); range with typical capacity payload and reserves, Series 475 1,865 miles (3001 km), Series 500 1,705 miles (2744 km)

Weights: (operating empty) Series 475 51,473 lb (23348 kg), Series 500 53,911 lb (24454 kg); maximum take-off, Series 475 98,500 lb (44680 kg), Series 500 104,500 lb (47400 kg)

Dimensions: span 93 ft 6 in (28.50 m); length, Series 475 93 ft 6 in (28.50 m), Series 500 107 ft 0 in (32.61 m); height 24 ft 6 in (7.47 m); wing area 1,031 sq ft (95.78 m²)

Operators include: Aer Lingus, Air Malawi, Air Pacific, Air UK, Austral Lineas Areas, Aviateca, Bahamasair, British Airways, British Caledonian Airways, Cayman Airways, Cyprus Airways, Dan-Air Services, Faucett, Hapag-Lloyd, Lacsa, Laker Airways, LAR-Romanian Airlines, Monarch Airlines, Philippine Airlines, Quebecair, TACA International Airlines, TAROM, and US Air

22 Entry door handle
23 Wing icing inspection light
24 Nosewheel doors
25 Twin nosewheels
26 Retractable airstairs
27 Folding handrail
28 Entry lobby
29 Cabin attendants folding seats
30 Starboard service door
31 Cabin bulkhead
32 Wardrobe
33 Communications aerials
34 Forward cabin seating
35 Window panel skin doubler plate
36 Freight hold door
37 Forward freight hold
38 Fuselage frame and stringer construction
39 ADF loop aerials
40 Floor beam support structure
41 Air conditioning distribution ducting
42 Forward/centre fuselage joint frame
43 Front wing spar main frame
44 Ventral air conditioning plant
45 Port emergency exit
46 Wing centre section fuel tank, 6,984-lb (3170-kg) capacity
47 Seat rail support beams
48 Starboard emergency exit window
49 Fuselage skin plating
50 Wing fence
51 Leading edge de-icing air duct
52 Starboard wing fuel tanks, 8,940-lb (4060-kg) capacity
53 Starboard navigation lights
54 Extended wing tip
55 Static dischargers
56 Starboard aileron
57 Aileron tab
58 Aileron hinge control mechanism
59 Spoilers open position
60 Spoiler jacks
61 Flap screw jacks and gearboxes
62 Flap track fairings
63 Starboard outboard slotted flaps, open position
64 Aerial cable
65 Cabin window trim panels
66 Rear wing spar main frame
67 Cabin floor panels
68 Centre/rear fuselage joint frame
69 Starboard three-abreast passenger seats
70 Overhead luggage lockers
71 Passenger overhead service unit
72 Fresh air delivery duct
73 Rail type aerial
74 Starboard engine nacelle
75 Cabin rear bulkhead
76 Starboard toilet
77 Rear entry door
78 Aft pressure bulkhead
79 Ejector cowl, closed
80 Eight lobe exhaust nozzle
81 Fin leading edge de-icing
82 Fin construction
83 VOR aerial
84 Twin pitot tubes
85 Tailplane bullet fairing
86 Tailplane trimming screw jack
87 Starboard tailplane
88 Static dischargers
89 Elevator tab
90 Starboard elevator
91 Communications aerial
92 Elevator control rods
93 Tail navigation light
94 Port aileron tabs
95 Port aileron construction
96 De-icing air outlet louvres
97 Tailplane construction
98 Leading edge de-icing
99 Rudder upper hinge
100 Rudder construction
101 Hydraulic rudder jacks
102 APU exhaust duct
103 Auxiliary power unit (APU)
104 Fireproof bulkhead
105 Fin mounting sloping frames
106 Engine nacelle pylon
107 Ejector cowl, open position
108 Cowl screw jack
109 Eight-lobe exhaust nozzle
110 Thrust reverser cascades
111 Reverser operating jacks
112 Rear ventral airstairs
113 Detachable engine cowlings
114 Engine bleed air ducting
115 Rolls-Royce Spey 25 Mk 512-14DW turbofan engine
116 Engine accessories
117 Engine mounting frame
118 Fire extinguisher bottles
119 Wash basin
120 Port toilet compartment
121 Engine intake
122 Port two-abreast passenger seats
123 Window panels
124 Rear freight hold
125 Trailing edge root fillet
126 Hydraulic reservoir
127 Flap operating motor and gearbox
128 Main undercarriage wheel well
129 Undercarriage retraction linkage
130 Main undercarriage pivot mounting
131 Automatic ground spoiler
132 Inboard slotted flap
133 Flap track fairings
134 Flaps down position
135 Flap shroud construction
136 Outboard flight spoilers
137 Flap guide rails
138 Aileron hinge control mechanism
139 Aileron tab
140 Port aileron
141 Static dischargers
142 Extended wing tip construction
143 Port navigation lights
144 Leading edge construction
145 Front spar
146 Fuel system piping
147 Centre spar
148 Port wing integral fuel tank, 8,940-lb (4060-kg) capacity
149 Rear spar
150 Wing fence/leading edge fillet
151 Machined wing skin panels
152 Main undercarriage leg strut
153 Automatic wheel brakes
154 Twin mainwheels
155 Leading edge de-icing air duct
156 Wing attachment joint strap
157 Wing root ventral fairing

British Aerospace (HS) 146

History and Notes

On 29 August 1973, Hawker Siddeley Aviation announced that the company was to receive support from the UK government for the development of a new short-range transport aircraft which had been given the designation HS 146. In its initial Series 100 version it was intended to provide accommodation for 71 to 88 passengers, to be capable of operation from short semi-prepared airstrips, and also to offer the benefits of comparatively low operating costs. The first flight of the first Series 100 pre-production aircraft was scheduled for December 1975.

This was not to be, for in the autumn of 1974 a worldwide recession resulted from the oil crisis of 1973-4, and in October Hawker Siddeley decided to suspend this programme. As it was a suspension rather than a termination, minimal funds were allocated each year to keep the project alive, with design and research continuing on a restricted basis. Then, on 29 April 1977, Hawker Siddeley was absorbed into the newly-formed British Aerospace Corporation: the project continues now, with work being carried out at several factories of what was known in 1981 as the British Aerospace Aircraft Group. The decision to reinstate the HS 146 as an active programme was reached on 10 July 1978, following intensive research into potential markets, and the roll-out of the Series 100 prototype of what was now designated the BAe 146 was achieved in June 1981.

Hawker Siddeley's HS 146 project had evolved through a series of designs embracing both high- and low-wing configurations, with a variety of engine layouts. As the BAe 146 it has been finalised as a high-wing cantilever monoplane of light alloy construction, the wing incorporating the company's own high-lift aerofoil section and Fowler type trailing-edge flaps. A basically circular-section fuselage of 11 ft 8 in (3.56 m) diameter will provide comfortable five-abreast seating for 71 passengers in a pressurised, air-conditioned environment. Alternative six-abreast seating will accommodate 88 passengers, and the planned Series 200 with a fuselage lengthened by 7 ft 3 in (2.21 m) will seat a maximum of 109 passengers.

The evaluation of suitable powerplants was extensive, covering wing- and aft-mounted installations, and both turbofan and turboprop engines. Final choice was the Avco Lycoming ALF 502R-3 high by-pass ratio turbofan, four of these being mounted in underwing pods. Designed for operation from surfaces which can include short semi-prepared airstrips, the hydraulically actuated landing gear has twin wheels on each unit, mounted on trailing axles. Heavy-duty brakes, anti-skid units, lift-dumpers and petal-type airbrakes forming the fuselage tailcone, combine to give the BAe 146 the necessary short-field landing performance.

Risk-sharing partners in this project include the Avco Corporation in the USA, and Saab-Scania in Sweden. The former not only provides the powerplant through the Avco Lycoming division, but is responsible also for manufacture of the wing boxes through its Avco Aerostructures division. Saab builds the tailplane and control surfaces. Sub-contractors include Short Brothers in the UK, responsible for construction of the pylon-mounted pods to house the engines. Certification and initial deliveries

BAe 146-100 of Lineas Aereas Privadas Argentinas.

of the first Series 100 aircraft are scheduled for the early summer of 1982, and the first Series 200 aircraft, which is intended for operation from paved runways only, was due to fly in the spring of 1982. The details which follow apply to the BAe 146-100.

Specification

Type: short-range commercial transport

Powerplant: four 6,700-lb (3039-kg) thrust Avco Lycoming ALF 502R-3 turbofans

Performance: (estimated) maximum cruising speed 500 mph (805 km/h) at 22,000 ft (6705 m); economic cruising speed 436 mph (702 km/h) at 30,000 ft (9145 m); range with maximum fuel, including reserves 1,647 miles (2651 km); range with maximum payload 668 miles (1075 km)

Weights: (estimated) operating empty 44,570 lb (20217 kg); maximum take-off 80,000 lb (36287 kg)

Dimensions: span 86 ft 5 in (26.34 m); length 85 ft 10 in (26.16 m); height 28 ft 3 in (8.61 m); wing area 832 sq ft (77.29 m²)

Operators: orders include three plus three options from Lineas Aereas Privadas Argentinas, two from an undisclosed US operator, and in late 1980 it was stated that some 12 other carriers were evaluating the potential of this new aircraft

British Aerospace (HS) 146 cutaway drawing key

1 Radome
2 Weather radar scanner
3 Radar mounting
4 ILS aerial
5 Oxygen bottle, capacity 400 Imp gal (1 812 l)
6 Sloping front pressure bulkhead
7 VOR flush aerial
8 Nose undercarriage wheel bay
9 Nosewheel leg strut
10 Twin nosewheels
11 Pitot tube
12 Rudder pedals
13 Instrument panel
14 Windscreen wipers
15 Instrument panel shroud
16 Windscreen panels
17 Overhead switch panel
18 First officer's seat
19 Centre control pedestal
20 Control column handwheel
21 Side console panel (area navigation system)
22 Cockpit floor level
23 Captain's seat
24 Direct vision window/flight deck emergency exit
25 Folding observer's seat
26 Flight deck bulkhead
27 Air conditioning ducting
28 Starboard galley unit
29 Forward service door
30 Main cabin divider
31 Port side forward toilet compartment
32 Forward entry door
33 Door latching handle
34 Escape chute stowage
35 Underfloor radio and electronics equipment bay

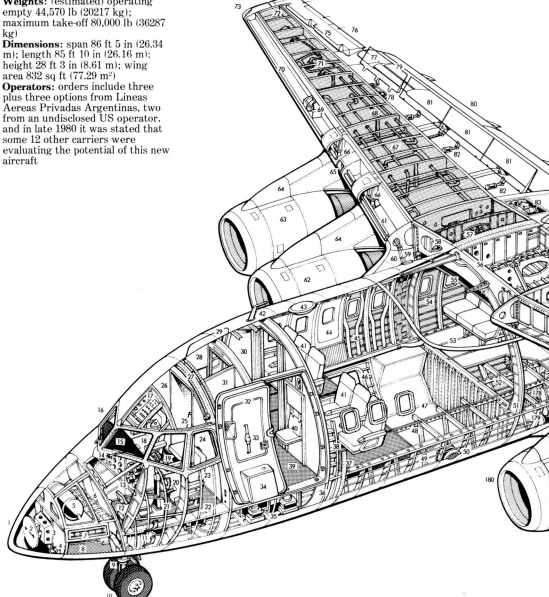

British Aerospace (HS) 146

36 Machined doorway cut-out main frames
37 Nose section/forward fuselage skin joint strap
38 Door frame support structure
39 Entry vestibule
40 Cabin attendant's folding seat
41 Six-abreast passenger seating
42 VHF aerial
43 D/F loop aerial
44 Cabin wall trim panels
45 Air conditioning ducting
46 Forward cargo hold door
47 Forward underfloor cargo hold
48 Seat rail support structure
49 Fuselage keel construction
50 Pressurisation air control valve
51 Fuselage/front spar attachment main frame
52 Floor beam construction
53 Honeycomb sandwich floor panels
54 Centre fuselage frame and Redux-bonded stringer construction
55 Wing fuel tank vapour barrier sealing diaphragm
56 Wing spar carry-through structure
57 Centreline skin panel joint
58 Anti-collision light
59 Wing spar/fuselage frame attachment joint
60 Engine control cable and hydraulic pipe runs
61 Leading edge de-icing air ducts

62 Inboard engine nacelle
63 Outboard engine nacelle
64 Nacelle pylons
65 Starboard landing/taxying lamp
66 Wing spar/pylon attachment joints
67 Starboard wing integral fuel tank; total usable fuel capacity 2,540 Imp gal (11 547 l)
68 Fuel system piping
69 Pressure refuelling connection
70 Outboard leading edge de-icing air duct
71 Fuel pump collector bay
72 Vent surge box
73 Starboard navigation light
74 Static dischargers
75 Starboard aileron
76 Aileron tabs
77 Roll control spoiler
78 Spoiler hydraulic jack and sequencing cam box
79 Flap slot behind roll spoiler
80 Starboard tabbed-Fowler flaps, down position
81 Lift spoilers
82 Spoiler hydraulic jacks
83 Flap drive hydraulic motor
84 Engine bleed air ducting
85 Flap pitch trim corrector
86 Cabin roof lighting panels
87 Overhead stowage bins
88 Passenger service units
89 Forward/rear fuselage skin joint strap
90 Wing root trailing edge fillet
91 Dorsal spine fairing
92 Hot air ducting

93 Rear cabin seating
94 Air system recirculation valve
95 Rear service door
96 Rear twin seats
97 Air conditioning system ram air intake
98 Leading edge de-icing air ducting
99 Fin front spar
100 Tailfin construction
101 Fin/tailplane attachment joints
102 De-icing air spill duct
103 Starboard tailplane
104 Starboard elevator

105 Elevator trim tab
106 Trim tab screw jack
107 Inboard servo tab
108 Elevator cable drive linkage
109 Port elevator rib construction
110 Static dischargers
111 Elevator horn balance
112 Fixed tailplane construction
113 Leading edge de-icing air duct
114 Rudder construction
115 Rudder hydraulic jacks
116 Yaw dampers and rudder trim jack
117 Split tailcone airbrake
118 Tail navigation lights
119 Port airbrake open position
120 Airbrake hydraulic jack
121 Garrett-AiResearch GTCP 36-100 auxiliary power unit (APU)
122 APU intake duct, exhaust to starboard
123 Fin root spar box
124 Sloping fin attachment frames

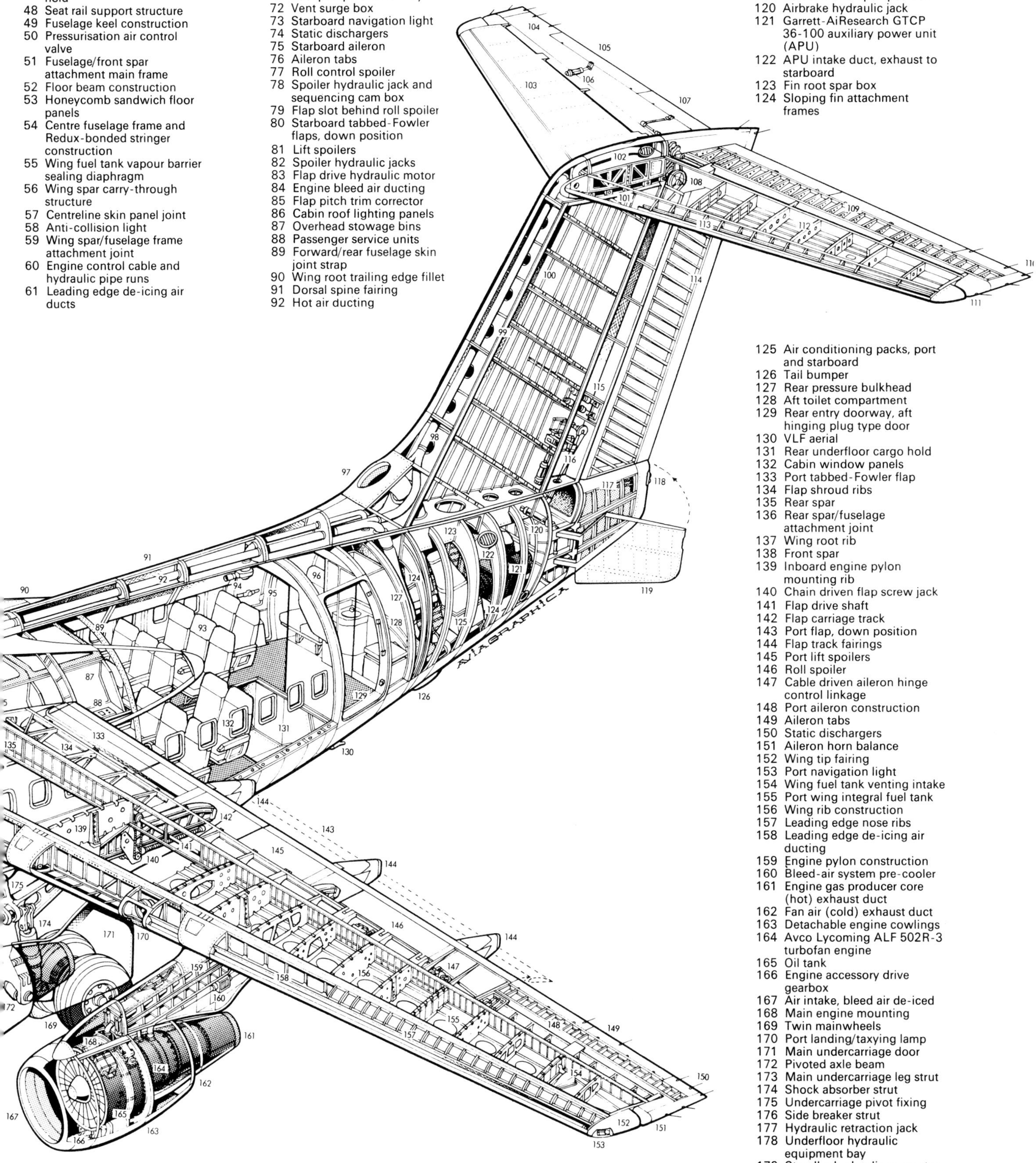

125 Air conditioning packs, port and starboard
126 Tail bumper
127 Rear pressure bulkhead
128 Aft toilet compartment
129 Rear entry doorway, aft hinging plug type door
130 VLF aerial
131 Rear underfloor cargo hold
132 Cabin window panels
133 Port tabbed-Fowler flap
134 Flap shroud ribs
135 Rear spar
136 Rear spar/fuselage attachment joint
137 Wing root rib
138 Front spar
139 Inboard engine pylon mounting rib
140 Chain driven flap screw jack
141 Flap drive shaft
142 Flap carriage track
143 Port flap, down position
144 Flap track fairings
145 Port lift spoilers
146 Roll spoiler
147 Cable driven aileron hinge control linkage
148 Port aileron construction
149 Aileron tabs
150 Static dischargers
151 Aileron horn balance
152 Wing tip fairing
153 Port navigation light
154 Wing fuel tank venting intake
155 Port wing integral fuel tank
156 Wing rib construction
157 Leading edge nose ribs
158 Leading edge de-icing air ducting
159 Engine pylon construction
160 Bleed-air system pre-cooler
161 Engine gas producer core (hot) exhaust duct
162 Fan air (cold) exhaust duct
163 Detachable engine cowlings
164 Avco Lycoming ALF 502R-3 turbofan engine
165 Oil tank
166 Engine accessory drive gearbox
167 Air intake, bleed air de-iced
168 Main engine mounting
169 Twin mainwheels
170 Port landing/taxying lamp
171 Main undercarriage door
172 Pivoted axle beam
173 Main undercarriage leg strut
174 Shock absorber strut
175 Undercarriage pivot fixing
176 Side breaker strut
177 Hydraulic retraction jack
178 Underfloor hydraulic equipment bay
179 Standby hydraulic generator
180 Port inboard engine nacelle

British Aerospace Trident

History and Notes

Beginning its history at approximately the same time as the aircraft known now as the British Aerospace One-Eleven, the Trident originated as the de Havilland D.H.121 proposal, which was drawn up to meet a British European Airways requirement of August 1956. BEA's specification called for a fast short/medium-range transport to accommodate about 100 passengers, to be suitable for operation from runways of approximately 6,000 ft (1830 m), and to be powered by rear-mounted turbojets. In all, de Havilland made three proposals, the D.H.119/120/121, but it was the last which was chosen from submissions received from Avro, Bristol and de Havilland. A contract for 24 D.H.121s, with an option on 12 more, was completed on 12 August 1959, and quantity production was initiated without the requirement for a prototype.

The resulting first aircraft (G-ARPA) made its maiden flight on 9 January 1962, piloted by John Cunningham with a crew of five, and in this initial Trident 1 form was powered by three 9,850-lb (4468-kg) thrust Rolls-Royce RB.163/1 Mk 505/5 Spey turbofans. The rear-mounted engines ensured that the swept low-set monoplane wing (with 35° of sweepback) was very clean: additionally the wing incorporated leading-edge nose droop, a Krueger leading-edge flap at each wing root, a spoiler on each wing surface to double as airbrake or lift dumper, conventional powered ailerons, and double-slotted trailing-edge flaps. The circular-section pressurised fuselage provided accommodation for a maximum of 103 passengers, and the T-tail also included powered controls. The landing gear had some unusual features: the twin-wheel nose unit was offset to port to allow for sideways retraction into the lower surface of the forward fuselage; each main unit had two twin-tyred wheels mounted on a common axle; and each unit rotated through 90° and extended by 6 in (0.15 m) before folding for stowage within the fuselage. It had been intended from an early stage that the Trident should have equipment that would enable it to operate efficiently in the often dubious weather conditions of Britain and Europe, this equipment including Smiths Autoland. Certification for automatic landing in Category II weather conditions was gained in September 1968.

For political reasons, production

of the Trident was to have been entrusted to a consortium that included de Havilland, Fairey and Hunting, and the title of The Aircraft Manufacturing Company (Airco) was ressurrected to cover this trio. However, this organisation was dissolved in late 1959 when de Havilland became a component of the Hawker Siddeley Group, and it was Hawker Siddeley that became responsible for later development and production of the Trident under the HS.121 designation.

Like the BAC One-Eleven, the Trident was also to experience deep-stall problems, the 23rd production aircraft (G-ARPY) being lost together with its crew of four during its first flight on 3 June 1966. However, the remainder of BEA's Trident 1s continued to give reliable service, but the somewhat restricted specification of this operator's requirements meant that the type was of little interest to other airlines. The first serious attempt to widen the scope of the Trident resulted in the Trident 1E, the first of which was flown on 2 November 1964. This introduced full-span leading-edge slats on each wing, in place of the leading-edge droop of the Trident 1, an increase of 5 ft 2 in (1.57 m) in wing span, increased fuel capacity, a revised internal layout to accommodate a maximum of 115 passengers, and the introduction of 11,400-lb (5171-kg) thrust R.B.163-25 Mk 511-5 Spey turbofans. A total of 15 were built, and of these four had an extra emergency exit and high-density seating layout for a maximum of 139 passengers.

A further-developed version, designated Trident 2E, flew for the first time on 27 July 1967. This introduced an additional increase of 3 ft 0 in (0.91 m) in wing span, low-drag wingtips, structural strengthening, increased fuel capacity, and 11,960-lb (5425-kg) thrust Mk 512-5W Spey turbofans. Trident 2Es for BEA were delivered with Smiths Autoland at full triplex level, and these airliners were the first in the world to have full all-weather operational instrumentation of this nature. A total of 15 of this version were built for

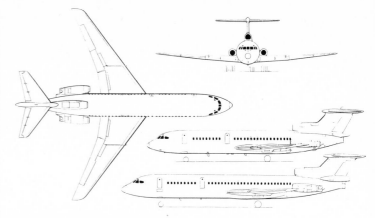

BAe Super Trident 3B of Central Aviation Administration of China (CAAC).

BAe (HS) Trident 2E (lower side view: Trident 3B)

BEA, two for Cyprus Airways, and 33 for CAAC, the national airline of the People's Republic of China.

The last major production version was designated Trident 3B, and 26 of these were built for service with BEA. Although basically a high-capacity short-range version of the Trident 1E, it had the same wing span and basic powerplant of the 2E, and introduced a fuselage lengthened by 16 ft 5 in (5.00 m) to provide seating for a maximum of 180 passengers. Wing area, wing incidence, and the span of the trailing-edge flaps, were all increased by comparison with the 2E, but more than this was needed to offset an increase of 6,500 lb (2948 kg) in maximum take-off weight. The short-range requirement meant that standard fuel capacity could be reduced by some 12 per cent and engine power was enhanced for take-off by the installation of a 5,250-lb (2381-kg) thrust Rolls-Royce RB.162-86 turbojet installed in the aircraft's tail, below the rudder. The first flight of a Trident 3B with all four engines operative for take-off was made on 22 March 1970, and on 1 April 1971 the first of the type entered service with BEA. This version also had full Autoland systems, and in December 1971 was certificated by the ARB for full

Category IIIa weather conditions. This includes take-off with a Runway Visual Range (RVR) of 295 ft (90 m), and a landing decision height of 12 ft (3.66 m). By the end of 1971, more than one million passengers had been landed automatically by the Smiths equipment installed in earlier versions of the Trident.

Final production consisted of two Super 3Bs for CAAC, these differing from the 3B in carrying additional fuel, having accommodation for 152 passengers, and being certificated for operation at a maximum take-off weight of 158,000 lb (71668 kg). Only these two examples were built, the first of them flown initially on 9 July 1975. Production terminated after a total of 117 aircraft had been built, comprising 24 Trident 1, 15 1E, 50 2E, 26 3B, and 2 Super 3B variants.

Specification

Type: short/medium-range transport

Powerplant (2E): three 11,960-lb (5425-kg) thrust Rolls-Royce RB.163-25 Mk 512-5W turbofans

Performance (2E): cruising speed 605 mph (974 km/h) at 25,000 ft (7620 m); economic cruising speed 596 mph (959 km/h) at 30,000 ft (9145 m); range with maximum fuel and reserves 2,500 miles (4023 km); range with typical payload 2,464 miles (3965 km)

Weights: operating empty, Trident 2E 73,200 lb (33203 kg), Trident 3B 81,778 lb (37095 kg); maximum take-off, Trident 2E 144,000 lb (65318 kg), Trident 3B 150,000 lb (68040 kg)

Dimensions: span, Trident 1 89 ft 10 in (27.38 m), Trident 1E 95 ft 0 in (28.96 m), Trident 2E and 3B 98 ft 0 in (29.87 m); length, Trident 1, 1E and 2E 114 ft 9 in (34.98 m), Trident 3B 131 ft 2 in (39.98 m); height, Trident 1, 1E and 2E 27 ft 0 in (8.23 m), Trident 3B 28 ft 3 in (8.61 m); wing area, Trident 1 1,358 sq ft (126.16 m²), Trident 1E 1,446 sq ft (134.33 m²), Trident 2E 1,456 sq ft (135.26 m²), Trident 3B 1,493 sq ft (138.70 m²)

Operators include: British Airways and CAAC.

An HS Trident 3B of British Airways climbs away after take-off. The airline has 56 Tridents, including 25 Trident 3Bs with an extra engine under the rudder.

Britten-Norman (Pilatus) Islander

History and Notes

Desmond Norman, and the late John Britten, had started their association in the development of crop-spraying equipment, and in 1964 began detail design work on a new lightweight feeder-line transport. Envisaged as a new-generation replacement for the ageing de Havilland Dragon Rapide, and for other aircraft in this class, the BN-2 started to take physical shape when construction of a prototype was initiated in September 1964. This aircraft (G-ATCT) flew for the first time on 13 June 1965, powered by two 210-hp (157-kW) Rolls-Royce/Continental IO-360-B engines, and with wings that spanned 45 ft 0 in (13.72 m). A number of changes resulted from flight testing, the most important being a 4 ft 0 in (1.22 m) increase in wing span, and the installation of 260-hp (194-kW) Avco Lycoming O-540-E engines. Engines of this type have remained the standard powerplant of the Islander, as the type was named, still being installed in production aircraft in its O-540-E4C5 version in 1980.

Initial production aircraft were BN-2 Islanders, of high-wing monoplane configuration with a functional rectangular-section fuselage, conventional tail unit, non-retractable tricycle type landing gear with twin wheels on the main units, and accommodation for a pilot and nine passengers. This 'high-density' seating arrangement had been contrived in a cabin that was only 3 ft 7 in (1.09 m) wide at its maximum by installing 'wall-to-wall' seats, with access via two doors on the port side, and one on the starboard side, making an aisle unnecessary. Exit in emergency can be made by removing the door windows. The first production example of the BN-2 made its initial flight on 24 April 1967, the type entering service less than four months later, on 13 August. The BN-2 Islander was superseded in mid-1969 by the improved BN-2A, which introduced detail aerodynamic and equipment improvements, in addition to a new side-loading baggage facility. Since 1978 the standard production version has the designation BN-2B. This differs primarily by having an increased maximum landing weight, improved internal design, and smaller

Britten-Norman BN-2A Islander of Northern Airlines, Australia.

diameter propellers.

Various items of alternative equipment have become available over the years to extend the usefulness of the Islander. These include 300-hp (224 kW) Avco Lycoming IO-540-K1BS piston engines, or 320-shp (239-kW) Allison 250-B17C turboprop engines, aircraft with this latter powerplant installation being designated BN-2T Turbine Islanders. Other options include an extended nose to provide an additional 22 cu ft (0.62 m³) of baggage space, raked wingtips containing auxiliary fuel tanks, and a Rajay turbocharger installation to enhance performance.

In addition to operation in a passenger-carrying capacity, the Islander can be used as a freighter with the passenger seats stored in the rear baggage bay, as an ambulance carrying three stretchers and two medical attendants, and for a variety of utility purposes when suitably equipped. Defender and Maritime Defender military versions are also available, and these can be adapted for casualty evacuation, patrol, transport, and search and rescue operations.

The success of this aircraft, which from the outset was intended to provide a low-cost reliable aircraft that could, if desired, be used in a number of differing roles, is highlighted by worldwide sales (in approximately 120 countries) by late 1980 approaching the 1,000 mark. Of this total more than 300 had been built under licence in Romania, and 35 were assembled in the Philippines

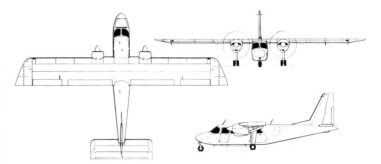

Britten-Norman BN-2B Islander II (dashed lines: optional unraked tips without tanks)

from components that had been manufactured by Britten-Norman. The details below apply to the standard BN-2B Islander.

Specification
Type: feeder-line transport
Powerplant: two 260-hp (194-kW) Avco Lycoming O-540-E4C5 horizontally-opposed piston engines
Performance: maximum cruising speed 160 mph (257 km/h) at 7,000 ft (2135 m); economic cruising speed 150 mph (241 km/h) at 12,000 ft (3660 m); service ceiling 14,600 ft (4450 m); range at economic cruising speed with full payload 870 miles (1400 km)
Weights: empty equipped 3,612 lb (1638 kg); maximum take-off 6,600 lb (2994 kg)
Dimensions: span 49 ft 0 in (14.94 m); length 35 ft 7¾ in (10.86 m); l height 13 ft 8¾ in (4.18 m); wing area 325.0 sq ft (30.19 m²)

Operators include: Aerovias del Valle, Air BVI, Air Condal, Air Inter Gabon, Air Guadeloupe, Air Liberia, A/S Norving, Bali Air, Bristow Helicopters Group, Civil Flying Services Pty, Dirgantara Air Service, Dorado Wings, Douglas Airways, Gulf Air, Jersey European Airways, Kanaf-Arkia Airlines, Lesotho Airways, Liat, Loganair, Malaysian Airline System, Maya Airways, Mount Cook Airlines, Pars Air Company, Société Guyane Air Transports, Sunbird Aviation, Transportes Aereos de Cabo Verde, Vaengir HF Airtransport, and Vieques Air Link

Numerically the most important civil aircraft produced in the UK since World War II, the Britten-Norman Islander has proved highly popular with small operators. The latest production variant is the BN-2B Islander II, which introduces a number of detail improvements.

Britten-Norman (Pilatus) Trislander

History and Notes

The solution to the requirement for a 'stretched' version of the Britten-Norman Islander needed rather more than the insertion of a new piece of hardware in the fuselage. Enquiries had shown that at least a 50 per cent increase in capacity was required to meet the needs of interested customers, leading in 1970 to evolution of the three-engine Trislander. The incorporation of a third engine always raises problems to ensure that there is no asymmetry of thrust. Sometimes this can be resolved by installing an engine in the aircraft nose, or at the centre of the wing, but neither of these solutions was acceptable in the case of the Islander configuration. Instead, it was decided to take a leaf from the book of much larger sisters, such as the Boeing 727, and install the third engine in the tail.

In the Islander's case the size of the tail unit meant that the engine could not be 'buried' within its structure, and considerable modification of the tail was necessary to make it possible for the fin to serve also to carry the engine mounting. Other changes included the insertion of a 7 ft 6 in (2.29 m) fuselage section forward of the wing, strengthening of the rear fuselage structure, the installation of new main landing gear units with larger wheels and tyres, and provision of an interior furnished to accommodate 17 passengers. Be-

Britten-Norman BN-2A Trislander of Trans Jamaican.

cause there was no change in size of the fuselage cross-section, the same 'wall-to-wall' seating arrangement pioneered in the Islander was retained, but access to these in the Trislander was via two port and three starboard doors.

The prototype Trislander was converted from the second Islander prototype (G-ATWU), and the conversion flew for the first time on 11 September 1970. Later the same day it was flown to Farnborough to take part in the 1970 SBAC Display. The first production Trislander was flown on 6 March 1971: this incorporated the extended-span wings that had been an optional feature of the Islander, and additional fin area had been provided above the rear engine. Certification was granted by the ARB on 14 May 1971, and the first airline to receive a Trislander was Aurigny Air Services on 29

June 1971.

Designation of the first production version was BN-2A Mk III, which retained the standard nose of the Islander. Current production versions include the BN-2A Mk III-2, which differs by having as standard the optional extended nose of the Islander; the Mk III-3 which incorporates a system to feather automatically the propeller of an engine which might fail on take-off; and the Mk III-4 which has a standby rocket

engine installed to provide extra thrust should there be an engine failure on take-off. Well over 80 Trislanders had been ordered by late 1980. The details below apply to the standard Mk III-2 Trislander.

Specification
Type: feeder-line transport
Powerplant: three 260-hp (194-kW) Avco Lycoming O-540-E4C5 flat-six piston engines
Performance: maximum cruising

Britten-Norman (Pilatus) Trislander cutaway drawing key

1 Static dischargers
2 Elevator tab
3 Mass balance
4 Starboard tailplane structure
5 Elevator hinge
6 Starboard elevator
7 Glass-fibre pylon tail cone
8 Elevator operating rod
9 Tail navigation light
10 VOR aerials
11 Upper fin structure
12 Port elevator
13 Elevator tab
14 Static dischargers
15 Tailplane tip
16 Aerial attachment
17 Port tailplane
18 Glass fibre engine cowling
19 Two-blade constant-speed propeller
20 Spinner
21 Intake
22 Lycoming IO-540-E4C5 engine
23 Steel-tube engine bearers
24 Exhaust
25 Firewall
26 Elevator control linkage
27 Rudder
28 Rudder trim tab
29 Glass-fibre tail cone (detachable)
30 Battery
31 Vent pipe
32 Rear fuselage/fin attachment frames
33 Rudder post
34 Rudder mass balance
35 Control linkage
36 Elevator control rods
37 Pylon frames
38 Rudder cables
39 Aft bulkhead
40 Baggage compartment
41 Passenger aft entry door (starboard)
42 External joint straps
43 Baggage compartment door (port)
44 External fuel lines (to rear engine)
45 Antenna
46 Passenger window
47 Flap linkage
48 Fuselage/rear spar attachment point
49 Passenger window
50 Main-leg top attachment
51 Starboard flap
52 Electric fuel pumps
53 Fuel sump
54 Filler cap
55 Starboard wing integral fuel tank
56 Aileron control
57 Aileron servo tab
58 Starboard aileron
59 Static dischargers
60 Starboard navigation light
61 Wing-tip integral fuel tank
62 Gravity filler
63 Starboard landing light
64 Pressed wing ribs
65 Rear spar
66 Spar web stiffeners
67 Front spar
68 Wing leading-edge construction
69 Leg fairing
70 Twin-wheel main undercarriage
71 Shock-absorber strut
72 Exhaust
73 Intake
74 Spinner
75 Starboard Lycoming IO-540-E4C5 engine
76 Nacelle/spar attachment
77 Fuselage/front spar attachment point
78 Aileron cables
79 Dorsal anti-collision beacon
80 Flap actuating mechanism
81 Port flap
82 Fuel lines
83 Electric fuel pumps
84 Unfeathering accumulator
85 Fuel sump
86 Port wing integral fuel tank
87 Aileron actuator
88 Aileron servo tab
89 Port aileron
91 Aerial
92 Static dischargers
93 Port navigation light
94 Wingtip integral fuel tank
95 Gravity filler

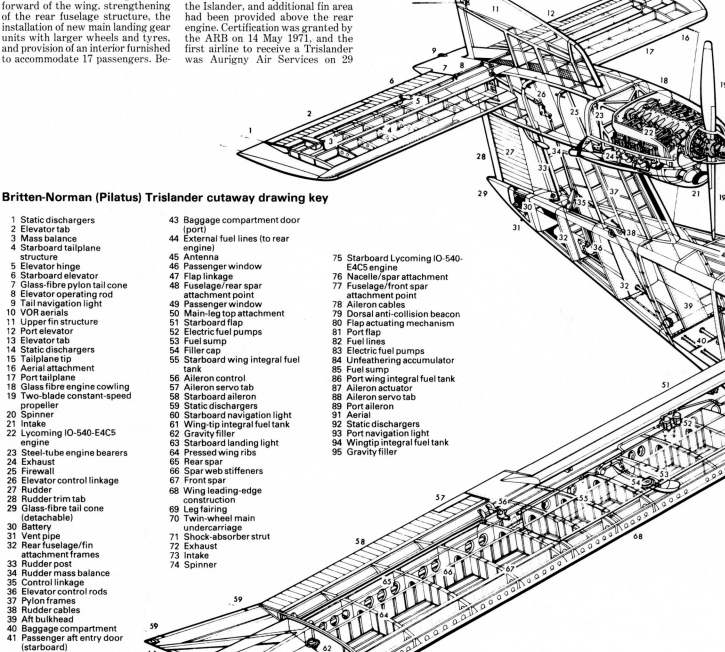

Britten-Norman (Pilatus) Trislander

speed 166 mph (267 km/h) at 6,500 ft (1980 m); economic cruising speed 150 mph (241 km/h) at 13,000 ft (3960 m); service ceiling 13,150 ft (4010 m); maximum range at economic cruising speed 1,000 miles (1609 km) **Weights:** empty equipped 5,843 lb (2650 kg); maximum take-off 10,000 lb (4536 kg) **Dimensions:** span 53 ft 0in (16.15 m); length 49 ft 3 in (15.01 m); height 14 ft 2 in (4.32 m); wing area 337.0 sq ft (31.31 m²) **Operators include:** Air Ecosse, Air Liberia, Air Martinique, Air Pacific, Air Seychelles, Air Tungaru, Aurigny Air Services, Bali Air, Bush Pilots Airways, Cayman Airways, Loganair, Sierra Leone Airways, TANA, and Uganda Airlines

The Britten-Norman Trislander has found extensive favour with small operators, such as the St. Vincent and the Grenadines Air Service, which uses this BN-2A Mk III on inter-island routes.

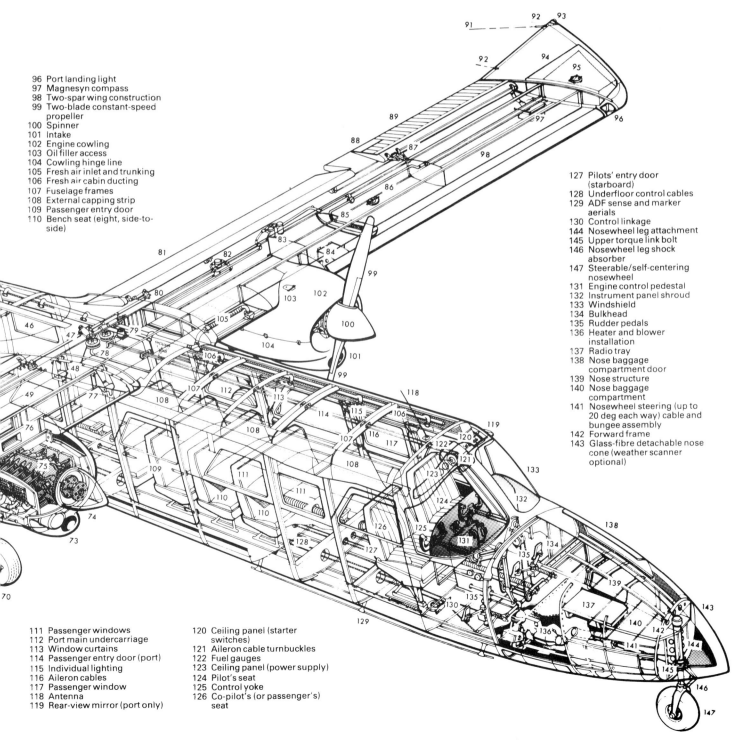

96 Port landing light
97 Magnesyn compass
98 Two-spar wing construction
99 Two-blade constant-speed propeller
100 Spinner
101 Intake
102 Engine cowling
103 Oil filler access
104 Cowling hinge line
105 Fresh air inlet and trunking
106 Fresh air cabin ducting
107 Fuselage frames
108 External capping strip
109 Passenger entry door
110 Bench seat (eight, side-to-side)

127 Pilots' entry door (starboard)
128 Underfloor control cables
129 ADF sense and marker aerials
130 Control linkage
144 Nosewheel leg attachment
145 Upper torque link bolt
146 Nosewheel leg shock absorber
147 Steerable/self-centering nosewheel
131 Engine control pedestal
132 Instrument panel shroud
133 Windshield
134 Bulkhead
135 Rudder pedals
136 Heater and blower installation
137 Radio tray
138 Nose baggage compartment door
139 Nose structure
140 Nose baggage compartment
141 Nosewheel steering (up to 20 deg each way) cable and bungee assembly
142 Forward frame
143 Glass-fibre detachable nose cone (weather scanner optional)

111 Passenger windows
112 Port main undercarriage
113 Window curtains
114 Passenger entry door (port)
115 Individual lighting
116 Aileron cables
117 Passenger window
118 Antenna
119 Rear-view mirror (port only)

120 Ceiling panel (starter switches)
121 Aileron cable turnbuckles
122 Fuel gauges
123 Ceiling panel (power supply)
124 Pilot's seat
125 Control yoke
126 Co-pilot's (or passenger's) seat

70

Canadair CL-44

History and Notes

In March 1954, Canadair Ltd negotiated a manufacturing licence for the Bristol Britannia from the British company. This covered, initially, a maritime reconnaissance version of the airliner for service with the Royal Canadian Air Force, the first being delivered in the autumn of 1957 under the designation CL-28 Argus. It differed from its parent aircraft in having a redesigned, unpressurised fuselage to make possible the inclusion of weapon bays, and had economical turbo-compound piston engines to give the long-range/endurance that is essential for a maritime role.

The RCAF had also a modest need for an aircraft which could be used in the freight/troop-carrying roles, and to meet this requirement Canadair proposed another version of the Britannia. To provide for the large capacity/payload that was needed, Canadair's design included increased wing span and a lengthened fuselage, and alternative powerplant proposals included Bristol Orion, Pratt & Whitney T34 or Rolls-Royce Tyne turboprops, and Wright R-3350 radial piston engines. The first of these was selected by the RCAF, but when development of this engine came to an end in Britain the Rolls-Royce Tyne was chosen instead. Designated Canadair CL-44D in this form, 12 were built for the RCAF, with which they served as the CC-106 Yukon, the last being delivered in 1961.

These RCAF aircraft had what was then conventional side-loading, with large cargo doors in the fuselage, forward and aft of the wing. While the CL-44D was under development and construction, Canadair's design team proposed a then revolutionary idea to simplify and speed cargo

Canadair CL-44 of ANDES (Aerolineas Nacionales del Ecuador).

loading: the provision of a hinged aft fuselage section which could be swung to one side, complete with tail unit, to permit straight-in loading or unloading of freight. This enabled large items of cargo, or palletised freight, to be transferred directly from trucks into the large cargo hold, and the CL-44D-4, as this version was designated, became the world's first cargo aircraft to introduce this capability on the production line.

The concept appealed to large cargo operators, and Canadair soon received orders from The Flying Tiger Line, Seaboard World Airlines and Slick Airways. The first CL-44D-4 flew on 16 November 1960, and FAA certification was gained seven months later. In July 1961, Flying Tiger and Seaboard flew the first services with these aircraft. A fourth customer was Loftleidir of Iceland, its initial order for three aircraft being completed as civil transports with seating accommodation for a maximum of 178 passengers. Used to provide low-cost transatlantic services, this fleet was supplemented by a fourth aircraft in 1966. It differed from the earlier trio by having a fuselage that was lengthened by 15 ft 1¾ in (4.62 m) to provide accommodation for a maximum of 214 passengers. Designated CL-44J, and known also as the Canadair 400, this type flew for the

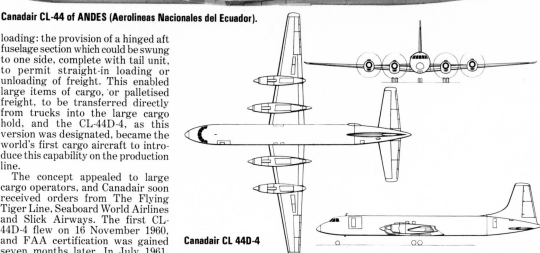

Canadair CL 44D-4

first time on 8 November 1965, and after it had entered service the company's three 178-seat airliners were retrospectively converted to CL-44J standard.

One other variant resulted when the Conroy Aircraft Corporation in the USA purchased a CL-44D-4 from Flying Tiger for conversion as a large volume cargo transporter. This company's founder, Jack Conroy, had developed the original Pregnant Guppy and its successors, and considered the CL-44 suitable for a similar exercise. In its completed form, designated CL-44-O, and first flown on 26 November 1969, it had a

maximum internal height of 11 ft 4 in (3.45 m) and a maximum width of 13 ft 11 in (4.24 m), while retaining the swing-tail loading capability.

Production of civil CL-44s totalled 27, and the RCAF's CC-106 Yukons eventually came on to the civil market. Although many of these have changed hands several times, more than 20 remained in service in 1980. The following details apply to the CL-44D-4.

Specification

Type: long-range cargo transport
Powerplant: four 5,730-hp (4273-kW) Rolls-Royce Tyne 515/10 turboprops
Performance: cruising speed 386 mph (621 km/h) at 20,000 ft (6100 m) with typical payload; service ceiling 30,000 ft (9145 m); range with maximum payload 2,875 miles (4627 km); range with maximum fuel 5,587 miles (8991 km)
Dimensions: span 142 ft 3½ in (43.37 m); length 136 ft 10¾ in (41.73 m); height 38 ft 8 in (11.79 m); wing area 2,075 sq ft (192.77 m²)
Weights: empty 88,950 lb (40348 kg); maximum take-off 210,000 lb (95256 kg)
Operators include: Aeronaves del Peru, Aer Turas, Air Gabon Cargo, ANDES, Bayu Indonesia Air, British Cargo Airlines, Cargosur, Cyprus Airways, SOACO, Tradewinds Airways, and Transvalair

The Flying Tiger Line no longer operates the Canadair CL-44D freighter, but 23 of the 39 built were in worldwide service in 1980 with 14 operators.

Canadair CL-215

History and Notes

The Canadair CL-215 was designed to meet a requirement for a firefighting amphibian which could replace the miscellany of types used in the 'water bomber' role in the 1960s. The basic parameters of the CL-215 design emerged from a symposium on forest fire protection held in Ottawa in December 1963. Early in 1966 it was decided to put the type into production. The Canadian Province of Quebec and the French *Protection Civile* were the first customers, ordering 20 and 10 CL-

215s respectively to undertake its primary role of forest fire detection and suppression. However, the robust and versatile amphibian was also available to military customers for the search and rescue and utility roles.

From the outset simplicity of design was a primary requirement, with ease of maintenance and reliability of equipment (achieved through the incorporation of already-proven systems wherever practicable) also receiving careful attention. Protection against salt-water cor-

rosion was achieved through the use of corrosion-resistant materials and by carefully sealing components during assembly.

The CL-215 is an aircraft of substantial size. It has a single-step hull, and fixed stabilizing floats are mounted just inboard of the wing tips. The tricycle undercarriage comprises a twin nosewheel and single mainwheels, the former retracting into the hull and the latter being raised to lie flat against the hull during operations from water. The high-mounted wing and tail-

plane are single-piece structures, with ailerons and flaps occupying the entire wing trailing edge. All fuel is carried in flexible wing cells, and the engine nacelles are integral with the wing structure.

For its firefighting role the CL-215 can lift 1,200 Imperial gallons (5,450 litres) of water or retardant fluid in two fuselage tanks. The water is scooped from a convenient lake or river through two retractable inlets mounted under the hull, while the CL-215 taxies across the surface. It then takes off and flies to the area

Canadair CL-215

of the fire where the load is jettisoned in under a second. The operation is repeated until the fire is under control. In most circumstances a load can be dropped at least every 10 minutes.

Configured for the search and rescue role, the CL-215 carries a crew of six. In addition to the pilot and co-pilot, a flight engineer is housed on the flight deck. The navigator's station is located farther back in the foreward fuselage, and two observers are carried in the rear fuselage. In the utility role the CL-215 can carry up to 19 passengers or an alternative freight load of 6,260 lb (2839 kg).

First flight of the CL-215 was on 23 October 1967, and deliveries to France began in May 1969. In March 1970 Quebec Province received the first of a reduced order of 15 CL-215s, the surplus machines going to France (2), Spain (2) and Greece (1). The Spanish Air Force was favourably impressed by an evaluation of the two CL-215s ordered by the Ministry of Agriculture and these machines, together with a new order for eight, formed the equipment of *Escuadron 404*.

The second-largest military operator of the CL-215 is Greece's Hellenic Air Force, which purchased a total of eight. Primarily operating in the forest protection role, the Greek CL-215s have nevertheless successfully demonstrated the aircraft's capability as a troop transport.

The Royal Thai Navy operates two CL-215s as patrol and search and rescue amphibians. The aircraft were delivered during the summer of 1978, the 10,000-mile (16094-km) ferry flight taking the aircraft across the Atlantic and then on to India.

Designed principally as a water-bomber, the Canadair CL-215 performs usefully as a general-purpose amphibian.

Specification
Type: twin-engined utility and firefighting amphibian
Powerplant: two 2,100-hp (1566-kW) Pratt & Whitney R-2800-83 radials
Performance: cruising speed at 10,000 ft (3050 m) 181 mph (290 km/h); rate of climb at sea level 1,000 ft (305 m) per minute;

range at maximum cruise power 1,150 miles (1851 km)
Weights: empty equipped 26,600 lb (12000 kg); maximum take-off (land) 43,500 lb (19730 kg); maximum take-off (water) 37,700 lb (17100 kg)
Dimensions: span 93 ft 10 in (28.6 m); length 65 ft ½ in (19.82 m); height (wheels extended) 29 ft 8 in (8.92 m); wing area 1,080 sq ft (100.33 m²)

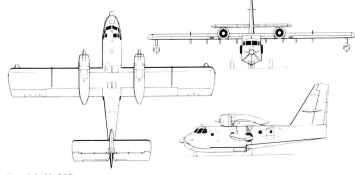

Canadair CL-215

Canadair Challenger

History and Notes
Originating from the drawing board of Bill Lear, designer of the Lear Jet, this executive aircraft was at first named LearStar 600. However, when Lear sold the exclusive production rights to Canadair in April 1976 it was redesignated CL-600, and later named Challenger. Canadair launched the programme on 29 October 1976 with 53 firm orders in hand and a $130 million government-authorised loan; changes were made in the design, the most noticeable being movement of the tailplane from its position at the bottom of the fuselage to a location near the top of the fin.

A market for 1,000 business aircraft in this category was forecast by Canadair for the following decade, and it was hoped that 400 of these would be Challengers; a unit price of $3.75 million was set for the first 60 aircraft at launch time, but inflation had increased this figure to $7.7 million by November 1980. A major selling point of the Challenger is its large cross-section fuselage, which offers a width of 8 ft 2 in (2.49 m) and height of 6 ft 1 in (1.85 m)—a real 'walk about' cabin not shared by other purpose-built executive jets.

Three pre-production Challengers

Canadair CL-600 Challenger

were built, flying on 8 November 1978, and on 17 March and 14 July 1979, while the first production aircraft flew on 21 September 1979. By mid-July 1980 these four aircraft had flown some 1,270 hours. Canadian certification was achieved in August 1980, with FAA certification following on 10 November that year. Both had temporary restrictions limiting gross weight to 33,000 lb (14969 kg) and speed to 365 mph 587 km/h; flight into known icing conditions and use of thrust reversers were prohibited.

A major weight problem caused Canadair to carry out a weight- and drag-reduction programme to enable the Challenger's range of 3,220 miles (5182 km) to be increased to at least

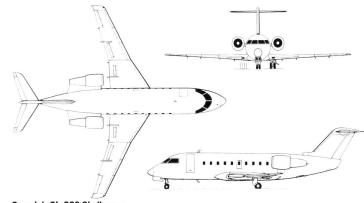

Canadair CL-600 Challenger

Canadair Challenger

54 Static dischargers
55 Aileron control jacks
56 Starboard aileron
57 Flap screw jacks
58 Outboard double slotted flap
59 Flap hinge fairings
60 Starboard spoileron
61 Starboard proportional spoiler
62 Wing/fuselage main frames
63 Starboard emergency exit
64 Rearward facing armchairs
65 Port emergency exit window
66 Three seater settee
67 Folding table
68 Cabin windows
69 Interior lighting and sound master control console
70 Two seater armchairs
71 Cabin roof air duct
72 Overhead service panel
73 Cabin rear bulkhead
74 Toilet compartment
75 Wash basin
76 Aft wardrobe
77 Baggage compartment
78 Aft pressure bulkhead
79 Starboard engine intake duct construction
80 Detachable engine cowlings
81 Main engine mounting

3,800 miles (6115 km), and customers have the option of either 7,500-lb (3402-kg) thrust Avco Lycoming ALF 502L or 8,650-lb (3924-kg) thrust General Electric CF34-1A turbofans.

By late 1980, Canadair held orders for 132 Challengers with the Avco Lycoming powerplant, and 48 with General Electric CF34s; the 32nd aircraft was on the production line at the year's end. Among the GE orders are a number of CL-610 Challenger Es, a lengthened version with two fuselage plugs totalling 8 ft 9 in (2.67 m) to increase the passenger capacity from 18 to 24. The wing

leading-edges will be modified to include high-lift devices and there will also be changes to the trailing-edge flaps. Go ahead for the E programme was given on 14 March 1980, and the first flight is expected to be early in 1982.

Specification
Type: business, cargo and commuter transport
Powerplant: two 7,500-lb (3402-kg) Avco Lycoming ALF 502L turbofans
Performance: maximum speed 562 mph (904 km/h); cruising

The Canadair Challenger is a competitor in the upper reaches of the 'bizjet' market, offering great comfort for up to 30 passengers carried over long ranges.

speed 495 mph (797 km/h); service ceiling 49,000 ft (14935 m); maximum range with maximum optional fuel 4,145 miles (6671 km)
Weights: empty 20,300 lb (9208 kg); maximum take-off 36,000 lb (16329 kg)
Dimensions: span 61 ft 10 in (18.85 m); length 68 ft 5 in (20.85 m); height 20 ft 8 in (6.30 m); wing area 450 sq ft (41.81 m²)

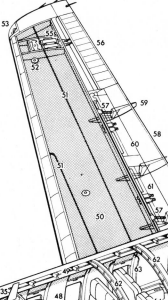

Canadair CL-600 Challenger cutaway drawing key

1 Radome
2 Weather radar scanner (RCA)
3 ILS Glideslope aerial
4 Emergency air driven generator (Sundstrand)
5 Radio and electronics equipment bay
6 Brake hydraulic valves
7 Nosewheel doors
8 Front pressure bulkhead
9 Pitot tube
10 Curved windscreen panels (Slerracin)
11 Instrument panel shroud
12 Rudder pedals
13 Nose undercarriage retraction mechanism (Dowty)
14 Steering jack
15 Twin nosewheels (Goodyear)
16 Nosewheel leg door
17 Cockpit floor level
18 Front fuselage frame construction
19 Transponder aerial
20 Air conditioning supply pipe
21 Pilot's seat (Teleflex Morse)
22 Control column
23 Engine throttle controls
24 Centre instrument console
25 Co-pilot's seat (Teleflex Morse)
26 Cockpit side console
27 Observer's seat, stowed
28 Cockpit bulkhead
29 Circuit breaker fuse panels
30 Galley
31 Wardrobe
32 Wing inspection light
33 Door actuator
34 Door hinge linkage
35 Communications aerial
36 Entry door, open
37 External door handle
38 Cabin bulkhead
39 Entry lobby
40 Retractable airstairs
41 Folding handrail
42 Wing leading edge fillet
43 Air conditioning supply duct
44 Floor beam construction
45 Wing centre section
46 Cabin floor
47 Swivelling armchairs
48 Cabin window trim panels
49 Cabin roof construction
50 Starboard wing fuel tanks, capacity 710 US gal (2 687 l)
51 Wing panel skin joints
52 Fuel tank filler caps
53 Starboard wing tip lighting

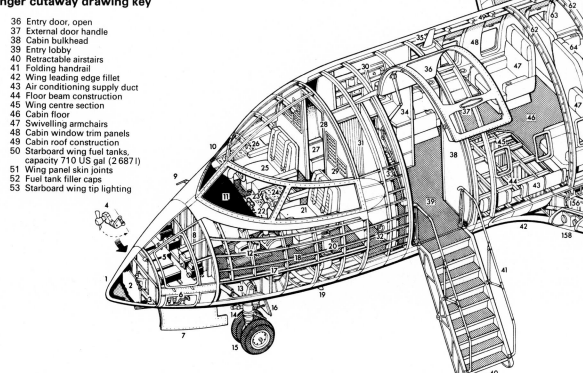

Canadair Challenger

82 Thrust reverser screw jack
83 Thrust reverser translating cowl, open position
84 Rear equipment bay
85 Engine mounting cross beam
86 Auxiliary power unit (AiResearch)
87 APU intake duct
88 Air conditioning plant (AiResearch)
89 Refrigeration packs
90 Ram air intake
91 Engine pylon fairing
92 Fin leading edge de-icing pipe
93 Fin spar construction
94 Tailplane trim screw jack
95 Elevator pitch feel simulator
96 Tailplane leading edge de-icing duct
97 Starboard tailplane
98 Static discharge wicks
99 Starboard elevator
100 Tailplane bullet fairing
101 Tailplane hinge fixing
102 Elevator hydraulic jacks
103 Port elevator
104 Static discharge wicks
105 Port tailplane construction
106 Elevator hinge control links
107 VOR aerial

108 Rudder hinge control links
109 Hydraulic jacks
110 Rudder construction
111 Tail navigation lights
112 Air louvres
113 Sloping fuselage/tailfin frames
114 Port engine pylon fairing
115 Air conditioning exhaust duct
116 Equipment bay access door
117 Core engine exhaust
118 Thrust reverser screw jack
119 Reverser cascade
120 Fan air exhaust duct
121 Core engine
122 Port engine cowlings
123 Avco Lycoming ALF 502L turbofan
124 Engine accessories
125 Oil tank
126 Fan blades
127 Intake de-icing
128 Port engine intake
129 Baggage door
130 Wing root trailing edge fillet
131 Hydraulic pump
132 Inboard double slotted flap
133 Main undercarriage leg (Dowty)
134 Retraction jack

135 Twin mainwheels
136 Lift dumper/inboard spoiler
137 Rear spar
138 Port outboard double slotted flap
139 Flap hinge fairings
140 Proportional spoiler
141 Outboard spoiler
142 Spoiler hydraulic jacks
143 Port aileron construction
144 Aileron hydraulic jacks
145 Wing tip static discharge wicks
146 Port anti-collision light

147 Port navigation lights
148 Lower surface wing skin/stringer panel
149 Fuel tank access panels
150 Wing rib construction
151 Front spar
152 Leading edge de-icing
153 Leading edge nose ribs
154 Port wing fuel tanks, capacity 710 US gal (2 687 l)
155 Fuel pumps
156 Wing attachment joints
157 De-icing air duct
158 Landing and taxying lights

CASA C-212C Aviocar

History and Notes

The primary reason for the design and development of a new light utility STOL (short take-off and landing) transport by Construcciones Aeronauticas SA (CASA), was the need to equip the Spanish air force with a standard aircraft. Before the evolution of this design, Spain's air force was using a variety of aircraft in the transport role, including such vintage types as the Douglas DC-3 and Junkers Ju 52/3m. Work on the design of a suitable replacement with multi-role capability began in the latter half of the 1960s, and from the outset the possibility of producing a civil transport version was given due attention. Designated C-212 by the company, a first prototype was flown initially on 26 March 1971. The first pre-production aircraft was flown on 17 November 1972, and the first C-212A was delivered to the air force on 20 May 1974.

A cantilever high-wing monoplane configuration was chosen to ensure that the wing structure did not restrict movement within the cabin, and wide-span double-slotted trailing-edge flaps are provided to facilitate STOL operations. The rear fuselage is upswept to allow for direct in-loading of cargo from the rear of the aircraft via a two-section loading ramp/door installed in the under-surface of the aft fuselage. Landing gear is of non-retractable tricycle type, and the powerplant consists of two neatly wing-mounted Garrett-AiResearch TPE331 turboprop engines.

The commercial passenger version, which has the designation C-212C Aviocar, was developed more or less simultaneously with the military aircraft. In the original C-212-5 series, as delivered first to the Indonesian company Pertamina on 16 July 1975, the powerplant comprised two 750-shp (559-kW) TPE331-5-251C turboprop engines, and accommodation was provided for a maximum of 19

CASA C-212 Aviocar of Bouraq Indonesian Airlines.

passengers. Two doors on the port side of the fuselage, one forward and one aft of the wing, provide access to the cabin. The underfuselage rear loading door is retained in this version, its interior providing additional baggage stowage.

Production of the C-212-5 series ended in 1978, after a total of 154 civil and military Aviocars had been built, since when the C-212 Series 200 versions have been developed. These introduce more powerful TPE331-10-501C engines, which have made possible an increase of some 12 per cent in maximum take-off weight. As a result the civil transport now has accommodation for a maximum of 26 passengers, and quick-change provisions have been introduced to make possible variations that range from all passenger, through different passenger/cargo to all-cargo configurations. Special VIP interior layouts are available also to any customer's requirements.

To expand the market potential for the type, CASA negotiated a deal by which Nurtanio Aircraft Industries of Bandung, Indonesia, are responsible for the operation of an assembly line in the Far East.

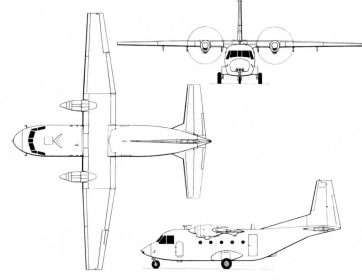

CASA C-212-200 Aviocar

The Spanish CASA C-212 Aviocar is a useful transport, offering STOL performance from unprepared strips a mere 437 yards (400 m) in length.

Specification

Type: STOL light transport
Powerplant: (Series 200) two 900-shp (671-kW) Garrett-AiResearch TPE311-10-501C turboprops
Performance: (Series 200) maximum cruising speed 240 mph (386 km/h) at 10,000 ft (3050 m); cruising speed 219 mph (353 km/h) at 10,000 ft (3050 m); service ceiling 28,000 ft (8535 m); range with maximum payload 472 miles (760 km); range with maximum fuel 1,007 miles (1620 km)
Weights: manufacturer's empty, 212-5 8,157 lb (3700 kg), Srs 200 8,631 lb (3915 kg); maximum take-off, C-212-5 14,330 lb (6500 kg), Srs 200 16,093 lb (7300 kg)
Dimensions: span 62 ft 4 in (19.00 m); length 49 ft 9 in (15.16 m); height 21 ft 11 in (6.68 m); wing area 430.56 sq ft (40.00 m²)
Operators include: Air Logistic Company, Bouraq Air Lines, Bursa Hava Yollari, Companie PT Deraya, Merpati Nusantara Air Lines, and Pelita Air Service

Cessna Model 150

History and Notes

A two-seat cabin monoplane, the Cessna Model 150 is one of the world's most popular light aircraft, well over 20,000 having been built in the U.S. and about 2,000 in France by Reims Aviation.

The prototype of the Model 150 first flew in September 1957, and was the aircraft with which Cessna re-entered the two-seat light aircraft market when production started in August 1958. In 1977 the Model 150 was being produced in Standard, Commuter, Commuter II and Aero-

bat versions. This last version embodies structural changes permitting a licence in the Aerobatic category for load factors of + 6g and –3g at full gross weight. The Aerobat combines the economy and versatility of the Standard model with an aerobatic capability permitting the execution of manoeuvres such as barrel and aileron rolls, snap rolls, loops, vertical reverses and chandelles.

Of all-metal construction, the high-set wing is braced by a single strut. The landing gear is of the non-retractable tricycle type, with toe-

operated single-disc hydraulic brakes on the main wheels. Nosewheel steering assists ground manoeuvring.

The enclosed cabin has side-by-side seating, and full dual controls can be fitted if required. Comprehensive standard equipment is fitted, including a stall-warning indicator. Extensive optional communications and navigational equipment is available, including systems such as the Cessna 300 Series nav/com (navigation and communication radio) with 360-channel com and 160-channel nav with remote VOR in-

dicator; 300 Series transceiver with 360 com channels; 300 Series nav/com with 360-channel com, 200 channel nav with remote VOR/LOC or VOR/ILS indicator; Series 300 ADF; marker beacon with three lights and aural signal; and transponder with 4096 code capability and slimline microphone. Other optional equipment includes blind-flying instrumentation; a rate of climb indicator; turn co-ordinator indicator; and outside air temperature gauge.

In 1977 the Cessna 150 range was replaced in production by the Cessna

152 series, basically similar but powered by the 110-hp (82-kW) Lycoming O-235 piston engine.

Specification

Type: two-seat cabin monoplane
Powerplant: one 100-hp (74.5-kW) Continental O-200-A flat-four piston engine
Performance: maximum design speed 162 mph (261 km/h); maximum cruising speed (75% power) at 7,000 ft (2135 m) 122 mph (196 km/h); economical cruising speed at 10,000 ft (3050 m) 95 mph (153 km/h); stalling speed (flaps down, power off) 48 mph (78 km/h)
Weights: empty equipped 1,000 lb (454 kg); maximum take-off 1,600 lb (726 kg)
Dimensions: span 32 ft 8½ in (9.97 m); length 23 ft 11 in (7.29 m); height 8 ft 6 in (2.59 m); wing area 157 sq ft (14.59 m²)

Introduced in 1977, the Cessna Model 152 replaced the classic Model 150, of which soime 23,836 had been built in a 19-year production life. The Model 152 differs in having a more powerful engine.

Cessna Model 170/172/175/182/Skylark/Skyhawk/Hawk/Skylane

History and Notes

The Cessna Model 170 and its immediate successors of the same family have the double distinction of being the best-selling series of lightplanes of all time, and also the most widely produced aircraft series yet developed, well over 30,000 examples having come off the production lines by the end of the 1970s.

The origins of the series stretch back to 1948, when Cessna introduced the Model 170, itself little more than a four-seat, re-engineered development of the earlier Model 120. The Model 170 proved popular, and was succeeded by the improved Model 170A. However, the type's real success started in 1953, when Cessna introduced the Model 170B: this was powered, like its predecessors, by the 145-hp (108-kW) Continental C-145-2 air-cooled piston engine, but incorporated the slotted Fowler flaps pioneered for Cessna's Model 305, widely produced for the US and other armed forces as the L-19 (later O-1) Bird Dog. With these efficient flaps, the field and low-speed performance of the Model 170 were improved radically, and all subsequent Cessna aircraft of the type have been designed round similar flaps.

The Model 170 family was selling moderately well, but Cessna felt that the true potential of the type had yet to be realised. In 1955, therefore, the company developed the Model 172, which was essentially a Model 170B with detail improvements and the tailwheel landing gear replaced by a spatted tricycle unit. The improved ground safety of the new variant proved immediately attractive, and in 1956 some 1,170 Model 172s were sold, compared with a mere 174 of the Model 170B, whose production was terminated.

In 1958 Cessna brought into production the Model 175. This was in effect the latest version of the Model 172 with a number of improvements (free-blown windscreen, glassfibre speed fairings, etc) and a 175-hp (131-kW) GO-300-C geared engine driving a constant-speed propeller. In 1959 a de luxe version of the Model 175A was introduced as the Skylark, but the Model 175/Skylark

type was dropped from production in 1963 as a result of constant problems with the engine gearing unit.

At the same time as the de luxe version of the Model 175 appeared as the Skylark, a similar de luxe version of the Model 172 was introduced under the name Skyhawk. Further improvements were made in 1960, with the provision of a new rear fuselage (slimmer and with rear windows) and a stylish swept vertical tail. These modifications were also applied to the Skyhawk and the Skyhawk II, which featured yet more comprehensive equipment, adding sophisticated navigation and com-

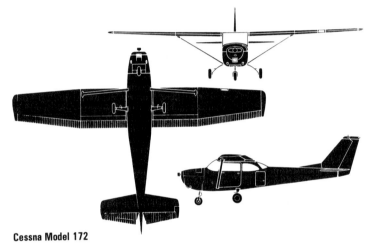

The Cessna Skylane started life as the de luxe version of the Model 182, itself a more powerful derivative of the highly successful Model 172/175 series.

Cessna Model 172

munication gear to blind-flying instrumentation found in the Skyhawk.

In 1963 the Cessna development programme had led to the R172E, which was in essence an up-engined version of the Model 172. Initial flight trials were conducted with the 180-hp (134-kW) Continental O-360 engine, but after type certification in 1964 production Model 172Es were powered by the higher-rated and fuel-injected IO-360-D of 210 hp (157 kW). Further improvements led to another two versions: in 1976 there appeared the Model R172 Hawk XP and in 1977 a basic but improved Model 172 Skyhawk. The former was powered by the 195-hp (145.5-kW) Continental IO-360-K, and was

available in a basic form and with IFR instrumentation as the Hawk XP/II; the latter had the 160-hp (119-kW) Lycoming O-320-H2AD running on low-lead 100-octane fuel.

The latest development of the standard, fixed-gear family had been the Model 182, powered by the 230-hp Continental O-470-S. This was available in three versions: the Model 182 basic production aircraft, the Skylane de luxe model, and the Skylane II with a factory-installed avionics outfit. However, the ultimate Cessna-developed version of the family had been the Cutlas RG introduced in 1979. This has a 180-hp (134-kW) engine and, most unusually, in a strut-braced high-wing mono-

plane, a retractable landing gear. There is also a Skylane RG, introduced in 1977, and available in two versions: the Skylane RG basic model, and the Skylane RG II with the extra equipment found in the Skylane II.

In France Reims Aviation has produced several variants under licence. These include the F172 Skyhawk 100, the FR-172K Hawk XP, F182 and FR182RG, plus the locally developed FR172 Reims Rocket with the 210-hp (157-kW) Continental IO-360-D driving a constant-speed propeller.

Specification
Type: (Model R172E) four-seat

cabin monoplane
Powerplant: one 210-hp (157-kW) Continental IO-360-D flat-six piston engine
Performance: maximum level speed 153 mph (246 km/h) at sea level; economical cruising speed 105 mph (160 km/h) at 10,000 ft (3050 m); initial climb rate 880 ft (268 m) per minute, service ceiling 17,000 ft (5180 m); range with maximum fuel at economical cruise 1,010 miles (1625 km)
Weights: empty 1,405 lb (637 kg); maximum take-off 2,550 lb (1156 kg)
Dimensions: span 35 ft 10 in (10.92 m); length 26 ft 11 in (8.20 m); height 8 ft 9½ in (2.68 m); wing area 174 sq ft (16.17 m²)

Cessna Model 177/Cardinal/Cardinal Classic Series

History and Notes
Expanding their range of single-engined aircraft in an attempt to satisfy what then appeared to be an insatiable market for this class of aeroplane, Cessna introduced the Model 177 at the end of September 1967. Generally similar in overall configuration to other members of the Cessna family in the four-seat class, it was distinguished easily by its cantilever monoplane wing. Other 'advanced' features included weight-saving integral wing fuel tanks, an improved version of Cessna's Land-O-Matic fixed tricycle landing gear, and what was regarded as an 'easy handling' control system. The Model 177 was, at the time of introduction, the designation of the basic model: a de luxe version was named Cardinal, and this included full blind-flying instrumentation, more extensive equipment, and luxury interior appointments as standard.

Powerplant of the initial version was a 150-hp (112-kW) Avco Lycoming O-320-E21D engine, but the Model 177A and Cardinal of 1969 introduced a 180-hp (134-kW) O-360. A year later the number of models increased to three, the Model 177B and Cardinal differing from their predecessors by having an O-360-A1F engine and constant-speed propeller. The third member of this range was the Cardinal RG, which introduced a

retractable landing gear actuated by an electrically powered hydraulic pump, and a more-powerful fuel injection engine. In 1971 Cardinal II and Cardinal RGII versions appeared, these differing by having more comprehensive equipment as standard. In 1976 the Model 177 was withdrawn, the Cardinal becoming regarded as the basic model of the remaining four versions. Two years later the Cardinal also disappeared, the Cardinal II being renamed as the Cardinal Classic. But by the end of 1978, at which time more than 4,000

177/Cardinals of all versions had been built, all Cardinal production was terminated. The details below apply to the high-performance Cardinal RG.

Specification
Type: four-seat cabin monoplane
Powerplant: one 200-hp (149-kW) Avco Lycoming IO-360-A1B6D flat-four piston engine
Performance: maximum cruising speed 170 mph (274 km/h) at 7,000 ft (2135 m); economic cruising speed 139 mph (224 km/h)

The Cessna Model 177 is a nicely proportioned high-wing monoplane, with accommodation for six persons.

at 10,000 ft (3050 m); service ceiling 17,100 ft (5210 m); maximum range with maximum fuel at economic cruising speed 1,030 miles (1658 km)
Weights: empty 1,703 lb (772 kg); maximum take-off 2,800 lb (1270 kg)
Dimensions: span 35 ft 6 in (10.82 m); length 27 ft 3 in (8.31 m); height 8 ft 7 in (2.62 m); wing area 174 sq ft (16.16 m²)

Cessna Model 180/185 Skywagon/AGcarryall Series

History and Notes
In 1953 Cessna introduced a more powerful partner for the Model 170: using the same wing and flap system as the Model 170B, the new Model 180 featured a completely new fuselage and tail unit, plus an additional 80 hp (60 kW) delivered by the 225-hp (168-kW) Continental O-470-A flat-six engine. At the same time a fully adjustable tailplane was introduced, obviating the need for elevator trim tabs. Most significantly, the additional power available for the Model 180 permitted an increase in maximum take-off weight from 2,200 to 2,550 lb (998 to 1157 kg) with the same wing area of 174 sq ft (16.16 m²), and a maximum speed of 165 mph (266 km/h) compared with the Model 170B's more modest 140 mph (225 km/h). In the late 1970s the Model 180 was still available, in two forms: the basic Model 180 Skywagon, and the improved Model 180 Skywagon II with a factory-fitted avionics

The Cessna 185 Skywagon has been built in substantial numbers, thanks to its 'no-frills' low price, adequate performance and general versatility. The Model 185 can operate on wheels, skis or floats.

package. By 1978 production of the Model 180 had reached some 5,900.

In July 1960 Cessna flew the prototype of the Model 185 Skywagon. This was in most respects similar to the Model 180 apart from the provision of extra power in the form of a 300-hp (224-kW) Continental IO-520 engine. Like its predecessor, the Model 185 was a six-seater, and was made available in basic form as the Model 185 Skywagon, and in more advanced form as the Model 185 Skywagon II. Greater versatility is conferred on the two Model 185 versions by their ability to carry under the fuselage the detachable glassfibre Cargo-Pack, capable of carrying some 300 lb (136 kg). The Model 185 Skywagons can also be fitted with Sorenson spraygear for agricultural work, and like the Model 180 Skywagons can be fitted with alternative ski or float landing gears. By 1978 production of the Model 185 Skywagons had reached some 3,400.

In 1971 Cessna introduced an extremely versatile version of the Model 185 in the form of the AGcarryall. This was designed principally for the agricultural role in the widest possible sense: the AGcarryall can demonstrate spraying procedures, ferry people and equipment, serve as an agricultural pilot trainer, and act as a backup spray aircraft in peak periods. The specification applies to the Model 185 Skywagon land plane.

Specification
Type: six-seat cabin monoplane
Powerplant: one 300-hp (224-kW) Continental IO-520-D flat-six piston engine
Performance: maximum level speed 178 mph (286 km/h) at sea level; maximum cruising speed 167 mph (269 km/h) at 7,500 ft (2285 m); initial climb rate 1,010 ft (308 m) per minute; service ceiling 17,150 m (5230 m); range with maximum fuel at economical cruise 829 miles (1334 km)

Cessna Model 185 Skywagon

Weights: empty 1,690 lb (766 kg); maximum take-off 3,350 lb (1519 kg)
Dimensions: span 35 ft 10 in (10.92 m); length 25 ft 9 in (7.85 m); height 7 ft 9 in (2.36 m); wing area 174 sq ft (16.16 m²)

Cessna Model 190/195 Series

History and Notes
The aircraft of the Cessna Models 190 and 195 series were unique amongst postwar Cessna single-engined lightplanes in being powered by radial engines. The two types were produced in parallel between 1947 and 1954.

The Model 190, of which 233 were built, was powered by the 240-hp (179-kW) Continental R-670-23. The two versions of the Model 195 were almost indistinguishable from the Model 190: the Model 195 was powered by the 300-hp (224-kW) Jacobs R-755A2, while the Model 195A had the 245-hp (183-kW) Jacobs R-744A2. Production of the Models 195 and 195A totalled 890, examples built in 1953 and 1954 being identifiable by their close-cowled engines, a small propeller spinner, and an increase of 50 per cent in the area of the flaps let into the undersurfaces of the high-set unbraced wings. The series is also notable for the fact that in introduced Cessna's now-celebrated spring-steel main landing gear legs. The specification applies to the Model 195A.

Specification
Type: four/five-seat cabin monoplane
Powerplant: one 245-hp (183-kW) Jacobs R-744-A2 radial piston engine

Performance: maximum speed 173 mph (278 km/h); cruising speed 155 mph (249 km/h); initial climb rate 1,050 ft (320 m) per minute; service ceiling 16,000 ft (4875 m); range 750 miles (1207 km)
Weights: empty 2,030 lb (921 kg); maximum take-off 3,350 lb (1520 kg)
Dimensions: span 36 ft 2 in (3.66 m); length 27 ft 4 in (8.33 m); height 7 ft 2 in (3.66 m); wing area 218.13 sq ft (20.26 m²)

Cessna Model 205/206 Super Skywagon, Super Skylane and Stationair 6/207 and Stationair 7 Series

History and Notes
The Cessna 205, introduced in 1962, was developed from the Model 182, although in appearance it was a fixed landing gear version of the Cessna 210. Indeed, FAA certification on 14 June 1962 was under the designation 210-5. Powered by a 260-hp (194-kW) Continental engine, the Model 205 was complementary to the tailwheel Model 185 Skywagon, having similar performance at slightly greater weight. Deliveries began in August 1962, and in December 1963 Cessna introduced the Model 205A with detail improvements; the six-seat passenger version was named Super Skylane.

Around 600 of the Model 205/205A series were built before the type was superseded at the end of 1963 by the Model 206 Super Skywagon, offering improvements in performance with a 285-hp (213-kW) Continental engine and a greater degree of flexibility. Double doors in the right side of the fuselage enabled long or awkward-shaped loads to be carried, and an optional underfuselage freight pack of 300-lb (136-kg) capacity could be installed.

Both the Model 205 and 206 series were available with agricultural equipment and could be flown, like most of the single-engine high-wing Cessna range, with floats, skis or various sizes of wheels. The specification applies to the Cessna 205A.

Specification
Type: six-seat passenger/utility monoplane
Powerplant: one 260-hp (194-kW) Continental IO-470-S flat-six piston engine
Performance: maximum speed 173 mph (278 km/h) at sea level; maximum cruising speed 162 mph (261 km/h) at 6,500 ft (1980 m); service ceiling 16,100 ft (4910 m); maximum range 1,015 miles (1633 km)
Weights: empty 1750 lb (794 kg); maximum take-off 3,300 lb (1497 kg)
Dimensions: span 36 ft 7 in (11.15 m); length 27 ft 9 in (8.46 m); height 9 ft 9 in (2.97 m); wing area 175.5 sq ft (16.30 m²)

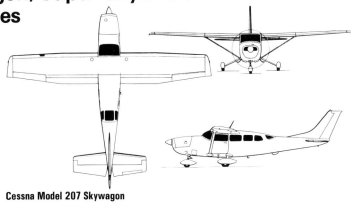

Successors to the Models 180 and 185, the prolific Cessna Models 205, 206 and 207 offer improved payload coupled with enhanced performance.

Cessna Model 207 Skywagon

Cessna Model 210 Centurion

History and Notes

Flown for the first time in January 1957, the Model 210 was the first of Cessna's high-wing range to feature retractable landing gear and swept fin and rudder. The first production aircraft flew in December 1959 powered by a 260-hp (194-kW) Continental IO-470-E engine, and since that time progressive improvements have been made each year.

The 1961 model, for instance, had two more cabin windows, additional headroom and an improved heating and ventilating system, and by 1963, when the 210C was introduced, an autopilot was offered as an option. By February of that year 1,143 Model 210s had been built, while by January 1965 the total had risen to 1,584 and the Model 210E Centurion had supplanted earlier versions. This had a 285-hp (213-kW) Continental IO-520-A.

The Model 210F followed in 1966, and in that year the first turbo-charged model became available, in the form of the T210F Turbo-System Centurion with a 285-hp (213-kW) Continental TSIO-520C. The extra power conferred a useful increase in performance, particularly at altitude; the Model 210F cruised at 198 mph (319 km/h) at sea level, while the Model T210F's cruising speed at 19,000 ft (5790 m) was 230 mph (370 km/h). Service ceilings were 19,900 ft (6070 m) for the Model 210F and 31,300 ft (9540 m) for the Model T210F. A new wing, first flown on a Model T210 in June 1965, was later introduced on production aircraft, and eliminated the need for the external struts.

By 1970, Cessna had dropped the suffix letter system and announced

two new models, the Centurion II and Turbo Centurion II, these going into production alongside the Centurion/Turbo Centurion I. The Centurion had grown to a six-seater, and now offered powerplant options of a 300-hp (224-kW) Continental IO-520-L or, in the Turbo version, a 285-hp (213-kW) Continental TSIO-520-H.

Turbocharged Centurions have established several world records in their class: they include time-to-height records, a round-the-world speed of 127 mph (204 km/h), and an altitude record of 42,344.16 ft (129065 m) established as long ago as 13 May 1967.

Production of the Model 210 topped the 5,000 mark in 1976, and in November 1977 a new pressurised model was announced. This was similar to the standard aircraft, but had a 310-hp (231-kW) Continental TSIO-520-P engine with a turbo-charger to support the pressurisation system.

By the beginning of 1981 total Cessna 210 Centurion deliveries were approaching the 8,000 mark.

Specification

Type: six-seat cabin monoplane
Powerplant: one 300-hp (224-kW) Continental IO-520-L flat-six piston engine
Performance: maximum speed 202

The Cessna 210 Pressurised Centurion has a somewhat unusual appearance with its combination of a cantilever high-set wing with retractable landing gear. Cabin pressurisation offers the equivalent of 12,125 ft at 23,000 ft.

mph (325 km/h) at sea level; maximum cruising speed 197 mph (317 km/h) at 6,500 ft (1980 m); service ceiling 17,300 ft (5275 m) range 1,226 miles (1973 km)
Weights: empty 2,198 lb (997 kg); maximum take-off 3,800 lb (1724 kg)
Dimensions: span 36 ft 9 in (11.20 m); length 28 ft 2 in (8.59 m); height 9 ft 8 in (2.95 m); wing area 175 sq ft (16.26 m²)

Cessna T303 Crusader

History and Notes

Cessna's direct competitor to the Piper Aztec and Beech Baron is the Crusader, flown in February 1978 as the Model 303. Designed originally as a four-seater with 160-hp (119-kW) engines, it introduced a number of new features including bonded construction and a supercritical wing section. However, the aircraft was redesigned and emerged as a six-seater, with 250-hp (186-kW) engines and normal construction.

For the redesigned form the designation T303 Clipper was applied, but the name was later changed to Crusader, the first of two prototypes flying on 17 October 1979. Prior to certification, planned for June 1981, it was intended to complete some 500 hours of flight testing, plus a similar time on service testing, with deliveries beginning in the late summer.

Little information on the Crusader has been released, but there will be a number of internal cabin layouts offered: the standard arrangement will be three seats on each side of a centre aisle. Baggage lockers with a total capacity of 590 lb (268 kg) will be situated in the nose, wing and rear of the cabin. Cessna is investing more than $2 million in 1981 to prepare for production of the Crusader at its Pawnee Division factory in Wichita.

Specification

Type: six-seat cabin monoplane
Powerplant: two 250-hp (186-kW) Teledyne Continental TSIO-520-AE flat-six piston engines
Performance: maximum speed 247 mph (398 km/h) at 20,000 ft (6100 m); cruising speed 207 mph (333 km/h) at 10,000 ft (3050 m); service ceiling 25,000 ft (7620 m);

range 921 miles (1482 km)
Weights: empty 3056 lb (1386 kg); maximum take-off 5025 lb (2279 kg)
Dimensions: span 38 ft 10 in (11.84 m); length 30 ft 5 in (9.27 m); height 12 ft 11 in (3.94 m); wing area 189 sq ft (17.56 m²)

The Cessna T303 Crusader is an advanced four-seater with a spacious cabin. The wing has the latest supercritical section, and extensive use is made of bonding techniques in the structure. A particularly useful feature of the type is the provision of an airstair door on the starboard side of the fuselage.

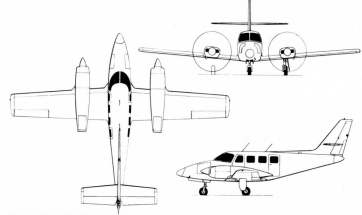

Cessna Model 303 Crusader

Cessna 336/337 Skymaster/Reims F337 Series

History and Notes

The push-pull concept, with engines driving one tractor and one pusher propeller, was not new when Cessna considered the idea in the late 1950s — a striking example was the World War II Dornier Do 335 — but it was unusual for a production light aircraft. The intention was to build a light, low cost, easy-to-fly twin, and one obvious advantage over a normal twin layout was that, in the event of an engine failure, there would be no asymmetric problems.

On 28 February 1961, the prototype Model 336 Skymaster flew and FAA certification followed 15 months later, with deliveries beginning in May 1963. Powered by two 210-hp (157-kW) Continental IO-360-A engines, the Model 336 was a four-seater with fixed tricycle landing gear, although alternative seating arrangements for up to six were available. However, fixed landing gear on light twins was becoming passé, and after 195 Model 336s had been built the type was replaced on the production line by the Model 337 Super Skymaster from February 1965. The increase in popularity of the Model 337 with retractable landing gear can be gauged from the fact that 322 had been delivered less than a year later. Additional baggage space was available in an optional glassfibre pack with a capacity of 300 lb (136 kg), which could be carried beneath the fuselage.

In 1969, Reims Aviation in France began licence assembly of the Model 337, with primary structures supplied by Cessna and Continental engines built in the UK under licence by Rolls-Royce. The US and French production lines continued in parallel, the French versions being classified F337. Detail improvements continued each year, and a turbocharged version, the Model 337 Turbo-System Super Skymaster, was introduced in 1970 with Continental TSIO-360-A engines each of 210 hp (157 kW).

Military versions designated O-2 were supplied to the US Air Force for various missions, including forward air control, and air-to-ground broadcasting.

The prototype of the pressurised T337 Skymaster, powered by 225-hp (168-kW) Continental TSIO-360 engines, flew in July 1971 (the word Super had then been dropped), and deliveries began the following May. Reims-built versions were FT337Ps, and by this time Reims Aviation was also offering the FA337, which had provision for STOL modifications, and the FTB337, a similar aircraft but with an ability to carry underwing stores. This later became the FTB337G and by January 1977 Reims had delivered 55 FTB337s in addition to 79 standard civil aircraft. US production by that time had reached 2,300 of all Model 337 versions, plus 544 military O-2s.

Production of the Model 337 series by Cessna ended in mid-1980; by the beginning of that year 1,821 Model 337s and 313 pressurised Model 337s plus 544 military O-2s had been delivered. Reims production figures were 66 Model F337s and 27 F337Ps before the French line moved over solely to the FTB-337G, 61 of which had been built by January 1980.

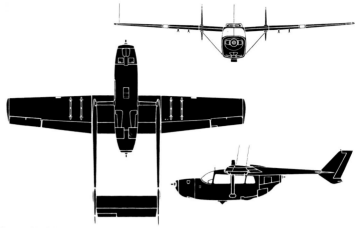

Cessna Model 337 Skymaster

Specification

Type: six-seat cabin monoplane
Powerplant: two 210-hp (157-kW) Continental IO-360-GB flat-six piston engines
Performance: maximum speed 206 mph (332 km/h) at sea level; maximum cruising speed 196 mph (315 km/h) at 5,500 ft (1675 m); service ceiling 18,000 ft (5485 m); range 1,422 miles (2288 km) at 10,000 ft (3050 m)
Weights: empty 2,787 lb (1264 kg); maximum take-off 4,630 lb (2100 kg)
Dimensions: span 38 ft 2 in (11.63 m); length 29 ft 9 in (9.07 m); height 9 ft 2 in (2.79 m); wing area 202.5 sq ft (18.81 m²)

Distinct oddities in the general-aviation world, the Cessna Models 336 and 337 offer twin-engine performance and safety without any problems of thrust asymmetry in the event of engine failure. The 337 has retractable gear.

Cessna 310/340/335 Series

History and Notes

Well over 3,000 Cessna 310 five/six-seat light twins had been built before the announcement of the Cessna 340 in December 1971, but the Model 340 was not intended merely as a step up into the six-seat class; it was also pressurised, and therefore a competitor to the similar sized, but slightly heavier and more powerful, Beech Duke.

Cessna's announcement on 8 December 1971, claiming that the Model 340 was the first pressurised aircraft in the light twin category (empty weight 3,697 lb:1677 kg) was strange, considering that the company had announced the lighter, pressurised Model 337 Skymaster (2,900 lb:1315 kg) on the same day, and that the Duke, which had been in production for five years, was only slightly heavier at 4,195 lb (1902 kg).

The Model 340 had wings with tip tanks and retractable tricycle landing gear similar to those of the Model 414, and a tail unit resembling that of the Model 310, but the pressurised fuselage was completely new. It entered production with 285-hp (213-kW) Continental TSIO-520-K turbocharged fuel-injection engines, and by January 1973 more than 220 had been delivered. The Model 340A II, introduced in 1976, was basically identical to the Model 340A, the standard production model, but had a factory-installed avionics pack. The

The Cessna Model 340 pressurised twin-engine business aircraft has proved very popular, and is available with the usual range of Cessna optional packages of avionics and other equipment.

earlier engines had given way to 310-hp (231-kW) Continental TSIO-520-Ns, and a pneumatic de-icing system was offered as an option. In 1978 the Model 340A III appeared with further additional avionics, improvements to the instrument layout, and detail changes. By the beginning of 1980, 1,026 Model 340s had been delivered, while production of the Model 310 had reached 5,298.

Complementing the range now is the Cessna 335, flown on 5 December 1978, with customer deliveries beginning in late 1979. This is basically a lighter and unpressurised Model 340A, and is available in the standard version and the Model 335 II with factory-installed avionics. The specification applies to the Model 340A.

Specification
Type: six-seat pressurised business transport
Powerplant: two 310-hp (231-kW) Continental TSIO-520-NB flat-six piston engines
Performance: maximum speed 281 mph (452 km/h) at 20,000 ft (6100 m); maximum cruising speed 264 mph (425 km/h) at 24,500 ft (7470 m); service ceiling 29,800 ft (9085 m); maximum range 1,586 miles (2552 km) at 10,000 ft (3050 m)
Weights: empty 3,911 lb (1774 kg); maximum take-off 5,990 lb (2717 kg)
Dimensions: span 38 ft 1 in (11.61 m); length 34 ft 4 in (10.46 m); height 12 ft 7 in (3.84 m); wing area 184 sq ft (1709 m²)

Cessna 401/402/AJI Turbo Star Series

History and Notes
On 1 November 1966, Cessna announced the Model 401 six/eight-seat executive transport, and the 10-seat Model 402 convertible passenger/freight aircraft. The airframes were identical, and the prototype had flown in August 1965, being certificated 13 months later. Both went into production and, like the rest of the Cessna range, featured detail improvements with each model, but production of the Model 401 was phased out in mid-1972 after 400 had been built, subsequent development being concentrated on the Model 402. In December 1971, the original Model 402 was renamed Utiliner, and another version was introduced, the Businessliner. This latter had six seats and an option for a further two, and filled the gap in the business market previously catered for by the Model 401.

With an eye to the new turboprop engines available, American Jet Industries (AJI) converted a Model 402 to turbine power in 1970 by installing two 400-shp (298-kW) Allison 250-B17s in place of the standard 300-hp (224-kW) Continentals. The result was a saving in weight of 380 lb (172 kg), an increase in cruising speed at 10,000 ft (3050 m) from 218 mph (351 km/h) to 275 mph (443 km/h) and in sea level rate of climb from 1,610 ft (491 m) per minute to 3,000 ft (914 m) per minute. AJI christened this model the Turbo Star.

Cessna continued to make improvements each year and by 1977 the Model 402 range covered four versions: the Model 402 Utiliner, Model 402 II Utiliner, the Model 402 Businessliner, and the Model 402 II

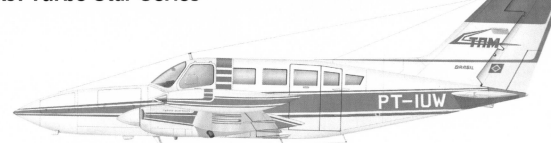

Cessna Model 402 of TAM, Brazil.

Businessliner, the Model IIs being versions with factory-installed equipment and electronics. Dual control is standard in the Model 402C II, and optional on the Model 402C. Most were delivered to civil customers, but 12 went to the Royal Malaysian air force in 1975. By January 1977, 911 Model 402s had been built, and this had risen to 1,220 three years later when the same four models were offered, now with C suffixes and 325-hp (242-kW) Continental TSIO-520-VB turbocharged engines. The C model marked the introduction of a 'wet' wing without tiptanks, and basic 1981 price was $282,000, with Series II models available from $304,950. The specification applies to the Model 402C.

Specification
Type: 10-seat passenger/freight transport
Powerplant: two 325-hp (242-kW) Continental TSIO-520-VB flat-six piston engines
Performance: maximum speed 266 mph (428 km/h) at 16,000 ft (4875 m); maximum cruising speed 245 mph (394 km/h) at 20,000 ft

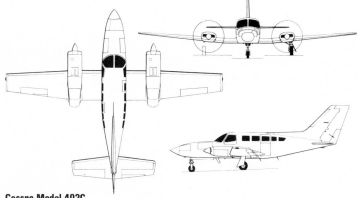

Cessna Model 402C

(6100 m); service ceiling 26,900 ft (8200 m); maximum range 1,132 miles (1822 km) at 20,000 ft (6100 m)
Weights: empty 4,074 lb (1848 kg); maximum take-off 6,850 lb (3107 kg)
Dimensions: span 44 ft 1½ in (13.45 m); length 36 ft 4½ in (11.09 m); height 11 ft 5½ in (3.49 m); wing area 225.8 sq ft (20.98 m²)

The Cessna 402 is based on the Model 411, and is available in two versions: the Business-liner commuter transport and the Utililiner light freighter. Some Model 402s have been converted by American Jet Industries into Turbo Star 402As by the replacement of the Continental piston engines by a pair of 400-shp (298-kW) Allison 250-B17 turboprops.

Cessna 404 Titan

History and Notes

Launched in July 1975, the Cessna 404 Titan flew in February of that year and deliveries began in October 1976. In appearance, the Titan was very similar to the turboprop Conquest which flew six months later, and the two aircraft shared a new feature for Cessna twins: a tailplane with 12° dihedral. Wings and landing gear were also similar to those of the Conquest. The Titan was powered by two 375-hp (280-kW) Continental GTSIO-520-M turbocharged engines, offering an increase of more than 30 per cent in ton/miles per gallon over the Cessna 402.

Initially two models were available: the Titan Ambassador passenger aircraft which offered an alternative executive interior, and the Titan Courier, a utility version for passengers or cargo, with seats for up to 10 passengers. By 1978 no fewer than eight versions were available, and by this time the model number was no longer quoted. Both Ambassador and Courier were offered in three versions, while the new Titan Freighter and Freighter II featured impact resistant polycarbonate interiors to protect the fuselage from damage by cargo. The new versions of earlier models differed mainly in the types of equipment installed.

Deliveries continued at the rate of about 80 Titans a year and by January 1980 the figure stood at 241. Engine time before overhaul is now 1,600 hours, and the 1981 Titan basic price was $415,000 for the Courier and Freighter, and $438,500 for the Series II models.

Specification

Type: passenger/cargo/executive transport
Powerplant: two 375-hp (280-kW) Continental GTSIO-520-M flat-six piston engines
Performance: maximum speed 267 mph (430 km/h) at 16,000 ft (4875 m); maximum cruising speed 250 mph (402 km/h) at 20,000 ft (6100 m); service ceiling 26,000 ft (7925 m); maximum range 2,119 miles (3410 km) at 20,000 ft (6100 m)
Weights: (Titan Ambassador) 4,816 lb (2185 kg); maximum take-off 8,400 lb (3810 kg)
Dimensions: span 46 ft 8 ¼ in (14.23 m); length 39 ft 6¼ in (12.04 m); height 13 ft 3 in (4.04 m); wing area 242 sq ft (22.48 m²)

The Cessna Titan was conceived as a versatile transport in three versions: the Titan Ambassador passenger carrier, the Titan Courier convertible passenger/freight transport, and the Titan Freighter cargo aircraft.

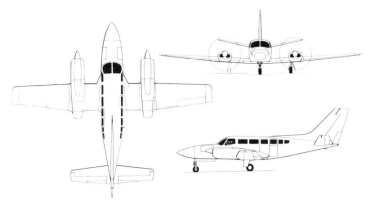

Cessna Model 404 Titan

Cessna 414 Chancellor

History and Notes

In order to provide a pressurised twin of slightly less capacity than its Model 421, Cessna married the basic fuselage of the Model 421 with the wing of the Model 401 and installed 310-hp (231-kW) Continental TSIO-520-J turbocharged engines. The result was the Model 414, flown on 1 November 1968, and certificated the following August. No less than eight seating layouts were available for up to seven people, and the new Cessna-developed Accru-Measure fuel monitoring system was said to provide an accuracy of plus or minus 3 per cent; the engine cowlings featured flush intakes to improve engine cooling.

Improvements made to the Model 402 continued to be reflected in the Model 414, and by January 1974 production of the latter had reached 261. In 1976, the Model 414 II with additional electronics and equipment was introduced alongside the standard model and the name Chancellor was adopted for the type. Major changes were made from 1978; the wingtip tanks were removed in favour of a redesigned 'wet' wing of greater span, a longer nose and extended baggage area were provided, and the designations became Model 414A Chancellor, Chancellor II and Chancellor III. Further detail improvements were introduced in 1980, and new options included a pneumatic de-icing system, and an electrically de-iced windscreen. From 1980 the manufacturer offered a 35-month or 1,400 hour engine repair or replacement warranty. Production exceeded 800 units by 1981. The specification applies to the Model 414A.

Specification

Type: six-seat pressurised light transport
Powerplant: two 310-hp (231-kW) Continental TSIO-520-NB flat-six piston engines
Performance: maximum speed 271 mph (436 km/h) at 20,000 ft (6100 m); maximum cruising speed 258 mph (415 km/h) at 24,500 ft (7470 m); service ceiling 30,800 ft (9390 m); maximum range 1,528 miles (2459 km)
Weights: 4,356 lb (1976 kg); maximum take-off 6,750 lb (3062 kg)

The Cessna Model 414.A Chancellor can seat up to seven passengers, while the fuel capacity of the 'wet' wing gives a range of some 1,500 miles.

Dimensions: span 44 ft 1½ in (13.45 m); length 36 ft 4½ in (11.09 m); height 11 ft 5½ in (3.49 m); wing area 225.8 sq ft (20.98 m²)

Cessna 441 Conquest

History and Notes

Announced in the same year as the Model 404 Titan, the Cessna 441 Conquest was designed for a different role: pressurised executive transport with accommodation for up to 11 people.

Flown on 26 August 1975, the prototype was powered by two Garrett TPE331-8-401 turboprops, each of 620 shp (462 kW), with Cessna hoping that this new aircraft would fill the slot between twin-piston engine and turbojet-powered business aircraft. In its size category immediate competitors were the Beech King Air 90 and the Rockwell Turbo Commander 690.

Misfortune came early in 1978, after only four Conquests had been delivered; a fatal crash occurred as the result of an elevator-tab actuator failure, and the type was grounded by the manufacturer. Another similar failure, which caused severe tailplane vibration in flight, fortunately did not lead to casualties, but the US Federal Aviation Administration withdrew the Model 441's certificate of airworthiness while investigations were made into the elevator and tailplane design.

Following redesign and testing, the Conquest was recertificated in September 1979, but a new tailplane had to be fitted to aircraft already completed. Deliveries had reached 115 by the beginning of January 1980, and subsequent production aircraft included a number of new items as standard, including an automatic engine torque and temperature limiting system. Among options offered was a Bendix colour weather radar.

An early European Conquest customer was Britain's Automobile Association, which operates the appropriately registered G-AUTO.

Specification

Type: pressurised executive transport
Powerplant: two 636-shp (474-kW) Garrett TPE331-8 turboprops
Performance: maximum speed 340 mph (547 km/h) at 16,000 ft (4875 m); maximum cruising speed 337 mph (542 km/h) at 24,000 ft

Cessna 441 Conquest

(7315 m); service ceiling 37,000 ft (11275 m); maximum range 2,545 miles (4096 km) at 33,000 ft (10060 m)
Weights: empty 5,666 lb (2670 kg); maximum take-off 9,850 lb (4468 kg)
Dimensions: span 49 ft 4 in (15.04 m); length 39 ft 0¼ in (11.89 m); height 13 ft 2 in (4.01 m); wing area 253.6 sq ft (23.56 m²)

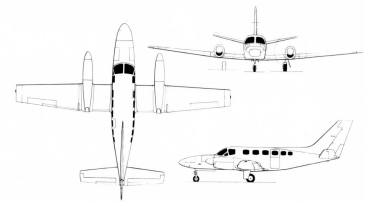

The Cessna Model 441 Conquest, which entered service in 1977, was the first Cessna aircraft to feature a turboprop powerplant, in the form of two Garrett-AiResearch TPE331s. Up to 10 passengers can be carried in fair comfort, the bleed-air pressurisation system permitting a cruise altitude of 33,000 ft (10060 m).

Cessna Model 441 Conquest

Cessna Citation I/II/III

History and Notes

Of the 'big three' of American general aviation manufacturers (Beech, Cessna and Piper), Beech was the first to introduce turbine power, with turboprops installed on the Model 90 King Air that was first flown in 1964. Cessna was the next, but it was not until October 1968 that the development of an eight-seat pressurised aircraft named Fanjet 500 was announced. The name was intended to reflect the use of a different type of turbine engine to that which powered the King Air, namely a turbofan. Presumably it was considered that this would not mean a great deal to potential passengers, and after a prototype had flown on 15 September 1969, Cessna's Model 500 became named Citation.

A number of changes were made to the basic configuration before certification was gained, on 9 September 1971, but this attractive aircraft is a fairly conventional low-wing monoplane with a pressurised fuselage, swept tail surfaces that incorporate tailplane dihedral, retractable landing gear, and a pod-mounted turbofan engine on each side of the rear fuselage. Citations began to enter service shortly after

Cessna Citation 1

certification, being followed in 1976 by the improved Citation I which introduced uprated JT15D-1A turbofans and a wing of increased span. A variant designated Citation I/SP, certificated for single-pilot operation, became available in early 1977.

The Citation II, first announced in September 1976, introduced a fuselage lengthened by 3 ft 9 in (1.14 m) to accommodate up to 10 passengers, a wing of greater span, increased fuel and baggage capacity, and more powerful JT15D-4 turbofans. As with the Citation I, a Citation II/SP single-pilot variant is also available. Certification of the Citation II was gained in March 1978, and by

early 1981 the combined sales of the first three Citation versions had exceeded 300 aircraft.

A very different Citation III was developed during 1978 to provide increased capacity and improved performance. This introduced a new supercritical wing with 25° of sweepback, a lengthened fuselage to accommodate a maximum of 13 passengers, a T-tail, and more powerful and fuel efficient Garrett TFE731-3B-100S turbofans, each of 3,650-lb (1656-kg) thrust. First flown in prototype form on 30 May 1979, certification is planned during 1982. The details that follow apply to the Citation II.

Specification

Type: twin-turbofan executive transport
Powerplant: two 2,500-lb (1134-kg) thrust Pratt & Whitney Aircraft of Canada JT15D-4 turbofans
Performance: cruising speed 443 mph (713 km/h); certificated ceiling 43,000 ft (13105 m); range with six passengers, 45-min reserves 1,969 miles (3169 m)
Weights: empty 7,181 lb (3257 kg); maximum take-off 13,300 lb (6033 kg)
Dimensions: span 51 ft 8 in (15.75 m); length 47 ft 2 in (14.38 m); height 14 ft 9 in (4.50 m²)

Compared with the Citation I, the Cessna Citation II introduced wings of greater span and higher aspect ratio, a longer fuselage, greater fuel capacity, and more powerful Pratt & Whitney Aircraft of Canada JT15D turbofans. The net effect of the changes has been to increase payload and performance, range with eight passengers being 430 miles (690 km) more than the Citation I with six passengers.

Champion Model 7/Challenger/Sky-Trac Series

History and Notes
In 1954, the Aeronca Manufacturing Corporation sold the manufacturing rights of its Model 7 Champion to Flyers Service Inc., which formed the Champion Aircraft Corporation and began building the Model 7EC towards the end of that year, the first aircraft being completed in February 1955.

A tandem two-seater, the aircraft was developed in a number of forms: the basic Model 7EC was named Traveler and had a 95-hp (71-kW) Continental C90 engine and tailwheel landing gear; the Model 7FC Tri-Traveler was identical apart from its tricycle gear; the Model 7JC Tri-Con was fitted with reversed tricycle gear; the Model 7GC Sky-Trac was a three-seater with a 140-hp (104-kW) Avco Lycoming O-290 engine; and the Model 7HC DX-er was a Sky-Trac with tricycle landing gear.

The Challenger, basically similar to the Model 7EC, had increased span, a 150-hp (112-kW) Avco Lycoming O-320-A engine and high-lift flaps; a de-luxe version offered more cabin luxury, improved instrumentation, and other cosmetic improvements.

The Sky-Trac was introduced in 1958 and, like the Traveler, could be easily adapted for agricultural work by installation of spraying gear. Wheel, float or ski landing gear was available optionally.

By the mid-1960s, production had been switched to a new model, the Citabria. The specification applies to the Champion Challenger.

Specification
Type: two-seat light monoplane
Powerplant: one 150-hp (112-kW) Avco Lycoming O-320-A flat-four piston engine
Performance: maximum speed 162 mph (261 km/h); cruising speed 125 mph (201 km/h); service ceiling 17,500 ft (5335 m); range 630 miles (1014 km)
Weights: empty 1,050 lb (476 kg); maximum take-off 1,650 lb (748 kg)
Dimensions: span 34 ft 5½ in (10.50 m); length 22 ft 1 in (6.73 m); height 6 ft 10½ in (2.10 m); wing area 170.22 sq ft (15.81 m²)

Convair CV-240/-340/-440

History and Notes
As elusive as the legendary crock of gold at the foot of the rainbow, but with a similar promise of potential riches to an astute aircraft manufacturer, is the creation of an effective DC-3 replacement. This promise of great financial reward is not surprising if one appreciates that, for a considerable number of years following World War II, DC-3s in commercial service outnumbered easily the total of all other transport aircraft in use worldwide. One of the contending manufacturers who hoped to make a 'killing' in this market was Consolidated Vultee Aircraft Corporation in the USA, which in the early 1950s began to identify its products as Convair types, and in 1954 became the Convair Division of General Dynamics Corporation. It is this division which now provides continuing product support for the Convair 240 and its derivatives.

In 1945, American Airlines issued their specification for an airliner to fulfil more effectively the operations being carried out by DC-3s. In due course this led to the construction by Consolidated Vultee of a prototype, designated Model 110, as the result of discussions which had been held between the company and American Airlines. This prototype was completed and flown for the first time on 8 July 1946. A twin-engined aircraft, powered by two 2,100-hp (1566-kW) Pratt & Whitney R-2800-S1C3-G radial piston engines, it had accommodation for 30 passengers. Before it was flown, however, American Airlines had already decided that greater capacity was necessary. This resulted in the development of the Model 240, known later as the Convair 240, or Convairliner. No prototype was built as such, all examples being completed to production standard using production jigs and tooling, and the first aircraft made its maiden flight on 16 March 1947. While retaining the same powerplant and overall configuration of the Model 110, the new aircraft introduced a number of changes to make possible a standard layout to seat 40 passen-

Convair CV-440 of American Inter-Island (Virgin Islands).

gers. Wing span was increased by only a few inches, but the slimmer-section fuselage (intended to reduce drag and improve performance), was lengthened by 3 ft 8 in (1.12 m). Convair 240s entered service with American Airlines on 1 June 1948, and of the total built (176 for the civil airlines) a considerable number served with the USAF as T-29 trainers and C-131 casualty evacuation transports.

Development of an improved version, known as the Convair 340, was initiated in early 1951. It differed by having R-2800-CB16 or -CB17 engines of 2,500 hp (1864 kW), and increased wing area to cater for a higher gross weight. A further 'stretch' of the fuselage, with two plugs totalling 4 ft 6 in (1.37 m) inserted one forward and one aft of the wing, increased standard accommodation to 44 passengers. The first example of this version flew first on 5 October 1951, and the initial delivery, to United Airlines, was made on 28 March 1952.

Further refinement of this design led to the generally similar Convair 440, which incorporated aerodynamic and comfort improvements. The introduction of a high-density seating arrangement on this version made possible the accommodation of a maximum of 52 passengers, and many of these airliners were equipped with weather radar, which increased the overall length by 2 ft 4 in (0.71 m). The first 440 was produced by the conversion of a Convair 340, and

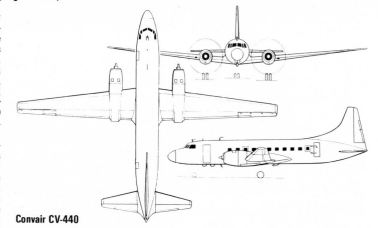

Convair CV-440

it was flown for the first time on 6 October 1955; subsequently 155 civil airliners were built as new to this standard.

Specification
Type: medium-range transport
Powerplant (Convair 340/440): two 2,500-hp (1864-kW) Pratt & Whitney R-2800-CB16 or -CB17 radial piston engines
Performance: (Convair 440) maximum cruising speed 330 mph (483 km/h) at 13,000 ft (3960 m); economic cruising speed 289 mph (465 km/h) at 20,000 ft (6100 m); service ceiling 24,900 ft (7590 m); range with maximum payload 470 miles (756 km); range with maximum fuel 1,930 miles (3106 km)

Weights: operating empty, Convair 240 27,600 lb (12519 kg), Convair 340 29,486 lb (13375 kg), Convair 440 33,314 lb (15111 kg); maximum take-off, Convair 240 41,790 lb (18956 kg), Convair 340 47,000 lb (21319 kg), Convair 440 49,000 lb (22226 kg)
Dimensions: span, Convair 240 91 ft 9 in (27.97 m), Convair 340/440 105 ft 4 in (32.11 m); length, Convair 240 74 ft 8 in (22.76 m), Convair 340/440 79 ft 2 in (24.13 m) or 81 ft 6 in (24.84 m) with weather radar; height, Convair 240 26 ft 11 in (8.20 m), Convair 340/440 28 ft 2 in (8.59 m); wing area, Convair 240 817 sq ft (75.90 m²), Convair 340/440 920 sq ft (85.47 m²)
Operators include: Aero B, Aero Caribe, Aerolineas de Guatemala Aviateca, Air-Sea Service, Air Sunshine, American Inter Island Airways, Astro Air Transport, Century Airlines, Combs Airways, Finnair, Kalahari Air Services, Kardair, Key Airlines, LACSA, LAGE, Mackey International Airlines, Music City International Airways, Norfly, North East Bolivian Airways, Oasis Air Transport, Pyramid Airlines, Red Carpet Flying Service, and Rutaca

A striking colour scheme enlivens this Convair CV-440 of the Mexican regional operator Aero Leon. Fuel economy, low capital cost and adequate passenger capacity still make the Convairliner an economic proposition for smaller lines.

Convair CV-540/-580/-600/-640

History and Notes

There have been many aircraft that have had powerplant conversions to improve performance and/or economy, and the Convair 240/340/440 series is no exception to this exercise. The turboprop, combining smooth power, and reliability of the turbine with the reduction gear and propeller of a piston engine, seemed attractive as soon as the development of such engines was proposed. However, many early applications of turboprops to replace the piston engines of aircraft from an earlier era were not entirely successful. In the case of the Convairliners the reverse applied, for the robust, well-designed structures of these aircraft were able to accept the considerably more powerful turboprop engines without undue airframe stress, giving the series a new lease of life.

The first of such conversion came in 1954, when D. Napier & Sons in Britain installed two of their 3,060-ehp (2282-ekW) Eland N.El.1 turboprop engines in a Convair 340, and this flew for the first time on 9 February 1955. This, and five similar aircraft, duly entered service with Allegheny Airlines in America, under the designation Convair 540. Subsequently, when development and production of the Eland came to an end in 1962, these particular aircraft were to revert to a piston engine powerplant. Canadair, in Canada, converted three Convair 440s to Eland turboprops as Canadair 540s, and later built 10 new aircraft with this powerplant for service with the Royal Canadian Air Force under the designation CC-109.

In the USA, PacAero Engineering Corporation of Santa Monica, California, also initiated a conversion programme for Convair 340/440 aircraft. This involved the installation of 3,750-shp (2796-kW) Allison 501-D13 turboprop engines, and the provision of greater area for the tail unit control surfaces. Designated Convair 580, and known sometimes as the Super Convair, it had accommodation for 52 passengers, as Convair 340 conversions included the installation of the additional 8 seats in the high-density arrangement. PacAero's first 580 made an initial flight on 19 January 1960, but it was not until June 1964 that the type began to enter airline service, with Frontier Airlines the first operator.

The last of these conversion programmes was that initiated by the type's original manufacturer, who selected the 3,025-ehp (2256-ekW) Rolls-Royce R.Da.10/1 Dart 542 turboprop for installation in 240/340/440 aircraft. In addition to the provision of these engines, the 240 was subjected also to airframe strengthening, and could be provided with a 48-seat interior arrangement, while the 330/440s could have a 56-seat layout. In their new form these aircraft were designated 240D, 340D, and 440D respectively, this being changed later to Convair 600 for the 240D, and to Convair 640 for each of the other two. The first 600 entered service with Central Airlines on 30 November 1965, and the first 640 with Caribair on 22 December 1965.

Under the designations Convair 580/600/640 about 240 conversions were carried out, and a considerable

number of these remain in service in 1980. The details below apply to the Convair 640.

Specification

Type: medium-range transport
Powerplant: two 3,025-ehp (2256-ekW) Rolls-Royce R.Da.10/1 Dart turboprops
Performance: cruising speed 300 mph (483 km/h); range with maximum payload 1,230 miles (1979 km); range with maximum fuel 1,950 miles (3138 km)
Weights: operating empty 30,275 lb (13733 kg); maximum take-off 57,000 lb (25855 kg)
Dimensions: span 105 ft 4 in (32.11 m); length 81 ft 6 in (24.84 m); height 28 ft 2 in (8.59 m); wing area 920 sq ft (85.47 m²)
Operators include: Aerolineas Colonia, Air Algérie, Aspen Airways, Avensa, Commuter Airlines, Evergreen International Airlines, Frontier Airlines, Gateway Aviation, Great Western Airlines, Midwest Air Express, Republic Airlines, SMB Stage Lines, Summit Airlines, Texas International Airlines, US Air, Viking International Air Freight, Worldways Airlines, Wright Air Lines, and Zantop International Airlines

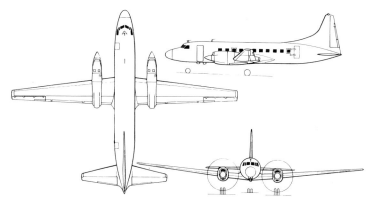

Convair CV-580

The postwar Convair CV-240/-340/-440 proved successful in their own right, but also formed the structural basis for an effective turboprop series, here epitomised by one of the 10 CV-580s of Aspen Airways.

Convair CV-880/-990

History and Notes

Having regard to overall production figures of civil transports during the first decade after World War II, Convair's sales of the Convair 240/340/440 could not be regarded as insignificant. There was then every reason to suppose that the company would continue to build for, and retain, a proportion of the US market for aircraft within this category. The news that Boeing and Douglas were building new-generation turbojet-powered airliners came as a challenge to Convair, and the company set out immediately to gain its share of this market. The company's interpretation of the results of its market research led to a design that would carry fewer passengers than the competing Boeing 707 and Douglas DC-8, but which would have better high-speed performance.

In April 1956 Convair announced publicly its intention to build this new aircraft, simultaneously giving the news that Delta Air Lines and TWA had ordered respectively 10 and 30. Few aircraft can have had as many designations, with the name Convair Skylark, later Golden Arrow, Convair 600, and finally Convair 880 for the initial version, whose prototype flew for the first time on 27 January 1959. In general appearance the new aircraft was very similar to the Boeing 707, with a low-set monoplane wing that had an equivalent 35° of sweepback, swept conventional tail surfaces, and a tricycle type landing gear with four-wheel bogies on each main unit. The powerplant consisted of four 11,200-lb (5080-kg) thrust General Electric CJ805-3 turbojet engines, and these were also mounted similarly to those of the 707. Advanced features of the wing included a double-skinned leading-edge to provide an anti-icing hot-air duct, wing upper-surface spoilers, and double-slotted trailing-edge flaps. The fuselage, however, was more slender than that of the production 707, limiting seating to a five-abreast layout that made provision for 88-110 passengers.

This original version of the Convair 880, known by the company as the Model 22, was intended for domestic

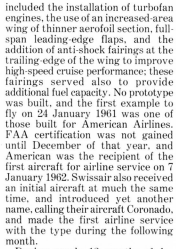

Convair CV-990A of Spantax Transportes Aereos (Spain).

use. Certification was gained on 1 May 1960, and Delta inaugurated its first service with the type exactly two weeks later. Despite a high cruising speed and range of close on 3,000 miles (4828 km) with full payload, its limited passenger capacity by comparison with the competing Boeing and Douglas jet-powered airliners made it a far less attractive proposition to potential operators, and by the time production ended only 48 had been built. Even with the introduction of the Model 31, with increased fuel capacity and several other improvements for intercontinental services, restricted seating capacity meant the Convair jet airliner family still had little appeal to airline operators. Designated Convair 880-M, only 17 of this version were built before production was terminated.

Even before the Convair 880 prototype was flown for the first time, the company had intended to build an increased-capacity higher-performance version, and this was known as the Model 30. It was perhaps unfortunate for Convair that an early order for this version from American Airlines signalled a go-ahead for its production. Had there been more time in which to judge customer reaction to the 880, it is possible that a major redesign of the fuselage might have received consideration. Instead, the Model 30 was given a fuselage 'stretch' of 9 ft 10½ in (3.01 m) to provide increased capacity, but retained a fuselage width that restricted the layout to the same five-abreast seating.

Other improvements incorporated in the design of this aircraft, which duly became designated Convair 990,

Convair 990 Coronado

included the installation of turbofan engines, the use of an increased-area wing of thinner aerofoil section, full-span leading-edge flaps, and the addition of anti-shock fairings at the trailing-edge of the wing to improve high-speed cruise performance; these fairings served also to provide additional fuel capacity. No prototype was built, and the first example to fly on 24 January 1961 was one of those built for American Airlines. FAA certification was not gained until December of that year, and American was the recipient of the first aircraft for airline service on 7 January 1962. Swissair also received an initial aircraft at much the same time, and introduced yet another name, calling their aircraft Coronado, and made the first airline service with the type during the following month.

During nearly 12 months of development flying which preceeded

certification, it was discovered that there were several aerodynamic shortcomings which eroded the planned performance of the 990. Research and development to overcome this was proceeding during the original certification flight programme, and the result of these investigations, as well as early operating experience, led to a number of aerodynamic improvements. These included a reduction in length of the outboard engine pylons, better streamlining of all engine pylons, and the introduction of full-span Krueger flaps to the undersurface of the wing leading-edge. These changes were carried out retrospectively to all 37 990s that were produced, modified aircraft receiving the designation Convair 990A.

Convair's 880/990 programme, together with its extended research and development exercise, and the modifications necessary for this aircraft to meet its performance guarantees, proved an extremely costly venture for the company. Since that time, the aviation divisions of General Dynamics Corporation have confined their activities within the field of military aviation. The details below relate to the Convair 990A.

Specification

Type: medium-range transport
Powerplant: four 16,050-lb (7280-kg) thrust General Electric CJ805-23B turbofans
Performance: maximum level speed 615 mph (990 km/h) at 20,000 ft (6100 m); cruising speed 556 mph (895 km/h) at 35,000 ft (10670 m); service ceiling 41,000 ft (12495 m); range with maximum payload 3,800 miles (6116 km); range with maximum fuel 5,400 miles (8690 km)
Weights: operating empty 120,900 lb (54839 kg); maximum take-off 253,000 lb (114759 kg)
Dimensions: span 120 ft 0 in (36.58 m); length 139 ft 2½ in (42.43 m); height 39 ft 6 in (12.04 m); wing area 2,250 sq ft (209.03 m²)
Operators include: Spantax

The CV-990 was one of the reasons for Convair's financial troubles. The 12 surviving Coronados are now operated by Spantax Transportes Aereos, of Madrid.

Curtiss C-46

History and Notes

Some evidence of the competence of the Douglas DC-3 is provided by the activities of aircraft manufacturers around the world, who have over a period of decades spared no efforts to design and develop an aircraft that would compete against and, at a later date, replace it. The fact that something like 300 of these remarkable aeroplanes remain in service in 1980, 45 years after the first flight of the prototype, suggests that competing manufacturers were not entirely successful.

One of the competitors was the Curtiss-Wright CW-20, design studies for which were originated in 1935, after the company had decided it was necessary to build an aircraft that would be superior to the Boeing Model 247 and Douglas DC-2/DC-3. As first flown on 26 March 1940, the CW-20 had a low-set monoplane wing, a double-lobe or 'double-bubble' fuselage, twin endplate fins and rudders, a retractable tailwheel type landing gear, and two 1,700-hp (1268-kW) Wright R-2600 Twin Cyclone piston engines, one mounted in a nacelle at the leading-edge of each wing. It was intended for operation by a crew of four, and there was to be accommodation for 36 passengers.

Early testing showed the desirability of introducing some changes in the design, the most significant being deletion of the twin tail and its replacement by a conventional tail unit with single fin and rudder. In this revised form the aircraft was known as the CW-20A, and but for the fact that World War II had already started, would almost certainly have gone into production as a civil airliner. Instead, the aircraft entered service with the USAAF under the designation C-46, later acquiring the name Commando. The first production example was completed in May 1942, and initial deliveries to the US Army began in July. There had been a change of powerplant to two 2,000-hp (1491-kW) R-2800-43 engines; there was

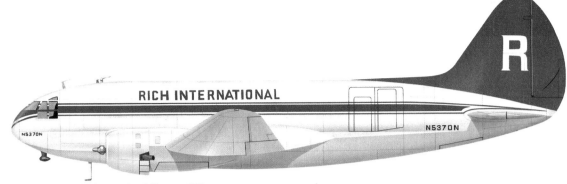

Curtiss C-46 of Rich International Airways, USA.

accommodation for 50 troops or, alternatively, 10,000 lb (4536 kg) of cargo; and there was little external difference except for the removal of most of the 20 windows of the original airline version. Production of C-46s, and R5Cs for the US Navy, totalled 3,182.

Large numbers of these aircraft were offered for sale to civil operators postwar, many of them being refurbished with civil interiors if intended for passenger carrying services. Some of these conversions were quite extensive, and included the provision of passenger doors with built-in airstairs and reinstatement of all cabin windows, but those intended purely as freight carriers were little changed from the military C-46. At the peak of their civil deployment, in the early 1960s, rather more than 90 operators had examples of these aircraft in their fleets.

Among these companies was Riddle Airlines of Miami, Florida, which evolved its own conversion programme for a fleet of 32 aircraft that, when modified, had the designation C-46R. The details below apply to this version.

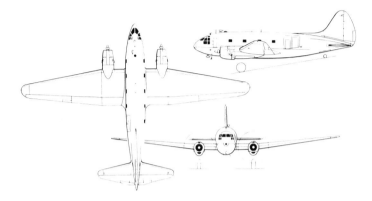

Curtiss C-46 Commando

Specification

Type: medium-range passenger/cargo transport
Powerplant: two 2,100-hp (1566-kW) Pratt & Whitney R-2800 C or CA series radial piston engines
Performance: maximum level speed 270 mph (435 km/h); maximum cruising speed 235 mph (378 km/h) at 9,000 ft (2745 m); service ceiling 22,000 ft (6705 m); range with maximum fuel 1,800 miles (2897 km)
Weights: empty 29,300 lb (13290 kg); maximum take-off 50,000 lb (22680 kg)
Dimensions: span 108 ft 0 in (32.92 m); length 76 ft 4 in (23.27 m); height 21 ft 9 in (6.63 m); wing area 1,358 sq ft (126.16 m²)
Operators include: Aeronorte, Aeropesca Colombia, Aerosucre, Aerovias Las Minas, Air Haiti, Astro Air Transport, Caribbean Air Services, Carib West Airways, Charter Airlines, LACSA, Lambair, LANICA, Latin Cargo, Lineas Areas La Urraca, North East Bolivian Airways, North Coast Air Services, Oasis Air Transport, Reeve Aleutian Airways, Rich International Airways, SAVA, SAVCO, Servicios Aereos Bolivianos, TABA, Trans Continental Airlines, Transportes Aereos San Martin

An aircraft that might have been a commercial rival for the DC-3, the Curtiss CW-20 was caught by World War II and built only as the C-46 military transport. Five of the 80 surviving in 1980 were operated by Air Haiti.

Dassault Mercure

History and Notes
The early sales success of its Mystère/Falcon 20 series led Dassault to investigate the market prospects for a new short-range airliner in very much the same class as the Boeing 737. Subsequent sales of this latter aircraft confirm the accuracy of the basic market research, but Dassault was unsuccessful in attracting more than one customer for its new venture, which became known as the Mercure.

Generally similar in size and external configuration to the Boeing 737, Dassault's new aircraft was a low-wing monoplane design, the wing swept 25° and incorporating leading-edge slots and slats. Three upper-surface spoilers and two airbrakes were included on each wing, the spoilers being used both for lateral control in conjunction with the ailerons, and as lift dumpers. Trailing-edge flaps were of the triple-slotted type. The conventional circular-section pressurised fuselage was given a maximum internal width 2 in (0.05 m) greater than that of the Boeing 737. This provided accommodation for 120-150 passengers, or a maximum of 162 in a high-density arrangement. The tail unit was entirely conventional, and the tricycle type landing gear had twin wheels on each unit. Again like the 737, the Mercure had two Pratt & Whitney JT8D turbofans, these being of the -15 series which was one of the options available for the 737.

The cost of launching such a project was formidable, certainly beyond the resources of Dassault, but the company was fortunate enough to obtain from the French government loan support amounting to 56 per

Dassault Mercure of Air Inter, France.

cent of the estimated initial cost of 1,000 million francs (£75 million). Dassault put in 14 per cent of the total, the balance coming from risk-sharing partners comprising Aeritalia (building the fuselage tailcone and tail unit), CASA (two fuselage sections), SABCA (ailerons, air-brakes, flaps and spoilers), and Switzerland's Federal Aircraft Factory (air intakes and cowling panels). Canadair, in Montreal, was also to build some assemblies under subcontract.

The initial prototype Mercure (F-WTCC) flew for the first time on 28 May 1971, the last three letters of this specially chosen registration representing Transport Court-Courrier (short-range transport). This aircraft was powered by two Pratt & Whitney JT8D-11 engines, each of 15,000-lb (6804-kg) thrust, but the second prototype (F-WTMD), flown on 7 September 1972, had the more powerful JT8D-15s.

It had been the initial intention to give the go-ahead for manufacture after receipt of orders for 50 aircraft. Somewhat imprudently, however,

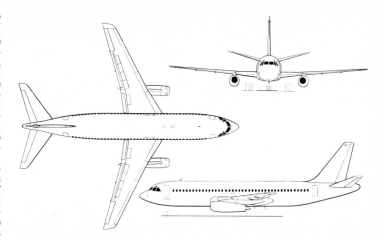

Dassault Mercure 100

production began after the receipt of an order for 10 aircraft from Air Inter, a French domestic airline, on 29 January 1972. This company, which received the first of its fleet on 16 May 1974, has remained the sole customer. The Mercures remain in

service in the 1980s, operating with an annual subsidy of some £850,000 from the French government to offset the extremely high cost of spares which resulted from production ending so rapidly.

Specification
Type: short-range transport
Powerplant: two 15,500-lb (7031-kg) thrust Pratt & Whitney JT8D-15 turbofans
Performance: maximum cruising speed 575 mph (925 km/h) at 20,000 ft (6100 m); economic cruising speed 533 mph (858 km/h) at 30,000 ft (9145 m); range with maximum payload 470 miles (756 km)
Weights: empty operating 70,107 lb (31800 kg); maximum take-off 124,561 lb (56500 kg)
Dimensions: span 100 ft 3 in (30.56 m); length 114 ft 3½ in (34.84 m); height 37 ft 3½ in (11.37 m); wing area 1248.65 sq ft (116.0 m²)
Operator: Air Inter

The Dassault Mercure was designed to compete with the Boeing 737 and McDonnell Douglas DC-9, but had neither the range nor the operating economy of the US twins.

Dassault Mystère/Falcon 20

History and Notes
In conjunction with Sud-Aviation (now part of Aérospatiale), Dassault initiated the design and development of a light twin-turbofan transport in the late 1950s. The new aircraft was intended for operation primarily in an executive transport role, but it was planned from the beginning that it would be convertible easily to fulfil a number of alternative duties. Manufacture of the prototype Mystère 20 began in January 1962, Dassault and Sud-Aviation sharing the construction, and the aircraft flew for the first time on 4 May 1963.

Of cantilever low-wing monoplane configuration, the Mystère 20 has a wing with 30° of sweepback, leading-edge slats, wing fences at approximately semi-span, airbrakes on the

wing upper surface, and single-slotted trailing-edge flaps. The fuselage is pressurised, the landing gear is of retractable tricycle type, and the tail unit has the tailplane mounted about half way up the fin to ensure that it is clear of the efflux of the rear-mounted turbofan engines. The prototype, however, was powered by two 3,300-lb (1497-kg) thrust Pratt & Whitney JT12A-8 turbojets. Powerplant of production aircraft consists of two General Electric CF700 turbofans, and the prototype was re-engined subsequently with these engines.

Accommodation is provided for a crew of two on the flight deck, and normal seating arrangements are for eight to 10 passengers, although a maximum of 14 can be carried in a

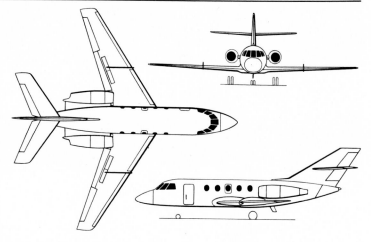

Dassault-Breguet Mystère/Falcon 20

Dassault Mystère Falcon 20

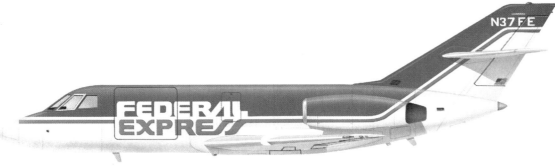

Dassault Falcon 20F Cargo of Federal Express, USA.

high-density layout. The cabin door, which incorporates built-in airstairs, is at the forward end on the port side. In addition to the normal passenger-carrying interior, a quick-change kit enables this aircraft to be converted to a cargo-carrying configuration with a total capacity of 235 cu ft (6.65 m³). Other easy conversions make it possible to utilise the Mystère 20 (generally known outside France as the Falcon 20) for roles which include airline crew training, the calibration of radio navigation aids, and high-altitude photographic survey.

The manufacture of production aircraft is shared between Aérospatiale and Dassault, the former carrying out construction of the fuselage and tail unit. Dassault builds the wings and is responsible for final assembly. The first production aircraft was flown on 1 January 1965, and the current basic production version in late 1980 has the designation Mystère 20 (Falcon 20) Series F. Series G aircraft for medium-range surveillance missions have been developed, the variant having, among other changes, more powerful Garrett-AiResearch turbofan engines. The introduction of these engines into the basic airframe, and the addition of a rear fuselage fuel tank, has resulted in the Series H aircraft which was completing its certification

programme during the second half of 1980. In this version the use of the more fuel efficient Garrett-AiResearch ATF 3-6-2C engines, each of 5,538-lb (2512-kg) thrust, plus the additional fuel capacity, gave the Series H some 40 per cent more range than the basic Series F.

Marketed by Dassault as the Mystère 20, the aircraft is sold in the USA as the Falcon 20 by the Falcon Jet Corporation, which was formed by Dassault-Breguet and Pan American World Airways. This latter organisation evolved a specialised cargo version of this aircraft under the name Falcon Cargo Jet, and the conversion can be incorporated retrospectively to any Mystère 20/Falcon 20. Primary changes include replacement of the standard cabin door by a cargo door measuring 6 ft 2 in by 4 ft 9 in (1.88 m by 1.45 m), and provision of a strengthened floor with suitable tie-down points.

Worldwide sales of this attractive aircraft were nearing 500 in 1980. The details below apply to the basic Series F.

Specification
Type: medium-range executive transport
Powerplant: two 4,500-lb (2041-kg) thrust General Electric CF700-2D-2 turbofans
Performance: maximum cruising speed 536 mph (863 km/h) at 25,000 ft (7620 m); economic cruising speed 466 mph (750 km/h) at 40,000 ft (12190 m); absolute ceiling 42,000 ft (12800 m); range with maximum fuel and 45-min reserves 2,080 miles (3347 km)

Weights: empty equipped 16,600 lb (7530 kg); maximum take-off 28,660 lb (13000 kg)
Dimensions: span 53 ft 5¾ in (16.30 m); length 56 ft 3 in (17.15 m); height 17 ft 5½ in (5.32 m); wing area 441.33 sq ft (41.00 m²)
Operators include: Air France, Air Taxi Company, Cimber Air A/S Denmark, Federal Express, Institut Géographique National, Japan Air Lines, and Korean Air Lines

The Mystère 20, marketed in North America as the Falcon 20, is the most successful civil aircraft yet produced by the Dassault-Breguet consortium. The type has been developed through a series of models with turbojet and then turbofan engines to increase operating efficiency while reducing noise emission.

Dassault Mystère/Falcon 50

History and Notes

The requirement for a business jet with transcontinental or transatlantic range led Dassault to study the Mystère/Falcon 20 twin-jet, to see what could be done to extend its range of around 2,000 miles (3218 km) to 4,000 miles (6437 km). The problem was solved by the introduction of a supercritical wing, and by using three engines of lower power, resulting in the Falcon 50 with three TFE731 turbofans each of 3,700-lb (1678-kg) thrust, compared with the Falcon 20's two CF700s each of 4,500-lb (2041-kg) thrust; many basic components from the Falcon 20 were used, and the same fuselage cross-section was retained.

The prototype Falcon 50 flew on 7 November 1976, followed by the second in February 1978, and the pre-production model in June 1978. French certification was achieved in February 1979 with the FAA following suit the next month. Aircraft no. 4, flown in March 1979, became the demonstrator with the US distributor, Falcon Jet, who had placed 70 of the 100 orders received by the end of 1979. Six months later the order book had reached 123, of which 13 had been delivered, the first going to a former Falcon 20 owner in July 1979. The second went to GLAM, the French air force unit which provides transport for the President and other high-ranking officials. A Falcon 50 was supplied to the King of Morocco. Three Falcon 50s a month were produced in 1980; by the end of the year, almost 150 had been ordered and 26 delivered.

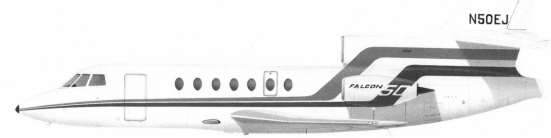

Dassault Mystère/Falcon 50

Specification

Type: long-range executive jet
Powerplant: three 3,700-lb (1678-kg) thrust Garrett TFE731-3 turbofans
Performance: maximum cruising 540 mph (870 km/h); service ceiling 45,275 ft (13800 m); range 4,038 miles (6500 km) at Mach 0.75 with 8 passengers
Weights: empty 19,842 lb (9000 kg); maximum take-off 38,801 lb (17600 kg)
Dimensions: span 61 ft 10½ in (18.86 m); length 60 ft 0½ in (18.30 m); height 22 ft 7½ in (6.90 m); wing area 504.1 sq ft (46.83 m²)

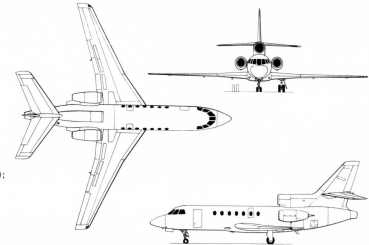

The Dassault-Breguet Mystère/Falcon 50 is an intercontinental-range version of the Mystère/Falcon 20 with wings of super-critical section, extra fuel tankage and three instead of two turbofans.

Dassault-Breguet Mystère/Falcon 50

De Havilland D.H. 104 Dove/Riley Turbo Executive 400/Carstedt Jet Liner 600 Series

History and Notes

To provide a postwar replacement for the D.H.89 Dragon Rapide biplane transport, which had also seen extensive service with the Royal Air Force and Royal Navy as the Dominie, the de Havilland design team under R.E.Bishop's leadership evolved a new low-wing monoplane which, with the exception of fabric-covered elevators and rudder, was of all-metal construction. The powerplant consisted of two de Havilland Gipsy Queen engines and their constant-speed fully-feathering and reversible-pitch propellers were to make the Dove, as the D.H.104 design was named, the first British transport aircraft to use reversible-pitch propellers for braking assistance. Standard accommodation as a transport was for 8 to 11 passengers.

First flown on 25 September 1945, the prototype soon demonstrated that there was little wrong with the basic design. Apart from the addition of a dorsal fin at an early stage of development, to improve stability with one engine out, and much later the introduction of a redesigned elevator, and a domed roof to give a little more headroom on the flight deck, production aircraft were generally similar to the original prototype.

The production Dove variants resulted from differing Gipsy Queen powerplants, these including the 330-hp (246-kW) 70 and 70-3 powering the prototype and Dove 1/2 respectively; 340-hp (254-kW) 70-4 in the Dove 1B/2B; 380-hp (283-kW) 70 Mk 2 in the Dove 5/6, and 400-hp (298-kW) 70 Mk 3 in the Dove 7/8. A number of Dove conversions carried out subsequently by Riley Aircraft in the USA as the Riley Turbo Executive 400 introduced 400-hp (298-kW) Avco Lycoming IO-720-A1A flat-eight horizontally-opposed engines. A more ambitious conversion by Carstedt Inc. at Long Beach, California, introduced two 605-ehp (451-ekW) Garrett AiResearch TPE 331 turboprop engines, and a lengthened fuselage to accommodate 18 commuter passengers. Named Jet Liner 600, the type was supplied primarily to Apache Airlines of Pheonix, Arizona.

Like the Rapide, which it superseded and supplemented (replaced is an unsuitable word, for Rapides just went on flying), the Dove proved to be reliable and popular, and well over 500 were built before production ended in 1968. Of these just over 100 were supplied under the name Devon to many air forces, including the RAF, and a small number went to the Royal Navy as Sea Devons. In addition to the light transport role for which they were intended, many

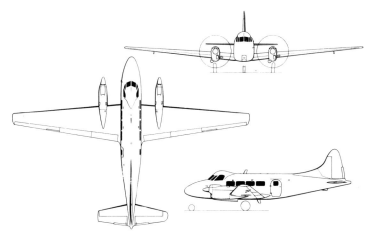

de Havilland D.H.104 Dove Series 8

have served as business, executive, and VIP aircraft. The following details apply to the Dove 7 and 8.

Specification
Type: light transport
Powerplant: two 400-hp (298-kW) de Havilland Gipsy Queen 70 Mk 3 inline piston engines
Performance: maximum speed 235 mph (378 km/h); cruising speed 162 mph (261 km/h); service ceiling 21,700 ft (6615 m); range 1,175 miles (1891 km)
Weights: empty 6,580 lb (2985 kg); maximum take-off 8,950 lb (4060 kg)
Dimensions: span 57 ft 0 in (17.37 m); length 39 ft 4 in (11.99 m); height 13 ft 4 in (4.06 m); wing area 335 sq ft (31.12 m²)
Operators include: many Doves remain in service in 1980 with military and civil operators, but none with scheduled airlines

---

De Havilland D.H.114 Heron/Riley Turbo Skyliner/Saunders ST-27 Series

History and Notes

The success of the Dove suggested to de Havilland that an enlarged version, with four engines, might prove an equally marketable replacement for the prewar 10 to 16-passenger D.H.86B. It was not until 10 May 1950, however, that the prototype of the resulting D.H.114 flew for the first time, incorporating many Dove assemblies and components. Named Heron, the initial production aircraft had non-retractable tricycle type landing gear, in order to reduce maintenance to a minimum, but the introduction of retractable gear on the Heron 2 resulted in greater speed and fuel economy and no further Heron 1s were built.

Of similar configuration to the Dove, except for dihedral on the tailplane, and all control surfaces being fabric-covered, the Heron had a longer fuselage which could accommodate 14 to 17 passengers. However, many of these aircraft saw service as luxury transports with a variety of special interiors, including those of The Queen's Flight based at RAF Benson, and other VIP aircraft included that of Saudi Arabia's Prince Talal al Saud, and the special military versions used by King Feisal of Iraq and by King Hussein of Jordan. Standard powerplant of both Heron 1 and 2 aircraft consisted of four de Havilland Gipsy Queen 30 Mk 2 engines but, as with the Dove, other manufacturers produced conversions with different powerplants. Riley Aircraft in the USA developed a version known as the Turbo Skyliner, with 290-hp (216-kW) Avco Lycoming engines and Rajay turbochargers, but Saunders Aircraft Corporation in Canada introduced more extensive modifications in a version known as the Saunders ST-27. The changes included a fuselage lengthened by 8

Most of the de Havilland D.H.114 Heron feeder-liners surviving in the USA are Series 2 aircraft with retractable landing gear, modified by the Riley Turbostream Corporation into Turbo Skyliners with Avco Lycoming engines.

de Havilland Heron/Riley Turbo Skyliner.

ft 6 in (2.59 m) to provide accommodation for up to 23 commuter passengers and a stewardess, the provision of a redesigned main wing spar to cater for the higher gross weight, and the installation of two 750-shp (559-kW) United Aircraft of Canada (Pratt & Whitney) PT6A-34 turboprop engines. An improved ST-28 was planned, but the company failed before production began.

A total of 148 Heron 1s and 2s (51 and 97 respectively) were built by de Havilland before production ended. Many went to air forces, five Sea Herons served with the Royal Navy, and airlines at different levels and private companies still operate a number of these reliable aircraft.

Specification
Type: light transport
Powerplant: four 250-hp (186-kW) de Havilland Gipsy Queen 30 Mk 2 inline piston engines
Performance (Mks 1 and 2): cruising speed 160 mph (257 km/h); service ceiling 18,500 ft (5640 m); range 805 miles (1296 km)
Weights: empty 7,960 lb (3611 kg); maximum take-off 13,000 lb (5897 kg)
Dimensions: span 71 ft 6 in (21.79 m); length 48 ft 6 in (14.78 m); height 15 ft 7 in (4.75 m); wing area 499 sq ft (46.36 m²)
Operators include: Air Atonabee (ST-27s), Affretair, Helitours, and Nationwide Air; many are still in service with air forces and private companies

De Havilland Canada DHC-2 Beaver

History and Notes

Design of the de Havilland Canada DHC-2 Beaver light transport was started in Toronto during late 1946. The concept behind this first of de Havilland Canada's line of effective STOL transports was influenced by the specific requirements of the Ontario Department of Lands and Forests, which suited the resulting DHC-2 Beaver also to the exacting requirements of 'bush' pilots in North America and elsewhere for an effective, rugged and reliable STOL utility transport.

The prototype was flown for the first time on 16 August 1947 with Russ Bannock at the controls, and the type was certificated in Canada during March 1948. Large-scale production plans had already been laid, and the Beaver Mk I was soon in service, powered by the 450-hp (336-kW) Pratt & Whitney R-985 radial. Of the 1,657 Beaver Mk Is built, no fewer than 968 were for the US Army and 46 for the British Army. There followed a single Beaver Mk II with the Alvis Leonides radial and, in 1964, a few 10-passenger Turbo-Beaver Mk IIIs powered by the 578-ehp (431-ekW) United Aircraft of Canada Ltd (later Pratt & Whitney Aircraft of Canada) PT6A-6 or -20 turboprop. Beaver production ended in the mid-1960s as de Havilland Canada concentrated on the development of more ambitious projects and products.

At the height of its career, the Beaver was to be found in some 50 countries, where it won universal

The de Havilland Canada DHC-2 Beaver is still in effective service with operators such as Tradewinds Aviation. The type is prized for its rugged reliability and great versatility, thanks to the possibility of wheel, ski or float landing gear.

acclaim for its performance, ground stability conferred by the wide-track tailwheel type landing gear, and versatility. Basic accommodation was provided for a pilot and seven passengers, the latter being replaceable by up to 1,500 lb (680 kg) of freight on the strengthened cabin floor with tie-down points. Great flexibility was bestowed on the Beaver by its ability to operate on wheel, ski, float or amphibious float landing gears.

Specification
Type: light utility transport
Powerplant: one 450-hp (336-kW) Pratt & Whitney R-985 Wasp Junior radial piston engine
Performance: maximum speed at 5,000 ft (1520 m) 163 mph (262 km/h); cruising speed at 5,000 ft (1520 m) 143 mph (230 km/h); initial climb rate 1,020 ft (311 m) per minute; service ceiling 18,000 ft (5485 m); cruising range on internal fuel 455 miles (732 km);

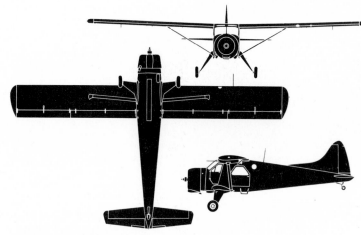

de Havilland Canada DHC-2 Beaver

maximum range 733 miles (1180 km)
Weights: empty 2,850 lb (1293 kg); maximum take-off 5,100 lb (2313 kg)

Dimensions: span 48 ft 0 in (14.63 m); length 30 ft 3 in (9.22 m); height 9 ft 0 in (2.74 m); wing area 250 sq ft (23.22 m²)

De Havilland Canada DHC-3 Otter

History and Notes

Its success with the DHC-2 Beaver persuaded de Havilland Canada in the late 1940s that there was room in the STOL utility market for a larger version of the Beaver, with cabin space for some 14 passengers or a freight load of up to 2,240 lb (1016 kg). The company therefore developed the DHC-3 Otter, which was essentially a scaled-up Beaver with an all-metal airframe and a 600-hp (448-kW) Pratt & Whitney R-1340 Twin Wasp radial. The lineage of the Otter is confirmed by the fact that it was originally known as the King Beaver. The choice of a single engine for an aircraft designed to operate in Canada's harsh climate and sparsely populated hinterland regions may seem lacking in forethought, but successful operations by the Beaver and other single-engined types had confirmed that the well proven radials of Pratt & Whitney design were more than adequate for the task: they possessed good power-to-weight ratios and, more importantly, were extremely reliable.

Notable for its parallel-chord wing with double-slotted flaps for good STOL performance, the Otter was an attractive high-wing monoplane with a single bracing strut on each side. The prototype first flew on 12 December 1951, and first deliveries were made in 1952. When production ceased in 1968, some 460 had been built, including 66 for the Royal Canadian Air Force and 227 for the US armed forces (223 U-1As for the US Army and four UC-1s [changed

to U-1Bs in 1962] for the US Navy). When released by military operators, many Otters found their way onto the civil market, where again the type found ready acceptance for its versatility. Like the Beaver, the Otter can operate on wheel, ski, float or amphibious float landing gears.

Specification
Type: STOL utility transport
Powerplant: one 600-hp (448-kW) Pratt & Whitney R-1340-S1H1-G Twin Wasp radial piston engine
Performance (landplane at maximum take-off weight, at sea level): maximum speed 153 mph (246 km/h); maximum cruising speed 132 mph (212 km/h); economical cruising speed 121 mph (195 km/h); initial climb rate 735 ft (224 m) per minute; service ceiling 18,000 ft (5485 m); range with 2,100-lb (953-kg) payload and reserves 875 miles (1410 km)
Weights (landplane): empty (4,431 lb (2010 kg); maximum take-off 8,000 lb (3629 kg)
Dimensions (landplane): span 58 ft 0 in (17.69 m); length 41 ft 10 in (12.80 m); height 12 ft 7 in (3.83 m); wing area 375 sq ft (34.83 m²)

One of the great aircraft of all time, the de Havilland Canada DHC-3 Otter first flew in 1951 and has since proved itself under all circumstances. Despite its single engine it is highly reliable, and can carry up to 14 passengers or 2,240 lb (1016 kg) of freight from difficult airstrips, thanks to its STOL performance. Large numbers are still in worldwide service.

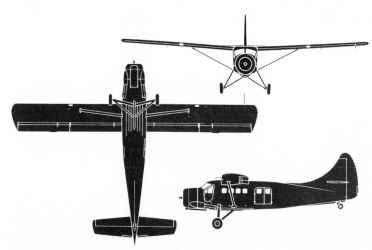

de Havilland Canada DHC-3 Otter

De Havilland Canada DHC-5E Transporter

History and Notes

On 9 April 1964, de Havilland Aircraft of Canada flew the prototype of a twin-turboprop STOL utility transport which was to acquire the designation DHC-5 and the name Buffalo. Like the beast after which it was named, the DHC-5 has proved to be rugged and enduring, although built in comparatively small numbers. It continued in production in 1981, with the current designation DHC-5D, and these aircraft serve with some 16 air forces.

A demonstration DHC-5E Transporter for civil passenger/cargo transport operations was exhibited at the Paris Air Show in 1979, and was scheduled for certification during 1981. Powered by General Electric CT64-820-4 turboprop engines, this will provide accommodation for 48 passengers in a standard utility layout, but will be available also with quick-change passenger/cargo, and VIP/executive interiors.

Specification

Type: twin-turboprop utility transport
Powerplant: two 3,133-shp (2336-kW) General Electric CT64-820-4 turboprops
Performance: maximum cruising speed 287 mph (462 km/h) at 10,000 ft (3050 m); economic cruising speed 210 mph (338 km/h) at 10,000 ft (3050 m); service ceiling 31,000 ft (9450 m); range

with maximum payload 115 miles (185 km); range with maximum fuel 1,980 miles (3187 km)
Weights: empty operating 25,200 lb (11431 kg); maximum take-off 41,000 lb (18597 kg)
Dimensions: span 96 ft 0 in (29.26 m); length 79 ft 0 in (24.08 m); height 28 ft 8 in (8.74 m); wing area 945 sq ft (87.79 m²)

The de Havilland Canada Transporter is a civil derivative of the well-proven DHC-5D Buffalo military freighter, and is admirably suited for the resources support market, being able to move up to 48 passengers in dire climatic regions, ranging from arctic to tropical.

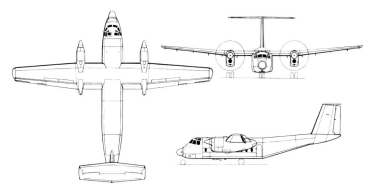

de Havilland Canada DHC-5D Buffalo

De Havilland Canada DHC-6 Twin Otter

History and Notes

Established in 1928 as a subsidiary of the British de Havilland Aircraft Company, The de Havilland Aircraft of Canada Ltd has, in more recent years, specialised in the design and development of short take-off and landing (STOL) utility and light transport aircraft. In 1964 this company announced that it was to begin development of a twin-turbo-prop high-wing monoplane with STOL capability and which would provide accommodation for 13 to 18 passengers. Identified as the DHC-6 Twin Otter, the first of an initial batch of five made its maiden flight on 20 May 1965.

Powerplant of the first three aircraft consisted of two Pratt & Whitney Aircraft of Canada PT6A-6 engines, each developing 579 ehp (432 ekW). However, the fourth and subsequent examples of the first production version, which became known as the Twin Otter Series 100, had similarly powered PT6A-20 engines. Design of this aircraft is quite conventional, the wings incorporating double-slotted trailing-edge flaps, and ailerons which can be drooped simultaneously with use of the flaps to enhance STOL characteristics. The landing gear is of the fixed tricycle type, and float or ski installations are optional to provide go-anywhere capability.

Intended primarily for service with commuter or third-level airlines, Twin Otters have seen fairly wide use with air forces and government agencies. They have also been put to a variety of other uses, including ambulance, cargo, maritime surveillance and survey duties.

The first Series 100 aircraft entered service with the Ontario Department of Lands and Forests in 1966, and since that time there has been a total of four production versions. Each successive model has improved the breed, and these comprise the Series 200, 300S, and the current production

de Havilland Canada DHC-6 Twin Otter of NorOntair, Canada.

Series 300. A total of 115 Series 100 aircraft were built, the Series 200 which followed differing by having greater baggage capacity. This was achieved by extending the rear baggage compartment further into the rear fuselage, and also by lengthening the fuselage nose, the resulting aircraft being duly certificated for operation at a higher gross weight. Production of Series 200 aircraft also totalled 115.

Construction of Series 300 aircraft began with the 231st aircraft off the line, this variant introducing the more powerful PT6A-27 engines which made possible an increase of almost 1,000 lb (454 kg) in maximum take-off weight. Well over 500 Series 300 aircraft had been sold by mid-1980, with production continuing. Six examples of a special version, identified as the Twin Otter Series 300S, were developed for use on a special experimental service between STOL airports in Montreal and Ottawa. Modifications to make these aircraft suitable for this exercise included the installation of an anti-skid braking system, emergency as well as high-capacity brakes, and wing spoilers, plus improvements to the electrical, fire protection and

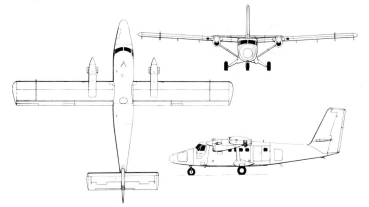

de Havilland Canada DHC-6 Twin Otter Series 300

hydraulic systems, and accommodation limited to 11 passengers in standard airline seats.

Current production aircraft retain the PT6A-27 engines, but have as standard interior a 20-seat commuter layout. All floatplane versions, irrespective of series, retain the shorter fuselage nose of the original Twin Otter Series 100, and other modifications associated with the float installation include wing fences and

small auxiliary fins.

To widen still further the scope of this aircraft, two items of specialised equipment have been developed. They consist of a ventral pod able to carry up to 600 lb (272 kg) of freight, and an expendable fabric membrane tank with a capacity of 400 Imperial gallons (1818 litres), which can be used for water-bombing fire-fighting operations. The following details apply to the Series 300.

De Havilland Canada DHC-6 Twin Otter

Specification

Type: utility STOL transport
Powerplant: two 652-ehp (486-ekW) Pratt & Whitney Aircraft of Canada PT6A-27 turboprops
Performance: maximum cruising speed 210 mph (338 km/h) at 10,000 ft (3050 m); service ceiling 26,700 ft (8140 m); range with 2,500-lb (1134-kg) payload 806 miles (1297 km); range with maximum payload 115 miles (185 km)
Weights: operating empty 7,415 lb (3363 kg); maximum take-off 12,500 lb (5670 kg)
Dimensions: wing span 65 ft 0 in (19.81 m); length, seaplane 49 ft 6 in (15.09 m), landplane 51 ft 9 in (15.77 m); height, seaplane 19 ft 10 in (6.05 m), landplane 19 ft 6 in (5.94 m); wing area 420 sq ft (39.02 m²)
Operators include: Air Alpes, Air Botswana, Air Burundi, Air Djibouti, Air Illinois, Air Madagascar, Air Mali, Air Mauritius, Air New England, Air North, Air Polynesie, Air Senegal, Air Tanzania, Austin Airways, Bradley Air Services, Brymon Airways, Burma Airways, CAAC, Command Airways, DLT, Eagle Air, Emirates Air Service, Ethiopian Airlines, Frontier Airlines, Golden Gate Airlines, Gronlandsfly A/S, Guyana Airways Corporation, Kenn Borek Air, Lesotho Airways, Lina Congo, Linea Aeropostal Venezolana, Lineas Aereas de Estado, Loganair, PT Merpati Nusantara Airlines, Metro Airlines, North Canada Air, Pilgrim Airlines, Rio Airways, Royal Nepal Airlines, Southwest Air Lines, Surinam Airways-SLM, TAME, TAP-Air Portugal, Time Air, Trans-Australia Airlines, Wideroe's Flyveselskap, and Windward Islands Airways International

The de Havilland Canada DHC-6 Twin Otter, a fuel-economical third-level airliner, has found renewed favour in the 1980s. The aircraft is seen here in the livery of TAP-Air Portugal, which operates two Twin Otters.

DHC-6 Twin Otter cutaway drawing key

1 Lightning protection rod — not used when weather radar is fitted
2 Weather radar (customer option)
3 Baggage compartment — FWD
4 FWD baggage compartment door
5 Avionics equipment
6 Instrument panel — pilot & co-pilot
7 Control columns — pilot & co-pilot
8 Engine power & propeller levers
9 Door to passenger cabin
10 Pulleys & cables — elevator & rudder tabs
11 Engine & propeller control cables
12 Airflow duct
13 Oil cooler
14 Air intake deflector
15 Hartzell constant speed, reverse pitch, fully feathering propeller
16 Pratt & Whitney PT6A-27 free-turbine powerplant
17 Engine exhaust nozzles
18 Engine air inlet
19 Engine oil tank filler
20 ADF loop antenna (two places, customer option)
21 Engine & propeller control cables
22 Engine & propeller control pulleys
23 Aileron control quadrant
24 Flap/elevator trim inter-connect screw jack
25 Wing flap actuator & control quadrants
26 VHF antennæ (two places, customer option)
27 ADF sense antennæ (two places, customer option)
28 Wing/fuselage attachment — FWD
29 Wing/fuselage attachment — AFT
30 Cabin door — right

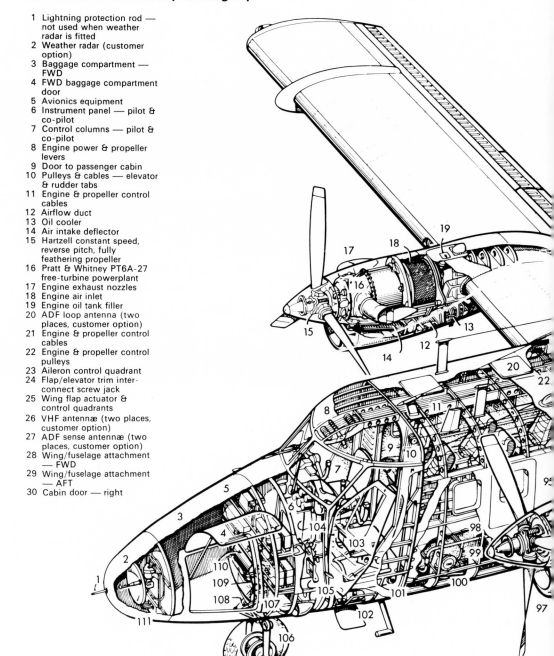

31 Door to aft baggage compartment
32 Baggage compartment — aft
33 Passenger oxygen cylinder — customer option
34 Pulleys & cables — elevator & rudder trim tabs
35 Aft baggage compartment extension
36 HF antenna — customer option
37 Rudder control pulleys
38 Elevator control quadrant
39 Elevator control rod
40 Elevator torque tube
41 VOR/ILS antenna (customer option)
42 Anti-collision light & lightning protection horn
43 Rudder
44 Rudder attachment point
45 Rudder trim tab
46 Rudder trim tab screw jack
47 Rudder trim cables
48 Rudder geared tab
49 Elevator/flap interconnect trim tab
50 Elevator trim tab
51 Elevator trim tab screw jack
52 Elevator attachment point
53 Elevator
54 Rudder lever
55 Rudder geared tab gearbox

de Havilland Canada DHC-6 Twin Otter

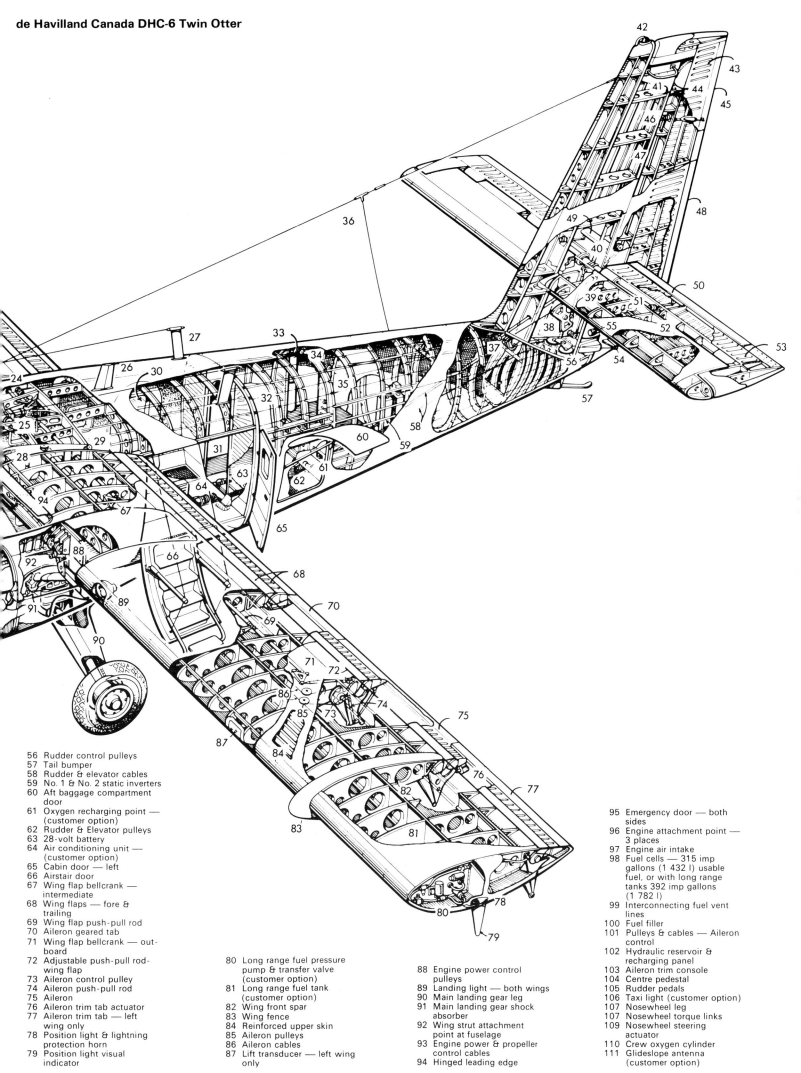

56 Rudder control pulleys
57 Tail bumper
58 Rudder & elevator cables
59 No. 1 & No. 2 static inverters
60 Aft baggage compartment door
61 Oxygen recharging point — (customer option)
62 Rudder & Elevator pulleys
63 28-volt battery
64 Air conditioning unit — (customer option)
65 Cabin door — left
66 Airstair door
67 Wing flap bellcrank — intermediate
68 Wing flaps — fore & trailing
69 Wing flap push-pull rod
70 Aileron geared tab
71 Wing flap bellcrank — outboard
72 Adjustable push-pull rod-wing flap
73 Aileron control pulley
74 Aileron push-pull rod
75 Aileron
76 Aileron trim tab actuator
77 Aileron trim tab — left wing only
78 Position light & lightning protection horn
79 Position light visual indicator

80 Long range fuel pressure pump & transfer valve (customer option)
81 Long range fuel tank (customer option)
82 Wing front spar
83 Wing fence
84 Reinforced upper skin
85 Aileron pulleys
86 Aileron cables
87 Lift transducer — left wing only

88 Engine power control pulleys
89 Landing light — both wings
90 Main landing gear leg
91 Main landing gear shock absorber
92 Wing strut attachment point at fuselage
93 Engine power & propeller control cables
94 Hinged leading edge

95 Emergency door — both sides
96 Engine attachment point — 3 places
97 Engine air intake
98 Fuel cells — 315 imp gallons (1 432 l) usable fuel, or with long range tanks 392 imp gallons (1 782 l)
99 Interconnecting fuel vent lines
100 Fuel filler
101 Pulleys & cables — Aileron control
102 Hydraulic reservoir & recharging panel
103 Aileron trim console
104 Centre pedestal
105 Rudder pedals
106 Taxi light (customer option)
107 Nosewheel leg
107 Nosewheel torque links
109 Nosewheel steering actuator
110 Crew oxygen cylinder
111 Glideslope antenna (customer option)

123

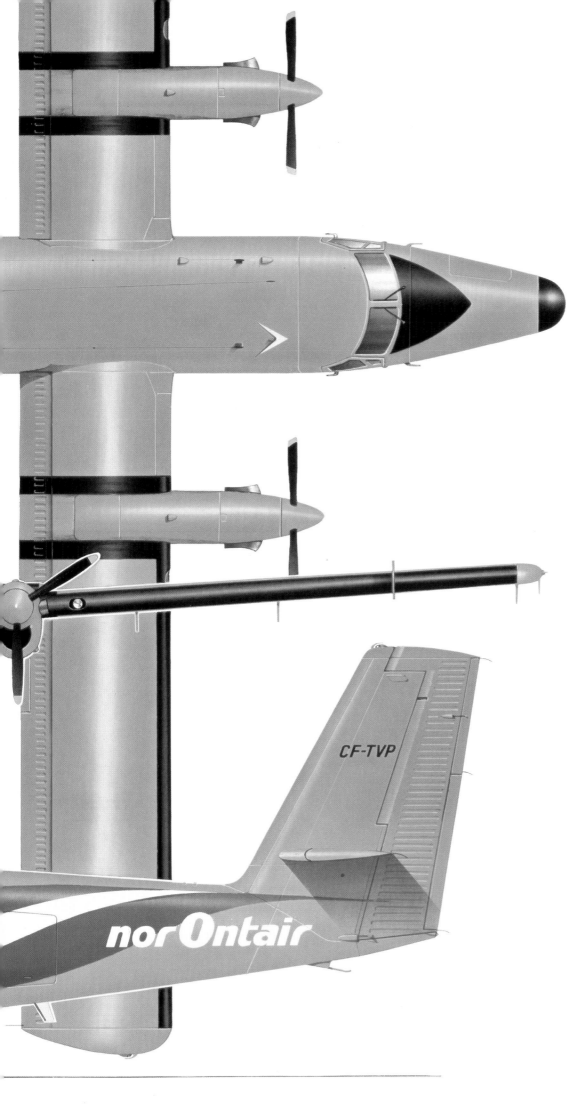

A de Havilland Canada DHC-6 Twin Otter of Norontair. A STOL commuter and utility transport, the Twin Otter entered production in 1966, the current Series 300 starting life in 1969. The type's versatility is enhanced by its ability to operate from wheel or float landing gear, and the Twin Otter's continued sales success is indicated by de Havilland Canada's decision to increase production to some six or seven aircraft per month during 1981. The main market for the Twin Otter has been American commuter airlines, but some European operators have adopted the type and negotiations were taking place during 1981 for licensed production in India by Hindustan Aeronautics Ltd.

De Havilland Canada DHC-7 Dash-7

History and Notes

The undoubted sales success of the Twin Otter led de Havilland Canada to initiate market research to estimate the interest in a large STOL aircraft which would incorporate the rugged reliability that had become associated with the products of this company. The intention was to develop a small airliner with advanced STOL capability, so that higher standards of comfort, comparable with much larger aircraft, would be available to those airlines which operate from runways about 3,000 ft (915 m) in length.

The necessary interest was forthcoming, and with backing from the Canadian government the construction of two pre-production DHC-7 aircraft began in late 1972, the first of these (C-GNBX-X) making its initial flight on 27 March 1975. Of high-wing monoplane configuration, the DHC-7 derives its essential STOL capability from wide-span double-slotted trailing-edge flaps that operate within the slipstream of the slow-turning propellers of the four wing-mounted turboprop engines. In addition, there are four spoilers in the upper surface of each wing. The inboard pair serve as spoilers or lift dumpers, the outboard pair as air spoilers which can also be operated differentially in conjunction with the ailerons to augment lateral control.

The fuselage is of fail-safe construction to permit pressurisation, and a very high T-tail places the tailplane and elevator well clear of the propeller slipstream. The landing gear is of the retractable tricycle type, with twin wheels on each unit, and the powerplant consists of four Pratt & Whitney Aircraft of Canada PT6A-50 turboprop engines. To reduce noise levels to a minimum, each drives a large-diameter (11 ft 3 in:3.42 m), slow-turning propeller.

Accommodation is provided for 50 passengers, with access to the main cabin via a single door, incorporating airstairs, at the rear of the cabin on the port side. There are provisions for optional mixed passenger/cargo or all-cargo operations, and a large freight door can be installed at the forward end of the cabin on the port side. In passenger service there is ample room within the cabin for a galley, toilet facilities, and one or two flight attendants. The flight crew of two is accommodated on a separate flight deck, and advanced avionics to enhance their efficiency includes an autopilot/flight director system which incorporates flight and air data computers, and weather radar.

The first operator to receive the Dash-7 was Rocky Mountain Airways, on 3 February 1978. All-cargo versions, designated DHC-7 Series 101, are also in service, and a maritime reconnaissance version known as the DHC-7R Ranger is under development. Production was at a rate of three aircraft per month in late 1981, and at which time sales were approaching the 100 mark.

Specification

Type: short/medium-range STOL transport
Powerplant: four 1,120-shp (835-kW) Pratt & Whitney Aircraft of Canada PT6A-50 turboprops
Performance: maximum cruising speed 266 mph (428 km/h) at 8,000 ft (2400 m); service ceiling 21,000 21,000 ft (6400 m); range with 50 passengers, IFR reserves 840 miles (1352 km)
Weights: operating empty 27,650 lb (12542 kg); maximum take-off

de Havilland Canada DHC-7 Dash-7 of Air Pacific.

44,000 lb (19958 kg)
Dimensions: span 93 ft 0 in (28.35 m); length 80 ft 7¾ in (24.58 m); height 26 ft 2 in (7.98 m); wing area 860 sq ft (79.89 m²)
Operators include: Air Niugini, Air Wisconsin, Alyemda-Democratic Yemen Airlines, Emirates Air Service, Golden Gate Airlines, Gronlandsfly A/S, Henson Aviation, Ransom Airlines, Rocky Mountain Airways, Spantax Transportes Aereos, Time Air, and Tyrolean Airways

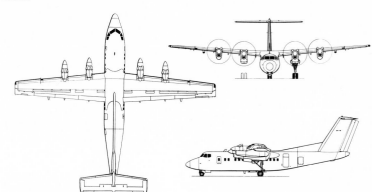

de Havilland Canada DHC-7 Dash-7

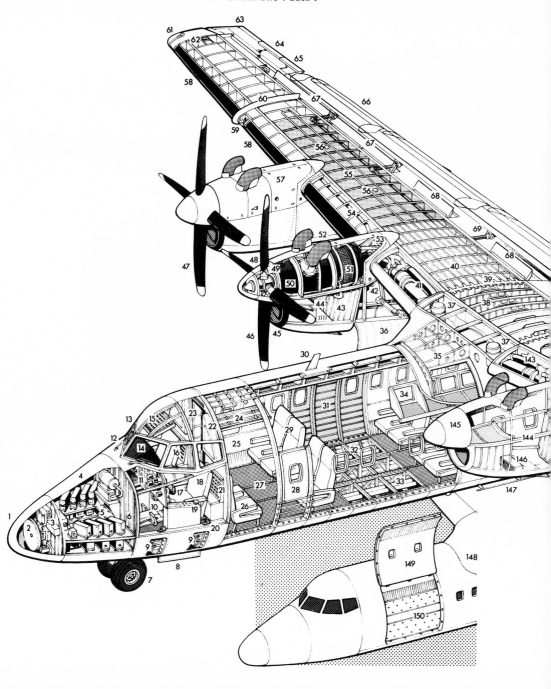

de Havilland Canada DHC-7 Dash-7

The de Havilland Canada DHC-7 Dash-7 has an excellent STOL performance coupled with airliner comfort, a combination that has considerable appeal for airlines such as Tyrolean Airways, which plans to have three.

de Havilland Canada DHC-7 Dash 7 cutaway drawing key

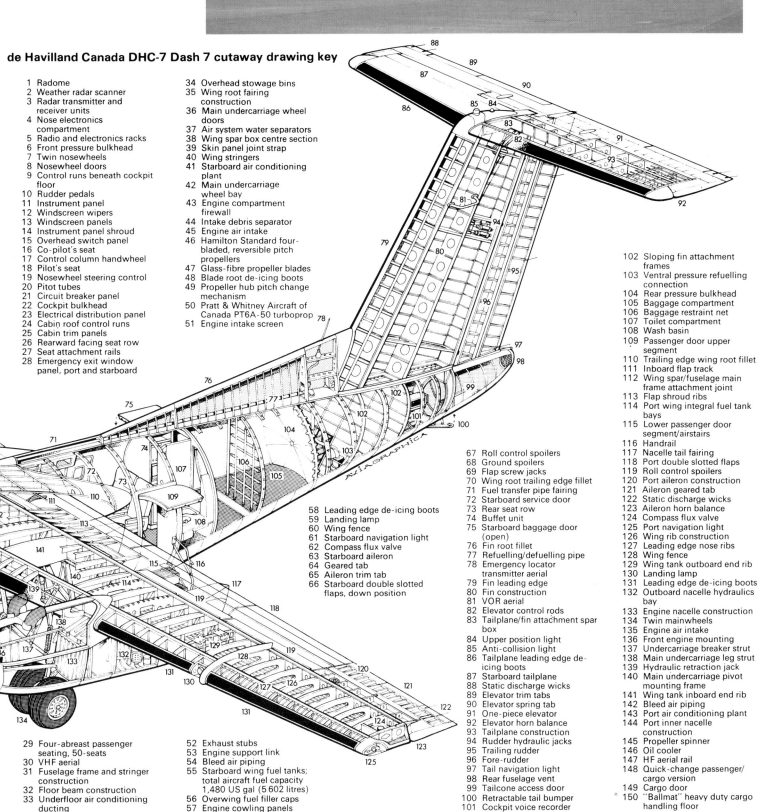

1 Radome
2 Weather radar scanner
3 Radar transmitter and receiver units
4 Nose electronics compartment
5 Radio and electronics racks
6 Front pressure bulkhead
7 Twin nosewheels
8 Nosewheel doors
9 Control runs beneath cockpit floor
10 Rudder pedals
11 Instrument panel
12 Windscreen wipers
13 Windscreen panels
14 Instrument panel shroud
15 Overhead switch panel
16 Co-pilot's seat
17 Control column handwheel
18 Pilot's seat
19 Nosewheel steering control
20 Pitot tubes
21 Circuit breaker panel
22 Cockpit bulkhead
23 Electrical distribution panel
24 Cabin roof control runs
25 Cabin trim panels
26 Rearward facing seat row
27 Seat attachment rails
28 Emergency exit window panel, port and starboard

34 Overhead stowage bins
35 Wing root fairing construction
36 Main undercarriage wheel doors
37 Air system water separators
38 Wing spar box centre section
39 Skin panel joint strap
40 Wing stringers
41 Starboard air conditioning plant
42 Main undercarriage wheel bay
43 Engine compartment firewall
44 Intake debris separator
45 Engine air intake
46 Hamilton Standard four-bladed, reversible pitch propellers
47 Glass-fibre propeller blades
48 Blade root de-icing boots
49 Propeller hub pitch change mechanism
50 Pratt & Whitney Aircraft of Canada PT6A-50 turboprop
51 Engine intake screen

29 Four-abreast passenger seating, 50-seats
30 VHF aerial
31 Fuselage frame and stringer construction
32 Floor beam construction
33 Underfloor air conditioning ducting

52 Exhaust stubs
53 Engine support link
54 Bleed air piping
55 Starboard wing fuel tanks; total aircraft fuel capacity 1,480 US gal (5 602 litres)
56 Overwing fuel filler caps
57 Engine cowling panels

58 Leading edge de-icing boots
59 Landing lamp
60 Wing fence
61 Starboard navigation light
62 Compass flux valve
63 Starboard aileron
64 Geared tab
65 Aileron trim tab
66 Starboard double slotted flaps, down position

67 Roll control spoilers
68 Ground spoilers
69 Flap screw jacks
70 Wing root trailing edge fillet
71 Fuel transfer pipe fairing
72 Starboard service door
73 Rear seat row
74 Buffet unit
75 Starboard baggage door (open)
76 Fin root fillet
77 Refuelling/defuelling pipe
78 Emergency locator transmitter aerial
79 Fin leading edge
80 Fin construction
81 VOR aerial
82 Elevator control rods
83 Tailplane/fin attachment spar box
84 Upper position light
85 Anti-collision light
86 Tailplane leading edge de-icing boots
87 Starboard tailplane
88 Static discharge wicks
89 Elevator trim tabs
90 Elevator spring tab
91 One-piece elevator
92 Elevator horn balance
93 Tailplane construction
94 Rudder hydraulic jacks
95 Trailing rudder
96 Fore-rudder
97 Tail navigation light
98 Rear fuselage vent
99 Tailcone access door
100 Retractable tail bumper
101 Cockpit voice recorder

102 Sloping fin attachment frames
103 Ventral pressure refuelling connection
104 Rear pressure bulkhead
105 Baggage compartment
106 Baggage restraint net
107 Toilet compartment
108 Wash basin
109 Passenger door upper segment
110 Trailing edge wing root fillet
111 Inboard flap track
112 Wing spar/fuselage main frame attachment joint
113 Flap shroud ribs
114 Port wing integral fuel tank bays
115 Lower passenger door segment/airstairs
116 Handrail
117 Nacelle tail fairing
118 Port double slotted flaps
119 Roll control spoilers
120 Port aileron construction
121 Aileron geared tab
122 Static discharge wicks
123 Aileron horn balance
124 Compass flux valve
125 Port navigation light
126 Wing rib construction
127 Leading edge nose ribs
128 Wing fence
129 Wing tank outboard end rib
130 Landing lamp
131 Leading edge de-icing boots
132 Outboard nacelle hydraulics bay
133 Engine nacelle construction
134 Twin mainwheels
135 Engine air intake
136 Front engine mounting
137 Undercarriage breaker strut
138 Main undercarriage leg strut
139 Hydraulic retraction jack
140 Main undercarriage pivot mounting frame
141 Wing tank inboard end rib
142 Bleed air piping
143 Port air conditioning plant
144 Port inner nacelle construction
145 Propeller spinner
146 Oil cooler
147 HF aerial rail
148 Quick-change passenger/cargo version
149 Cargo door
150 "Ballmat" heavy duty cargo handling floor

After a slow sales start, the de Havilland Canada DHC-7 Dash-7 STOL commuter-liner has begun to attract considerable interest. A significant Canadian operator is Time Air, whose main services are operated by a trio of Dash-7s. Amongst the type's impressive performance parameters is a runway requirement of only 2,300 ft (700 m) for take-off at maximum weight.

De Havilland Canada DHC-8 Dash-8

History and Notes
To meet growing demands for a quiet short-range transport in the 30/40-seat category, de Havilland Aircraft of Canada has initiated the development of such an aircraft under the designation DHC-8 and name Dash-8. Of high-wing monoplane configuration, with a fuselage that incorporates a cargo-loading door as standard, retractable tricycle landing gear with twin-wheel units, and a large-span T-tail, the Dash-8 will have fuel-efficient turboprop engines, driving large-diameter slow-turning four-blade propellers to ensure very low noise levels.

Standard accommodation will be provided for a crew of two on the flight deck, a cabin attendant, and 32 passengers. Alternative layouts will seat up to 36 passengers, or varying mixes of passengers/cargo in an easily convertible interior. Development of the airframe is in progress, and by the end of 1980 de Havilland had received letters of intent to purchase almost 100 examples. The powerplant is also under development by Pratt & Whitney Aircraft of Canada, the PT7A-2R turboprop selected for this new aircraft representing an advanced-technology engine that is expected to offer considerable improvement in fuel efficiency. The first production air-craft are scheduled for delivery in mid-1984.

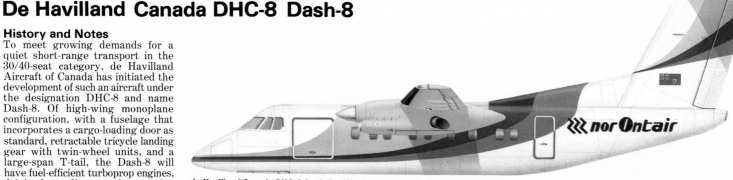
de Havilland Canada DHC-8 Dash-8 of NorOntair, Canada.

Specification
Type: twin-turboprop short-range transport
Powerplant: two 1,800-shp (1342-kW) Pratt & Whitney Aircraft of Canada PT7A-2R turboprops
Performance: (estimated) maximum cruising speed 300 mph (483 km/h); maximum operating altitude 25,000 ft (7620 m); normal range with reserves 691 miles (1112 km); maximum range with reserves 1.266 miles (2037 km)
Weights: none available
Dimensions: span 84 ft 0 in (25.60 m); length 75 ft 6 in (23.01 m); height 25 ft 0 in (7.62 m)

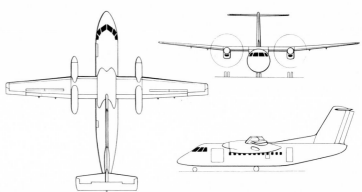
de Havilland Canada DHC-8 Dash-8

Dornier Do 27

History and Notes
The Dornier Do 27 was the first aircraft to enter production in Germany after World War II. Claudius Dornier recommenced activities in Spain in 1949, his Oficinas Tecnicas Dornier working closely with the Spanish CASA. The initial fruits of this collaboration were evident with the first flight of the Do 25 in June 1954. Prepared to meet a Spanish air ministry specification, the STOL transport was powered by a single 150-hp (112-kW) ENMA Tigre engine; 50 similar aircraft subsequently appeared under the designation CASA C-127.

Developed from this, the prototype Do 27 was flown on 8 April 1955. Production took place in Germany at Dornier-Werke, the first example flying in October 1956. With a large 'wraparound' windscreen and generous five-seat layout, the Do 27A proved popular. Deliveries began at 20 aircraft per month.

The main military Do 27A and dual-control Do 27B differed little.

The strutless, high wing provided ease of access for loading passengers or freight. Large flaps gave an amazing STOL capability. By far the largest user was the Federal German Republic, with well over 400. Another early customer was the Swiss *Flug-waffe*, whose initial seven aircraft sported a wheel-and-ski under-carriage. A prototype floatplane, the Do 27S, was built and flown, another was re-engined with the Turboméca Astazou turboprop. Production of the standard Do 27 exceeded 600 units in all its sub-versions before the line closed in 1965.

Specification
Type: STOL liaison and utility transport
Powerplant: one 275-hp (205-kW) Lycoming GO-480 air-cooled piston engine
Performance: maximum speed at 3,280 ft (1000 m) 155 mph (250 km/h); cruising speed at 3,280 ft (1000 m); 127 mph

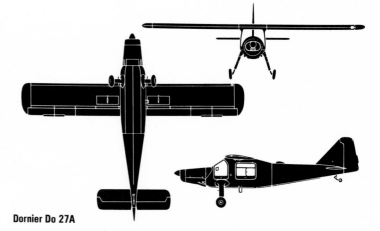
Dornier Do 27A

(205 km/h); cruising range 540 miles (870 km); service ceiling 18,400 ft (5500 m); climb to 3,280 ft (1000 m) 2 minutes 36 seconds; take-off to clear 50-ft (15-m) obstacle (maximum fuel, no wind) 558 ft (160 m); landing from 50 ft (15 m)

525 ft (170 m)
Weights: empty 2,167 lb (983 kg); loaded 3,460 lb (1570 kg)
Dimensions: span 39 ft 4½ in (12.0 m); length 31 ft 4 in (9.54 m); height 8 ft 10¾ in (3.28 m); wing area 208.8 sq ft (19.4 m²)

Dornier Do 28 D and Do 128 Skyservant and Turbo-Skyservant/Do 228 Series

History and Notes
Germany's famous Dornier company has a lineage which stretches back over the years of aviation history to the Zeppelin Werke Lindau, which linked Graf von Zeppelin and Claudius Dornier to design and build heavier-than-air craft. After the end of World War II, when Germany was prohibited from building aircraft, Professor Dornier developed in Spain a utility monoplane designated Do 25.

When it became possible to resume aircraft construction in Germany, the Dornier company produced first a developed version of the Do 25 under the designation Do 27. In the mid-1960s, this development was taken more than one step ahead in the Do 28 design. While the Do 28 retained the same basic configuration as the Do 27 it was, in fact, a completely new aircraft with a twin- instead of single-engine powerplant.

The prototype of the Do 28 D Sky-servant (D-INTL) first flew on 23 February 1966, and features of its design were a cantilever monoplane wing set high on the fuselage, a non-retractable tailwheel type landing gear with fairings over the main wheels, and an unusual location of the powerplant. Accommodation was provided for the pilot and co-pilot or one passenger on the flight deck, and a maximum of 13 passengers in the main cabin. The powerplant consisted of two 380-hp (283-kW) Avco Lycoming IGSO-540 piston engines, these and the main landing gear units being mounted on stub wings extending laterally from the lower fuselage.

Since that time there has been considerable development of this aircraft through Do 28 D, D-1 and D-2 versions. More than 260 had been sold, the majority for military use, before the current production version, redesignated Do 128-2 Sky-servant, became available in 1980. In this version the main cabin can accommodate eight passengers as standard, and alternative interiors provide for

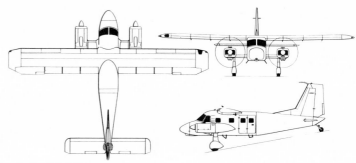
Dornier Do 28D-2 Skyservant

ambulance, cargo and survey roles.

The prototype (D-IBUF) of a turbo-prop-powered version was flown on 9 April 1978. This has the designation Do 128-6 Turbo-Skyservant, and production examples with Pratt

Dornier Do 28 D and Do 128 Skyservant and Turbo-Skyservant/Do 228 Series

& Whitney Aircraft of Canada PT6A-110 turboprops, de-rated to 400 shp (298 kW) in this application, were scheduled for delivery in early 1981. Also in 1980, the company was evaluating an advanced-technology wing which it is planned to use on increased-capacity commuter/general purpose aircraft which will have the designation Do 228. Prototypes of 15-seat and 19-seat Do 228-100 and Do 228-200 aircraft were unveiled in 1981. These retain the basic fuselage of the Skyservant, lengthened appropriately for the desired capacity, but introduce retractable landing gear and more powerful Garrett AirResearch turboprop engines. The details below apply to the current production Do 128-2.

Dornier Do 28 D-2 Skyservant of Corsair, France.

Specification

Type: STOL transport and general-purpose aircraft
Powerplant: two 380-hp (283-kW) Avco Lycoming IGSO-540-A1E flat-six piston engines.
Performance: maximum level speed 202 mph (325 km/h) at 10,000 ft (3050 m); maximum cruising speed 189 mph (304 km/h) at 10,000 ft (3050 m); economic cruising speed 131 mph (211 km/h) at 10,000 ft (3050 m); service ceiling 25,200 ft (7680 m); range with maximum fuel and payload 708 miles (1139 km)
Weights: empty 5,172 lb (2346 kg); maximum take-off 8,852 lb (4015 kg)
Dimensions: span 51 ft 0¼ in (15.55 m); length 37 ft 5¼ in (11.41 m); height 12 ft 9½ in (3.90 m); wing area 312.16 sq ft (29.00 m²)
Operators include: Europe Aero Service, Ilford Riverton Airways, and Linhas Aereas da Guiné-Bissau

The Dornier Do 28 D-series Skyservant was in the early 1980s redesignated the Do 128, but the aircraft still faithfully performs its role as a 14-passenger STOL transport.

The prototype Dornier Do 228-200 STOL utility transport shows little grace, but offers great flexibility and economy thanks to the special features of its TNT advanced-technology wing.

Douglas DC-3/Conroy Tri Turbo-3

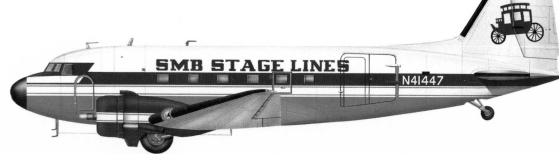

History and Notes

Undoubtedly a classic airliner, and almost certainly as well known to travellers all over the world as to the aviation enthusiasts, by the end of 1980 the Douglas DC-3, as a type, will have been in service continuously for 45 years. Few can have appreciated the potential longevity of this design when, in 1934, the Douglas Company was requested by American Airlines to develop an enlarged version of the DC-2 to provide a 'sleeper' that could be used on US transcontinental flights.

This resulted in the Douglas DST (Douglas Sleeper Transport) with 16 sleeping berths, first flown on 17 December 1935. It was, however, the 24-seat day version of this airliner, designated DC-3, which was to become so important a part of aviation history. Before US involvement in World War II, the DC-3 had gained a dominant position in the nation's airlines and the type's rugged reliability was to appeal to military planners as soon as the requirement for large numbers of transport aeroplanes was appreciated.

By the end of the war nearly 11,000 of these aircraft had been built in the US, and a further 2,000 or so were also built under licence in Russia with the designation Lisunov Li-2. The DC-3's robust construction meant that very large numbers of the type survived the war, and when these were disposed of as war surplus items, at better than bargain prices, operators all over the world acquired them as fast as they could lay hands on them. Used in the passenger-carrying and utility roles, DC-3s played a significant part in establishing many new airlines and air services. In such tasks they have plodded along nobly, awaiting the evolution of a replacement that would be superior in performance, economy and comfort, and yet retaining the virtues displayed by this Douglas masterpiece. The search for an effective DC-3 replacement has been going on for the past 35 years: there can be few experts who will admit that these efforts have been crowned with success.

Of cantilever low-wing configuration, the DC-3 is of all-metal construction except for fabric-covered control surfaces. A feature of the wing is its multi-spar structure, derived from the DC-1, which has played a significant part in the long service life of these aircraft. The all-metal fuselage is almost circular in cross-section, and an attractive feature of this at the date of introduction into service was its internal height, making it possible for most passen-

Douglas DC-3 of SMB Stagelines, USA.

gers to stand upright in the offset aisle. The landing gear is of the retractable tailwheel type, with a fully-castoring tailwheel, and the cantilever tail unit is of metal construction.

Civil DC-3s delivered to US airlines before the nation became involved in World War II played a most important part in the development of reliable national air routes. It has been recorded that in the period 1936-41 national passenger mileage in the USA increased by almost 600 per cent, a growth that was very largely due to the DC-3, which was the primary equipment of most US airlines in this period whose safety record has become almost legendary.

US participation in World War II saw large-scale production of these aircraft for the USAAF as C-47s and the USN as R4Ds. Aircraft in service with US airlines were impressed for military service, and civil aircraft under construction by Douglas were completed for delivery to the armed services.

Throughout the entire period of production there was little significant change in airframe design. The same was not true of powerplants, for as improved and/or more powerful engines became available they were installed to provide enhanced performance or load-carrying capability. Manufacturer's lists show 13 variants of the Wright SGR-1820 Cyclone, with ratings from 920 to 1,200 hp (686 to 895 kW). There were also 11 civil and military Pratt & Whitney Twin Wasp engines installed in prewar and wartime production aircraft, these having ratings between 1,050 and 1,200 hp (783 and 895 kW).

When these DC-3/C-47 variants came on to the market after the war, there was such an acute shortage of aircraft suitable for the initiation of civil passenger and cargo services that many were operated without any alteration to the military interior. The majority, however, were sub-

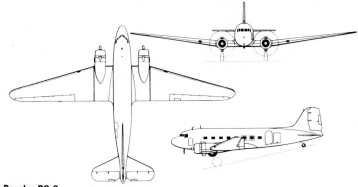

Douglas DC-3

jected to modification schemes which brought internal furnishings and equipment up to an acceptable airline standard. Some were provided with executive and VIP interior layouts. The development of turbine engines was not overlooked by several companies who tend to specialise in conversions of aircraft produced by other companies, and DC-3s have served also as test-beds for some engines. One of the most recent and most ambitious schemes was that known as the Tri Turbo-3 developed by Jack M. Conroy in the USA. In its most advanced state this prototype conversion had two 1,174-ehp (875-ekW) Pratt & Whitney Aircraft of Canada PT6A-45 turboprop engines replacing the conventional piston engines, plus the installation of a third, similar engine, in the nose of the fuselage. By comparison with the original powerplant this offered improved performance in terms of cruising speed and range, and made possible operations (often with greater payloads) under previously unacceptable high-altitude/high-temperature conditions.

So far, however, there have been no significant sales of these re-engined DC-3s. This is not really surprising, for it must be remembered that the installation of new, advanced-technology engines does not instantly and automatically confer a new lease of life upon the airframe. At the same time, the capital cost of these new turboprop engines very considerably exceeds the price at which airlines acquired their DC-3s, and it would need a computerised crystal ball to decide whether such an expenditure would pay off in the long term.

Continuing use and the popularity of DC-3s and their derivatives encouraged Douglas to evolve a suitable replacement. To save time and cost it was decided to modernise existing aircraft, and two secondhand DC-3s were acquired for this exercise. These

had the fuselage extended and strengthened to provide a 30-seat interior, extra windows were added and an airstair cabin door installed. Some changes were made to aerofoil surfaces to improve handling and stability, and the retracted main wheel units were totally enclosed in neat fairings. The powerplant of the first prototype comprised two 1,475-hp (1100-kW) Wright R-1820-C9HE Cyclones; the second had two 1,450-hp (1081-kW) Pratt & Whitney R-2000-D7 radials.

Designated DC-3S, or Super DC-3, the first of these revised aircraft flew on 23 June 1949. Testing gave excellent results, demonstrating much improved performance over the basic DC-3. It was too late, however, for faster and more comfortable aircraft of more modern design were already in service, or about to begin operations, and the company's gamble failed to pay off.

About 100 years ago the British poet, Alfred, Lord Tennyson, wrote a poem entitled *The Brook*. Some verses terminate with the words: 'For men may come, and men may go, but I go on for ever.' It almost seems that this could be applied to the ubiquitous DC-3, but inevitably the day will come when these superb aeroplanes will be seen only in museums, be recorded in history, or remain alive in the memory of those who flew in them.

In early 1980 almost 300 were in service with airlines of varying sizes. The details which follow apply to a typical postwar conversion of an ex-military C-47.

The justified fame of the Douglas DC-3 makes comment almost superfluous, but it is worth noting the type's reliability and economy, good structural record and relative independence from the need for modern repair facilities.

Specification

Type: short/medium-range transport

Powerplant: two 1,200-hp (895-kW) Pratt & Whitney R-1830-S1C3G Twin Wasp radial piston engines

Performance: maximum speed 230 mph (370 km/h) at 8,500 ft (2590 m); cruising speed 207 mph (333 km/h); service ceiling 23,200 ft (7070 m); range with maximum fuel 2,125 miles (3420 km)

Weights: empty 16,865 lb (7650 kg); maximum take-off 25,200 lb (11430 kg)

Douglas DC-3

Dimensions: span 95 ft 0 in (28.96 m); length 64 ft 5½ in (19.65 m); height 16 ft 11½ in (5.17 m); wing area 987 sq ft (91.69 m²)

Operators include: Academy Airlines, Aero Virgin Islands, Air BVI, Air Cape, Air Indiana, Alyemeda-Democratic Yemen Airlines, Basler Flight SVC, Bo-S-Aire, Bouraq Indonesia, Bradley Air Services, Bush Pilot Airways, Caprivi Airways, Comair Ltd, Connair, COPA, Ethiopian Airlines, Faucett, Florida Air Lines, Gateway Aviation, Hang Khong Vietnam, Ilford Riverton Airways, Jersey European Airways, Kenn Borek Air, LA La Urraca, LAGB, Lambair, LANSA Airlines, Mannion Air Charter, Merpati Nusantara, Millardair, Nevada Airlines, Norcanair, Northern Wings, NWT Air, Ontario Central, PACS, PAL, Provincetown-Boston Airlines, Red Carpet Flying Services, Rutaca, Satena, Skyways Cargo, SMB Stage Line, Southern Flyer, and Yemen Airways Corporation

More than 500 Douglas DC-3s remained in service in the early 1980s, including this example modified for geological survey in the colours of the Finnish operator Kar-Air.

Douglas DC-4/Canadair DC-4M Series

History and Notes

Even before the DC-3 had flown, United Air Lines (UAL) and Douglas had started discussions regarding the development of a more advanced airliner of larger capacity. At the outset this seemed unlikely to materialise, for neither the airline nor the manufacturer had the money to back the design and construction of such an aircraft. However, UAL's president was considerably impressed by the company's proposals, and by early 1936 had induced four other airlines to help finance the construction of a prototype.

Designated originally DC-4 (later DC-4E, the E standing for experimental), it was an impressive aeroplane in those prewar days, with projected accommodation for 42 passengers in a pressurised and air-conditioned cabin. Other advanced ideas included the use of powered controls, the installation of an auxiliary power unit, and the introduction of an AC electrical system. The aircraft's configuration was that of a low-wing monoplane, with a retractable tricycle type landing gear, and a tail unit featuring triple fins and rudders. The powerplant consisted of four wing-mounted Pratt & Whitney R-2180 radial engines, each developing a maximum of 1,450 hp (1081 kW). First flown on 7 June 1938, the DC-4 on subsequent test and proving flights revealed that its advanced systems were too complicated and its operating economics disappointing. Cutting its losses, Douglas decided instead in 1939 to proceed with a more simple, smaller and unpressurised version of this aircraft, also designated DC-4. It was at this time that the original project was re-designated DC-4E.

The DC-4 of 1939 was virtually a new design, considerably lighter in construction, having a new high-aspect ratio wing, and a conventional tail unit with a single fin and rudder. The landing gear was of the retractable tricycle type, the main units carrying twin wheels and retracting forward and upward into the inboard engine nacelles. The

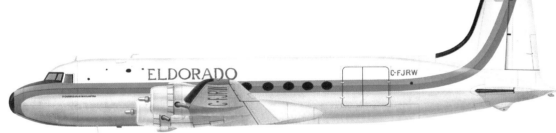

Douglas DC-4 of Eldorado Airlines.

initial powerplant selection had been for four engines, each of around 1,000 hp (746 kW), but after discussion with interested airlines the type was put into production (without construction of a prototype) with four 1,450-hp (1081-kW) Pratt & Whitney R-2000-2SD1-G Twin Wasp radials.

Before the first aircraft had flown, the USA was embroiled in World War II. This meant that the aircraft on the production line were completed for the USAAF under the designation C-54 Skymaster, the first flying with military markings on 14 February 1942. The type was to prove a most valuable long-range military transport, and more than 1,000 were built for the armed forces during the war. At the end of military production Douglas built 79 civil DC-4s and these, together with large numbers of de-militarised C-54s, were to give valuable service on long-range passenger carrying and cargo routes until the new-generation airliners became available.

Specialised derivatives of the DC-4 included 24 aircraft with 1,725-hp (1286-kW) Rolls-Royce Merlin engines, developed by Canadair Ltd in Montreal for service with the RCAF, which allocated the aircraft the name North Star. There followed production of DC-4M-2s with Merlin engines, a pressurised fuselage, and square cabin windows. Some 42 were built, 20 for service with Trans-Canada Air Lines, and 22 for the London-Far East routes of British Overseas Airways Corporation, which called its aircraft Argonauts. One other derivative was evolved by

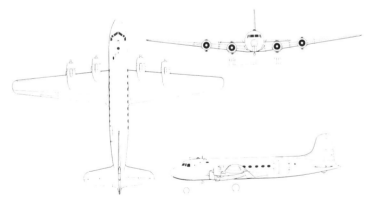

Douglas DC-4

Aviation Traders (Engineering) Ltd in Britain, by the addition of 8 ft 8 in (2.64 m) to the forward fuselage and a hydraulically operated swing-nose to allow the direct in-loading of vehicles. Known as the Carvair, these aircraft, modified for service with the Channel Air Bridge car ferry, could accommodate five cars and 23 passengers.

Accommodation of these various DC-4s varied considerably. The basic version provided for a crew of four and 44 passengers with plenty of room between the seats, and this enabled some operators to introduce as many as 86 seats in high-density layouts. DC-4M-1 and DC-4M-2s carried up to 62 economy-class passengers.

Apart from many record-breaking flights, DC-4s are remembered in aviation history for their very con-

siderable contribution to the Berlin Airlift of 1948-9. Their use by major airlines dwindled fairly rapidly as more advanced aircraft became available, but about 40 remained in service in early 1980.

Specification
Type: long-range transport
Powerplant: four 1,450-shp (1081-kW) Pratt & Whitney R-200-2SD-13G Twin Wasp radial piston engines
Performance: maximum speed 280 mph (451 km/h) at 14,000 ft (4265 m); cruising speed 227 mph (365 km/h) at 10,000 ft (3050 m); service ceiling 22,300 ft (6800 m); range 2,500 miles (4023 km) with 11,440-lb (5189-kg) payload
Weights: empty 43,300 lb (19640 kg); maximum take-off 73,000 lb (33112 kg)

Douglas DC-4 Canadair DC-4M Series

Dimensions: span 117 ft 6 in (35.81 m); length 93 ft 10 in (28.60 m); height 27 ft 6 in (8.38 m); wing area 1,460 sq ft (135.63 m²)
Operators include: Aero Medellin, Air Chad, Air Mauritanie, Air Niger, Airworks India, Eldorado Aviation, Falcon Airways, Hang Khong Vietnam, Millardair, Nationwide Air Transport, Satena, and Zaïre Aero Service

Produced almost exclusively to meet military requirements, the Douglas DC-4 has soldiered on as a freighter workhorse, some 65 of the type still performing usefully in the early 1980s with African and South American lines.

Douglas DC-6

History and Notes

With major involvement in a war (1941-5) that was centred at the far side of the Pacific Ocean, USAAF interest in long-range landplanes is understandable. The DC-4, or C-54, proved to be a valuable tool, and a glowing tribute to its reliability is provided by a total of almost 80,000 wartime ocean crossings (Atlantic/Pacific) during which only three aircraft were lost. Such a record induced the USAAF to look for a larger-capacity transport from the same source, and the first of these to fly, on 15 February 1946, had the designation XC-112A. By then, of course, it was too late for participation in World War II, and the new type was developed instead for service with postwar airlines under the company identification DC-6. DC-6As were, however, to serve with the USAF at a later date, under the designation C-118A.

By comparison with its predecessor, the DC-6 retained the same wing, but had a pressurised fuselage that was lengthened by 6 ft 9 in (2.06 m) to give increased passenger capacity. Seating for 48 to 52 was standard, but a high-density layout could accommodate 86. The powerplant of the initial DC-6 comprised four 2,100-hp (1566-kW) Pratt & Whitney R-2800-CA15 Double Wasp engines, and the first of 50 civil airliners ordered by American Airlines made its initial flight on 29 June 1946. The DC-6 began to enter service in April 1947, initially on the New York-Chicago route of American Airlines, but grounding of the type came later in that year after two aircraft had suffered in-flight fires. Investigation and remedy occupied some four months, with services being resumed on 21 March 1948, from which time the DC-6 provided reliable and most economical operation.

In this same year the company began development of an increased-capacity version, with the fuselage lengthened by 5 ft 0 in (1.52 m), powered by 2,400-hp (1790-kW) Double Wasp engines. Offered initially in an all-cargo version as the DC-6A, with two freight doors on the port side (one forward and one aft of the wing), no windows, and strengthened flooring, the DC-6A was followed by the generally similar DC-6B passenger transport. In early production examples the standard seating capacity was 54, but high-density layouts for up to 102 passengers were introduced subsequently.

Last of the civil designations was

Douglas DC-6A of Zantop International Airlines, USA.

DC-6C, this applying to a convertible cargo/passenger version that was generally similar to the DC-6A, but with standard cabin windows. Construction of DC-6 civil and XC-112A/C-118A and R6D-1 military aircraft totalled 704. Among variants were two DC-6Bs modified by Sabena, these being given swing-tails to simplify the direct in-loading of bulky cargo. There were also a number of DC-6Bs provided with a 3,000-US gallon (11356-litre) capacity under-fuselage tank to carry fire-retardant chemicals, and these saw considerable

Low capital cost, combined with adequate payload and great fuel economy has made it possible for some 130 Douglas DC-6s to survive into the 1980s.

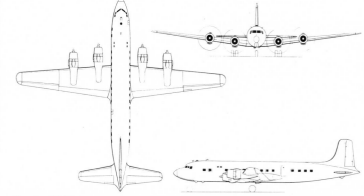

Douglas DC-6B

Douglas DC-6

service in Canada and the USA during periods of high fire risk in national timberlands.

The DC-6 came to be regarded as a worthy example of the reliable and efficient piston-engine airliners that were soon to be displaced by first-generation turboprop-and turbojet-powered aircraft. As DC-6s became surplus to the requirements of major users they were eagerly sought by operators in the lower echelons of air transport. They, too, were to

benefit from their excellence, and in early 1980 more than 100 remained in service. The details below apply to a later version DC-6B.

Specification
Type: long-range transport
Powerplant: four 2,500-hp (1864-kW) Pratt & Whitney R-2800-CB17 Double Wasp radial piston engines
Performance: cruising speed 315 mph (507 km/h); service ceiling 25,000 ft (7620 m); range with

maximum payload 3,005 miles (4836 km); range with maximum fuel 4,720 miles (7596 km)
Weights: empty 55,357 lb (25110 kg); maximum take-off 107,000 lb (48534 kg)
Dimensions: span 117 ft 6 in (35.81 m); length 105 ft 7 in (32.18 m); height 28 ft 8 in (8.74 m); wing area 1,463 sq ft (135.91 m²)
Operators include: Aerocarga SA, Aerotransporte de Espana, Air Atlantique, Air Gabon, Aviateca,

Balair, Cayman Airways, Dominicana, Faucett, Guyana Airways Corporation, Hang Khong Vietnam, Iscargo HF, Kar-Air, LASA, Lineas Aereas del Caribe, Northern Air Cargo, Pacific Alaska Airlines, Pan African Airlines, Petroleum Air Transport, Rich International Airways, SOACO, Syrian Arab Airlines, TAMPA, Transportes Aereos La Cumbre, Yemen Airways, and Zantop International Airlines

Douglas DC-7

History and Notes
The first decade following World War II brought intense competition in the USA between the Douglas and Lockheed aircraft companies, the market for long-range civil airliners then being dominated by the piston-engine aircraft evolved by these two manufacturers. It is generally accepted that the Douglas DC-7 and its derivatives, and Lockheed's Constellation and its derivatives, represented the pinnacle of development of piston-engine airliners.

Design and development of the DC-7, as it became known, was prompted by American Airlines' desire for an aircraft superior in performance to the Super Constellations being used by TWA. The Super 'Connie' had the advantages accruing from the installation of new Wright Turbo-Compound engines developed from the standard R-3350 Cyclone 18-cylinder radial piston engine in military use. Each of these engines had three exhaust-driven turbines disposed equally around its circumference, giving a power output some 20 per cent greater than the standard engine. To meet the requirement of American Airlines, it was decided to evolve an improved version of the DC-6B using these new engines.

The initial DC-7 was a direct development of the DC-6B, with the fuselage lengthened by 3 ft 4 in (1.02 m) to allow for the inclusion of an additional row of seats. Installation of the 3,250-hp (2424-kW) R-3350 Turbo-Compound engines made possible an increase in gross weight of 15,200 lb (6895 kg), this in turn requiring a strengthening of the landing gear structure. There were also some minor changes in detail, but externally the DC-7 appeared little different from the DC-6B.

Some 105 DC-7s were built, and the 112 DC-7Bs which followed showed only minor changes. The powerplant was generally similar, each engine having the same power output as those of the DC-7, but the engine nacelles were extended further aft to permit the installation of saddle tanks within the rear of the nacelles for those operators who required maximum range. Some structural strengthening was added, and the DC-7B was certificated at a new gross weight increased by 3,800 lb (1724 kg), most of this being additional fuel.

Not all operators opted for this additional fuel capacity, but those who did, such as Pan American which inaugurated non-stop London-New York services with the DC-7B on 13 June 1955, were soon to discover that fuel capacity was marginal for North Atlantic services. In fact, with a full load and normal headwinds, DC-7Bs which were used to operate the westward service frequently had to divert for a refuelling stop. This was clearly unsatisfactory, and potentially dangerous, so Douglas set about

the task of developing a version of the DC-7B with greater range.

The third version, designated DC-7C had, therefore, wings of increased span to provide greater fuel capacity. This was achieved by inserting a new parallel-chord wing section between the fuselage and the inboard engine nacelles, an arrangement which had the added advantage of improving the cabin environment by reducing engine noise. During the development of the DC-7C, Curtiss-Wright was able to offer a further increase in engine power and, as a result, the fuselage was lengthened by the insertion of a 3 ft 4 in (1.02 m) plug, so providing accommodation for up to 105 passengers. Among other changes, the areas of the fin and rudder were increased; de-icing equipment was provided; and the most advanced weather radar, coupled with new avionics, were installed.

Production of the DC-7C totalled 120, and the alphanumeric suffix of this version became corrupted most appropriately to provide the name Seven Seas, for this aircraft was able to take the oceans in its stride without any problems. Not only were DC-7Cs used on North Atlantic and Pacific Ocean services, but they also made possible non-stop scheduled operations across the continental USA, and were used additionally by SAS to inaugurate a route from Europe to the Far East over the North Pole. An improved DC-7D was planned, to be powered by four 5,730-eshp (4273-ekW) Rolls-Royce Tyne turboprop engines, but the emergence of the Boeing 707 and the

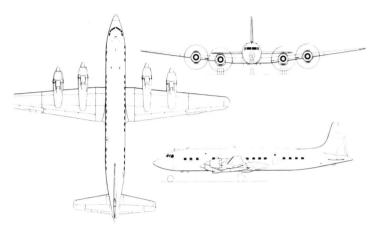

Douglas DC-7C

Douglas Company's purpose-built DC-8 jetliner meant that this remained an unfulfilled project.

Because the Turbo-Compound engine increased operating costs, these fine airliners disappeared quickly from the aviation scene when replaced by the first turboprop- and turbojet-powered airliners. At the beginning of 1980, less than 10 remained in service. The details below apply to the DC-7C.

Specification
Type: long-range transport
Powerplant: four 3,400-hp (2535-kW) Wright R-3350-18EA-1 Turbo-Compound radial piston engines
Performance: maximum speed 406 mph (653 km/h) at 21,700 ft (6615 m); average cruising speed 355

mph (571 km/h); service ceiling 21,700 ft (6615 m); range with maximum payload 4,605 miles (7411 km)
Weights: empty 72,763 lb (33005 kg); maximum take-off 143,000 lb (64864 kg)
Dimensions: span 127 ft 6 in (38.86 m); length 112 ft 3 in (34.21 m); height 31 ft 10 in (9.70 m); wing area 1,637 sq ft (152.08 m²)
Operators include: Cia Sudamericana, Fleming International Airways, and Talingo Airlines

Very few Douglas DC-7s remain in airline service in the 1980s, but a few survivors are used for special tasks: the DC-7B illustrated is a specialised firefighting aircraft with an underfuselage tank.

Douglas DC-8

History and Notes

The aircraft turbine engine which had been developed during World War II, almost simultaneously in the UK and Germany by Frank Whittle and Dr Pabst von Ohain respectively, offered in the long term power output far beyond the capability of the piston engine/propeller propulsion units that had served as aircraft powerplants until that time. The turbines additionally promised to have far fewer moving parts, and therefore to be more reliable and less costly to maintain. It was also reasonably certain that, in the process of development, completely new figures for power/weight ratio would be realised.

How true were these beliefs can be illustrated by just a few figures: the Whittle W.1 turbojet which had powered the Gloster E.28/39, Britain's first jet aircraft to fly, on 15 May 1941, developed only 860-lb (390-kg) thrust; modern-technology turbofans such as the General Electric CF6, Pratt & Whitney JT9D and Rolls-Royce RB.211, are available with ratings in excess of 54,000-lb (24494-kg) thrust. As an example of power/weight ratio, the Rolls-Royce Gnome H.1400-1 has a contingency rating of 1,600 shp (1238 kW) at a dry weight of only 326 lb (148 kg). This represents an output in excess of 5 hp (3.7 kW) per 1 lb (0.45 kg) of engine weight, yet the R-3350 Turbo-Compound engine that powered the DC-7C produced a maximum of 3,400 hp (2535 kW) for a dry weight of 3,645 lb (1653 kg), representing 0.93 hp (0.70 kW) per 1 lb (0.45 kg). These latter figures do not include the hefty metal propeller which was an all-essential component of the powerplant.

Even in their early development stage, it was clear that a combination of the turbine engine with a propeller (turboprop) would be more fuel efficient than a turbojet. As a next stage of evolution, therefore, beyond the highly successful DC-7C, Douglas looked carefully at a turboprop-powered development of the DC-7. This included not only the DC-7D project, but also examined the design of a larger-capacity transport with turboprop power.

Although this seemed to the Douglas company to be the most desirable method of progress, the drawback was that Britain's initial turbojet-powered de Havilland Comet had demonstrated that such a powerplant provided completely new standards of high-speed cruising flight.

McDonnell Douglas DC-8-50 of UTA (Union de Transports Aériens), France.

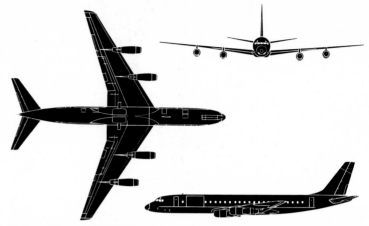

McDonnell Douglas DC-8-50CF

A turboprop powerplant, however good and however powerful, was performance-limited by its propeller. Douglas was aware that Boeing was well advanced with its Model 707, and that Lockheed was interested in both large-capacity turboprop-powered and small-size turbojet-powered transports. If Douglas wished to maintain its hold on the market for civil transports then, sooner or later, there would have to come the design of a turbojet-powered large-capacity transport. Once the board had reached this conclusion, then the sooner that hardware was available the better. Thus the DC-8 project was launched.

Market research was initiated, the company announcing on 7 June 1955 its intention of developing a turbojet-powered airliner to supersede the DC-7, and design went ahead without delay. One prototype/demonstrator was built, and when this first aircraft flew, on 30 May 1958, it was seen to be externally very similar to the Boeing 707. It was of the same basic configuration: a low-wing monoplane with four pylon-mounted turbojets, and a tail unit with all-swept surfaces, comprising a single fin and rudder, and tailplane with dihedral. Like the 707, the DC-8's wing was swept, but the Douglas design team had opted for a more modest 30° of sweep to provide good handling characteristics at low speeds.

As flown originally, the wing incorporated powered ailerons and double-slotted trailing-edge flaps. In addition, a series of spoilers on the upper surface of each wing, forward of the flaps, served as lift-dumpers, being actuated automatically as soon as the nosewheel contacted the runway during the landing phase. The landing gear, of the tricycle type, had a steerable nose unit with twin wheels, and each main unit carried a four-wheel bogie, the aft pair of wheels on each being free-castoring to make possible small-radius turns.

From the outset the company had

planned to offer a number of versions that would be suitable for domestic or intercontinental services, and accordingly there was a diversity of cabin accommodation. This ranged initially from 118 seats for first-class domestic services, to a maximum of 176 in a high-density economy-class layout. Because of this variation in roles, which it was hoped would appeal to a broad spectrum of airlines, it was decided also to offer a variety of alternative powerplants. Thus, the nine aircraft that took part in the certification programme comprised three with Pratt & Whitney JT3C turbojets, four with JT4As, and two with Rolls-Royce Conways.

It may seem surprising that nine aircraft were involved in the development and certification programme but, conscious of Boeing's lead, the Douglas company wanted to gain FAA approval for the DC-8 at the earliest possible date. This was awarded on 31 August 1959, when Delta Air Lines and United Airlines became the recipients of the first aircraft. Both initiated revenue services on 18 September 1959, just over four years after the company's decision to develop this aircraft.

During the next nine years Douglas built a total of 294 examples of these transports, produced in five series. All, however, had the same basic fuselage, which meant they were less flexible than the Boeing jetliner in meeting the requirements of different airlines. Boeing's Model 707 had been made available with three differing fuselage lengths, and permutation of these variables meant that most operators could select a suitable aircraft from the Boeing range. This, more than any other factor, was responsible for the comparatively poor initial sales record of the DC-8, but significant also was the fact that the 707 was earlier in the market. The attempts which Douglas made to redeem this situation are described under the heading DC-8 Super Sixty series.

Early examples were designated DC-8 Series 10, which was regarded as the basic domestic version, and 28 of these were built for service with Delta and United. The powerplant of these aircraft consisted of four Pratt & Whitney JT3C-6 turbojets, each rated at 13,000-lb (5897-kg) thrust for take-off with water injection. The use of this latter technique had been developed many years earlier, to cool the petrol/air mixture charge in a piston engine's cylinders and so delay the onset of detonation. In the case of a turbine engine the water is injected into the compressor or combustion chambers to cool the air, resulting in a higher mass flow and increased thrust. There were also some aerodynamic changes introduced on the Series 10, the first being installation of two leading-edge slots on each wing, inboard of each engine pylon, to improve low-speed flight characteristics. New wingtips were also provided, these reducing drag, and thereby increasing range.

The Series 20 version which followed was also intended for domestic use but was powered typically by JT4A-3 turbojets, each of which developed a maximum thrust, without water injection, of 15,800 lb

UTA is a major European operator of the McDonnell Douglas DC-8, with three -62s, two -63s, one -63CF and three -50s.

Douglas DC-8

Cargolux operates freight services with its three DC-8-63Fs, soon to be updated to -73F standard with CFM58 turbofans.

(7167 kg). Apart from the changed powerplant the Series 20 aircraft was identical to the Series 10, but the increased engine power was intended to make the type suitable for operation from hot and/or high airfields. The 34 built were certificated for take-off at a gross weight 3,000 lb (1361 kg) higher than that of Series 10 aircraft, and the increased thrust available reduced the sea cent. Subsequently, 15 of United Airlines' Series 10s were converted to Series 20 standard.

Series 30 aircraft were the first intended specifically for intercontinental services. These retained the same basic airframe as their predecessors, but had more powerful engines, typically JT4A-9s of 16,800-lb (7620-kg) thrust. The greater range requirement was met by an increase of some 5,900 US gallons (22334 litres) in fuel capacity, with certification at higher gross weights resulting. Such gains could not be achieved without some loss in another area, and the sea level take-off run was 18 per cent greater than that of the Series 20. To offset this to some extent, all but four of the 57 Series 30 aircraft were provided with ailerons which had a droop capability to increase total lift.

The installation of Rolls-Royce Conway 509 turbofans, each of 17,500-lb (7938-kg) thrust, which had been specified by certain operators, resulted in the Series 40 intercontinental version. This, in all important respects, was otherwise identical to the Series 30. Shortly after certification of this Conway-powered version, on 24 March 1960, the original DC-8 prototype/demonstrator was prepared for the installation of new turbofan engines developed by Pratt & Whitney. Designated JT3D, this had evolved from the JT3C, but had higher take-off ratings coupled with greater fuel efficiency.

Certification of the DC-8 with JT3D-1 turbofans, each of 17,000-lb (7711-kg) thrust, was achieved on 1 May 1961, and the resulting aircraft was designated Series 50. In addition to the powerplant change, this version had its maximum seating capacity increased to 189 without any change in external fuselage dimensions. This was achieved by the repositioning of the aft bulkhead, and so increasing the overall internal length of the cabin. Later Series 50 aircraft had

more powerful JT3D-3 or -3B engines, and despite a gross weight of 325,000 lb (147418 kg), just over 3 per cent higher than that of the Series 30 with identical fuel capacity, the version was able to demonstrate a full-load range increase of some 800 miles (1287 km). Production of Series 50 passenger aircraft totalled 88, while six Series 10 and four Series 30 aircraft were converted retrospectively to this configuration.

Other specialist requirements were met by the production of 39 Series 50CF and 15 Series 50AF aircraft,

these being convertible passenger/freight and all-freight aircraft respectively. Both had a large cargo door installed on the port side of the forward fuselage, plus floor reinforcement, cargo-handling equipment and adequate tie-down facilities. JTD-3 or -3B engines were standard in both, but the Series 50AF differed by having no passenger facilities, being devoid of seats, galleys and cabin windows.

Production of these standard DC-8s totalled 294, and in mid-1980 about half of them remained in

service. The details which follow apply to the DC-8 Series 50.

Specification

Type: long-range intercontinental transport

Powerplant: four 18,000-lb (8165-kg) thrust Pratt & Whitney JT3D-3 turbofans

Performance: maximum cruising speed 579 mph (932 km/h) at 30,000 ft (9145 m); range with maximum payload 5,720 miles (9205 km)

Weights: empty operating 132,325 lb (60022 kg); maximum take-off 325,000 lb (147418 kg)

Dimensions: span 142 ft 5 in (43.41 m); length 150 ft 6 in (45.87 m); height 43 ft 4 in (13.21 m); wing area 2,883 sq ft (267.83 m²)

Operators include: Aeral, ANDES Airlines, Aeromexico, Aeronaves del Peru, Aero Peru, ARCA Airlines, Affretair, Air Afrique, Air Canada, Air Gabon Cargo, Airlift International, Air New Zealand, Aviaco, Capitol International Airways, Delta Air Lines, Evergreen International Airlines, InterContinental Airways, Japan Air Lines, KLM, Philippine Airlines, TAE, UTA, United African Airlines, United Airlines, Viasa, Worldways Airlines, and Zantop International Airlines

The national airline Air New Zealand has three McDonnell Douglas DC-8-50s for lower-density intercontinental routes.

Douglas DC-8 Super Sixty Series

History and Notes

When Douglas had first initiated development of the DC-8, it had been the company's intention to provide a degree of flexibility in operation. This resulted in the five series of aircraft described under the DC-8 heading, but this approach did not have the broad outlook that Boeing had given to initial developments of the Model 707.

Fortunately, the basic design of the DC-8 provided potential for the evolution of growth versions. This included an upswept rear fuselage, and landing gear that was tall enough to allow fuselage lengthening without the likelihood of endangering the rear fuselage during take-off and landing operations. Accordingly, the company announced on 5 April 1965 its intention of developing larger-capacity, improved variants of the DC-8 under the Super Sixty (Series 60) designation.

First of these new aircraft was the Super 61, which was intended for high-capacity domestic services, and could therefore be evolved with the minimum amount of change from the DC-8 Series 50. Thus it retained the same wing, tail unit, landing gear and powerplant of late-production Series 50 aircraft, but introduced a fuselage which had been 'stretched' by 36 ft 8 in (11.18 m). This had been achieved by inserting a plug 20 ft 0 in (6.10 m) long in the fuselage forward of the wing, and one of 16 ft 8 in (5.08 m) aft of the wing. This made possible the accommodation of a maximum of 259 passengers in a high-density seating arrangement, and at the same time increased the capacity of the underfloor cargo hold by almost 80 per cent. Fuel capacity was unchanged from that of the Series 50, which meant that as the maximum take-off weight of Series 50 and 61 aircraft was identical, the greater payload necessitating a lower fuel uplift. Maximum range with full payload was, therefore, reduced by more than 30 per cent, but as this version was intended purely for domestic services this did not matter.

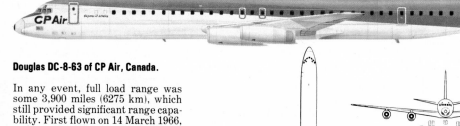

Douglas DC-8-63 of CP Air, Canada.

In any event, full load range was some 3,900 miles (6275 km), which still provided significant range capability. First flown on 14 March 1966, and certificated on 2 September of that year, 78 of this version were built.

The Super 62 was developed to provide services over extra long range, and this requirement meant that the version incorporated several changes. These included increased wingspan, and redesigned engine pods and pylons, all intended to reduce drag. The fuselage was lengthened by only 6 ft 8 in (2.04 m) by comparison with the Series 50, plugs of 3 ft 4 in (1.02 m) being inserted in the fuselage both fore and aft of the wing. In addition, fuel capacity was increased, and there were a number of system changes. Standard accommodation was provided for 189 passengers, and while the JT3D-3B engines were retained as basic powerplant, 19,000-lb (8618-kg) thrust JT3D-7 turbofans were obtainable optionally. Production of this version totalled 51.

Last of the series was the Super 63, a combination of its two predecessors, with the long fuselage of the Series 61, and the other improvements introduced on the Series 62. Standard seating capacity was for 180 to 220 passengers, but like the Series 61 it could accommodate a maximum of 259 in a high-density layout. Production of this version totalled 41 aircraft, the last of them being delivered on 12 May 1972.

As with the original series DC-8s, all-cargo (AF) and convertible passenger/cargo (CF) variants of the Super Sixty series were available. Some of these had wing structure

Douglas DC-8-61

and landing gear strengthening to permit operations at higher gross weights, and the Series 63AFs of The Flying Tiger Line were able to carry the greatest maximum payload, amounting to no less than 114,700 lb (52027 kg). Production of these AF and CF variants comprised: 61CF (10), 62AF (6), 62CF (10), 63AF (7) and 63CF (53). In addition six all-passenger aircraft were completed to Series 63 standard with the reinforcing of the 63AF/CF, and these received the designation Series 63PF. When production ended, 262 Super Sixty aircraft had been built.

In early 1980 more than 90 per cent of these aircraft remained in service. The company had in operation a programme, initiated in 1976, to convert DC-8 passenger versions into specialised freighters. This work involves the installation of heavy-duty freighter flooring, and the provision of cargo doors on the main

deck. More recent proposals by the Douglas company cover the installation of new-technology engines in Series 61, 62 and 63 aircraft, to produce the Super Seventy series, numbered 71, 72 and 73 respectively. Modification of a Series 61 aircraft to Series 71 standard, by the installation of General Electric/SNECMA CFM56 turbofan engines was completed in 1980, with certification planned for late 1981. It has been claimed that these Super Seventy series aircraft will not only be very considerably quieter than existing DC-8s, but will also offer improvements in performance and operating costs. The details below apply to the DC-8 Super 63.

Specification

Type: long-range transport
Powerplant: four 19,000-lb (8618-kg) thrust Pratt & Whitney JT3D-7 turbofans
Performance: maximum cruising speed 600 mph (966 km/h) at 30,000 ft (9145 m); economic cruising speed 523 mph (842 km/h); range with maximum payload 4,500 miles (7242 km)
Weights: operating empty 153,749 lb (69739 kg); maximum take-off 350,000 lb (158760 kg)
Dimensions: span 148 ft 5 in (45.24 m); length 187 ft 5 in (57.12 m); height 42 ft 5 in (12.93 m); wing area 2,927 sq ft (271.92 m²)
Operators include: Air Afrique, Air Algérie, Air Bahama, Air Canada, Air-India, Air Jamaica, Air Japan, Airlift International, Air Zaïre, Alitalia, Balair, Braniff International, Capitol International Airways, Cargolux Airlines International, CP Air, Delta Air Lines, Evergreen International Airlines, Finnair, Flying Tiger Line, Iberia, Japan Air Lines, Japan Asia Airways, Mackey International, Saudia, Scanair, Scandinavian Airlines System, Seaboard World Airlines, Spantax, Supair, Surinam Airways-SLM, Swissair, Thai International, Transamerica Airlines, UTA, United Airlines, Viasa, and World Airways

One of the keys to the success of Delta Air Lines is the company's constant quest for efficiency and economy: to this end Delta is having its 13 McDonnell Douglas DC-8-61s upgraded to DC-8-71 standard with General Electric CFM56 turbofans.

Douglas DC-9

History and Notes

With orders for all versions of the DC-9 exceeding comfortably the 1,000 mark in 1980, there is no doubt that, to date, this short/medium-range airliner represents the company's most successful turbine-powered commercial transport. There was little hint that this might be so when, in 1962, Douglas gave details of its design study for a short-range turbine-powered transport. This was not really surprising, for there was already a fair degree of competition in this field with the Aérospatiale (Sud-Aviation) Caravelle established in service, and the BAe (BAC) One-Eleven under development.

At that date there was no suggestion that Boeing was to develop a short-haul version of the successful 707/727 family, and by the time Boeing's 737 entered service, in early 1968, the first production DC-9s had been in airline use for more than two years. In that period they had proved themselves to be reliable in service and economical to operate, gaining a market lead over the 737 which has been maintained. This does not imply that one or the other of these two excellent aircraft is technically superior. It just happened that the DC-9 was first on the market, with a two-year lead over its principal competitor. In addition, the Douglas company had gained from experience with the DC-8 to be prepared, from the beginning of production, to have a flexible approach to the needs of individual airlines.

The decision of the Douglas company to invest in the design and development of a short-haul turbofan-powered airliner had not been reached easily or quickly. There had been an attempt to interest operators in a four-engined short-range derivative of the DC-8, but this proposal was not well received. It was decided, therefore, to evolve a design which would be tailored specifically for the short-range operator, with the object of providing a fast, reliable and economic vehicle for use in this important sector of the market.

Without the benefit of initial orders to provide a degree of financial support, the company initiated construction of the new DC-9 on 26 July 1963. Fortunately, orders began to flow in during the early construction period, but these had reached only 58 by the time the first aircraft made its maiden flight on 25 February 1965. This was no development of the earlier DC-8, but a completely new design. Of low-wing monoplane configuration, the DC-9 had wings which were moderately swept at 24°, and incorporated wide-span double-slotted trailing-edge flaps, inboard (high speed) and outboard (low speed) ailerons, air brakes on the wing upper surfaces and a boundary-layer fence beneath the wing. Subsequent versions, after the initial Series 10, were also to have leading-edge slats.

The fuselage was of fail-safe construction to allow for pressurisation, and the cantilever T-tail raised the tailplane and elevator well clear of the efflux of the rear-mounted turbofan engines. The retractable landing gear was of the tricycle type, with twin wheels on each unit. Initial powerplant comprised two 12,000-lb (5443-kg) thrust Pratt & Whitney JT8D-5 turbofans, but versions of the Series 10 also appeared with 14,000-lb (6350-kg) thrust JT8D-1 or JT8D-7 engines. All-passenger models, which had standard accommodation for 80 and maximum seating for 90, were known as Series 10 Model 11 aircraft, but Model 15s were also built for Trans-Texas Airways under the designation DC-9-15MC, and for Continental Airlines under the designation DC-9-15RC. The MC (Multiple Change) aircraft had reinforced flooring, a cargo door on the port side of the fuselage, plus folding seats aft and cargo stowage forward; RC (Rapid Change) aircraft were similar, except that the seating was pallet-mounted.

The first Series 10 gained certification on 23 November 1965, and two weeks later, on 8 December, Delta Air Lines inaugurated its first revenue service with the type. Production of Series 10s totalled 137, and they were to demonstrate excellent standards of reliability. By comparison with competing BAC One-Elevens, however, their operating cost per seat/mile was higher, emphasising to the company the

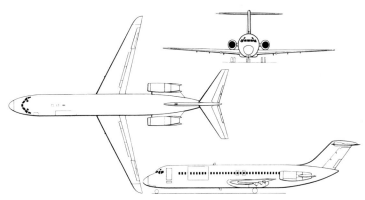

McDonnell Douglas DC-9-50 of Hawaiian Airlines.

McDonnell Douglas DC-9-30

Swissair operates a large European network with its McDonnell Douglas DC-9 fleet: one DC-9-30F; 20 DC-9-30s, 12 DC-9-50s (one illustrated) and 15 DC-9-80s on order.

Douglas DC-9

urgent need to develop and introduce into service a higher-capacity version.

It had been intended to develop 'stretched' versions from the earliest design stage, so the evolution of a higher capacity cabin was not long delayed. It was achieved by the insertion of a fuselage plug 14 ft 10¾ in (4.54 m) in length, to give standard accommodation for 105 passengers, or maximum seating for 119. Other changes were incorporated at this stage, however, including an increase of 4 ft 0 in (1.22 m) in wing span, the introduction of full-span wing leading-edge slats, and the installation of 14,000-lb (6350-kg) thrust JT8D-7 turbofans as standard.

Designated as the Series 30, the first of these was flown on 1 August 1966, and initial services were operated by Eastern Air Lines on 1 February 1967. Optional powerplants have included 14,500-lb (6577-kg) thrust JT8D-9s, 15,000-lb (6804-kg) thrust JT8D-11s, 15,500-lb (7031-kg) JT8D-15s, and 16,000-lb (7257-kg) JT8D-17s. In addition to the standard passenger carrying Series 30, AF (All Freight), CF (Convertible Freighter) and RC (Rapid Change) configurations were available.

To meet the requirement for a version that would be suitable for the shorter runways of the network operated by Scandinavian Airlines System, Douglas evolved the Series 20, which retained the fuselage of the Series 10, but combined with this the increased-span, more-advanced wing that had been developed for the Series 30. Accommodation is provided for 90 passengers, and powerplant consists of 14,500-lb (6577-kg) thrust JT8D-9 turbofans. The first Series 20 aircraft was flown on 18 September 1968, and began revenue service with SAS on

McDonnell Douglas DC-9-30 of Iberia (Lineas Aereas de Espana).

23 January 1969.

SAS was the stimulus also for initial development of the Series 40, a high-capacity short-range version. Generally similar to the Series 30 in overall configuration, it differs in having a fuselage lengthened by 6 ft 3¾ in (1.92 m) to provide maximum seating capacity for 132 passengers. Fuel capacity is increased, and the Series 40 is available with JT8D-9, -15 or -17 engines, later versions having engine nacelles that incorporate advanced sound suppression materials and techniques. The first of these aircraft made its initial flight on 28 November 1967, and SAS introduced the type into revenue service on 12 March 1968.

Since 1976 the major production version has been the DC-9 Series 50, first announced on 5 July 1973. This is also a 'stretched' development of the Series 30, but originating at a much later time it benefits from a more modern approach to interior layout and decor. The Series 50 retains the wing of the Series 30, but has the fuselage lengthened by an additional 14 ft 3 in (4.34 m), which represents an increase in length of almost 28 per cent by comparison with the original Series 10. Standard accommodation is for 122 passengers, with a maximum of 139 in a high-density seating arrangement. The interior of Series 50 aircraft has what Douglas calls a 'new look',

which by skilful design gives the cabin a more spacious appearance, intended to have greater appeal for those passengers accustomed to the 'wide-body' of the Boeing 747, and other later aircraft featuring such large-capacity cabins. JT8D-15 or JT8D-17 engines are available for the Series 50, and the engine nacelles are acoustically treated to reduce noise emission to the lowest figure so far possible for this powerplant installation.

All current versions of the DC-9 are available also in freight (F), convertible (CF), and passenger/freight (RC) configurations. In addition specialised conversions of the Series 30 have been supplied: to the USAF under the designation C-9A Nightingale, as an aeromedical transport; to the USN as the C-9B Skytrain II, as a fleet logistic support transport; and to the USAF as the VC-9C for duties with the Special Air Missions Wing. The details below apply to the DC-9 Series 50.

Specification

Type: short/medium-range transport
Powerplant: two 15,500-lb (7031-kg) thrust Pratt & Whitney JT8D-15 turbofans
Performance: maximum speed 575 mph (925 km/h); economic cruising speed 510 mph (821 km/h); range with reserves and payload of 97

passengers 2,065 miles (3323 km)
Weights: empty 61,880 lb (28068 kg); maximum take-off 121,000 lb (54885 kg)
Dimensions: span 93 ft 5 in (28.47 m); length 133 ft 7¼ in (40.72 m); height 28 ft 0 in (8.53 m); wing area 1,000.75 sq ft (92.97 m²)
Operators include: Aerolinee Itavia, Aeromexico, Aero Trasporti Italiana, Air Canada, Air Florida, Air Jamaica, Alisarda, Alitalia, Ansett Airlines of Australia, ALM Antillean Airlines, Austral Lineas Aereas, Avensa, Austrian Airlines, Aviaco, Balair, British Midland Airways, BWIA International, Delta Air Lines, Eastern Air Lines, Evergreen International Airlines, Finnair, Garuda Indonesian Airways, Hawaiian Airlines, Hughes Airwest, Iberia, Inex-Adria Airways, Jugoslovenski Aerotransport, KLM, LAV, Martinair Holland, Midway Airlines, Ozark Airlines, Republic Airlines, SAS, Swissair, Texas International, Toa Domestic Airlines, Trans-Australian Airlines, TWA, Turk Hava Yollari, and US Air

The first major 'stretch' of the McDonnell Douglas DC-9 family came with the Series 30, with a fuselage some 14 ft 11 in (4.60 m) longer than that of the Series 10. Austrian Airlines has a fleet of 14 DC-9s, including nine Series 30 aircraft.

Douglas DC-9 Super 80 Series

History and Notes

The DC-9-50 has proved to be an efficient and reliable short/medium-range transport, endorsed by airlines with significant numbers of these aircraft such as Eastern Air Lines, Republic Airlines and Swissair. However, these and other users appreciated that a version with even greater capacity would be more fuel-efficient, and with fuel costs rising at an alarming rate, even minor economies can represent a very large overall saving when spread across a year of operations.

The development of a larger-capacity DC-9 was related, of course, to the availability of a suitable powerplant. This was not only required to provide greater thrust, but low noise emission was essential to meet the more stringent regulations intended to reduce significantly the noise pollution by transport aircraft. Pratt & Whitney had been involved in the development of an improved version of the well-proven JT8D turbofan. One aspect of this work was the introduction of a new low pressure compressor: this was of increased diameter but had fewer compression stages, and NASA research had shown that such a configuration would provide reduced noise levels and more economy in operation.

Known as the JT8D Series 200 engines, their design has enjoyed the benefits of the experience with the company has gained in the evolution of new-generation powerplants, and flight development of a prototype engine began in March 1977. This was to show that a three- rather than two-fold advance had been gained. Not only was the JT8D-209 some 15 per cent more powerful than the JT8D-17, but it was also quieter and demonstrated a specific

fuel consumption about 10 per cent below that of the earlier engine. One new benefit had also accrued: the standard thrust rating of the -209 engine is 18,500 lb (8391 kg), but each has an emergency thrust reserve of 750 lb (340 kg); in the event of an engine failure, this additional thrust is available automatically on the remaining operating powerplant.

Clearly, the availability of this engine meant that Douglas could proceed with the development of an increased capacity DC-9, one which would offer significantly improved standards of performance. By comparison with the DC-9-50, the basic DC-9 Super 81 has a number of

structural changes. These include an increase in wing span of 14 ft 5 in (4.39 m), an increase in tailplane span, and a fuselage 'stretch' totalling 14 ft 3 in (4.34 m), of which 12 ft 8 in (3.86 m) is forward of the wing. With this lengthened fuselage, accommodation is provided for 137 mixed-class passengers, or a maximum of 172 in a high-density layout. Like the DC-9-50, the Super 81 has the Douglas 'new look' interior, decor and lighting, to enhance the impression of spaciousness in what is now a large cabin, measuring 101 ft 0 in (30.78 m) from front to rear. It is interesting to note that the equivalent measurement in the original DC-9-

The McDonnell Douglas DC-8 Super Eighty series is the third major derivative of the basic DC-9, the world's best selling transport twin-jet. The Super Eighty was developed as a short/medium-range airliner of high capacity, and among the airlines to have ordered the type is Austral, which plans to have five.

The McDonnell Douglas DC-9 Super 80 series is a classic example of the 'stretch' that can be built into aircraft. Compared with Series 50 aircraft, the fuselage is lengthened by 14 ft 3 in (4.34 m) to seat a maximum of 172 instead of 139 passengers, and wing span is increased by 14 ft 5 in (4.39 m). The first Super 80 went to Swissair in 1980.

Douglas DC-9 Super 80 Series

10 was only 55 ft 9 in (16.99 m). The volume of the Super 81's underfloor cargo hold is more than doubled compared with that of Series 10 aircraft.

In addition to the foregoing changes, the Super 81 has a number of system improvements that not only help to improve performance and on-board environment, but are intended also to reduce the workload of the flight crew. The first Super 81 was flown for the first time on 18 October 1979, receiving FAA certification on 26 August 1980, and the first of 15 on order for Swissair was

Another major operator of the McDonnell Douglas DC-9 Super Eighty series is the important Japanese line, Toa Domestic Airlines, which plans a fleet of eight. Operating a taut network of services to 35 Japanese cities, Toa has an extensive fleet (more than 60 fixed-wing aircraft) including 22 DC-9-40s. The Super Eighty's maximum seating capacity is 172.

McDonnell Douglas DC-9 Super 80 cutaway drawing key

1 Radome
2 Weather radar scanner
3 Front pressure bulkhead
4 Pitot tube
5 Radio and electronics bay
6 Nosewheel well
7 Twin nosewheels
8 Rudder pedals
9 Instrument panel
10 Instrument panel shroud
11 Windscreen wipers
12 Windscreen panels
13 Cockpit eyebrow windows
14 First officer's seat
15 Overhead switch panel
16 Captain's seat
17 Nosewheel steering control
18 Underfloor electrical and electronics bay
19 Nose strake
20 Retractable airstairs
21 Door mounted escape chute
22 Forward passenger door, open
23 Entry lobby
24 Starboard service door
25 Forward galley
26 Toilet compartment
27 Wash hand basin
28 First-class seating compartment, 12 passengers four-abreast
29 D/F loop aerials
30 VHF aerial
31 Curtained cabin divider
32 Cabin window panel
33 Pressurisation valves
34 Fuselage lower lobe frame construction
35 Wardrobe
36 Tourist class seating, 125 passengers five-abreast
37 Overhead stowage bins
38 Cabin roof frames
39 Air conditioning ducting
40 Cabin roof trim panels
41 Floor beam construction
42 Forward freight hold, capacity 849 cu ft (24,04 m³)
43 Forward freight hold rear door
44 Port overhead stowage bin rack
45 Fuselage frame and stringer construction
46 Leading edge slat central hydraulic jack control
47 Wing panel centreline joint
48 Floor beam construction
49 Centre fuselage construction
50 Cable drive to leading edge slats
51 Starboard wing integral fuel tank; total system capacity 5,779 US gal (21 876 l)

52 Fuel system piping
53 Ventral wing fence ("vortilon")
54 Pressure refuelling connections
55 Leading edge slat segments, open
56 Overwing fuel filler cap
57 Starboard navigation lights
58 Extended wing tip
59 Rear navigation and strobe lights
60 Static dischargers
61 Starboard aileron
62 Aileron tabs
63 Starboard outer double-slotted flap, down position
64 Flap hydraulic jacks
65 Flap hinge brackets
66 Outboard spoilers
67 Inner double-slotted flap, down position
68 Inboard spoiler
69 Starboard emergency exit windows
70 Pressure floor above wheel bay
71 Port emergency exit windows
72 Hydraulic reservoir
73 Main undercarriage wheel well
74 Rear cabin tourist class seats
75 Cabin attendant's folding seat
76 Rear service door/emergency exit
77 Rear underfloor freight hold door
78 Cabin wall trim panels
79 Overhead stowage bins

80 Starboard engine intake
81 Detachable engine cowlings
82 Cabin rear bulkhead
83 Rear galleys, port and starboard
84 Toilet compartments, port and starboard
85 Rear pressure bulkhead
86 Rear entry door
87 Engine thrust reverser, open position
88 Fin root fillet
89 Air conditioning ram air intake
90 Fin construction
91 VOR aerials
92 Rudder feel system pressure sensor
93 Tailplane trim jack
94 Starboard tailplane
95 Elevator horn balance
96 Starboard elevator
97 Elevator tabs
98 Tailplane bullet fairing
99 Elevator hinge controls
100 Tailplane pivot mounting
101 Port elevator
102 Tailplane construction
103 Rudder construction
104 Rudder tab
105 Static dischargers
106 Tailcone, jettisonable for emergency exit
107 Air conditioning louvres
108 Sloping fin attachment frames

109 Tailplane de-icing air duct
110 Rear entry airstairs tunnel
111 Air conditioning plant
112 Engine pylon
113 Port engine thrust reverser doors, closed
114 Radial lobe engine silencer
115 Nacelle strake
116 Bleed air piping
117 Pratt & Whitney JT8D-209 turbofan engine
118 Engine accessory gearbox
119 Port engine intake
120 Rear underfloor freight hold, capacity 445 cu ft (12,60 m³)
121 Wing root trailing edge fillet
122 Port inner double-slotted flap
123 Flap rib construction
124 Flap vane
125 Main undercarriage mounting
126 Main undercarriage leg strut
127 Inboard spoiler
128 Flap down position
129 Outer double-slotted flap
130 Outboard spoilers
131 Aileron tabs
132 Port aileron
133 Fixed portion of trailing edge
134 Static dischargers

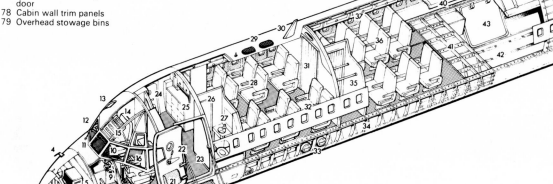

Douglas DC-9 Super 80 Series

delivered just over two weeks later, on 12 September. At that date, orders and options for Super 80s totalled 115.

About five months before the first flight of the Super 81, Douglas announced the intention to develop a 'hot-and-high' version of this aircraft under the designation DC-9 Super 82. Generally similar to the DC-9-81, this will have JT8D-217 turbofans, each rated at 20,000-lb (9072-kg) thrust, and each with an emergency thrust reserve of 850 lb (386 kg). In addition to its attraction for airlines which operate from above average

altitude/temperature airports (Aeromexico was the first buyer), the Super 82 will appeal also to airlines operating in more standard conditions, for the increased thrust makes possible the uplift of a greater payload, and if this comprises more fuel, then greater full-capacity range can result.

Other versions have been proposed, including a short-field Super 80SF, and a Super 83 for European charter operations, but no decision to proceed with their development had been reached in the summer of 1980.

The details below apply to the DC-9 Super 81.

Specification

Type: short/medium-range transport

Powerplant: two 18,500-lb (8391-kg) thrust Pratt & Whitney JT8D-209 turbofans, each with an emergency thrust reserve of 750 lb (340 kg)

Performance: maximum speed 576 mph (927 km/h); normal cruising speed Mach 0.76; range with maximum fuel 3,060 miles (4925 km)

Weights: empty 79,757 lb (36177 kg); maximum take-off 140,000 lb (63503 kg)

Dimensions: span 107 ft 10 in (32.87 m); length 147 ft 10 in (45.06 m); height 29 ft 8 in (9.04 m); wing area 1,279 sq ft (118.82 m²)

Orders include: Aeromexico, Air California, Austral Lineas Aereas, Austrian Airlines, Hawaiian Airlines, Inex-Adria Airways, North Central Airlines, Republic Airlines, Pacific Southwest Airlines, Swissair, and Toa Domestic Airlines

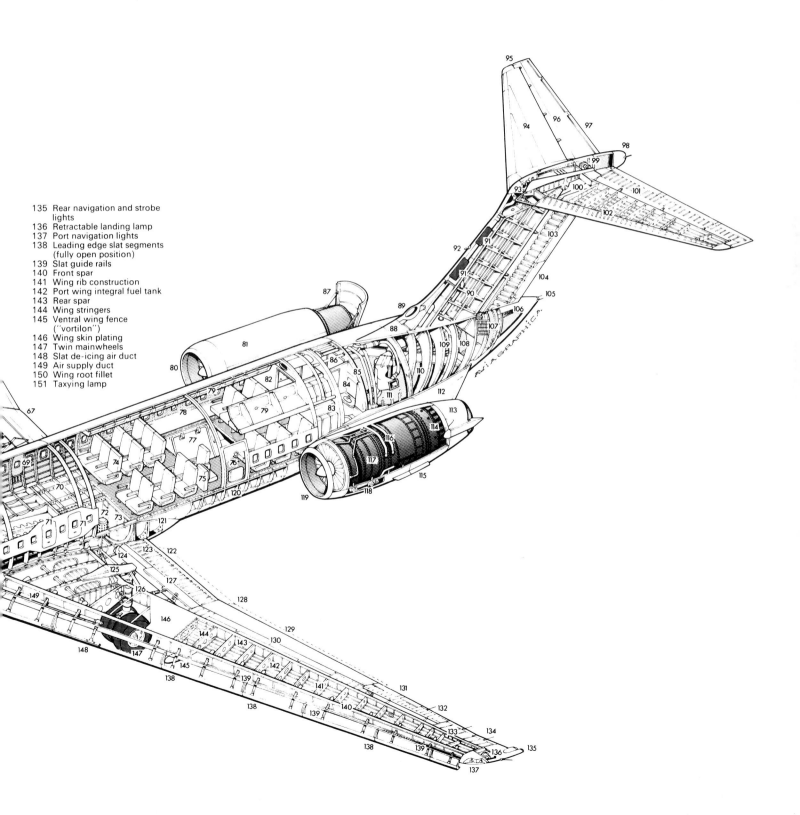

135 Rear navigation and strobe lights
136 Retractable landing lamp
137 Port navigation lights
138 Leading edge slat segments (fully open position)
139 Slat guide rails
140 Front spar
141 Wing rib construction
142 Port wing integral fuel tank
143 Rear spar
144 Wing stringers
145 Ventral wing fence ("vortilon")
146 Wing skin plating
147 Twin mainwheels
148 Slat de-icing air duct
149 Air supply duct
150 Wing root fillet
151 Taxying lamp

Hawaiian Airlines runs an inter-island passenger network, and the company plans to extend this both to the Pacific island groups to the south-east and to the continental USA. Hawaiian's fleet is based on 10 DC-9-50s and eight DC-9-30s, and the company is also receiving six of the Super Eighty series, one of these being illustrated.

Douglas DC-10

History and Notes

In July 1966, The Boeing Company had committed the Boeing Model 747 to production. The information that a giant, wide-body, turbofan-powered long-range transport was in the process of construction was received in a variety of ways. These ranged from the scaremongering of the more lurid journalists, who felt compelled to point out that an aircraft accident could involve up to 500 passengers; at the other end of the spectrum this was offset by air traffic controllers who were quick to appreciate that wide-scale use of such aircraft could very considerably ease their heavy workload.

Information regarding Boeing's plans, at whatever date this became known to the Lockheed Corporation and Douglas Aircraft Company Inc., must have come as something of a shock. This does not imply that the two companies had not been working along similar lines, but with Boeing having started production, it was necessary for them both to decide quickly whether or not they intended to compete in the same league. As a result, Douglas went into production with the DC-10 in April 1968, Lockheed following with its L-1011 (later named TriStar) in July 1968.

The Douglas design team was very conscious, from the earliest days of study and planning, that the aircraft which was to materialise from their drawing boards would need to have a basic design that would allow for growth versions and variants suitable for a variety of roles. The Douglas project, and Lockheed's also, began in March 1966, when American Airlines outlined their requirement for a large-capacity twin-engined aircraft. Both manufacturers were to propose a rather larger aircraft than that envisaged by American Airlines, and both opted for a three-engine powerplant. The Douglas proposal proved the more attractive, and on 19 February 1968 American Airlines ordered 25 DC-10 aircraft, and reserved options on a further 25. This, however, was not regarded by Douglas as a safe launching order, and it was not until United Airlines

McDonnell Douglas DC-10-30 of Laker Airways, UK.

ordered 30 plus 30 options, in late April 1968, that the decision was made to put the aircraft into production.

The initial version, designated DC-10 Series 10, was intended for service on domestic routes. Most importantly for such utilisation, it was expected to provide economical operation over a wide range of stage lengths, from as little as 300 miles (483 km) to a maximum of 3,600 miles (5794 km). The low-set wing is, therefore, swept 35° to provide good high-speed cruise performance. Good low-speed characteristics are also required, and the wing therefore incorporates full-span leading-edge slats, double-slotted trailing-edge flaps, inboard (high-speed) and outboard (low-speed) ailerons, and five spoilers on each wing that can be used differentially in the air for roll control, collectively in the air as speed brakes, or collectively on the ground as lift-dumpers. The fuselage is a fail-safe structure of circular cross-section, and the tail unit is conventional for aircraft with a third engine installed at the base of the fin; the remaining two engines are pylon-mounted, one beneath each wing. The tricycle type landing gear of the Series 10 is also conventional, with a twin-wheel steerable nose unit, and a four-wheel bogie on each main unit. However, the company had realised this would be inadequate for future versions to be certificated at higher gross weights, and thus planned for the main units to be supplemented by a third central unit with twin wheels.

The flight deck is intended for a

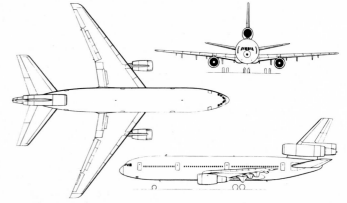

McDonnell Douglas DC-10-30

crew of three, though two additional seats are provided for the use of observers, as and when required for check purposes. Standard accommodation in the main cabin can vary from 255 to 270 for mixed-class configurations, and with a high-density seating arrangement a maximum of 380 passengers can be carried.

The powerplant of the basic Series 10 comprises three 40,000-lb (18144-kg) thrust General Electric CF6-6D turbofans, but 41,000-lb (18597-kg) CF6-6D1s are available optionally for airlines operating from 'hot-or-high' airports. Other series DC-10s are in service with General Electric or Pratt & Whitney engines, and it has been company policy from the early days of DC-10 development to allow customers to specify the powerplant required.

The first Series 10 aircraft made its maiden flight on 29 August 1970, with FAA certification being awarded on 29 July 1971. The first revenue flight, on their non-stop Los Angeles-Chicago service, was made by American Airlines a week later, on 5 August 1971, representing a period of three years and four months between the decision to begin production and entry into scheduled service. In this respect, McDonnell Douglas won the development race, for Boeing's 747 required three years and six months, and Lockheed's L-1011 TriStar three years and nine months between these two milestones.

Continental Airlines, which was to acquire eight basic DC-10-10s, also had the need for a convertible passenger/cargo variant, of which eight were built for this operator. Designated DC-10-10CF, these have strengthened flooring, and an 8 ft 6 in by 11 ft 8 in (2.59 m by 3.56 m) cargo loading door installed in the port side of the fuselage at the forward end of the cabin.

A variant of the DC-10-10, with 52,000-lb (23587-kg) thrust General Electric CF6-50C2F engines, was ordered by Aeromexico and Mexicana, in the summer of 1979. Apart from the differing powerplant installation, intended to simplify for these airlines their operations under 'hot-and-high' conditions, these Series 15 aircraft are virtually identical to the basic Series 10. Each airline has ordered two DC-10-15s, plus two options for Mexicana, and the four covered by firm orders were scheduled for delivery during 1981.

The next version to be evolved, an extended-range aircraft for intercontinental operation, was developed initially to meet the requirements of Northwest Orient Airlines. This company ordered 22 aircraft towards the end of 1968, specifying the installation of Pratt & Whitney JT9D-15 turbofans. This powerplant was in

A McDonnell Douglas DC-10-10F of Federal Express. Based at Memphis Airport, this unique airline runs a nocturnal parcels service within the USA.

Douglas DC-10

A McDonnell Douglas DC-10-10 of Western Air Lines. This is the oldest US airline, having been founded in 1925 as Western Air Express, and operates 12 DC-10-10s on its longer routes.

use in Northwest's Boeing 747s, and this standardisation of engine was considered a worthwhile contribution to economical maintenance simplification. Designated originally as Series 20 aircraft, the DC-10-20 prototype was flown for the first time on 28 February 1972, but this version was later redesignated Series 40, and no Series 20 aircraft were built as such. With this change in designation of the aircraft, that of the powerplant became JT9D-20, and each of these engines was rated at 49,400-lb (22407-kg) thrust with water injection. Other changes to suit this version for its intercontinental role included increased wing span and area, a slight increase in overall length resulting from the JT9D engine installation, the introduction of the third main landing gear unit, and increased fuel tankage with almost 68 per cent more capacity than that of the Series 10. As a result of these changes the maximum take-off weight is some 22 per cent higher, and maximum payload range is increased from 2,706 miles (4355 km) to 4,030 miles (6485 km). Japan Air Lines were subsequently to order Series 40 aircraft, but these have more powerful JT9D-59A turbofans, each developing 53,000-lb (24040-kg) thrust. They permit a maximum take-off weight of 572,000 lb (259455 kg), just over 3 per cent higher than Northwest's Series 40s, but increase the maximum

The Scandinavian Airlines System (SAS) has a mixed fleet with five McDonnell Douglas DC-10-30s, fitted with uprated engines and the third main landing gear leg, for long-haul operations.

payload range by almost 16 per cent to 4,663 miles (7504 km).

The major production variant by the end of 1980 was the Series 30, an extended-range intercontinental aircraft with General Electric CF6-50A, -50C, -50C1 or -50C2 engines. First flown on 21 June 1972, it is generally similar to the Series 40 apart from the different turbofans, and is available also in convertible passenger/cargo configuration as the DC-10-30CF. An extended-range version of the DC-10-30, known as

the Series 30ER, was ordered by Swissair in the summer of 1980. This will have additional fuel capacity, provided by an extra tank in the rear of the cargo compartment, giving an increase of 800 miles (1287 km) in range by comparison with the standard Series 30.

The DC-10 was also selected by the USAF to satisfy its requirement for an Advanced Tanker/Cargo Aircraft. The first of these was scheduled to enter service in 1981, designated KC-10A Extender, and each is able

to carry about 18,075 US gallons (68420 litres) of fuel in addition to the standard fuel system capacity of 34,955 US gallons (132315 litres). All of this total can be transferred in refuelling operations, except that quantity which the tanker requires to regain its base.

Used extensively on US domestic services, DC-10s with General Electric CF6 turbofans have proved reliable and economical aircraft for operations over a wide range of stage lengths. Orders and options

Modern airline operations are balanced on the knife-edge of profitability, placing great emphasis on the low fuel consumption of modern types that must be airborne as much as possible. Swissair is a major operator of the McDonnell Douglas DC-10-30, which has recently been made available in an Extended Range model with extra fuel.

Douglas DC-10

for these wide-body airliners totalled 390 in mid-1980. The details below apply to the DC-10-30.

Specification

Type: commercial transport
Powerplant: three 52,500-lb (23814-kg) thrust General Electric CF6-50C1 or -50C2 turbofans
Performance: maximum cruising speed 564 mph (908 km/h) at 30,000 ft (9145 m); service ceiling 33,400 ft (10180 m); range with maximum payload 4,606 miles (7413 km); range with maximum fuel 7,490 miles (12054 km)
Weights: basic empty 267,197 lb (121199 kg); maximum take-off 572,000 lb (259455 kg)
Dimensions: span 165 ft 4½ in (50.41 m); length 182 ft 1 in (55.50

By the mid-1980s, CP Air plans to have six McDonnell Douglas DC-10-30s for its high-density long-haul routes, operating alongside four Boeing 747s and 11 DC-8s (five -63s and six -40/50s).

McDonnell Douglas DC-10 Series 30 CF cutaway drawing key

1 Weather radar
2 Windshield
3 Instrument console
4 Flight deck
5 Captain's seat (Aircraft Mechanics Inc)
6 First Officer's seat (ditto)
7 Flight Engineer's position
8 Supernumary crew seat
9 Flight deck door
10 Forward starboard toilet
11 Forward port toilet
12 Crew and passenger forward entry door
13 Twin wheel nose gear (Abex or Dowty Rotol; Goodyear tyres)
14 Air conditioning access doors
15 Forward cargo bulkhead
16 Air conditioning bay (Garrett AiResearch equipment)
17 Forward lower galley area (used for containerized cargo)
18 Air conditioning trunking
19 Cargo deck lateral transfer area (omni-caster rollers)
20 Cargo deck pallet channels (rollers)
21 Main cargo door (fully open position)
22 VHF antenna
23 Frame-and-stringer fuselage construction
24 Main deck cargo (ten 88 x 125-in, 2,23 x 3,17-m (pallets), capacity 4,958 cu ft (140,4 m³)
25 Passenger door
26 Forward lower compartment (five 88 x 125-in, 2,23 x 3,17-m pallets), capacity 1,890 cu ft (53,5 m³)
27 Centre-section fuselage main frame
28 Centre-section front beam
29 Sheer-web floor support over centre-section fuel tank

30 Cargo/passenger compartment dividing bulkhead
31 Starboard engine pod (Rohr subcontract)
32 Engine intake
33 Nacelle pylon
34 Leading-edge slats
35 Integral wing fuel tank
36 Starboard navigation lights
37 Low-speed outboard aileron
38 Fuel ventpipe
39 Wing spoilers/lift dumpers
40 Double-slotted flaps
41 All-speed inboard drooping aileron
42 Passenger doors
43 Centre-section fuselage mainframe
44 Cabin air ducts
45 Centre undercarriage bay
46 Keel box structure
47 Fuselage/wing attachment points
48 Wing torsion-box construction
49 Leading-edge structure
50 Nacelle pylon
51 Engine intake
52 General Electric CF6-50 turbofan
53 Exhaust outlet
54 Four-wheel main undercarriage (Menasco Manufacturing; Goodyear tyres and brakes)
55 Leading-edge slats
56 Outboard slat extended
57 Port navigation lights
58 Low-speed outboard aileron
59 Fuel vent pipe
60 Outboard flap hinge fairings
61 Fuel pipes
62 All-speed inboard drooping aileron
63 Inboard flap hinge actuator and fairing
64 Undercarriage support structure
65 Flap construction

66 Wing root fairing
67 Fuselage-attached flap track
68 Centre cargo compartment, capacity 1,280 cu ft (36,25 m³)
69 Cabin floor support
70 Overhead luggage lockers
71 Eight-abreast coach-class seating (147 passengers)
72 Baggage containers
73 Bulk cargo hold door
74 Rear passenger door (port and starboard)
75 Rear toilet (port and starboard)
76 Three toilets/washrooms
77 Underfloor bulk cargo hold capacity 805 cu ft (22,79 m³)
78 Rear pressure bulkhead
79 Tailplane centre-section (AiResearch APU below)
80 Tailplane leading-edge
81 Tailplane construction (LTV subcontract)
82 Elevator actuators
83 Dual elevators (LTV subcontract)
84 Tail cone (Mitsubishi subcontract)
85 Exhaust outlet
86 General Electric CF6-50 turbofan
87 Intake trunking
88 Intake hot-air duct
89 Engine intake
90 Starboard tailplane
91 Dual elevators
92 Tailfin leading-edge
93 Rudder actuator
94 Tail fin torsion box construction
95 VOR
96 Upper rudder sections (Aerfer subcontract)
97 Lower rudder sections
98 Tail pylon

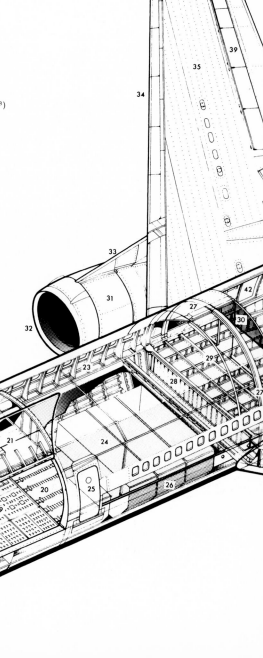

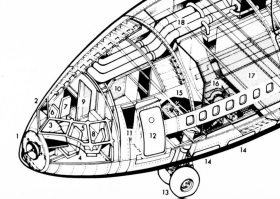

Douglas DC-10

m); height 58 ft 1 in (17.70 m); wing area 3,958 sq ft (367.70 m²)

Operators include: Aeromexico, Air Afrique, Air Florida, Air New Zealand, Air Zaïre, Alitalia, American Airlines, CP Air, Federal Express, Garuda Indonesian Airways, Iberia, Japan Air Lines, Jugoslovenski Aerotransport, KLM, Korean Air Lines, Laker Airways, Lufthansa, Malaysian Airlines System, Martinair Holland, National Airlines, Nigeria Airways, Northwest Orient Airlines, Pakistan International Airlines, Philippine Airlines, Sabena, SAS, Singapore Airlines, Swissair, Thai Airways International, THY, UTA, United Airlines, Varig, Viasa, Wardair Canada, Western Air Lines, and World Airways

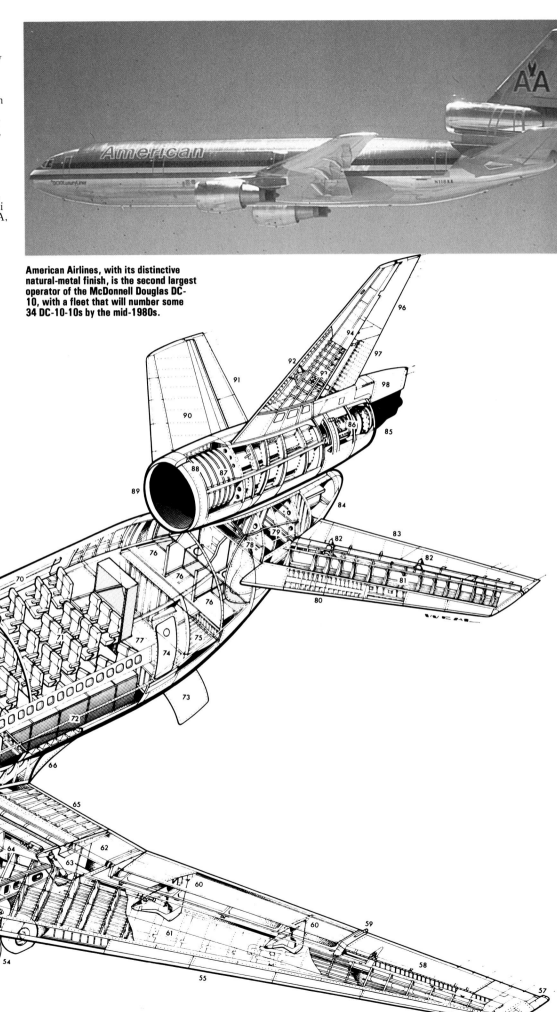

American Airlines, with its distinctive natural-metal finish, is the second largest operator of the McDonnell Douglas DC-10, with a fleet that will number some 34 DC-10-10s by the mid-1980s.

Douglas DC-10

A McDonnell Douglas DC-10-30 of the Dutch national carrier KLM. This airline has run continuous scheduled services since 1919, and from its base in Amsterdam it currently operates to most parts of the free world. The airline has a mixed fleet, its long-range element deploying 13 Boeing 747s (seven 747-200Bs and six 747-200B Combis), 14 McDonnell Douglas DC-8s (11 DC-8-63s and three DC-8-50Fs) and seven McDonnell Douglas DC-10-30s. The DC-10 series is notable for its third engine, located wholly in the vertical tail surfaces, while the DC-10-30 intercontinental version introduces a twin-wheel supplementary leg on the fuselage centre-line between the two four-wheel bogies under the wings, as well as extended-span wings and uprated engines. For training KLM has one CAE DC-10-30 simulator with another on order, thus keeping non-productive flying hours to a minimum.

EMBRAER EMB-110 Bandeirante

History and Notes

To promote the development of Brazil's aircraft industry, the company known as Empresa Brasileira de Aeronáutica SA was formed in 1969, its name being abbreviated in general use to EMBRAER. Under this title the company began operations at the beginning of January 1970, and since that time has made almost enviable progress. In addition to the design and development of indigenous aircraft, EMBRAER also builds under licence products of the US Piper Aircraft Corporation.

Among a number of highly successfull designs one must include the Bandeirante (Pioneer), a twin-turboprop aircraft that was developed to meet the requirements of Brazil's Ministry of Aeronautics for a multi-purpose light transport. Designed under the guidance of well-known French designer Max Holste, the first of three prototypes, designated YC-95, flew for the first time on 26 October 1968, and production of this aircraft became one of the first tasks of the EMBRAER company.

A low-wing monoplane of light alloy construction, the Bandeirante has a wing incorporating double-slotted trailing-edge flaps and Frise type ailerons. The semi-monocoque fuselage and mixed-construction tail unit are entirely conventional; and the landing gear is of the retractable tricycle type with a single wheel on each unit. The powerplant comprises two Pratt & Whitney Aircraft of Canada PT6A turboprops, each driving a constant-speed and reversible propeller. Accommodation is provided for a pilot and co-pilot on the flight deck, with seating for a maximum of 21 passengers in the main cabin.

The Bandeirante has successfully met the requirements of Brazil's Ministry of Aeronautics, serving in both civil and military roles. Civil transport versions include the EMB-110C, with basic accommodation for

15 passengers; the seven-passenger EMB-110E(J) executive transport; the EMB-110P 18-passenger commuter transport; and the EMB-110P2 21-passenger commuter version. There is also an EMB-110P1 quick-change version of the 21-passenger - 110P2, intended for cargo and passenger operations. A new EMB-110P3 Bandeirante with a pressurised fuselage, T-tail, twin-wheel landing gear, more powerful PT6A-65 turbo-props, and accommodation for 19 passengers, was scheduled to make a first flight in early 1982.

All versions have a wide range of standard equipment, including such features as an engine fire-detection system and propeller synchrophasers, but there is also an extensive range of optional equipment and avionics available. The Bandeirante has gained an excellent reputation in service for reliability and economy of operation, and in late 1980 sales figures were creeping past the 300 mark. The details below relate to the EMB-110P2.

Specification
Type: general-purpose light transport
Powerplant: two 750-shp (559-kW) Pratt & Whitney Aircraft of Canada PT6A-34 turboprops
Performance: maximum speed 286 mph (460 km/h) at 8,000 ft (2440 m); maximum cruising speed

EMBRAER EMB-110P1 Bandeirante of TABA (Transportes Aereos da Bacia Amazonica), Brazil.

EMBRAER EMB-110P3 Bandeirante

259 mph (417 km/h) at 10,000 ft (3050 m); economic cruising speed 203 mph (327 km/h); service ceiling 24,100 ft (7345 m); range with standard payload at 10,000 ft (3050 m) and with 45-min reserves 309 miles (497 km); range with maximum fuel at 10,000 ft (3050 m) and with 45-min reserves 1,180 miles (1900 (1900 km)
Weights: empty equipped 7,751 lb (3516 kg); maximum take-off 12,500 lb (5670 kg)
Dimensions: span 50 ft 3¼ in (15.32 m); length 47 ft 10½ in (14.59 m); height 16 ft 1¾ in (4.92

m); wing area 313.24 sq ft (29.10 m²)
Operators include: Air Affaires Gabon, Air Ecosse, Air Pacific, Air UK, Jersey European Airways, Kar-Air, Mountain West Airlines, Royale Airlines, Transportes Aereos Regionais, TABA, and Votec Servicios Aereos Regionais

One of the most remarkable successes of recent years has been the way in which the EMBRAER EMB-110 Bandeirante has broken into the commuter market. Shown is an EMB-110P1 of Imperial, a Brazilian third-level operator.

EMBRAER EMB-120 Brasilia

History and Notes
Encouraged by the successful penetration of the commuter market by its EMB-110 Bandeirante, in September 1979 EMBRAER initiated design studies for a completely new pressurised twin-turboprop 30-passenger aircraft, to be known as the EMB-120 Brasilia. The prototype is due to fly in mid-1982 and certification to US FAR25 is scheduled for 1984. Design objective is the carriage of a full 30-passenger payload for up to three 115-mile (185-km) sectors without refuellilng. The fuselage will have an interior diameter of 7 ft 1 in (2.16 m) and an aisle height of 5 ft 9 in (1.75 m), the aisle being offset by the two-and-one seating arrangement. In cargo configuration the aircraft will have a maximum available cabin volume of 848 cu ft (24.01 m³) and a 79.7 by 63 in (2.02 by 1.60 m) cargo door.

The selected engine is the advanced-technology Pratt & Whitney Aircraft of Canada PT7A, now being developed for the 30/40-passenger short-haul market and offering a claimed 20 per cent improvement in specific fuel consumption when compared with current turboprop engines in its class. Four-blade Hamilton Standard 14RF-1 propellers will be fitted but, to facilitate speedier turnrounds, the engines can be ground-run without turning the propellers, obviating the need to shut down during loading or unloading. The starboard engine will act as an auxiliary power unit, to provide ground electrical power and cabin air-conditioning.

Options for approximately 60 aircraft have been taken by the Brasilian air force and domestic operator TABA, by US commuter operators Aeromech, Provincetown-Boston Airways, Metro Airlines, Cascade Airways, and by Fairflight Charters/Air Ecosse in Britain.

Specification
Type: twin-engined 30-passenger transport
Powerplant: two 1,500-ehp (1119-ekW) Pratt & Whitney Aircraft of Canada PT7A turboprops
Performance: (estimated) maximum speed 338 mph (544 km/h); cruising speed 288 mph (463 km/h); service ceiling 33,500 ft (10210 m); range with 30 passengers, allowances, and 45-min reserves 403 miles (649 km)
Weights: (estimated) empty 11,618 lb (5270 kg); maximum take-off 20,000 lb (9072 kg)

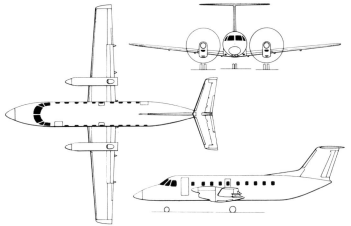

EMBRAER EMB-120 Brasilia of TAM (Brazil).

EMBRAER EMB-120 Brasilia

Dimensions: span 64 ft 10¼ in (19.77 m); length 64 ft 4¾ in (19.63 m); height 19 ft 10¼ in (6.05 m); wing area 409.35 sq ft (38.03 m²)

The progress of the Brazilian company EMBRAER in the light transport category has been remarkably rapid, and should be maintained by the fuel-economical EMB-120 Brasilia commuter-liner.

EMBRAER EMB-121 Xingu

History and Notes
EMBRAER's EMB-121 owes much to the design philosophy and detailed engineering of the EMB-110 Bandeirante but is, in fact, the first of the Brazilian company's -12 series of light cabin twins. Of this new group of models, the EMB-120 Araguaia and EMB-123 Tapajos are pressurised commuter airliners, and the EMB-121 Xingu is a smaller aircraft with a shortened fuselage equipped to carry up to 9 passengers.

The prototype EMB-121 made its first flight on 10th October, 1976. The aircraft was intended primarily to compete with the Beech King Air 90 and Mitsubishi MU-2 as a business and commercial transport; however, the initial demand came from the Brazilian air force who ordered five for use as VIP transports. Carrying the designation VU-9, these aircraft were delivered to the Grupo de Transporte Especial in Brasilia during 1978.

In FAB service the VU-9 is equipped with comfortable seating for five passengers in the main cabin. The two crew members are accommodated in a screened-off cockpit area; cockpit controls and instruments are similar in layout to those of the FAB's C-95 transports. The standard avionics include dual RCA VHF tranceivers, Collins ADF and Sunair HF units, a Sperry SPZ-200 autopilot and Bendix Weather-vision radar. The dish aerial for the latter unit is housed in a hinged dielectric nosecone.

The wings of the EMB-121 are very similar to those of the Bandeirante but are reduced in span and have modified wingtips. The short fuselage has necessitated a large vertical tail unit which is swept and has the stabiliser mounted on top. The Xingu is powered by PT6A-28 engines in Bandeirante nacelles, and the tricycle undercarriage is also the same as that of the EMB-110. A full de-icing system is fitted and the pressurised fuselage has an airstair door aft of the port wing root for main cabin access.

Specification
Type: seven-seat light communications aircraft
Powerplant: two 680-shp Pratt & Whitney Aircraft of Canada PT6A-28 turboprops
Performance: maximum speed 294 mph (473 km/h) at 15,000 ft (4575 m); long range cruising speed 247 mph (398 km/h) at 20,000 ft (6100 m); stalling speed (flaps down) 81 mph (131 km/h); maximum rate of climb at sea level 1900 ft (580 m) per minute; take-off run at take-off gross weight 1706 ft (520 m); service ceiling 27,300 ft (8,320 m); maximum range at long range cruising speed and altitude with 45-min reserves 1646 miles (2650 km)
Weights: empty equipped 7663 lbs (3476 kg); maximum take off 12346 lb (5600 kg)
Dimensions: span 46 ft 4¾ in (14.14 m); length 40 ft 5 in (12.32 m); height 16 ft 2½ in (4.94 m); wing area 296.0 sq ft (27.50 m²)

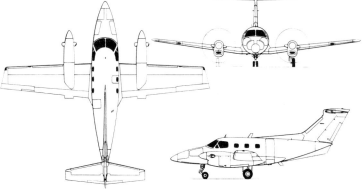

EMBRAER EMB-121 Xingu

EMBRAER's first pressurised aircraft, the EMB-121 Xingu, is a light utility transport capable of carrying up to nine passengers over a range of 1,480 miles (2380 km) at 280 mph (450 km/h).

Fairchild FH-227

History and Notes
The excellent and reliable Fokker F.27 Friendship, which has been in production in the Netherlands since 1958, was the subject of a licence agreement in April 1956 between Fokker and the Fairchild Engine and Airplane Corporation in the USA. This latter company, which for some years had been building Fokker trainers in America, was to become responsible for construction and marketing of the F.27 on that side of the Atlantic. Built under the designation F-27, the type underwent development of a pattern similar to that of the F.27 in Holland. When the development of the lengthened F.27 Mk 500 began in the 1960s, the American company, known by then as the Fairchild Hiller Corporation, produced its own 'stretched' version under the designation FH-227.

A cantilever high-wing monoplane on the same general lines as the Fokker F27, Fairchild's FH-227 had a fuselage lengthened by 6 ft 0 in (1.83 m) to provide accommodation for 44 to 52 passengers, and the first of two prototypes made its initial flight on 27 January 1966. More powerful versions of the Rolls-Royce Dart turboprops were installed, while engine variations and revised structure to cater for higher operating weights accounted for the five variants built. The FH-227 was followed by the FH-227B, which was structurally strengthened for operation at higher weights; the FH-227C retained the original operating weights of the FH-227, but incorporated some of the FH-227B improvements; and the introduction of Dart Mk 532-7L engines on FH-227s and FH-227Bs brought the resulting designations of FH-227E and FH-227D respectively.

The first FH-227s entered service with Mohawk Airlines in April 1966, this airline changing its entire fleet subsequently for the higher-weight FH-227B. A total of 78 of these

The Fokker F.27 underwent parallel production in the Netherlands and in the USA, where Fairchild produced the F-27 and FH-227 series. Illustrated is the sole FH-227B of the Aerolineas Centrales de Colombia (ACES).

Fairchild FH-227B of Touraine Air Transport, France.

'stretched' versions were built by Fairchild before production ended. The details which follow apply to the FH-227B.

Specification
Type: medium-range transport
Powerplant: two 2,050-shp (1529-kW) Rolls-Royce Dart RDa.7 Mk 532-7 turboprops
Performance: maximum cruising speed 294 mph (473 km/h) at 15,000 ft (4575 m); economic cruising speed 270 mph (435 km/h) at 25,000 ft (7620 m); service ceiling 28,000 ft (8535 m); range with maximum payload and 45-min reserves at 10,000 ft (3050 m) 606 miles (975 km); range with maximum fuel and same reserves 1,580 miles (543 km)
Weights: empty 23,200 lb (10523 kg); maximum take-off 45,500 lb (20639 kg)
Dimensions: span 95 ft 2 in (29.01 m); length 83 ft 8 in (25.50 m); height 27 ft 7 in (8.41 m); wing area 754 sq ft (70.05 m²)
Operators include: Aerochaco, Aerolineas Centrales de Colombia SA, Air New England, Air Service Company, Ecuavia, Nordair, Ozark Air Lines, and Pan Adria

FFA AS.202 Bravo

History and Notes
Originally conceived as a joint Swiss/Italian production, the Flug-und Fahrzeugwerke AG Altenrhein (FFA) Bravo was to have been built in both countries—as the AS.202 in Switzerland and as the SA.202 in Italy—but in the event SIAI-Marchetti constructed the second prototype only and it was decided because of shortage of production space to produce the type exclusively in Switzerland. The first prototype was Swiss-built and flew on 7 March 1969. A production line was established by FFA at Altenrhein, on Lake Constance, the former Swiss branch of the Dornier company.

A third prototype was built, and the first production Bravo flew on 22 December, 1971. Two versions were initially available, the AS.202/15 and AS.202/18A, powered respectively by 150-and 180-hp (122-and 134-kW) Lycoming engines. The latter had an inverted-flight oil system.

The /15 achieved Swiss certification on 15 August 1972, and FAA certification on 16 November 1973. By early 1978, 28 of the 32 ordered had been delivered.

The first /18 flew on 22 August 1974 and was certificated in Switzerland on 17 December, 1976.

Flown in 1978 and making its overseas public debut at the SBAC display at Farnborough in September of that year, the AS.202/26A is powered by a 260-hp (194-kW) Lycoming O-540 engine giving a greatly improved performance, including a maximum speed of 240 mph (386 km/h), maximum rate of climb at sea level 1,240 ft (348 m) per minute and ceiling of 22,000 ft (6700 m). The increased performance has however resulted in a range penalty, reducing this to 560 miles (900 km).

Specification
Type: two/three-seat light touring or training aircraft
Powerplant: (AS.202/15) one 150-hp (112-kW) Lycoming O-320-E2A flat-four piston engine; (AS.202/18A) one 180-hp Lycoming AEIO-360-B1F flat-four piston engine
Performance: (AS.202/15) maximum speed at sea level 131 mph (211 km/h); cruising speed at 8,000 ft (2440 m) 131 mph (211 km/h); maximum rate of climb at sea level 633 ft (193 m) per

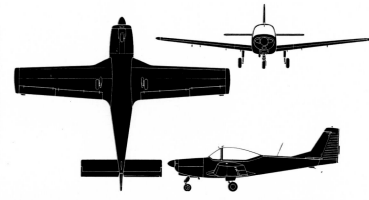

FFA AS.202 Bravo

minute; service ceiling 14,000 ft (4265 m); range (no reserves) 533 miles (890 km)
Performance: (AS.202/18) maximum speed at sea level 150 mph (241 km/h); cruising speed at 8,000 ft (2440 m) 141 mph (227 km/h); maximum rate of climb at sea level 922 ft (281 m) per minute; service ceiling 18,000 ft (5490 m); range (no reserves) 704 miles (1134 km)
Weights: (AS.202/15) empty 1,388 lb (630 kg); maximum take-off 2,202 lb (999 kg); (AS.202/18) empty 1,466 lb (665 kg); maximum take-off 2,315 lb 91050 kg)
Dimensions: (both versions) span 32 ft 0 in (9.75 m); length 24 ft 7 in (7.50 m); height 9 ft 3 in (2.81 m); wing area 149 sq ft (13.86 m²)

Fokker F.27 Friendship/Fairchild F-27 Series

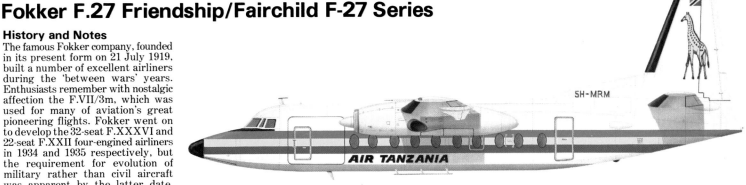

History and Notes

The famous Fokker company, founded in its present form on 21 July 1919, built a number of excellent airliners during the 'between wars' years. Enthusiasts remember with nostalgic affection the F.VII/3m, which was used for many of aviation's great pioneering flights. Fokker went on to develop the 32-seat F.XXXVI and 22-seat F.XXII four-engined airliners in 1934 and 1935 respectively, but the requirement for evolution of military rather than civil aircraft was apparent by the latter date. There was thus to be a break of virtually 17 years before, once again, the Fokker design team began to consider seriously the production of a new airliner.

Early postwar association with European airlines emphasised to Fokker the need for a modern airliner in a similar class to the Douglas DC-3. So in 1950 there followed a design study for a 32-seat transport to be powered by two Rolls-Royce Dart turboprop engines. Known as the P.275 project, this was enlarged slightly and modified to incorporate a circular-section pressurised fuselage by 1952, when Dutch government backing was sought for construction and development of the design which had by then become identified as the F.27.

The first of two prototypes (PH-NIV) made its maiden flight on 24 November 1955, powered by two Rolls-Royce Dart 507 turboprops. Of high-wing monoplane configuration, it had a conventional tail unit, a retractable tricycle type landing gear, and accommodation for 28 passengers. The second prototype was of similar configuration to the intended first production version, having a fuselage lengthened by 3 ft 0 in (0.91 m) to accommodate 32 passengers, and this was powered by Dart 511 engines when it flew for the first time on 31 January 1957. Between the initial flights of these two prototypes, Fokker had concluded an agreement with Fairchild Aircraft Division of the Fairchild Engine and Airplane Corporation in the USA. This company was to build and market the F.27 on the American side of the Atlantic under the designation F-27, later Fairchild Hiller FH-

Fokker F.27 Friendship Mk 600 of Air Tanzania.

227 after the company was renamed the Fairchild Hiller Corporation in 1964 in the wake of Fairchild's acquisition of the Hiller Aircraft Company.

Fokker's F.27 was given the name Friendship, which proved most appropriate, for this reliable airliner has made for itself a host of friends since the first F.27 entered service with Aer Lingus in December 1958. Fairchild had been a little quicker in getting its first F.27s certificated and into service, with West Coast Airlines in September 1958. In the process, Fairchild had increased basic seating capacity to 40, provided more fuel capacity, and made provision for weather radar in a lengthened fuselage nose. Fokker adopted similar changes in due course.

The initial Fokker production version was designated F.27 Mk 100 (Fairchild F-27), and was powered by two 1,715-shp (1279-kW) Rolls-Royce Dart RDa.6 Mk 514-7 turboprops. It was followed by the similar F.27 Mk 200 (F-27A), with 2,050-shp (1529-kW) Dart RDa.7 532-7 engines. Both of these airliners had standard seating accommodation for 40 passengers, but rearrangement of cabin facilities and a high-density layout made it possible to carry 52. An executive version of the Mk 200 was also available, and the interior could be furnished to virtually any customer specification. For those with money, but little imagination, a basic three-section layout was available, comprising conference room, lounge, and rest room.

The F.27 Mk 300 Combiplane (F-27B) introduced a reinforced cabin

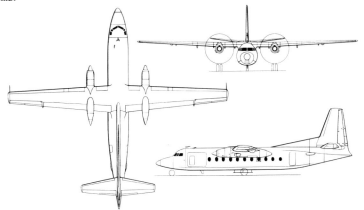

Fokker F.27 Friendship Mk 500

floor, cargo tie-down rings, and a 5 ft 10 in by 7 ft 7½ in (1.78 m by 2.32 m) cargo door forward of the wing on the port side. This version retained the powerplant of the Mk 100, and was intended for combined passenger/cargo. A similar Combiplane conversion of the Mk 200 was redesignated Mk 400, but there was no equivalent version produced by Fairchild in America. Fairchild were to develop subsequently F-27F, F-27J, and F-27M aircraft, primarily with different engine/propeller combinations, and when they ended production in the early 1970s a total of 128 F-27s of all versions had been built.

Fokker next proposed a lengthened-fuselage (by 4 ft 11 in:1.50 m) variant of the Mk 200 under the designation Mk 500. This, however, failed to appeal initially to airline

operators, but 15 were ordered by the French government in 1966 for service with the nation's highly specialised *Postale de Nuit*. In addition to the lengthened fuselage, these Air France aircraft were also provided with special large doors on each side of the fuselage. Mk 500 Friendships in airline service have standard accommodation for 52 passengers, with maximum seating for 60. The idea of this further fuselage 'stretch' appealed also to Fairchild in America, which went on to produce a variant known as the FH-227.

In 1978 the New Zealand National Airways Corporation (NAC) was merged with Air New Zealand under the latter name. Amongst the holdings of the new state airline are 15 Fokker F.27 Friendships (nine Mk 100s and six Mk 500s).

Pilgrim Airlines run services in the north-east USA and into Canada. The company's largest aircraft is the Fokker F.27 Friendship, in the form of four Mk 200s, the second production model featuring uprated Dart turboprops. Despite the age of the air frame and engine, airlines of the 1980s were still ordering the F.27 for its reliability and fuel economy.

Fokker F.27 Friendship

The latest production version is the F.27 Mk 600 which, though generally similar to the Mk 200, has the large cargo door of the Mk 300/400 Combiplanes but does not have the reinforced cargo flooring. However, a roller-track quick-change interior is available optionally for the Mk 600, making the aircraft suitable for passenger or cargo services, with palletised seats or cargo. A single example of the above, with the lower rated engines of the Mk 100, was sold to Icelandair, and this carries the designation Mk 700. Other versions comprise Mk 400M and Mk 500M military aircraft, a Mk 400M aerial-survey variant with wide angle cameras and inertial navigation, and an F.27 Maritime suitable for coastal patrol, fishery protection, and search and rescue.

Current production aircraft have an updated flight deck and cabin interior, and manufacture is shared also by Dassault-Breguet (mid and aft fuselage sections), SABCA (outer wing panels), and VFW (ailerons, flaps and dorsal fin). Overall sales by Fokker exceeded 520 in early 1981, and a further 215 F-27/FH-227s had been built by Fairchild in America before their production ended. Details below apply to the current Mk 200 Friendship.

Specification
Type: medium-range transport
Powerplant: two Rolls-Royce Dart Mk 536-7R turboprops, each with a maximum take-off rating of 2,320 ehp (1730 ekW)
Performance: normal cruising speed 298 mph (480 km/h) at 20,000 ft (6100 m); service ceiling 29,500 ft (8990 m); range with 44 passengers and reserves 1,197 miles (1926 km)
Weights: operating empty 24,612 lb (11164 kg); maximum take-off 44,996 lb (20410 kg)
Dimensions: span 95 ft 1¾ in (29.00 m); length 77 ft 3½ in (23.56 m); height 27 ft 10½ in (8.50 m); wing area 753.50 sq ft (70.00 m²)
Operators include: Air Alpes, Air Executive-Norway, Air France, Air Inter, Air New Zealand, Air Niugini, Air Tanzania, Air UK, Air Zaïre, Ansett Airlines of Australia, Ansett Airlines of New South Wales, Ansett Airlines of South Australia, ATI, Aviaco, Aviateca, Bangladesh Biman, Burma Airways Corporation, East-West Airlines, Gulf Air, Iberia, Indian Airlines, Korean Air Lines, Libyan Arab Airlines, LADE, Luxair, Malaysian Airline System, PT Merpati Nusantara Airlines, Nederlandse Luchtvaart Maatschappij, Nigeria Airways, PIA, Pilgrim Airlines, Sudan Airways, TAAG-Angola Airlines, and Trans-Australia Airlines

Three Fokker F.27 Friendships are operated by Luxair, the national airline of Luxembourg. The aircraft are two F.20 Mk 100 and one Mk 600, the latter being illustrated.

Fokker F.28 Fellowship

History and Notes
Relationships developed by Fokker during early sales negotiations for the F.27 showed that airlines also had a requirement for a higher-performance airliner of slightly greater capacity. In 1960, therefore, the company initiated design studies for a turbofan-powered short/medium-range airliner that would be complementary to the F.27. In April 1962 the first details were released of this new aircraft, which was to become designated F.28 Fellowship, and in 1964 a decision was made to start development and production of this new airliner. Financial backing was provided by the Netherlands government, with support coming also from Fokker and a number of risk-sharing international manufacturers. These included MBB in West Germany which builds the mid-fuselage section, engine nacelles and their mounting supports; Shorts in the UK which manufactures the wings and other components; and VFW in West Germany responsible for a small forward-fuselage section, the rear fuselage and tail unit.

The first of three prototypes (PH-JHG) made its maiden flight on 9 May 1967, with certification and delivery of the first production aircraft effected simultaneously, on 24 February 1969. This initial Mk 1000 short-fuselage version was of low-wing monoplane configuration, the wing incorporating powered ailerons, double-slotted Fowler flaps and lift dumpers to provide good short-field performance. The pressurised fuselage was of circular cross-section, the tail unit incorporated a T-tailplane to avoid the efflux of the rear-mounted engines, and the landing gear was of the retractable tricycle type with twin wheels on each unit. The powerplant comprised two 9,850-lb (4468-kg) thrust Rolls-Royce RB.183-2 Spey Mk 555-15 turbofans. In this version accommodation was provided for 55 to 65 passengers, according to seat pitch, but it was available optionally as the Mk 1000C for all-cargo or mixed passenger/cargo operations; this latter variant included a large cargo door in the forward fuselage on the port side, aft of the standard passenger door.

A generally similar Mk 2000 differed only in having the fuselage lengthened by 7 ft 3 in (2.21 m), to provide accommodation for a maximum of 79 passengers. Current production versions are the Mk 3000 and Mk 4000. These both have 9,900-lb (4491-kg) thrust Spey Mk 555-15H turbofans, but the former has the fuselage length of the Mk 1000, the latter that of the Mk 2000, to accommodate a maximum of 65 and 85 passengers respectively. The Mk 3000 is also available optionally in a 15-seat executive layout.

A Mk 6000 prototype flew for the first time on 27 September 1973, this retaining the fuselage length of the Mk 2000/4000, but introducing a 4 ft 10¾ in (1.49m) increase in wing span, wing leading-edge slats and Spey Mk 555-15H turbofans. Only two examples of the version were built, and a similar Mk 5000, which retained the Mk 1000/3000 short fuselage, failed to gain any orders. A Mk 6600 was projected for service with Japanese domestic airlines, but this also failed to receive support. This would have had the fuselage lengthened by a further 7 ft 3 in (2.21m) by comparison with the Mk 6000, to accommodate 100 passengers, and would have been powered by Spey Mk 555-15K engines with automatic performance reserve.

Sales of the Fellowship were approaching 170 in the autumn of 1980, and Fokker anticipates that demand for this aircraft will continue on a steady basis for a number of years ahead. The details below apply to the current Mk 3000.

Fokker F.28 Fellowship Mk 1000 of AeroPeru (Empresa de Transporte Aero del Peru).

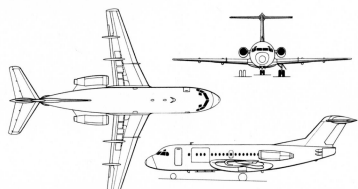

Fokker F.28 Fellowship Mk 1000

Though sales of the Fokker F.28 Fellowship have been unspectacular, they have been rising steadily to a highly respectable level. Seen is an F.28 Mk 4000 of KLM's City Hopper Service.

Fokker F.28 Fellowship

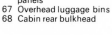

The Turkish national airline, Turk Hava Yollari (THY) operates its local routes with the aid of three Fokker F.28 Mk 1000 Fellowships, supplemented for slightly longer operations by nine McDonnell Douglas DC-9-30s.

Specification

Type: short/medium-range airliner

Powerplant: two 9,900-lb (4491-kg) thrust Rolls-Royce RB.183-2 Spey Mk 555-15H turbofans

Performance: maximum cruising speed 524 mph (843 km/h) at 23,000 ft (7010 m); economic cruising speed 421 mph (678 km/h) at 30,000 ft (9145 m); maximum cruising altitude 35,000 ft (10670 m); range with maximum fuel, reserves and 65 passengers 1,611 miles (2593 km)

Weights: operating empty 36,641 lb (16620 kg); maximum take-off 72,995 lb (33110 kg)

Dimensions: span 82 ft 3 in (25.07 m); length 89 ft 10¾ in (27.40 m); height 27 ft 9½ in (8.47 m); wing area 850.38 sq ft (79.00 m²)

Operators include: Aerolineas Argentinas, Aerolinee Itavia, AeroPeru, Air Alsace, Air Gabon, Air Ivoire, Air Niugini, Air UK, Braathens SAFE, Burma Airways Corporation, Cimber Air, Garuda Indonesian Airways, LADE, Linjeflyg AB, MacRobertson Miller Airline, Nederlandse Luchtvaart Maatschappij, Nigeria Airways, Touraine Air Transport, and THY.

Fokker F.28 Fellowship Mk 4000 cutaway drawing key

1 Radome
2 Weather radar scanner
3 Front pressure bulkhead
4 Radar equipment mounting
5 Windscreen wipers
6 Windscreen frame
7 Instrument panel shroud
8 Back of instrument panel
9 Rudder pedals
10 Ram air intake
11 Cockpit roof control panel
12 Overhead window
13 Co-pilot's seat
14 Pilot's seat
15 Control column
16 Pilot's side console
17 Air conditioning plant
18 Nosewheel doors
19 Nose undercarriage leg
20 Twin nosewheels
21 Cockpit roof construction
22 Radio and electronics rack
23 Radio rack cooling duct
24 Galley
25 Stewardess' seat
26 Curtained doorway to passenger cabin
27 Handrail
28 Entrance vestibule
29 Entry stairway
30 VHF aerial
31 Main passenger door
32 Upper VHF aerial
33 Air conditioning duct
34 Forward cabin passenger seating
35 Seat rails
36 Freight and baggage hold door
37 ADF loop aerials
38 Fuselage frame and stringer construction
39 Soundproofing panels
40 Underfloor freight and baggage hold
41 Window panels
42 Cabin floor construction
43 Hot air duct
44 Wing centre section front spar
45 HF aerial fixing
46 Leading edge fence
47 Starboard wing integral fuel tank
48 Fuel filler
49 Starboard navigation light

50 Static discharge wicks
51 Starboard aileron
52 Aileron tab
53 Flap mechanism fairings
54 Starboard outer flaps
55 Outboard spoilers (open)
56 Starboard inboard flaps
57 Inboard spoilers (open)
58 Centre section main fuselage frames
59 Air distribution duct
60 Wing centre section construction
61 Emergency escape windows
62 Mainwheel well pressurised cover
63 Port mainwheel well
64 Cabin window trim panels
65 Rear cabin seating
66 Passenger overhead service panels
67 Overhead luggage bins
68 Cabin rear bulkhead

69 Starboard engine cowling
70 Toilet
71 Wash basin
72 Air intake to APU
73 Fin root fairing
74 Fuselage sloping frames
75 De-icing air duct
76 HF aerials
77 Fin leading edge de-icing
78 Fin construction
79 Tailplane hydraulic jacks
80 Tailplane de-icing air duct
81 Anti-collision light

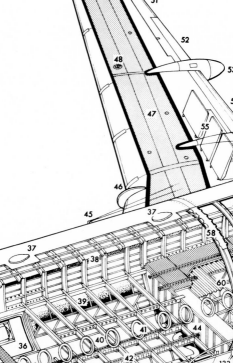

Fokker F.28 Fellowship

82 Starboard tailplane
83 Starboard elevator
84 Tailplane pivot fairing
85 Elevator hinge controls
86 Tailcone fairing
87 Tail navigation light
88 Port elevator
89 Tailplane construction
90 Leading edge de-icing
91 Tailplane pivot
92 Rudder
93 Rudder hydraulic jack
94 Port airbrake (open)
95 Airbrake jack housing
96 Rear fuselage construction
97 Hydraulic accumulators
98 Exhaust silencer nozzle
99 Engine pylon fairing
100 Bleed air ducting
101 Rolls Royce Mk 555-15 Spey Junior engine
102 Engine mountings
103 Engine cowlings
104 Auxiliary power unit (APU)
105 Engine mounting beam
106 Air intake
107 Five-abreast passenger seating
108 Underfloor air duct

109 Trailing edge wing root fairing
110 Inboard flap track fairing
111 Port inboard spoilers
112 Port flaps
113 Flap mechanism fairings
114 Port outboard spoilers
115 Flap construction
116 Aileron tab
117 Port aileron
118 Static discharge wicks
119 Port wingtip
120 Port navigation light
121 Outer wing rib construction
122 Leading edge de-icing air ducts
123 Leading edge construction
124 Lattice ribs
125 Wing integral fuel tanks
126 Twin mainwheels
127 Main undercarriage leg
128 Leading edge fence
129 Undercarriage retraction jack fixing
130 Wing panel bolted joint
131 Corrugated inner wing skin
132 Wing spar attachment frame
133 Leading edge de-icing air duct

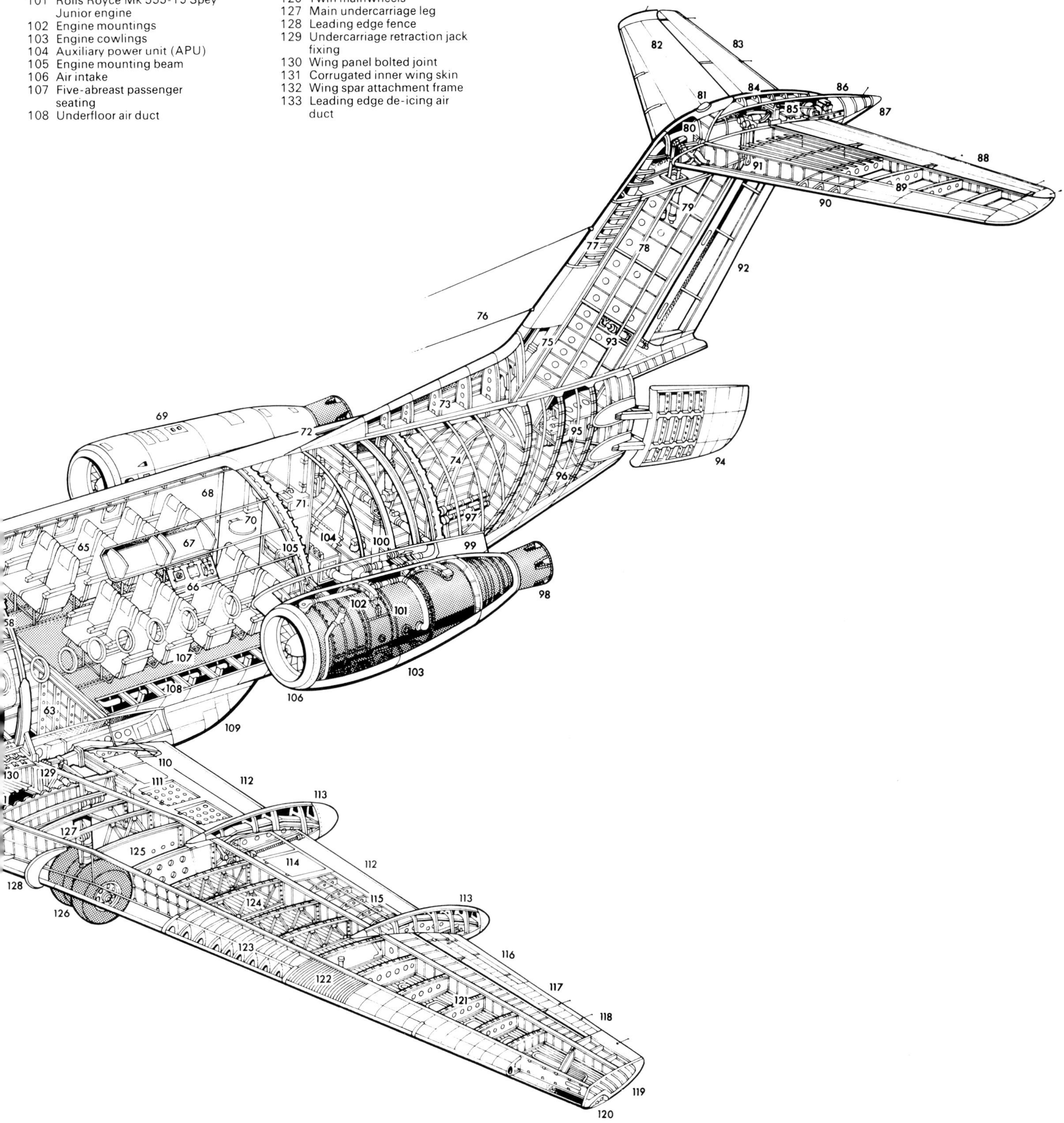

Found FBA-2/Centennial

History and Notes

Found Brothers Aviation was formed at Malton, Ontario in 1948 to build a four-seat cabin monoplane designed by Captain S R Found and designated FBA-1A. It flew for the first time on 13 July 1949, powered by a 140-hp (104-kW) de Havilland Gipsy Major engine, and was much later developed into the four/five-seat FBA-2. Of all-metal construction, the FBA-2 was flown as a prototype on 11 August 1960, originally fitted with a fixed tricycle landing gear which was proposed for the production FBA-2B (not in fact built). In spring 1961 the prototype was converted to test a set of Edo floats, offered as an option

for the production FBA-2C, which was normally fitted with conventional tailwheel landing gear. It could also operate on Edo amphibious floats or Federal wheel-skis. Powered by a 250-hp (186-kW) Avco Lycoming O-540-A1D engine, the FBA-2C featured a 6-in (15.24-cm) increase in cabin length and a 25 per cent enlargement of the rear cabin doors to improve access for freight. The initial order, for two aircraft, was placed by Georgian Bay Airways, Ontario, and the first flew on 9 May 1962. Thirty-four had been built when production ceased in favour of an improved version known as the Found 100 Centennial.

The six-seat Centennial was originally conceived in August 1966 and detail design work started in October. The prototype, powered by a fuel-injected 290-hp (216-kW) Avco Lycoming IO-540-G1D5 engine, flew on 7 April 1967. Over the next 22 months, three prototypes and two production aircraft took part in a 1,000-hour flight test programme, which culminated in FAR23 certification by the Canadian Department of Transport in July 1968. The specification applies to the FBA-2.

Specification
Type: single-engined four/five-seat cabin monoplane

Powerplant: one 250-hp (186-kW) Avco Lycoming O-540-A1D flat-six piston engine
Performance: maximum speed 147 mph (237 km/h) at 5,000 ft (1525 m); cruising speed 142 mph (229 km/h); service ceiling 16,000 ft (4875 m); range 600 miles (966 km)
Weights: empty 1,550 lb (703 kg); maximum take-off 2,950 lb (1338 kg)
Dimensions: span 36 ft 0 in (10.97 m); length 25 ft 6 in (7.77 m); height 7 ft 9½ in (2.37 m); wing area 180 sq ft (16.72 m²)
Operators: BC Airlines, Georgian Bay Airways, Pacific Western Airlines.

Fournier RF-6B

History and Notes

In December 1970 M. René Fournier began the design of a side-by-side two-seater with tricycle landing gear, a departure from his earlier 'avion planeur' series built by Alpavia in France and by Sportavia-Pützer in Germany. This aircraft was designated RF-6 and was later developed into the four-seat Sportavia RS 180 Sportsman.

Fournier established his own organisation, Avions Fournier, at Nitray, near Montlouis, and there developed a slightly smaller and aerodynamically cleaner version, still seating two side-by-side but under a

low-profile bubble canopy. The prototype, first flown in 12 March 1974, was powered by a 90-hp (67-kW) Rolls-Royce O-200-E engine driving a fixed-pitch metal propeller, and certification was achieved in April 1975 as the RF-6B.

The intended roles for the RF-6B were those of training and aerobatics, and the wood and Dacron-covered structure was stressed to limits of +6g and -3g. on 4 March 1976 the first of five pre-production aircraft flew for the first time, powered by a 100-hp (75-kW) Rolls-Royce Continental O-200-A engine with a fixed-pitch wooden propeller, as adopted for all

subsequent production examples.

Production ceased after 45 RF-6Bs had been built, the last of these being a development aircraft with a 118-hp (88-kW) Avco Lycoming O-235-L2A engine. Responsibility for development and production has been taken over by Slingsby Engineering in the UK, and the first British-built RF-6B was scheduled to fly in May 1981. A small batch of wooden aircraft was followed by a glassfibre version.

Specification
Type: two-seat aerobatic, touring and training monoplane
Powerplant: one 100-hp (75-kW)

Rolls-Royce Continental O-200-A flat-four piston engine
Performance: maximum speed 124 mph (200 km/h) at sea level; cruising speed 112 mph (180 km/h) at sea level; service ceiling 13,125 ft (4000 m); range with maximum fuel 404 miles (650 km)
Weights: empty 1,102 lb (500 kg); maximum take-off 1,653 lb (750 kg)
Dimensions: span 34 ft 5½ in (10.50 m); length 22 ft 11¾ in (7.00 m); height 8 ft 3 in (2.52 m); wing area 139.9 sq ft (13.00 m²)

Fuji FA-200 Aero Subaru

History and Notes

Successor to the Nakajima Aircraft Company, Fuji Heavy Industries was formed in July 1953 and, just over a year later, delivered the first of 161 licence-built Beech Mentors which were supplied to the Japan Self-Defense Forces, to the Philippine air force, and the Indonesian air force. The company evolved a number of derivatives which were built in small numbers, and in 1964 embarked upon the design of an entirely new four-seat light aircraft, the FA-200 Aero Subaru.

Of all-metal construction, the FA-200 prototype was flown for the first time on 12 August 1965, and subsequently went into production at Fuji's Utsunomiya factory, initially

as the FA-200-160 powered by a 160-hp (119-kW) Avco Lycoming O-320-D2A engine. In its basic four-seat configuration, the FA-200 was awarded a Normal category type certificate by the Japan Civil Aviation Bureau on 1 March 1966; certification as a three-seater in the Utility category, and as a two-seater in the Aerobatic category followed on 6 July 1966 and 29 July 1967, respectively. United States FAA Type Approval in all three categories was awarded on 26 September 1967.

The installation of the 180-hp (134-kW) Avco Lycoming IO-360-B1B engine, driving a constant-speed propeller, resulted in the introduction of the FA-200-180, which received Japanese Type Approval in the

Normal, Aerobatic and Utility categories on 28 February 1968. In the latter case, approval was for full four-seat use. With a fixed-pitch propeller, the aircraft became the FA-200-180 AO, certificated in Japan on 27 September 1973. US certification for the FA-200-180 and -180 AO was received on 25 April 1968 and 1 February 1974, respectively.

During 1980, after 294 had been completed, Fuji temporarily suspended production to concentrate on joint development with Rockwell of the Fuji 300 light twin. Deliveries of the FA-200 recommenced early in 1981, initially from a stock of uncompleted airframes.

Specification
Type: single-engined four-seat aerobatic, touring and training monoplane
Powerplant: (FA-200-160) one 160-hp (119-kW) Avco Lycoming O-320-D2A flat-four piston engine
Performance: maximum speed 138 mph (222 km/h) at sea level; economic cruising speed 102 mph (164 km/h) at 5,000 ft (1525 m); service ceiling 11,400 ft (3475 m); range with maximum fuel 755 miles (1215 km)
Weights: empty 1,366 lb (620 kg); maximum take-off 2,333 lb (1059 kg)
Dimensions: span 30 ft 11 in (9.42 m); length 26 ft 9½ in (8.17 m); height 8 ft 6 in (2.59 m); wing area 150.7 sq ft (14.00 m²)

GAF Nomad

History and Notes

Australia's Government Aircraft Factories (GAF) is the main producer of aircraft in that country, and since World War II has been regarded traditionally as a source of aircraft for the armed forces. As there were only limited military requirements, however, it was decided to develop a small turboprop-powered STOL aircraft that would be suitable for both military and civil use, in the hope that it would be possible to maintain some continuity of aircraft production.

Development began in the late 1960s, and the first of two N2 prototypes (VH-SUP) made its initial flight on 23 July 1971. Of high-wing monoplane configuration, the N2 has wings braced by a strut on each side and this strut is attached at the lower end to a small stub wing which also carries a fairing for the main landing gear unit. STOL performance is provided by full-span double-slotted flaps and drooping ailerons. The semi-monocoque fuselage is basically of rectangular cross-section, the tail

GAF N22B Nomad of Douglas Airways

unit is conventional, and the landing gear is of the retractable tricycle type. The powerplant consists of two Allison turboprop engines, each driving a constant-speed propeller with reversible capability to enhance short-field landing peformance.

Versions of the aircraft, named Nomad, have included the initial production N22 with accommodation for up to 12 passengers, and the N24 with a fuselage lengthened by 3 ft 9 in (1.14 m) to seat a maximum of 15. Current production versions include

the 13-passsenger N22B, and 17-seat N24A. A twin float N22F was certificated in the USA during 1979, and an amphibious version was due to complete its certification programme during 1980. There is also a short-fuselage military version which

GAF Nomad

has the name Mission Master, a basic coastal-patrol Search Master B, and a more sophisticated Search Master L. All of these aircraft share a common capability of being adaptable for a variety of roles, and following a slow start sales of about 130 Nomads have been made. About half of these have gone to military services. Details below apply to the N22B.

Specification
Type: STOL utility aircraft
Powerplant: two 400-shp (298-kW) Allison 250-B17B turboprops
Performance: normal cruising speed 193 mph (311 km/h); service ceiling 21,000 ft (6400 m); range with standard fuel and reserves 840 miles (1352 km) at 10,000 ft (3050 m)
Weights: operating empty 4,741 lb (2150 kg); maximum take-off 8,500 lb (3855 kg)
Dimensions: span 54 ft 2¼ in (16.52 m); length 41 ft 2½ in (12.56 m); height 18 ft 1½ in (5.52 m); wing area 324.00 sq ft (30.10 m²)
Operators include: Aeroco, Douglas Airways, Independent Air Transport, Northern Territory Aeromedical Service, and Rhine-Air

Unusually for a modern light transport, the GAF N22B Nomad can be fitted with floats, in this instance by Wipline of Minneapolis, Minnesota.

Lear Jet 23

History and Notes
The Swiss FFA P-16 jet fighter, cancelled by the federal government in the late 1950s, nevertheless caught the attention of Bill Lear Snr, who saw in it the basis for a twin-jet executive aircraft. To this end preliminary design work commenced at St Gallen, Switzerland, in November 1959. Lear sold his interest in his electronics company to the Siegler Corporation and formed the Swiss American Aviation Corporation to develop the aircraft, known originally as the SAAC Lear Jet 23. Lear's objective was to keep the Lear Jet's gross weight below 12,500-lb (5670-kg) so that it would qualify for single-pilot operation under FAA CAR 3 regulations and for air taxi operations without requiring CAB approval.

In August 1962, after the design had been finalised and tooling was in progress, Lear transferred the project to Wichita, Kansas and renamed the organisation the Lear Jet Corporation. The prototype Lear Jet made its first flight on 7 October 1963, in the hands of Henry G. Beaird, and the second and third aircraft followed it into the air on 5 March and 15 May 1964, respectively. Certification trials began on 1 April 1964, and the FAA Type Certificate was awarded on 31 July. The first production Lear Jet 23 was delivered to the Chemical and Industrial Corporation of Cincinnati, Ohio on 13 October 1964.

Despite the fact that the Lear Jet was considerably smaller than the piston-engined aircraft that it was designed to replace, it very much made up for this in performance. With an initial rate of climb of 6,900 ft (2105 m) per minute, it could reach its normal cruising height of 40,000 ft (12190 m) in a little over 9 minutes and could cruise at 526 mph (846 km/h) for approximately 1,800 miles (2895 km). Although designed for a single-pilot operation, the basic layout was for a crew of two and five/seven passengers. The first 30 aircraft were powered by two General Electric CJ610-1 engines, each of 2,850-lb (1293-kg) thrust, and the remainder of the total production run of a little over 100 Lear Jet 23s by CJ610-4s.

Specification
Type: five/seven-passenger executive transport
Powerplant: two 2,850-lb (1293-kg) thrust General Electric CJ610-4 turbojets
Performance: maximum speed 561 mph (903 km/h) at 24,000 ft (7315 m); economic cruising speed 485 mph (781 km/h) at 40,000 ft (12190 m); service ceiling 45,000 ft (13715 m); range with maximum fuel at economic cruising speed 1,830 miles (2945 km)
Weights: empty 6,150 lb (2790 kg); maximum take-off 12,500 lb (5670 kg)
Dimensions: span 35 ft 7 in (10.85 m); length 43 ft 3 in (13.18 m); height 12 ft 7 in (3.84 m); wing area 231 sq ft (21.46 m²)

Gates Learjet 24

History and Notes
The 12,500 lb (5670 kg) gross weight limit to which the original Lear Jet 23 had been developed proved in practice to be an unnecessary constraint, as most operators flew with two-man crews and CAB licensing requirements for low-capacity jet aircraft were eased. Lear was able, therefore, to take advantage of the basic strength of the design and to develop a new model, to FAR25 standards, with a gross weight of 13,500 lb (6123 kg). Announced in October 1965, the Model 24 incorporated a number of improvements, including a bird-proof windscreen and increased cabin pressure differential for higher altitude operation. The first aircraft flew on 24 February 1966, and type

The Gates Learjet 24 is a versatile aircraft, and in addition to its standard role as a 'bizjet' can be delivered as a multi-role paramilitary machine with equipment to suit it for target-towing, sea patrol and aerial mapping, etc.

certification in the air transport category was received on 17 March.

Announced on 25 September 1968 and delivered from January 1969, the Learjet 24B introduced uprated 2,950-lb (1338-kg) thrust General Electric CJ610-6 engines, and was certificated on 17 December 1968. Development of the stripped-down, lighter Learjet 24C was abandoned in December 1970, the Model 24D having been introduced. This offered increased range, as a result of the provision of additional fuel tankage, and a higher payload. The non-

structural bullet at the junction of horizontal and vertical tail surfaces was deleted on the Model 24D and all subsequent Learjets, and the original rounded cabin windows were replaced by square units. With maximum take-off weight restricted to 12,499-lb (5669-kg) the Learjet 24D became the Model 24D/A. Both models were superseded in 1976 by the Learjet 24E and 24F, both in the Century III series announced by the manufacturer on 28 October 1975. A new cambered wing and other improvements reduced stall and app-

roach speeds, and balanced field length requirements, the basic difference between the two aircraft being fuel capacity: 715 US gallons (2707 litres) in the Model 24E, and 840 US gallons (3180 litres) in the Model 24F. The specification applies to the Model 24F.

Specification
Type: twin-engined six-passenger business transport
Powerplant: two 2,950-lb (1338-kg) thrust General Electric CJ610-8A turbojets

Performance: maximum speed 547 mph (880 km/h) at 25,000 ft (7620 m); economical cruising speed 493 mph (793 km/h) at 47,000 ft (14 325 m); service ceiling 51,000 ft (15 545 m); range with four passengers, maximum fuel, plus 45-min reserves 1,697 miles (2731-km)
Weights: empty 7,064 lb (3204 kg); maximum take-off 13,500 lb (6123 kg)
Dimensions: span 35 ft 7 in (10.85 m); length 43 ft 3 in (13.18 m); height 12 ft 3 in (3.73 m); wing area 231.77 sq ft (21.53 m²)

Gates Learjet 25/28/29

History and Notes
With a fuselage stretch of 4 ft 2 in (1.27 m) to provide a cabin large enough to accommodate eight passengers and a crew of two, the Learjet 25 was flown in prototype form on 12 August 1966 and certification to FAR 25 was awarded on 10 October 1967. An improved model, designated Learjet 25B, received FAA Type Approval on 4 September 1970, as did the Learjet 25C. The latter had an additional then 193-US gallon (731-litre) fuel tank, located in the fuselage, to confer a range of about 2,500 miles (4023 km). In 1976 the Century III series modifications, including a new wing for improved low-speed and balanced field length performance, were incorporated in both models which then became the Learjet 25D and 25F. Both complied with FAR36 noise standards without suppressors, and both were initially offered with the 2,950-lb (1338-kg) thrust CJ610-6 engines, as installed in the Learjet 24. They were later available with the CJ610-8A, type-approved in April 1977 for operation

up to 51,000 ft (15 545 m), the Learjet 24E and F and the 25D and F being the first business aircraft certificated to operate at this height.

On 24 August 1977 the prototype Learjet 28 was flown for the first time: this was basically a Model 25 with a new long-span wing, with supercritical winglets at the tips in place of the usual wingtip fuel tanks. FAA Type Approval was received on 30 January 1979 and just five aircraft were delivered that year. With accommodation for a crew of two and 10 passengers, and a total usable fuel capacity of 702 US gallons (2657 litres) the Learjet 28 thus differed from the otherwise similar Learjet 29 which traded two passengers for an additional 100 US gallons (379 litres) of fuel. Both aircraft were approved for high-altitude operation and were powered by CJ610-8A engines.

Specification
Type: twin-engined 10-passenger business transport

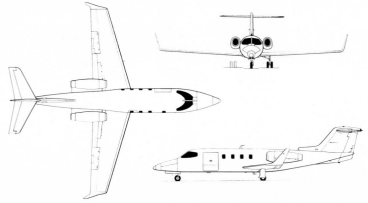

Gates Learjet 28/29 Longhorn

Powerplant: two 2,950-lb (1338-kg) thrust General Electric CJ610-8A turbojets
Performance: maximum speed 549 mph (884 km/h) at 25,000 ft (7620 m): economical cruising speed 470 mph (756 km/h) at 51,000 ft (15 545 m); service ceiling 51,000 ft (15 545 m); range with four passengers, maximum fuel,

plus 45-min reserves 1,416 miles (2279 km)
Weights: empty 8,268 lb (3750 kg); maximum take-off 15,000 lb (6804 kg)
Dimensions: span 43 ft 9½ in (13.35 m); length 47 ft 7½ in (14.52 m); height 12 ft 3 in (3.73 m); wing area 264.5 sq ft (24.57 m²)

Gates Learjet 35/36

History and Notes
The development of the Garrett-AiResearch TFE731 turbofan engine, promising lower noise levels and lower specific fuel consumption than the General Electric CJ610 turbojet which had been the standard Learjet engine, led to the introduction of the Learjets 35 and 36 in 1973. In fact, the original intention had been to develop the aircraft as versions of the Model 25, designated Learjet 25B-GF (Garrett fan) and 25C-GF. A Learjet 25 test aircraft was converted for use as an engine test-bed, mounting a 3,500-lb (1588-kg) static thrust TFE731-2 engine to starboard and retaining the CJ610 in the port nacelle. It flew on 12 May 1971 and was joined in the test programme by a second Learjet 25 (with two TFE731-2s) on 4 January 1973, and by a definitive Learjet 35 prototype on 22 August 1973.

Compared with the Learjet 25 series, the two new models both featured a 1 ft 1 in (0.33 m) increase in length and a 2 ft (0.61m) extension to each wingtip, outboard of the ailerons. Both were certificated at 17,000 lb (7711 kg) maximum weight, and differed in fuel and seating capacity. Some 921 US gallons (3486 litres) of fuel gave the eight-passenger Model 35 transcontinental range, while the Model 36 traded two passengers for an additional fuel tank in the rear fuselage, bringing total capacity up to 1,109 US gallons (4198 litres) and conferring non-stop transatlantic capability. In May 1976 the golf professional and Learjet pilot Arnold Palmer used a Learjet 36 to set a new round-the-world

Gates Learjet 35A of Wards Express, Australia.

speed record for business jets, covering 22,984.55 miles (36990 km) in an elapsed time of 57 hours 25 minutes 42 seconds, at an average speed of 400.23 mph (644.11 km/h). Certification was achieved in July 1974 and initial deliveries were made in November of that year.

The Century III package of product improvements including, notably, a new wing designed to improve low-speed handling, led to the introduction of the Models 35A and 36A in 1976. In 1978 a thrust reverser package, developed by Aeronca Inc., became available on new Learjet 35As and 36As, or as a retrofit on earlier aircraft. In the following year the Raisbeck Group achieved FAA approval for another Model 35/36 retrofit package, the Mk IV Stall Characteristics Improvement System (SCIS), the modifications including the addition of two leading-edge wing fences which alter the airflow patterns and reduce stalling speed by several knots. The removal of the wing vortex-generators provides a 7-10 per cent improvement in cruising drag and a consequent increase in range. Gates Learjet achieved similar results with its Softflite package,

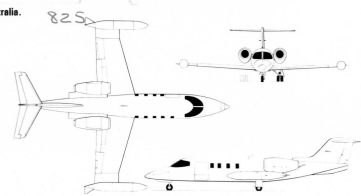

Gates Learjet 35A

fitted to all production aircraft delivered after 1 July 1979. In the same year a further enhancement became available for the Learjet 35A, in the form of a fifth cabin window on the port side and a sixth to starboard.

A special missions version of the Models 35 and 36 is the Learjet Sea Patrol, the prototype making appearances at the 1979 Paris Air Show and at the 1980 Farnborough Show. With a dash capability of about 500

mph (805 km/h) and low-speed manoeuvrability down to 130 mph (209 km/h), Gates claims that the Sea Patrol can provide twice the coverage, in the maritime patrol role, of a conventional medium-size twin-turbo-prop maritime surveillance aircraft. Equipment which can be specified includes Litton AN/APS-504(V)2 sea surveillance radar, low-light-level television with video facility, forward-looking infra-red sensors and the Daedalus DS-1210 multi-spectral

infra-red and ultra-violet line scanner with its associated data processing peripherals. ASW sonobuoy equipment can be carried, and under each wing there is a hardpoint which can take survival equipment pods, flares or other loads up to 485 lb (220 kg). The following details apply to the longer-range Learjet 36A.

Specification
Type: twin-turbofan executive transport
Powerplant: two 3,500-lb (1588-kg) thrust Garrett TFE731-2-2B turbofans
Performance: maximum cruising speed 528 mph (850 km/h) at 41,000 ft (12 495 m); economic

cruising speed 481 mph (774 km/h) at 45,000 ft (13 715 m); service ceiling 45,000 ft (13 715 m); range with maximum fuel, four passengers and 45-min reserves 3,290 miles (5295 km)
Weights: empty 9,154 lb (4152 kg); maximum take-off 18,000 lb (8165 kg)

Undoubtedly one of the most handsome 'bizjets' available, this Gates Learjet 35/36 is registered in Chile.

Dimensions: span over tiptanks 39 ft 6 in (12.04 m); length 48 ft 8 in (14.83 m); height 12 ft 3 in (3.73 m); wing area 253.3 sq ft (23.53 m²)

Gates Learjet 54/55/56 Longhorn

History and Notes
In June 1977, at the Paris Air Show, Gates Learjet released details of the Learjet 50 series, specifying increases in cabin dimensions and the installation of a more powerful version of the Garrett TFE731 turbofan engine. In September came a further announcement, of the introduction of wing modifications which involved adding a 4-ft (1.22-m) section at each wingtip and fitting NASA-developed winglets, giving rise to the Longhorn designation. The modifications were first flown on 24 August 1977, using an aerodynamic prototype wing fitted to a Learjet 25 fuselage. The aerodynamic effects are complex, but the principal benefit is that of increased range, arising from a reduction in induced drag normally produced by the wingtip vortex.

The new wing was certificated on the General Electric CJ610-8A powered Learjet 28 on 30 January 1979, but in October 1978 it had been flown on a Learjet 35, to test its compatibility with the TFE731 engine selected for the Learjet 50 series. Construction of a prototype Longhorn 50 had commenced at Wichita, Kansas in April 1978 and it flew on 19 April 1979, to be joined by a second prototype on 15 November. The first production aircraft was rolled

out on 28 March 1980, from the new manufacturing facility at Tucson, Arizona, a second final assembly line having been made necessary by a growing order book for all Learjet models.

All three models of the Longhorn 50 series have the same basic fuselage, the cabin increased in width by 12 in (0.30 m) at shoulder height and

in headroom by 16 in (0.41 m) over the central aisle. Cabin length has been increased by 6 ft 6 in (1.98 m) to accommodate up to 11 passengers. External dimensions for all three models are identical but they vary in fuel capacity, range and maximum take-off weight. The Longhorn 54, certificated at 18,500 lb (8391 kg) has a range of 2,424 miles (3901 km)

The Gates Learjet 54/55/56 series was announced in 1977 at the Paris Air Show. Designed to capitalise on the latest aerodynamic and engine improvements, the type also features a larger cabin.

and a capacity of 867 US gallons (3282 litres), while the Longhorn 55 achieves 2,859 miles (4601 km), uplifting 1,028 US gallons (3891 litres)

Gates Learjet 54/55/56 Longhorn

at a gross weight of 19,500 lb (8845 kg). Top of the range is the Longhorn 56 which has a maximum take-off weight of 20,500 lb (9299 kg) and a range of 3,468 miles (5581 km) on 1,236-US gallons (4679 litres). The specification applies to the Model 56 Longhorn.

Specification

Type: twin-engined 11-passenger business transport
Powerplant: two 3,700-lb (1678-kg) thrust Garrett TFE731-3-2B turbofans
Performance: maximum speed 534 mph (859 km/h) at 30,000 ft

(9145 m); economical cruising speed 462 mph (744 km/h) at 49,000 ft (14 935 m); service ceiling 51,000 ft (15 545 m); range with four passengers, maximum fuel plus 45-min reserves 3,468 miles (5581-km)
Weights: empty 11,119 lb (5043

kg); maximum take-off 20,500 lb (9299 kg)
Dimensions: span 43 ft 9½ in (13.35 m); length 55 ft 1¼ in (16.80 m); height 14 ft 8¼ in (4.48 m); wing area 264.5 sq ft (24.57 m²)

Two of the keys to the first-class flight performance of the Gates Learjet 54/55/56 series is the combination of fuel-economical Garrett AiResearch turbofans and low-drag wings with winglets. In the Learjet 55 this means that up to 10 passengers can be carried over distances of 3,000 miles (4830 km) at a cruising speed of 508 mph (818 km/h) and at altitudes of 51,000 ft (15545 m).

Gates Learjet Series 50 Longhorn cutaway drawing key

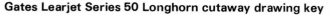

1 Radome
2 Weather radar scanner
3 Radar tracking mounting
4 Nose compartment structure
5 Baggage compartment fire extinguisher
6 Windscreen de-icing alcohol tank
7 Nose compartment access doors
8 Radio and electronics compartment
9 Nose undercarriage wheel well
10 Forward baggage compartment
11 Underfloor emergency oxygen bottle
12 Nosewheel doors
13 Nosewheel
14 Incidence vane
15 Pitot tube
16 Forward pressure bulkhead
17 Windscreen de-icing air ducts
18 Curved windscreen panels
19 Instrument panel shroud
20 Instrument panel
21 Rudder pedals
22 Control linkages
23 Cockpit floor level
24 Seat adjusting handle
25 Pilot's seat
26 Control column handwheel
27 Centre radio and instrument console
28 Engine throttles
29 Co-pilot's seat
30 Cockpit roof construction
31 Cabin bulkhead
32 Cabin roof frames
33 Seat mounting rails
34 Folding table
35 Handrail
36 Entry doorway
37 Upper door segment
38 Lower door segment/integral steps
39 Door handles
40 Fuselage frame and stringer construction
41 Cabin window panel
42 Door hinge torque tube
43 Passenger seating, eight-seat layout

44 Cabin wall trim panels
45 Three-seat settee
46 Cabin sidewall heater duct
47 Drinks cabinet
48 Wash basin
49 Toilet compartment, optional rear cabin position
50 Toilet compartment folding doors
51 Cabin roof air conditioning duct
52 Baggage door/emergency exit
53 VHF aerial
54 Baggage door open position
55 Inboard starboard wing fence
56 Wing integral fuel tank, capacity 430 US gal (1 628 l)
57 Fuel system piping
58 Outboard starboard wing frame
59 Fuel filler cap
60 Starboard navigation light, green
61 Starboard winglet
62 Winglet honeycomb construction
63 Static dischargers

64 Fixed portion of trailing edge
65 Starboard aileron
66 Aileron servo tab
67 Cable control linkage
68 Starboard single slotted flap
69 Flap guide rail
70 Starboard spoiler/speedbrake
71 Fuselage skin plating
72 Air conditioning system evaporator
73 Wing attachment, fuselage double frames
74 Baggage compartment, volume 52 cu ft (1,47 m³) Model 54; 33 cu ft (0,93 m³) Model 55; 23 cu ft (0,65 m³) Model 56
75 Pressurisation valve
76 Cabin air blower
77 Area ruled fuselage centre section

78 Rear pressure bulkhead
79 Fuselage fuel tank
80 Fuel filler cap
81 Engine pylon construction
82 Starboard engine intake
83 Garrett-AiResearch TFE 731-3A turbofan engine
84 Engine fire extinguisher bottle
85 Bleed air ducting
86 Engine mounting beam
87 Fan air exhaust duct
88 Core engine "hot-stream" exhaust

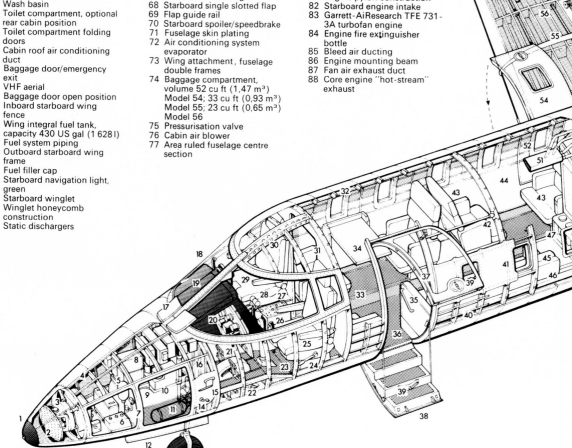

Gates Learjet 54/55/56 Longhorn

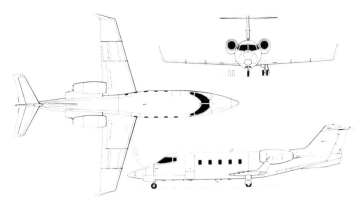

131 Flap hydraulic jack linkage
132 Port spoiler/speedbrake
133 Port single slotted flap construction
134 Aileron trim tab
135 Servo tab
136 Aileron cable control
137 Port aileron construction
138 Fixed portion of trailing edge
139 Port winglet
140 Static dischargers
141 Wing tip strobe light, white
142 Winglet rib construction

143 Port navigation light, red
144 Fuel filler cap
145 Eight-spar wing construction
146 Outboard port wing frame
147 Port wing integral fuel tank
148 Inboard port wing fence
149 Twin mainwheels
150 Main undercarriage leg strut
151 Landing/taxying lamp
152 Leading-edge stall strip
153 Leading-edge de-icing air duct

Gates Learjet 55 Longhorn

89 Pylon tail fairing
90 Ram air intake
91 Hydraulic reservoir
92 Batteries
93 Air conditioning plant
94 Dorsal fillet
95 Five-spar fin construction
96 VOR/ILS aerial
97 Elevator hinge control links
98 HF transceiver aerial cable
99 VHF aerial
100 Tailplane trim jack
101 Anti-collision light
102 Starboard tailplane
103 Leading-edge electrical de-icing
104 Elevator horn balance
105 Starboard elevator
106 Tail navigation light
107 Tailplane pivot mounting
108 Elevator torque tube
109 Port elevator construction
110 Static dischargers
111 Elevator horn balance

112 Tailplane construction
113 Balance tab
114 Rudder construction
115 Rudder trim tab
116 Tailcone
117 Ventral fin
118 Rudder hinge control
119 Venting air louvres
120 Tailcone access door
121 Rear baggage bay, 18·5 cu ft (0,52 m³)
122 Pylon engine mountings
123 Detachable engine cowlings
124 Rear baggage door, open position
125 Port engine intake duct
126 Intake lip bleed air de-icing
127 Wing root trailing edge fillet
128 Wing spar/fuselage attachment joints
129 Undercarriage hydraulic retraction jack
130 Main undercarriage mounting rib

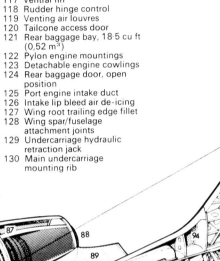
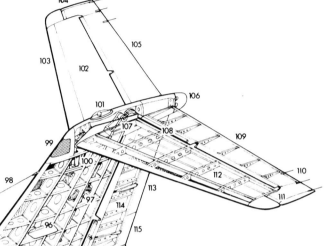
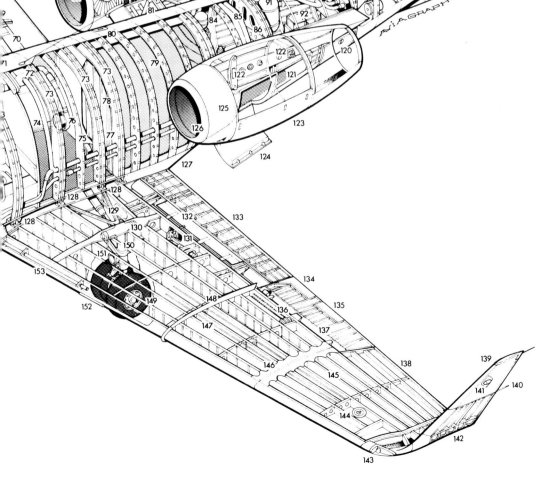

169

General Avia F-20 Pegaso

History and Notes

In January 1970 Dott. Ing. Stelio Frati, renowned as a freelance designer of a series of successful light aircraft built by manufacturers such as Ambrosini, Aviamilano, Caproni, Pasotti, Procaer and SIAI Marchetti, established Construzioni Aeronautiche General Avia to construct prototypes of his designs. The first new type to be developed at the Milan workshops was the F-20 Pegaso, a six-seat twin-engined light executive transport aircraft. Work on the first prototype commenced in September 1970: it was first flown on 21 October 1971, and a second prototype, slightly larger and heavier than the first, flew on 11 August 1972.

Contemporaneously with the establishment of General Avia, publisher Dr. Gianni Mazzocchi was setting up Italair SpA to provide development, manufacturing and marketing facilities for light single- and twin-engined aircrft, and this organisation took over the two prototypes to conduct the certification programme in anticipation of production. Type approval was granted by the RAI on 19 November 1974, and by the FAA on 14 May 1975. By agreement, production was handed back to General Avia and the first aircraft flew on 17 December 1979, incorporating a number of minor changes which included improved cabin heating and sound-proofing, and the substitution of three-blade Hartzell propellers for the original two-blade units.

A four-seat military version is available as the F-20 Condor, which can be fitted with three stores pylons under each wing, the central carrier accepting a 50-Imp gallon (250-litre) auxiliary fuel tank. Military roles include long-range maritime surveillance, search and rescue, and weapon training. The specification applies to the General Avia F-20 Pegaso.

Specification
Type: twin-engined six-seat light executive transport
Powerplant: two 300-hp (224-kW) Rolls-Royce Continental IO-520-K flat-six piston engines
Performance: maximum speed 249 mph (400 km/h) at sea level; economical cruising speed 211 mph (340 km/h) at 12,000 ft (3660 m); service ceiling 20,500 ft (6250 m); range with maximum payload of 1,134 lb (514 kg) 630 miles (1014 km)
Weights: empty 3,330 lb (1510 kg); maximum take-off 4,960 lb (2250 kg)
Dimensions: span 33 ft 11 in (10.34 m); length 26 ft 11½ in (8.22 m); height 11 ft 5¾ in (3.49 m); wing area 172.4 sq ft (16.02 m²)

Great Lakes Sport Trainer

History and Notes

The Great Lakes Aircraft Corporation, founded at Cleveland, Ohio on 2 January 1929, designed and manufactured a two-seat biplane known as the Sport Trainer, supplied with a variety of engines including Cirrus and Menasco power units. During the mid-1960s Andrew Oldfield designed the Baby Great Lakes, a scaled-down, single-seat version of the Sport Trainer. The Great Lakes Aircraft Company re-appeared to market kits of parts and plans for this aircraft and, later, for the full-scale Sport Trainer, for which drawings were produced for the installation of several modern engines in the range between 125 and 240 hp.

On 23 February 1972, company president Harvey Swack sold the organisation to Douglas Champlin and activities were transferred to Wichita, Kansas. In May 1973 certification was received for the Sport Trainer 2T-1A-1, powered by a 140-hp (104-kW) Avco Lycoming O-320-E2A engine, and production deliveries commenced in October 1973. In July 1974 there became available the first examples of an improved version designated 2T-1A-2 and powered by a 180-hp (134-kW) Avco Lycoming IO-360-B1F6. A constant-speed Hartzell propeller replaced the fixed-pitch McCauley propeller of the earlier model, an inverted fuel system was fitted as standard, and other changes included the fitting of ailerons to all four mainplanes. Control of the company passed to R. Dean Franklin and it was re-established at Eastman, Georgia. The specification applies to the Great Lakes 2T-1A-2.

Specification
Type: two-seat sporting biplane
Powerplant: one 180-hp (134-kW) Avco Lycoming AEIO-360-B1G6 flat-four piston engine
Performance: maximum speed 125 mph (201 km/h) at 10,000 ft (3050 m); cruising speed 118 mph (190 km/h); service ceiling 17,000 ft (5180 m); range with maximum fuel 300 miles (483 km)
Weights: empty 1,230 lb (558 kg); maximum take-off 1,800 lb (816 kg)
Dimensions: span 26 ft 8 in (8.13 m); length 21 ft 2 in (6.45 m); height 7 ft 8 in (2.34 m); wing area 187.6 sq ft (17.43 m²)

Grumman G-21 Goose/McKinnon Turbo-Goose and Turboprop Goose

History and Notes

In 1937 Grumman produced a twin-engine amphibian flying-boat known as the G-21 Goose. Powered by two 450-hp (336-kW) Pratt & Whitney R-985 radial engines, it was of high-wing monoplane configuration, the wing serving also to mount the engines and carry underwing floats to balance the flying-boat on the water. The deep two-step hull was of conventional construction, and the tail unit included a braced tailplane. Amphibious capability was provided by the tailwheel type landing gear, all three units of which retracted into the hull. Built prewar for commercial use as the G-21A, which had accommodation for up to seven passengers the Goose continued in production during World War II for service with the USAAF, US Coast Guard and US Navy, some of this latter service's aircraft serving also with the US Marine Corps.

Surviving commercial and war-surplus aircraft which came on to the market were to prove of value for certain postwar air services, and McKinnon Enterprises in the USA began to specialise in Goose refurbishment and the development of improved versions. These have included an early modification which replaced the two R-985s with four 340-hp (254-kw) Avco Lycoming engines, but the majority of conversions have been to the G-21C and -21D Turbo-Goose standard with two Pratt & Whitney Aircraft of Canada PT6A turboprops in place of the original radials. A number of improvements are incorporated during this conversion including the introduction of retractable wingtip floats and the provision of larger cabin windows. A G-21G Turbo-Goose is also available, this being a generally similar conversion but provided with a somewhat higher standard of equipment and some cabin improvements. There is also a Turboprop Goose, this involving only the change to turboprop power without any of the airframe improvements of earlier conversions.

The G-21G Turbo-Goose and Turboprop Goose conversions are available currently, but the work is now carried out by McKinnon-Viking Enterprises of Canada. The details below apply to the G-21G Turbo-Goose

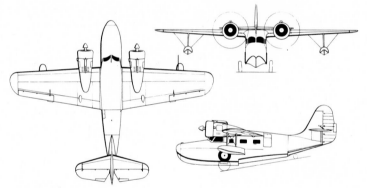

Grumman G-21 Goose

Specification
Type: light amphibian transport
Powerplant: two 680-shp (507-kW) Pratt & Whitney Aircraft of Canada PT6A-27 turboprops
Performance: maximum speed 243 mph (391 km/h); service ceiling 20,000 ft (6100 m); range with standard fuel 1,600 miles (2575 km)
Weights: empty equipped 6,700 lb (3039 kg); maximum take-off 12,500 lb (5670 kg)
Dimensions: span 50 ft 10 in (15.49 m); length 39 ft 7 in (12.06 m); wing area 377.64 sq ft (35.08 m²)
Operators include: Airwest Airlines, Antilles Air Boats, Catalina Airlines, Golden West Airlines, Haida Air, Kodiak Western Alaska Airlines, Parsons Airways Northern, Rainy Lake Airways, Reeve Aleutian Airways, Sea Bee Air, Trans-Provincial Airlines, and West Coast Air Services

The Grumman Goose has proved to be a remarkably versatile aircraft capable of accepting a wide variety of powerplants: the original pair of 450-hp (336-kW) radials, or four 340-hp (254-kW) horizontally-opposed inlines, or even a pair of 680-shp (507-kW) Pratt & Whitney PT6A turboprops.

Grumman G-64 Albatross/G-111

History and Notes

Experience with the Grumman Goose, which served throughout World War II with great reliability, prompted the US Navy to procure a somewhat larger amphibian with greater range capability. In 1944 Grumman initiated design of this aircraft, which was to be named Albatross, and which saw service with the US Air Force, Coast Guard and Navy. The prototype was flown first on 24 October 1947, and was seen to be of generally similar configuration to its predecessor. Fixed underwing floats were retained, but these and the entire structure had been considerably refined to reduce drag.

Accommodation was provided for a crew of four to six, and the cabin could accommodate 10 passengers, stretchers, or cargo, according to requirements. These factors, plus the use of more powerful and fuel-hungry engines, meant that when surplus aircraft become available for civil use they were not such an attractive proposition to airline operators as the Goose, despite a much greater range capability. Only small numbers remain in civil use in 1980. However, in that year Gruman achieved certification of a G-111 commuter version designed to meet the requirements of Chalk's

Air Service. The first 'production' aircraft was delivered in May 1981, and features a new wing centre-section, a commuter interior for 28 passengers plus inflight attendant and toilet and numerous other improvements. The availability of this revised model may spur further orders, and Grumman is considering a version re-engined with General Electric CT7, or Pratt & Whitney PW117 or Garrett AiResearch TPE331-15 turboprops.

Specification
Type: general-purpose amphibian
Powerplant: two 1,425-hp (1063-kW) Wright R-1820-76A or -76B radial piston engines
Performance: maximum speed 236 mph (380 km/h); cruising speed 150 mph (241 km/h); service ceiling 21,500 ft (6555 m); range with maximum internal and external fuel 2,850 miles (4587 km)
Weights: empty 22,883 lb (10380 kg); maximum take-off 35,700 lb

Civil success has eluded the Grumman Albatross, which has too low a capacity combined with too high a power.

(16193 kg)
Dimensions: span 96 ft 8 in (29.46 m); length 61 ft 3 in (18.67 m); height 25 ft 10 in (7.87 m); wing area 1,035.00 sq ft (96.15 m²)
Operators include: Antilles Air Boats, and Chalk's Air Service

Grumman G-73 Mallard

History and Notes

In the early years following World War II, Grumman developed, under the company designation G-73 and the name Mallard, a twin-engined commercial amphibian that benefitted from the company's extensive experience of the design of military aircraft in this category. A high-wing cantilever monoplane of all-metal construction, with a stressed-skin two-step hull, the G-73 had an upswept tail unit, and retractable tricycle landing gear to provide amphibious capability. Balancer floats were mounted beneath the wings to provide stability on the water, and these could double also as auxiliary fuel tanks. The powerplant comprised two Pratt & Whitney Wasp radial piston engines, wing-mounted in 'clean' streamlined nacelles.

The hull provided air-conditioned, heated, and sound-proofed accommodation for up to 10 passengers in two compartments, with the crew of two situated on a separate flight deck. Interior furnishings and equipment were to a high standard but some VIP examples, such as that equipped specially for the personal use of King Farouk of Egypt, were finished with the most luxurious appointments.

Specification
Type: twin-engined amphibian flying-boat
Powerplant: two 600-hp (447-kW) Pratt & Whitney R-1340-S3H1 Wasp radial piston engines
Performance: maximum speed 215 mph (346 km/h) at 6,000 ft (1830 m); cruising speed 180 mph (290 km/h) at 8,000 ft (2440 m); service ceiling 23,000 ft (7010 m); range with maximum fuel 1,380 miles (2221 km)
Weights: empty 9,350 lb (4241 kg); maximum take-off 12,750 lb (5783 kg)
Dimensions: span 66 ft 8 in (20.32 m); length 48 ft 4 in (14.73 m); height, on landing gear 18 ft 9 in (5.72 m); wing area 444 sq ft (41.25 m²)

A fine example of the Grumman design philosophy for twin-engine amphibians, the Mallard was built only in small numbers and bought for luxury conversion. Only a few survive into the 1980s.

Grumman Mallard of Chalk's Air Service.

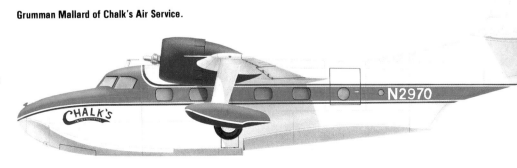

Gulfstream American AA-1/T-Cat/Lynx

History and Notes

Jim Bede's BD-1 was designed as a low-cost two-seat sporting aircraft with a structure that made extensive use of aluminium honeycomb construction and metal-to-metal bonding. Design definition commenced in June 1962 and construction of a prototype began in October, the first flight following on 11 July 1963. Bede Aviation Corporation was formed at Cleveland, Ohio in 1964, being renamed American Aviation Corporation in September 1967, to assume responsibility for the development, certification and manufacture of the aircraft as the AA-1 Yankee. An FAA Type Certificate for the production AA-1 was granted on 16 July 1968, the first example having flown on 30 May 1968.

Development of a training version was started in October 1969 and the prototype, on which work had begun on 1 February 1970, made its first flight on 25 March of that year.

Designated AA-1A, it retained the 108-hp (81-kW) Avco Lycoming O-235-C2C engine of the AA-1, but incorporated a modified wing, minor equipment changes, and dual controls as standard. The first production AA-1A flew on 6 November 1970 and type certification was awarded on 14 January 1971.

The Grumman Corporation acquired American Aviation in 1972 and minor design and equipment changes introduced in 1974 resulted in redesignation as the AA-1B, further updating in 1977 producing the AA-1C. Dual-purpose touring/training variants of the AA-1B and AA-1C, with enhanced equipment and interiors, were manufactured as the Tr 2 and T-Cat, respectively; a de luxe version was produced as the Lynx. The specification applies to the AA-1.

Specification
Type: two-seat touring and

training monoplane
Powerplant: one 108-hp (81-kW) Avco Lycoming O-235-C2C flat-four piston engine
Performance: maximum speed 144 mph (232 km/h) at sea level; cruising speed 135 mph (217 km/h) at 8,000 ft (2440 m); service ceiling 11,200 ft (3415 m); range with maximum fuel 512 miles (824 km)

The Gulfstream American Lynx and T-Cat are identical apart from the former's de luxe interior and wheel fairings.

Weights: empty 940 lb (426 kg); maximum take-off 1,500 lb (680 kg)
Dimensions: span 24 ft 5½ in (7.45 m); length 19 ft 2¾ in (5.86 m); height 6 ft 5¾ in (1.97 m); wing area 98.11 sq ft (9.11 m²)

Gulfstream American AA-5A/Cheetah and AA-5B/Tiger

History and Notes

In June 1970 American Aviation began work on an enlarged four-seat version of the AA-1 designated AA-5 Traveler. Wing span was increased by 7 ft (2.13 m), tail surfaces were increased in area and the fuselage was lengthened by 2 ft 9 in (0.84 m) to accommodate the second pair of seats. Usable fuel capacity was increased from 24 to 37 US gallons (91 to 140 litres), supplying a 150-hp (112-kW) Avco Lycoming O-320-E2G engine. The prototype flew on 21 August 1970 and FAA Type Approval was received on 12 November 1971.

The 1974 model introduced a new fin and ventral fillet, a 1 ft 0 in (0.30 m) extension of the rear cabin windows and an enlarged baggage compartment with a port-side external door. In 1976 the standard AA-5, with minor improvements such as

an enlarged tailplane and increased propeller ground clearance, became the AA-5A while the de luxe version of the same aircraft was named Cheetah. The AA-5B, in its de luxe version the Tiger, was introduced late in 1974, powered by a 180-hp (134-kW) Avco Lycoming O-360-A4K engine. The specification applies to the AA-5A.

Specification
Type: four-seat cabin monoplane
Powerplant: one 150-hp (112-kW) Avco Lycoming O-320-E2G flat-four piston engine
Performance: maximum speed 157 mph (253 km/h) at sea level; economic cruising speed 136 mph (219 km/h) at 8,500 ft (2590 m); service ceiling 12,560 ft (3830 m); maximum range with standard fuel 647 miles (1041 km)

Weights: empty 1,303 lb (591 kg); maximum take-off 2,200 lb (998 kg)
Dimensions: span 31 ft 6 in (9.60 m); length 22 ft 0 in (6.71 m); height 7 ft 6 in (2.29 m); wing area 139.7 sq ft (12.98 m²)

The Gulfstream American Cheetah is the de luxe model of the AA-5A with superior internal finish and more advanced instrumentation/avionics. The Cheetah was named Traveler up to 1976, and has been little altered since that time.

Gulfstream American GA-7/Cougar

History and Notes

The discerned need for an economical lightweight four-seat twin to equip flying schools offering multi-engine conversion courses, and to meet the requirements of private pilots looking for natural progression from high-performance single-engined aircraft, led Grumman American to develop the GA-7. The prototype made its first flight on 20 December 1974, powered by two 160-hp (119-kW) Avco Lycoming O-320-D1D engines, and a production-standard trials aircraft flew on 14 January 1977. Deliveries commenced in February 1978, continuing after the take-over by American Jet Industries which resulted in the company being renamed Gulfstream American on 1 September 1978. In 1980, however, production of the GA-7 (and of the Gulfstream American single-engined range) was suspended pending transfer to another manufacturing facility.

The GA-7 is the basic production version, equipped to a lower standard than the de luxe Cougar which includes dual controls as standard, together with tinted windscreen and cabin windows, and communication and navigation avionics. Other standard Cougar equipment includes turn indicator, vertical speed indicator, directional and horizon gyros, landing and strobe lights. An integral fuel tank in each wing provides a total capacity of 118 US gallons (447 litres) to confer a range of more than 1,300

miles (2092 km). The specification applies equally to the GA-7 and Cougar.

Specification
Type: four-seat cabin monoplane
Powerplant: two 160-hp (119-kW) Avco Lycoming O-320-D1D flat-four piston engines

Performance: maximum speed 193 mph (311 km/h) at sea level; economic cruising speed 131 mph (211 km/h) at 8,500 ft (2590 m); service ceiling 18,300 ft (5580 m); range with maximum fuel 1,336 miles (2150 km) at 8,500 ft (2590 m)
Weights: empty 2,515 lb (1141 kg); maximum take-off 3,800 lb (1724 kg)

Dimensions: span 36 ft 10¼ in (11.23 m); length 29 ft 10 in (9.09 m); height 10 ft 4¼ in (3.16 m); wing area 184 sq ft (17.09 m²)

The Gulfstream American GA-7 was designed to replace the Piper Comanche four-seater, and is also available in a de luxe version as the Cougar.

Gulfstream American G-159 Gulfstream I/G-1C

History and Notes

In the mid-1950s Grumman began the design of a twin-turboprop executive transport which was intended for a crew of two and 10-14 passengers in typical corporate versions. An alternative high-density seating layout could accommodate a maximum of 24 passengers. Because of its proven reliability in operation, the Rolls-Royce Dart turboprop engine was selected by Grumman, and two of these engines, driving Rotol four-blade constant-speed propellers, comprised the powerplant of this G-159 Gulfstream I aircraft. The overall layout is that of a conventional low-wing monoplane transport, with a retractable tricycle landing gear with twin wheels on each unit. The entire accommodation is pressurized by a system able to maintain a 5,500-ft (1675-m) cabin altitude up to 25,000 ft (7620 m), the baggage compartment also being pressurized. An auxiliary power unit (APU) is installed to provide electrical power and air-conditioning prior to main-engine starting. The prototype of the Gulfstream I flew for the first time on 14 August 1958, and FAA certification was awarded on 21 May 1959.

Most of the 200 Gulfstream Is built went to North American customers, and in the 1980s several are being converted into G-1C commuter airliners. The fuselage is 'stretched' by 10 ft 8 in (3.25 m) to provide seating for 37 passengers, but is otherwise basically unaltered. However, the G-1C suffers, in comparison with newer commuter airliners, from a higher structure weight, excessive fuel capacity and relatively inefficient engines, so Grumman is thinking hard about the profitability of restarting production, even with more efficient PT7A or CT7 turboprops.

The specification applies to the G-1C.

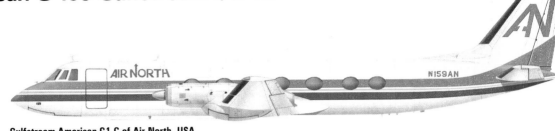

Gulfstream American G1-C of Air North, USA.

Specification

Type: commuter airliner
Powerplant: two 2,100-eshp (1647-ekW) Rolls-Royce Dart Mk 529 turboprops
Performance: maximum cruising speed 300 mph (556 km/h) at 30,000 (9145 m); range with 7,400-lb (3357-kg) payload 521 miles (838 km); maximum fuel range 2,300 miles (3701 km)
Weights: empty operating 24,850 lb (11272 kg); maximum take-off 36,000 lb (16300 kg)
Dimensions: span 78 ft 4 in (23.88 m); length 75 ft 4 in (22.97 m); height 23 ft 0 in (7.01 m); wing area 632 sq ft (58.7 m²)

Comparison of the Gulfstream American Gulfstream I (background) and G-1C (or G-159C, foreground) reveals the fuselage 'stretch' of 10 ft 8 in (3.25 m) and the presence of two more windows to port.

Gulfstream American Gulfstream II

History and Notes

Encouraged by pressure from existing Gulfstream I operators, early in 1975 Grumman began work on preliminary studies for a turbofan-engined version of its very successful corporate turboprop. Market research indicated a requirement for an aircraft with the cabin volume of the Gulfstream I but with high-speed transoceanic capability, while at the same time enjoying good short-field performance. By the time the planned full-scale mock-up had been completed Grumman had received 30 firm orders, and the programme was given the go-ahead on 5 May 1965. There was no prototype as such and the first aircraft took off on its 52-minute maiden flight from Bethpage, New York on 2 October 1966, flown by Bob Smyth and Carl Alber.

With two Rolls-Royce Spey Mk 511-8 engines, each producing 11,400-lb (5171-kg) thrust in an airframe some 65 per cent of the weight of similarly-powered aircraft such as the BAC One-Eleven and Fokker F.28, the Gulfstream II met the short-field performance requirement with ease and enjoyed a maximum-fuel range of more than 3,800 miles

(6115 km). It provided accommodation for a crew of three and up to 19 passengers in a cabin 34 ft (10.36 m) long and 6 ft 1 in (1.85 m) high.

All Gulfstream IIs were fitted with avionics and custom interiors at distributors, and in December 1967 the fifth aircraft was handed over to AiResearch Inc. for completion prior to becoming the first to reach a customer, in this case National Distillers and Chemical Corporation of New York.

The introduction of the more stringent requirements of FAR25, and more particularly FAR36, necessitated the development of an engine hush-kit. This was certificated in May 1975, fitted to production aircraft from airframe number 166, and became available as a retrofit on earlier aircraft. Grumman also developed a tip tank installation which provided a further 3,500 lb (1588 kg) of fuel, extending the NBAA IFR range by 460 miles (740 kw) at the optimum cruise speed of Mach 0.72. Maximum ramp weight and maximum take-off weight increased to 66,000 lb (29937 kg) and 65,500 lb (29710 kg) respectively. This version was certificated in September 1976. Aircraft number 258, one of four

delivered in December 1979, was the last Gulfstream II to be built.

Specification

Type: twin-engined 19-passenger executive transport
Powerplant: two 11,400-lb (5171-kg) thrust Rolls-Royce Spey Mk 511-8 turbofans
Performance: economic cruising speed 483 mph (777 km/h) at 43,000 ft (13105 m); service ceiling 43,000 ft (13105 m); VFR range with maximum fuel and 2,000-lb (907-kg) payload 3,744 miles

The Gulfstream American Gulfstream II has seating for up to 19 passengers, and is thus one of the largest 'bizjets' in the world. Just as significantly, the capacity is matched by the performance, especially over transcontinental ranges.

(6025 km)
Weights: empty 30,938 lb (14033 kg); maximum take-off 65,000 lb (29710 kg)
Dimensions: span 68 ft 10 in (20.98 m); length 79 ft 11 in (24.36 m); height 24 ft 6 in (7.47 m); wing area 809.6 sq ft (75.21 m²)

Gulfstream American Gulfstream III

History and Notes

Grumman first announced an intention to develop the Gulfstream III in November 1976, but the programme was temporarily suspended in spring 1977, to be resumed a year later. By comparison with the Gulfstream II, fuselage length was increased by 3 ft 11 in (1.19 m) to incorporate a redesigned, more pointed nose, improve cockpit visibility through a revised windscreen, and provide a longer passenger cabin. Key to the improved performance of the aircraft was to be the new supercritical wing, with its NASA Whitcomb wingtip winglets, which was increased in span by 9 ft (2.74 m) and featured integral tankage totalling 4,400 US gallons (16656 litres).

The first aircraft was converted from Gulfstream II airframe number 249, taken from the production line. After roll-out on 21 September 1979, this machine made its first flight at Savannah, Georgia on 2 December. Pilots were Bob Smyth of Grumman Aerospace, who had flown the Gulfstream II 13 years earlier, and Morgan Cobb of Gulfstream American, the renamed company which resulted from American Jet Indus-

Gulfstream American Gulfstream III.

tries' acquisition of Grumman's American Aviation Corporation on 1 September 1978. The second aircraft joined the flight test programme on 24 December.

In executive transport configuration eight passengers can be carried over an NBAA IFR range of 4,330 miles (6968 km) at a long-range cruising speed of 512 mph (824 km/h), but the Gulfstream III is a multi-mission aircraft, equally capable of operating in the navaid checking, aeromedical/casevac, priority cargo and administrative transport roles. Three Gulfstream IIIs, ordered by the Royal Danish air force, will be called upon to perform several of

these tasks, although their primary role will be that of fishery patrol. Texas Instruments AN/APS-127 sea surveillance radar will replace the RCA Primus weather radar of the civil transport, and other features will include a 63 in by 83 in (1.60 m by 2.11 m) cargo door in the starboard side of the front fuselage, a rear fuselage flare-launcher system, an overhead hook-up system for parachute release lanyards, and a cargo roller conveyor system at the rear of the cabin. Emergency supplies will be airdropped through the rear-fuselage baggage door, the aperture being shielded by a hydraulically operated air deflector.

Specification

Type: twin-engined 19-passenger executive transport
Powerplant: two 11,400-lb (517-kg) thrust Rolls-Royce Spey Mk 511-8 turbofans
Performance: maximum cruising speed 581 mph (935 km/h); maximum VFR range, with 30-min reserves 4,842 miles (7792 km)
Weights: empty 38,300 lb (17373 kg); maximum take-off 68,200 lb (30935 kg)
Dimensions: span 77 ft 10 in (23.72 m); length 83 ft 1 in (25.32 m); height 24 ft 4½ in (7.43 m); wing area 934.6 sq ft (86.82 m²)

Gulfstream American Hustler 500

History and Notes

On 24 October 1975 American Jet Industries announced the launch of a STOL seven-seat executive transport on which design work had commenced in December 1974. Novel features included the lack of ailerons, lateral control being maintained by the use of wing spoilers, and the combination of turboprop and turbojet power. Prime power source was to be an 850-shp (634-kW) Pratt & Whitney Aircraft of Canada PT6A-41 turboprop mounted in the nose, supplemented by a Williams Research Corporation 718-lb (362-kg) thrust WR19-3-1 turbofan in the tail. The latter power unit was intended to

provide standby emergency propulsion, being started automatically by a torque-sensing device fitted to the main engine, or allowed to idle if field-length or temperature conditions led the pilot to anticipate the need for extra power at take-off.

The prototype, designated Hustler 400, flew on 11 January 1978 and the original intention was to seek certification as a single-engined aircraft pending availability of a type-approved version of the Williams engine. Later, however, the manufacturer (which had become Gulfstream American after the acquisition of Grumman American on 1 September 1978) decided to obtain

approval as a full twin. As a result the Williams engine was replaced by a 2,200-lb (998-kg) thrust Pratt & Whitney Aircraft of Canada JT15D-1 turbofan, this necessitating the insertion of a 2 ft 8 in (0.81 m) plug in the forward fuselage, the relocation of the main cabin door forward of the wing, the addition of wingtip fuel tanks, and the reduction of the flaps to two-thirds span to allow conventional ailerons to be fitted. The intake for the rear engine was moved from the lower rear fuselage to a new position at the base of the fin.

A further change, announced in April 1979, was the substitution of a 900-shp (671-kW) Garrett TPE331-

10-501 turboprop for the PT6A, and in this form the aircraft was redesignated Hustler 500. The prototype completed taxiing trials at Van Nuys, Los Angeles in December 1980 and the first flight took place in February 1981. A version with twin rear-mounted turbofan engines is being studied.

Specification

Type: twin-engined five/seven-seat executive/utility transport
Powerplant: one 900-shp (671-kW) Garrett TPE331-10 turboprop and one 2,200-lb (998-kg) thrust Pratt & Whitney Aircraft of Canada JT15D-1 turbofan
Performance: maximum speed 402 mph (647 km/h); normal cruising speed, both engines 402 mph (647 km/h) at 38,000 ft (11580 m); service ceiling 38,000 ft (11580 m); range at normal cruising speed 2,303 miles (3706 km)
Weights: empty 5,430 lb (2463 kg); maximum take-off 10,000 lb (4536 kg)
Dimensions: span 34 ft 5 in (10.49 m); length 41 ft 3 in (12.57 m); height 13 ft 2½ in (4.03 m); wing area 190.71 sq. ft. (1772 m²)

The American Jet Industries Hustler Model 500 has undergone an extended development phase, the result largely of its highly unusual powerplant configuration: a Pratt & Whitney Aircraft turboprop and turbofan.

Gulfstream Commander Jetprop 840/980/1000

History and Notes

Mergers of aircraft manufacturers have become increasingly common: some are simple, some are not. The latter category applies to the progression of American Jet Industries Inc., founded in 1951, which on 1 September 1978 acquired the Grumman Corporation's Grumman American Aviation Corporation. The new major company name then became Gulfstream American Corporation, which at the end of 1980 acquired Rockwell International's General Aviation Division with its Com-

mander line of aircraft. This is now named as the Commander Division of Gulfstream American Corporation.

Since acquiring the Commander line, Gulfstream American had decided to discontinue production of all but the two aircraft known formerly as the Rockwell Jetprop Commander 840 and Jetprop Commander 980. These are now designated respectively as the Gulfstream Commander Jetprop 840 and Commander Jetprop 980. In addition to the continued improvement and production of these two aircraft, the company has under

development a new Commander Jetprop 1000.

Developed from the Turbo Commander 690B, the Commander Jetprop 840 is generally similar in overall configuration: a cantilever high-wing monoplane with conventional swept tail surfaces, retractable tricycle landing gear, and two wing-mounted turboprop engines. It differs from the Model 690B by an increase in wing span and introduction of shallow winglets at each wingtip, an increase in fuel capacity, and the introduction of Dowty Rotol supercritical propel-

lers for the 840-shp (626-kW) Garrett TPE331-5-254K turboprops which, in this application, are flat rated at 700 shp (522 kW). First flown on 17 May 1979, the Jetprop 840 gained FAA certification on 7 September 1979. Deliveries began shortly after this, and a total of 57 had been completed by the beginning of 1981. It is planned to produce about 70 of these aircraft during 1981.

The Commander Jetprop 980 shares the same heritage, and differs primarily in the powerplant installation. The engines are 980-hp (730-kW)

Gulfstream Commander Jetprop 840/980/1000

Garrett TPE331-10-501K turboprops, which in this case are flat rated to 715 shp (533-kW), and there is increased fuel capacity resulting from the inclusion as standard of 59 US gallons (223 litres) of fuel in two bladder cells that are optional on the Model 840. The prototype Jetprop 980 flew for the first time on 14 June 1979, and FAA certification was gained on 1 November 1979. A total of 55 had been delivered by the beginning of 1981, during which year it is planned to produce 31 examples.

The new Commander Jetprop 1000, first flown in prototype form on 12 May 1980, is also in the same mould. It has increased cabin space resulting from a reduction in baggage area, the cabin volume being increased by some 25 per cent. The cabin pressurisation differential has also been increased, as a result of which it is planned to gain certification for operation at a higher altitude and higher gross weight to gain greater economy of operation from the installed powerplant. Certification

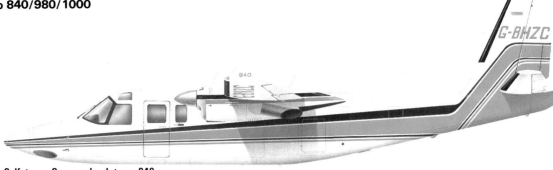

Gulfstream Commander Jetprop 840.

was achieved in the early summer of 1981, with some 25 units manufactured by the end of the year.

All three Commander Jetprops have maximum accommodation for a pilot and 10 passengers, but are generally used to carry six or seven passengers in a very comfortable and well appointed cabin. This is pressurised, air-conditioned, heated, and ventilated. A full de-icing system is standard, and a wide range of optional communication and naviga-

tion systems can be complemented by more sophisticated avionics that include autopilot/flight director systems and weather radar. The details that follow apply to the Commander Jetprop 980.

Specification
Type: twin-turboprop light transport
Powerplant: two 980-shp (730-kW) Garrett TPE331-10-501K turboprops
Performance: maximum cruising speed 356 mph (573 km/h) at

22,000 ft (6705 m); economic cruising speed 287 mph (462 km/h) at 31,000 ft (9450 m); service ceiling 35,000 ft (10 670 m); range with maximum fuel, 45-min reserves 2,350 miles (3782 km)
Weights: empty 6,727 lb (3051 kg); maximum take-off 10,325 lb (4683 kg)
Dimensions: span 52 ft 1½ in (15.89 m); length 42 ft 11¾ in (13.10 m); height 14 ft 11½ in (4.56 m); wing area 279.37 sq ft (25.95 m²)

Handley Page H.P.R.7 Herald

History and Notes
Designed by the Handley Page company's Reading, Berkshire, division (formerly the Miles Aircraft company), the first Herald prototype (G-AODE) made its maiden flight on 25 August 1955. Looking not unlike an enlarged and modernised Miles Marathon, which had originated from the same stable, it was of high-wing monoplane configuration with four 870-hp (649-kW) wing-mounted Alvis Leonides Major radial piston engines. The circular-section fuselage was pressurised, the landing gear of retractable tricycle type, and the tail unit of conventional design. Standard accommodation was for 36 passengers, with a maximum of 44.

The Herald had been expected to appeal to operators in Asia, Australia and South America as a feeder-liner suitable for operation from undeveloped airfields. Market research had shown that operators in these areas wanted an aircraft that was simple and easy to maintain, without the complication of turbine engines. An initial production batch of 25 aircraft was started, to meet orders totalling 29 aircraft, but none of these was completed with the powerplant that had been planned. Three years of experience with the Vickers Viscount had demonstrated, most effectively, that the 'new-fangled' turboprop engines which powered it were not only extremely reliable, but also most economical in operation.

With potential operators expressing their doubts about the wisdom of holding to their contracts, and with the similarly sized turboprop-powered Fokker F.27 undergoing its development/certification programme, it was decided in May 1957 to develop a Dart-powered version as an alternative. In fact, only the original prototypes were flown with piston engines, and these were converted subsequently to turboprop power, both flying in their revised form during 1958.

The initial production version was the Herald Series 100, with accommodation for a maximum of 47 passengers. The Series 200, with the fuselage lengthened by 3 ft 7 in (1.09 m), had seating for up to 56. By the time that the Handley Page company collapsed in 1970, production had totalled four Series 100 and 38 Series 200 aircraft, plus eight Series 400s (which was a military variant of the

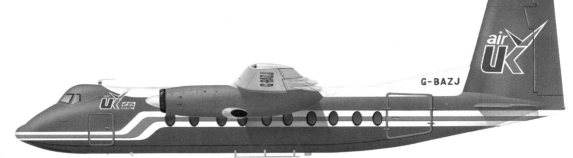

Handley Page Herald of Air UK.

Series 200) for the Royal Malaysian Air Force. No further examples were built after the liquidation of this once great company. The details below apply to the Series 200.

Specification
Type: medium-range transport
Powerplant: two 2,105-ehp (1570-ekW) Rolls-Royce Dart 527 turboprops
Performance: maximum cruising speed 274 mph (441 km/h) at 15,000 ft (4570 m); economic cruising speed 265 mph (426 km/h) at 23,000 ft (7010 m); service ceiling 27,900 ft (8500 m); range with maximum payload 1,110 miles (1786 km); range with maximum fuel 1,620 miles (2607 km)
Weights: operating empty 25,800 lb (11703 kg); maximum take-off 43,000 lb (19504 kg)
Dimensions: span 94 ft 9 in (28.88 m); length 75 ft 6 in (23.01 m); height 24 ft 1 in (7.34 m); wing area 886.00 sq ft (82.31 m²)

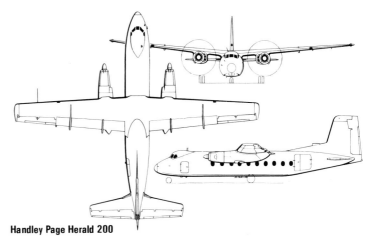

Handley Page Herald 200

Operators include: Air Manila International, Air UK, British Air Ferries, Brymon Airways, Europe Aero Service, Jersey European Airways, Nile Valley Aviation, and Uracca Airlines

The elderly Handley Page Herald is still in profitable service. British Air Ferries has the second-largest fleet: one Series 100, two Series 200 and three Series 400, the last being ex-Royal Malaysian Air Force machines.

Harbin C-11

History and Notes
Responsibility for aircraft and aero engine manufacture in China is the responsibility of the Third Ministry of Machine Building and there are a number of design and development centres, with main manufacturing facilities located at Shenyang in Liaoning Province and at Harbin in Heilungkiang Province. Harbin's products have included licence-built Ilyushin Il-28 bombers (Harbin B-5), Mil Mi-4 helicopters (H-5) and Antonov An-2 general-purpose bi-

planes (C-5). Currently in production, however, is a twin-engined utility aircraft of indigenous design, designated C-11 (Type 11 Transport Aeroplane) which is intended as a replacement for more than 1,000 Harbin C-5s believed to be in use in China for agricultural and general transport duties.

The prototype is believed to have flown in 1975, and the initial production model was powered by a radial engine believed to be related to the 285-hp (213-kW) Hou-sai-6, which is

based on the Russian Ivchenko AI-14RF and installed in the Shenyang BT-6 two-seat basic trainer. Later aircraft may have licence-built Pratt & Whitney Aircraft of Canada PT6A-100 turboprops. The C-11 is believed to be in the six/eight-passenger class and to be of similar size to the GAF Nomad.

Specification
Type: six/eight-passenger transport
Powerplant: two 280-hp (213-kW) Hou-sai-6 radial piston engines

Performance: maximum speed 137 mph (220 km/h); cruising speed 102 mph (164 km/h); service ceiling 13,225 ft (4030 m)
Weights: empty 4,519 lb (2050 kg); maximum take-off 7,715 lb (3500 kg)
Dimensions: span 55 ft 9¼ in (17.00 m); length 39 ft 5⅛ in (12.02 m); height 15 ft 2¾ in (4.64 m); wing area 365.97 sq ft (34.00 m²)

Helio Courier/Stallion Series

History and Notes
The Helio Courier has its origins in the remarkable Koppen-Bollinger Helioplane of 1949. With full-span automatic leading-edge slats and dual-purpose ailerons, the Helioplane's slow flight performance soon attracted the US Army's interest, resulting in an evaluation order for one YL-24. The YL-24 was delivered in 1952; it was of mixed construction with a fabric-covered rear fuselage and powered by a 145-hp (108-kW) Continental C-145-4 engine. Despite the type's versatility, however, the US Army did not order L-24s, and Helio Aircraft tackled the commercial market with the all-metal H-391 Courier, which was certificated in 1954. Later developments were the five-seat H-395 Super Courier of 1958, with a 295-hp (220-kW) Lycoming GO-480-C1D6, the six-seat H-250 of 1964, and the six-seat improved H-295 of 1965. Only the H-295 remained in production by the end of the 1970s, with future production

uncertain. The H-295 has a tailwheel landing gear, while the HT-295 has fixed tricycle gear.

The ultimate expression of Helio's current design philosophy is the H-550A Stallion, a 10-seater powered by the 680-ehp (507-ekW) Pratt & Whitney Aircraft Canada PT6A-27 turboprop. The first H-550 flew in 1965. The specification applies to the H-295 model.

Specification
Type: six-seat STOL communications and utility aircraft
Powerplant: one 295-hp (220-kW) Avco Lycoming GO-480-G1A6 flat-six piston engine
Performance: maximum speed at sea level 167 mph (269 km/h); maximum cruising speed at 75% power at 8,500 ft (2600 m) 165 mph (265 km/h); rate of climb at sea level 1,150 ft (350 m) per minute; standard range 660 miles (1062 km)
Weights: empty 2,080 lb (943 kg);

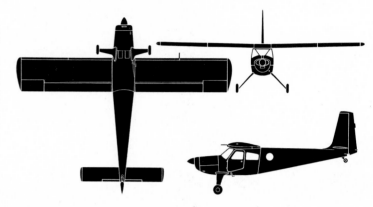

Helio Super Courier

maximum take-off 3,400 lb (1542 kg)
Dimensions: span 39 ft 0 in (11.89 m); length 31 ft 0 in (9.45 m); height 8 ft 10 in (2.69 m); wing area 231 sq ft (21.46 m²)

Hughes Model 269/300/300C

History and Notes
Hughes Helicopters are something of a specialist in the design of light helicopters. The first successful example was the Model 269, of which development began in 1955. The first Model 269 flew in October 1956, and the type was then re-engineered as the Model 269A with the 180-hp (134-kW) Lycoming O-360. Deliveries to civil operators began in 1961.

The basic design has undergone many changes over the years. The first three-seat variant, the Model 300, appeared in 1963. Five years later, in July 1968, construction began of the Model 300C. Powered by a 190-hp (142-kW) Lycoming piston engine, this three-seat aircraft first flew in August 1969 and offered a 45% increase in payload. The 300CQ is 75% quieter than earlier models. Adoption of a larger engine called for a number of structural changes, including enlarging the tail rotor and fin and lengthening the tailboom and rotor mast to accommodate the longer and heavier main rotor blades. Huges has also experimented with alternative powerplants.

The Model 300C is also built under licence in Italy by BredaNardi as the NH-300C. The specification applies to the Hughes Model 300C.

Specification
Type: light utility helicopter
Powerplant: one 190-hp (142-kW) Lycoming HIO-360-D1A flat-four piston engine piston engine
Performance: maximum cruising speed 94 mph (151 km/h) at sea level; initial climb rate 750 ft (229 m) per minute; service ceiling 10,200 ft (3110 m); range 230 miles (370 km)

Weights: empty 1,050 lb (476 kg); maximum take-off 2,050 lb (930 kg)
Dimensions: main rotor diameter 26 ft 0 in (8.18 m); length overall, rotor blades fore and aft 30 ft 11 in (9.42 m); height 8 ft 9 in (2.67 m); main rotor disc area 565.5 sq ft (52.5 m²)

The Hughes Model 300 is a versatile light helicopter which first flew in 1956. In 1969 Hughes introduced the more advanced Model 300C, with an extra 10-hp (7.46-kW) of power and larger-diameter rotor blades to boost payload by some 45 per cent. This latter model is characterised by a quadri-lateral rather than triangular ventral fin.

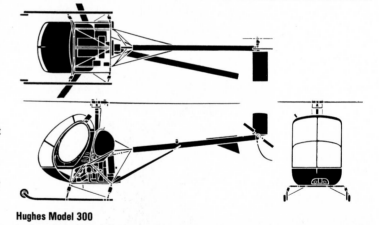

Hughes Model 300

Hughes Model 500/500D

History and Notes

Hughes announced on 21 April 1965 that it was the company's intention to market a commercial equivalent of the military OH-6A. Three versions were to be available: the basic Model 500, a five-seat executive aircraft; the utility Model 500U (later 500C), which would carry seven persons or up to 1,710 lb (776 kg) of freight; and a military Model 500M, basically the same as the US Army's OH-6A, but configured for sale to foreign military customers. These variants differed from the military OH-6A mainly in their powerplant. The Models 500 and 500M retained the same basic Allison T63-A-5A, but in these applications rerated to 278 shp (207 kW) for take-off, and with a maximum continuous rating of 243 shp (181 kW). The 500C had the commercial 400-shp (298-kW) Allison Model 250-C20 turboshaft, derated to the same levels as the T63-A-5A, but giving improved 'hot and high' performance. Deliveries of these helicopter models began in 1968, and the 500M proved an attractive buy for many foreign air forces, including those of Colombia, Denmark, Mexico, the Philippines, and Spain. In addition, licence manufacture of the Model 500 has been undertaken by BredaNardi in Italy, Kawasaki in Japan and RACA in Argentina.

The development of a more advanced version began in 1974, introducing a number of changes to enhance performance. The more powerful Allison 250-C20B was introduced: this develops a maximum of 420 shp (313 kW), but is derated in this application to 375 shp (280 kW) for take-off, and has a maximum continuous rating of 350 shp (261 kW). There are two readily noticeable external changes, the first being the provision of a T-tail, with a small-span horizontal stabilizer, with diminutive end-plate fins, mounted at the tip of the dorsal fin. This replaces the earlier unit which had a similar ventral/dorsal fin arrangement, but had also a fixed stabilizer with considerable dihedral mounted on the starboard side of the fin. The other major external change is the introduction of a five-blade main rotor similar to that installed on the experimental OH-6C. In fact, as early as April 1976 Hughes had been

working on a modified OH-6A which was known as 'The Quiet One', and it was for this aircraft that the slower-rotating five-blade main rotor had originally been developed. This latter aircraft also had a four-blade tail rotor, but to avoid excessive weight that of the 500D, as this new helicopter is known, has only two blades of slightly increased diameter, plus a longer and strengthened tail boom to cater for the increased torque. Other changes include strengthening of the lower fuselage and landing gear, and the introduction of a small fairing over the rotor hub to eliminate a slight problem of buffeting with the prototype. This flew for the first time in August 1974, followed by the first flight of a production aircraft on 9 October 1975, initial deliveries being made in December 1976. The specification applies to the Model 500D.

Though it has some resemblance to the Model 300, the Hughes Model 500 is an altogether more advanced machine with superior performance and payload thanks to the use of a turboshaft powerplant.

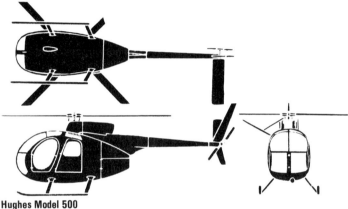

Hughes Model 500

Specification
Type: light utility helicopter
Powerplant: one 420-shp (313-kW) Allison 250-C20B turboshaft
Performance: maximum cruising speed 160 mph (258 km/h) at sea level; initial climb rate 1,700 ft (518 m) per minute; service ceiling 15,000 ft (4570 m); range 335 miles (539 km)
Weights: empty 1,320 lb (598 kg); maximum take-off 3,000 lb (1361 kg)
Dimensions: main rotor diameter 26 ft 5 in (8.05 m); length overall, rotors fore and aft 30 ft 6 in (9.30 m); height 8 ft 3½ in (2.53 m); main rotor disc area 547.8 sq ft (50.89 m²)

IAR 823

History and Notes

In May 1970 work on the design of the IAR 823 all-metal, two/five-seat light aircraft began at the Institute of Fluid Mechanics and Aerospace Construction in Bucharest, the research and development centre for the Romanian aviation industry. The design team was led by Dipl. Ing. Radu Manicatide, who had designed the IAR 811 trainer, the first postwar aircraft to be built by Industria Aeronautica Romana at Brasov. Although the Brasov factory was redesignated Intreprinderea de Constructii Aeronautice (ICA) in 1968, the products retained the IAR type numbering system and manufacture of the IAR 823 prototype began there in autumn 1971. The first flight took place in July 1973 and the first of the initial production batch flew in the following year. Powered by a 290-hp (216-kW) Avco Lycoming IO-540-G1D5 engine, the IAR 823 is fully aerobatic as a two-seater but with a bench seat for three in the rear of the cabin it can also be used for air taxi and general communications duties. Deliveries have been made to state aero clubs and the Romanian air force.

Specification
Type: two/five-seat cabin monoplane
Powerplant: one 290-hp (216-kW) Avco Lycoming IO-540-G1D5 flat-six piston engine
Performance: maximum speed 192 mph (309 km/h) at sea level; economical cruising speed 180 mph (290 km/h) at 10,000 ft (3050 m); service ceiling 18,375 ft (5600 m); range with maximum fuel 1,118 miles (1800 km)
Weights: empty 2,006 lb (910 kg); maximum take-off 3,042 lb (1380 kg)
Dimensions: span 32 ft 9¾ in (10.00 m); length 27 ft ¼ in (8.24 m); height 8 ft 3¼ in (2.52 m); wing area 161.5 sq ft (15.00 m²)

ICX Aviation X-Avia LC-3

History and Notes

In December 1979 ICX Aviation of Washington, DC announced an agreement with Aviaexport, the Russian trade agency, to cover the building of a modified version of the Yakovlev Yak-40 short-range transport aircraft. The prototype Yak-40 flew on 21 October 1966 and many hundreds were built for Aeroflot and for export to civil and military operators before production ended in the USSR. Design changes to meet Western certification requirements were initiated in December 1975 and ICX has been working on plans to re-engine the aircraft with three Garrett TFE731-3 turbofans, each of 3,700-lb (1678-kg) thrust, in place of the three 3,500-lb (1588-kg) thrust Ivchenko AI-25s originally installed. A pre-production prototype was due to fly in 1981 and the LC-3 is to be offered in three versions. These are the basic LC-3A, with a three-man crew and accommodation for 30 passengers; the LC-3B 40-passenger version with high-density seating; and the LC-3C cargo aircraft with a payload of 10,000 lb (4536 kg).

Specification
Type: twin-engined 30/40-passenger transport
Powerplant: two 3,700-lb (1678-kg) thrust Garrett TFE731-3 turbofans
Performance: maximum speed 408 mph (657 km/h) at 30,000 ft (9145 m); economical cruising speed 345 mph (555 km/h) at 36,000 ft (10975 m); service ceiling 40,000 ft (12190 m); range with 10,000-lb (4536-kg) payload 600 miles (966 km)
Weight: maximum take-off 38,500 lb (17463 kg)
Dimensions: span 82 ft ¼ in (25.00 m); length 66 ft 9½ in (20.36 m); height 21 ft 4 in (6.50 m); wing area 753.50 sq ft (70.00 m²)

Ilyushin Il-14

History and Notes

Like other nations developing national and international air routes in the years immediately before World War II, the Soviet Union was to discover the value of the Douglas DC-3. So much so, indeed, that some 2,000 examples were to be licence-built in Russia under the designation Lisunov Li-2, and the survivors of these, plus converted C-47s supplied by America, represented the mainstay of Aeroflot's fleet during the early postwar years.

In due course came the time when, as in the West, a DC-3 replacement was needed. So followed the design and production of the Ilyushin Il-12. This was a conventional low-wing monoplane of the period with retractable tricycle type landing gear, powered by two wing-mounted Shvetsov radial piston engines. Although slightly larger than the DC-3, and with maximum accommodation for 27 passengers, the bulk of these aircraft operating on long-range routes were equipped to seat 21.

The Il-12 was followed by an improved version designated Il-14, with new wings of more efficient aerofoil section, many drag-reducing refinements, and more powerful engines. Entering service with Aeroflot in 1954-5, these Il-14P (passenger) aircraft had improved accommodation for 18 passengers. A lengthened fuselage Il-14M (modified), which was 'stretched' by 3ft 3¼ in (1.00 m), entered service in 1956 with standard seating for 24. Some two years later high-density layouts were introduced, and Il-14P and Il-14M aircraft were in service with maximum seating for 24 and 36 passengers respectively. Cargo versions were also built with double doors on the port side, with the designations Il-14T and Il-14G, and these are believed to relate to the short- and long-fuselage versions respectively.

Production of the Il-14 in the Soviet Union, for civil and military use, and for export, is believed to have reached more than 3,500 aircraft. In addition, a small number were built under licence in Czechoslovakia by Avia as the Avia-14, and by VEB Flugzeugwerke in East Germany as the VEB Il-14P.

It is interesting to record that a number of Il-14s were presented by the Soviet Union to several heads of state, and among well-known recipients were President Nasser, Prime Minister Nehru, President Tito, and the Shah of Iran. The details below apply to the Il-14M.

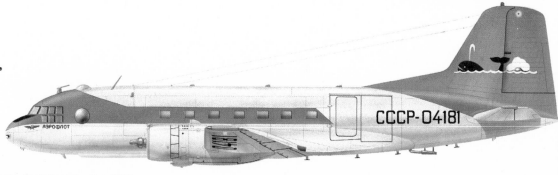

Ilyushin Il-14 of Aeroflot, USSR.

Specification

Type: short-range transport
Powerplant: two 1,900-hp (1417-kW) Shvetsov ASh-82T radial piston engines
Performance: maximum cruising speed 217 mph (350 km/h) at 9,840 ft (3000 m); economic cruising speed 199 mph (320 km/h) at 9,840 ft (3000 m); service ceiling 24,280 ft (7400 m); range with maximum payload and 1-hour reserves 249 miles (400 km); range with maximum fuel and 1-hour reserves 1,087 miles (1750 km)
Weights: empty equipped 27,778 lb (12600 kg); maximum take-off 38,581 lb (17500 kg)
Dimensions: span 104 ft 0 in (31.70 m); length 73 ft 2¼ in (22.31 m);

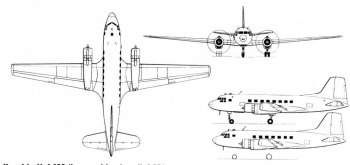

Ilyushin Il-14M (lower side view Il-14P)

height 25 ft 7 in (7.80 m); wing area 1,076.43 sq ft (100.00 m²)
Operators include: Aeroflot, CAAC, Choson Minhang Civil Aviation Company, Cubana, and Mongolian Airlines

A few hundred venerable Ilyushin Il-14s remain in service, mostly with Aeroflot, but seen here is an example operated by the Polish airline Aeropol on internal services. Up to 28 passengers can be accommodated.

Ilyushin Il-18

History and Notes

To meet Aeroflot's requirements for an economic medium-range 75/100-seat transport, both the Antonov An-10 and the Ilyushin Il-18 were developed, each flying for the first time in 1957 and entering service in 1959. Ilyushin's Il-18 was of low-wing monoplane configuration with a pressurised circular-section fuselage, conventional tail unit, and a retractable tricycle type landing gear with a twin nosewheel unit and a four-wheel bogie on each main unit. The powerplant of the prototype (SSSR-L5811), which flew for the first time on 4 July 1957, comprised four wing-mounted Kuznetsov SN-4 turboprops, each developing 4,000 eshp (2983 ekW). Early production aircraft were also equipped with these engines, but the similarly-powered Ivchenko AI-20 turboprop was available as an optional alternative. However, the 21st and subsequent production aircraft were to have AI-20s as the standard installation.

The prototype aircraft had been named *Moskva* (Moscow), but this was not retained as a type name. The first Il-18s to enter service had accommodation for 75 passengers, the initial passenger services being flown by Aeroflot on 20 April 1959 on the Moscow-Adler and Moscow-Alma Ata routes. These first Il-18s were followed into service after only a short period by generally-similar Il-18Bs, these differing primarily by having the seating layout rearranged to accommodate 84 passengers as standard.

An improved Il-18V began to enter service with Aeroflot in 1961, the main change by comparison with Il-18Bs in service resulting from a revised seating layout to accommodate 90 to 100 passengers. Because this represented a rather different arrangement to that of the original 75-seat version, some cabin windows were repositioned. With Il-18Vs established in production and in service, development work was carried out to improve the breed still further. This resulted in a development aircraft identified initially as the Il-18I.

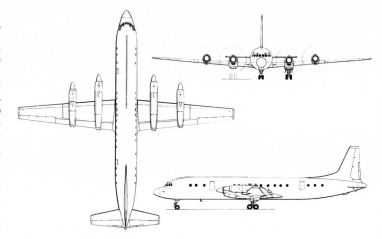

Ilyushin Il-18 'Coot'

Ilyushin Il-18

which introduced more powerful AI-20M turboprop engines, increased fuel capacity and, by deletion of the unpressurised tail cargo hold, a pressurised cabin extended aft to provide for a maximum of 122 passengers in the summer months. This capacity was possible because the extensive storage for outer clothing, imposed by the Russian winter, could be deleted; when the coat storage space was needed, passenger capacity was reduced to 110.

Put into production as the Il-18D, or Il-18E without the increased fuel tankage, these aircraft began to enter service with Aeroflot in 1965. Loss of the tail cargo hold meant that the APU, installed in that area on earlier versions, needed a new home. This was found in the under-surface of the centre fuselage, the APU being covered by a streamlined fairing and providing an external feature by which Il-18D/-18E aircraft can be identified.

It is believed that something in excess of 700 of these aircraft were built, the majority of them for commercial operations. In Aeroflot use Il-18s were reported, after 20 years in service, to have carried some 235 million passengers during approximately 505 million flights. Only small numbers went into military operation, primarily for VIP transport. In 1978 an ECM or electronic intelligence version of the Il-18 was identified, and it seems possible that as these turboprop aircraft are replaced in civil operations by new-generation turbofan airliners, more examples of the Il-18s may appear in military support roles. The details below apply to the Il-18D.

Specification
Type: long-range transport
Powerplant: four 4,250-ehp (3169-ekW) Ivchenko AI-20M turboprops
Performance: maximum cruising

Ilyushin Il-18 of Interflug (East Germany).

speed 419 mph (675 km/h); operating altitude 26,250-32,810 ft (8000-10000 m); range with maximum payload and 1-hour reserves 2,299 miles (3700 km); range with maximum fuel and 1-hour reserves 4,039 miles (6500 km)
Weights: empty equipped (90 seats) 77,162 lb (35000 kg);

maximum take-off 141,096 lb (64000 kg)
Dimensions: span 122 ft 8½ in (37.40 m); length 117 ft 9¼ in (35.90 m); height 33 ft 4¼ in (10.17 m); wing area 1,507.00 sq ft (140.00 m²)
Operators include: Aeroflot, Air Guinée, Air Mali, Balkan Bulgarian Airlines, CAAC, Ceskoslovenske

Aerolinie, Choson Minhang Civil Aviation Company, Cubana, Hang Khong Vietnam, Interflug, LOT, Malév, and Tarom

The Ilyushin Il-18, the Russian equivalent of the Lockheed Electra, was built in moderately large numbers and most are still in service. Illustrated is one of Balkan Bulgarian Airlines' seven Il-18s.

Ilyushin Il-62

History and Notes
While there had been unconfirmed reports that the Soviet Union was constructing the prototype of a long-range turbojet-powered transport, this was not made public knowledge until 24 September 1962, when the then incomplete aircraft was seen by a number of Soviet leaders, including the late Premier Krushchev. First flown in January 1963, one of the prototypes was exhibited at the Paris Air Show in 1965.

Designed to complement and partially to replace the turboprop-powered Tupolev Tu-114 on long-range domestic and intercontinental routes the Il-62, as this new Ilyushin design was identified, was of low-wing configuration, with four rear-mounted engines. The wing, like that of the Boeing 707, was swept 35° at quarter-chord, and incorporated such features as three-section ailerons, double-slotted trailing-edge flaps, and two upper-surface spoilers forward of the flaps on each wing. Flight testing was to show that, in common with many T-tail aircraft, only limited control was maintained at low flight speeds, and as a result the leading-edge of each wing ws provided with a fixed drooping leading-edge extension on the outer two-thirds of the span.

As already mentioned, the tail unit was of T-type, with all surfaces swept, and the retractable tricycle type landing gear had a twin-wheel nose unit and a four-wheel bogie on each main unit. The fuselage was

Ilyushin Il-62/62M of Ceskoslovenske Aerolinie, Czechoslovakia.

basically of circular cross-section, with the whole of the cabin and two of the baggage/freight compartments pressurised. The powerplant was mounted, like that of the Vickers (BAC) VC10, in horizontal pairs on each side of the rear fuselage. Planned engines were four Kuznetsov turbofans, but these had not reached a sufficiently advanced stage of development by the time the prototype was ready to fly, and four 16,535-lb (7500-kg) thrust Lyulka AL-7 turbojets were installed as a temporary measure. The production Kuznetsov engine was not long delayed, however, and was ready in the time to power some of the later development aircraft. Thrust-reversers were provided, to reduce the landing run, but only on the two outboard engines.

Because of the Il-62's long-range role, the flight deck was planned for a standard flight crew of five, but there is provision for the accommodation of two additional crew members for check or training purposes. Several different cabin layouts are available, but all of these have a

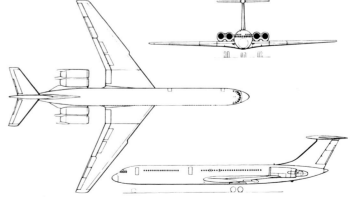

Ilyushin Il-62M

fore-and-aft cabin with access doors on the port side, one door being forward of the forward cabin, the other between the two cabins. Alternative layouts include 72 seats forward and 114 rear, 66 forward and 102 rear, and 45 forward and 69 rear. There is also a de luxe version

which provides 45 seats forward and 40 sleeper-chairs in the aft cabin.

As might be expected in a long-range aircraft of this class, avionics are to a high standard and, in addition to normal communications and navigation radio systems, the Il-62 has an autopilot, air data system, navigation computer and weather radar.

When, on 15 September 1967, Aeroflot introduced this aircraft on its Moscow-Montreal route, it represented the Soviet Union's first long-range four-engine intercontinental jet transport. Before that, of course, the Il-62 had entered service on domestic routes earlier in the year. Initial operations had been on cargo services, but on 10 March passenger/mail services were inaugurated on the Moscow-Khabarovsk and Moscow-Novosibirsk routes.

Developed versions have since appeared, the first being the Il-62M which was displayed publicly at the 1971 Paris Air Show, and which entered service on Aeroflot's Moscow-Havanna route in 1974. This retains the same basic structure and dimensions as the earlier production aircraft, but introduces many improvements. These include differential use of the wing spoilers to improve roll control; increased fuel capacity; more economical Soloviev D-30KU turbofan engines, the outer engine of each pair having improved thrust reversers of clamshell type; and better cabin facilities. The two main underfloor baggage holds have been modified to introduce a containerised system with mechanised handling. There is also an improved layout of the flight deck, and more advanced avionics.

In 1978 there was announced a variant of the Il-62M intended for operation at higher gross weights, and with the cabin revised to provide accommodation for a maximum of

195 passengers. This has the designation Il-62MK, and while retaining the same dimensions as earlier versions differs in having a strengthened wing structure, and de-rated engines. The details below apply to the Il-62M.

Specification
Type: long-range transport
Powerplant: four 25,353-lb (11500-kg) thrust Soloviev D-30KU turbofans

Performance: cruising speed 559 mph (900 km/h) at optimum altitude; economic cruising speed 528 mph (850 km/h) at optimum altitude; range with maximum payload and reserves 4,971 miles (8000 km)
Weights: empty operating 153,001 lb (69400 kg); maximum take-off 363,763 lb (165000 kg)
Dimensions: span 141 ft 8¾ in (43.20 m); length 174 ft 3¼ in (53.12 m); height 40 ft 6¼ in

The USSR has so far failed to develop a successor to the Ilyushin Il-62 long-range airliner, a contemporary of the UK's Vickers VC10, 50 Russian clients such as Cuba are therefore compelled to keep in service this now obsolescent and economically unviable aircraft.

(12.35 m); wing area 3,037.67 sq ft (282.20 m²)
Operators include: Aeroflot, Ceskoslovenske Aerolinie, Cubana, Interflug, LOT, and Tarom

Ilyushin Il-76

History and Notes
With the Soviet air force requiring a heavy transport aircraft that would be suitable for operation in the Siberian regions, the Ilyushin design team initiated in the late 1960s studies of a large-capacity turbofan-powered transport that would be capable of operation from short unprepared strips. Intended to replace the four-turboprop Antonov An-12 in service, the new aircraft was required to be faster, and also easier to maintain.

Designated Il-76, the prototype (CCCP-86712) flew for the first time on 25 March 1971, and two months later this aircraft was displayed at the Paris Air Show, appearing in Aeroflot insignia. Of high-wing monoplane configuration, to ensure that the wing structure does not compromise cabin volume, the Il-76 has wings incorporating wide-span triple-slotted trailing-edge flaps, upper-surface spoilers forward of the flaps, and almost full-span leading-edge slats to ensure that the requisite short-field performance can be achieved. To enhance the type's go-anywhere capability, the nosewheel type landing gear has a nose unit incorporating four wheels, and each main wheel bogie carries two rows of four wheels, making a total of 20 wheels with low-pressure tyres to distribute the total loaded weight of the aircraft over as great a surface area as possible. Tyre pressures which can be adjusted in flight, heavy-duty brakes, and thrust reversers on each of the four Soloviev turbofan engines, which are mounted in wing pods, make short landings possible on a variety of surfaces.

The all-important cargo loading takes place from the rear of the fuselage, which has two large clamshell type doors, an upward-hinged panel, and a downward-hinged loading ramp to provide clear access.

Ilyushin Il-76T of Iraqi Airways.

The cabin floor is reinforced for heavy loads, is able to accept a variety of tracked or wheeled vehicles that can be driven up the ramp, and has advanced mechanical handling systems to simplify the task of loading or unloading containerised or palletised freight. The aircraft is designed to be operated by a crew of seven, which includes two specialised freight handlers. The flight crew's task is simplified by advanced avionics equipment for day or night all-weather operation (including automatic landing approaches), and a large APU can provide all essential services (including engine starting) on the ground, making the aircraft capable of operation without recourse to local facilities.

Testing was to show that the design requirements had been met most adequately, and at low operating costs. In 1975 the type established no fewer than 25 officially recognised records for speed and altitude with payload, and the improved Il-76T, with greater cargo capacity and operating at a higher gross weight, began to enter service with Aeroflot. Its use on domestic routes was initiated in early 1978, and on the international Moscow-Japan service

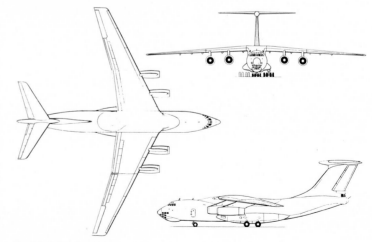

Ilyushin Il-76T 'Candid'

on 5 April 1978. It was believed that more than 40 of these transports were in service with Aeroflot by late 1980, and their potential for heavy cargo lift is of growing interest to other airlines. Considerably larger numbers are understood to be in service with the Soviet air force, by whom the Il-76 is used also for the transport and deployment of para-

troops, as well as for strategic heavy freighting. The Il-76 has also been evaluated for other military roles, including that of a flight refuelling tanker.

Specification
Type: medium/long-range freight transport
Powerplant: four 26,455-lb

Ilyushin Il-76

(1200-kg) thrust Soloviev D-30KP turbofans
Performance: maximum speed 528 mph (850 km/h); maximum cruising speed 497 mph (800 km/h); economic cruising speed 466 mph (750 km/h); cruising ceiling 42,650 ft (13000 m); range with maximum payload 3,107 miles 500 km); maximum range with reserves 4,163 miles (6700 km)
Weight: maximum take-off 374,786 lb (170000 kg)
Dimensions: span 165 ft 8¼ in (50.50 m); length 152 ft 10½ in (46.60 m); height 48 ft 4¾ in (14.75 m); wing area 3,229.28 sq ft (300.00 m²)
Operators include: Aeroflot, Iraqi Airways, and Libyan Arab Airlines

Nominally operated by Iraqi Airways, this one of four Ilyushin Il-76 heavy freighters clearly has a paramilitary role, as indicated by the retention of the tail gunner's position, which would have a pair of 23-mm cannon in time of war.

Ilyushin Il-86

History and Notes
The rapid growth of demand in the Soviet Union for civil air transport, to speed the carriage of passengers, mail and freight over the very long-range internal routes of the nation, as well as for international communications, has caused Aeroflot to initiate the development of many new types of aircraft during the postwar years. The evolution of civil aircraft has followed very much the same pattern as that of European and United States products, and it therefore caused little surprise when it was learned, at the 1971 Paris Air Show, that a wide-body turbofan-powered transport was to be developed for service with Aeroflot.

Proposals were sought from the Antonov, Ilyushin and Tupolev design bureaux, but it was Ilyushin's design which appealed to Aeroflot and was selected for development. A model of this proposal was displayed in Moscow, showing that it was in some respects following the successful configuration of the Il-62, including a similar powerplant of four rear-mounted engines. However, when the first pictures of the prototype (this flying for the first time on 22 December 1976) were seen, it became clear that the aircraft had been subjected to a number of design changes and now had a general configuration and size somewhat similar to the European Airbus, save that it had four, instead of two, pylon-mounted turbofan engines.

Of low/mid-wing monoplane configuration the Il-86, as the aircraft is designated, has a number of interesting features. The wing has 35° of sweep at quarter-chord, and incorporates full-span leading-edge flaps, upper-surface spoilers forward of wide-span double-slotted trailing-edge flaps, and conventional ailerons. The circular-section fuselage has a maximum internal width of approximately 18 ft 8½ in (5.70 m), providing adequate room for nine-abreast seating, divided by two aisles. The tail unit is a conventional structure with all surfaces swept, but each control surface is constructed in two sections. The tricycle type landing gear is reminiscent of that carried by Douglas DC-10 Series 30 and 40 aircraft, the nose unit having twin wheels, but with two conventional and one central main unit, all three units carrying a four-wheel bogie.

Ilyushin Il-86 of Aeroflot, USSR.

The powerplant comprises four Kuznetsov NK-86 turbofan engines, pylon-mounted under the wings so that they are forward of the leading-edge, and each having thrust reversers.

Accommodation is provided for a crew of three or four on the flight deck, and there is seating for a maximum of 350 passengers, split between three cabins which are separated by wardrobes. Access to this aircraft is unique, being via three lower-deck airstair type doors which enable the aircraft to dispense with conventional airport loading/unloading bridges. These airstairs reach down to ground level, and after boarding passengers can deposit their baggage in lower-deck stowage positions before climbing an internal fixed staircase to the passenger cabin.

As might be expected, avionics and equipment are to a very high standard, and the flight control and navigation systems are such that automatic climb and descent can be selected, and automatic landing capability is included.

It is believed that the first pro-duction example made its initial flight on 24 October 1977. It was planned that the Il-86 would be in service with Aeroflot in sufficient time to carry passengers to the 1980 Olympic Games in Moscow. This schedule was not achieved, although it is known that the type entered service on Aeroflot's Moscow-Mineralnye Vody route in September 1978. Although this was some months ahead of the anticipated date for first deployment, there is no confirmation whether this was of any exploratory nature, or if the service is still in operation.

Following full-scale acceptance of the Il-86 into Aeroflot service, there seems every likelihood that the Soviet air force will also show interest in this large-capacity aircraft. It has even been suggested that the Soviet Union may be interested in the development of an airborne warning and control system (AWACS) version of this aircraft which, like the US AABNCP and AWACS, require ample cabin space for control and data consoles, advanced avionics equipment, and the not inconsiderable staff needed to make possible the utmost use of these costly aircraft.

Specification
Type: medium/long-range transport
Powerplant: four 28,660-lb (13000-kg) thrust Kuznetsov NK-86 turbofans
Performance: (estimated) cruising speed 559-590 mph (900-950 km/h) at 29,530-36,090 ft (9000-11000 m); range with maximum payload 2,237 miles (3600 km); range with maximum fuel 2,858 miles (4600 km)
Weights: (estimated) maximum take-off 454,152 lb (206000 kg)
Dimensions: span 157 ft 8¼ in (48.06 m); length 197 ft 6½ in (60.21 m); height 51 ft 5¼ in (15.68 m); wing area 3,44.56 sq ft (320.00 m²)
Operator: Aeroflot

The Ilyushin Il-86, the USSR's first wide-body airliner, was to have been in full service by 1980 but had not achieved this status even in 1981.

IAI 1124/1124A Westwind 1/2

History and Notes

The Aero Commander Bethany Division of Rockwell Standard Corporation announced, in early 1961, the development of a new high-speed executive transport to be known as the Jet Commander 1121. It was of cantilever mid-wing monoplane configuration, with a fail-safe pressurised fuselage, retractable tricycle landing gear, a conventional tail unit with swept surfaces, and two 2,850 lb (1293 kg) thrust General Electric turbojet engines, one mounted on each side of the aft fuselage. Its 19 ft (5.79 m) long cabin provided accommodation for a pilot and up to eight passengers in a well-equipped and comfortable interior. The prototype was first flown on 27 January 1963, and after gaining certification, the first production delivery was made on 11 January 1965.

The merger which joined North American Aviation and Rockwell Standard in 1967 brought a sales conflict of similar aircraft: North American's Sabreliner and Rockwell's Jet Commander. It was decided to continue production of the longer established Sabreliner, and all tooling and production rights for the Jet Commander were sold to Israel Aircraft Industries. Production by IAI was initially under the original designation, though IAI Jet Commanders introduced increased fuel capacity and a higher gross weight, and plans were made to build an 1121A with a gross weight increase and all-weather equipment, an 1121B with more powerful engines, and an advanced development to be known as the 1122. A name change to Commodore Jet was made, and production of the above mentioned versions proceeded as planned, except that the 1122 emerged as the 1121C. The designation 1122 was applied to two development aircraft that led to the Commodore Jet, later Westwind 1123, from which the current 1124 Westwind 1 has derived. The primary change in the 1124 was the introduction of Garrett TFE731-3 turbofan engines, but throughout the progressive developments that have led to this version there has been continuous product improvement. By comparison with the Commodore Jet 1123, the Westwind 1 with five passengers has an improvement in range capability of almost 33 per cent. In addition, standard seating now accommodates a crew of two and 10 passengers. A maritime reconnaissance version, the 1124 Sea Scan, is also available.

First flown on 24 April 1979 was the prototype of an advanced version that has the designation 1124A Westwind 2: it includes a new 'Sigma' wing of IAI design. This incorporates a supercritical wing section and wingtip winglets to enhance performance, to the extent that it will carry double the number of passengers over the same range. There are other refinements, but basically it has the same powerplant and two crew/10 passenger capacity of its immediate predecessor. The first delivery of a production Westwind 2 was made in the autumn of 1980. The details that follow apply to the 1124 Westwind 1.

Specification

Type: twin-turbofan business transport
Powerplant: two 3,700-lb (1678-kg) thrust Garrett TFE731-3-1G turbofans
Performance: maximum level speed 542 mph (872 km/h) from sea level to 19,000 ft (5915 m);

IAI 1124A Westwind 2.

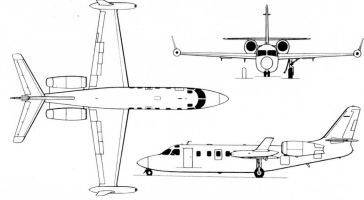

IAI 1124 Westwind 2

economic cruising speed 460 mph (740 km/h) at 41,000 ft (12 495 m); certificated ceiling 45,000 ft (13 715 m); range with 7 passengers, maximum fuel and reserves 2,475 miles (3983 km)
Weights: empty operating 12,700 lb (5761 kg); maximum take-off 23,500 lb (10659 kg)
Dimensions: span 43 ft 2 in (13.16 m); length 52 ft 3 in (15.93 m); height 15 ft 9½ in (4.81 m); wing area 308.26 sq ft (28.64 m²)

IAI Westwind 2 cutaway drawing key

1 Radome
2 Weather radar scanner
3 Radar tracking mechanism
4 Nosewheel leg door
5 Twin nosewheels
6 Nose undercarriage leg strut
7 Radio and electronics equipment
8 Oxygen bottle
9 Nose compartment access doors
10 Batteries
11 Front pressure bulkhead
12 Pitot tube
13 Cooling air intake
14 Rudder pedals
15 Instrument panel
16 Windscreen wipers
17 Instrument panel shroud
18 Curved windscreen panels
19 Overhead switch panel
20 Co-pilot's seat
21 Engine throttles
22 Control column
23 Nosewheel steering control
24 Pilot's seat
25 Cockpit eyebrow windows
26 Cockpit bulkhead
27 Entry door
28 Door latch
29 Folding boarding step
30 Entry lobby
31 Three-seat settee
32 VHF aerial
33 Sea Scan, maritime patrol version
34 Litton AN/APS-504(V)2 search radar
35 Observation window
36 Fuselage mounted stores pylon
37 Flare launcher/sensor pod
38 Fuselage skin plating
39 Galley unit
40 Drinks cabinet
41 Fuselage frame construction
42 Folding table
43 Cabin window panel
44 Fuselage main longeron
45 Individual swivelling seats, seven-seat executive layout
46 Starboard emergency exit window
47 D/F loop aerial
48 Radio telephone
49 Fold-out table stowage
50 Port emergency exit window
51 Cabin wall trim panels
52 Rearmost forward-facing seats
53 Magazine rack

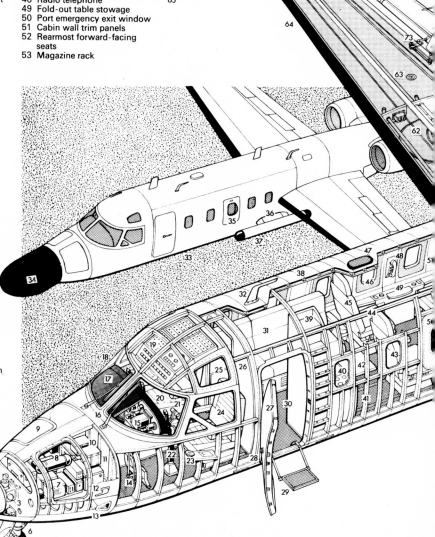

IAI 1124/1124A Westwind 1/2

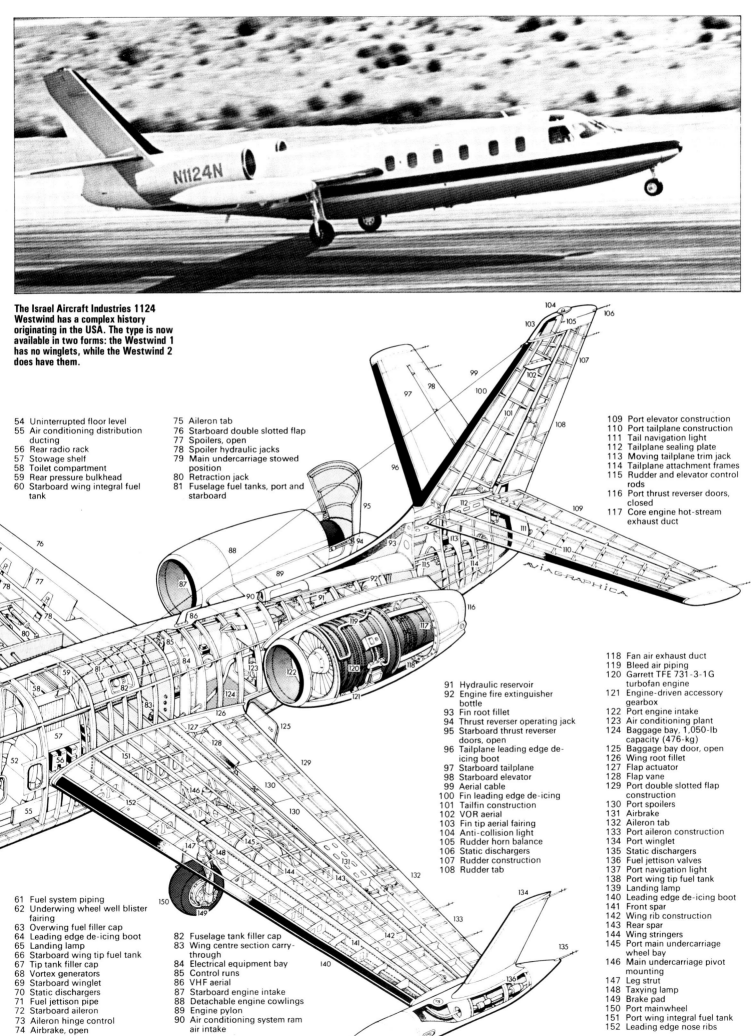

The Israel Aircraft Industries 1124 Westwind has a complex history originating in the USA. The type is now available in two forms: the Westwind 1 has no winglets, while the Westwind 2 does have them.

54 Uninterrupted floor level
55 Air conditioning distribution ducting
56 Rear radio rack
57 Stowage shelf
58 Toilet compartment
59 Rear pressure bulkhead
60 Starboard wing integral fuel tank

75 Aileron tab
76 Starboard double slotted flap
77 Spoilers, open
78 Spoiler hydraulic jacks
79 Main undercarriage stowed position
80 Retraction jack
81 Fuselage fuel tanks, port and starboard

91 Hydraulic reservoir
92 Engine fire extinguisher bottle
93 Fin root fillet
94 Thrust reverser operating jack
95 Starboard thrust reverser doors, open
96 Tailplane leading edge de-icing boot
97 Starboard tailplane
98 Starboard elevator
99 Aerial cable
100 Fin leading edge de-icing
101 Tailfin construction
102 VOR aerial
103 Fin tip aerial fairing
104 Anti-collision light
105 Rudder horn balance
106 Static dischargers
107 Rudder construction
108 Rudder tab

109 Port elevator construction
110 Port tailplane construction
111 Tail navigation light
112 Tailplane sealing plate
113 Moving tailplane trim jack
114 Tailplane attachment frames
115 Rudder and elevator control rods
116 Port thrust reverser doors, closed
117 Core engine hot-stream exhaust duct
118 Fan air exhaust duct
119 Bleed air piping
120 Garrett TFE 731-3-1G turbofan engine
121 Engine-driven accessory gearbox
122 Port engine intake
123 Air conditioning plant
124 Baggage bay, 1,050-lb capacity (476-kg)
125 Baggage bay door, open
126 Wing root fillet
127 Flap actuator
128 Flap vane
129 Port double slotted flap construction
130 Port spoilers
131 Airbrake
132 Aileron tab
133 Port aileron construction
134 Port winglet
135 Static dischargers
136 Fuel jettison valves
137 Port navigation light
138 Port wing tip fuel tank
139 Landing lamp
140 Leading edge de-icing boot
141 Front spar
142 Wing rib construction
143 Rear spar
144 Wing stringers
145 Port main undercarriage wheel bay
146 Main undercarriage pivot mounting
147 Leg strut
148 Taxying lamp
149 Brake pad
150 Port mainwheel
151 Port wing integral fuel tank
152 Leading edge nose ribs

61 Fuel system piping
62 Underwing wheel well blister fairing
63 Overwing fuel filler cap
64 Leading edge de-icing boot
65 Landing lamp
66 Starboard wing tip fuel tank
67 Tip tank filler cap
68 Vortex generators
69 Starboard winglet
70 Static dischargers
71 Fuel jettison pipe
72 Starboard aileron
73 Aileron hinge control
74 Airbrake, open

82 Fuselage tank filler cap
83 Wing centre section carry-through
84 Electrical equipment bay
85 Control runs
86 VHF aerial
87 Starboard engine intake
88 Detachable engine cowlings
89 Engine pylon
90 Air conditioning system ram air intake

Issoire IA 80/Wassmer WA.80 Piranha

History and Notes

Wassmer Aviation, at its Issoire factory, developed a series of all-plastics light aircraft which were based on the prototype WA50, a four-seater which first flew on 22 March 1966. The production version was the WA51 Pacific, which differed in detail from the prototype and in having non-retractable landing gear. In 1975 Wassmer announced the WA.80 Piranha, which was to be a two-seat training and touring aircraft with a fuselage very similar to that of the WA51, but with a 100-hp (75-kW) Rolls-Royce Continental O-200-A engine in place of the earlier aircraft's 150-hp (112-kW) Avco Lycoming O-320-E2A. A new feature was the one-piece laminated polyester resin spring which mounted the main wheels. The first prototype flew in November 1975, and the second underwent static tests at CEAT Toulouse in spring 1976. Certification in the Utility category followed and production began against initial orders for 20 examples. On 16 September 1977 Wassmer went into liquidation and its premises and industrial assets, including the Piranha, were taken over by the Société Issoire Aviation, formed on 1 February 1978.

Specification

Type: two-seat trainer
Powerplant: one 100-hp (75-kW) Rolls-Royce Continental O-200-A flat-four piston engine
Performance: maximum speed 149 mph (240 km/h) at sea level; cruising speed 118 mph (190 km/h) at sea level; service ceiling 13,125 ft (4000 m); range 435 miles (700 km)
Weights: empty 1,102 lb (500 kg); maximum take-off 1,763 lb (800 kg)
Dimensions: span 30 ft 10 in (9.40 m); length 24 ft 7¼ in (7.50 m); height 6 ft 10¾ in (2.10 m); wing area 133.5 sq ft (12.40 m²)

Kamov Ka-26

History and Notes

It was announced in January 1964 that the Kamov design bureau was involved in the development of a new helicopter, and that a prototype was due to fly in the following year. This first flight was made as planned, but it was not until September that the Ka-26, as the new helicopter was designated, was seen publicly for the first time. A casual observer might have thought that its design left a great deal to be desired: in fact, the reverse was very much the case, for an enormous amount of work must have been devoted to finalise this very practical attempt to develop a multi-role helicopter that would be comparatively cheap to operate.

Its basic structure comprises a two-seat fully enclosed cabin at the forward end, united with the tailplane and twin fins and rudders by twin tailbooms. The non-retractable four-wheel landing gear has main units below the engine support structure, and castoring nosewheel units below the forward end of the cabin. Powerplant consists of two piston engines mounted in pods on high-set short stub wings: they drive, via the combining transmission, two contra-rotating three-blade rotors, and in emergency either engine can drive both rotors.

The Ka-26 is intended primarily to fulfil an agricultural role, and this requirement promoted certain features of the design: piston engines for economical operation; extensive use of plastics materials for light weight and non-corrosive features; and considerable use of bonding techniques to prevent the degree of chemical ingress that can occur with riveted structures.

Most ingenious of all, perhaps, was the solution of the multi-role requirement. Immediately aft of the forward control cabin is an area, on the aircraft's centre of gravity, in which can be mounted agricultural equipment, an open cargo platform, or a six-passenger/cargo/equipment pod. This has made it possible for the Ka-26 to meet almost any role so far demanded of it. These include agricultural dispersal of dry or liquid chemicals, air ambulance, fire reconnaissance, fish and ice patrol, passenger and cargo carrying, pipeline/powerline patrol, rescue, and survey. It has been reported that a more advanced version, presumably with turbine engines, is under development. The details below apply to the Ka-26 available in 1981.

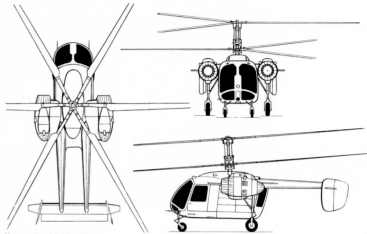

Kamov Ka-26 'Hoodlum'

Specification

Type: multi-role helicopter
Powerplant: two 325-hp (242-kW) Vedeneev M-14V-26 radial piston engines
Performance: maximum cruising speed 93 mph (150 km/h); economic cruising speed 56-68 mph (90-110 km/h); service ceiling 9,840 ft (3000 m); range with pilot/seven passengers, 30-min reserves 248 miles (400 km)
Weights: empty operating, stripped 4,300 lb l(1950 kg); maximum take-off 7,165 lb (3250 kg)
Dimensions: rotor diameter (each) 42 ft 8 in (13.00 m); length of fuselage 25 ft 5 in (7.75 m); height 13 ft 3½ in (4.05 m); total rotor disc area 2,857.5 sq ft (265.46 m²)

Kawasaki (Boeing Vertol) KV-107

History and Notes

As long ago as 1956, Boeing Vertol in the USA initiated the design of a new twin-rotor transport helicopter. The powerplant selected for this aircraft comprised two of the lightweight turboshaft engines that were then coming on to the market, the availability of which was to prove of great value to all helicopter manufacturers. The turboshafts' weight was such that they could be mounted above the cabin, providing greater airframe volume for the carriage of passengers, goods or equipment, with the additional advantage of the simplification of the rotor transmission systems.

Boeing Vertol's Model 107, as the new helicopter was designated, first flew in prototype form on 22 April 1958, and was manufactured subsequently in a variety of commercial and military versions. In Japan, Kawasaki Heavy Industries negotiated a licence to manufacture and market the aircraft, under the designation KV-107, and the first Japanese-built example was flown in May 1962. Three and a half years later, in November 1965, Kawasaki obtained from Boeing Vertol worldwide sales rights for the KV-107, and since that time has developed more advanced versions for both civil and military use.

In the current form manufactured by Kawasaki, each of the three-blade rotors has blades of composite steel, aluminium and glassfibre construction. The transmission is so arranged that, in the event of failure of one engine, both rotors can be driven by the surviving engine. Kawasaki's basic airline helicopter, which has the designation KV-107/II-2, has a fuselage that is of square cross-section, and which is sealed to permit operation from and to water surfaces if desired. The landing gear is of the fixed tricycle type, with twin wheels on each unit. Standard powerplants for this version are two 1,250-shp (932-kW) General Electric CT58-110-1, or Ishikawajima-Harima CT58-IHI-110-1 turboshaft engines mounted side-by-side adjacent to the rear rotor pylon. Accommodation is provided for a flight crew of two, two stewar-

The sole rights for the manufacture and marketing of the Boeing Vertol 107 are now vested in Kawasaki, whose KV-107/II and KV-107/IIA models are produced in a variety of sub-variants.

desses, and 25 passengers. A KV-107/II-7 version is also available, this being equipped as a VIP transport with seating layouts which can accommodate 6 to 11 persons.

An improved model has also been developed and certificated with more powerful turboshaft engines, this having the designation KV-107/IIA-2, and there are in addition KV-107/IIA-SM-1 and KV-107/IIA-SM-2 variants equipped for firefighting and aero-medical/rescue operations

respectively. The use of these more powerful engines gives improved performance for vertical take-off missions, or for use in 'hot-and-high' situations, and these versions are available optionally with greater fuel capacity to increase range capability. For self-ferry flights the -SM-1 and -SM-2 special-purpose aircraft have provision for an additional fuel tank inside the cabin.

The details below apply to the KV-107/IIA-2.

Specification
Type: transport helicopter
Powerplant: two 1,400-shp (1044-kW) General Electric CT58-140-1, or Ishikawajima-Harima CT58-IHI-140-1 turboshafts
Performance: maximum speed 158 mph (254 km/h) at sea level; cruising speed 150 mph (241 km/h) at 5,000 ft (1525 m); service ceiling 17,000 ft (5180 m); range with standard fuel 222 miles (357 km); range with maximum fuel 682

miles (1098 km)
Weights: empty equipped 11,576 lb (5251 kg); maximum take-off 21,400 lb (9707 kg)
Dimensions: rotor diameter, each 50 ft 0 in (15.24m); length, blades turning 83 ft 4 in (25.40 m); height 16 ft 8½ in (5.09 m); rotor disc area, total 3,925 sq ft (364.63 m²)
Operators include: Airlift Inc., Columbia Helicopters, and Saudi Arabian Government

Lake LA-4 Buccaneer/Colonial Skimmer

History and Notes
In August 1946 the Colonial Aircraft Corporation began work on the design of the C-1 Skimmer, a three-seat light amphibian to be powered by a 125-hp (93-kW) Avco Lycoming O-290-D engine. Construction of the prototype commenced in January 1947 and the first flight took place on 17 July 1948. The Type Certificate was awarded on 19 September 1955 and the Skimmer was put into production with the 150-hp (112-kW) Avco Lycoming O-320-A1A engine. In 1957 Colonial introduced the four-seat C-2 Skimmer IV, powered by a 180-hp (134-kW) Avco Lycoming O-360-A1A, and the production rights for this model were acquired by Lake Aircraft Corporation in October 1959.

A Lake-built prototype, designated LA-4P, flown in November 1959 and certificated on 21 June 1960, was followed by two LA-4As which incorporated a 4 ft (1.22 m) increase in wing span, with each aileron increased in length by 1 ft (0.30 m), modified wing/fuselage attachment

points, and structural strengthening to allow operation at a higher all-up weight. The production LA-4, with the same improvements as the LA-4A but with the addition of a 1 ft 5 in (0.43 m) bow extension, was awarded Type Approval on 25 July 1960. Lake became a division of Consolidated Aeronautics following a merger in 1962, and the LA-4 continued in production until 1970 when FAA certification was received for the current production version, the LA-4-200 Buccaneer, which is powered by a 200-hp (149-kW) Avco Lycoming IO-360-A1B engine. The specification applies to the LA-4-200.

Specification
Type: four-seat amphibian
Powerplant: one 200-hp (149-kW) Avco Lycoming IO-360-A1B flat-four piston engine
Performance: maximum speed 146 mph (235 km/h) at sea level; cruising speed 150 mph (241 km/h) at 8,000 ft (2440 m); service ceiling 14,700 ft (4480 m); range with maximum fuel 825 miles (1328 km)

Weights: empty 1,555 lb (705 kg); maximum take-off 2,690 lb (1220 kg)
Dimensions: span 38 ft 0 in (11.58 m); length 24 ft 11 in (7.59 m); height 9 ft 4 in (2.84 m); wing area 170 sq ft (15.79 m²)

An enduring design of widespread operator appeal, the Lake Buccaneer amphibian has been in production in one form or another since 1948. The current production model is the LA-4-200.

Lapan XT-400

History and Notes
LAPAN (Lembaga Penerbangan Dan Antariksa Nasional) is the Indonesian National Aeronautics and Space Institute, which was established in Jakarta in 1963. A team under Dipl. Ing. Suharto began work on the design of an eight-seat light transport aircraft which clearly owes some of its features to the Britten-Norman Islander, including its STOL capability. Designed to meet the requirements of FAR23 and 25 in the Utility

Category, the XT-400 is intended for up-country operations and can be flown from grass or semi-prepared strips. Clamshell doors in the upswept rear fuselage permit the loading of freight into the 150 cu ft (4.25 m³) cabin which, in passenger configuration, provides accommodation in four pairs of seats for the pilot and seven passengers. The ambulance version, also making use of the clamshell doors, can take two stretchers and a medical attendant. The XT-400 is

powered by two 250-hp (186-kW) Avco Lycoming IO-540-C engines, and the total fuel capacity of 130 US gallons (492 litres) confers a maximum fuel range of 600 miles (966 km).

Specification
Type: eight-seat utility transport
Powerplant: two 250-hp (186-kW) Avco Lycoming IO-540-C flat-six piston engines
Performance: maximum speed 170 mph (274 km/h); economic cruising

speed 145 mph (233 km/h); service ceiling 15,300 ft (4665 m); range with maximum payload 300 miles (483 km)
Weights: empty 3,136 lb (1422 kg); maximum take-off 5,600 lb (2540 kg)
Dimensions: span 47 ft 10½ in (14.59 m); length 33 ft 5½ in (10.20 m); height 14 ft 1¼ in (4.30 m); wing area 272.97 sq ft (25.36 m²)

Let L-410 Turbolet

History and Notes
Designed at the Let Narodni plant at Kunovice, by a team under chief designer Ladislav Smrcek, the L-410 Turbolet twin-turboprop light transport was developed for local service and feeder operations, including those from grass airfields. The project began in 1966 and the first prototype took off on its maiden flight on 16 April 1969, powered by two 715-ehp (533-ekW) United Aircraft of Canada PT6A-27 engines, driving Hamilton Standard three-blade propellers. Four-blade Hartzell propellers were flown on the second of three further PT6A-27-engined prototypes, in a programme aimed at reducing the noise level in the cabin. The Canadian engine was retained for the 27 L-410As built during 1971-4, and for the L-410AF, an aerial survey version with a glazed nose, one example of which was supplied to Hungary in 1974.

The prototype L-410M, powered by indigenous 735-ehp (548-ekW) Walter M-601A turboprops fitted with Avia V508 propellers, flew for

Let L-410UVP of Aeroflot (USSR).

the first time in 1973, and the first of 109 production aircraft was delivered in 1976. The current production version, being built at a rate believed to be in the order of 100 a year for operation on Aeroflot's internal services, is the L-410UVP. The first of three prototypes flew on 1 November 1977, incorporating a number of changes which included

an increase of 1 ft 6 in (0.46 m) in fuselage length, and increases in wing span and in fin and rudder area. Tailplane dihedral angle of 7° was introduced, as were auto-feathering for the Avia V508B propellers, spoilers, and automatic bank control surfaces, the last operating in engine-out conditions and reducing the lift on the side of the engine

which is still running.

In basic airline configuration the Turbolet seats 15 passengers, but other internal arrangements include one for ambulance operation with accommodation for six stretcher cases, five seated patients and a medical attendant. Double upward-opening doors at the rear of the aircraft provide a 4 ft 9½ in by 4 ft

1¼ in (1.46 m by 1.25 m) aperture for loading freight in the all-cargo configuration. The specification applies to the L-410UVP.

Specification
Type: 15-passenger transport
Powerplant: two 730-ehp (544-ekW) Walter M 601 B turboprops
Performance: economic cruising speed 186 mph (300 km/h); service ceiling 29,360 ft (8950 m); range with maximum fuel and 1,874-lb (3015-kg) payload 646 miles (1040 km)
Weights: empty 8,212 lb (3725 kg); maximum take-off 12,566 lb (5700 kg)
Dimensions: span 63 ft 10¾ in (19.48 m); length 47 ft 5½ in (14.47 m); height 19 ft 1½ in (5.83 m); wing area 378.67 sq ft (35.18 m²)
Operators: Slov Air, Aeroflot

Lockheed Constellation/Super Constellation/Starliner Series

History and Notes

Aviation enthusiasts of an earlier vintage will recall with considerable nostalgia those halcyon days of the late 1950s when, at airports around the world, they could feast their eyes upon the piston-engined airliner at the peak of its development, and upon the first of the new and exciting turbojet-powered aircraft. High among the ranks of the former category were Lockheed's superb Constellations and Super Constellations. Their operators appreciated their sterling qualities of economy and reliability, while their passengers enjoyed the comfortable travel conditions that they provided; and enthusiasts delighted in their lines and grace, especially those of the Super Constellation.

Design of the Lockheed L-49 had originated in 1939, to meet the requirements of Pan American Airways and Transcontinental & Western Air (now Trans World Airlines), for a 40-passenger airliner for use on domestic routes. Like several other contemporary transport aircraft, the L-49 was fated to begin its flying life as a military aircraft after the production lines had been commandeered for the USAAF. The first C-69, as the L-49 had been redesignated, made its maiden flight on 9 January 1943, and 22 were supplied to the USAAF before VJ-Day brought cancellation of the outstanding contracts. Of these one was a 49-seat C-69C with VIP interior.

The first civil Constellations had the designation L-049, being constructed from the components that were in hand for the manufacture of C-69s, but with the interior completed to airline standard. The first of these was certificated for civil operations on 11 December 1945, and this version was to enter service first with Pan American and TWA. Of low-wing monoplane configuration, the Constellation had a wing which incorporated wide-span Lockheed-Fowler trailing-edge flaps. The fuselage was of circular cross-section and pressurised, and the tail unit consisted of a tailplane and elevators mounted on the fuselage upper surface, with two

Lockheed L-749 Constellation of Aerolineas Argo, Dominican Republic.

inset fins and rudders, and a third fin and rudder on the fuselage centre-line. The landing gear was of the retractable tricycle type, with dual wheels on all units. The powerplant comprised four wing-mounted 2,200-hp (1641 - kW) Wright R - 3350 - 745C18BA-1 radial piston engines. Basic accommodation of this version was for 43 to 48 passengers, but a maximum of 60 seats could be provided in a high-density layout. L-049s of TWA were used on the first regular US-Paris service, inaugurated on 6 February 1946.

The first true civil Constellations were identified by Lockheed as L-649s. Built from the beginning as commercial aircraft they had far more luxurious interiors, and 2,500-hp (1864-kW) Wright GR-3350-749C 18BD-1 engines. These had accommodation for 48 to 64 passengers as standard, but could also be supplied with high-density seating for a maximum of 81. The L-649 was replaced in production in 1947 by the L-749, a long-range version of the L-649, which carried additional fuel that increased its range by 1,000 miles (1609 km) while carrying the same payload as the earlier Constellation.

By the end of 1949 the demand for air travel was beginning to rise rapidly, and to meet the requirements of operators for aircraft of greater capacity, Lockheed began development of a lengthened-fuselage version of the L-749. Identified as the L-1049, and duly given the name Super Constellation, this aircraft had the fuselage 'stretched' by the insertion of new fuselage sections both fore and aft of the wing. The total increase in length was 18 ft 4 in (5.59 m), and Super 'Connies' entered service

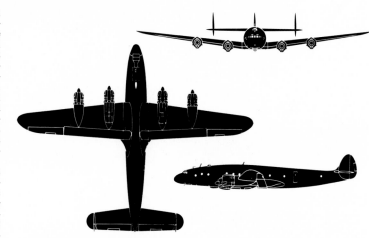

Lockheed L-749 Constellation

during their production life with a variety of seating layouts that could accommodate a maximum of 109 passengers.

While the design detail of the L-749 was being reappraised to include the above-mentioned fuselage 'stretch', the opportunity was taken to update the overall design. This resulted in strength reinforcement of the entire airframe to permit operation at a higher gross weight, the introduction of larger cabin windows, the provision of increased fuel capacity, and the installation of 2,700-(2013-kW) R-3350-956C18CB-1 engines. All of these changes, plus many detail refinements, were incorporated in the original prototype, and this was flown in its L-1049 form on 13 October 1950, the first of the type entering service with Eastern

Air Lines on its New York-Miami route on 17 December 1951.

It did not take long to discover that in this L-1049 configuration the Super Constellation was underpowered, so 3,250-hp (2424-kW) Wright R-3350-972TC18DA-1 Turbo-Cyclone turbocompound engines were installed in the next civil version, the L-1049C. The first of these higher-powered civil Super 'Connies' was flown on 17 February 1953, and service with them was inaugurated by KLM some six months later.

Subsequent civil versions have included the L-1049D, a commercial cargo transport generally similar to the L-1049C, except for the provision of two large cargo doors, fore and aft. With the standard airline interior removed, the total cargo volume of these transports amounted to 5,568 cu ft (157.69 m³). The L-1049E was generally similar to the L-1049C, except for structural strengthening to permit operation at a higher gross weight when suitable, more powerful engines became available. The L-1049G, sometimes known as the 'Super G', had 3,400-hp (2535-kW) R-3350-)72TC18DA3 engines and, optionally, additional fuel contained in wingtip tanks. last of the basic Super Constellations was the L-1049H, which could be converted easily from all-cargo to all-passenger configuration, or *vice versa:* it had the fore and aft cargo doors of the L-1049D, and the same cargo volume in all-cargo configuration; as a passenger carrier it could accommodate a maximum of 109 passengers.

A classic of its time, the Lockheed Constellation series was in 1981 represented in airline service by a mere 10 aircraft, comprising five Constellations and five Super Constellations. Illustrated is the single L-749A operated by Aerolineas Argo.

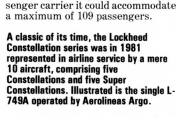

Last of the civil Constellation-derived airliners was the L-1649A Starliner, with a completely new wing of increased span and far greater fuel capacity to provide a range considerably in excess of any of its predecessors. Some 43 of these were built, and evolved originally at the request of TWA for an airliner that could compete against the Douglas DC-7C. In addition to the civil Constellations/Super Constellations/Starliners, there were also a number of specialised variants produced for service with the US armed forces. The details below apply to the L-1049E.

Specification
Type: medium/long-range transport
Powerplant: four 3,250-hp (2424-kW) Wright R-3350-972TC18DA-1 Turbo-Cyclone turbocompound radial piston engines
Performance: cruising speed 331 mph (533 km/h) at 23,000 ft (7010 m); service ceiling 27,200 ft (8290 m); range with maximum fuel and no reserves 4,820 miles (7757 km)
Weights: empty equipped 76,423 lb (34665 kg); maximum take-off 133,000 lb (60328 kg)
Dimensions: span 123 ft 0 in (37.49 m); length 113 ft 4 in (34.54 m) without weather radar; height 24 ft 9 in (7.54 m); wing area 1,650 sq ft (153.29 m²)
Operators include: Aerotours Dominicano, Aerovias Quisqueyanas, Air Cargo Support, and Central American Airways Flying Services

Lockheed Model 1329 Jetstar I/II

History and Notes
In March 1957 Lockheed announced the development of a new light utility transport with turbojet powerplant. Its design, like that of North American's Sabreliner, had been triggered by the USAF's stated interest of being able to buy an 'off-the-shelf' transport aircraft in this category. No doubt, both manufacturers hoped to recover the development and launching costs from military procurement, but in Lockheed's case sales to such sources proved to be limited.

From the outset, Lockheed was determined that its mini-jet should combine high performance with worthwhile range. This required plenty of power and fuel, outlining what appeared to be an unusual configuration for a transport that had standard accommodation for a crew of two and 10 passengers. The Model 1329's cantilever monoplane wing, low set, incorporated a large streamlined fuel tank on each side and these, together with four integral wing tanks, provided a total capacity of nearly 2,700 US gallons (10220 litres). The powerplant, comprising two Bristol Siddeley Orpheus turbojets in the prototypes, gave place in production JetStars to four Pratt & Whitney JT12As, mounted two on each side of the aft fuselage.

Although only 16 of these transports were procured by the USAF (five C-140As and 11 VC-140Bs), the JetStar continued to be a steady seller for corporate and private users. It was superseded in 1973 by an improved JetStar II, which introduced Garrett TFE731 turbofans and detail refinements to the airframe

Lockheed JetStar II of Iraqi Airways

and its equipment. Certification of the JetStar II was attained on 14 December 1976, and retrospective conversions of JetStars to the JetStar II turbofan powerplant became available at the same time.

Production of the JetStar II was suspended in 1980, but with the recession that has resulted from the tremendous increase in fuel costs, it seems unlikely in 1981 that manufacture will again be resumed. The details that follow apply to the Model 1329-25 JetStar II.

Specification
Type: four-turbofan light utility transport
Powerplant: four 3,700-lb (1678-kg) thrust Garrett TFE731-3 turbofans
Performance: maximum cruising speed 547 mph (880 km/h) at 30,000 ft (9145 m); economic cruising speed 504 mph (811 km/h) at 35,000 ft (10670 m); service ceiling 43,000 ft (13105 m); range with maximum payload, 30-min reserves 2,995 miles (4818 km)

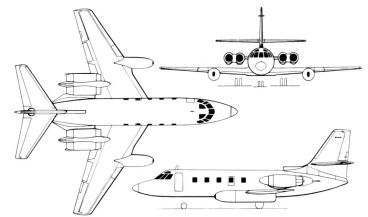

Lockheed Model 1329-25 JetStar II

Weights: operating empty 24,900 lb (11294 kg); maximum take-off 44,500 lb (20185 kg)
Dimensions: span 54 ft 5 in (16.59 m); length 60 ft 5 in (18.41 m); height 20 ft 5 in (6.22 m); wing area 542.5 sq ft (50.40 m²)

The turbojet-powered Lockheed JetStar was supplanted by the turbofan-engined JetStar II in 1975-6.

Lockheed L-100 Commercial Hercules

History and Notes

In 1951, after the US Air Force had decided to procure turboprop-powered transport aircraft for service with the Military Air Transport Service (MATS), now Military Airlift Command (MAC), proposals from Douglas and Lockheed resulted in design and production of the C-133 Cargomaster and C-130 Hercules respectively. Only comparatively small numbers of the Cargomaster were built, but the Hercules seems to have become an integral component of the USAF, and many other air forces, built in large numbers and seemingly endless variety to fulfil a wide range of missions.

The first USAF transport to be evolved to the new 'weapon system' concept, it was identified initially as the SS-400L medium cargo support system by the US Air Force. Lockheed allocated the model number 82 to its design, which was submitted in the late spring of 1951. Lockheed's proposal was rewarded by a contract, placed on 11 July 1951, for two prototypes under the designation YC-130. The first of these was flown just over three years later, on 23 August 1954, but long before that date, in September 1952, Lockheed had been awarded a contract for the first production version under the designation C-130A. A production line for the Hercules was established at Marietta, Georgia, where in due course the C-130A was followed by a developed C-130B with more powerful engines, increased fuel capacity and strengthened landing gear. The next major version was the C-130E, an extended-range version of the C-130B, from which the first Model 382 civil transport was developed.

The conspicuous success of the C-130 Hercules was beginning to be appreciated by Lockheed after the first military version had been in service for only just over two years, when production of the C-130A ended after 231 had been built. Contracts for continued military versions and variants wre building up, and it seemed reasonable to suppose that a civil version of the Hercules would appeal to those operators with large or heavy cargoes to carry over medium to long ranges. Accordingly, Lockheed prepared a civil demonstrator, which was basically a C-130E without military equipment, and this was flown for the first time on 21 April 1964.

Like the military Hercules, it was of high-wing monoplane configuration, the wings unswept but tapered on the trailing-edge of the outer wing panels. Trailing-edge flaps were of the Lockheed-Fowler type, and the ailerons, like the tail unit control surfaces, were hydraulically boosted by duplicated systems to relieve the pilot's controls of aerodynamic forces. The fuselage was a fail-safe semi-monocoque structure, the undersurface of the upswept rear fuselage comprising a hydraulically actuated door which served as the main loading door/ramp. The tail unit was conventional in configuration, but the retractable tricycle type landing gear was a little unusual, for although each unit carried two wheels, those of the main units were in tandem.

The powerplant of the C-130E, from which the Model 382 was derived, consisted of four wing-mounted Allison T56-A-7 turboprop engines, each developing 4,050 ehp (3020 ekW). In the Model 382 these were replaced by Allison 501-D22 engines, the commercial counterpart of the T56-A-7, with the same power output. Accommodation was provided for a flight crew of four or five, and the flight deck and main cargo hold were both pressurised and air-conditioned.

The Model 382 demonstrator (N1130E) was used for the certification programme of this civil version, which was gained on 16 February 1965, and initial deliveries of production examples began very shortly after that date. Sales were not as successful as had been anticipated, the availability of this larger-volume (4,300 cu ft:121.75 m³) freighter being a little ahead of its time on the civil market, where operating economics were far more critical than for military services. The basic Model 382 commercial transport, which is no longer available, was followed by the Model 382B, which was the first to have the designation L-100 Hercules. Generally similar to its predecessor, except for variations in the cargo loading system, this version was certificated on 5 October 1965 and duly entered service. This model is also no longer available.

During 1967 Lockheed decided that if it was to enjoy any real success with the Hercules in the civil market it would need to show better economy in operation. Accordingly, the original Model 382 demonstrator was given a fuselage extension of 8 ft 4 in (2.54 m), by the insertion of two fuselage plugs, this increasing the internal capacity to 5,307 cu ft (150.26 m³) representing almost 24 per cent more volume. Simultaneously the powerplant was changed, the four Allison 501-D22s being replaced by four 501-D22As, each developing 4,508 ehp (3362 ekW). In this form designated the Model 382E, or L-100-20, the civil Hercules was flown for the first time on 19 April 1968, being certificated almost six months later, on 4 October. Two Model 382Bs were subsequently given this fuselage 'stretch,' but retained the 501-D22 engines under the designation Model 382F, and retained the L-100-20 identification. In addition to these two 382Fs, several 382Bs were subsequently converted to Model 382E L-100-20 configuration, their improved operating economics making the cost of the conversion worthwhile.

In October 1969 a new increased-capacity version was proposed, this having the designation of Model 382G or L-100-30. Once again the fuselage was lengthened, this time by 6 ft 8 in (2.03 m), to provide an internal volume of 6,057 cu ft (171.50 m³). At the same time, the rear cargo hold windows were removed, and the JATO (jet-assisted take-off) provision carried over from the military versions was eliminated. The first L-100-30 was flown initially on 14 August 1970, and following certification on 7 October of that year the first of the type was delivered to Saturn Airways (now Trans International Airlines). This company required L-100-30s specifically to fly powerplant sets for the Lockheed TriStar, comprising three Rolls-Royce RB.221 turbofans, from the UK to Lockheed's production line in California. Since then other operators have shown interest in the L-100-30 which, with a cargo hold that has a length of 56 ft 0 in (17.07 m), is able to accept a wide range of commercial loads.

By comparison with the market for military versions of the Hercules which, acquired by armed forces and governments, had notched up more than 1,500 sales in 1980, the demand for civil versions, which totalled only 78 at the same time, must be regarded as very small. Civil Hercules are, however, manufactured on the same production line and, presumably, considered a profitable proposition by the company which was working on a new version in early 1980.

To be known as the L-100-50 Hercules Regional Airfreighter, this is a still higher capacity version for operation over short/medium ranges. By comparison with the L-100-30 it will have a fuselage lengthened by an additional 21 ft 8 in (6.60 m), to provide an internal capacity of 7,948 cu ft (225.04 m³), and this represents an increase in internal volume of 85 per cent by comparison with the original L-100 Hercules. With a maximum take-off weight estimated at 175,000 lb (79379 kg), this corresponds to the maximum overload take-off weight of the current military C-130H. The details below apply to the L-100-20 Hercules.

Specification

Type: medium/long-range transport

Powerplant: four 4,508-ehp (3362-ekW) Allison 501-D22A turboprops

Performance: maximum cruising speed 361 mph (581 km/h) at 20,000 ft (6100 m); range with maximum payload and 45-min reserves 2,417 miles (7871 km)

Weights: operating empty 72,607 lb (32934 kg); maximum take-off 155,000 lb (70307 kg)

Dimensions: span 132 ft 7 in (40.41 m); length 106 ft 1 in (32.33 m); height 38 ft 3 in (11.66 m) wing area 1,745.0 sq ft (162.11 m²)

Operators include: Alaska International Air, Northwest Territorial Airways, Pacific Western Airlines, Safair Freighters, Southern Air Transport, TAAG-Angola Airlines, Trans International Airlilnes, and Uganda Airlines

The Lockheed L-100 civilian version of the Hercules has been produced in several models for transport and resources support, but has not sold well.

Lockheed L-100 Commercial Hercules of Air Botswana.

Lockheed L-188 Electra

History and Notes

The success which Lockheed had gained in the design, development and early production of the turbo-prop-powered C-130 Hercules for the USAF undoubtedly influenced the company's choice of this basic powerplant for turbine-engine airliners to enter service in the late 1950s. Two proposals for aircraft with such engines were drawn up but these, identified as CL-303 and CL-310, failed to arouse any enthusiasm. However, in early 1955 American Airlines issued to manufacturers its specification for a short/medium-range airliner for use on US domestic routes, and Lockheed succeeded in June 1955 in gaining from American Airlines an initial order for 35 of these aircraft. Designated L-188 Electra this was, in fact, a development of Lockheed's CL-310 proposal, and the receipt of a second order, for 40 of these aircraft for service with Eastern Air Lines, was considered sufficient indication of potential airline interest to warrant the start of production.

Although construction had started in 1955, it was not until 6 December 1957 that the first prototype (N1881) was flown. By that time, however, Lockheed had accumulated orders for 144 production aircraft, and it must have seemed that they were set for a long production run. This, unfortunately, was not the case: like other similar ventures of the period, in the transition between piston- and turbine-engine aircraft, they were to take second place to faster turbojet-powered airliners. This was not really surprising for, though less economical to operate, passenger preference was for the fastest means of travel between A and B, and the higher utilisation of the pure jet-liners soon more than offset the higher operating cost of turbojet engines.

The Electra's configuration was that of a low-wing monoplane, with a conventionally constructed fuselage of circular cross-section, and a tricycle type retractable landing gear with twin wheels on each unit. The powerplant comprised four wing-mounted Allison 501-D13 turboprops.

Lockheed L-188 Electra of Great Northern.

The initial version, designated L-188A, entered service with Eastern Air Lines on 12 January 1959, and with American Airlines on 23 January. It was to be followed by the L-188C, with increased fuel capacity to offer greater range, and this entered service later in 1959. KLM was the only European user of the Electra, its first services flown in December 1959.

Electras had been in service for little over nine months when one was lost in unexplained circumstances. When a second fatal accident occurred some six months later, speed restrictions were imposed until investigations were able to establish the cause. Strengthening of the engine nacelles, mountings, and adjacent wing structure were carried out retrospectively to in-service aircraft, and constructional modifications were introduced on the production line. The problem was resolved, but it was not until January 1961 that it was possible to dispense with the speed regulations. During this period, however, sales had stagnated and were never to recover.

The majority of Electras were retired from first-line service by 1975, but their economic operation and reliability meant that most were retained on secondary duties of one sort or another. From 1967 Lockheed Aircraft Services modified 41 aircraft for use in convertible passenger/cargo, or all-cargo roles, this involving the installation of completely new flooring, and a large cargo door forward of the wing on the port side. The details below apply to the L-188A.

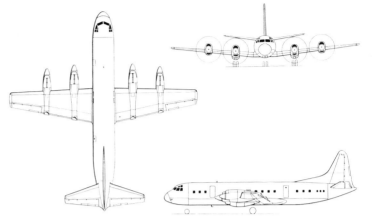

Lockheed Electra

Specification

Type: short/medium-range transport
Powerplant: four 3,750-ehp (2796-ekW) Allison 501-D13A turboprops
Performance: maximum cruising speed 405 mph (652 km/h) at 22,000 ft (6705 m); economic cruising speed 374 mph (602 km/h) at optimum altitude; service ceiling 27,000 ft (8230 m); range with maximum payload 2,200 miles (3541 km); range with maximum fuel 2,500 miles (4023 km)
Weights: empty operating 61,500 lb (27896 kg); maximum take-off 116,000 lb (52617 kg)
Dimensions: span 99 ft 0 in (30.18 m); length 104 ft 6 in (31.85 m); height 32 ft 10 in (10.01 m); wing area 1,300 sq ft (120.77 m²)
Operators include: Aerocondor,

Air California, Ansett Airlines of Australia, Copa, Evergreen International Airlines, Fred Olsens Flyveselskap, Hawaiian Air, Iscargo HF, Lacsa, Lineas Aereas Paraguayas, Nordair, Northwest Territorial Airways, Reeve Aleutian Airways, SAHSA, Taca International Airlines, TAME, Transamerica Airlines, TAN Airlines, and Zantop International Airlines

The L-188 Electra was a commercial failure for Lockheed, with structural problems compounded by customer reluctance to buy turboprop-powered aircraft at the time turbojet-powered airliners were just coming into their own. The type has however soldiered on in large numbers with smaller operators; illustrated is an Electra of Mandala Airlines.

Lockheed L-1011 TriStar

History and Notes

Lockheed's wide-body airliner, which was to become identified as the L-1011 TriStar, originated as did the McDonnell Douglas DC-10 to meet the requirements of American Airlines for a large-capacity short/medium-range transport. Lockheed's design team was to reach a similar decision to that of the Douglas company, that three engines were necessary to provide the essential load-carrying capability and performance, resulting in a similar configuration of a pylon-mounted engine on each wing and a third combined with the tail unit.

In more ways than one the TriStar was an important aircraft for the Lockheed company, which had commanded a significant proportion of the US market for civil airliners in the years before and immediately following World War II. Since production of the Electra ended in 1962, the company's long relationship with civil operators had been dormant except for continued support of earlier products. It was, therefore, considered essential that this new airliner must satisfy the requirements of operators in terms of economy of operation and ease of maintenance. Equally important, it would have to appeal to air travellers, providing speed and comfort. Lockheed devoted its considerable expertise to achieving these aims. It was necessary that Lockheed should look long and hard at the options, for the fact that the company was not at that moment busily building civil airliners for operators around the world was due, basically, to the selection of the wrong powerplant for the Electra. Lockheed had consequently suffered a considerable financial loss, for sales, and consequently production, had come to an end long before the financial break-even point had been reached.

At the stage of development which turbine engines had reached in the early/mid-1950s, there was then little doubt that the combination of turbine engine and propeller in the turboprop powerplant represented the most efficient source of propulsion for civil transports. The Electra was but one of many projects that relied upon the turboprop, gaining in efficiency of operation, but losing ticket sales to the less-efficient turbojet which offered much faster travel.

Lockheed L-1011-1/200 TriStar of Saudia (Saudi Arabian Airlines).

And it had been proved, time and time again, that the air traveller almost invariably opted for the fastest means of travel over any particular route. Lockheed had failed to recognise this factor in their choice of turboprops for the Electra and had either overlooked, or deliberately decided to ignore at that time the fact that, in their continued use and development, turbojets would become more fuel efficient. This was especially true when the first by-pass turbojets, or turbofans, became practical hardware.

Market research, prior to the production of a proposal to meet the requirements of American Airlines, led to a number of design objectives. Foremost was the fact that the new airliner must be able to operate from and to existing airports without requiring any special facilities. High safety standards, easy maintenance, and automatic landing capability were considered to be essentials. So were other factors that related very much to the final decision on powerplant: higher cruising speeds, double the payload of current airliners over short-range stages, and lower noise levels. And no less important was passenger comfort and the overall ambience; a subtle combination of design, colour, facilities and spaciousness that would have an immediate appeal to the fare-paying customer.

In this particular respect, it is interesting to record some of the thoughts that finalised just one interior detail: the width of the cabin. No fewer than eight full-scale cabin mock-ups were built, to allow evaluation of the factors that would make the interior more, or less, appealing to the passengers. Cabin width is, of course, critical in more than one way: it not only determines the number of aisles and the number of

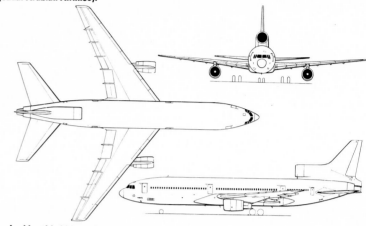

Lockheed L-1011-1 TriStar

seats in each row, but very considerably affects the gross weight of the aircraft. In the case of the TriStar the difference of 2 ft 8 in (0.81 m), between what was considered the minimum and the most desirable fuselage width would have added rather more than 7,000 lb (3175 kg) to the empty weight. The minimum width would have been 18 ft 8 in (5.69 m), allowing for a maximum of eight-abreast seating with two aisles. Something more flexible was desired, leading to the final selection of a 19 ft 7 in (5.97 m) fuselage width, giving a maximum cabin width of 18 ft 11 in (5.77 m) which carries eight seat tracks, allowing 6-, 8-, 9- or 10-abreast seating with two full-length aisles.

No less critical was the choice of powerplant, but in this respect Lockheed left it very much to the big three — General Electric, Pratt & Whitney, and Rolls-Royce — to make proposals based on new-technology turbofan engines currently under

development. The final decision favoured the Rolls-Royce RB.211, a new turbofan derived from the larger RB.207, which was lighter in weight and offered a better specific fuel consumption than its competitors. It was also cheaper, because of the strong dollar/weak pound situation that applied at the time. In an attempt to secure the contract for its CF6, General Electric put in a special bid, making Rolls-Royce cut its price per engine below that which was to prove a realistic production cost. This secured the contract for the British engine manufacturer, but was to have later, almost devastating, complications for both companies.

Eventually, the way was clear for construction to begin (there was to be no prototype), after a joint announcement by Lockheed and Rolls-Royce, on 29 March 1968, stating that initial orders totalled 144 aircraft and that the TriStar was to enter production. A first flight was planned for late 1970, with initial deliveries about 12 months later. The first stage of this plan was achieved when, on 17 November 1970, the TriStar made its maiden flight. Unfortunately, the enthusiasm generated by this event was to evaporate quickly as both Lockheed and Rolls-Royce became involved in major financial problems. In the UK, development costs of the RB.211 had worked out at more than double the figure that had been estimated originally; even worse, the company could not meet the delivery programme, and it was clear that production engines would be sold at a loss. This resulted in bankruptcy for the engine builder, and the formation of a new state-owned Rolls-Royce (1971) Ltd.

Lockheed, also, was involved in problems that originated primarily from large financial losses on its C-5-A Galaxy military transport programme. The news of the Rolls-

Cathay Pacific Airways, based in Hong Kong and operating services throughout the Far East and to Australia and the UK, has seven Lockheed TriStars, comprising seven L-1011-1s and two L-1011-100s. A Redifon simulator is used for training.

Lockheed L-1011 TriStar

Royce difficulties, and the inevitable delay in the production of engines, meant that the company had to lay off its work force until a real solution had been realised. British and US government aid was necessary before it became possible to continue with production, and new contracts had to be negotiated with airline customers. Thus, it was not until 14 April 1972 that certification was gained, with the first revenue service flown by Eastern Air Lines on 26 April 1972.

In its original L-1011-1 form, as intended for short/medium-range routes, the TriStar's basic configuration is that of a low-wing monoplane, with the wings swept back 35°, and incorporating on each wing seven leading-edge slats, outboard (low-speed) and inboard (high-speed) ailerons, and six upper-surface spoilers forward of the trailing-edge flaps, the latter being of double-slotted Fowler type. All control surfaces are powered by hydraulic actuators that have four independent and separate sources of hydraulic power. The fail-safe fuselage structure is of circular cross-section, and the unit has all swept surfaces, with the controls powered by the four same independent hydraulic systems. The landing gear is of the retractable tricycle type, with twin wheels on the nose unit, and two twin-wheel units, mounted in tandem, on each main gear. The three Rolls-Royce turbofans are mounted one to each wing, carried in pods on underwing pylons, with the third in the fuselage tailcone, its air intake located on the fuselage upper surface, forward of and faired into the fin. The engines powering this initial L-1011-1 production version consisted of 42,000-lb (19051-kg) thrust RB.211-22B turbofans.

Accommodation is provided for a flight crew of two to four, to meet the requirements of different airlines, and 256 passengers are carried in the standard mixed-class configuration. A maximum of 400 can be seated in a high-density economy-class configuration. There are three

doors and an emergency exit on each side of the cabin, replaced by an arrangement with four doors on each side if a 10-abreast seating arrangement is installed.

As might be expected the TriStar, as with most new complex aircraft, suffered some early teething troubles, principally with the powerplant, which required engines to be taken out of service for inspection at very frequent intervals. But apart from these comparatively short-term problems, Lockheed's new wide-body transport was soon demonstrating efficient operation, and impressing operators, passengers, and the long-suffering public with the comparative low noise-levels of its Rolls-Royce engines.

The L-1011-1 was followed into service by the longer-range L-1011-100, which carried additional fuel, and was certificated for operation at a maximum take-off weight some 8 per cent greater than that of the -1. To provide better performance from 'hot-and-high' airfields, the L-1011-200 was developed with 48,000-lb (21772-kg) thrust RB.211-524 engines, but in other respects is similar to

the L-1011-1. It is available also with the increased fuel tankage of the -100, the improved performance of the -524 engine offering slightly longer range, and is certificated for operation at a higher gross weight. An L-1011-200 with -524 engines was flown for the first time on 10 April 1976, certification being gained on 26 April 1977. The first production examples were delivered to Saudi Arabian Airlines, entering service in the summer of that year.

By late 1980, about 170 of the above versions had been delivered, with orders and options for about 75 aircraft outstanding. The details below apply to the L-1011-200 TriStar.

Specification

Type: wide-body transport
Powerplant: three 48,000-lb (32883-kg) thrust Rolls-Royce RB211-524 turbofans
Performance: maximum cruising speed 610 mph (982 km/h) at 30,000 ft (9145 m); economic cruising speed 558 mph (898 km/h) at 35,000 ft (10670 m); service ceiling 42,000 ft (12800 m); range

with maximum passengers 4,238 miles (6820 km); range with maximum fuel 5,619 miles (9043 km)
Weights: operating empty 245,800 lb (111493 kg); maximum take-off 477,000 (216364 kg)
Dimensions: span 155 ft 4 in (47.35 m); length 177 ft 8½ in (54.17 m); height 55 ft 4 in (16.87 m); wing area 3,456.0 sq ft (321.06 m²)
Operators include: Aero Peru, Air Canada, All Nippon Airways, British Airways, Cathay Pacific Airways, Delta Air Lines, Eastern Air Lines, Gulf Air, Lufttransport Unternehmen, Saudia, Trans Caribair, and Trans World Airlines

Lockheed L-1011-500 TriStar

History and notes

The first Lockheed TriStar to be built (N1011), although not truly a prototype has virtually served as such, being widely used by Lockheed to flight-test new ideas and features. It had been the original intention to refurbish it to airline standard for delivery to an operator requiring an L-1011-1, but the company has found the need to keep this aircraft in use to date, and as configured in mid-1980 was identified as the Advanced TriStar. It has as a powerplant three 50,000-lb (22680-kg) thrust RB.211-524 turbofans and introduces extended wingtips which reduce drag. To overcome the necessity of strengthening the wing structure, new automatically controlled ailerons have been incorporated at the same time, these being deflected to offset additional loads on the increased-span structure which can occur during certain manoeuvres and operating conditions. Early testing of this feature has indicated fuel savings in the order of 3 per cent. Other features of the Advanced TriStar include automatic thrust control, which provides a reserve of power to offset an engine failure during take-off; automatic brakes that ensure optimum braking efficiency under all runway conditions; and this aircraft serves also as a test bed for new avionics and flight control systems.

Airlines had shown interest in a long-range version of the TriStar, leading to the development of such an aircraft under the designation L-1011-500. This has 50,000-lb (22680-kg) thrust RB.211-524B or -524B4 engines and the fuselage length reduced by 13 ft 6 in (4.11 m), a combination which provides a payload decrease of one-third by comparison with the -200, allowing for increased fuel capacity. Other changes include location of the galley on the main deck, instead of the lower deck/food elevator arrangement of the medium-range versions, and introduction of an improved fairing for the junction of the fuselage and rear engine air intake. And, of course, the shorter fuselage makes changes in passenger accommodation: a typical mixed-class configuration allows for 24 first-class and 222 economy-class passengers in six- and nine-abreast seating respectively, or can provide for a maximum of 330 in a high-density layout.

The wingtip extensions/automatic aileron system, and automatic brakes, first tested on the Advanced TriStar, were also flown on the L-1011-500 in late 1979, and were being introduced on some production aircraft in 1980-1.

Specification

Type: long-range transport
Powerplant: three 50,000-lb (22680-kg) thrust Rolls-Royce RB.211-52B or -524B4 turbofans
Performance: maximum cruising speed 605 mph (974 km/h) at 30,000 ft (9145 m); economic cruising speed 558 mph (898 km/h) at 35,000 ft (10670 m); service ceiling 42,000 ft (12800 m); range with maximum passengers 5,998 miles (9653 km); range with maximum fuel 7,082 miles (11397 km)
Weights: operating empty 240,963 lb (109299 kg); maximum take-off 496,000 lb (224982 kg)
Dimensions: span 155 ft 4 in (47.35 (47.35 m) without extended wingtips, 164 ft 4 in (50.09 m) with extended wingtips; length 164 ft 2½ in (50.05 m); height 55 ft 4 in (16.87 m); wing area 3,456 sq ft

Lockheed TriStar 500 cutaway drawing key

1 Radome
2 VOR localiser aerial
3 Radar scanner dish
4 ILS glideslope aerial
5 Front pressure bulkhead
6 Curved windscreen panels
7 Windscreen wipers
8 Instrument panel shroud
9 Rudder pedals
10 Cockpit floor level
11 Ventral access door
12 Forward underfloor radio and electronics bay
13 Pitot tubes
14 Observer's seat
15 Captain's seat
16 First officer's seat
17 Overhead panel
18 Flight engineer's station
19 Cockpit roof escape hatch
20 Air conditioning ducting
21 Forward galley units
22 Starboard service door
23 Forward toilet compartments
24 Curtained cabin divider
25 Wardrobe
26 Forward passenger door
27 Cabin attendant's folding seat
28 Nose undercarriage wheel bay
29 Ram air intake
30 Heat exchanger
31 Nose undercarriage leg strut
32 Twin nosewheels
33 Steering jacks
34 Nosewheel doors
35 Air conditioning plant, port and starboard
36 Cabin window panel
37 Six-abreast first-class seating, 24 seats
38 Forward underfloor freight hold
39 Forward freight door
40 VHF aerial
41 Curtained cabin divider
42 Overhead stowage bins
43 Nine-abreast tourist class seating, 222 seats
44 Baggage/freight containers, twelve LD3 containers forward
45 Fuselage frame and stringer construction
46 Wing root fillet
47 Taxying lamp
48 Bleed air system ducting
49 Escape chute and life raft stowage
50 Mid-section entry door
51 Centre section galley units
52 Fuselage centre section construction
53 Wing centre section carry-through structure
54 Dry bay
55 Centre section fuel tanks, capacity 8,060 US gal (30 510 l)
56 Floor beam construction
57 Fuselage/front spar attachment main frame
58 Anti-collision lights
59 Starboard inboard fuel tank bay, capacity 7,985 US gal (30 226 l)
60 Thrust reverser cascade, open
61 Starboard engine nacelle
62 Nacelle pylon
63 Fixed portion of leading edge
64 Fuel surge box and boost pump reservoir
65 Fuel system piping
66 Outboard fuel tank bay, capacity 3,806 US gal (14 407 l)
67 Pressure refuelling connections
68 Screw jack drive shaft
69 Slat screw jacks
70 Leading-edge slat segments, open
71 Extended wing tip fairing
72 Starboard navigation light
73 Wing tip strobe light
74 Static dischargers
75 Starboard "active control" aileron
76 Aileron hydraulic jacks
77 Fuel jettison pipe
78 Outboard spoilers

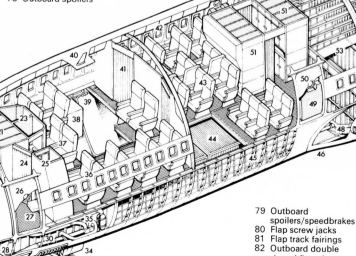

79 Outboard spoilers/speedbrakes
80 Flap screw jacks
81 Flap track fairings
82 Outboard double slotted flap, down
83 Inboard aileron
84 Inboard double slotted flap, down
85 Flap vane

Lockheed L-1011-500 TriStar

(321.06 m²) with standard wings
Operators include: British
Airways, Delta Air Lines and Pan
American World Airways; the type
has been ordered also by Aero
Peru, Air Canada, Alia, BWIA
International, LTU and TAP

Lockheed L-1011-500 TriStar of Pan American World Airways, USA.

Increased weights and range
performance are made possible on the
Lockheed L-1011 TriStar 500 by
additional tankage, active controls and
extended wingtips. Delta Air Lines has
three such aircraft among its 38 TriStars
(on order or delivered).

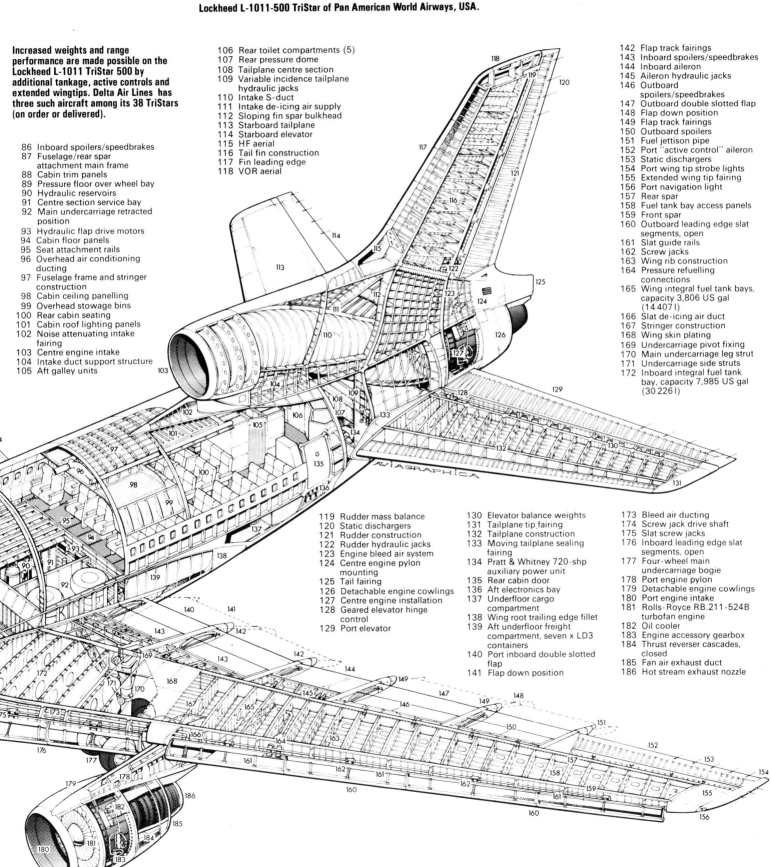

86 Inboard spoilers/speedbrakes
87 Fuselage/rear spar
   attachment main frame
88 Cabin trim panels
89 Pressure floor over wheel bay
90 Hydraulic reservoirs
91 Centre section service bay
92 Main undercarriage retracted
   position
93 Hydraulic flap drive motors
94 Cabin floor panels
95 Seat attachment rails
96 Overhead air conditioning
   ducting
97 Fuselage frame and stringer
   construction
98 Cabin ceiling panelling
99 Overhead stowage bins
100 Rear cabin seating
101 Cabin roof lighting panels
102 Noise attenuating intake
   fairing
103 Centre engine intake
104 Intake duct support structure
105 Aft galley units

106 Rear toilet compartments (5)
107 Rear pressure dome
108 Tailplane centre section
109 Variable incidence tailplane
   hydraulic jacks
110 Intake S-duct
111 Intake de-icing air supply
112 Sloping fin spar bulkhead
113 Starboard tailplane
114 Starboard elevator
115 HF aerial
116 Tail fin construction
117 Fin leading edge
118 VOR aerial

119 Rudder mass balance
120 Static dischargers
121 Rudder construction
122 Rudder hydraulic jacks
123 Engine bleed air system
124 Centre engine pylon
   mounting
125 Tail fairing
126 Detachable engine cowlings
127 Centre engine installation
128 Geared elevator hinge
   control
129 Port elevator

130 Elevator balance weights
131 Tailplane tip fairing
132 Tailplane construction
133 Moving tailplane sealing
   fairing
134 Pratt & Whitney 720-shp
   auxiliary power unit
135 Rear cabin door
136 Aft electronics bay
137 Underfloor cargo
   compartment
138 Wing root trailing edge fillet
139 Aft underfloor freight
   compartment, seven x LD3
   containers
140 Port inboard double slotted
   flap
141 Flap down position

142 Flap track fairings
143 Inboard spoilers/speedbrakes
144 Inboard aileron
145 Aileron hydraulic jacks
146 Outboard
   spoilers/speedbrakes
147 Outboard double slotted flap
148 Flap down position
149 Flap track fairings
150 Outboard spoilers
151 Fuel jettison pipe
152 Port "active control" aileron
153 Static dischargers
154 Port wing tip strobe lights
155 Extended wing tip fairing
156 Port navigation light
157 Rear spar
158 Fuel tank bay access panels
159 Front spar
160 Outboard leading edge slat
   segments, open
161 Slat guide rails
162 Screw jacks
163 Wing rib construction
164 Pressure refuelling
   connections
165 Wing integral fuel tank bays,
   capacity 3,806 US gal
   (14 407 l)
166 Slat de-icing air duct
167 Stringer construction
168 Wing skin plating
169 Undercarriage pivot fixing
170 Main undercarriage leg strut
171 Undercarriage side struts
172 Inboard integral fuel tank
   bay, capacity 7,985 US gal
   (30 226 l)

173 Bleed air ducting
174 Screw jack drive shaft
175 Slat screw jacks
176 Inboard leading edge slat
   segments, open
177 Four-wheel main
   undercarriage bogie
178 Port engine pylon
179 Detachable engine cowlings
180 Port engine intake
181 Rolls-Royce RB.211-524B
   turbofan engine
182 Oil cooler
183 Engine accessory gearbox
184 Thrust reverser cascades,
   closed
185 Fan air exhaust duct
186 Hot stream exhaust nozzle

Lockheed L-1011-500 TriStar

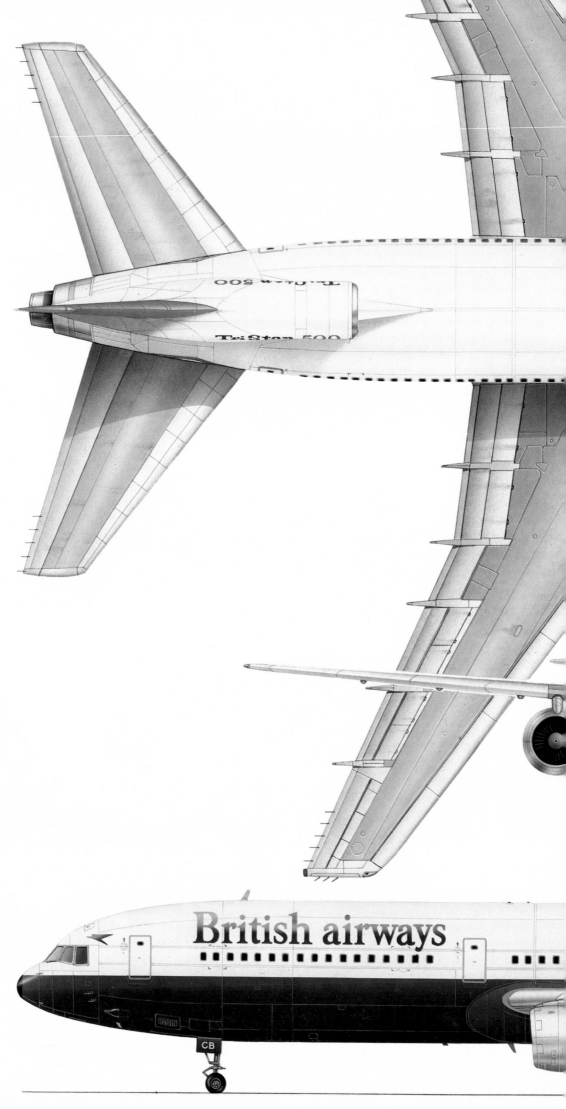

Among its fleet of 21 Lockheed TriStars, British Airways numbers six of the advanced long-range version, the L-1011-500. This has a shorter fuselage and reduced payload, but the greater fuel load provided enhanced range. Other improvements include more advanced versions of the Rolls-Royce RB.211 turbofan engine, and a number of aerodynamic modifications. These last are centred on extended wingtips, which reduce drag by a significant factor, and active controls to reduce airframe stresses resulting from loads imposed by gusts acting on the longer-span wings. First tested on the company-owned Advanced Tristar, the active controls and extended wings can be retro-fitted on earlier TriStar 500s, and are being incorporated on current production aircraft.

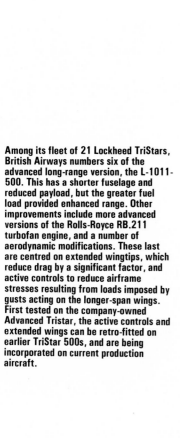

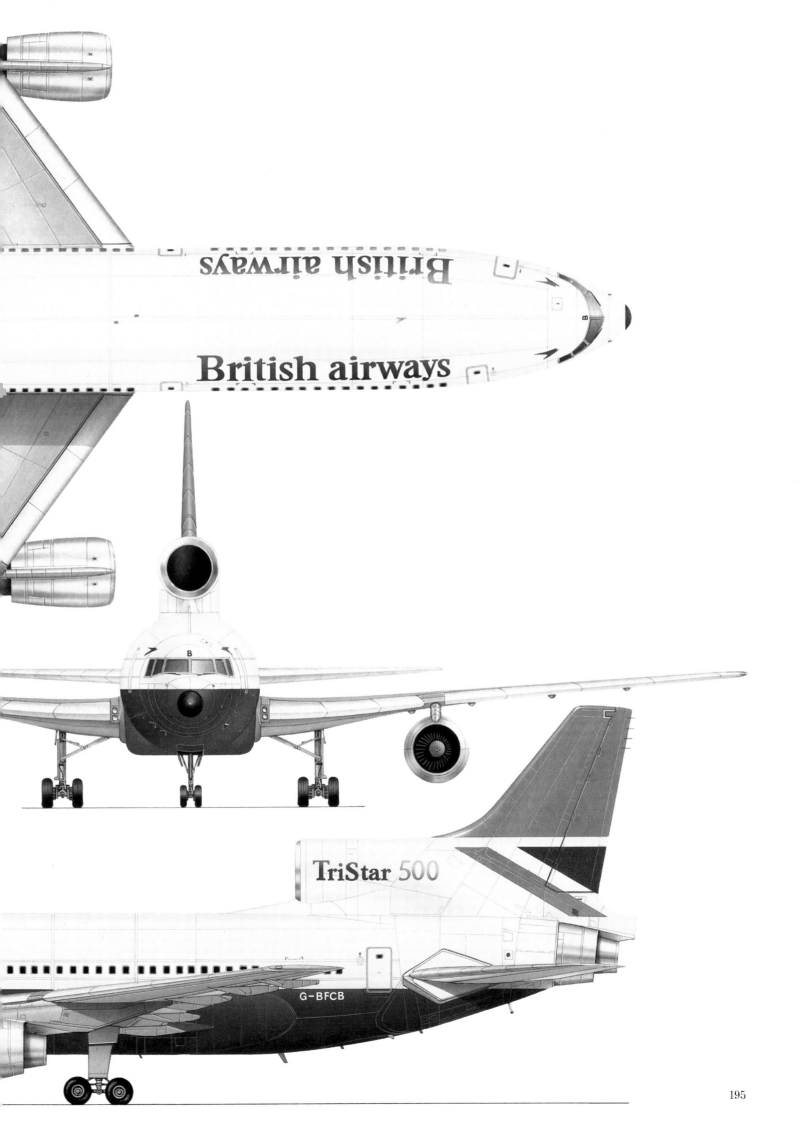

British airways

British airways

TriStar 500

G-BFCB

Martin 4-0-4

History and Notes
The Glenn L. Martin Company, which long ago lost its original identity as a manufacturer of civil transport aircraft when it became a part of the Martin Marietta Corporation, retains a significant position in the aviation history of the USA. Glenn Martin, one of America's aviation pioneers, had been associated with Orville Wright in the Wright-Martin Aircraft Corporation, but left to form his own company in 1917.

This company was, in the years immediately following World War II, to design and produce the Martin 2-0-2, a 36/40-seat transport which had the distinction of being the first twin-engine airliner of US post-war design to gain certification. The prototype, which flew first on 22 November 1946, was of low-wing monoplane configuration, with an unpressurised circular-section fuselage, conventional tail unit, retractable tricycle type landing gear, and powerplant consisting of two wing-mounted Pratt & Whitney R-2800 Double Wasp engines.

The first of these aircraft entered service in October 1947, but the loss of one in 1948 led to investigations that located some weakness in the wing structure, and no additional new aircraft were built as such. Essential modifications were carried out to in-service aircraft, but before this the company had proposed new passenger and cargo versions under the designations Martin 3-0-3 and 3-0-4 respectively. Although a prototype of the former was flown on 20 June 1947, the need to redesign the wing structure led to these two models being dropped in favour of an improved Martin 4-0-4. This was generally similar in configuration to the 2-0-2, but had a new pressurised fuselage structure that had been lengthened by 3 ft 3 in (0.99 m), and introduced a number of detail improvements. Standard accommodation was for a crew of three or four, plus 40 passengers, and R-2800 Double Wasp engines were retained.

Some 103 of these 4-0-4s had been delivered when production ended in early 1953, supplied to Eastern Air Lines (60). Trans World Airlines (41) and the US Coast Guard (2), these last aircraft being designated RM-1. The 4-0-4s changed hands subsequently many times, after their initial users had replaced them with new-generation aircraft, and only

Some 30 Martin 4-0-4s remain in service with smaller operators such as CAMBA, a Bolivian company with two such aircraft for local services.

Martin 4-0-4 of Marco Island Airways, USA.

about a dozen remained in service in 1980.

Specification
Type: short/medium-range transport
Powerplant: two 2,400-hp (1790-kW) Pratt & Whitney R-2800-CB16 Double Wasp radial piston engines
Performance: maximum speed 312 mph (502 km/h) at 14,500 ft (4420 m); cruising speed 280 mph (451 km/h) at 18,000 ft (5485 m); service ceiling 29,000 ft (8840 m); range with maximum payload 1,080 miles (1738 km); range with maximum fuel 2,600 miles (4184 km)
Weights: empty equipped 29,126 lb (13211 kg); maximum take-off 44,900 lb (20366 kg)
Dimensions: span 93 ft 3 in (28.42 m); length 74 ft 7 in (22.73 m); height 28 ft 5 in (8.66 m); wing area 864 sq ft (80.27 m²)

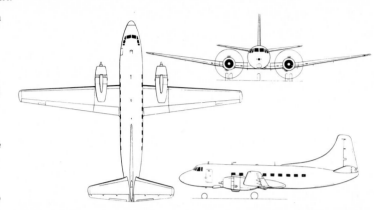

Martin 4-0-4

Operators include: Aerovias Quisqueyanas, Atlantic Southeast Airlines, Florida Airlines, Marco Island Airways, Petroleum Air Transport, and Provincetown-Boston Airlines

Maule M-4 Jetasen and Rocket Series

History and Notes
The Maule Aircraft Corporation was established by B. D. Maule to develop and market a four-seat home-build aircraft known originally as the Bee Dee M-4. Design was initiated in 1956 and the prototype M-4 was flown on 8 September 1960. Type certification was obtained in August 1961 and Maule decided to manufacture the aircraft himself. Notable features of the M-4 were its short-field performance, and a link between ailerons and a rudder tab so that full control could be maintained using only the control wheel, the rudder pedals not being needed in flight.

The initial production version was the M-4 Jetasen, identified by its 145-hp (108-kW) Continental O-300-A engine and McCauley fixed-pitch propeller. A 180-hp (134-kW) Franklin

6A-335-B1A, driving a McCauley constant-speed propeller, was fitted to the de luxe M-4 Astro-Rocket, which also introduced cambered wingtips, which became standard on all models but the Jetasen. On 24 September 1964 Maule received FAA Type Approval for the M-4 Rocket, powered by a 210-hp (157-kW) Continental IO-360-A driving a McCauley constant-speed propeller, and this model was available as a floatplane from 1967. The de luxe version was the M-4 Strata-Rocket, which was

Conceived as a high-performance four-seater for homebuilders, the Maule M-4 appeared in five production forms, and was also available as the Jetasen and Rocket with 145- and 210-hp (108- and 157-kW) engines respectively. The type is also the basis of the M-5.

fitted with a 220-hp (164-kW) Franklin 6A-350-C1 engine. On 31 October 1973 FAA approval was given for the optional installation of a 11½-US gallon (43.5-litre) fuel tank in each outer wing panel. Production of all M-4 models ceased in 1975. The specification applies to the M-4 Rocket.

Specification
Type: four-seat cabin monoplane
Powerplant: one 210-hp (157-kW) Continental IO-360-A flat-six piston engine
Performance: maximum speed 170 mph (274 km/h) at sea level; economic cruising speed 150 mph (241 km/h); service ceiling 18,000 ft (5485 m); range with 45-min reserves 680 miles (1094 km)

Weights: empty 1,190 lb (540 kg); maximum take-off 2,300 lb (1043 kg)
Dimensions: span 29 ft 8 in (9.04 m); length 22 ft 0 in (6.71 m); height 6 ft 2 in (1.88 m); wing area 152.5 sq ft (14.17 m²)

Maule M-5 Lunar Rocket Series

History and Notes
In order to improve further the rate of climb and short-field performance of the M-4 Strata-Rocket, it was modified into the M-5 Lunar Rocket by the provision of enlarged tail surfaces and a 30 per cent increase in flap area. The first of two prototypes was flown on 1 November 1971, with the designation M-5-220C, and powered by a 220-hp (164-kW) Franklin 6A-350-C1 engine. The second, flown on 16 October 1973, was the M-5-210C with a 210-hp (157-kW) Continental IO-360-D engine. FAA Type Approval was received on 28 December 1973.

The later unavailability of the Franklin engine led to the withdrawal of the M-5-220 and on 6 April 1976 Maule completed the certification programme of the M-5-235C with a 235-hp (175-kW) Avco Lycoming O-540-J1A5D, driving a larger-diameter Hartzell constant-speed propeller in place of the McCauley propeller of the earlier models. The prototype of the M-5-180C, powered by a 180-hp (134-kW) Avco Lycoming O-360-C1F engine, flew on 18 May 1978, followed on 7 August 1978 by the first M-5-

210TC, a cargo version with a 210-hp (157-kW) turbocharged Avco Lycoming TO-360-C1A6D engine. All versions have a cargo-carrying capability, as indicated by the C in the designations, and the centre and rear of the three starboard-side cabin doors can be opened together to provide an opening 4 ft 1 in (1.24 m) in width. Also produced for civil patrol duties, with any of the engines approved for other models, the Maule Patroller can have Plexiglas doors and a port-side rear observation window, public address system and siren, and an underfuselage manually operated searchlight.

All M-5 models can accept auxiliary fuel tanks in the outboard wing bays, to provide an additional usable capacity of 23 US gallons (87 litres). FAA approval for this installation was given on 31 October 1973. The details that follow apply to the M-5-235C Lunar Rocket.

Specification
Type: four-seat cabin monoplane
Powerplant: one 235-hp (175-kW) Avco Lycoming O-540-J1A5D flat-six piston engine

Performance: maximum speed 172 mph (277 km/h); economic cruising speed 160 mph (257 km/h); service ceiling 20,000 ft (6100 m); range with standard fuel 550 miles (885 km)
Weights: empty 1,400 lb (635 kg); maximum take-off 2,300 lb (1043 kg)

The Maule M-5 Lunar Rocket series offers good STOL performance with the wheel, ski or float landing gear.

Dimensions: span 30 ft 10 in (9.40 m); length 23 ft 6 in (7.16 m); height 6 ft 2½ in (1.89 m); wing area 157.9 sq ft (14.67 m²)

Messerschmitt-Bölkow-Blohm BO 105

History and Notes
Rigid non-articulated rotor, two engines, compact size—all these combine to make the Messerschmitt-Bölkow-Blohm BO 105 a particularly impressive helicopter. It is fully aerobatic and highly manoeuvrable, but also comparatively expensive. Its safety and versatility have made the BO 105 a successful civil helicopter, and a few military forces find the type equally suitable. It is assigned multiple roles and can operate in all weathers. Nap-of-the-earth flying is a speciality to which the BO 105 is well suited, the rigid rotor allowing it to hug contours like a leach. A conventional helicopter can tolerate no negative-g, restricted as it is by a much more mobile rotor assembly, but the BO 105 can be pushed down the other side of such obstacles as trees, having been pulled up over them conventionally.

The BO 105 started life in 1962, the radical rotor system having been tested earlier on a ground rig. Government contracts covered this initial testing and also the construction of prototypes in 1964. Dipl. Ing. E. Weiland conceived the rotor, which in its developed, production form uses rigid, glass-fibre, folding blades.

Sud-Aviation (now part of Aérospatiale) was involved, and it was one of this company's helicopters, a Turboméca Astazou-powered Alouette II, which was used as a test bed for the initial trials. The first prototype BO 105 was fitted with a conventional rotor assembly (from the Westland Scout) and a pair of Allison

250-C18 turboshafts but was destroyed following resonance during ground trials; the second aircraft, similarly powered, pioneered the rigid rotor on the BO 105. MTU-München Turbo 6022 engines were tried on the third development aircraft, but production machines are now all powered by the Allison turboshaft. Customers previously had the option of two versions of this engine: the 317-shp (236-kW) C18, now out of production, or the 400-shp (298-kW) C20. The current production model is the BO 105CB with 420-shp (313-kW) 250-C20B engines; other versions are the

BO 105CBS with seating for six in a fuselage stretched by 9.8 in (0.254 m) and the BO 105D for the British market.

Boeing Vertol has developed a stretched version, called the Executaire, for the civil market in America.

Specification
Type: light general-purpose helicopter
Powerplant: two 420-shp (313-kW) Allison 250-C20B turboshafts
Performance: maximum speed at sea level 167 mph (270 km/h); maximum cruising speed at sea level 144 mph (232 km/h); range

with standard fuel and no reserves 363 miles (585 km) at sea level, 388 miles (625 km) at 5,000 ft (1525 m); maximum range with auxiliary tanks at sea level 621 miles (1000 km), at 5,000 ft (1525 m); 658 miles (1060 km); maximum rate of climb at sea level 1,870 ft (570 m) per minute.
Weights: empty equipped 2,645 lb (1200 kg); maximum take-off 5,070 lb (2300 kg)
Dimensions: rotor diameter 32 ft 2¾ in (9.82 m); length (rotors turning) 38 ft 10¾ in (11.84 m); height 9ft 9½ in (2.98 m); main rotor disc area 811.2 sq ft (75.4 m²)

The MBB BO 105's rigid rotor system makes it a helicopter capable of extreme precision in flight. This means that although the machine is expensive, it is cost-economical for operators requiring a craft able to get into tight corners.

Messerschmitt-Bölkow-Blohm Bö 208C Junior

History and Notes
Working in the United States, Swedish freelance designer Bjorn Andreasson evolved a light all-metal two-seater under the designation BA-7. Powered by a 75-hp (56-kW) Continental A-75 engine, the prototype was first flown on 10 October 1958, originally with one-piece, all-moving tail surfaces, although a fixed fin with a conventional rudder was later substituted. The aircraft was developed for production by AB Malmö Flygindustri in Sweden as the MFI-9 Junior, fitted with a 100-hp (75-kW) Rolls-Royce Continental O-200 engine, and the first Swedish-built production Junior flew on 9 August 1962.

Bölkow Apparatebau GmbH, at Nabern/Teck in Germany, acquired a manufacturing licence in 1961 and the first German-built example, designated Bölkow 208, flew in April 1962. German certification was awarded on 22 April 1963 and in May 1964 the Model 208B was introduced, identified by its electrically operated flaps; an optionally-available wing increased both span and area. The Model 208C was certificated on 20 May 1965, and production of all models ceased in mid-1969 after a run of 210 aircraft, making way for the Bölkow 209 Monsun. The specification applies to the Bö 208C.

Specification
Type: two-seat light monoplane
Powerplant: one 100-hp (75-kW) Continental O-200-A flat-four piston engine
Performance: maximum speed 143 mph (230 km/h) at sea level; cruising speed 127 mph (204 km/h); service ceiling 14,100 ft (4300 m); range 620 miles (998 km)
Weights: empty 835 lb (379 kg); maximum take-off 1,375 lb (624 kg)
Dimensions: span 26 ft 3½ in (7.10 m); length 19 ft 0 in (5.79 m); height 6 ft 6 in (1.98 m); wing area 100.9 sq ft (9.37 m²)

The Bö 208 ultralight was the West German equivalent of the MFI-9 Junior, designed by Björn Andreasson. About 200 were built by Bölkow under licence, while the parent company produced only 25 civil models.

Messerschmitt-Bölkow-Blohm 209 Monsun

History and Notes
In 1965 Bölkow Apparatebau's technical director, Dr Hermann Mylius, began work on the design of a light all-metal two-seat training, aerobatic and glider-towing aircraft, under the designation MHK-101. Clearly owing much to the Bö 208 Junior, with some commonality of components, the MHK-101 had a completely new wing and a wider fuselage to provide more room in the cabin. The prototype took off on its maiden flight on 22 December 1967, powered by a 115-hp (86-kW) Lycoming O-235-C2A engine. It was developed as the Bölkow 209 Monsun and manufacture of a prototype began in January 1969, this making its first flight on 28 May.

The main production variants were the Bö 209-150, powered by a 150-hp (112-kW) Avco Lycoming O-320-E1C engine driving a McCauley fixed-pitch or optional Hartzell constant-speed propeller, and the Bö 209-160 with a 160-hp (119-kW) Avco Lycoming IO-320-D1A fuel injection-equipped engine fitted with the Hartzell propeller as standard. Both models had folding wings to reduce hangar space requirements and to facilitate towing of the aircraft behind a car; they also had retractable nosewheels and fixed main wheels.

The Monsun was also available as the Bö 209S two-seat trainer, with non-folding wings and non-retractable landing gear. Production of all models totalled 102, ceasing in 1971.

Specification
Type: two-seat light monoplane
Powerplant: one 160-hp (119-kW) Avco Lycoming IO-320-D1A flat-four piston engine
Performance: maximum speed 170 mph (127 km/h) at sea level; economic cruising speed 151 mph (113 km/h) at 8,000 ft (2440 m); service ceiling 18,100 ft (5515 m); range 745 miles (556 km)
Weights: empty 1,067 lb (484 kg); maximum take-off 1,807 lb (820 kg)

The MBB Bö 209 Monsun is an interesting design, of which relatively few were built in three versions. The two Lycoming-engined models featured an optionally retractable nosewheel leg.

Dimensions: span 27 ft 6¾ in (8.40 m); length 21 ft 7¾ in (6.60 m); height 7 ft 2½ in (2.20 m); wing area 110 sq ft (10.20 m²)

Messerschmitt-Bölkow-Blohm HFB 320 Hansa

History and Notes
West Germany entered the business-jet field when the first prototype HFB 320 Hansa flew on 21 April 1964. Design had begun three years before at Hamburger Flugzeugbau's factory at Hamburg/Finkenwerder Airport. HFB was part of the North European group of aircraft manufacturers who were at that time licence-producing the Lockheed F-104G Starfighter and other projects; the Hansa was the company's first design.

The first prototype was lost in a crash during May 1965, but a second prototype had been flying since the previous October and the type was in production. The first production Hansa flew on 2 February 1966, and an initial batch of 10 was laid down, with a similar number to follow. The first 15 Hansas had General Electric CJ610-1 engines, the following 20 the more powerful CJ610-5, and subsequent production the CJ610-9.

In addition to its executive role, the Hansa was offered for a wide variety of military duties including VIP transport, liaison, casualty evacuation, navigation training, radio and radar reconnaissance and light freighting.

Competition was extremely strong, and although the Hansa with the unusual swept-forward wing (passing at the mid-position behind the cabin) attracted some attention it did not attract many orders. A few went to civil operators in the USA and Italy; three were supplied to the RLS (Rijksluchtvaartschool) in the Netherlands for training and calibration work but the biggest user, and the only military one, was the West German Luftwaffe, which accepted 16 of approximately 40 Hansas built.

Messerschmitt-Bölkow-Blohm HFB 320 Hansa

Specification
Type: twin-jet executive transport
Powerplant: two 3,100-lb (1406-kG) General Electric CJ610-9 turbojets.
Performance: maximum cruising speed at 25,000 ft (7620 m) 513 mph (825 km/h); rate of climb at sea level 4,250 ft (1295 m) per minute; range 1,472 miles (2370 km) with 1,200 lb (545 kg) load and 45 minutes reserves; service ceiling 40,000 ft (12200 m)
Weights: empty (passenger version) 11,960 lb (5425 kg), empty (freighter version) 11,874 lb (5386 kg); maximum take-off 20,280 lb (9200 kg)
Dimensions: span 47 ft 6 in (14.49 m); length 54 ft 6 in (16.61 m); height 16 ft 2 in (4.94 m); wing area 324.4 sq ft (30.14 m²)

Mil Mi-4

History and Notes
Developed to flight-test status in only seven months following a personal edict from Stalin, the Mil Mi-4 'Hound' was at first considered to be a Soviet copy of the Sikorsky S-55 until it was realised that it was considerably larger than the later S-58. It was thus the first of a long line of large Mil helicopters.

The first prototype Mi-4 was completed in April 1952. It shared the basic layout of the S-55, with the powerful radial engine in the nose and quadricycle landing gear, but added a pair of clamshell loading doors capable of admitting a small military vehicle or most light infantry weapons such as anti-tank guns. It was thus a far more capable military transport than its Western contemporaries, and several thousand of the type were built.

The Mi-4 entered service in 1953. Early production aircraft had wooden-skinned rotor blades of very short life, but later aircraft had all-metal blades. Special versions include an amphibious development, tested in 1959, and the Mi-4V for high-altitude operations with a two-stage supercharger fitted to the ASh-82FN engine. The Mi-4 was also put into production at the Shenyang plant in China, as the Whirlwind-25 or H-5.

The standard Mi-4 can be used as freighter, and there are two basic civil variants: the Mi-4P passenger/ambulance helicopter, with accommodation for up to 11 passengers or eight litters and one attendant, and the Mi-4S agricultural helicopter, with 352 Imperial gallons (1600 litres) of chemicals and the necessary spray bars or dust spreader. In the freight role the Mi-4 can carry up to 3,527 lb (1600 kg).

Though seen here in the markings of the Finnish air force, the Russian Mil Mi-4 helicopter has a number of civil roles, including passenger-carrying (Mi-4P) and carrying the type has clamshell rear doors.

Specification
Type: utility helicopter
Powerplant: one 1,700-hp (1268-kW) Shvetsov ASh-82V two-row radial air-cooled piston engine
Performance: maximum speed 130 mph (210 km/h) at 4,920 ft (1500 m); cruising speed 99 mph (160 km/h); service ceiling 19,685 ft (6000 m); range 367 miles (590 km)
Weights: empty 11,805 lb (5355 kg); maximum take-off 17,195 lb (7800 kg)
Dimensions: rotor diameter 68 ft 11 in (21.00 m); fuselage length 55 ft 1 in (16.79 m); height 14 ft 5¼ in (4.40 m); main rotor disc area 3,728 sq ft (346.36 m²) 3,724 sq ft (346 m²)

Mil Mi-6/-10/-26 Series

History and Notes
When the first of five prototypes of the Mil Mi-6 'Hook' was flown in September 1957, it was by far the largest helicopter in the world; what is more surprising is that with one exception (the same design bureau's apparently abortive Mi-12) it has retained that distinction and seems likely to do so into the foreseeable future.

The Mi-6 was the result of a joint military and civil requirement for a massive helicopter that would not only bring a new dimension to mobile warfare, with the ability to transport light armoured vehicles, but would also help in the exploitation of previously uncharted areas of the Soviet Union.

The requirement was met by the first use of turbine power in a Soviet helicopter, and also by the provision of variable-incidence wings, first fitted in 1960 to the 30 pre-series aircraft, which carry 20% of the weight of the aircraft in cruising flight. Unusually, the Mi-6 can make a rolling take-off at a weight greater than that at which it can take off vertically. The engineering problems were formidable—the R-7 gearbox and rotor head alone weigh 7,055 lb (3200 kg), more than both the engines.

Like the Mi-4, the Mi-6 has clamshell doors at the rear of the cabin and can accommodate small armoured vehicles. Even larger loads can be lifted by the specialized flying-crane derivative of the Mi-6, the Mi-10 'Harke'; this features a much shallower fuselage than the Mi-6, and in its initial version is fitted with a vast quadricycle landing gear which allows it to straddle and lift loads as large as a motor-coach or a prefabricated building. The later Mi-10K has a shorter, lighter landing gear and a rear-facing gondola beneath the nose for a crewman to direct lifting.

Specification
Type: heavy transport helicopter and (Mi-10) crane helicopter
Powerplant: two 5,500-shp (4103-kW) Soloviev D-25V turboshafts.
Performance: maximum speed 186 mph (300 km/h); cruising speed 155 mph (250 km/h); range with 26,455-lb (12000-kg) payload 125 miles (200 km); range with 8,818-lb (4000-kg) payload 620 miles (1000 km); service ceiling at maximum gross weight 14,500 ft (4400 m); hovering ceiling 8,200 ft (2500 m)
Weights: empty 60,050 lb (27240 kg); maximum internal payload 26,500 lb 812000 kg); normal take-off 89,300 lb (40500 kg); maximum vertical take-off 93,700 lb (42500 kg)
Dimensions: main rotor diameter 114 ft 10 in (35.0 m); fuselage length 108 ft 10¼ in (33.18 m); wing span 50 ft 2½ in (15.3 m); height on ground 30 ft 1 in (9.16 m); main rotor disc area 10,356.8 sq ft (962 m²)

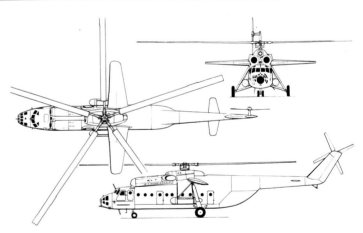

Mil Mi-6 'Hook'

The Mil Mi-6 is one of the world's most significant heavy lift helicopters and is widely used by the military as well as by Aeroflot, in whose livery the example illustrated is seen. Up to 65 passengers can be carried.

Mil Mi-8

History and Notes

Mikhail Mil was involved in the design and development of rotary-wing aircraft from the early 1930s, his own design bureau being established shortly after the end of World War II. The initial product of the Mil bureau was a light general-purpose helicopter designated Mi-1, first flown in 1950, and since that time successive designs have been built in very large quantities. The Mi-1 was to become the far superior Mi-2 when powered by turboshaft engines, and in a similar way the Mi-4 has a relationship to the current Mi-8 transport helicopter.

While the Mi-8 is derived from the Mi-4, and uses a number of common components, the similarity really ends there, for the single 1,700-hp (1268-kW) piston engine which powered the Mi-4 was replaced by a 2,700-shp (2013-kW) Soloviev turboshaft engine in the prototype Mi-8, this considerable increase in power making it possible to design a larger fuselage with greatly increased cabin area. Work on the development of the Mi-8 (then identified as V-8) began in 1960, and this flew first in 1961.

Since that time there has been continuing improvement of this extensively-built helicopter, of which it is believed that more than 6,000 have been delivered. It continued in production in 1980, reportedly at a production-rate of 700 examples per year. In its current form it has a five-blade main rotor and a three-blade anti-torque rotor, all blades being of light-alloy construction. The fuselage is of conventional helicopter pod-and-boom type, which in basic airline configuration accommodates a crew of two or three on the flight deck, and 28 passengers with adequate wardrobe space. Without the wardrobe a maximum of 32 passengers can be accommodated in four-abreast seating. The landing gear is of non-retractable tricycle type, and the single Soloviev turboshaft engine has now been displaced by two 1,700-shp (1268-kW) Isotov TV2-117A turboshaft engines, thus providing this latest model with double the power of the parent Mi-4.

Standard access is via a sliding door at the forward end of the cabin on the port side, or by means of a ventral airstair door at the rear. The rear end of the cabin incorporates large clamshell doors, to permit the loading of bulky freight. In addition to the standard Mi-8 passenger version there is also a general utility Mi-8T which is intended for operation primarily as a freight carrier, but can be equipped also to carry 24 passengers on tip-up seats mounted along the cabin walls. Both of the above can be operated in an alternative ambulance role, able to carry 12 stretcher cases plus a medical attendant. There is also a de luxe version which has the designation Mi-8 Salon, available in 11-seat or, optionally, nine-seat layouts.

Large numbers of Mi-8s are used by Aeroflot in the transport role, but also for ice reconnaissance, rescue operations, and logistic support. Even greater numbers are in use with the Soviet air force and have been supplied also to the armed forces of many other nations. The military version, which has the NATO codename 'Hip-E', was at one time described as the world's most heavily

A powerful and versatile medium-lift helicopter, the Mil Mi-8 has achieved only one sale to a company outside the Soviet bloc, in this instance Asahi Helicopter of Japan.

Mil Mi-8 of Instal, Poland.

armed helicopter. The details below apply to the basic passenger-carrying Mi-8.

Specification

Type: transport helicopter
Powerplant: two 1,700-shp (1268-kW) Isotov TV2-117A turboshafts
Performance: maximum level speed 155 mph (250 km/h) at sea level; maximum cruising speed 140 mph (225 km/h); service ceiling 14,765 ft (4500 m); range with 28 passengers and 20-min reserves 311 miles (500 km) at 3,280 ft (1000 m)
Weights: empty 14,991 lb (6800 kg); maximum vertical take-off 26,455 lb (12000 kg)
Dimensions: main rotor diameter 69 ft 10¼ in (21.29 m); tail rotor diameter 12 ft 9½ in (3.90 m); length, rotors turning 82 ft 9¾ in (25.24 m); height 18 ft 6½ in (5.65 m); main rotor disc area 3,821 sq ft (355.00 m²)
Operators include: Aeroflot, and Asahi Helicopter

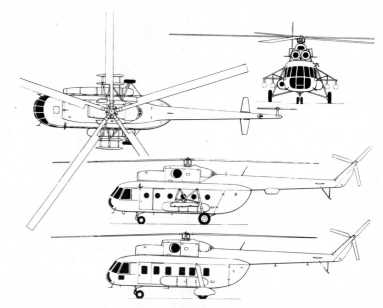

Mil Mi-8 'Hip' (lower side view: Mi-8 civil version)

Mooney M-20/M-20D Ranger

History and Notes

Formed at Wichita, Kansas on 18 June 1948, Mooney Aircraft designed and manufactured the single-seat M-18 Mite, later renamed Wee Scotsman which was developed into the four-seat M-20. The prototype M-20 flew on 10 August 1953 and the production version, powered by the 150-hp (112-kW) Avco Lycoming O-320, was fitted with wings of pressure-bonded laminated spruce construction, as was the M-20A with its 180-hp (134-kW) Avco Lycoming O-360-A engine.

In 1961 Mooney undertook extensive redesign, and an all-metal version emerged as the M-20C Mk 21, first flown on 23 September 1961. FAA Type Approval was received on 7 November 1961. The basically similar M-20D Master had fixed landing gear, and was first flown as a prototype on 22 September 1962, receiving Type Approval on 15 October 1962 and entering production in January 1963.

The Mk 21 became the Mooney Ranger and then, after the company had been renamed Aerostar Aircraft Corporation on 1 July 1970, the Aerostar Ranger, acquiring new vertical tail surfaces with a large dorsal fillet. Production was suspended early in 1972 and restarted after Republic Steel Corporation acquired the company in October 1973, restoring the Mooney name. Manufacture of the Ranger ceased in 1979 after more than 2,000 had been built. The specification applies to the Mooney Ranger.

Specification

Type: four-seat light monoplane
Powerplant: one 180-hp (134-kW) Avco Lycoming O-360-A1D flat-four piston engine
Performance: maximum speed 179 mph (288 km/h) at sea level; cruising speed 172 mph (277 km/h) at 7,500 ft (2285 m); service ceiling 17,200 ft (5245 m); range 1,043 miles (1679 km)
Weights: empty 1,566 lb (710 kg); maximum take-off 2,575 lb (1168 kg)
Dimensions: span 35 ft 0 in (10.67 m); length 23 ft 2 in (7.06 m); height 8 ft 4½ in (2.55 m); wing area 167 sq ft (15.51 m²)

The Mooney 201 is an attractive development of the Mooney Ranger, originally designated M-20C Mark 21. The 201 offers higher performance as a result of increased power coupled with superior aerodynamics.

Mooney M-20E/-20K Statesman

History and Notes

On 10 September 1963, Mooney flew the first production example of the more powerful M-20E Super 21, powered by a 200-hp (149-kW) Avco Lycoming IO-360-A1A engine. The prototype had flown on 6 July 1963 and FAA Type Approval had been awarded on 1 September. The type was further developed as the M-20F Executive 21 with a 13 in (0.33 m) fuselage 'stretch' to provide more leg room in the cabin, which introduced a third window on each side, and improved soundproofing. Wing root integral fuel tanks were increased in capacity from 52 to 64 US gallons (197 to 242 litres). Introduced during 1968, the M-20G Mooney Statesman was similar to the M-20C Mooney-Ranger, but with the longer fuselage of the Mooney Executive 21.

After the manufacturer's reorganisation as Aerostar Aircraft Corporation on 1 July 1970, the Super 21 and the Executive 21 continued in production as the Aerostar Chaparral and Aerostar Executive, both with new vertical tail surfaces and a dorsal fillet. When the company adopted the Mooney name once more, on take-over by the Republic Steel Corporation, the Mooney Executive remained in production until phased out in 1978. An improved and aerodynamically cleaner version, the M-20J Mooney 201 flew for the first time in June 1976 and is a current production model, together with the M-20K Turbo Mooney 231 first flown in October 1976, certificated on 10 November 1978 and powered by a 210-hp (157-kW) Continental TSIO-360-GB turbocharged engine. The specification applies to the Mooney Statesman.

Specification

Type: four-seat light monoplane
Powerplant: one 200-hp (149-kW) Avco Lycoming IO-360-A1A flat-four piston engine
Performance: maximum speed 178 mph (286 km/h) at sea level; cruising speed 169 mph (272 km/h) at 7,500 ft (2285 m); service ceiling 17,000 ft (5180 m); range 1,000 miles (1609 km)
Weights: empty 1,585 lb (719 kg); maximum take-off 2,575 lb (1168 kg)
Dimensions: span 35 ft 0 in (10.67 m); length 24 ft 3 in (7.39 m); height 8 ft 4½ in (2.55 m); wing area 167 sq ft (15.51 m²)

Mudry CAP 20 L

History and Notes

Although externally similar to the earlier CAP 20, used by the French air force Equipe de Voltige Aerienne, the CAP 20 L is structurally a new design. The wing planform is more angular, with a reduced dihedral angle of 1.5°, and the fuselage has a rectangular cross section with a rounded top decking, replacing the triangular section of the earlier aircraft. Slightly smaller than its forebear, the CAP 20 L is some 300 lb (136 kg) lighter (the L designation deriving from *léger* or light).

The prototype flew for the first time on 15 January 1976 at Bernay, in the hands of Mudry test pilot Louis Pena. Powered by a 180-hp (134-kW) Avco Lycoming IO-360-RCF engine, it completed initial manufacturer's trials before beginning the official certification programme at the Centre d'Essais en Vol at Istres, interrupted by an appearance in the 8th World Aerobatic Championships in Kiev. The airframe was used for structural tests at CEAT Toulouse from mid-October 1976 and did not fly again.

The first of five pre-production aircraft, flown on 6 November 1976, was powered by a 200-hp (149-kW) AIO-360-B1B engine, driving a Hartzell constant-speed metal propeller. This and all subsequent aircraft were designated CAP 20 LS-200. Production was suspended in July 1979, after delivery of the 12th CAP 20 LS-200 to the Aero Club d'Italia in Turin, to await development of a new wing. In fact, the CAP 20 L was superseded by the CAP 21. The specification applies to the CAP 20 L.

Specification

Type: single-seat light monoplane
Powerplant: one 200-hp (149-kW) Avco Lycoming AIO-360-B1B flat-four piston engine

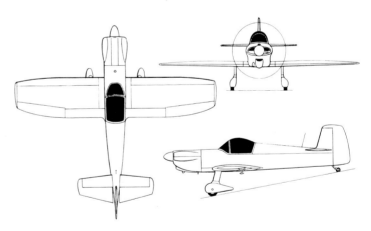

Mudry CAP 20 L

Performance: maximum cruising speed 186 mph (299 km/h)
Weights: empty 1,102 lb (500 kg); maximum take-off 1,433 lb (650 kg)
Dimensions: span 24 ft 10 in (25.14 m); length 21 ft 2½ in (6.46 m); height 5 ft 0 in (1.53 m); wing area 112.7 sq ft (10.47 m²)

Mudry CAP 21

History and Notes

Following the 1978 World Aerobatic Championships, the Avions Mudry design team initiated studies to improve the competitiveness of the CAP 20 LS and, in co-operation with Aérospatiale, developed a new wing, of V16F profile. In order to lessen control column forces and to provide improved effectiveness in rolling manoeuvres, the ailerons were increased in size, to cover 86 per cent of the wing span and 19 per cent of chord. This wing, which also improves performance in snap manoeuvres, was mated to the standard CAP 20 LS-200 fuselage and tail surfaces, and new glassfibre landing gear legs were designed. The 200-hp (149-kW) Avco Lycoming AEIO-360-A1B was retained, but fitted with a Hartzell variable-pitch propeller.

Work on the prototype started in 1979, but completion was delayed and the aircraft did not fly until 23 June 1980, making two flights of 12 and 15 minutes duration, Louis Pena carrying out some simple aerobatic manoeuvres. A three-week intensive flying programme followed, not only to complete preliminary clearance trials, but also to provide practice for Pena and Swiss aerobatic champion Eric Müller. These two pilots were scheduled to fly the aircraft in the 1980 World Championships, which took place at Oshkosh, Wisconsin in the fortnight 17-30 August. On its return the prototype undertook certification trials at CEV Istres, and a structural test programme at CEAT Toulouse. A pre-production batch of five CAP 21s was authorised and the CAP 20 L was finally abandoned.

Specification

Type: single-seat light monoplane
Powerplant: one 200-hp (149-kW) Avco Lycoming AEIO-360-A1B flat-four piston engine
Performance: maximum cruising speed 199 mph (320 km/h); endurance 2 hours
Weights: empty 1,080 lb (490 kg); maximum take-off 1,323 lb (600 kg)
Dimensions: span 26 ft 6 in (8.08 m); length 21 ft 2½ in (6.46 m); height 5 ft 0 in (1.52 m); wing area 99 sq ft (9.20 m²)

Mitsubishi MU-2/Marquise/Solitaire Series

History and Notes

Mitsubishi, which by the end of World War II had built an estimated 80,000 aircraft in its 25-year history, had also become a leading aero-engine manufacturer. It thus had a wealth of experience with which to face postwar markets when, in 1952, a resumption of manufacturing activities followed completion of the Peace Treaty. Work began with overhauls for the USAF, and in 1956 the company began licence construction of 300 North American F-86F Sabres for the Japan Air Self-Defense Force. Almost simultaneously, Mitsubishi initiated the design of a light utility transport to be powered by two turboprop engines.

It was nearly seven years before the first of four prototypes was flown, on 14 September 1963. Designated MU-2, it was a cantilever high-wing monoplane with a pressurised fuselage, conventional tail unit, retractable tricycle landing gear, with main units housed in fuselage side fairings when retracted, and wing-mounted turboprop engines. It has proved to be a successful design, with orders approaching the 700 mark in early 1981, and many versions have been built.

First production version was the MU-2A with Turboméca Astazou turboprops (three built), followed by the MU-2B with Garrett TPE331 turboprops (34 built), a similar MU-2D (18 built), an unpressurised multi-role MU-2C for the JGSDF (four built), a search and rescue MU-2E (16 built), and the MU-2F with uprated TPE331 engines (95 built). The MU-2G was the first of the 'stretched' versions, with a fuselage lengthened by 6 ft 3 in (1.91 m) and the powerplant of the -2F (46 built) and this was followed by the MU-2J with more powerful engines (108

Mitsubishi MU-2N of Gateway Aviation, Canada.

built), the MU-2K with -2F's fuselage and -2J's powerplant (83 built), the MU-2L higher-weight version of the -2J (36 built), the MU-2M higher-weight version of the -2K (29 built), MU-2N that is similar to the -2L but with Garrett TPE331-5-252M engines (39 built), and the MU-2P, a similarly engined version of the -2M (40 built).

In 1965, Mitsubishi had established a facility at San Angelo, Texas for the assembly of MU-2s for the North American market. This now represents the continuing production facility for worldwide distribution, and in early 1981 manufacture was concentrated on the Marquise and Solitaire. The former is generally similar to the MU-2N, but with TPE331-10-501M engines, and while the Solitaire also has this powerplant, it is otherwise similar to the MU-2P. Under this production plan, basic airframe components are constructed in Japan and shipped to San Angelo where they are used on a production line which incorporates such American-built items as avionics, brakes, engines, furnishings, propellers and tyres. The details that follow apply to the longer-fuselage 11-seat Marquise.

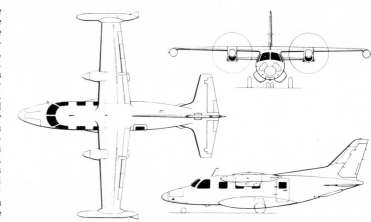

Mitsubishi MU-2L

Mitsubishi MU-2J cutaway drawing key

1 Nose cone
2 Hinged nose doors (left and right)
3 Hinged landing and taxi lamps (left and right)
4 Nosewheel doors
5 Forward-retracting twin nosewheels
6 Nosewheel leg
7 Landing gear access panel
8 Forward electronics compartment
9 Forward battery
10 Bulkhead
11 Control column
12 Rudder pedals
13 Windshield wiper
14 Instrument console shroud
15 Windshield de-icing installation
16 Two-piece curved windshield
17 Control yoke
18 Second pilot's seat
19 First pilot's seat
20 Seat adjustment mechanism
21 Circuit breaker panel
22 Floor support structure
23 Main undercarriage fairing
24 Underfloor control runs
25 Main passenger cabin floor
26 Three-a-side cabin windows
27 Strengthened anti-ice panel
28 Frame and longeron fuselage construction
29 Fuselage skinning
30 Aerial mast
31 Wingroot fairings
32 Leading-edge relay panel
33 Fuselage/front spar attachment points
34 Emergency escape window (right-hand rear)
35 Wing carry-through surface
36 Centre-section fuel tank
37 No 1 right-hand fuel tank
38 Fuel lines

39 Garrett AiResearch TPE331-6-251M turboprop
40 Intake
41 Airscrew spinner
42 Three-blade Hartzell propeller
43 Pneumatic leading-edge de-icer
44 Leading-edge ribs
45 No 2 right-hand fuel tank
46 Auxiliary tip tank
47 Tip tank fin
48 Spoilers (extended)
49 Trim aileron section
50 Flap track fairing
51 Aerial
52 Inner section double-slotted flap
53 Centre-section anti-collision beacon
54 Spoiler mechanism
55 Fuselage/rear spar attachment points

56 Flap actuator mechanism
57 Wingroot fillet
58 Cabin entry door
59 Air-conditioning ducts
60 Dorsal fillet
61 Pneumatic fin leading-edge de-icer
62 Aerial (to right-hand tailplane)
63 Fin main spar
64 Rudder tab mechanism
65 Antenna
66 Anti-collision beacon

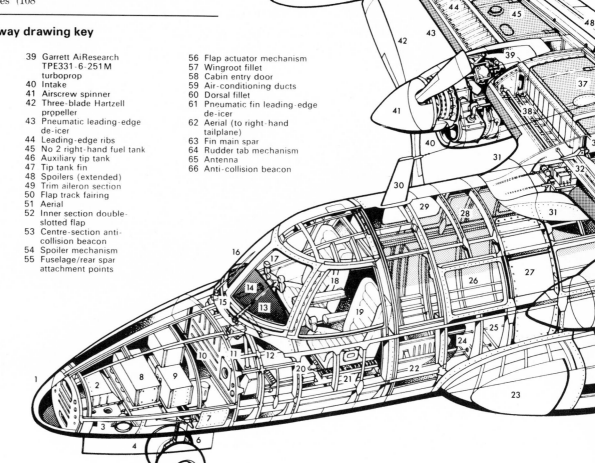

Mitsubishi MU-2 Marquise/Solitaire Series

Specification

Type: twin-turboprop business aircraft

Powerplant: two 715-shp (533-kW) Garrett TPE331-10-501M turboprops

Performance: maximum cruising speed 355 mph (571 km/h) at 16,000 ft (4875 m); economic cruising speed 340 mph (547 km/h) at 20,000 ft (6100 m); service ceiling 29,400 ft (8960 m); range with maximum fuel and 45-min reserves 1,606 miles (2585 km)

Weights: empty equipped 7,650 lb (3470 kg); maximum take-off 11,575 lb (5250 kg)

Dimensions: wing span over tiptanks 39 ft 2 in (11.94 m); length 39 ft 5 in (12.01 m); height 13 ft 8 in (4.17 m); wing area 178 sq ft (16.54 m²)

The Mitsubishi MU-2P is marketed in the USA as the Solitaire, and one of its strongest selling points is its high cruising speed of 370 mph (592 km/h).

67 Static dischargers
68 Rudder hinge fairing
69 Rudder construction
70 Rudder tab control
71 Rudder post main beam
72 Rudder tab
73 Tail cone
74 Rear navigation light
75 Elevator tab
76 Tab mechanism
77 Port elevator
78 Tailplane construction
79 Pneumatic leading-edge de-icer
80 Tailplane fillet
81 Control runs
82 Ventral strake (left and right)
83 Electronics access panel
84 Air-conditioning and pressurisation installation

85 Aft electronics compartment (main junction box and batteries)
86 Aft cabin coat closet space
87 Door handle
88 Door hinges
89 Fuel dump line (left and right)
90 Undercarriage retraction mechanism
91 Mainwheel door
92 Mainwheel leg
93 Axle
94 Port mainwheel
95 Wing ribs
96 Outer-section flap profile
97 Port auxiliary tip tank
98 Wingtip lights (navigation and strobe)
99 Tip tank fin
100 Tip tank strake

NAMC YS-11

History and Notes

The Nihon Aircraft Manufacturing Company (NAMC) was created on 1 June 1959 from the earlier Transport Aircraft Development Association, which had been established in May 1957 to design and develop an indigenous medium range civil airliner in Japan. This later association incorporated six established companies (Fuji, Kawasaki, Mitsubishi, Nippi, Shin Meiwa, and Showa), all involved in the design of this aircraft, which became finalised as a short/medium-range transport that was slanted mainly to satisfy the requirements of Japan's domestic airlines.

Immediately after its formation, NAMC began the task of building two prototypes and two static test airframes, with the component companies involved in the manufacture of different airframe assemblies. Thus Fuji was responsible for the tail unit; Kawasaki for the wings and engine nacelles; Mitsubishi for the forward fuselage, equipment, and final assembly; Nippi for the ailerons and flaps; Shin Meiwa for the rear fuselage; and Showa for light-alloy honeycomb structural components. NAMC was the overall controlling and co-ordinating unit, and concerned also with sales.

The first of the two prototypes made its initial flight on 30 August 1962, the second in December of that year, and these aircraft completed the certification programme, with the Japanese Type Certificate awarded on 25 August 1964. By that time the production line was established, and the first production aircraft flew on 23 October 1964. In April 1965 the first revenue operations were initiated by Toa Airways.

The initial production version of the new YS-11 was identified as the YS-11-100. Of low-wing monoplane configuration, the aircraft had a wing fitted with Fowler type trailing-edge flaps; the fuselage was of circular-section fail-safe construction to allow for cabin pressurisation; the tail unit was conventional; and the retractable tricycle type landing gear carried twin wheels on each unit. Accommodation was provided for a crew of two and 60 passengers. Of the 47 production aircraft that were built six went to Japan's armed forces, four as 32/48-seat VIP transports and two in all-cargo configuration.

The choice of powerplant had been finalised only after a fairly extensive evaluation of available turboprop engines. British Napier and Rolls-Royce, and US Allison powerplants were among the final competitors, with the Rolls-Royce RDa.10/1 Dart being chosen for installation, and this version was to power all of the 182 aircraft built.

To promote export sales, the YS-11A was developed. This retained the same overall dimensions and

NAMC YS-11 of Toa Domestic Airlines, Japan.

powerplant, but was certificated at a higher gross weight, resulting in a payload increase of 2,976 lb (1350 kg). Initial version was the YS-11A-200, a basic passenger version with standard seating for 60 passengers, followed by the YS-11A-300 and YS-11A-400, which were respectively cargo/passenger and all-cargo versions. The former introduced an 8 ft 1½ in by 6 ft 0 in (2.48 m by 1.83 m) cargo door in the port side of the forward fuselage, and aft of the forward cargo area was standard accommodation for 46 passengers. The all-cargo -400 had a 10 ft 0 in by 6 ft 0 in (3.05 m by 1.83 m) cargo door in the port side of the rear fuselage. Three versions with the maximum take-off weight increased by 1,102 lb (500 kg) were also made available under the designations YS-11A-500, -600, and -700, but apart from their higher operating weights these correspond respectively to the -200, -300, and -400. The details below apply to the YS-11A-200.

Specification

Type: short/medium-range transport
Powerplant: two 3,060-ehp (2282-ekW) Rolls-Royce Dart Mk 542-10K turboprops
Performance: maximum cruising speed 291 mph (468 km/h) at

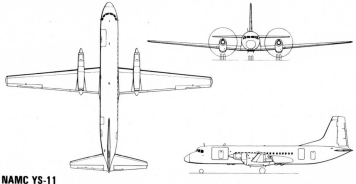

NAMC YS-11

15,000 ft (4570 m); economic cruising speed 281 mph (452 km/h) at 20,000 ft (6100 m); service ceiling 22,900 ft (6980 m); range with maximum payload, no reserves 680 miles (1094 km); range with maximum fuel, no reserves 2,000 miles (3219 km)
Weights: operating empty 33,993 lb (15419 kg); maximum take-off 54,013 lb (24500 kg)
Dimensions: span 104 ft 11¾ in (32.00 m); length 86 ft 3½ in (26.30 m); height 29 ft 5½ in (8.98 m); wing area 1,020.45 sq ft (94.80 m²)
Operators include: All Nippon Airways, China Airlines, Lapa,

Nihon Kinkyori Airways, Olympic Airways, Philippines Airlines, Piedmont Aviation, Pinehurst Airlines, Pyramid Airlines, Reeve Aleutian Airways, Southwest Air Lines, Toa Domestic Airlines, and Tramaco

Although NAMC YS-11s are used by a number of operators in the Far East and the USA, the main fleets are in Japan. All Nippon Airways has no fewer than 30 YS-11As, the only larger operator being Toa Domestic Airlines with 40 YS-11As. The only European operator is Olympic Airways, which has six YS-11As.

Nash Petrel

History and Notes

Developed from the single-seat Procter Kittiwake light aircraft, the Petrel two-seater in its original form was intended to use a number of similar components, but was improved and simplified. The first Petrel to fly was built by British Aerospace apprentices at Preston, and had a 130-hp (97-kW) Rolls-Royce Continental O-240 engine, but this aircraft is not representative of the current version being built by Nash Aircraft Ltd at Farnham.

Founded originally by Roy Proc-

ter, Procter Aircraft Associates Ltd had its name changed to Nash Aircraft Ltd in 1980, when Alan Nash acquired a controlling interest. Both Alan Nash and Roy Procter are directors of the company, a subsidiary of Kinetrol Ltd.

The prototype Nash-built Petrel was exhibited at the Farnborough Air Show in September 1980, and made its first flight the following month. Operating on a Permit to Fly, it had put in some 20 hours by the beginning of April 1981 from its base at Lasham, and was due to

begin glider-towing tests. Handling had proved satisfactory, and CAA certification was awaited.

A batch of five Petrels was under construction at Farnham, with the first due to fly by the end of 1981. The prototype had a 160-hp (119-kW) Avco Lycoming O-320-D2A engine; production aircraft will be offered with a choice of powerplants between 118-180 hp (88-134 kW) with prices beginning at £17,250.

Specification

Type: two-seat light monoplane

Powerplant: one 160-hp (119-kW) Avco Lycoming O-320-D2A flat-four piston engine
Performance: (provisional figures) cruising speed 111 mph (179 km/h) at sea level; service ceiling 16,000 ft (4875 m); range with standard fuel 262 miles (422 km)
Weights: empty 1,180 lb (535 kg); maximum take-off 1,886 lb (855 kg)
Dimensions: span 29 ft 4 in (8.94 m); length 20 ft 5 in (6.22 m); height 7 ft 6 in (2.29 m); wing area 136 sq ft (12.63 m²)

Neiva 360 Regente/420 Lanceiro Series

History and Notes
In 1959 Neiva started work on the design of an all-metal four-seat light aircraft, initially designated Neiva 360C. The prototype flew on 7 September 1961 and the Brazilian Ministry of Aeronautics granted a Type Certificate on 12 November 1963. Powered by a 180-hp (134-kW) Continental O-360-A1D engine with a Hartzell constant-speed propeller, the aircraft was put into production, as the Regente 360C, against an order for 80 examples from the Brazilian air force. In military service it became the U-42 (later C-42) and the first delivery was made in February 1975.

Neiva also developed for the Brazilian air force a liaison and observation version of the Regente, to replace the Neiva L-6s and Cessna O-1 Bird Dogs then in service. The rear fuselage was lowered to provide improved all-round visibility from the cabin, which contained three seats, and underwing carriers could be fitted for the attachment of light stores. The prototype Regente 420L or YL-42, powered by a 210-hp (157-

kW) Continental IO-360-D, made its first flight in January 1967 and 40 production L-42s were ordered. The first of these flew in June 1969 and production was terminated in March 1971. During the following year, however, the company flew the prototype of a four-seat civil version which was to become known as the Lanceiro. The first production Lanciero flew on 5 September 1973 and manufacture ceased in 1976. The specification applies to the Lanceiro.

Specification
Type: four-seat light monoplane
Powerplant: one 210-hp (157-kW) Continental IO-360-D flat-four piston engine
Performance: maximum speed 153 mph (246 km/h) at sea level; maximum cruising speed 142 mph (229 km/h) at sea level; service

The Neiva Lanceiro is a Brazilian light-plane, but shows marked American influence in its basic design. One unusual feature of the Lanceiro is the sharp taper on both the leading- and trailing-edges of the wingtips.

ceiling 15,810 ft (4820 m); range with maximum fuel 590 miles (950 km)
Weights: empty 1,642 lb (745 kg); maximum take-off

2,517 lb (1142 kg)
Dimensions: span 33 ft 0 in (10.06 m); length 23 ft 7¾ in (7.21 m); height 9 ft 7¼ in (2.93 m); wing area 158.34 sq ft (14.71 m²)

North American Navion/Navion Rangemaster Series

History and Notes
The basic design of the all-metal, four-seat Navion was evolved by North American Aviation in 1945, and the first of two prototypes flew early in 1946. The production Navion received its Type Certificate on 28 January 1947 and approximately 1,100 were built, powered by the 185-hp (138-kW) Continental E-185-3 or 205-hp (153-kW) E-185-9 engines. On 15 April 1947, with 280 unsold aircraft on hand, design and production rights were sold to Ryan Aeronautical Corporation. Eighty-three of the stock aircraft were supplied to the US Army as L-17As, and by the time production was suspended, in 1951, Ryan had completed 1,238 Navions. These included some 600 Navion As, mostly with 250-hp (187-kW) engines, and more than 220 Navion Bs with the 260-hp (194-kW) Avco Lycoming GO-435-C2. Navions D, E and F were conversions produced during the late 1950s by the Tusco Corporation, respectively powered by 240-hp (179-kW), 250-hp (187-kW) and 260-hp (184-kW) versions of the Continental O-470 engine.

In 1960 Tusco established Navion

Aircraft Co. at Harlingen, Texas to build the Rangemaster, a modernised five-seat version with a revised cabin, the original sliding canopy being replaced by conventional doors. The line of the rear fuselage was raised, taller vertical tail surfaces were fitted, and wingtip fuel tanks added. The prototype flew on 10 June 1960 and production, which commenced in October 1961, comprised 20 Rangemaster Gs and 101 G-1s, all powered by the 260-hp (194-kW) Continental IO-470 engine, before suspension in 1964. In 1965 all rights were sold to the American Navion Society, a Navion owners' organisation which set up Navion Aircraft Co. at Seguin, Texas. The Rangemaster H was introduced and 51 of these aircraft, powered by 285-hp (213-kW) Continental IO-520 engines, were manufactured before the company went into liquidation in 1972. The assets were acquired by Cedric Kotowicz late in 1972, and the Navion Rangemaster Aircraft Company was formed at Wharton, Texas. One Rangemaster H was built in 1974 and Consolidated Holding Inc., also at Wharton, manufactured two in 1975 and six in

1976. The specification applies to the Rangemaster G.

Specification
Type: five-seat light monoplane
Powerplant: one 260-hp (194-kW) Continental IO-470-H flat-six piston engine
Performance: maximum speed 180 mph (290 km/h) at sea level; cruising speed 173 mph (278 km/h); service ceiling 20,500 ft (6250 m);

The Navion Rangemaster Model H is merely the latest in a long series of variants, produced by several manufacturers, going back to the mid-1940s.

range 1,858 miles (2990 km)
Weights: empty 1,950 lb (885 kg); maximum take-off 3,317 lb (1504 kg)
Dimensions: span 34 ft 9 in (10.59 m); length 27 ft 6 in (8.38 m); height 8 ft 4 in (2.54 m); wing area 184.4 sq ft (17.13 m²)

Oberlerchner JOB 15

History and Notes
Drawing on past experience in the design and production of gliders and sailplanes, Josef Oberlerchner Holz-industrie built its first powered design in 1957. Of wooden construction, the prototype JOB 5 was a side-by-side two-seater powered by a 95-hp (71-kW) Continental C90-12F engine and, after completion of more than 100 hours of development flying during 1958-9, the decision to embark upon series production was taken. A number of design alterations were incorporated, however, and the JOB 15 was evolved, larger than the prototype and with a third seat added. The original all-wood fuselage was replaced by a steel-tubular structure with glassfibre and fabric covering, enlarged vertical tail surfaces were fitted, and the selected engine was the 135-hp (101-kW) Avco Lycoming O-290-D2B. A hook was fitted to add glider-towing to the original roles of training, touring and limited aerobatics. The prototype

Though designed by a company specialising in wooden structures, the Oberlerchner JOB 15 has a composite structure. Only a relatively small number were built by this little-known Austrian manufacturer.

JOB 15 flew late in 1960 and two more were completed in 1962 before the JOB 15-150 was introduced, powered by a 150-hp (112-kW) Avco Lycoming O-320-A2B engine. Eleven were built, together with 10 JOB 15/2s, before the production ceased in June 1966. The specification applies to the JOB 15.

Specification
Type: three-seat light monoplane
Powerplant: one 150-hp (112-kW) Avco Lycoming O-320-A2B flat-four piston engine
Performance: maximum speed 146 mph (235 km/h); maximum

cruising speed 121 mph (195 km/h); range 510 miles (821 km)
Weights: empty 1,314 lb (596 kg); maximum take-off 2,050 lb (930 kg)

Dimensions: span 33 ft 1½ in (10.10 m); length 25 ft 2½ in (7.68 m); height 6 ft 6½ in (1.99 m); wing area 158.2 sq ft (14.70 m²)

Partenavia P.64 Oscar/P.66B Oscar/P.66C Charlie Series

History and Notes

Partenavia's P.57 Fachiro II-f, built in small numbers between 1959 and 1966, was a four-seater powered by a 180-hp (134-kW) Avco Lycoming C-360 B2A engine. it was of mixed construction with wooden wings and a fabric-covered steel-tube fuselage. Development of an all-metal replacement, the P.64 Oscar, began late in 1964 and the prototype flew on 2 April 1965. In November 1966 work began on an improved version, designated P.64B Oscar B, which flew in the first half of 1967. To improve all-round vision, the rear fuselage was lowered and a panoramic rear cabin window added. It was later renamed Oscar 180 and, in addition to production in Italy, was also built in South Africa. AFIC (Pty) Ltd was formed for the purpose in 1967 and a prototype, assembled from Italian-built components, flew late in 1967. After certification by the South African Department of Civil Aviation early in 1968, the aircraft was put into production as the RSA 200 Falcon, differing from the Italian aircraft mainly in internal equipment, cabin furnishing and instrument layout.

The Oscar 200 derived its improved performance from the installation of 200-hp (149-kW) fuel-injection Avco Lycoming IO-360-A1A engine, driving a Hartzell variable-pitch propeller. Developed from the P.64B, the P.66 Oscar 100 and 200 were introduced as two- and three-seat versions, respectively, powered by a 115-hp (86-kW) Avco Lycoming O-235-C1B and a 150-hp (112-kW) 0-320-E2A engine. Intended as a replacement for the earlier models, the prototype two/four-seat P.66C-150 Charlie flew in January 1976, powered by a 150-hp (112-kW) Lycoming O-360-A1A. Certificated in the FAR23 Utility category and cleared for positive-g aerobatics and six-turn spins, production P.66C-160 Charlies are being built for the Aero Club d'Italia which has selected the type as the standard basic trainer for Italian aeroclubs. Engine is the 160-hp (119-kW) Avco Lycoming O-320-H2AD driving a Hoffmann fixed-pitch propeller. The specification applies to the P.66C-160.

Specification

Type: two/four-seat light monoplane
Powerplant: one 160-hp (119-kW) Avco Lycoming O-320-H2AD flat-four piston engine
Performance: maximum speed 150 mph (241 km/h) at sea level; economic cruising speed 128 mph (206 km/h) at 9,000 ft (2740 m); service ceiling 15,000 ft (4570 m); range at economic cruising speed, with reserves 486 miles (782 km)

The Oscar and Charlie series now comprises five basically similar Partenavia aircraft: the high-powered P.64B Oscar-180 and -200, the lower-powered P.66B Oscar-100 and -150, and the P.66C-160 Charlie.

Weights: empty 1,322 lb (600 kg); maximum take-off 2,183 lb (990 Kg)
Dimensions: span 32 ft 9¾ in (10.00 m); length 23 ft 9 in (7.24 m); height 9 ft 1 in (2.77 m); wing area 144.2 sq ft (13.40 m²)

Partenavia P.68 Victor

History and Notes

The prototype of Luigi Pascale's P.68 six/seven-seat light twin flew for the first time on 25 May 1970, powered by two 200-hp (149-kW) Avco Lycoming IO-360 engines. RAI certification was awarded on 17 November 1971, and FAA Type Approval followed on 7 December. The last of 13 pre-production aircraft was completed at Partenavia's original Arzano factory in February 1974, and manufacture was transferred to a new production facility at Capodichino Airport, Naples where the improved P.68B was introduced. Changes included a 6 in (0.15 m) fuselage 'stretch,' made behind the crew seats and immediately in front of the wing leading-edge, effectively widening the cockpit area by moving forward the point at which the fuselage curved into the nose.

Partenavia later added the P.68C to its model range, this having a lengthened nose to take weather radar, single 125-Imp gallon (568-litre) integral fuel tanks in each wing to replace those of 90-Imp gallon (409-litre) capacity, a third cabin window level with the wing trailing-edge, and a number of interior improvements. The P.68C-TC, with turbocharged 210-hp (157-kW) Avco Lycoming TO-360-C1A6D engines, was certificated in June 1980.

A specialised patrol and observation version, known as the P.68 Observer, was developed by Sportavia-Pützer in Germany. Fitted with a new front fuselage with a Plexiglas nose which is claimed to provide a forward and downward view equal to that of a helicopter, the prototype was flown on 20 February 1976. Production was later undertaken by Partenavia at Capodichino and certification was achieved in June 1980. Currently under development in association with Aeritalia is the turboprop AP.68/8, a nine-seat version which can also have underwing and fuselage-side hardpoints for external stores. The prototype, designated AP.68TP, was first flown on 11 September 1978, powered by two Allison 250-B17C engines. The specification applies to the P.68C.

Specification

Type: six/seven-seat monoplane
Powerplant: two 200-hp (149-kW)

Partenavia P. 68B Victor.

Avco Lycoming IO-360-A1B6 flat-four piston engines
Performance: maximum speed 200 mph (322 km/h) at sea level; cruising speed 185 mph (298 km/h) at 11,000 ft (3350 m); service ceiling 19,200 ft (5850 m); range at 11,000 ft (3350 m) with 45-min reserves 1,312 miles (2111 km)
Weights: empty 2711 lb (1230 kg); maximum take-off 4,387 lb (1990 kg)
Dimensions: span 39 ft 4½ in (39.68 m); length 31 ft 4 in (9.55 m); height 11 ft 1¾ in (3.40 m); wing area 200.2 sq ft (18.60 m²)

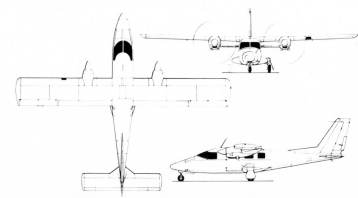

The Partenavia P.68B Victor exemplifies Italian design flair, with sleek lines and neatly faired fixed landing gear.

Partenavia P.68 Turbo

Piaggio P.166

History and Notes

Italy's long-enduring light twin-engined transport, designated as the Piaggio P.166 when the prototype flew for the first time on 26 November 1957, continues in production in 1981 in the P.166-DL3 version. This reflects in its performance the refinements introduced during 23 years of development, especially the progressive changes from the 340-hp (254-kW) piston engines of the prototype to the current powerplant of 587-shp (438-kW) Avco Lycoming LTP101-600 turboprops.

The shoulder gull-wing monoplane configuration is a legacy of the P.136 amphibian from which the type was derived. The P.166 has an all-metal semi-monocoque fuselage, upswept at the rear and mounting a conventional tail unit. Landing gear is of the retractable tricycle type, with main units that also reflect amphibian ancestry by retracting outward to stow neatly in the undersurface of the wing root. Standard accommodation is for a crew of two and eight passengers. The engines, mounted in nacelles at the trailing-edge of each wing, are unusual for most transports in this class in that they drive pusher propellers. In addition to the standard P.166-DL3, a maritime surveillance version is also available. It differs primarily by the installation of specialised equipment for this role, and carries the designation P.166-DL3-MAR.

Despite the longevity of the P.166's manufacturing programme, comparatively small numbers have been built, approaching a total of 120 in early 1981. The following details apply to the P.166-DL3.

Specification
Type: twin-turboprop light transport
Powerplant: two 587-shp (438-kW) Avco Lycoming LTP101-600 turboprops
Performance: maximum cruising speed 236 mph (380 km/h) at 10,000 ft (3050 m); economic cruising speed 186 mph (300 km/h) at 10,000 ft (3050 m); service ceiling 29,000 ft (8840 m); range at

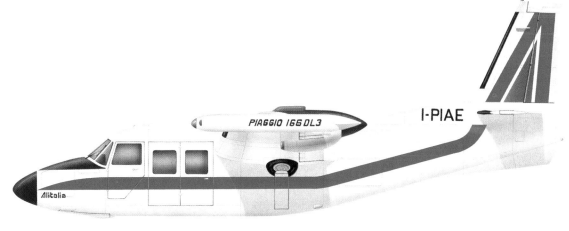

Piaggio P.166 of Alitalia.

economic cruising speed with 30-min reserves 994 miles (1600 km)
Weights: empty equipped 5,732 lb (2600 kg); maximum take-off 9,480 lb (4300 kg)
Dimensions: span over tiptanks 48 ft 2½ in (14.69 m); length 39 ft 3 in (11.96 m); height 16 ft 5 in (5.00 m); wing area 285.9 sq ft (26.56 m²)

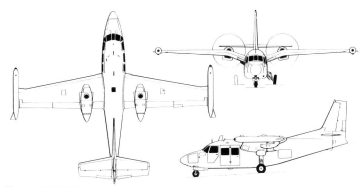

Displaying its flying-boat lineage in its cranked wings and pusher engines, the Piaggio P.166 has enjoyed a steady if unspectacular production run, the latest version being the turboprop-powered P.166 DL3 version with larger windows.

Piaggio P.166-DL3

Pilatus PC-6 Turbo-Porter

History and Notes

Pilatus recognised that a turboprop-powered derivative of the Porter would confer a better 'hot and high' performance. The economy and reliability was expected to outweigh the increased technology required for servicing. Thus, 2 May 1961 saw the first flight of the Turbo-Porter, a standard airframe with a 563-shp (420-kW) Turboméca Astazou. Performance proved superior in all flight regimes. Later several turboprops were offered to customers.

The 700-shp (522-kW) Astazou XII was fitted to the PC-6-A1/H2. The PC-6B1-H2 used a 550-shp (410-kW) Pratt & Whitney PT6A-20 and flew for the first time in May 1966. This variant was built in parallel by Fairchild Industries of the USA. Fairchild was also responsible for the AiResearch TPE331-powered PC-6C1/H2 and C2/H2 Turbo-Porters, the former leading to the Fairchild AV-23 Peacemaker for the US Air Force. All models can have an H1 or H2 suffix to their designations, denoting an improved model with higher gross weights.

In the late 1970s the standard production model was the PC-6/B2-H-2 powered by the 550-shp (410-kW) PT6A-27 turboprop. Both the

B1 and B2 versions can be fitted with a Q-STOL kit to reduce airfield noise by some 10 per cent. The Turbo-Porter can also be outfitted as an agricultural aircraft capable of dispensing liquid or dust.

Specification
Type: STOL utility transport
Powerplant: one 550-shp (410-kW) Pratt & Whitney Aircraft of Canada PT6A-27 turboprop
Performance: maximum design speed 174 mph (280 km/h); maximum cruising speed at 10,000 ft (3050 m) 151 mph (259 km/h); range on internal fuel 644 miles (1036 km); service ceiling 30,025 ft (9150 m); rate of climb at sea level 1,580 ft (482 m) per minute
Weights: empty 2,678 lb (1215 kg); loaded 4,850 lb (2200 kg)
Dimensions: span 49 ft 8 in (15.13 m); length 35 ft 9 in (10.9 m); height 10 ft 6 in (3.2 m); wing area 310 sq ft (28.8 m²)

A Pilatus PC-6 Turbo-Porter displays its remarkable STOL performance, which enables it to clear a 50-ft (15-m) obstacle only 770 ft (220 m) from brakes-off.

Pilatus PC-7 Turbo-Trainer

History and Notes

The Pilatus PC-7 Turbo-Trainer stems from an aircraft first flown in 1953. This was the P-3, whose immediate predecessor, the P-2, had utilised assemblies salvaged from scrapped Messerschmitt Bf 109 fighters.

Intended to fulfil the roles of both *ab initio* and advanced training, the P-3 was powered by a 240-hp (179-kW) Lycoming GO-235 engine, which conferred a top speed of 193 mph (310 km/h). Major operator was Switzerland's *Flugwaffe*, which flew a total of 72 examples from 1958. The type completed 20 years' continuous incident-free service, although a tendency to flat-spin when handled carelessly had proved troublesome. A large ventral fin was added beneath the rear fuselage to remedy this.

Following its success with the Turbo-Porter, Pilatus produced the P-306, flown on 12 April 1966, with a Pratt & Whitney PT6A turboprop, flat-rated to 550 shp (410 kW) for improved hot-and-high performance.

A lengthy period of development followed. The aircraft's designation was changed to P-3B and finally to PC-7. The frame canopy was replaced by a Plexiglas 'bubble' assembly.

Specification
Type: trainer
Powerplant: one 550-shp (410-kW) Pratt & Whitney Aircraft of Canada PT6A-25A turboprop
Performance: maximum design speed 310 mph (500 km/h); maximum cruising speed 276 mph (445 km/h); range 683 miles (1100 km); service ceiling 31,175 ft (9500 m); rate of climb at sea level 2,065 ft (630 m) per minute.
Weights: empty 2,866 lb (1300 kg); normal loaded 4,188 lb (1900 kg).
Dimensions: span 34 ft 1½ in

The Pilatus PC-7 Turbo-Trainer offers high standards of performance for a trainer.

(10.4 m); length 32 ft 0 in (9.75 m); height 10 ft 6½ in (3.21 m); wing area 178.7 sq ft (16.6 m²)

Piper PA-18 Super Cub

History and Notes

Many of the chestnuts of aviation humour grew up alongside the longer living of the Wright brothers, Orville, who died in 1948 at the age of 77. Opening gambits or punchlines based on 'As I said to Orville' were commonplace at one time, but it is fascinating to record that Orville Wright lived very nearly long enough to have seen the earliest Piper PA-18 Super Cub 95, which attained FAA certification in 1949.

You can, if you wish, still buy a new Super Cub in 1981, and while powerplants have changed, refinements been made, and improvements introduced, the Super Cub's basic configuration has remained unchanged throughout the years. It was, and still is, a braced high-wing monoplane, with a welded steel-tube structure for the fuselage and tail unit. Its covering is almost entirely fabric, and the only significant change is invisible externally: a substitution of aluminium for spruce wing spars. The tailwheel landing gear relies upon rubber cord shock-absorption for its main units, and the enclosed cabin seats two in tandem, provided with dual controls as standard. Of course, the radios that could be installed if required in 1949 have given place to avionics in 1981. These provide communications and navigation facilities that represent almost as much of a revolution as does a comparison of the Wright 'Flyer' with the Super Cub. What, one conjectures, would the Wright brothers have given for the 90-hp (67-kW) Continental C90 engine that powered the first example?

In between the Super Cub extremes of 1949 and 1981, there has been the Super Cub 105 with a 108-hp (81-kW) Avco Lycoming O-235, followed by the PA-18-150 Super Cub with a 150-hp (112-kW) Avco Lycoming O-320. This latter designation and powerplant have stood the test of time, being current today. There was a comparatively short-lived PA-18-A agricultural version, and Super Cubs have been re-equipped by their owners with different engines and

landing gear. But the Super Cub still endures, proving there was little wrong with its original basic design.

Specification
Type: two-seat cabin monoplane
Powerplant: one 150-hp (112-kW) Avco Lycoming O-320 flat-four piston engine
Performance: maximum level speed 130 mph 9209 km/h); maximum cruising speed 115 mph (185 km/h) at 5,000 ft (1525 m); service ceiling 19,000 ft (5790 m); range with maximum fuel and payload 460 miles (740 km)
Weights: empty 983 lb (446 kg); maximum take-off 1,750 lb (794 kg)
Dimensions: span 35 ft 2½ in (10.73 m); length 22 ft 7i in (6.88 m); height 6 ft 8½ in (20.4 m); wing area 178.5 sq ft (16.58 m²)

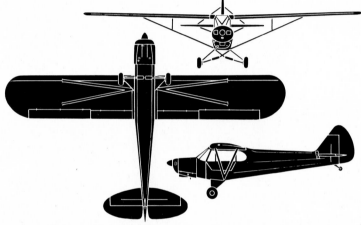

Piper PA-18 Super Cub

One of light aviation's most enduring designs, the Piper PA-18 Super Cub has been produced since 1949 but, despite numerous detail improvements, has remained substantially unaltered.

Piper PA-23 Apache/Aztec Series

History and Notes

In 1949 Piper decided that the time was ripe for the company to enter the competitive, but potentially very lucrative, market for twin-engined lightplanes. The possibility of building the Smith Twin (later produced as the Aero Commander) was at first investigated, but the company opted instead to develop its own design. This was the Twin Stinson, which first flew on 2 March 1952. The prototype had a metal airframe with fabric covering, endplate twin vertical tail surfaces, and a powerplant comprising two 125-hp (93-kW) Lycoming flat-four piston engines. Flight trials revealed a number of shortcomings, but these were eliminated and the first production aircraft was completed in December 1953. By this time the design had been renamed PA-23 Apache, the airframe was all metal, power had been increased to a total of 300 hp (224 kW), and the original tail unit replaced by the more conventional unit of the earlier Piper Sky Sedan design. It soon became clear that Piper had found the right niche between the somewhat limited single-engined types and the more expensive twin-engined models offered by Beech and Cessna. By the end of 1954 Piper had delivered 100 Apaches, and another 200 were on order. Various Apache models followed, the most significant being the Apache F of 1958, with 160-hp (119-kW) engines, and the Apache G of 1960, with seating for five rather than four. The final Apache model of the initial series was the Apache H of 1961. The final appearance of the name came in 1963, when Piper introduced the shortlived Apache 235, in fact a short-nosed PA-23 Aztec with 235-hp (175-kW) engines.

By the late 1950s Piper were becoming aware of the Apache's relative lack of seating, range and power, and somewhat dated appearance. The result was the PA-23-250 Aztec, which differed from the Apache mainly in having 250-hp (186.5-kW) Lycoming O-540-A1D5 engines and modish swept vertical tail surfaces. FAA type certification of the Aztec A was granted in 1959, with deliveries beginning at the end of the year. The Aztec A was soon replaced, however, by the more modern-looking Aztec B with a lengthened nose (providing greater baggage space) and modified instrumentation. The Aztec C of 1964 had a revised landing gear system and IO-540-C4B5 engines in nacelles of revised shape, and further improvements were brought in with the Aztec D. Like the other Aztecs other than the Aztec A, which was a five-seater, the Aztec D was a six-seater with accommodation on two pairs of individual seats and a bench seat at the rear of the cabin, and was available in a number of models depending on instrumentation, equipment and finish. And like its predecessors, it was also available in Turbo Aztec form, with turbocharged engines able to provide full power up to an altitude of about 20,000 ft (6100 m).

The Aztec E was also available in a multitude of forms, but additionally introduced a nose lengthened by 1 ft 0 in (0.305 m) to provide yet more baggage volume, extra internal features such as inertia-reel shoulder harness for the front seats, and automatic flight capability. In 1976 there appeared the Aztec F, with a considerable number of improvements: a reduction in control forces, interconnection of the flaps and tailplane, more advanced instrumentation, better brakes, a more effective fuel system and a restyled cabin. The Aztec F is available in four basic forms: Custom, the basic model: Sportsman, with an external power socket and de luxe interior; Professional, as for the Sportsman but with pneumatic de-icing for the wings and tail, and electrical de-icing of the propellers; and Turbo, as for the other variants apart from the provision of TIO-540-C1A engines with AiResearch turbocharging, which

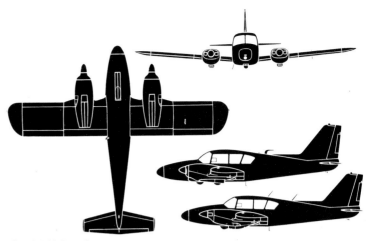

Piper PA-23 Aztec D

enables the engines to maintain their rated power up to 22,000 ft (6705 m). The Aztec is still in production, more than 5,000 of this important light aviation workhorse having been delivered. The specification applies to the PA-23-250 Custom Aztec F.

Specification
Type: six-seat light transport
Powerplant: two 250-hp (186.5-kW) Lycoming IO-540-C4B5 flat-six piston engines
Performance: maximum level speed 215 mph (346 km/h); normal cruising speed 210 mph (338 km/h) at 4,000 ft (1220 m); initial climb rate 1,400 ft (426 m) per minute;

absolute ceiling 18,950 ft (5775 m); range with maximum fuel at long-range cruising speed of 172 mph (278 km/h) at 10,200 ft (3110 m) 1,519 miles (2445 km)
Weights: empty 3,221 lb (1461 kg); maximum take-off 5,200 lb (2359 kg)
Dimensions: span 37 ft 2½ in (11.34 m); length 31 ft 2¾ in (9.52 m); height 10 ft 4 in (3.15 m); wing area 207.6 sq ft (19.28 m²)

The striking colour scheme of this Piper PA-23 Aztec operated by Lease Air somewhat obscures the fine lines of this popular business twin, one of the prolific Apache/Aztec series.

Piper PA-24 Comanche Series

History and Notes

With the PA-24 Comanche, Piper turned away from the traditional high-wing cabin monoplane design on which the company had made its name, introducing a relatively high-performance four-seat, low-wing all-metal aircraft with retractable landing gear and a 180-hp (134-kW) Avco Lycoming O-360-A1A engine. The prototype was first flown on 24 May 1956 and production began to flow from the Lock Haven lines in October 1957. The Comanche 180 was offered in Standard, Custom and Super Custom versions, according to equipment standard, and the Autoflite Comanche 180 was the Super Custom aircraft with addition of the AutoControl two-directional control automatic flight system. A full triple-axis Piper Altimatic, auto-pilot was offered as an optional extra. Between 24 and 26 November 1959, in a standard Comanche 180 with additional tankage to bring the total to 370 US gallons (1,400 litres), the late Max Conrad set a world distance record of 6,976 miles (11227 km) by flying non-stop from Casablanca in Morocco to El Paso, Texas in 56 hours 26 minutes.

Piper later introduced the Comanche 250, fitted with a 250-hp (186-kW) Avco Lycoming O-540-A1A5 engine and with standard fuel capacity raised from 50 to 60 US gallons (189 to 227 litres). FAA Type Approval was received on 7 March 1958. The Comanche 250 was superseded in August 1958 by the Comanche 260, with a 260-hp (194-kW) Avco Lycoming IO-540 engine and revised landing gear. With the addition of the engine cowling developed for the Twin Comanche, and a number of interior and equipment enhancements, Piper introduced the PA-24-260 Comanche C in June 1969, also available in turbocharged form from May 1970 as the Turbo Comanche C.

The most powerful of the Comanches, the Model 400, flew as a prototype in March 1961, and received FAA Type Approval on 28 January 1964. Some structural changes were made to allow operation at increased gross weight and higher speeds, resulting from the installation of a 400-hp (298-kW) Avco Lycoming IO-720-A1A engine. Standard fuel capacity was raised to 100 US gallons (379 litres) and a new tail unit with all-moving horizontal surfaces was fitted. A Comanche 400 was flown experimentally as an engine test-bed, fitted with a Garrett TPE331 turboprop engine, rated at 605 shp (451 kW). Piloted by Mr J. T. Womack, on 15 May 1968 it established a world altitude record of 41,320 ft (12594 m) for aircraft in Class C-1-c Group II.

The British pilot Miss Sheila Scott used a standard Comanche 260B, modified only by the installation of two additional 65-US gallon (246-litre) fuel tanks in the cabin, to set a Class 3 round-the-world record, flown between 18 May and 20 June 1966 and covering 29,055 miles (46759 km). The specification applies to the PA-24-260B Comanche B.

Specification
Type: four-seat light monoplane
Powerplant: one 260-hp (194-kW) Avco Lycoming IO-540 flat-six piston engine
Performance: maximum speed 194 mph (312 km/h) at sea level; maximum cruising speed 182 mph (293 km/h) at 7,000 ft (2135 m); service ceiling 20,000 ft (6100 m); range at maximum cruising speed with standard fuel 712 miles (1162 km)
Weights: empty 1,728 lb (784 kg); maximum take-off 3,100 lb (1406 kg)
Dimensions: span 35 ft 11¾ in (10.97 m); length 25 ft 0 in (7.62 m); height 7 ft 6 in (2.29 m); wing area 178 sq ft (16.54 m²)

Piper PA-28 Cherokee Series

History and Notes

The Piper Cherokee was developed as a replacement for the PA-22 Tri-Pacer, as a low-cost all-metal four-seater engineered with the minimum number of parts to facilitate economical volume production. The prototype flew on 14 January 1960, and the first production aircraft on 10 February 1961. Initial production versions were the PA-28-150 with a 150-hp (112-kW) Lycoming O-320-A2A engine, the PA-28-160 with a 160-hp (119-kW) O-320-D2A, and the PA-28-180 with a 180-hp (134-kW) O-360-A2A. They were offered in Standard, Custom, Super Custom and Autoflite models, with variations in equipment. The 1,000th Cherokee was delivered on 24 January 1963.

In August 1963 Piper announced the Cherokee 235, structurally strengthened to take the 235-hp (175-kW) Avco Lycoming O-540-B2B5 engine. An additional fuel tank in each wingtip increased total capacity from 50 to 84 US gallons (189 to 318 litres), at the same time resulting in a 2 ft (0.61 m) increase in wing span. A feature of the Cherokee 235, first flown on 9 May 1962 and FAA type-approved on 16 June 1963, was its ability to carry a payload greater than its own empty weight.

Just as the Tri-Pacer had been produced in two-seat trainer form as the PA-22-108 Colt, so the Cherokee was built as a two-seater, designated PA-28-140 and powered by a 140-hp (104-kW) Avco Lycoming O-320-A2B engine. Its type certificate, in the FAA Utility category, was awarded on 14 February 1964, and in the autumn of the following year Piper

announced the Cherokee 140-4, convertible into a full four-seater with an Avco Lycoming O-320 uprated to 150 hp (112 kW). From March 1971 Piper delivered a low-cost, limited option two-seat trainer, the Cherokee Flite Liner, for the company-sponsored Flite Center flying schools. In 1972 the Cherokee 140-4 was replaced by the very similar Cherokee Cruiser 2 Plus 2 which became simply Cherokee Cruiser in 1974. The specification applies to the PA-28 Cherokee 180.

Specification
Type: two/four-seat light monoplane
Powerplant: one 150-hp (112-kW) Avco Lycoming O-320 flat-four piston engine
Performance: maximum speed 144 mph (232 km/h) at sea level; cruising speed 135 mph (217 km/h) at 7,000 ft (2135 m); service ceiling 14,900 ft (4540 m); range with standard fuel at 7,000 ft (2135 m) 535 miles (861 km)
Weights: empty 1,250 lb (567 kg);

A popular series thanks to its sturdiness and low price, the Piper PA-28 Cherokee family has been produced to a number in excess of 20,000 by the parent company and licensees in Argentina and Brazil.

maximum take-off 2,150 lb (975 kg)
Dimensions: span 30 ft 0 in (9.14 m); length 23 ft 6 in (7.16 m); height 7 ft 3½ in (2.22 m); wing area 160 sq ft (14.86 m²)

Piper PA-28 Cherokee Warrior/Warrior II

History and Notes

On 26 October 1973 Piper announced that its 1974 range would include the PA-28-151 Cherokee Warrior, to be powered by a 150-hp (112-kW) Avco Lycoming O-320-E3D engine, and combining the longer fuselage of the Cherokee Challenger/Archer with a new long-span wing. Marking a departure from standard Piper practice by abandoning the constant-chord planform, the new wing introduced taper on the outer panels, and its value was to improve performance in a number of areas, principally in that of maximum take-off weight which was 175 lb (79 kg) greater than that of the similarly-powered Cherokee Cruiser. Design began in June 1972 and the prototype flew on 17 October in that year, followed by FAA certification on 9 August 1973. Minor improvements introduced in 1976 included a new cabin door with modifications to the latching mechanism, and in the basic structure to achieve a reduction in cabin noise. On 27 August 1976, Piper flew the first example of the PA-28-161 Warrior II with a 160-hp (119-kW) Avco Lycoming O-320-D3G engine using 100-octane low-lead fuel. It superseded the original Warrior in 1977. The specification applies to the PA-28-161 Warrior II.

Specification
Type: four-seat light monoplane
Powerplant: one 160-hp (119-kW) Avco Lycoming O-320-D3G flat-four piston engine
Performance: maximum speed 140 mph (225 km/h) at sea level; cruising speed 135 mph (217 km/h) at 9,000 ft (2745 m); service ceiling 13,000 ft (3960 m); range at 9,000 ft (2745 m) 651 miles (1048 km)

Weights: empty 1,336 lb (606 kg); maximum take-off 2,325 lb (1055 kg)
Dimensions: span 35 ft 0 in (10.67 m); length 23 ft 9½ in (7.25 m); height 7 ft 3½ in (2.22 m); wing area 170 sq ft (15.79 m²)

The Piper PA-28 Warrior II is typical of the company's policy of producing four-seaters of limited cost and adequate performance. The basic aircraft has fixed landing gear and a 160-hp (119-kW) engine, but there are eight optional electronics packages for the two main versions. These latter are the Custom Warrior II standard aircraft, and the Executive Warrior II with superior interior finish and equipment.

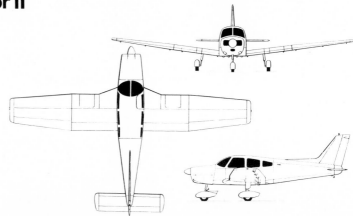

Piper PA-28 Warrior II

Piper PA-28 Cherokee Archer/Archer II

History and Notes

A replacement for the Cherokee 180 was announced by Piper in October 1972, and was originally known as the Cherokee Challenger. The fuselage was lengthened to provide more room in the cabin, the greater length requiring compensation in the form of a larger all-moving tailplane. The wings were also increased in span by 2 ft (0.61 m), which produced a 6 per cent increase in wing area and allowed the useful load to be increased. New and aerodynamically-efficient glass-fibre wingtips were also added. The Challenger became the PA-28-180 Archer in 1974 and in 1976 the PA-28-181 Archer II was introduced, fitted with the tapered wing developed for the Cherokee Warrior. The specification applies to the PA-28-181 Archer II.

Specification

Type: four-seat light monoplane
Powerplant: one 180-hp (134-kW) Avco Lycoming O-360-A4M flat-four piston engine
Performance: maximum speed 147 mph (237 km/h) at sea level; cruising speed 142 mph (229 km/h) at 9,000 ft (2745 m); service ceiling 13,650 ft (4160 m); range at 9,000 ft (2745 m) 645 miles (1038 km)
Weights: empty 1,416 lb (642 kg); maximum take-off 2,550 lb (1157 kg)
Dimensions: span 35 ft 0 in (10.67 m); length 23 ft 9½ in (7.25 m); height 7 ft 3½ in (2.22 m); wing area 170 sq ft (15.79 m²)

In 1974 the Piper Cherokee Challenger was replaced by the Cherokee Archer, which introduced many detail refinements. In 1976 it became the Cherokee Archer II.

Piper PA-28-235 Pathfinder/PA-28-236 and PA-28-201T Dakota Series

History and Notes

Announced in October 1973 as a replacement for the Cherokee 235, the Piper PA-28-235 Cherokee Pathfinder incorporated the airframe and interior enhancements introduced the previous year in the Cherokee Challenger. The fuselage was increased in length by 5 in (0.13 m) to provide more room in the cabin; wider cabin doors were fitted, including increased window area, and this eased access to the rear seats, the occupants of which enjoyed a 50 per cent increase in leg-room. New aerodynamically-efficent glassfibre wingtips were fitted and wing span was increased by 2 ft (0.61 m) to accommodate additional fuel tanks which raised total usable capacity from 48 to 82 US gallons (182 to 310 litres). To compensate for the longer fuselage, larger, all-moving horizontal tail surfaces were fitted, and to ease servicing of the 235-hp (175-kW) Avco Lycoming O-540-B4B5 engine a new easily-removable two-piece glassfibre cowling was introduced, incorporating a landing light located directly beneath the spinner. After Piper production had ended, Pathfinders continued to be manufactured under licence in Brazil as the EMBRAER EMB-710C Carioca. The Brazilian line closed in 1979 after 264 had been built.

In 1978 Piper introduced the PA-28-236 Dakota, which combined the fuselage of the PA-28 Archer/Arrow line with the increased-span tapered wing that had been a feature of the PA-28 Warrior of 1973. Powerplant comprised a 235-hp (175-kW) Avco Lycoming O-540 engine, and increased capacity fuel tanks were incorporated in the wings to cater for this more powerful engine. In the same way that the Pathfinder was superseded by the Dakota in the USA, EMBRAER in Brazil planned to replace the EMB-710C by an EMB-710D that is essentially the same as the Dakota. The Turbo Dakota, introduced in the following year, is not directly derived from the Dakota, but from the Cherokee Arrow, and this is reflected by the PA-28-201T designation. Its powerplant is a 200-

The Piper Dakota is a member of the Warrior, Archer and Arrow family, but has a more powerful engine for better performance, and greater fuel capacity to maintain range.

hp (149-kW) Continental TSIO-360-FB turbocharged engine.

All three PA-28s described were available with different packages of optional equipment, those for the currently-produced Dakota and Turbo Dakota marketed as Custom and Executive packages. But despite the permutations of wing and fuselage, and the confusion of names, all of these PA-28s are four-seaters. The details that follow apply to the PA-28-236 Dakota.

Specification
Type: four-seat cabin monoplane **Powerplant:** one 235-hp (175-kW) Avco Lycoming O-540-J3A5D flat-six piston engine **Performance:** maximum speed 170 mph (274 km/h) at sea level; cruising speed 166 mph (267 km/h) at optimum altitude; service ceiling 17,500 ft (5335 m); range at economic cruising speed 933 miles (1502 km) at optimum altitude **Weights:** empty 1,602 lb (727 kg); maximum take-off 3,000 lb (1361 kg) **Dimensions:** span 35 ft 0 in (10.67 m); length 24 ft 8¾ in (7.54 m); height 7 ft 2 in (2.18 m); wing area 170 sq ft (15.79 m²)

Piper PA-28R Cherokee Arrow Series

History and Notes
A retractable landing gear version of the Cherokee 180 was announced on 19 June 1967, to be known as the PA-28-180R Cherokee Arrow. Structurally similar to the fixed-gear aircraft, it was fitted with a fuel-injection 180-hp (134-kW) Avco Lycoming IO-360 engine, with a constant-speed propeller as standard, and also introduced a third cabin window on each side. As an accident-prevention device, Piper provided an automatic gear extension system, actuated by a probe located in the propeller slipstream, to lower the landing gear in the event of airspeed dropping below 105 mph (169 km/h) with power reduced. A free-fall extension system was also incor-

porated. The changes resulted in an approximate increase of 16 per cent in maximum cruising speed and 10 per cent in range.

A later model, the PA-28-200 Cherokee Arrow 200, was powered by a 200-hp (149-kW) Avco Lycoming IO-360-C1C engine; this was retained in the Cherokee Arrow II, which incorporated the longer fuselage originally introduced with the Cherokee Challenger in October 1972. The tapered wing of the Cherokee Archer II was fitted to the Arrow II fuselage to produce the PA-28R-201 Arrow III, which was flown as a prototype on 16 September 1975, and followed by the first production example on 7 January 1977. The first production turbocharged Turbo

Arrow III had flown on 1 December 1976. Both models were provided with increased usable fuel capacity, totalling 72 US gallons (273 litres). Latest Arrow model, introduced in 1979, is the PA-28-201RT Arrow IV with an all-moving tailplane mounted at the top of the fin, complemented by the Turbo Arrow IV with a turbocharged 200-hp (149-kW) Continental TSIO-360-F engine. The specification applies to the PA-28R-201 Arrow III.

Specification
Type: four-seat light monoplane **Powerplant:** one 200-hp (149-kW) Avco Lycoming IO-360-C1C flat-four piston engine

Performance: maximum speed 175 mph (282 km/h) at sea level; cruising speed at optimum altitude 175 mph (282 km/h); service ceiling 16,200 ft (4940 m); range at optimum altitude 1,047 miles (1685 m) **Weights:** empty 1,622 lb (736 kg); maximum take-off 2,750 lb (1247 kg) **Dimensions:** span 35 ft 0 in (10.67 m); length 25 ft 0 in (7.62 m); height 8 ft 0 in (2.44 m); wing area 170 sq ft (15.79 m²)

Piper PA-30/PA-39 Twin Comanche Series

History and Notes
The buoyant market for four/five-seat private aircraft prompted Piper to believe that there could be a worthwhile demand for a twin-engined aircraft in this category. On the credit side of any decision to go ahead were the factors that twin engines would offer better performance, and safety, since the aircraft would be operable with full load on the power of only one engine. On the debit side were higher capital and operating costs, plus the complexity for a private pilot of flying a multi-engine aircraft. Subsequent consideration suggested that this latter factor would probably have considerable sales value, presenting a challenge to a competent private pilot who, in many cases, would have a single-engine aircraft to trade in.

The decision was made to launch the twin-engined PA-23 Apache, with two 150-hp (112-kW) engines, and the company discovered very quickly that it had made the correct decision. Several models of the PA-23 were built before the introduction in 1963 of a much superior replacement, the PA-30 Twin Comanche, the prototype of which had flown for the first time on 7 November 1962. A cantilever low-wing monoplane of all metal construction, the PA-30 was provided with retractable tricycle landing gear, and was powered by two 160-hp (119-kW) flat-four engines. Accommodation, which was heated and ventilated, had four seats as standard, but could optionally have two additional seats.

As has become standard practice with Piper aircraft, there was a

basic Twin Comanche, plus Custom, and Sportsman versions which included additional factory-installed equipment. In any event, the basic model was very well equipped, and a wide range of optional avionics and equipment was available to meet individual requirements. Shortly after launching the Twin Comanche, the company announced the introduction of a generally similar Turbo Twin Comanche powered by turbocharged engines to offer improved performance.

This is not to suggest that any of the Twin Comanches were lacking in capability, as pointedly demonstrated by the late Max Conrad. During 24-26 December 1964, he flew a Twin Comanche non-stop from Cape Town, South Africa to St Petersburg, Florida, a distance of 7,878.26 miles

(12678.83 km) to establish a new world distance record in the FAI's Class C-1-e.

The PA-30 series of Twin Comanches remained in production until 1970, by which time 2,000 had been produced. In that year it was superseded by an improved PA-39 Twin Comanche C/R which introduced new engines with counter-rotating propellers. Advantages claimed for such a powerplant installation included the elimination of many trim adjustments during the various stages of flight; equal performance from either engine in the event of one engine failing and improved flight characteristics. As with the earlier PA-30s, the PA-39 C/Rs were available in Standard, Custom, and Sportsman versions, and there was also a Turbo Twin Comanche C/R. Production ended in 1972 when 144 had been built, the type being superseded by new and improved developments. The details which follow apply to the PA-39 Twin Comanche C/R.

Specification
Type: four/six-seat cabin monoplane **Powerplant:** two 160-hp (119-kW) Avco Lycoming IO-320-B1A flat-four piston engines **Performance:** maximum level speed 205 mph (330 km/h) at sea level; cruising speed 198 mph (319 km/h); economic cruising speed 188 mph (303 km/h); service ceiling 20,000 ft (6100 m); range with standard fuel, at economic cruising speed 1,110 miles (1786 km) **Weights:** empty 2,270 lb (1030 kg); maximum take-off 3,600 lb (1633 kg) **Dimensions:** span 36 ft 0 in (10.97 m); length 25 ft 2 in (7.67 m); height 8 ft 3 in (2.51 m); wing area 178 sq ft (16.54 m²)

The Twin Comanche series is based structurally on the Comanche series. The PA-30 initial model was supplanted in 1970 by the PA-39 with counter-rotating propellers. Both models were available in Turbo form with Rajay turbochargers.

The Piper PA-28R Turbo Arrow IV is the latest member of the family descended from the Archer series but fitted with retractable landing gear. The Arrow IV introduces a T-tail and other updatings.

Piper PA-31 Navajo/Chieftain Series

History and Notes

Piper's PA-31-350 Chieftain, first announced on 11 September 1972, was developed from a very much earlier and successful series of aircraft, the PA-31 Navajo introduced in 1964. The Navajo was described as the first of a planned new range of corporate/commuter aircraft that, with six/eight-seat accommodation, were a little larger than anything the company had produced previously. Clearly, Piper appreciated the buoyant market that existed for this category of aircraft but was, in fact, following a line that had been exploited rather earlier by Beech Aircraft Corporation.

The Navajo has proved a most successful aeroplane, and versions that have been developed in addition to the basic model include the Turbo Navajo with turbocharged engines, the Navajo C/R with counter-rotating propellers, and the Pressurised Navajo. This last variant had limited appeal and was discontinued in 1977. In 1981 the basic Navajo continues in production, now having turbocharged engines as standard, and is complemented by the Navajo C/R.

When first introduced, the derivation of the Chieftain from the Navajo was apparent to all, because it was called the Navajo Chieftain: since that time the qualifying Navajo has been dropped. The Chieftain combines a more powerful version of the turbocharged counter-rotating engines of the Navajo C/R, with a fuselage which has been lengthened by 2 ft 0 in (0.61 m). Additionally, the Chieftain has a strengthened floor so that, without seating installed, it can serve as a cargo carrier.

Of low-wing cantilever monoplane configuration, this all-metal aircraft has electrically actuated trailing-edge flaps, hydraulically actuated tricycle landing gear, and is available with a six-seat Standard, or 10-seat Commuter interior. The installed equipment is comprehensive, and an extensive range of optional avionics includes a flight director system/autopilot, and weather radar.

Specification

Type: six/ten-seat corporate/commuter/cargo aircraft
Powerplant: two 350-hp (261-kW) Avco Lycoming TIO/LTIO-540-J2BD flat-six piston engines
Performance: maximum level speed 266 mph (428 km/h); maximum cruising speed 254 mph (409 km/h) at 20,000 ft (6100 m); economic cruising speed 199 mph (320 km/h) at 12,000 ft (3660 m); service ceiling 27,200 ft (8290 m); range with maximum fuel, allowances and 45-min reserves 1,094 miles (1761 km)
Weights: empty 4,221 lb (1915 kg);

Piper Navajo of Chaparral Airlines, USA.

maximum take-off 7,000 lb (3175 kg)
Dimensions: span 40 ft 8 in (12.40 m); length 34 ft 7½ in (10.55 m); height 13 ft 0 in (3.96 m); wing area 229 sq ft (21.27 m²)

The Piper PA-31 Navajo C/R is basically similar to the standard Navajo apart from having, in common with many other modern light twins, counter-rotating engines to mitigate torque problems at high power settings. Seven passengers can be accommodated in corporate or commuter interiors, and the versatility of the type is enhanced by the availability of optional co-pilot instrumentation and de-icing equipment, plus avionics.

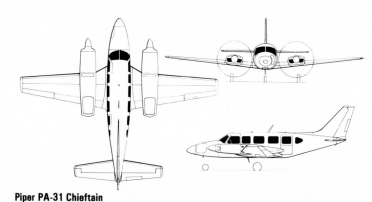

Piper PA-31 Chieftain

Piper PA-31T Cheyenne I/II

History and Notes

Similar in general configuration to the Navajo family from which it was developed, the prototype of the Piper PA-31T Cheyenne was flown for the first time on 20 August 1969. The letter T suffix in the company designation denoted that this aircraft had a turboprop powerplant and the Cheyenne, as it came to be named, was the first Piper aircraft to benefit from turbine power. It shared the fail-safe pressurised fuselage structure that had been developed for the Pressurised Navajo, with six/eight-seat accommodation, and to give this aircraft increased range the standard fuel system was supplemented by

permanently attached wingtip tanks. The introduction of a lower-cost model of this aircraft in 1978 led to designation changes, the new aircraft becoming PA-31T-1 Cheyenne I, the original version retaining the company designation of PA-31T, but with its name changed, oddly, to Cheyenne II.

The reduced cost of the Cheyenne I comes from the installation of lower-powered Pratt & Whitney Aircraft of Canada PT6A-11 turboprop engines, and less extensive standard installed equipment. This is, of course, obtainable optionally if required by individual customers. Standard and Executive interior

options are available for both aircraft, these including cabin equipment as well as seating. In addition to the standard passenger-carrying Cheyenne II, Piper has developed also a version that is suitable for such roles as airways calibration, geological survey, map making, maritime reconnaissance, and other special missions. This has the designation Maritime Surveillance Cheyenne II. The description which follows applies to the standard Cheyenne II.

Specification

Type: six/eight-seat executive transport
Powerplant: two 620-ehp (462-

ekW) Pratt & Whitney Aircraft of Canada PT6A-28 turboprops
Performance: cruising speed 325 mph (523 km/h) at 11,000 ft (3355 m); cruising speed 287 mph (462 km/h) at 29,000 ft (8840 m); service ceiling 31,600 ft (9630 m); range at long-range power with maximum fuel, allowances and 45-min reserves 1,737 miles (2795 km) at 29,000 ft (8840 m)
Weights: empty 4,980 lb (2259 kg); maximum take-off 9,000 lb (4082 kg)
Dimensions: span over wingtip tanks 42 ft 8¼ in (13.01 m); length 34 ft 8 in (10.57 m); height 12 ft 9 in (3.89 m); wing area 229 sq ft (21.27 m²)

Piper PA-32 Cherokee SIX/Cherokee Lance/Saratoga Series

History and Notes

The Piper PA-32-301 Saratoga, which entered production in late 1979, represents the latest member of a family of single-engine six/seven-seat aircraft that stretches back to the Cherokee SIX, of which the prototype flew for the first time on 6 December 1963. Deliveries of the original Cherokee SIX began during 1965, and this initial member of the series had accommodation for only six passengers, but the improved version that was produced from late 1966 could have an optional seventh seat installed.

The Cherokee SIX was generally similar in configuration to the two/four-seat PA-28 Cherokees, but had increased dimensions and a more powerful engine to cater for the extra passengers. A cantilever low-wing monoplane of all-metal construction, it had non-retractable tricycle landing gear, and was available with a 260-hp (194-kW) Avco Lycoming O-540-E flat-six engine as standard, but could be powered optionally by a 300-hp (224-kW) IO-540-K. These two versions were designated respectively PA-32-260 and PA-32-300. Throughout its production period, the Cherokee SIX gained from steady improvement of detail, and was available with a variety of optional equipment and avionics packages. Its seats could be removed easily to accommodate

cargo, or a stretcher and one or two attendants, and options included a three-axis auto pilot, and an air-conditioning system.

In 1974, the Cherokee SIX was complemented by the introduction of the PA-32R-300 Cherokee Lance. Generally similar to its predecessor, it introduced a new fuselage, retractable tricycle landing gear, and had the 300-hp (224-kW) engine as standard. In 1978 the conventional unit of the Lance was replaced by a T-tail, the aircraft then becoming redesignated PA-32RT-300 Lance II, and it was available also with a turbocharged engine as the PA-32RT-300T Turbo Lance II.

At the end of 1979, however, both the Cherokee SIX and the Lance II/Turbo Lance II were replaced by a new PA-32-301 Saratoga and PA-32-301T Turbo Saratoga, both with non-retractable tricycle landing gear, and a reversion to the conventional tail unit; plus the PA-32R-301 Saratoa SP and PA-32R-201T Turbo Saratoga SP with hydraulically retractable tricycle gear. All four versions introduce a new tapered wing of increased span, and in addition to changed landing gear, the Turbo Saratoga SP can be equipped with an optional factory installed de-icing package. All of the Saratogas are extensively equipped as standard, and have a wide range of optional avionics and equipment to suit the

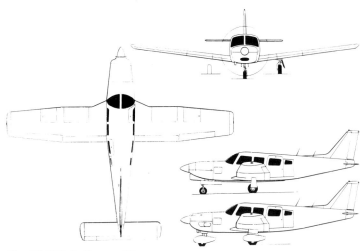

Piper PA-32 Turbo Saratoga SP

requirements of individual owners. The details which follow apply to the Saratoga SP with standard two-blade propeller.

Specification

Type: six/seven-seat cabin monoplane
Powerplant: one 300-hp (224-kW) Avco Lycoming IO-540-K1G5D flat-six piston engine
Performance: maximum level speed 189 mph (304 km/h);

cruising speed 183 mph (295 km/h) at optimum altitude; economic cruising speed 162 mph (261 km/h) at optimum altitude; service ceiling 16,700 ft (5090 m); range with maximum fuel, allowances and 45-min reserves 1,132 miles (1822 km)
Weights: empty 1,986 lb (901 kg); maximum take-off 3,600 lb (1633 kg)
Dimensions: span 36 ft 2 in (11.02 m); length 28 ft 4 in (8.64 m); height 9 ft 6 in (2.90 m); wing area 178.3 sq ft (16.56 m²)

Piper PA-34 Seneca II

History and Notes

Piper first announced in September 1971 the availability of a new light aircraft which had the designation PA-34 Seneca. It introduced twin-engined power to what was basically a Cherokee SIX airframe, an installation that had been tried out on a Cherokee SIX in 1965 as part of the company's continuous research and development programme. During the experiment, the Cherokee was flown with two additional wing-mounted Avco Lycoming engines, and on some occasions had been tested with all three engines operating. In the case of the Seneca the new engines were counter-rotating, and the non-retractable tricycle landing gear was replaced by hydraulically retractable units generally similar to the incorporated in the Cherokee Lance in 1974.

In 1975 some significant modifications were made to the Seneca, leading to the II suffix in the designation of the PA-34. Most important new feature was a switch from normally-aspirated to turbocharged engines, these being installed in newly-designed low-drag nacelles. Other alterations included strengthened landing gear to cater for operation at a higher gross weight, and detail changes in flying controls to improve the low-speed handling characteristics.

The Seneca II is available with special equipment packages under the name of Executive and Sportsman, plus a number of factory-installed avionics packages. As with most Piper aircraft, there is also an impressive list of both avionics and equipment to meet the special requirements of individual owners and operators.

The Piper PA-34 Seneca III is the latest model of this low-priced seven-seat light twin-engined transport, available in Executive and Sportsman models.

Specifications

Type: six/seven-seat cabin monoplane
Powerplant: two 200-hp (149-kW) Continental TSIO-360-E flat-four piston engines.
Performance: maximum level speed 225 mph (362 km/h) at 12,000 ft (3660 m); maximum cruising speed 219 mph (352 km/h) at 20,000 ft (6100 m); economic cruising speed 190 mph (306 km/h) at 25,000 ft (7620 m); service ceiling 25,000 ft (7620 m); range with maximum standard and optional fuel, allowances, and 45-min reserves 1,019 miles (1640 km) at 20,000 ft (6100 m)
Weights: empty 2,841 lb (1289 kg); maximum take-off 4,570 lb (2073 kg)
Dimensions: span 38 ft 10¾ in

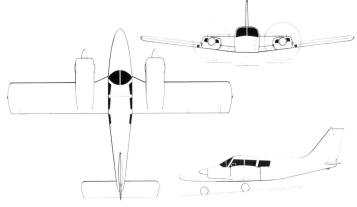

Piper PA-34 Seneca II

(11.86 m); length 28 ft 7½ in (8.72 m); height 9 ft 10¾ in

(3.02 m); wing area 208.7 sq ft (19.39 m²)

Piper PA-38 Tomahawk

History and Notes

During the late 1970s, Piper began design and development of a new two-seat lightweight cabin monoplane that was intended primarily to serve in a training role, but which would be suitable also for a variety of utility purposes that could be fulfilled by a small two-seater. Its design combined typical Piper light-alloy constructional techniques with a fuselage that was wide enough to provide comfortable seating for a pupil and instructor, in the side-by-side arrangement that is regarded as ideal for *ab initio* training.

With training considered to be the main role of this aircraft, design concentration was on such features as visibility and handling, both in the air and on the ground. Thus, excellent all-round view is afforded to both pupil and instructor by the provision of a large windscreen and even larger rear window which, together with good side windows, are combined in a high-strength roll-over support structure. Ailerons extend to semi-span, the other half of each wing trailing-edge being occupied by manually actuated flaps. The landing gear, which is of fixed tricycle type, incorporates very wide-track main legs to simplify ground handling of this attractive aircraft. Well equipped in basic form for both utility and elementary training, there is also available a special optional package that provides suitable equipment and avionics to enhance the training capability.

A measure of Piper's success in the design of the Tomahawk is indicated by sales of more than 1,000 aircraft within 12 months of certification gained on 20 December 1977.

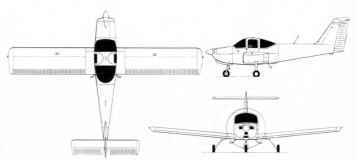

Piper PA-38 Tomahawk

Specification

Type: two-seat trainer/utility aircraft
Powerplant: one 112-hp (84-kW) Avco Lycoming O-235-L2C flat-four piston engine
Performance: maximum level speed 126 mph (203 km/h) at sea level; cruising speed 115 mph (185 km/h) at 10,500 ft (3200 m); service ceiling 13,000 ft (3960 m); optimum range with maximum fuel, allowances and 45-min reserves 539 miles (867 km)
Weights: empty 1,108 lb (503 kg); maximum take-off 1,670 lb (757 kg)
Dimensions: span 34 ft 0 in (10.36 m); length 23 ft 1¼ in (7.04 m); height 9 ft 0¾ in (2.76 m); wing area 124.7 sq ft (11.58 m²)

The Piper PA-38 Tomahawk was introduced in 1978 as a side-by-side trainer with a wide-track landing gear for good ground stability, and excellent fields of vision from the extensively glazed cockpit. Seen here is the Tomahawk II.

Piper PA-42 Cheyenne III

History and Notes

Introduced on 26 September 1977, the PA-42 designation of this third member of the Piper Cheyenne family is sufficient to suggest that fairly comprehensive changes have been made from the Cheyenne II from which it is derived. This is indeed the case, for the excellent performance of the Cheyenne II left Piper in little doubt that this aircraft could be developed to serve as an economical corporate/commuter aircraft if the capacity was increased.

To achieve this aim, the fuselage has been extended by 8 ft 8¾ in (2.66 m) to provide accommodation for a crew of two and up to nine passengers. To cater for the increased gross weight, the wing span and area have been increased, more powerful engines installed, and a T-tail introduced to improve handling characteristics.

The Cheyenne III is available with the same standard and optional equipment as the Cheyenne II, except that a de-icing package which is optional for this latter aircraft, is incorporated as standard equipment on the Cheyenne III.

Piper PA-42 Cheyenne III.

Specification

Type: six/eleven-seat corporate/commuter transport
Powerplant: two 720-shp (537-kW) Pratt & Whitney Aircraft of Canada PT6A-41 turboprops
Performance: maximum level speed 336 mph (541 km/h); cruising speed 333 mph (536 km/h) at 21,000 ft (6400 m); cruising speed 311 mph (501 km/h) at 33,000 ft (10060 m); service ceiling 33,000 ft (10060 m); range at long-range power with maximum fuel, allowances and 45-min reserves 2,347 miles (3777 km) at 33,000 ft (10060 m)
Weights: empty 6,240 lb (2830 kg); maximum take-off 11,000 lb (4990 kg)
Dimensions: span over wingtip tanks 47 ft 8 in (14.53 m); length 43 ft 4¾ in (13.23 m); height 14 ft 9 in (4.50 m); wing area 293 sq ft (27.22 m²)

The most advanced aircraft yet produced by Piper, the PA-42 Cheyenne III is an 11-seat corporate or commuter transport. It differs from the Cheyenne I and II in having extended-span wings, a longer fuselage, a T-tail, more powerful Pratt & Whitney Aircraft of Canada PT6A turboprops and a number of other improvements. A wide variety of avionics and interior furnishings are available.

Piper PA-44 Seminole

History and Notes

In May 1976 Piper flew the prototype of a new twin-engined light aircraft, the PA-44-180 Seminole, first announced in February 1978 soon after successfully completing its certification programme. It had been designed specifically to provide an economically-priced four-seat lightweight cabin monoplane that provided the benefits of twin-engined power. Yet it can become, if desired, a sophisticated aircraft if equipped with optional factory-installed equipment packages. In addition, available avionics offer a permutation of navigation/communication systems that can include automatic direction finders, distance-measuring equipment, encoding and radar altimeters, glideslope and marked beacon receivers, horizontal situation indicators, area navigation, and transponders.

Of low-wing cantilever monoplane configuration, the all-metal Seminole has plain ailerons, manually actuated trailing-edge flaps, a T-tail, hydraulically retractable tricycle landing gear, and the counter-rotating engines which are now used on the major proportion of the company's twin-engined aircraft. A turbocharged version, the PA-44-180T Turbo Seminole, was introduced in the spring of 1980. This has engines of the same power as the Seminole, but because it has a certificated ceiling of 20,000 ft (6100 m), has provision for the installation of an optional oxygen system to

permit of more efficient high-altitude operation if and when desired. The details that follow apply to the Turbo Seminole.

Specification

Type: four-seat cabin monoplane
Powerplant: two 180-hp (134-kW) Avco Lycoming TO/LTO-360-E1 flat-four piston engines
Performance: maximum level speed 224 mph (360 km/h) at optimum altitude; maximum cruising speed 210 mph (338 km/h) at optimum altitude; cruising speed 192 mph (309 km/h) at 10,000 ft (3050 m); certificated ceiling 20,000 ft (6100 m); range with maximum fuel, allowances and 45-min reserves 943 miles (1518 km)
Weights: empty 2,435 lb (1104 kg); maximum take-off 3,925 lb (1780 kg)

The Piper PA-44 Seminole is a lightweight four-seat twin, and is also available in the Turbo-Seminole form illustrated for operators wanting better high-altitude performance. The engines are counter-rotating to improve controllability at high power settings.

Dimensions: span 38 ft 7 in (11.76 m); length 27 ft 6¼ in (8.39 m); height 8 ft 6 in (2.59 m); wing area 180 sq ft (16.72 m²)

Piper Aerostar 600/601/601P Series

History and Notes

In 1967 a new company, known as the Ted Smith Aerostar Company, began limited production of the first two of what was intended to be a series of light transport aircraft. They were of very clean design, and the company claimed that the constructional method chosen for these aircraft meant that, by comparison with similar-sized models from other manufacturers, almost 50 per cent fewer components were involved. This was achieved by the extensive use of monocoque construction and, for example, the wing was a simplified structure comprising only the spars, a few bulkheads and stringers, with heavy gauge skins carrying much of the load.

But despite excellent design, there was a great deal of competition from large manufacturers in the particular

market in which the Aerostar Company was looking for customers. By 1970 the assets had been acquired by Butler Aviation International and, soon after this, production was suspended. In 1972 Ted R. Smith and Associates re-acquired the business, putting the Models 600 and 601 back into production. A pressurised Model 601P was also developed and certificated in late 1972, but less than six years later, in March 1978, the Piper Aircraft Corporation acquired all the assets and liabilities of what had become the Ted Smith Aerostar Corporation.

Under the overall control of Piper, within what is known as the company's Santa Maria Division, production of the Aerostars continues in 1981. The basic version is the Model 600, with two 290-hp (216-kW) Avco Lycoming IO-540-K1J5 engines;

the Model 601 has increased wing span and similarly powered turbocharged engines; and the Model 601P is very similar except that it incorporates cabin pressurisation. All three have an extensive range of equipment as standard, and a wide range of optional avionics equipment is available to meet the personal requirements of individual customers.

These mid-wing monoplane Aerostars offer luxurious travel for a pilot and five passengers, or crew of two and four passengers, and represent a distinctive expansion of the Piper product line.

Specification

Type: twin-engined light transport
Powerplant (Model 610P): two 290-hp (216-kW) Avco Lycoming IO-540-S1A5 flat-six piston engines with high capacity turbochargers

Performance: cruising speed 296 mph (476 km/h) at 25,000 ft (7620 m); economic cruising speed 231 mph (372 km/h) at 15,000 ft (4570 m); service ceiling 25,000 ft (7620 m); maximum range with maximum fuel, allowances and 45-min reserves 1,375 miles (2213 km) at 20,000 ft (6100 m)
Weights: empty 4,056 lb (1840 kg); maximum take-off 6,000 lb (2722 kg)
Dimensions: span (600) 34 ft 2 in (10.41 m), (601/601P) 36 ft 8 in (11.18 m); length 34 ft 9¾ in (10.61 m); height 12 ft 1½ in (3.70 m); wing area (600) 170 sq ft (15.79 m²), (601/601P) 178 sq ft (16.54 m²)

The Aerostar 600 series was developed by the Ted Smith Aerostar Corporation before its acquisition by Piper in 1978. Seen here is the basic Model 600A.

Pitts Model S-2S

History and Notes
Curtis Pitts is well known as one of the US designers responsible for the development of new high-performance light aircraft. Immediately after World War II he became active in this field, later designing and building aerobatic biplanes for such internationally known aerobatic display pilots as Caro Bailey, Joyce Case, and Betty Skelton. Following the successes gained in national- and world-class aerobatic contests from 1966 to date, these small high-performance biplanes have become known to enthusiasts of every nation. Many of them have been homebuilt from the detailed construction drawings which have been marketed for some years.

Two-seat Pitts S-2As equipped the British aerobatic display team, which was financed originally by the Rothman Tobacco Company, and the Carling Black Label team which operated in Canada. The superb demonstrations given by these teams had a worldwide impact, creating wider interest in Pitts designs, and leading to the single-seat S-2S which

the Pitts Aerobatics Company put into production in late 1978. The S-2A is available only as a production aircraft, but the S-2S is available also in kit form so that it can be built by amateurs if you so wish.

The design varies little from one model to another, the principal differences being concerned with powerplant, single- or two-seat capacity, open or enclosed cockpit, and built on the production line or by an enthusiastic amateur. All share a very similar biplane configuration and fixed tailwheel type landing gear. What is impressive is the superb finish imparted by many of the homebuilders: it makes it almost impossible to judge between production or homebuilt, and if you guess the odds are that you will be wrong. The Model S-2S is powered by a 260-hp (194-kW) Avco Lycoming AEIO-540-D4A5 flat-six piston engine, giving it a top speed of 181 mph (291 km/h). No other details of this version were available in early 1981, so those which follow apply to the single-seat S-1S Special.

Specification
Type: single-seat sporting biplane
Powerplant: one 180-hp 9134-kW) Avco Lycoming IO-360-B4A flat-four piston engine
Performance: maximum level speed 176 mph (283 km/h) at sea level; cruising speed at sea level 141 mph (227 km/h); service ceiling 22,300 ft (6795 m); range 315 miles (507 km)

The Pitts S-2S single-seat aerobatic biplane is one of the ultimates in flying, but suitable only for good pilots.

Weights: empty 720 lb (327 kg); maximum take-off 1,150 lb (522 kg)
Dimensions: span 17 ft 4 in (5.28 m); length 15 ft 5½ in (4.71 m); height 6 ft 3½ in (1.92 m); wing area 98.5 sq ft (9.15 m²)

Procaer F15 Picchio

History and Notes
In the late 1950s Dott. Ing. Stelio Frati designed a number of attractive light aircraft that were subsequently built and marketed by different companies. Examples include the Falco and Nibbio by Aviamilano and Aeromare, and the F.250/SF.260 series, the latter currently in production as a very successful military trainer by SIAI-Marchetti.

The Procaer F15 Picchio (Woodpecker) was a typical example of Frati's style, and the prototype flew in May 1959. It was a three-seater fully aerobatic, of wooden construction with a thin aluminium outer skin. An initial production series of five was built with 160-hp (119-kW) Avco Lycoming engines, and these were followed by 10 F15As with 180-

hp (134-kW) Avco Lycomings and four seats.

The F15B, of which 20 were built, was generally similar but featured an increased wing area; production of the F15B ended in September 1961 and things slowed down somewhat at Procaer: the next variant, the F15C, did not appear until 1964. It had a 260-hp (194-kW) Continental engine and demonstrated longer range than its predecessors, but only two were built, converted from F15B airframes.

A proposed variant, the F15D with a 250-hp 9186-kW) turbocharged Franklin 6AS-350 engine, remained a project only, but an F15E was flown on 15 December 1968 with a 300-hp (224-kW) Continental IO-520-F. This was an all-metal version of

the F15C, the prototype being acquired for a while by Ambrosini who proposed to build it under the title NF15. But by 1971, when the type had been certificated, ownership had reverted to Procaer.

In 1970, Stelio Frati established his own company, General Avia, and eventually built and flew a prototype of the F15F Delfino (Dolphin) with a 200-hp (149-kW) Avco Lycoming IO-360-A. Intended as a basic trainer, it had a bubble canopy and no tip tanks, and first flew on 20 October 1977; Procaer was to undertake manufacture of the first batch, but no production examples had been registered by 1980. A brochure on the Picchio issued by Procaer in that year claimed that 72 had been manufactured, but constructor's num-

bers up to 39 and the prototype F15F are all that can be traced. The specification applies to the F15E.

Specification
Type: four-seat light monoplane
Powerplant: one 300-hp (244-kW) Continental IO-520-F flat-six piston engine
Performance: maximum speed 200 mph (322 km/h); cruising speed 190 mph (306 km/h); service ceiling 17,390 ft (5300 m); range 994 miles (1600 km)
Weights: empty 1,856 lb (842 kg); maximum take-off 3,000 lb (1360 kg)
Dimensions: span 32 ft 5¾ in (9.90 m); length 24 ft 7¼ in (7.50 m); height 9 ft 2½ in (2.80 m); wing area 143.2 sq ft (13.30 m²)

Rhein-Flugzeugbau RS 180 Sportsman

History and Notes
Rhein-Flugzeugbau, known more usually as RFB, was founded in 1956. In 1976 this company acquired the assets and liabilities of Sportavia-Pützer, which had been formed 10 years earlier to take over from Alpavia SA the manufacture of a series of lightplanes designed by René Fournier. Production began soon afterwards and in late 1970 René Fournier started the design of a new four-seat cabin monoplane which was given the name Sportsman. This flew in its original prototype form on 1 March 1973, but the

second prototype, which did not fly until 28 April 1976, was a completely redesigned aircraft designed by Sportavia. This had the designation RF6C Sportsman when it entered production in late 1976, being redesignated RS 180 Sportsman when a new tail-unit layout was adopted in early 1978.

The Sportsman, which has a basic structure of wood, is of low-wing cantilever monoplane configuration. All surfaces have a GRP outer skin, which gives this aircraft a beautiful external finish to match very clean lines. Landing gear is of the non-

retractable tricycle type, with wheel speed fairings as standard, and the roomy four-seat accommodation is enhanced by a large transparent bubble canopy.

At the end of 1980, Sportavia-Pützer was integrated into the RFB organisation, the RS 180 being redesignated RFB RS 180 Sportsman, and in early 1981 its production was temporarily suspended.

Specification
Type: four-seat cabin monoplane
Powerplant: one 180-hp (134-kW) Avco Lycoming O-360-A3A flat-four piston engine
Performance: cruising speed 140 mph (225 km/h) at 8,500 ft (2590 m); service ceiling 17,715 ft (5400 m); range with maximum fuel 864 miles (1390 km)
Weights: empty 1,411 lb (640 kg); maximum take-off 2,425 lb (1,100 kg)
Dimensions: span 34 ft 5½ in (10.50 m); length 223 ft 5½ in (7.15 m); height 8 ft 4½ in (2.55 m); wing area 156.08 sq ft (14.50 m²)

Robin DR.400

History and Notes
Avions Pierre Robin was formed in 1957 as Centre Est Aéronautique at Dijon, changing its name in 1969 to the present title. The company manufactured a series of light aircraft based on the original Jodel designs and in 1967 flew its first design with tricycle landing gear, the four-seat DR.253 Regent with a 180-hp (134-kW) Avco Lycoming O-360-A2A engine.

The Regent was followed by a series of broadly similar designs: the DR.315 Cadet with a 115-hp (86-kW) Avco Lycoming O-235; DR.330 with a 130-hp (97-kW) Rolls-Royce Continental O-240-A; DR.340 Major with

a 140/150-hp (104/112-kW) Avco Lycoming O-320-E; DR.360 Chevalier with a 160-hp (119-kW) Avco Lycoming O-320-D; and DR.380 Prince, with a 180-hp (134-kW) Avco Lycoming O-360-D. All were basically of wooden structure and led eventually to a new series, the DR.400, prototype construction of which began in 1971.

First of the new series to fly, in May 1972, was the DR.400/125 Petit Prince with a 125-hp (93-kW) Avco Lycoming O-235-F2B, a three/four-seater certificated in December 1972. In the same month the DR.400/180 Regent was flown; this was the most powerful of the series with a 180-hp

(134-kW) Avco Lycoming O-360-A, and was a replacement for the DR.253 and DR.380. In June the DR.400/160 Chevalier flew, its 160-hp (119-kW) Avco Lycoming O-320-D making it a DR.360 replacement.

The remaining three new models also appeared in 1972: the DR.400/140 Major with a 140-hp (104-kW) Avco Lycoming O-320-E in October, the DR.400/180R Remorqueur glider-tug with a 180-hp (134-kW) Avco Lycoming O-360-A in November, and the smallest of the range, the DR.400/2+2 with a 180-hp (134-kW) Avco Lycoming O-235-C20 in December. This was a two-seater with two extra small seats for children. All six

of the new series featured a canopy which slid forward over the engine cowling to give access to the cabin in place of the hinged canopies of earlier versions. Lower cabin walls gave easier access and also improved visibility. By 1980, production of the DR.400/2+2 had ended; and the DR.400/120 Dauphin 80 with a 112-hp (84-kW) Avco Lycoming O-235-L2A engine had replaced the DR.400/120 Petit Prince, itself introduced in 1975. The remainder of the range still in production comprised the DR.400/160 Major 80, DR.400/180 Regent and DR.400/180R Remorqueur.

Total production of light aircraft

Robin DR.400

by Avions Robin at the beginning of 1981 stood at 2,350. The specification applies to the DR400/180.

Specification
Type: four/five-seat light monoplane
Powerplant: one 180-hp (134-kW) Avco Lycoming O-360-A flat-four piston engine
Performance: maximum speed 173 mph (278 km/h) at sea level; cruising speed 166 mph (267 km/h) at 8,000 ft (2440 m); service ceiling 15,475 ft (4715 m); range 900 miles (1448 km)
Weights: empty 1,322 lb (600 kg); maximum take-off 2,425 lb (1100 kg)

Dimensions: span 28 ft 7¼ in (8.72 m); length 22 ft 10 in (6.96 m); height 7 ft 3¾ in (2.23 m); wing area 152.8 sq ft (14.20 m²)

The Robin DR.400 series of French lightplanes has been produced in a number of forms to meet customer requirements, with the main differences in the powerplants. All models are notable for their forward-sliding one-piece canopies, and the low sides to the cabin walls.

Robin HR.100/R.1180 Series

History and Notes
When Avions Pierre Robin began to consider using an all-metal structure for its light aircraft range in the mid-1960s, this 'innovation' was evaluated on the prototype DR.253 Regent by building it with metal wings. It flew in this form on 3 April 1969 and was designated HR.100/180, the engine being a 180-hp (134-kW) Avco Lycoming O-360.

Three pre-production aircraft were built in 1970, while construction of the first definitive version, the HR.100/200 with a 200-hp (149-kW) Avco Lycoming IO-360 engine, began in January 1971. In this first batch of 31, deliveries were made to customers in Bangui, Belgium, France, Germany, Luxembourg, Switzerland and the UK. One of the prototypes, designated HR.100/320/4+2, was a six-seater, but standard production aircraft were four-seaters.

A disastrous fire in the Dijon factory in April 1972 destroyed 10 aircraft (c/ns 131 to 137 and 139 to 141). Aircraft from no. 142 onwards were completed as HR.100/210s, with 210-hp (157-kW) Continental engines. First flown in April 1971, the HR.100/210 was manufactured until February 1976, a total of 75 production aircraft

being built.

The need for a higher-power version with retractable landing gear led to substantial redesign of the airframe, the prototype HR.100/285 being flown in November 1972 with a 320-hp (239-kW) Teledyne Continental Tiara engine. Certification and initiation of production followed in July 1974, these aircraft having the 285-hp (213-kW) Tiara 6-285B engine and 15 being delivered to the SFACT at Montpelier for training. Construction of an alternative HR.100/250TR with the 250-hp (186-kW) Avco Lycoming IO-540 engine began in 1975, and the two versions were built on a common production line. A total of 57 HR.100s of the two types were built, including some HR.100/285Cs which had a slightly higher maximum take-off weight.

Following the HR.100 came the first of a new series, the R.1180 Aiglon, an all-metal four-seater with fixed tricycle landing gear, the prototype of which flew in 1976. The first production model was certificated in September 1978, and by the end of 1980 about 60 had been delivered, including 18 for French civil aviation training schools. The specification applies to the R.1180.

Specification
Type: four-seat light monoplane
Powerplant: one 180-hp (134-kW) Avco Lycoming O-360-A3 AD flat-four piston engine
Performance: maximum speed 156 mph (251 km/h) at sea level; cruising speed 146 mph (235 km/h); service ceiling 16,500 ft (5030 m); range 1,009 miles (1624 km)

Weights: empty 1,433 lb (650 kg); maximum take-off 2,535 lb (1150 kg)
Dimensions: span 29 ft 9½ in (9.08 m); length 23 ft 9¾ in (7.26 m); height 7 ft 9¾ in (2.38 m); wing area 162.5 sq ft (15.10 m²)

A typical four-seater of the Robin type, the R 1180 Aiglon was designed as a replacement for the HR 100/210 Safari II.

Robin HR.200/R.2000 Series

History and Notes
The requirement for a two-seat all metal aircraft for flying clubs and training schools prompted the Robin HR.200 series, whose prototype flew on 29 July 1971. The basic version was the HR.200/100 Club with a 108-hp (81-kW) Avco Lycoming O-235-H2C engine, but also offered were the HR.200/120 with a 125-hp (93-kW) Avco Lycoming O-235-J2A, the HR.200/140 with a 140-hp (104-kW) Avco Lycoming O-320-E, and the HR.200/160 with a 160-hp (119-kW) Avco Lycoming IO-320D. Deliveries began towards the end of 1973 and by February 1974 totalled 15.

As the design progressed a basic low-cost variant, the HR.200/100S, was introduced. This was generally similar to the HR.200/100, but had less equipment and no wheel fairings. The HR.200/120 was phased out in favour of the HR.200/120B with a 118-hp (88-kW) Avco Lycoming O-235-L2A. Production of the HR.200 series ended in 1976 after a total of 108 had been built, and a new range was introduced: the R.2000 series of two-seaters.

The prototype, designated R.2160, flew in September 1976, and the initial Robin range in this series covered three models: the R.2100A with a 108-hp (81-kW) Avco Lycoming O-235-H engine, and the R.2160 and

R.2160 Acrobin, both of which were powered by the 160-hp (119-kW) Avco Lycoming O-320-D. The new range was derived from the HR.200, using the basic fuselage and fin married to a new wing, and since it was intended that all variants would get aerobatic certification, there was a larger rudder and under-fuselage strake to aid spin recovery. An early customer was SFA, the French government flying training school, which ordered 17 Acrobins in the spring of 1978.

A new variant, the R.2112 Alpha with a 112-hp (84-kW) Avco Lycoming engine, was introduced in 1979, and by then the R.2160A Rafale with a 160-hp (119-kW) Avco Lycoming AEIO-320 engine had also been announced. However, by 1980 the series had become established with two variants only, the R.2112 Alpha and R.2160 Alpha Sport, this latter being the Rafale renamed. Deliveries by the end of that year had reached almost 100.

For the future, Robin is developing a new 3000 series with engines

The Robin R.2160 is essentially an aerobatic version of the HR 200. The cockpit is extremely spacious for a two-seater, and also notable are the long ventral spin-control strake and the large-area rudder.

between 100-180 hp (75-134 kW), a T-tail, and some with fixed and others with retractable landing gear. The specification applies to the R.2160.

Specification
Type: two-seat aerobatic monoplane
Powerplant: one 160-hp (119-kW) Avco Lycoming O-320-D flat-four piston engine
Performance: maximum speed 160 mph (257 km/h) at sea level; cruising speed 150 mph (241 km/h) at 7,500 ft (2285 m); service ceiling 15,000 ft (4570 m); range 495 miles (796 km)
Weights: empty 1,213 lb (550 kg); maximum take-off 1,764 lb (800 kg)
Dimensions: span 27 ft 4 in (8.33 m); length 23 ft 3½ in (7.10 m); Agusta A 109C (7.10 m); height 7 ft 0 in (2.13 m); wing area 140 sq ft (13.00 m²)

Rockwell 112/Alpine Commander Series

History and Notes
North American Aviation, famous for its World War II P-51 Mustang fighter, and for postwar designs such as the X-15 research aircraft and F-86 Sabre/F-100 Super Sabre turbojet fighters, merged in 1967 with the Rockwell Standard Corporation to form the North American Rockwell Corporation. General aviation was separated from the corporation's military aviation activities in the autumn of 1969 by the formation of a General Aviation Division with several components. One of the first new products of the Aero Commander division was the four-seat Model 112, whose design was initiated immediately after the division had been established. The first of five prototypes made its maiden flight on 4 December 1970. A cantilever low-wing monoplane of all-metal construction, the Model 112 had retractable tricycle landing gear, and its powerplant comprised a 180-hp (134-kW) flat-four engine. A leading point in the marketing of this aircraft was the internal accommodation, which the company claimed to be the most spacious of all four-

seat single-engined aircraft available worldwide.

In January 1974, almost 12 months after the company had been re-organised as Rockwell International Corporation, the Model 112 was upgraded to a 200-hp (149-kW) power-plant, given a higher gross weight, and detail improvements, under the designation Model 112A. Two years later two additional versions were made available: the Commander 112TC with a 210-hp (157-kW) turbocharged engine, and the Commander 114 with 260-hp (194-kW) normally aspirated engine. This latter aircraft was to initiate a separate line of development at a later date, and the original Commander 112 with normally aspirated engine disappeared, production becoming centred upon the turbocharged version which became available in three variants with differing standards of installed equipment. Finally, all variants were merged into an extensively equipped Alpine Commander, manufactured in this form and under this designation for about 12 months before production was ended during 1979.

Specification
Type: four-seat cabin monoplane
Powerplant: one 210-hp (157-kW) Avco Lycoming TO-360-C1A6D flat-four piston engine
Performance: maximum level speed 196 mph (315 km/h) at 20,000 ft (6100 m); maximum cruising speed 188 mph (303 km/h) at 20,000 ft (6100 m); certificated ceiling 20,000 ft (6100 m); range with maximum standard and optional fuel 1,038 miles (1670 km)

Of quite portly but nevertheless sleek lines, the Rockwell Alpine Commander was a fine example of the single-engine high-performance lightplane. But it could not break into the US market.

at 15,000 ft (4570 m)
Weights: empty 2,035 lb (923 kg); maximum take-off 2,950 lb (1338 kg)
Dimensions: span 35 ft 7¼ in (10.85 m); length 25 ft 0½ in (7.63 m); height 8 ft 5 in (2.57 m); wing area 163.8 sq ft (15.22 m²)

Rockwell 114/Gran Turismo Commander

History and Notes
In 1976 Rockwell International introduced a more powerful version of the Model 112. This, unlike the turbo-charged Model 112TC which had been announced simultaneously, had a normally aspirated engine that, by comparison with that of the standard Model 112, provided improved low-altitude performance, a higher rate of climb, and an increase of over 10 per cent in maximum take-off weight.

The Model 114, as this higher powered version was designated, was otherwise generally similar to the aircraft from which it derived and, in this slightly changed form, had only limited appeal. In 1978, therefore, it became known as the Gran Turismo Commander, introducing as standard a more extensive range of equipment in an attempt to attract an increased number of buyers prepared to pay more for a combination of high performance and a luxuriously appointed aircraft.

Sharing with the Alpine Com-

mander (formerly the Model 112TC) such features as electrically actuated wide-span single-slotted trailing-edge flaps, a constant-speed propeller, steerable nosewheel, hydraulic brakes, a heated and ventilated cabin, and windscreen defrosting, a Gran Turismo assured its owner of good handling characteristics both in the air and on the ground. It also had double pane windows and high-quality soundproofing to ensure a good cabin environment, dual controls and blind-flying instrumentation, and standard avionics included communications and navigation equipment, plus digital ADF and DME, and full autopilot.

Production of the Gran Turismo ended during 1979, at which time the company rationalised its product line with concentration on general aviation aircraft for which it was considered there would be a continuing steady demand, despite the recession then being experienced.

Specification
Type: four-seat cabin monoplane
Powerplant: one 260-hp (194-kW) Avco Lycoming IO-540-T3B5D flat-four piston engine
Performance: maximum level speed 191 mph (307 km/h) at sea level; maximum cruising speed 181 mph (291 km/h) at 7,000 ft (2135 m); service ceiling 16,500 ft (5030 m); optimum range with maximum fuel and 45-min reserves

The Rockwell 114 Gran Turismo Commander was the ultimate single-engined light-plane produced by the company.

813 miles (1308 km)
Weights: empty 2,070 lb (939 kg); maximum take-off 3,260 lb (1479 kg)
Dimensions: span 35 ft 7¼ in (10.85 m); length 25 ft 0½ in (7.63 m); height 8 ft 5 in (2.57 m); wing area 163.8 sq ft (15.22 m²)

Rockwell/Fuji Commander 700/710

History and Notes
In collaboration with Fuji Heavy Industries in Japan, Rockwell International's General Aviation Division was involved in the development of a twin-engined six/eight-seat light transport aircraft. Design began in Japan in 1971, the aircraft then having the designation FA-300, and on 28 June 1974, Fuji and Rockwell signed an agreement covering its development as a joint venture, with Rockwell designating the aircraft Commander 700 for marketing in North America.

Of cantilever low-wing monoplane configuration, the Commander 700 had a fuselage constructed for pressurisation, the tail unit being conventional with swept surfaces and the landing gear of retractable tricycle type. Powerplant comprised two Avco Lycoming turbocharged engines, these being wing-mounted in well streamlined nacelles. Standard accommodation was for a pilot and co-pilot plus four passengers, all in a pressurised, air-conditioned, heated and ventilated environment. The first of five prototypes made its

initial flight in Japan on 13 November 1975, and the second which was assembled by Rockwell, flew on 25 February 1976. Japanese JCAB certification was gained on 19 May 1977, and US FAA certification on 31 October 1977.

Development of a generally similar aircraft, designated Commander 710, was proceeding simultaneously. This differed mainly by the installation of more powerful (450-hp:335-kW) engines. The first of two prototypes was flown in Japan on 22 December 1976, and JCAB certification was gained in early 1979. Later in the year it was reported that development was being continued, the Model 710 then being flown with winglets installed at the wingtips.

Rockwell's decision in late 1979 to sell off its General Aviation Division to Gulfstream American Corporation resulted in terminating of the agreement with Fuji. At this time Rockwell had delivered 25 Commander 700s. The Japanese company now has worldwide manufacturing and marketing rights for these aircraft, but it is believed that if production is initiated

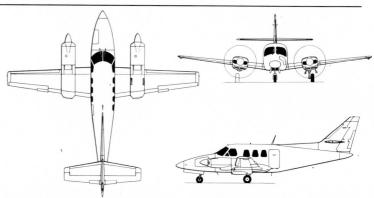

Rockwell Commander 700

it will be concentrated on the Model 710. The details that follow apply to the Commander 700.

Specification
Type: six/eight-seat light transport
Powerplant: two 340-hp (254-kW) Avco Lycoming TIO-549-R2AD flat-six piston engines
Performance: maximum level speed 254 mph (409 km/h) at weight of 6,350 lb (2880 kg) at

17,000 ft (5180 m); cruising speed 244 mph (393 km/h) at weight of 6,350 lb (2880 kg) at 21,500 ft (6555 m); service ceiling 27,400 ft (8350 m); maximum range with maximum fuel, allowances and 45-min reserves 1,384 miles (2227 km)
Weights: empty 4,704 lb (2134 kg); maximum take-off 6,947 lb (3151 kg)
Dimensions: span 42 ft 5½ in (12.94 m); length 39 ft 5¾ in (12.03 m); height 13 ft 3½ in (4.05 m); wing area 200.2 sq ft (18.60 m²)

Rockwell Darter Commander

History and Notes

The Aero Commander Darter Commander four-seat light aircraft started life as the Volaire Model 1050, a product of Volaircraft Corporation of Aliquippa, Pennsylvania, which produced the type in small numbers. Volaircraft was acquired by Rockwell Standard in July 1965, and production continued initially under the name Aero Commander 100.

The company had big plans for the 100, and hoped to build about 180 by the end of 1965, with at least 500 the following year. Although these figures were impressive the Aero Commander 100, with its 150-hp (112-kW) Lycoming engine, came into direct competition with the well-established Cessna range and Rockwell was unable to make a significant dent in the market.

Improvements were introduced from May 1968 when, in common with North American Rockwell's policy of using bird names, the 100 became the Darter Commander and 120 were sold during that year. But by that time the aircraft's shape was beginning to look dated, and following the lead already set by other general aviation manufacturers, the company cleaned up the design, incorporated a swept fin and rudder, and installed a 180-hp (134-kW) Avco Lycoming O-360-A2F engine. In this guise the aircraft became the Lark Commander, and first deliveries were made in April 1968; 62 were sold during the year, but only a few more were built before Rockwell decided to concentrate on development of its new Model 112.

Specification
Type: four-seat light monoplane
Powerplant: one 150-hp (112-kW) Lycoming O-320-A flat-four engine
Performance: maximum speed 133 mph (214 km/h); cruising speed 128 mph (206 km/h) at 7,500 ft (2285 m); service ceiling 13,000 ft (3960 m); range 510 miles (821 km)
Weights: empty 1,280 lb (581 kg); maximum take-off 2,250 lb (1021 kg)
Dimensions: span 35 ft 0 in (10.67 m); length 22 ft 6 in (6.86 m); height 9 ft 4 in (2.84 m); wing area 181 sq ft (16.81 m²)

Rockwell Lark Commander

History and Notes

A product of North American Rockwell's Aero Commander division, the Lark Commander was developed during 1967 with deliveries beginning in 1968. Derived from the Aero Commander Darter Commander it differed as a result of the company's intention to provide a basic sporting/training/business four-seat aircraft that, because of improved performance, would appeal to a far wider range of users than the sportsman and weekend private pilot.

To achieve this standard, the Lark Commander differed from the Darter Commander by introducing a more powerful engine, swept vertical tail surfaces that immediately 'modernised' its appearance, improved landing gear design to enhance operation from rough strips, the introduction of refinements to reduce drag, and the provision of a more luxurious interior.

A braced high-wing monoplane, with non-retractable tricycle landing gear, the Lark Commander was very much in the likeness of the Cessna Model 150, differing mainly by having a much more powerful engine. The Model 150 was, however, formidable competition, for in the year that the Lark Commander was being developed Cessna delivered its 10,000th Model 150. But North American Rockwell was also to introduce competition that hastened the demise of the Lark Commander, for production ended when deliveries of the cantilever low-wing Aero Commander Model 112 began in 1972.

Specification
Type: four-seat light cabin monoplane
Powerplant: one 180-hp (134-kW) Avco Lycoming O-360-A2F flat-four piston engine
Performance: maximum level speed 138 mph (222 km/h) at sea level; maximum cruising speed 132 mph (212 km/h) at 7,500 ft (2285 m); service ceiling 11,100 ft (3385 m); range with maximum fuel at 7,500 ft (2285 m) 560 miles (901 km)
Weights: empty 1,532 lb (695 kg); maximum take-off 2,475 lb (1123 kg)
Dimensions: span 35 ft 0 in (10.67 m); length 27 ft 2 in (8.28 m); height 10 ft 1 in (3.07 m); wing area 180 sq ft 916.72 m²)

Rockwell Shrike Commander/Turbo Commander 681/Turbo Commander 690/Commander 685 Series

History and Notes

In March 1969 North American Rockwell flew the prototype of a new member of the Commander family. Designated Turbo Commander 690, this derived from the earlier four/seven-seat Shrike Commander and Turbo Commander 681B. This latter aircraft differed from the Shrike Commander by substituting 605-eshp (451-ekW) Garrett TPE331-43BL turboprops for the Shrike's 290-hp (216-kW) Avco Lycoming IO-540-E1B5 piston engines, and simultaneously introducing cabin pressurisation, a reduction of almost 5 ft 0 in (1.52 m) in wing span, and an increase of 6 ft 4¾ in (1.95 m) in length to provide accommodation for six/nine persons. Following what was then the company's policy of allocating names to their products, it was known for a period as the Hawk Commander before being redesignated Turbo Commander 681B. The prototype first flew on 31 December 1964.

The prototype of the improved Turbo Commander 690 enjoyed the benefits derived from almost five years of experience with the Hawk/681, as well as from development that had been taking place over that same period. It was flown initially with 665-eshp (496-ekW) TPE331 turboprops, but production examples delivered after certification in July 1971 had more powerful engines. Other changes included an increase in wing span, the engines being mounted further outboard and driving larger-diameter propellers. Fuel capacity was increased, and new cabin layouts made it possible to accommodate between seven and 11 persons.

Two aircraft were developed from the Turbo Commander 690 during 1971. One was the Commander 685, which was generally similar except for the installation of 435-hp (324-kW) Continental GTSIO-520-F turbocharged piston engines. Although this powerplant reduced the high-altitude performance demonstrated by its predecessor, and restricted accommodation to a maximum of nine seats, the Model 685 had an optimum range of 1,766 miles (2842 km) compared with the Model 690's maximum of 1,567 miles (2522 km), and this was achieved with a fuel saving of 62 US gallons (234 litres). The second development was the Turbo Commander 690A, differing by having an increase in cabin pressure differential, which resulted in certification at a higher operational ceiling. There were also a number of system improvements introduced simultaneously.

Production of the Commander 685 ended during 1976, and of the final version of the Turbo Commander 690, the 690B, in 1979. The latter had left behind an altitude record that was still retained in FAI records in early 1981, that of 42,404.8 ft (12567.5 m) gained on 27 April 1978. The following details apply to the Turbo Commander 690B.

Specification
Type: 11-seat business aircraft
Powerplant: two 700-shp (522-kW) Garrett TPE331-5-251K turboprops.
Performance: maximum cruising speed 327 mph (526 km/h) at

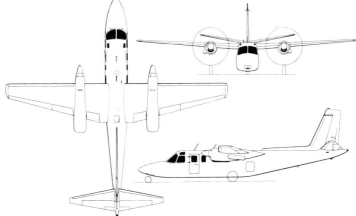

Rockwell Turbo Commander 690A

17,000 ft (5180 m); economic cruising speed 288 mph (463 km/h) at 31,000 ft (9450 m); service ceiling 32,800 ft (9995 m); maximum range with maximum fuel and 45-min reserves at 31,000 ft (9450 m) 1,689 miles (2718 km)
Weights: empty (Executive I) 6,733 lb (3054 kg); maximum take-off 10,325 lb (4683 kg)
Dimensions: span 46 ft 8 in (14.22 m); length 44 ft 4¼ in (13.52 m); height 14 ft 11¼ in (4.56 m); wing area 266.0 sq ft (24.71 m²)

Powered by a pair of 980-eshp (731-ekW) AiResearch TPE331-5-501 turboprops, the Jetprop 980 (illustrated) and its sister, the more luxurious Jetprop 1000, are the leaders in Rockwell's executive series.

Rockwell Sabreliner 40/60/75 Series

History and Notes

In the same way that Lockheed had developed the JetStar to meet USAF interest in a light jet-powered transport that would be available 'off-the-shelf', North American Aviation began the development of a similar aircraft in 1956. Named Sabreliner, the prototype flew for the first time on 16 September 1958.

Of low-wing monoplane configuration, with a pressurised fuselage, conventional tail unit, and retractable tricycle landing gear, the Sabreliner was powered initially by two General Electric J85 turbojets, one mounted on each side of the aft fuselage. The Sabreliner appealed to the USAF, which in October 1958 ordered two versions as T-39A and T-39B, both with Pratt & Whitney J60 turbojets. The US Navy also ordered two Sabreliners as T-39Ds, and later CT-39Es brought total military production to 200.

First of the civil versions to be produced were equivalents of the T-39A/B and D, but powered by the JT12A civil equivalent of the military J60 turbojet. These led to the exclusively civil model NA282 with 3,000-lb (1361-kg) thrust JT12A-6As, and thence to the Sabreliner Series 40 and Series 60, introduced in 1967. The Series 40, powered by 3,300-lb (1497-kg) thrust JT12A-8s, had accommodation for a crew of two and nine passengers; the Series 60 was generally similar except for a fuselage 'stretch' of 3 ft 2 in (0.97 m) to provide more comfortable accommodation for two crew plus 10 passengers. Earlier production Sabreliners could be modified retrospectively to Series 40 or 60 configuration.

These were followed by the Sabre (later Sabreliner) 75 first demonstrated in 1971. This had the same accommodation as the Series 60, in a fuselage that was 1 ft 2 in (0.51 m) shorter, and this latter factor necessitated an increase in fin and rudder area. The same powerplant was retained, but with an increase of 1,000 lb (454 kg) in maximum take-off weight, the main landing gear units were provided with twin wheels instead of a single wheel on each main unit. In 1973 the Sabre 75 was complemented, and later superseded, by the Sabre (later Sabreliner) 75A. This introduced more powerful General Electric CF700 turbofans, and airframe improvements included improved cabin furnishings and equipment, increased tailplane span, and new anti-skid and air-conditioning systems. The type became available in 1978 with a Raisbeck Mark Five improvement kit that provided improved performance and payload. However, production terminated in May 1979 after 72 had been built.

Specification

Type: twin-turbofan business transport
Powerplant: two 4,500-lb (2041-kg) thrust General Electric CF700-2D-2 turbofans
Performance: maximum cruising speed 563 mph (906 km/h); economical cruising speed 480 mph (772 km/h) at 40,000 ft (12190 m); certificated ceiling 45,000 ft (13715 m); maximum range with four passengers and 45-min reserves 1,972 miles (3174 km)
Weights: empty equipped 13,200 lb (5987 kg); maximum take-off 23,000 lb (10433 kg)
Dimensions: span 44 ft 8 in (13.61 m); length 47 ft 2 in (14.38 m); height 17 ft 3 in (5.26 m); wing area 342.05 sq ft (31.78 m²)

The Rockwell Sabreliner series has been evolved through a number of versions. Seen here is the Sabreliner 75, which is also available with the Mark Five System improvements developed by the Raisbeck Group, notably a supercritical wing.

Rockwell Sabre 75A cutaway drawing key

1 Radome
2 Radar scanner dish
3 Bendix RDR-1200 weather avoidance radar.
4 Nose structure
5 Electrical equipment compartment
6 Batteries
7 Avionics compartment (Collins flight director and autopilot)
8 Nosewheel well
9 Equipment access doors
10 Nosewheel door
11 Twin steerable nosewheels. Goodrich Type VII
12 Fuselage front bulkhead
13 Windscreen panels
14 Windscreen wipers
15 Instrument panel shroud
16 Back of instrument panel
17 Control linkages
18 Cockpit roof windows
19 Co-pilot's seat
20 Throttles
21 Control column
22 Opening side window
23 Pilot's seat
24 Lower VHF aerial
25 Flight deck bulkhead
26 Electrical equipment rack
27 Upper VHF aerial

28 Forward baggage and coat locker
29 Passenger door
30 Buffet and bar locker
31 Fuselage top longeron
32 Cabin roof structure
33 Fuselage main frames
34 Starboard escape hatch
35 Starboard integral wing fuel tank, capacity 452 US gal (1 710 l)
36 Leading edge slat segments
37 Leading edge de-icing
38 Starboard wingtip
39 Navigation light
40 Static dischargers
41 Starboard aileron
42 Aileron trim tab
43 Starboard flap
44 Cabin windows

45 Three-a-side seating
46 Folding table
47 Starboard engine intake
48 Starboard nacelle
49 Rear baggage and coat locker
50 Toilet compartment
51 Cabin rear bulkhead
52 Air system intake

Rockwell Sabreliner 75A.

53 Fuselage bladder fuel tank, capacity 199 US gal (753 l)
54 Air trunking
55 Air cycling and air conditioning plant
56 Auxiliary power unit
57 Fuel dump pipe
58 Fin root fairing
59 Fin spar fixing
60 Fin structure
61 Leading edge de-icing
62 Pressure and temperature sensors
63 Starboard tailplane
64 Starboard elevator
65 Fin VHF navigation aerial
66 Anti-collision light
67 Static dischargers
68 Rudder structure
69 Trim tab mechanism
70 Rudder trim tab
71 Tailcone
72 Fuel jettison
73 Port elevator
74 Elevator hinge connection

75 Port all-moving tailplane structure
76 Leading edge de-icing
77 Autopilot rudder servo control
78 Elevator controls
79 Tailplane interconnection
80 Autopilot tailplane servo control
81 Moving tailplane jack
82 Hydraulic pressure accumulator
83 Rear fuselage structure
84 Control cables
85 Hydraulic reservoir
86 Port jet efflux
87 Cascade-type vertically-orientated thrust reverser mechanism
88 Nacelle fireproof bulkhead
89 General Electric CF700-2D-2B engine
90 Aft fan casing
91 Engine gearbox and equipment

92 Rear engine mounting
93 Fan air duct
94 Front engine mounting
95 Core engine intake
96 Removable engine cowlings
97 Air intake
98 Engine pylon fairing
99 Wash hand basin
100 Fuselage skin panel
101 Cabin roof air and lighting duct
102 Cabin air distribution duct
103 Fire extinguisher
104 Flap electric motors
105 Seat rails
106 Port mainwheel well
107 Fuselage lower fairing

108 Port flap
109 Flap drive shaft
110 Flap control jack
111 Flap rails
112 Aileron controls
113 Port aileron
114 Aileron trim tab
115 Static dischargers
116 Port wing tip strakes
117 Navigation light
118 Fuel filler
119 Wing structure
120 Port wing fuel tank, capacity 452 US gal (1 710 l)
121 Fuel system pipes
122 Port main undercarriage leg
123 Twin mainwheels, Goodrich 10-ply tyres
124 Leading edge slat sections
125 Leading edge structure
126 Leading edge de-icing
127 Spar root fixing
128 Fuel pump
129 Centre box structure
130 Port escape hatch
131 Cabin floor structure
132 Fuel in inboard leading edge (part of main wing integral tank)
133 Handrail
134 Folding entry steps
135 Under fuselage airbrake
136 Twin airbrake jacks
137 Airbrake hinges

Saab Safari TS

History and Notes

The Saab Safari can trace its ancestry back to the BA-7 two-seat light aircraft designed by Björn Andreasson, and built by him in the USA in 1958. Malmö Flygindustri in Sweden took up the design and put it into production as the MFI-9 Junior, and MBB in Germany also produced it as the Bö 208 Junior. Both military and civil versions were produced in Sweden, while German production concentrated solely on the civil market; about 200 were built by MBB between April 1962 and October 1969, while Swedish production totalled 70.

Among the latter was two MFI-9B Mili-trainers for evaluation by the Swedish air force in 1964. As a result of the evaluation, an air force and army requirement was issued for two types of light aircraft, one as a pre-selection trainer and one for artillery spotting. These subsequently appeared as the MFI-15A and -15B respectively, the former with tricycle landing gear and the latter with a tailwheel. Flown in prototype form on 11 July 1969 with a 160-hp (119-kW) engine, the type was later re-engined with a 200-hp (149-kW) Avco Lycoming IO-360-A1B and put into production with tricycle landing gear; a tailwheel layout was available optionally.

By August 1978 about 250 had been built, civil versions being named Safari and military aircraft Supporter; in that month the Avco Lycoming engine was replaced by a turbocharged 210-hp (157-kW) Con-

tinental and the designation became Safari TS, the name Supporter being dropped. Six underwing hardpoints can carry a total of 1,540 lb (700 kg) of stores, which can include machine-gun pods, rockets, or anti-tank missiles, and the Safari can operate with optional float or ski landing gear.

Military users of the Safari/Supporter include Pakistan and Denmark. The specification applies to the Safari TS.

Specification

Type: two/three-seat light monoplane
Powerplant: one 210-hp (157-kW) Continental horizontally opposed piston engine
Performance (aerobatic category): maximum speed 163 mph (262 km/h) at sea level; cruising speed 160 mph (257 km/h) at 12,000 ft (3660 m); service ceiling 20,000 ft (6100 m)
Weights: (aerobatic category) empty 1,499 lb (680 kg); maximum take-off 1,984 lb (900 kg)
Dimensions: span 29 ft 0½ in (8.85 m); length 23 ft 3½ in (7.10 m); height 8 ft 6½ in (2.60 m); wing area 128.1 sq ft (11.90 m²)

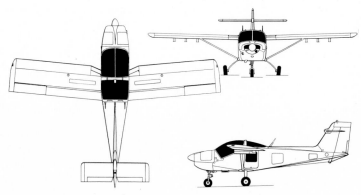

Saab Supporter/MFI 17

The Saab Safari has an almost futuristic appearance, thanks largely to its T-tail and swept-forward wings. A highly versatile aircraft, the Safari can accommodate a stretcher inside the cabin, or alternatively carry up to 661 lb (300 kg) of stores (famine relief, firefighting etc) on underwing racks.

Saab-Fairchild Model 340 Commuter

History and Notes

Saab-Scania of Sweden and Fairchild Industries in the USA announced in early 1980 their intention to develop a new turboprop-powered commuter aircraft. Following technical and market studies by the two companies, design emphasis is intended to optimise this aircraft for simple and economic operation, and one that will be able to be used without any need for airport ground-handling equipment. Advanced-technology turboprop engines are expected to offer new low fuel and operating costs, coupled with very quiet operation.

Drawings released in 1980 show that in its current design form the Model 340 is a cantilever low-wing monoplane with pronounced wing dihedral. The fail-safe pressurised fuselage is intended to accommodate a crew of three and up to 34 passengers, but it has been suggested that alternative interior layouts will be developed. The tail unit is quite conventional, and the retractable tricycle landing gear has twin wheels on each unit. Selected powerplant consists of two General Electric CT7 turboprops, mounted in streamlined nacelles on the leading-edge of each wing.

It is intended that final assembly will take place in Sweden, and if development proceeds as planned a first flight is scheduled for late 1982 or early 1983, with entry into service following during 1984.

Specification

Type: twin-turboprop commuter transport
Powerplant: two 1,650-shp (1230-kW) General Electric CT7 turboprops
Performance (estimated, ISA): maximum cruising speed 300 mph (483 km/h; range with maximum

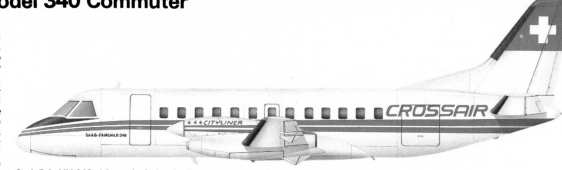

Saab-Fairchild 340 of Crossair, Switzerland.

payload and reserves 920 miles (1480 km)
Weights (estimated): empty operating 14,550 lb (6600 kg); maximum take-off 25,020 lb

(11350 kg)
Dimensions: span 70 ft 4 in (21.44 m); length 63 ft 9 in (19.43 m); height 21 ft 8¼ in (6.61 m²)

When Saab and Fairchild launched their SF-340 34-seat airliner, the order for five aircraft by the Swiss operator Crossair was one of the first two received.

Shorts Skyliner/Skyvan

History and Notes

The Shorts SC.7 Skyvan, which can trace its ancestry back to the Miles Aerovan of the immediate post-World War II years, was started as a private venture by Shorts in 1959, with construction of the prototype beginning in 1960. This Series 1 Skyvan (G-ASCN) flew for the first time on 17 January 1963, powered by two wing-mounted 390-hp (291-kW) Continental GTSIO-520 horizontally opposed piston engines.

From the outset it had been planned to build a comparatively low-cost aircraft of functional construction, and this was of braced high-wing monoplane configuration to ensure that the fuselage capacity was in no way restricted by the wing structure. The fuselage was of particular interest at that time, for while the forward curved-contour section that contained the flight deck was a conventional semi-monocoque, the main fuselage was of an experimental nature. This comprised double-skin panels, the square-section of the fuselage being maintained by light alloy frames; the unusual nature of these skin panels lay in their construction, with two light gauge sheets of light alloy (one flat, one corrugated in a special way) bonded together by Redux to form strong and rigid panels of extremely light weight. The curved rear bottom panel of the fuselage was hinged to serve as the loading door to the cargo hold, permitting direct in-loading of freight.

Although the protype had flown initially with Continental engines, it had been intended to power the type with Turboméca Astazou turboprops. When G-ASCN re-emerged from the works in May 1963 it had acquired two 520-eshp (388-ekW) Astazou II engines, resulting in the designation Series 1A. Later, in March 1965, this same aircraft appeared with a modified rear fuselage and tail unit, and two 666-eshp (497-ekW) Astazou X engines, and in this overall configuration it was close to the first true production aircraft which, with 730-eshp (544-ekW) Astazou XII turboprops, flew for the first time on 29 October 1965. Since that time Series 3 and 3A civil production versions have been built and are still available, plus a military version designated Series 3M. Current Series 3/3A/3M aircraft are powered by two 715-shp (533-kW) Garrett AiResearch TPE331-201 turboprops, and in passenger configuration the SC.7 has seats for 19 persons, plus a crew of one or two.

A special de-luxe all-passenger version was developed during 1969-70, and displayed publicly for the first time at the 1970 SBAC Air Show at Farnborough. While gener-

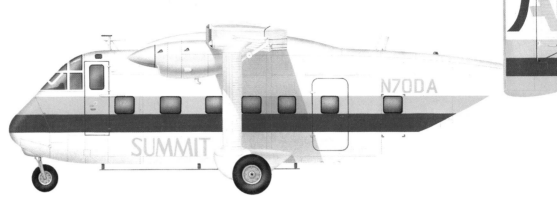

Shorts SC.7 Skyvan of Summit Airlines, USA.

ally similar to the passenger versions of the Skyvan, this Skyliner, as it was named, had a purpose-designed, more luxurious cabin interior for the same number of passengers, but incorporated overhead baggage lockers. A galley for buffet meals, toilet, and airstair door, are available as optional installations.

More than 130 Skyvans/Skyliners had been sold by mid-1980 and the type continues in production. The details below apply to the Skyvan Series 3.

Specification

Type: light utility transport
Powerplant: two 715-shp (533-kW) Garrett AiResearch TPE331-201 turboprops
Performance: maximum cruising speed 203 mph (327 km/h) at 10,000 ft (3050 m); economic cruising speed 173 mph (278 km/h) at 10,000 ft (3050 m); service ceiling 22,500 ft (6850 m); range at economic cruising speed, 45-min reserves 694 miles (1117 km)
Weights: operating empty 7,344 lb (331 kg); maximum take-off 12,500 lb (5670 kg)
Dimensions: span 64 ft 11 in (19.79 m); length 40 ft 1 in (12.22 m); height 15 ft 1 in (4.60

(4.60 m); wing area 373.0 sq ft (34.65 m²)
Operators include: Air Executive Norway A/S, Gulf Helicopters, Olympic Airways, Summit Airlines, Taiwan Airlines, and Wien Air Alaska

A good load-carrier with first-class STOL performance, thanks to the combination of a bulky fuselage with a highly efficient wing, the Shorts Skyvan has failed to attract really large orders because of its small size. Nevertheless, the type is in service with Olympic Aviation.

Shorts 330

History and Notes

In the early days of the Short SC.7 Skyvan, one of its first highly-enthusiastic supporters was to predict that in achieving such a practical, reliable aircraft that was easy to operate and maintain, and one which had a low initial cost, it could not fail to attract sales. He even predicted that Shorts might have to build well in excess of 1,000 examples.

With sales totalling between 130 and 140 aircraft in late 1980, some 14 years after the type first entered service, it seems unlikely that such an ambitious figure will ever be realised. What went wrong? So far as the basic aircraft was concerned,

the answer must be nothing at all. It has continued to operate reliably and economically, and operators of Skyvans, in whatever capacity, consider them to be a worthwhile investment. The key to the situation is really performance or size, the market for a 19-seat aircraft being somewhat limited in the performance category of the Skyvan. The 19/20-passenger Swearingen Metro, for example, which entered service in 1974 and has since sold almost 200 examples, has an economic cruising speed almost double that of the Skyvan.

Market research indicated to Shorts that an aircraft which retained the

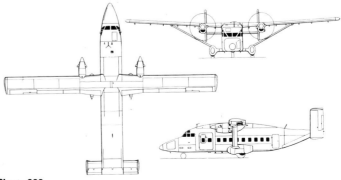

Shorts 330

same design philosophy, but offered seating capacity for about 30 passengers, would appeal to a wider field, so the company initiated the design of what is basically an improved and enlarged Skyvan. To cater for this increased capacity, and consequently a higher gross weight, the new design, which was known originally as the SD3-30, differs in several ways. Wing span is increased by 9 ft 9 in (2.97 m) by the introduction of a new wing centre-section, the former wings being retained with but little change as outer panels. The fuselage is of the same basic construction as that of the Skyvan, the size of the internal cross-section being only very slightly reduced by lining and soundproofing. The length, however, differs considerably, with a 'stretch' of 12 ft 5 in (3.78 m) making it possible to accommodate as standard 30 passengers with improved facilities. The non-retractable tricycle type landing gear of the Skyvan is replaced by a retractable system, the main units supported from short sponsons into which they retract, leaving only a small portion of the tyre of each wheel exposed.

The Garrett AiResearch TPE331s have been deleted from this version, the powerplant installation now comprising two Pratt & Whitney Aircraft of Canada PT6A-45B turboprops, these each having a maximum continuous rating of 1,020 shp (761 kW). Each drives a large-diameter low-speed five-blade propeller, and these contribute to low external and internal noise levels. Fuel capacity has been increased by about 63 per cent.

In addition to the basic 30-seat passenger configuration, a mixed passenger/freight interior is available, with a cabin divider to separate the forward freight hold from, typically, an 18-seat passenger cabin at the rear. A large cargo door is standard, located at the forward end of the cabin at the port side, and a passenger access door is at the rear of the cabin on the same side. This aircraft, which is now known as the Shorts 330, can also be operated in an all-cargo role, the cabin accommodating up to seven standard 'D' type containers. Uncontainerised freight can be secured to the seat rails by special attachments.

The first of two prototypes (G-BSBH) made its initial flight on 22 August 1974. Deliveries of early production aircraft were made in June 1976, and Time Air of Alberta, Canada, initiated the first revenue service with the type on 24 August 1976. Since that time, more than 70 Shorts 330s have been sold, and there seems every likelihood that the market prospects for this light transport are better than those of the Skyvan/ Skyliner.

A military SD3-M has been proposed, and this would be able to carry 32 troops, or cargo, and would be suitable also for such roles as casualty evacuation, search and rescue, and supply dropping. Another proposal is for a maritime patrol version designated SD3-MR Seeker. Much increased range would be provided by the installation of fuselage fuel tanks, offering an endurance of some 12 hours, and advanced communication, navigation and radar equipment could be accommodated easily in the large cabin, leaving adequate space for crew rest facilities.

The details below apply to the standard Shorts 330.

Shorts SD3-30 cutaway drawing key

1 Glass-fibre nose cone
2 Weather radar installation
3 Nose skin panelling
4 Forward baggage compartment, 45 cu ft/400 lb (1,27 m³/ 181 kg) max
5 Upward-hinged baggage door, 30·5 in × 37·7 in (77,5 cm × 95,8 cm)
6 VHF 2 aerial
7 Hydraulically steerable rearward-retracting nosewheel
8 Nosewheel fork
9 Nosewheel oleo
10 Nosewheel pivot point
11 Nosewheel box
12 Nosewheel retraction mechanism and jack
13 Undercarriage emergency actuation accumulator
14 Hydraulics bay
15 Rudder circuit linkage
16 Avionics bay (port and starboard)
17 23 Amp/hr batteries (port and starboard)
18 Seat adjustment lever
19 Seat belt
20 Heated pitot head
21 Underfloor avionics equipment
22 Elevator circuit linkage
23 Control column
24 Pilot's seat
25 Rudder pedals
26 Windscreen wipers
27 Windscreen panels (electrically heated)
28 Instrument panel coaming
29 Central control console (trim wheels)
30 Co-pilot's seat
31 Overhead panel (AC/DC power supply)
32 Fuel cocks
33 Crew escape/ditching hatch
34 Flight deck/cabin sliding door
35 Aileron circuit linkage
36 Control cable conduit (rudder and elevator trim circuits)
37 Flight deck conditioned/ heating/de-misting air supply

42 Heat exhanger
43 Air cycle installation
44 Engine bleed-air supply
45 Pre-cooler
46 Pre-cooler intake
47 Cabin conditioned/fresh air supply
48 Doorway-surround doubler plate
49 Cabin forward emergency exits, port 37 in × 24·5 in (94 cm × 62 cm); starboard 42 in × 27 in (107 cm × 68,6 cm)
50 Forward freight door, 65·6 in × 55·6 in (167 cm × 141 cm)
51 Freight door hinges
52 Honeycomb-sandwich floor panels
53 Corrugated inner skin
54 Cabin air distribution duct
55 Seat mounting rails
56 Rudder circuit
57 ADF sense aerials (port and starboard)
58 Rectangular fuselage section frames
59 Chemically-milled window panel
60 12-a-side cabin windows, 18·5 in × 14·4 in (74 cm × 36,6 cm)
61 Passenger accommodation: 30 seats, 3-abreast (single port/double starboard) arrangement
62 Engine bleed-air supply duct

38 Ambient-air intake
39 Combined VOR/ Localiser/ILS glide-slope aerials
40 Blow-in door (ground running)
41 Turbine-blower intake

63 Fuel tank mounting lugs
64 Forward multiple fuel tank (Cell 1)
65 Class II sealed tank dividing bulkhead
66 Fuel gravity filler

67 Forward multiple fuel tank (Cell 2)
68 Class I sealed tank dividing bulkhead
69 Forward multiple fuel tank (Cell 3)
70 Sealed containment area (tank seepage)
71 Tank/fuselage attachment
72 Wingroot fairing
73 Engine-propeller control cable runs

74 Hydraulics reservoir
75 Wing centre-section
76 Chemically-milled centre-section skinning
77 Dorsal anti-collision beac
78 Centre-section front spar
79 Leading-edge access pan
80 Oil coller
81 Engine firewall
82 Engine mounting ring
83 Exhaust ducts
84 Air intake duct (with debris deflector)
85 Propeller pitch-change mechanism
86 Hartzell constant-speed five-bladed auto-featherin propeller, 9 ft (2,75 m) diameter

Shorts 330

The Shorts 330 is having greater success than the smaller-capacity Skyvan. Apart from increased load, the 330 has been refined with a higher aspect ratio wing, semi-retractable landing gear and other improvements.

Specification

Type: light transport
Powerplant: two 1,156-shp (862-kW) Pratt & Whitney Aircraft of Canada PT6A-45B turboprops, each having a continuous rating of 1,020 shp (761 kW)
Performance: maximum cruising speed 219 mph (352 km/h) at 10,000 ft (3050 m); economic cruising speed 184 mph (296 km/h) at 10,000 ft (3050 m); range with 30 passengers, no reserves 500 miles (805 km); range with maximum fuel 872 miles (1403 km)
Weights: empty equipped 14,750 lb (6690 kg); maximum take-off 22,600 lb (10251 kg)
Dimensions: span 74 ft 8 in (22.79 m); length 58 ft 0½ in (17.69 m); height 16 ft 3 in (4.95 m); wing area 453.0 sq ft (42.08 m²)
Operators include: Air North, ALM Antillean Airways, Chautauqua Airlines, Command Airways, DLT, Golden West Airlines, Hawaiian Airlines, Henson Aviation, Loganair, Metro Airlines, Mississippi Valley Airlines, Royale Airlines, Surburban Airlines, and Time Air

Shorts 330 of Command Airways, USA.

200 Port landing/taxying lamp
201 Hydraulic ground service panel (fairing hinged aft section)
202 Wing outer-section front spar
203 End ribs
204 Outer/inner wing pin joints
205 Port inner flap section
206 Outrigged flap hinge arms
207 Aileron trim tab cables
208 Port centre flap section
209 Hinged trailing-edge (controls) access panels
210 Port outer flap section
211 Aileron control rods
212 Support strut box
213 Multi-angle section diffusion members
214 Pressed ribs
215 Corrugated inner skin panels
216 Aileron actuating rod
217 Cable-operated trim tab jack
218 Trim tab actuating rod
219 Aileron trim tab
220 Port aileron
221 Outer-section rear spar

222 Aileron mass-balance weights
223 Wing skin outer panelling
224 Outer-section front spar
225 Outer-section leading-edge spar
226 End rib structure/tip attachments
227 Glass-fibre port wing-tip fairing
228 Port navigation light

137 Rudder extension fairing
138 Static dischargers
139 Rudder trim tab
140 Starboard rudder
141 Trim tab actuating rod
142 Rear navigation light (starboard lower fin only)
143 Elevator trim tab
144 Trim tab actuating rod
145 Three-section elevator
146 Elevator actuation quadrant
147 Rudder control linkage

165 Baggage restraint net
166 Stepped aft baggage compartment, 100 cu ft/ 600 lb (2,83 m³/272 kg) max
167 Bulkhead
168 Doorway-surround doubler plate
169 Passenger entry door, 56·5 in × 28·4 in (143,5 cm × 72 cm)
170 Cabin electrics and communications panel
171 Buffet unit heated water container/cup stowage/ trash bin
172 Cabin attendant's tip-up seat (lowered)
173 Contoured inner window surrounds
174 Cabin seating rearmost row (port seat omitted for clarity)
175 Rudder circuit linkage
176 Damper strut
177 Flap actuating rod
178 Centre-section ribs
179 Centre-section front spar
180 Firewall/bulkhead
181 Engine support structure
182 Engine mounting ring (with four dynafocal resilient mounts)
183 Exhaust duct
184 Spinner
185 Intake lip electrical de-icing
186 Oil cooler intake scoop
187 Aft gearbox integral oil tank
188 Fuselage main frames (wing/undercarriage carrying)
189 Rudder circuit
190 Stub wing front and rear spars
191 Undercarriage mounting beam
192 Undercarriage retraction jack
193 Wing support strut attachment
194 Undercarriage pivot point
195 Undercarriage levered suspension leg
196 Port main landing-gear fairing
197 Retractable mainwheel
198 Shock-absorber strut
199 Port wing support strut

87 Propeller de-icing boots
88 Pratt and Whitney PT6A-45 turboprop engine
89 Oil filler cap
90 Outer/inner wing pin joints
91 Outer-section front spar
92 Outer wing support strut
93 Starboard landing/ taxying lamp
94 Support strut pin joints
95 Strut attachment bracket
96 Fluid de-iced leading-edge (tank and pump unit mounted at rear of starboard mainwheel well)
97 Starboard navigation light
98 Glass-fibre wing-tip fairing
99 Starboard aileron
100 Aileron trim tab
101 Aileron hinge rib
102 Support strut box
103 Flap hinge ribs
104 Starboard outer flap section
105 Starboard centre flap section

106 Centre-section end rib
107 Starboard inner flap section
108 Flap actuating rod mechanism (mounted on spar rear face)
109 Water-methanol tank and pump
110 Gravity fuel filler
111 Aft fuel tank (Cell 4)
112 Sealed containment area (tank seepage)
113 Tank/fuselage attachment
114 Elevator circuit
115 Cabin concealed ceiling lighting
116 Fuselage (detachable) top fairings
117 Overhead passenger hand-baggage lockers
118 Service door/emergency exit, 56·5 in × 28·4 in (143,5 cm × 72 cm)

119 Buffet unit storage compartment (sandwiches/ biscuits etc)
120 Cabin furnishing profile
121 Coat closet
122 Toilet compartment
123 VHF 1 aerial
124 Skin outer panelling
125 Corrugated inner skin panelling
126 HF sense aerial
127 Rudder/elevator circuits
128 Emergency locator antenna
129 Rectangular section aft frame
130 Tailplane spar pin joint strip
131 Tailplane structure
132 Rudder actuation lever
133 Rudder trim tab jack
134 Leading-edge de-icing fluid lines
135 Fin skin panels
136 Rudder aerodynamic balance

148 Elevator spring strut
149 Trim cable pulleys
150 Port tailplane spar pin joints
151 Fluid de-iced leading-edge
152 Fin structure
153 Rudder aerodynamic balance
154 Rudder extension fairing
155 Port rudder
156 Rudder trim tab
157 Rudder actuation lever fairing
158 Fin attachment access panels
159 Fin lower section
160 De-icing system access
161 Fluid de-iced leading-edge
162 Aft fuselage structure
163 Aft baggage door, 43 in × 57 in (109 cm × 145 cm)
164 Baggage door (open)

Shorts 360

History and Notes

In mid-1980, Short Brothers announced the intention to develop a 'stretched' version of the Shorts 330 (originally SD3-30) which, with more than 60 ordered at that time, was beginning to be regarded as a commercial success. However, the new Shorts 360, as it is to be known, represents rather more than a simple fuselage extension to accommodate an extra six passengers. The opportunity is being taken to introduce simultaneously more powerful and more economic engines, to replace the twin fins and rudders of the Shorts 330 by a new tail unit with single fin and rudder, and to provide more baggage space.

The 'stretch' involves the insertion of a 3 ft 0 in (0.91 m) plug in the fuselage forward of the wings, but the changed lines of the aft fuselage to accept the new tail unit have extended the internal length of the cabin by 5 ft 1 in (1.55 m), while the overall fuselage length is increased by 12 ft 5½ in (3.80 m). The result of

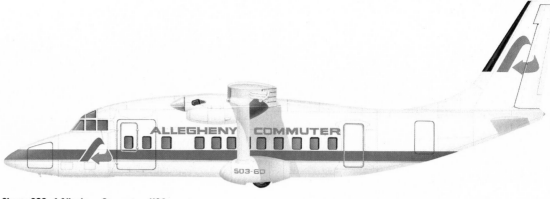

Shorts 360 of Allegheny Commuter, USA.

this is to transform the distinctive, but somewhat ugly ducking 330, into a far more graceful bird, although not all will agree that it can yet be called a swan.

A prototype was under construction in early 1981, with a first flight achieved in the early summer of the year, and initial entry into service expected towards the end of 1982.

Specification
Type: twin-turboprop commuter transport
Powerplant: two 1,294-shp (965-kW) Pratt & Whitney Aircraft of Canada PT6A-65R turboprops
Performance: (estimated) cruising speed 243 mph (391 km/h); range with maximum passengers and

reserves 265 miles (426 km) at 10,000 ft (3050 m)
Weights: (estimated) empty operating 16,490 lb (7480 kg); maximum take-off 25,700 lb (11657 kg)
Dimensions: span 74 ft 8 in (22.76 m); length 70 ft 6 in (21.49 m); height 22 ft 7 in (6.88 m); wing area 453.0 sq ft (42.08 m²)

Shorts Belfast

History and Notes

Short Brothers, which has the distinction of being a manufacturer of aircraft with a record that stretches back to 1909, was a well-known constructor of transport flying-boats during the 'between wars' years. World War II saw flying-boats supplanted increasingly by landplanes for the long-distance ocean flights which had once been the province of these sea-going aircraft.

Realising that this market was no longer available to them. Shorts began to investigate the prospect of breaking into the utility transport field. A number of projects were proposed, evaluated and rejected before, in February 1959, the company's design team began work on a large military transport under the identification Shorts SC.5/10. This was to become the RAF's Belfast C.Mk 1, able to carry the largest guided missiles, guns, and vehicles of the British Army and Royal Air Force, and convertible to carry from 150 to 250 troops. When the Belfast entered service, with No.53 Squadron on 20 January 1966, it was then the largest aircraft ever to have served with the RAF.

Of high-wing monoplane configuration, the Belfast had a circular-section pressurised fuselage, its main cargo hold having the maximum internal dimensions of 16 ft 1 in (4.90 m) in width and 13 ft 5 in (4.09 m) in height, and a usable volume of 11,000 cu ft (311.49 m³). To cater for heavy loads the retractable tricycle type landing gear had no fewer than 18 wheels: a nose unit with two wheels, and each main unit consisting of an eight-wheel bogie. The powerplant comprised four wing-mounted Rolls-Royce Tyne turboprops. First flown on 5 January 1964, the type was certificated initially for military use only, as no interest in this aircraft was shown by civil operators. In fact, production totalled only the 10 aircraft which had been ordered by the RAF. When, in due course, these became surplus to service requirements, they were acquired by civil

Designed as a military freighter for the carriage of bulky loads, the Shorts Belfast had only a meagre service career. Following a prolonged civil certification process, the type is now in operation with TAC Heavylift, which owns five such aircraft but keeps only three airworthy.

Shorts Belfast of TAC Heavylift, UK.

operators for the transport of large size or heavy cargoes.

Specification
Type: heavy transport
Powerplant: four 5,730-ehp (4273-ekW) Rolls-Royce RTy.12 Tyne turboprops
Performance: maximum cruising speed 352 mph (566 km/h); economic cruising speed 336 mph (541 km/h) at 24,000 ft (7315 m); service ceiling 30,000 ft (9145 m); range with maximum payload and 20 per cent reserves 1,000 miles (1609 km); range with maximum fuel and 20 per cent reserves 5,300 miles (8530 km)
Weights: empty operating 127,000 lb (57606 kg); maximum take-off 230,000 lb (104326 kg)

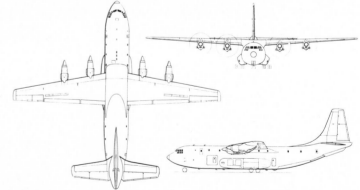

Shorts Belfast

Dimensions: span 158 ft 9½ in (48.40 m); length 136 ft 5 in (41.58 m); height 47 ft 0 in (14.33 m);

wing area 2,466.0 sq ft (229.09 m²)
Operators include: British Cargo Airlines, and TAC Heavylift

SIAI-Marchetti SF.260

History and Notes
Designed by Stelio Frati as a compact, fast and flamboyant private aircraft, the SIAI-Marchetti SF.260 has found favour with a large number of armed forces, but only relatively few private purchasers because of its comparatively high price. The prototype flew on 15 July 1964, and was at the time designated as the F.250. Built by Aviamilano, it was powered by a 250-hp (186.5-kW) Lycoming O-540 flat-six piston engine. From this prototype Aviamilano developed a production model to be built under licence by SIAI-Marchetti as the SF.260 and powered by a 260-hp (194-kW) Lycoming O-540. SIAI-Marchetti has since acquired all rights in the type, which received its FAA certification on April 1966.

The first production variant was the SF.260A, similar in most respects other than the powerplant to the F.250 prototype. In 1969 the variant, which was sold in the USA as the Waco Meteor, established two Class C-1-b records for speed over 100- and 1000-km (62.1- and 621.4-mile) closed

circuits. Production of the SF.260A was small, however, and the variant was replaced by the SF.260B, which incorporated many of the aerodynamic and structural improvements developed for the highly successful SF.260M military version. The more-than-adequate performance and handling characteristics of the SF.260B are indicated by the fact that several airlines, including Air France and Sabena, ordered the type for pilot training.

The current production model is the SF.260C based on the continuously improved SF.260M, SF.260 W Warrior and SF260 SW Sea Warrior military aircraft, but of course without specifically military equipment. Like its predecessors, the SF.260C is fully aerobatic, and the specification applies to this model.

Specification
Type: aerobatic three-seat light aircraft
Powerplant: one 260-hp (194-kW) Lycoming O-540-E4A5 flat-six piston engine

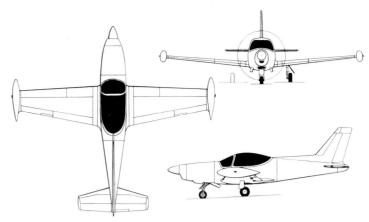

SIAI-Marchetti SF.260TP

Performance: maximum speed 215 mph (347 km/h) at sea level; maximum cruising speed 205 mph (330 km/h) at 10,000 ft (3050 m); initial climb rate 1,791 ft (546 m) per minute; service ceiling 19,000 ft (5790 m); range with maximum

fuel 1,274 miles (2050 km)
Weights: empty 1,664 lb (755 kg); maximum take-off 2,430 lb (1102 kg)
Dimensions: span over tiptanks 27 ft 4¾ in (8.35 m); length 23 ft 3½ in (7.10 m); height 7 ft 11 in (2.41 m); wing area 108.7 sq ft (10.10 m²)

Sikorsky S-58/Westland Wessex Series

History and Notes
In mid-1952 the US Navy issued a requirement for an anti-submarine helicopter with greater capabilities than the Sikorsky S-55 (service designation HO4S) then in service. Sikorsky responded with its S-58, which was essentially a scaled-up version of the S-55 with more than double the power of the earlier helicopter. The prototype flew on 8 March 1955, and production HSS-1 (later SH-34 Seabat) helicopters for the US Navy began to enter service in August 1955. Production continued up to January 1970, when the last of 1,821 examples was delivered. The majority of S-58s went to military operators, but on 2 August 1956 Sikorsky received FAA certification for civil S-58s. These were produced as the general-purpose S-58B with seats for up to seven passengers, and the airliner S-58C with seats for up to 12 passengers. Like the military H-34 variants, the civil S-58s were powered by the 1,525-hp (1138-kW) Wright R-1820-84 radial piston engine.

The S-58 was also built under licence in the UK by Westland. However, the British manufacturer immediately updated the design to reap the benefits offered by turboshaft power: the Westland Wessex was powered, therefore, by either one 1,450-shp (1082-kW) Napier Gazelle or two Rolls-Royce (Bristol) Gnomes coupled to provide 1,550-shp (1156-kW) at the rotor head. The twin-engined powerplant offered significant safety advantages, and was selected for the sole civil variant, the Wessex 60 derived from the RAF's Wessex HC.2 introduced in 1964. The Wessex 60 could accommodate 10 passengers at airline standard, or eight litters, two sitting casualties and one attendant, or 15 survivors.

With the end of S-58 production in 1970, Sikorsky also turned its attention towards a turboshaft conversion of the basic helicopter, offering a kit-form modification of existing S-58s into S-58Ts. The selected powerplant was the 1,800-shp (1342-kW) Pratt & Whitney Aircraft of Canada PT6T-3 Twin Pac coupled turboshaft, later superseded by the higher-rated PT6T-6. Such a conversion permitted the S-58T to carry up to 16 passengers at a maximum speed some 16 mph (26 km/h) higher than the S-58C's

122 mph (196 km/h) over slightly longer ranges, with the additional safety of a twin-engined powerplant. More than 125 S-58Ts were subsequently produced, FAA certification having been gained in April 1971. There was also an S-58T Mk II kit coupling the PT6T-6 installation with a number of airframe improvements.

Another turboshaft conversion is that offered by the Helitec Corporation, whose modifications result in the Helitec (Sikorsky) S-58T. This is a simpler conversion, the Wright piston engine being replaced by an 840-shp (626-kW) AiResearch TSE331-3U-303 turboshaft derated to 650-shp (485-kW). Unlike the Sikorsky S-56T, which has nasal inlets in the top half of the nose and a rearward-facing exhaust outlet on the port side of the nose, the Helitec (Sikorsky) S-58T has its inlet under the nose and the exhaust outlet facing to starboard right in the nose so as to offload the tail rotor. The lesser power available from the TSE331 means that the Helitec conversion is less capable than the Sikorsky modification. The specification applies to the Sikorsky S-58T Mk II.

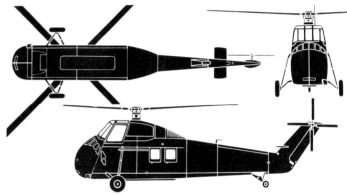

Sikorsky S-58

Specification
Type: general-purpose helicopter
Powerplant: one 1,875-shp (1399-kW) Pratt & Whitney Aircraft of Canada PT6T-6 Twin Pac coupled turboshaft
Performance: maximum level speed 138 mph (222 km/h) at sea level; cruising speed 127 mph (204 km/h); hovering ceiling out of ground effect 6,500 ft (1980 m); range 278 miles (447 km)
Weights: empty 8,354 lb (3789 kg);

maximum take-off 13,000 lb (5896 kg)
Dimensions: main rotor diameter 56 ft 0 in (17.07 m); fuselage length 47 ft 3 in (14.40 m); height 15 ft 11 in (4.85 m); main rotor disc area 2,460 sq ft (228.54 m²)

One of Court Helicopters' four Sikorsky S-58T Mk IIs is seen hovering over one of the same airline's three Sikorsky S-62As. Court specialises in offshore support work with its 19 helicopters.

Sikorsky S-61

History and Notes

Igor Sikorsky, pioneer aircraft designer, was of Russian origin and there, on 13 May 1913, he flew the *Le Grand*, the world's first four-engined aircraft. He was to develop from this the *Il'ya Muromets* four-engined bomber which, although built in comparatively small numbers (about 80) was to have a significant impact during World War I, when flown against German targets by crews of the Imperial Russian Air Service. Even at this early period of aviation history Sikorsky had been interested in the potential of rotary-wing aircraft, but his early experiments were unsuccessful and, being a practical engineer, he decided without too much hesitation that far more knowledge and improved power-plants would be necessary before a really practical helicopter could become reality.

Following the Russian revolution, Sikorsky emigrated to the USA where, after a period of abject poverty, he managed to establish on 5 March 1923, in conjunction with several other Russian emigrés, a small company known as the Sikorsky Aero Engineering Corporation to build fixed-wing aircraft. His interest in the potential of the helicopter was undiminished, and on 14 September 1939 he flew his VS-300 design, which was developed into the world's first practical single-rotor helicopter. The fundamental secret of Sikorsky's success was the introduction of the tail rotor, this overcoming the problems induced by the torque of the main rotor. From that moment, the development and introduction into service of small rotary-wing aircraft was fairly rapid. None saw service in World War II, other than for evaluation purposes in the closing stages of the war, and it was the Korean War which began in 1950 that brought the first real understanding of just how valuable this comparatively slow, go-anywhere aircraft could be.

In these postwar years, the US Navy had discovered that a pair of helicopters, one equipped with suitable search equipment, the other with homing torpedoes, made an excellent hunter/killer team to combat the growing menace of deep-diving, long-endurance submarines. Practical experience showed that the use of two helicopters, one dependent on the other, had limitations. It was realised that a single large helicopter, able to combine the two roles, would prove far more effective, and this resulted in a US Navy contract of 24 December 1957 for the development and production of such an aircraft. Designated SH-3 Sea King from September 1962 under

Sikorsky S-61L of Okanagan Helicopters, Canada.

the unified tri-service designation system, the first of these aircraft had entered service with US Navy squadrons VHS-3 and VHS-10 a year earlier.

Sikorsky's model number for this helicopter was S-61, which with S-61A military amphibious transports, S-61B navy anti-submarine, and later S-61R military transports for the USAF and US Coast Guard, has been built in considerable numbers. The early success of these aircraft during military trials convinced the company that they had created a design which combined reliability and safety, two factors which led to the decision to develop also a civil transport version.

First to be built was the S-61L, a non-amphibious version, which flew for the first time in prototype form on 6 December 1960. This retained the rotor system and drive designed for the military S-61s, consisting of five-blade main and tail rotors of all-metal construction. The main rotor is fully articulated, incorporates a rotor brake as standard but, unlike the military versions, has no blade-folding capability. The two General Electric CT58 turboshaft engines, mounted on the upper surface of the fuselage, each drive the main gearbox through free wheeling units, which means that both or each engine is able to drive both rotors.

The semi-monocoque metal fuselage has a basic boat-hull form, sealed so that in an emergency the helicopter can land on water without any danger of sinking. The landing gear is of the non-retractable tailwheel type, each main unit carrying twin wheels. The tail rotor is mounted on the uptilted extension of the fuselage, on its port side, and on the opposite side of this fixed structure is a stabiliser surface. Accommodation is provided for a flight crew of two, plus a steward/stewardess, and a total of 28 passengers can be carried. Facilities can include a galley and toilet, and access to the cabin is through two doors on the starboard side, the aft door incorporating an airstair. The forward

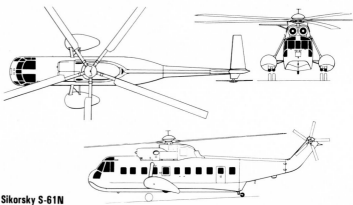

Sikorsky S-61N

half of the cabin can be provided optionally with folding seats and tiedown facilities for cargo, enabling the helicopter to be used also for mixed passenger/cargo operations. These aircraft have full blind-flying instrumentation, but avionics are to customer's requirements.

The S-61L was certificated on 2 November 1961, entering service with Los Angeles Airways which, on 1 March 1962, became the first operator to use S-61s on revenue service. The S-61N which followed is generally similar to the non-amphibious S-61L, but the fixed landing gear is replaced by main units which retract hydraulically into stabilising floats mounted on each side of the hull. The powerplant comprises two 1,350-shp (1007-kW) General Electric CT58-140 turboshafts, and there is seating for up to 26 passengers. Late production aircraft, designated S-61N Mk II, have more powerful CT58-140-1.2 turboshafts, and the mark can carry a maximum of 30 passengers. These Mk II aircraft also have better baggage accommodation and handling facilities and improved damping to minimise rotor-induced vibration. Both the S-61L and S-61N are equipped for all-weather service, and when both versions received FAA certification on 6 October 1964 for full IFR operation, they were the first tran-

sport helicopters to receive such endorsement from the FAA.

In addition to the standard S-61N, a heavy-lift version for such operations as general construction, logging, and powerline installation was developed under the name Payloader. This reverted to the non-retractable landing gear of the S-61L, and was stripped of all non-essential equipment and fittings to make this version capable of lifting a payload in excess of 11,000 lb (4990 kg).

Production of commercial S-61L and S-61N helicopters ended on 19 June 1980, after a total of 13 and 123 respectively had been built. The details below apply to the S-61N Mk II.

Specification

Type: all-weather helicopter transport

Powerplant: two 1,500-shp (1119-kW) General Electric CT58-140-1/2 turboshafts

Performance: maximum cruising speed 150 mph (241 km/h); economic cruising speed 138 mph (222 km/h); service ceiling 12,500 ft (3810 m); range with maximum fuel, 30-min reserves 495 miles (797 km)

Weights: empty 12,510 lb (5674 kg); maximum take-off 20,500 lb (9299 kg)

Dimensions: main rotor diameter 62 ft 0 in (18.90 m); tail rotor diameter 10 ft 7 in (3.23 m); length, rotors turning 72 ft 10 in (22.20 m); height 17 ft 5½ in (5.32 m); main rotor disc area 3,019.0 sq ft (280.47 m²)

Operators include: Ansett Airlines of Australia, Bow Helicopters, Bristow Helicopter Group, British Airways, British Caledonian Airways, Carson Helicopters, Court Helicopters, Era Helicopters, Evergreen Helicopters, Greenlandair Helikopter Services, Irish Helicopters, KLM Helicopters, Management Aviation, Okanagan Helicopters

The Sikorsky S-61N has a watertight boat hull and stabilizing floats to allow emergency landings on water, and can carry some 30 passengers. The S-61L can be used for land operations only.

Sikorsky S-76 Spirit

History and Notes

There have been few major airlines which have used helicopters for scheduled operations, and the majority of these were equipped with the Sikorsky S-61N. Nevertheless, there has been an expanding market for transport helicopters, especially since the large-scale offshore exploration for and exploitation of underwater natural gas and oil fields, and Sikorsky was anxious to design and produce a transport helicopter that would secure for the company a share of these growing sales.

Prudently, Sikorsky initiated extensive worldwide market research, not only to discover the sales potential, but also to sound-out the requirements of operators, particularly in regard to capacity. On completion of this stage of the programme, during which the configuration was finalised as operators' needs were established, Sikorsky announced on 19 January 1975 that the company was to put into production this new commercial transport helicopter under the designation S-76; since that time it has also acquired the name Spirit.

The first of four prototypes (N762SA) was flown initially on 13 March 1977, and by comparison with the S-61 which was getting close to the end of its production run, the design incorporates the most recent advances resulting from research and development to produce new-generation high-performance military helicopters. Of conventional configuration (main rotor plus anti-torque tail rotor), the S-76 has a four-blade main rotor with blades of composite construction, based on the use of a titanium spar, but employing also such materials as glassfibre, nickel and nylon; the tail rotor is also a four-blade composite structure. The transmission of power from the twin turbines to the rotors follows standard practice, with free-

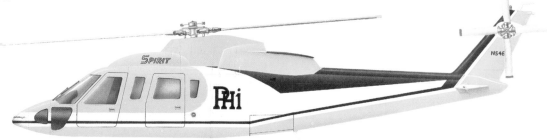

Sikorsky S-76A Spirit of Petroleum Helicopters, USA.

wheeling units to ensure that each engine can drive both rotors.

To combine weight-saving and strength of structure, the fuselage incorporates composite materials that include glassfibre, Kevlar and light alloy honeycomb. The fuselage carries at its rear an all-moving tailplane, and a tail rotor pylon with the rotor mounted on the port side. The landing gear is of retractable tricycle type, and the two Allison turboshaft engines are mounted above the cabin. Standard accommodation is provided for a crew of two with a maximum of 12 passengers, but the S-76 can be furnished optionally in a variety of executive layouts. In any configuration, easy access to the cabin is provided by two doors on each side of the fuselage.

Standard equipment includes such features as engine fire detection and extinguishing systems, and there is a wide range of optional equipment and avionics available to broaden the applications for this helicopter. The first IFR-certificated aircraft were delivered to Air Logistics of Lafayette, Louisiana on 27 February 1979. By the end of 1980 well over 400 Spirits had been sold, and about 100 had been delivered. These sales indicate most effectively the impact of offshore energy sources on helicopter utilisation, for more than half

Sikorsky S-76 Spirit

of sales recorded to date are for use by operators who provide support to these installations.

Specification

Type: general-purpose all-weather helicopter
Powerplant: two 650-shp (485-kW) Allison 250-C30 turboshafts
Performance: maximum cruising speed 167 mph (269 km/h); economic cruising speed 144 mph (232 km/h); service ceiling 15,000 ft (4570 m); range with 12 passengers and 30-min reserves 465 miles (748 km)
Weights: empty equipped 5,475 lb (2483 kg); maximum take-off 10,000 lb (4536 kg)
Dimensions: diameter of main

rotor 44 ft 0 in (13.41 m); diameter of tail rotor 8 ft 0 in (2.44 m); length, rotors turning 52 ft 6in (16.00 m); height, tail rotor turning 14 ft 5¾ in (4.41 m); main rotor disc area 1,257.0 sq ft (116.78 m²)
Operators include: Bow Helicopters, Bristow Helicopters Group, British Airways, Carson Helicopters, Island Helicopter Corporation, KLM Helicopters, Management Aviation, Okanagan Helicopters, and Votec Servicios Aereos Regionais

The Sikorsky S-76 Spirit was designed specifically for the high-performance support of offshore resources operators, with high levels of safety and capability.

Socata GY-80 Horizon

History and Notes

A subsidiary of Aérospatiale, which itself was formed by a merger of Sud-Aviation, Nord-Aviation, and SEREB in 1970, Socata is responsible for development and production of all the organisation's light aircraft. Before the formation of Aérospatiale, Sud-Aviation had acquired from France's well-known designer Yves Gardan a licence to build and market a four-seat all-metal light aircraft of his design. Known as the GY-80 Horizon, the prototype had flown for the first time on 21 July 1960, and Socata was to build more than 250 before production ended in 1969.

A cantilever low-wing monoplane, the Horizon had a wing the whole of whose trailing-edge was made up of two Frise type ailerons and four electrically actuated Fowler type flaps. The landing gear was of semi-retractable tricycle type, rather more than half of each wheel remaining exposed when retracted. Standard powerplant was a 160-hp (119-kW) Avco Lycoming O-320-D engine driving a fixed-pitch two-blade propeller, but a more powerful engine and three-blade constant-speed propeller were optional. The resulting basic day-flying aircraft was more competitively priced, but could have more sophistication in the form of higher-performance powerplant, night-flying equipment, and nav/com radio if the customer so required.

Specification

Type: four-seat light cabin monoplane
Powerplant: (optional) one 180-hp (134-kW) Avco Lycoming O-360-A flat-four piston engine
Performance: (with optional O-360-A and c/s propeller) maximum level speed 155 mph (250 km/h) at sea level; cruising speed 152 mph (245 km/h) at 8,200 ft (2500 m); service ceiling 15,420 ft (4700 m); range with maximum optional fuel 777 miles (1250 km)
Weights: empty 1,378 lb (625 kg); maximum take-off 2,535 lb (1150 kg)
Dimensions: span 31 ft 9¾ in (9.70 m); length 21 ft 9½ in (6.64 m); height 8 ft 6¼ in (2.60 m); wing area 139.9 sq ft (13.0 m²)

Designed by Yves Gardan, the GY-80 Horizon was produced under licence by Socata, an Aérospatiale subsidiary. The design is typical of French light aircraft, with tall vertical surfaces and a capacious fuselage.

Socata Rallye Series

History and Notes

Socata's association with light aircraft construction had begun with a tourer designed by the old Morane-Saulnier company which, as Gérance des Etablissements Morane-Saulnier, became a subsidiary of Sud-Aviation during 1965. On 10 June 1959 Morane-Saulnier had flown successfully the prototype of its new MS 880A Rallye-Club. Certification was gained during 1961, and some 20 years later the Rallye series continues in production. These excellent lightplanes have formed the major proportion of Socata's production programme since the company's formation in 1966, with a total of close on 3,000 built by them.

Until early 1979 the original Rallye names were retained, but with the start of a new production programme in May of that year, Socata bestowed a new set of names on these aircraft, the current basic version being the Galopin (formerly Rallye 110ST) with a 110-hp (82-kW) Avco Lycoming O-235-L2A flat-four engine. Typical of the Rallye series, the Galopin has low-set all-metal cantilever monoplane wings that incorporate full-span automatic leading-edge slats, wide-chord slotted ailerons, and wide-span trailing-edge flaps. Such wing features mean that the series as a whole has enjoyed, and continues to demonstrate, good reliable flight characteristics, based upon inherent stability and safety. The fuselage and conventional tail unit are also of light alloy construction. The landing gear is of non-retractable tricycle type, this being standard to all except one variant of the Gabier (Rallye 235 C) which has tailwheel type gear.

The Galopin can be operated as a three/four-seat aircraft if spins are prohibited, but the remainder of the series are full four-seaters. Primary differences between the various Rallyes are a combination of powerplant and role, and the second member of the family is the higher-performance Garnament (Rallye 160 ST) with a 155-hp (116-kW) Avco Lycoming O-320-D2A engine. It is followed by the glider- or banner-towing Galerien (Rallye 18 T), which has a 180-hp (134-kW) Avco Lycoming O-360-A3A, and the improved glider-towing and similarly powered Gaillard (Rallye 180 GT), which has a strengthened structure and detail improvements for operation at a higher gross weight.

The details which follow apply to the high-performance Gabier (Rallye 235 GT) which has a constant-speed propeller as standard and, as mentioned earlier, is available with both tricycle or tailwheel type non-retractable landing gear.

Specification

Type: two/four-seat light cabin monoplane
Powerplant: one 235-hp (175-kW) Avco Lycoming O-540-B4B5 flat-six piston engine
Performance: maximum level speed 171 mph (275 km/h) at sea level; cruising speed 152 mph (245 km/h); economic cruising speed 144 mph (232 km/h); service ceiling 14,760 ft (4500 m); range with maximum fuel, allowances and reserves 677 miles (1090 km)
Weights: empty 1,530 lb (694 kg); maximum take-off 2,646 lb (1200 kg)
Dimensions: span 31 ft 11½ in (9.74 m); length 23 ft 9½ in (7.25 m); height 9 ft 2¼ in (2.80 m); wing area 137.35 sq ft (12.76 m²)

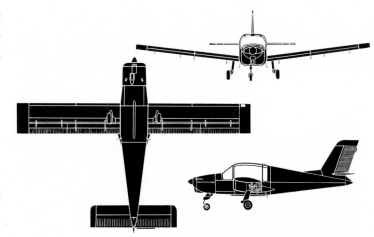

Socata Rallye

The Rallye series has been in production for 20 years, and in the early 1980s was available in no less than 11 versions with different equipment and engines, and in two-, three- or four-seat forms. More than 3,000 have been built.

Socata ST 10 Diplomate

History and Notes

On 7 November 1967, Socata flew the prototype of a four-seat cabin monoplane of its own design which was derived from the GY-80 Horizon. Known originally as the Super Horizon 2000, and later as the Provence, it was finally designated as the ST 10 Diplomate in its production form when deliveries began in late 1969. It retained a generally similar wing, but differed by having a fuselage lengthened by 2 ft 0¼ in (0.62 m), a redesigned tail unit, a slightly more powerful engine as standard, and an almost fully retractable tricycle landing gear. The aft-retracting main gear of the Horizon had been replaced by conventional units that were completely enclosed within the wing when retracted, but the nose unit still had about 25 per cent of the wheel exposed when it was in the up position.

Certification was gained in late November 1969, with the first deliveries beginning very shortly afterwards. But despite the considerably improved performance by comparison with the Horizon from which it was developed, the Diplomate failed to attract any worthwhile volume of sales. When production terminated during 1975, a total of only 56 had been delivered.

Specification

Type: four-seat cabin monoplane
Powerplant: one 200-hp (149-kW) Avco Lycoming IO-360-C1B flat-four piston engine
Performance: maximum level speed 174 mph (280 km/h) at sea level; cruising speed at sea level 165 mph (265 km/h); service ceiling 16,405 ft (5000 m); range with maximum standard fuel 860 miles (1385 km)
Weights: empty 1,594 lb (723 kg); maximum take-off 2,690 lb (1220 kg)
Dimensions: span 31 ft 9¾ in (9.70 m); length 23 ft 9¾ in (7.26 m); height 9 ft 5½ in (2.88 m); wing area 139.9 sq ft (13.0 m²)

Swearingen Merlin II/III

History and Notes

Swearingen Aircraft gained a high reputation in the early-1960s with their powerplant conversions of Beech Twin Bonanzas and Queen Airs. As a natural development the company rebuilt a Queen Air with a new streamlined, pressurized fuselage and a pair of 400-hp (298-kw) Lycoming TIGO-541 piston engines. As testing advanced, it became clear that this aircraft—the Merlin I—was an ideal mount for turboprop engines. The Merlin I was therefore shelved, and the production version was the SA-26T Merlin IIA powered by two Pratt & Whitney Aircraft of Canada PT6A turboprops. The first aircraft flew on 13th April, 1965 with FAA certification being granted on 15th July, 1966.

In 1971, with brisk Merlin II sales in hand, Swearingen announced the SA-226T Merlin III. The gross weight was increased from 10,000 lb (4536 kg) to 12,500 lb (5670 kg), the engines were changed to Garrett AiResearch TPE331s in redesigned nacelles, the vertical tail surfaces were redesigned and the tailplane was raised to a mounting on the fin. The Merlin III got a new landing gear with forward-retracting nose leg and twin-wheel main units and an extra starboard cabin window. Later, after Swearingen had been acquired by Fairchild Industries, the Merlin was further developed as the IIIA with detailed changes and improved performance. The specification applies to the Merlin IIIA.

Specification

Type: 11-seat light transport
Powerplant: two 840-shp (626-kW) Garrett AiResearch TPE331-3U-303G turboprops
Performance: maximum cruising speed at 16,000 ft (4877 m) 325 mph (520 km/h); maximum rate of climb at gross weight 2,530 ft (771 m) per minute; maximum standard range with 45 minutes reserve 2,860 miles (4576 km); service ceiling 28,900 ft (8810 m)
Weights: empty 7,400 lb (3357 kg); maximum take-off 12,500 lb (5670 kg)
Dimensions: span 46 ft 3 in (14.10 m); length 42 ft 2 in (12.85 m); height 16 ft 10 in (5.13 m); wing area 227.5 sq ft (25.78 m²)

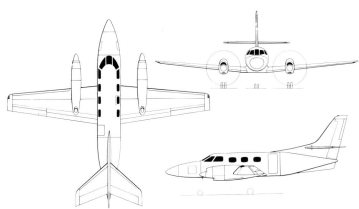

Swearingen Merlin III

The Swearingen Merlin IIIB is derived from Beech (wings from the Queen Air and landing gear from the Twin Bonanza) with a totally new presurised fuselage of Swearingen origins. The result is great comfort, high performance and more than adequate range.

Swearingen Metro and Metro II/III

History and Notes

In the late 1960s Swearingen initiated the design of a transport that would carry 19 or 20 passengers in a commuter configuration. Construction of the prototype of this aircraft began in August 1968, and the aircraft flew for the first time on 26 August 1969. So far as the Swearingen company was concerned it was a unique aircraft, representing the first completely new product to be designed by them. Before then, their work had been confined primarily to the modification or rebuilding of airframes designed for other purposes.

Of low-wing monoplane configuration this SA-226 TC Metro, as it was designated, had a fairly conventional structure. The wings incorporated double-slotted trailing-edge flaps; the fuselage was a fail-safe light-alloy structure of circular-cross section stressed to provide a pressurised environment for crew and passengers; the tail unit had all swept surfaces and a large dorsal fin; the landing gear was of the retractable tricycle type with twin wheels on each unit; and the powerplant consisted of two Garrett AiResearch TPE331 turboprops, one mounted on each wing, each driving a reversible-pitch propeller to assist short-field operations.

Accommodation was provided for a crew of two on a flight deck that was separated from the cabin only by a curtain, and there was standard seating for 20 passengers. To make operations as flexible as possible for the smaller commuter airlines, seating could be folded to make space for cargo, and a movable bulkhead could be used to separate cargo and passengers according to requirements. A door with an integral airstair gave access to the cabin at the forward end on the port side, and at the rear of the cabin on the same side a 4 ft 3¼ in by 4 ft 5 in (1.30 m by 1.35 m) cargo door was installed as standard.

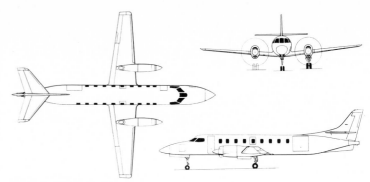

Swearingen Metro II of Tavina (Colombia).

Following certification in June 1970, there was a decided pause before this graceful transport made a significant impact on potential operators. Commuter Airlines of Binghampton, New York, were the first to use Metros on revenue service in 1973, but since that time many operators have learned to value the operational capability and reliability of the aircraft. An improved Metro II is currently available, this introducing larger cabin windows and a number of detail changes. There is also a 12-seat corporate version of this design which is designated Merlin IV, which is generally similar except for the changed accommodation.

Total deliveries of Metro/Metro IIs were in excess of 130 in mid-1980, at which time sales were approaching the 200 mark. In addition to these deliveries/sales, more than 60 cooperate Merlin IV/IVA aircraft have been delivered, and Swearingen's slow starter is beginning to notch up a real success in the commuter airliner market.

The production version of the mid-1980s will be the Metro III. Compared with the Metro II, this will have wings of 10 ft 9 in (3.27 m) more span and 11 per cent greater area; more powerful TPE331s will drive advanced-technology Dowty-Rotol propellers, the net effect of the improvements being to improve performance (especially range) while reducing fuel consumption and noise. The specification applies to the Metro II.

Swearingen Merlin 4 (Metro II)

Specification

Type: commuter transport
Powerplant: two 940-shp (701-kW), with water/methanol injection, Garrett-AiResearch TPE331-3UW-304G turboprops
Performance: maximum cruising speed 294 mph (473 km/h) at 10,000 ft (3050 m); economic cruising speed 279 mph (449 km/h) at 20,000 ft (6100 m); service ceiling 27,000 ft (8230 m); range at maximum cruising speed with 19 passengers and 45-min reserves 215 miles (346 km); maximum ferry range, 45-min reserves 2,456 miles (3953 km)
Weights: empty 7,450 lb (3379 kg); maximum take-off 12,500 lb (5670 kg)
Dimensions: span 46 ft 3 in (14.10 m); length 59 ft 4¾ in (18.10 m); height 16 ft 9¾ in (5.12 m); wing area 277.50 sq ft (25.78 m²)

Operators include: Air Balear, Air Midwest, Air Wisconsin, Austrian Air Services, Bush Pilots Airways, Commuter Airlines, Consolidated Airways, Crossair, Empire Airlines, Golden Gate Airlines, Kanif-Arkia Airlines, Midstate Air Commuter, Mississippi Valley Airlines, Republic Airlines, Rio Airways, Tejas Airlines, and Trans Adria

The Swearingen Metro II, although not unique among civil aircraft in having an auxiliary powerplant to boost take-off performance, shares with only the Britten-Norman Trislander the distinction of having provision for a rocket engine. The aircraft shown has such a provision, as indicated by the protruding pipe under the rudder, and belongs to Empire Airlines, a third-level operator in northeastern states of the USA.

Taylorcraft Model F-19 Sportsman

History and Notes

The name of C.G. Taylor who, with his brother, formed Taylor Brothers Aircraft Corporation in 1929, is one that is well known among the light-plane builders of the United States. In the years prior to World War II he designed and built a variety of aircraft, but the most important of these prewar designs were the Taylorcraft Models B,C, and D. The C and D were to form a basis for the establishment of Taylorcraft Aeroplanes (England) Ltd, which eventually became Auster Aircraft Ltd.

In the USA the Model D went to war as the L-2 Grasshopper, of which nearly 2,000 were built for the US Army Air Force, and postwar nearly 3,000 derivatives of the Model B were built before the company went bankrupt. Reformed in 1947 as Taylorcraft Inc., the company produced a variety of lightplanes for 11 years until 1958, when the company closed down. This time there was a break of 10 years before a new Taylorcraft Aviation Corporation was formed, initially to provide support for the many aircraft of Taylorcraft origin which remained in use.

In 1973 this company began the construction of an aircraft based on the Model B, now named Model F-19 Sportsman 100, and this duly entered production. A braced high-wing monoplane, it shared the composite wood/metal/fabric-covered construction of its predecessor, its non-retractable tailwheel type landing gear, and enclosed two-seat accommodation. Its 100-hp (75-kW) powerplant provided better performance than that of the earlier aircraft and the F-19 could, optionally, have a range of radios and equipment that could make it a day- or night-flying aircrft suitable for sporting or training activities. Production of the Sportsman ended in early 1980 after 120 had been built, and the company's efforts are now concentrated on a new, generally similar aircraft, which is designated as the Model F-21. It differs primarily in having a 115-hp (86-kW) Avco Lycoming O-235-L2C engine.

Specification

Type: two-seat training and sports aircraft
Powerplant: one 100-hp (75-kW) Continental O-200-A flat-four piston engine
Performance: maximum level speed 127 mph (204 km/h) at sea level; cruising speed 115 mph (185 km/h); service ceiling 18,000 ft (5485 m); range with maximum fuel 400 miles (644 km)
Weights: empty 900 lb (408 kg); maximum take-off 1,500 lb (680 kg)

The Taylorcraft F-19 Sportsman is at base a reworking of the prewar Taylorcraft Plus D, a fact which explains the F-19's somewhat dated appearance.

Dimensions: span 36 ft 0 in (10.97 m); length 22 ft 1¼ in (6.74 m); height 6 ft 6 in (1.98 m); wing area 183.71 sq ft (17.07 m²)

Transall C-160

History and Notes

The original Transall manufacturing group was formed in January 1959 and comprised, as now, Aérospatiale in France with the German companies Messerschmitt-Bölkow-Blohm and Vereinigte Flugtechnische Werke. This group was established to build the Transall C-160 transport for the air forces of France and Germany, and production ended in 1972 after the construction of 90 C-160Ds for Germany, 50 C-160Fs for France, 20 C-160Ts for Turkey, and nine C-160Zs for South Africa. In 1973 four C-160 Fs were modified for nocturnal mail operations by Air France for the Centre d'Exploitation Postal Metropolitan under the designation C-160P.

The industrial agreement was resumed in October 1976 to restart production, and the manufacture of a batch of 75 aircraft was authorised in 1977. In 1980 a total of 16 aircraft were being assembled, with initial deliveries planned to the French air force in late 1981 and to Indonesia in 1982. Only 28 of the production batch of 75 had been ordered in early 1981, but it is anticipated that when aircraft become available for prompt delivery in 1983-4 there will be little difficulty in finding buyers for them.

A high-wing monoplane, with a pressurised fuselage that incorporates a hydraulically operated door/ramp in the upswept aft fuselage, and a paratroop deployment door on each side of the fuselage, aft of the mainwheel fairings, the C-160 has a cabin/cargo compartment with reinforced flooring to cater for a wide variety of loads. Typical loads could comprise 93 troops, 61-88 fully-equipped paratroops, 62 stretchers with four attendants, or vehicles and/or cargo to a maximum weight of 37,478 lb (1700 kg). The tail unit is conventional, but the retractable tricycle landing gear has twin weels on the nose unit, and twin wheels in tandem on each main unit. All wheels can be raised on the ground to adjust the fuselage height to simplify loading.

Air France operates four specially modified Transall C-160 transports. Designated C-160Ps, these are used for the bulk carriage of mail within metropolitan France.

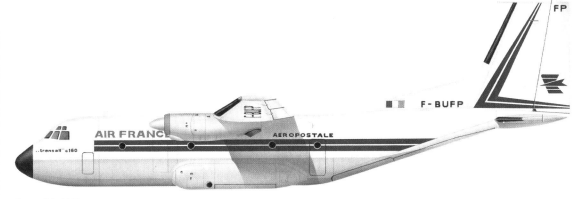

Transall C-160P of Air France.

Specification

Type: twin-turboprop transport
Powerplant: two 6,100-eshp (4549-ekW) Rolls-Royce Tyne RTy.20 Mk 22 turboprops
Performance: maximum level speed 319 mph (513 km/h) at 16,000 ft (4875 m); service ceiling 28,000 ft (8535 m) at 99,208 lb (45000 kg) AUW; range with maximum payload 1,151 miles (1852 km)
Weights: empty operating 63,934 lb (29000 kg); maximum take-off 112,435 lb (51000 kg)
Dimensions: span 131 ft 3 in (40.00 m); length 106 ft 3½ in (32.40 m); height 38 ft 2¾ in (11.65 m); wing area 1,722.3 sq ft (1600.00 m²)

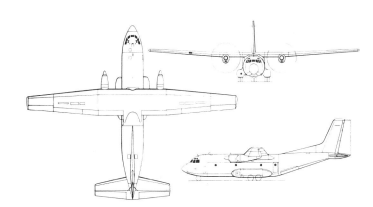

Transall C-160

Tupolev Tu-104

History and Notes

In the midst of the UK's almost six-year involvement in World War II, the government established a committee under the chairmanship of Lord Brabazon of Tara to investigate and advise upon the types of civil aircraft most likely to be required in the immediate post-war years. Five types were recommended, including the Type IV jet transport intended to capitalise upon the turbojet engine, first proposed in practical form and developed by Frank (later Sir Frank) Whittle. The Type IV materialised as the de Havilland Comet I, the world's first turbojet airliner to enter service when it inaugurated BOAC's first turbojet-powered airline service, between London and Johannesburg, on 2 May 1952.

At that time the UK had a very considerable technological lead, and it can be conjectured that had the Comet I followed a conventional development sequence, Britain might have gained a substantial share of the now very large worldwide fleet of turbine-powered transport aircraft. Instead, the structural failures suffered by three of these aircraft, the last on 8 April 1954, led to grounding of the type, and it was not until 1958 that BOAC was able to inaugurate transatlantic jet services, followed by other routes, with the Comet 4. Just over four years had been lost, and in that period Britain's one-time lead in the category of turbojet-powered transport aircraft had gone forever.

First of the other nations to develop and introduce into service a civil airliner in this same category was the Soviet Union, the prototype of the Tupolev Tu-104 flying for the first time on 17 June 1955. This had been developed at high speed; not, so far as is known, with any intention of capturing a world market, but because of the need to cope with an ever-growing volume of passengers and cargo to be carried over the long-range domestic routes of the Soviet Union.

Designed in 1953 by a team led by Andrei N.Tupolev, the Tu-104 was planned round a turbojet powerplant to cater not only for greater capacity, but also to provide much higher cruising speeds. From the beginning

Tupolev Tu-104 of Aeroflot, USSR.

the project was regarded as being sufficiently urgent to warrant any legitimate short cuts in design, construction, and development, and Tupolev decided to base the design on the utilisation of as many assemblies and components as possible of the Tu-16 twin-turbojet bomber which was being developed almost simultaneously. In fact, the Tu-104 utilised the wings, fuselage nose, tail unit, landing gear and powerplant of the Tu-16, all of which were integrated with a completely new fuselage incorporating a pressurised cabin to allow the new airliner to operate at the high altitudes necessary to make possible the economic operation of the turbojet engines.

A low-wing monoplane, with wings that had a sweepback of 35° at quarter-chord, the design incorporated some advanced features. These included the use of Fowler-type trailing-edge flaps, extending outboard from the landing gear fairings to the ailerons, with additional short span flaps between the landing gear fairings and the engine nacelles, the engines being mounted within the wing roots. Other wing features included boundary-layer fences, and the use of engine bleed air for wing leading-edge anti-icing. The hydraulically retractable tricycle type landing gear had a twin-wheel nose unit, main units each carrying a four-wheel bogie, and an anti-skid braking system. The tail unit included a powered rudder, and leading-edges of the aerofoil surfaces were electrically de-iced. An unusual feature for a civil airliner was the inclusion of dual braking parachutes.

The powerplant of the early Tu-104s, of which about 20 were built, comprised two 14,881-lb (6,750-kg) thrust Mikulin AM-3 (RD-3) turbojet engines. Since the accommodation

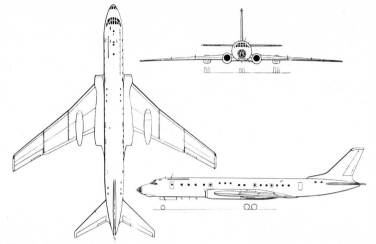

Tupolev Tu-104B

provided for only 50 passengers, this powerplant provided excellent performance when these aircraft began to enter service with Aeroflot in the summer of 1956, the first domestic service, on the Moscow—Irkutsk route, being inaugurated on 15 September 1956. The Soviet Union was, therefore, the second nation to provide scheduled passenger services with turbojet-powered civil transport aircraft, for it was not until just over a year later that Pan American introduced the Boeing 707 on its New York—London route.

It was very soon appreciated that these early Tu-104 aircraft had an abundance of power, so there was rapid development of the Tu-104A with rearranged cabin seating to accommodate a maximum of 70 passengers. The first example was used during September 1957 to set a number of new speed, load-carrying,

and altitude records for turbojet-powered aircraft, and this version, which was the most extensively built, entered service with Aeroflot in 1957. Its powerplant comprised two 19,180-lb (8,700-kg) thrust AM-3M engines, and the following Tu-104B had more powerful RD-3M-500 turbojets This latter version, which introduced a number of improvements, had also a fuselage that was lengthened by 3 ft 11½ in (1.21 m), and the cabin rearranged in a five-abreast layout to provide seating capacity for a maximum of 100 passengers. In addition, it utilised the improved fuselage and trailing-edge flaps which had by then been designed and developed for the four-engine Tu-110. The Tu-104B version began to enter service with Aeroflot in April 1959, and many Tu-104As were modified subsequently to carry 100 passengers without the benefit of the 'stretched' fuselage, these converted aircraft having the designation Tu-104V.

When these first Russian turbine-powered transports were seen in the West there was much derogatory criticism of their 'Victorian' interior decor, but this could not detract from the fact that the Soviet Union had introduced into commercial service a thoroughly reliable aircraft. Something like 200 of all versions are believed to have been built, and about half of these remained in service with Aeroflot in 1980. Attempts to market the Tu-104 to other nations met with little success, for only six aircraft were sold outside the Soviet Union, these entering service with Czechoslovakia's Ceskoslovenské Aerolinie in 1957; these were no longer in use in 1980. An unusual use of the Tu-104 by the Soviet air force is worth recording: it is flown in a parabolic pattern to provide trainee cosmonauts with some experience of weightless conditions.

Whatever the shortcomings of

The Tupolev Tu-104 was the world's second turbojet-engined airliner to enter service, and despite its lack of operating economy provided Aeroflot with the high-speed transport it needed, as well as with experience of jet airliners.

this aircraft, its impact on Soviet long-range domestic routes was little short of dramatic, as it reduced flight times by as much as 60 per cent by comparison with the piston-engine airliners which it replaced, and pointed the way to the future for Aeroflot's growing services. For Andrei Tupolev it earned in 1957 a Lenin Prize, the Fédération Aéronautique Internationale's Gold Medal in 1959, and Honorary Fellowship of Britain's Royal Aeronautical Society in 1970. 'Victorian' or not, the Tu-104 has an assured place in aviation history.

Specification
Type: medium-range airliner
Powerplant (Tu-104B): two 21,384-lb (9,700-kg) thrust Mikulin RD-3M-50 turbojets
Performance: maximum speed 590 mph (950 km/h) at 32,810 ft (10000 m); cruising speed 446-497 mph (750-800 km/h); service ceiling 37,730 ft (11500 m); range with maximum payload 1,647 miles (2650 km); range with maximum fuel 1,926 miles (3100 km)
Weights: empty 91,711 lb (41600 kg); maximum take-off 167,551 lb (76000 kg)
Dimensions: span 113 ft 4 in (34.54 m); length 131 ft 5 in (40.06 m); height 39 ft 0½ in (11.90 m); wing area 1,975.2 sq ft (183.50 m²)
Operators: Aeroflot, Ceskoslovenské Aerolinie, and the Soviet air force

Tupolev Tu-114

History and Notes
In 1953 Aeroflot embarked on a major programme of re-equipment, this leading to the Tupolev Tu-104 that revolutionised air travel in the Soviet Union, and to the Tu-114 which, when it appeared at the Paris Air Show in June 1959, was the world's largest and heaviest commercial transport aircraft. First flown on 3 October 1957, at the time of the 40th anniversary of the Russian Revolution, the Tu-114 was named *Rossiya* (Russia) for a short period.

The Tu-114 derived from the Tu-20 military bomber, which had first been seen at Tushino in 1955, and retained similar wing, tail unit, and landing gear structures wedded to a completely new fuselage. By comparison with the Tu-20, both wing and tailplane were set low on the fuselage, which was of circular cross-section and provided accommodation for a maximum of 220 passengers. Standard seating layout was, however, for 170 passengers, or only 120 on long-range non-stop routes. Pressurisation and air-conditioning was standard, and electric lifts were provided to carry food from lower-deck galleys to serving positions in the main cabin. Landing gear was of retractable tricycle type, each main unit consisting of a massive four-wheel bogie and the nose unit carrying twin-wheels. The main units retracted aft to be housed in very conspicuous fairings that projected well aft of the wing trailing-edge.

The powerplant was wing-mounted, and comprised four Kuznetsov turboprops in long nacelles extending forward of the wing leading-edge. Each of these engines was rated initially at 12,000 eshp (8952 kW), but later benefitted from an uprating of almost 25 per cent. Each engine had two contra-rotating propellers 18 ft 4½ in (5.60 m) in diameter, which not only highlights the size of the transport, but also helps to explain how this giant aircraft remains in early 1981 the fastest propeller-driven aeroplane in the world, having established the record on 9 April 1960, when a 55,115-lb (25000-kg) payload

was carried over a 3,107-mile (5000-km) circuit at a speed of 545.07 mph (877.212 km/h).

During the spring of 1960 Ivan Sukhomlin, who piloted the Tu-114 when the above speed record was set, also established a series of height-with-payload records which remained unbeaten in early 1981. No less impressive was a New York—Moscow flight time of 9 hr 48 min which the prototype recorded on a first proving flight at the end of June 1959. On 24 April 1961 the type entered service with Aeroflot on the airline's 4,225-mile (6800-km) route between Moscow and Khabarovsk.

Despite such achievements, only about 30 entered service with Aeroflot, very long-range routes for which the Tu-114 was intended. One variant, of which only two or three examples appear to have been built, had the designation Tu-114D. Generally similar to the basic Tu-114, and intended to carry a small number of passengers, mail, or urgent cargo over long ranges, it differed mainly in having a fuselage very much like that of the military Tu-20 bomber. So far as is known, none of these Tu-114/Tu-114Ds remain in service.

Specification
Type: long-range commercial transport
Powerplant (Tu-114): four 14,795-eshp (11033-kW) Kuznetsov NK-12MV turboprops
Performance: maximum level speed 541 mph (870 km/h) at 26,245 ft (8000 m); maximum cruising speed 478 mph (770 km/h) at 29,530 ft (9000 m); service

The Tupolev Tu-114 may have been something of an aerial oddity, but it was a magnificent one, with four enormous engines requiring massive contra-rotating propellers to turn the turbines' power into effective motive force.

ceiling 39,370 ft (12000 m); range with maximum payload and fuel reserves 3,853 miles (6200 km); range with maximum fuel, fuel reserves and 33,069-lb (15000-kg) payload 5,561 miles (8950 km)
Weights: empty 200,620 lb (91000 kg); maximum take-off 376,990 lb (171000 kg)
Dimensions: span 167 ft 7¾ in (51.10 m); length 177 ft 6 in (54.10 m); height 50 ft 10¼ in (15.50 m); wing area 3,348.8 sq ft (311.10 m²)
Operator: Aeroflot when in service

Tupolev Tu-124

History and Notes
The undoubted success of the Tupolev Tu-104 resulted in Aeroflot indicating their need for a turbine-powered short/medium-range airliner to replace the piston-engined Ilyushin Il-14 in service on such routes. A capability for the new aircraft to operate from shorter length or unpaved runways was an essential part of the requirement.

To cater for this, Tupolev's bureau initiated the design of what was, in effect, a reduced-scale version of the Tu-104. Two areas needed special attention: the provision of short/rough-field capability, and the introduction of more economical engines. The first requirement was met by an extension of the wing trailing-edge

between the engines and landing gear fairings; the introduction of double-slotted trailing-edge flaps and, immediately forward of them, spoilers that are used conventionally in the air, but which extend automatically as the wheels touch the ground to act as lift-dumpers; the provision of a large under-fuselage airbrake used both to steepen the angle of approach and to reduce the landing run; and the introduction of short-stroke tricycle landing gear (with twin nose-wheels and four-wheel main bogies) with fast-operating hydraulic retraction to reduce to a minimum landing gear drag from the moment the aircraft becomes airborne.

One of the criticisms levelled against the Tu-104 was that its

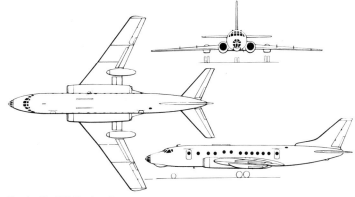

Tupolev Tu-124 'Cookpot'

powerplant was not economically viable, and if the Tu-104 had been evaluated purely on an economic basis this was almost certainly a valid comment: it was, however, capacity and speed with made this first turbojet-powered airliner so valuable to Aeroflot. The major shortcoming of all early turbojet engines was their high specific fuel consumption, and operation at high altitude was then the only real palliative available. Engine designers were to discover that improved combustion chambers and increased compression ratios offered lower specific fuel consumptions, but it was the development of turbofan engines that changed significantly the economics of pure jet engines and, at the same time, reduced considerably the noise pollution of airport environments. The Soloviev D-20Ps installed in the Tu-124 were of this latter class of engine, being of two-spool configuration, and the first powerplant of this type to equip any of the world's short/medium-range small jet-powered transports, antedating any similar installation in any other nation by more than two years.

Tu-124s entered service with Aeroflot on the Moscow—Ul'yanovsk route on 10 November 1962. These aircraft provided accommodation for 44 passengers; the standard version, however, was the 56-seat Tu-124V introduced at a later date, and there were also the Tu-124K and Tu-124K2 with de luxe accommodation seating 36 and 22 passengers respectively. It is believed that about 100 were built: of these three were supplied to Ceskoslovenské Aerolinie, two to East Germany's Interflug, and other examples to the air forces of East Germany, India and Iraq. By mid-1980 about 80 remained in service

with Aeroflot, and three and one respectively with the air forces of East Germany and India.

Specification
Type: short/medium-range twin-turbofan airliner
Powerplant: two 11,905-lb (5400-kg) thrust Soloviev D-20P turbofans
Performance: maximum speed 603 mph (970 km/h) at 26,250 ft

540 mph (870 km/h); economic (8000 m); maximum cruising speed 497 mph (800 km/h) at 32,800 ft (10000 m); service ceiling 38,385 ft (11700 m); range with maximum payload 758 miles (1220 km); range with maximum fuel 1,305 miles (2100 km)
Weights: empty 49,604 lb (22500 kg); maximum take-off 83,776 lb (38000 kg)
Dimensions: span 83 ft 9¾ in

The Tupolev Tu-124 was developed from the larger Tu-104 to provide Aeroflot with a short-range turbine-engined airliner for important routes.

(25.55 m); length 100 ft 4 in (30.58 m); height 26 ft 6 in (8.08 m); wing area 1,280.9 sq ft (119 m²)
Operators: Aeroflot, Ceskoslovenské Aerolinie, Interflug, and the air forces of East Germany, India and Iraq

Tupolev Tu-134

History and Notes
Although the Tupolev Tu-104 and Tu-124 had proved revolutionary aircraft so far as Aeroflot's domestic operations were concerned, their very limited success in the export market seemed to underline the fact that by comparison with the products of other nations they were less attractive to prospective customers. Certainly this was true of interior layout which was, after all, the aspect most likely to affect acceptance by the fare-paying public, to whom the niceties of one or another technological device meant little. So a decision was made to develop a new short-haul medium-capacity airliner for use by Aeroflot and, hopefully for the export market.

Work began soon after the Tu-124 had entered service and the new aircraft, similar in size and capability requirements to the Tu-124, was designated provisionally Tu-124A. This, however, was soon altered, for although the wings, fuselage and landing gear were generally similar to those of the earlier aircraft, there were some fundamental changes which justified the allocation of the entirely new designation Tu-134.

The principal change related to the adoption of a rear-engine layout of the type pioneered by the Sud-Aviation Caravelle, and this in turn dictated the replacement of the Tu-124's conventional tail unit by a high-mounted T-tail to ensure that the horizontal surfaces would be unaffected by the efflux from the turbofan engines. The need for the Tu-134 to operate into and out of similar short/rough fields as the Tu-

Tupolev Tu-134A of LOT (Polskie Linie Lotnicze), Poland.

124 meant that it retained the same high-lift wing features, landing gear, and fuselage-mounted airbrake.

The powerplant of the prototype is believed to have been the same as that of production Tu-124s, but the five pre-production aircraft and subsequent production examples were powered by two Soloviev D-30 turbofans. Interior configuration varied: the early production Tu-134 which entered service with Aeroflot in September 1967 could accommodate 72 passengers in a four-abreast layout, but alternatives included 68 passengers in a one-class or 64 in a dual-class (8 first-class and 56 tourist-class) arrangement. A lengthened fuselage Tu-134A was introduced in the autumn of 1970, with accommodation for 76 to 80 passengers, and power provided by a pair of the improved Soloviev D-30-2 turbofans with thrust-reversers. This model also had an APU for ground air-conditioning or self-contained start capability. Some late versions of the Tu-134A dispensed with the glazed fuselage nose, which had been a distinctive feature of the Tu-104 and Tu-124 also, adopting instead a 'solid' nose with weather radar.

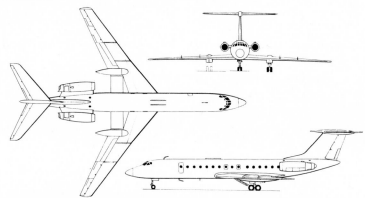

Tupolev Tu-134A 'Crusty'

Apparently the Tupolev team had arrived at an acceptable airliner so far as export customers were concerned for in addition to those which were built for Aeroflot (estimated as about 250), the Tu-134 was supplied also to Aviogenex, Balkan Bulgarian, Ceskoslovenské Aerolinie, Interflug, LOT, and Malev. Of the total of approximately 520 which have been built since the type first entered service in late 1967, the majority

remained in airline use in 1980.

Specification
Type: short/medium-range airliner
Powerplant (Tu-134A): two 14,990-lb (6800-kg) thrust Soloviev D-30-2 turbofans
Performance: maximum cruising speed 550 mph (885 km/h) at 32,800 ft (10000 m); normal cruising speed 466-528 mph (750-850 km/h); service ceiling 39,040 ft

Tupolev Tu-134

(11900 m); range with maximum payload 1,174 miles (1890 km); range with 11,025-lb (5000-kg) payload 1,876 miles (3020 km)
Weights: operating empty 63,934 lb (29000 kg); maximum take-off 103,617 lb (47000 lg)
Dimensions: span 95 ft 2 in (29.01 m); length 121 ft 6½ in (37.05 m); height 30 ft 0 in (9.14 m); wing area 1,370.3 sq ft (127.30 m²)
Operators: Aeroflot, Aviogenex, Balkan Bulgarian Airlines, Československé Aerolinie, Interflug, LOT, and Malev, plus several air forces which have predominantly Soviet equipment

Malév, the Hungarian state airline, has six Tupolev Tu-134 short/medium-range transports, including this Tu-134A. Aeroflot has some 400 Tu-134s, and small numbers are operated by other Eastern European communist states, while Hang Khong Vietnam's fleet includes two of the stretched Tu-134As.

Tupolev Tu-144

History and Notes
When, on 14 October 1947, the USAF's Captain Charles ('Chuck') Yeager piloted the Bell X-1 rocket-powered research aircraft at a speed in excess of Mach 1 for the first time, he had initiated a new dimension in the capability of heavier-than-air craft. Under the entry for the Aéro-spatiale/British Aerospace Concorde, this event and its repercussions are dealt with in greater detail, but it led, in civil affairs, to the development of the Anglo/French Concorde and Soviet Tupolev Tu-144 supersonic transport (SST) aircraft.

The potential value of such aircraft on the civil transport scene has been amply demonstrated by Concorde, which has brought communication links between Britain/France and the United States to a time scale that would have staggered the pioneers of aviation. This is no place to argue the real need for such aircraft, their effects on pollution of the environment, or their thirst for rapidly diminishing hydrocarbon fuels. And while we have no figures available to confirm or deny the economic viability of the Tu-144, there is little doubt that Concorde services are prestigious rather than profitable. None of these comments is intended to denigrate the technological miracle of these SSTs which have, despite the complexity of their design and systems, shown remarkable despatch reliability and high standards of safety.

We know why Concorde was designed, developed and put into production; we do not have any reason to believe that the Tu-144 was built as a result of radically different conclusions. It has, of course, been suggested that development of an SST in the Soviet Union was necessary to keep face with the West, but in view of this nation's technological achievements in conventional aircraft and spacecraft this would seem a somewhat illogical suggestion. Far more valid a reason for the development of a Soviet SST had surely been given by the Tupolev Tu-104, which had virtually revolutionised air transport over the long internal air routes of the Soviet Union. If an aircraft with a cruising speed of 500 mph (805 km/h) had achieved so much, what was the potential value of a civil transport with a cruising speed three times that figure? There was only one way

to find out: design and build it.

The Tupolev design bureau began this process in the early 1960s, exhibiting a model at the Paris Air Show in 1965. Between that time and construction of the prototype there was considerable refinement of the design, and this first prototype (CCCP-68001) was flown into aviation history by Eduard Elyan and his crew on 31 December 1968, recording the first flight of a supersonic airliner anywhere in the world. It was flown at a speed in excess of Mach 1 for the first time on 5 June 1969, and on 26 May 1970 became the first commercial transport to exceed Mach 2. Since then it is reported to have flown at a speed in excess of Mach 2.4.

There have been many comments in the past regarding the Tu-144's similarity to the Anglo/French Concord and, in fact, some journalists were to highlight this by dubbing the Tu-144 as Concordski. In fact, both aircraft were designed quite independently to have a similar flight envelope and, by the nature of modern design techniques, were therefore likely to be very similar in appearance. For example, a design cruising speed of around Mach 2.0 was chosen in both East and West so that the airframe could be constructed largely of conventional materials. A normal cruising speed much in excess of Mach 2.3 would have meant that titanium, or other metals and synthetic materials, would have had to be used, despite cost or complexity, to overcome the problems caused by kinetic heating of the airframe.

An ogival delta wing was chosen by both manufacturing sources for similar reasons, because the wing needs to be thin to keep drag to a minimum, and that is also why each aircraft has its powerplant grouped at the rear of the wing. And because the large angle of attack necessary for such a wing at take-off and landing puts the aircraft into an attitude which limits severely the pilot's view, each aircraft has a drooping nose to improve this vision problem.

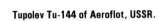

Tupolev Tu-144 of Aeroflot, USSR.

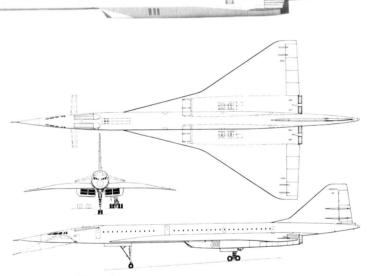

Tupolev Tu-144 'Charger'

In detail, of course, the Tu-144 differs considerably from Concorde. The wing is of double-delta planform, with the inboard (or forward) section swept 76°, and the outer (or rear) panels swept 57°. Four separate powered elevons are provided at the trailing-edge of each wing, these serving for control in both pitch and roll. The rudder is built in two sections, and both of these are power operated. Small foreplanes are incorporated in the fuselage structure immediately aft of the flight deck, and are retracted into the fuselage except for take-off and landing, when they are extended to enhance low-speed control characteristics.

The landing gear is of retractable tricycle type, the steerable nose unit carrying twin wheels. Each main unit on production aircraft carries an eight-wheel bogie (the prototype had 12-wheel bogies) and an interesting feature is that the wheels are thermally insulated during flight to prevent deterioration of the tyres by kinetic heating.

The powerplant consists of four Kuznetsov NK-144 turbofan engines, and the prototype had these mounted side by side in a large single under-

wing fairing with a bifurcated air intake, each side feeding two engines. The prototype's engines were each rated at 28,660-lb (13000-kg) thrust without afterburning, and at 38,580-lb (17500-kg) thrust with full afterburning. The engines of production aircraft differ in their installation, being paired in two separate ducts, and have a full afterburning rating of 44,092-lb (20000-kg) thrust. In both prototype and production aircraft the intake ducts are divided so that each engine receives an independent flow of air, this being controlled by fully automatic movable ramps that ensure the optimum flow of air to the engines at all speeds and altitudes.

Accommodation is provided for a flight crew of three, and production aircraft have seating for 140 passengers as standard. Baggage and freight are contained within the aft fuselage, more or less in line with the engines.

Little positive detail is known of operational use of the Tu-144. The first route proving trials began during 1974, and on 26 December 1976 Aeroflot began a regular freight/mail service with these aircraft between

Moscow and Alma Ata. This route of some 1,864 miles (3000 km) required a flight time of approximately 2 hours. Similar route-proving flights were carried out over the Moscow—Khabarovsk route during 1977, and it is believed that twice-weekly passenger flight were inaugurated between Moscow and Alma Ata in late 1977, continuing until mid-June 1978 when all flights were suspended after an accident involving a Tu-144 making a non-commercial flight.

A developed version, which has the designation Tu-144D, has been reported to have made a proving flight of 3,843 miles (6185 km) on 23 June 1979, in a flight time of 3 hours 21 minutes. Little is known of the improvements, but it is believed to be powered by newly-developed Kolesov turbojet engines. The details below apply to the basic Tu-144.

Specification
Type: supersonic transport
Powerplant: four Kuznetsov NK-144 turbofans, each developing 44,092-lb (20000-kg) thrust with full reheat
Performance: maximum cruising speed, 1,553 mph (2500 km/h); normal cruising speed 1,305-1,429 (2100-2300 km/h); cruising altitude between 52,495 and 59,055 ft (16000 and 18000 m); maximum range with 140 passengers 4,039 miles (6,500 km)
Weights: operating empty

187,393 lb (85000 kg); maximum take-off 396,832 lb (180000 kg)
Dimensions: span 94 ft 5¾ in (28.80 m); length 215 ft 6½ in

(65.70 m); height, wheels up 42 ft 2 in (12.85 m); wing area 4,714.75 sq ft (438.00 m²)
Operator: Aeroflot

The Tupolev Tu-144 supersonic transport bears a close resemblance to the Anglo-French Concorde, perhaps reflecting almost identical requirements;

Tupolev Tu-154

History and Notes
First information that a new three-engined commercial transport was being developed in the Soviet Union was released in the spring of 1966. The new aircraft was intended to replace the earlier-generation turbojet powered Tu-104, and the turbo-prop-powered Antonov An-10 and Ilyushin Il-18 on medium/long-range routes. With the release of this news came also the information that prototype and pre-production aircraft were then under construction.

In some respects, this new design from the Tupolev bureau was to required to combine features of all three aircraft that it was intended to replace: the capability of the An-10 to operate from and to secondary airfields where the best surface to be expected was packed earth and gravel; it needed also to have the speed of the Tu-104, for this aircraft had revolutionised Aeroflot's operations by reducing flight time by more than half over any routes; and no less important, it must have the range capability of the Il-18, for even on Aeroflot's domestic routes very long stages could be required, especially in what was then a period of rapid expansion. Another desired feature was an ability to operate at a high flight level, for this would reduce air traffic congestion over the Soviet Union's network of domestic routes. By ensuring that when it came into service the new Tu-154 would be able to fly economically, and with good separation above the bulk of the Soviet Union's air traffic, the additional flight control burden would be kept to a minimum.

All of these requirements helped shape the prototype aircraft which flew for the first time on October 1968. Of cantilever low-wing configuration, it shares with several other commercial transports a wing swept at 35° for high-speed performance and one of comparatively large area for cruising flight at a

Tupolev Tu-154B of Malév (Magyar Légiközlekedési Vállalat), Hungary.

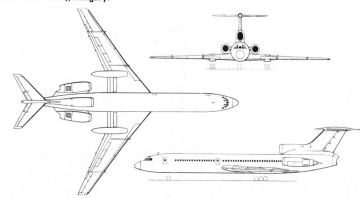

Tupolev Tu-154 'Careless'

level of around 36,090-39,370 ft (11000-12000 m). For the short-field performance needed at secondary airfields each wing incorporates leading-edge slats over about 80 per cent of the span, and triple-slotted trailing-edge flaps. Forward of the flaps are four-section upper-surface spoilers which, in a number of differing modes, serve as airbrakes, or lift dumpers, or to supplement the conventional ailerons for roll control.

The fuselage is of circular-section semi-monocoque fail-safe construction incorporating pressurisation of the flight-deck, cabin, and two under-floor baggage holds. The T-tail has all-swept surfaces, and the retractable tricycle type landing gear is designed to cater for the sub-standard surface of secondary airfields. This means that there are a total of 14 wheels to support the aircraft's weight: twin nosewheels, and a six-wheel bogie on each main unit. Accommodation caters for a standard flight crew of four, with provision for additional check or training personnel, and from 128 to 167 passengers can be seated in a variety of layouts.

Although slightly larger in overall dimensions, the Tu-154 is in very much the same class of transport as Boeing's Model 727. Its three-engine configuration was chosen for very much the same reasons, and was regarded also as giving better than two-engine reliability with better than four-engine economy. The powerplant comprises three 20.945-lb (9500-

kg) thrust Kuznetsov NK-8-2 turbofan engines, one pod-mounted on each side of the rear fuselage, the third in the fuselage tailcone with its inlet on the upper surface of the fuselage, forward of the fin. Avionics are to a high standard, and include automatic flight control and automatic navigation systems. Automatic landing equipment has also been standard, but its scope has been developed progressively, with full Category III capability thought to be due for introduction in 1980-1.

Six prototype/pre-production aircraft were built to speed the development programme. The seventh aircraft entered service with Aeroflot in early 1971 for evaluation and route-proving. Subsequent deliveries were used for initial mail and cargo

flights, with the first domestic revenue services being established on a regular basis on 8 February 1972. The first international services were flown later that year.

Since the entry into service of the Tu-154, improved Tu-154A and Tu-154B versions have been developed. Both have increased-power Kuznetsov NK-8-2U turbofans, greater fuel capacity, and introduce improvements to enhance performance and reliability. The internal configuration of the Tu-154A is little changed from that of the original version, but the Tu-154B has a slightly lengthened cabin, without any change in fuselage external dimensions, to accommodate a maximum of 169 passengers without any reduction in cabin facilities. The first Tu-154As are believed to have entered service in 1975, and production of Tu-154Bs began in 1977. Total construction, for Aeroflot and for export, was believed to be approaching about 400 aircraft in late 1980. The details below apply to the Tu-154B.

Specification
Type: medium/long-range transport
Powerplant: three 23,150-lb (10500-kg) thrust Kuznetsov NK-82U turbofans
Performance: cruising speed 560-590 mph (901-950 km/h) at 39,370 ft (12000 m); range with 160 passengers 2,019 miles (3250 km); range with maximum payload 1,709 miles (2750 km)
Weights: empty operating 111,940 lb (50775 kg); maximum take-off 211,644 lb (96000 kg)
Dimensions: span 123 ft 2¼ in (37.55 m); length 157 ft 1¾ in (47.90 m); height 37 ft 4¾ in (11.40 m); wing area 2168.46 sq ft (201.45 m²)
Operators include: Aeroflot, Balkan Bulgarian Airlines, Choson Minhang Civil Aviation Company, Malév, and Tarom

The Tupolev Tu-154 is used by the airlines of some Russian satellites, some nine Tu-154Bs being operated by the Romanian national airline, Tarom.

UTVA-56/60

History and Notes
The Yugoslav company Fabrika Aviona Utva designed and constructed the prototype of a four-seat utility aircraft which flew for the first time on 22 April 1959. Of braced high-wing monoplane configuration, this was powered by a 260-hp (194-kW) Avco Lycoming GO-435 piston engine, and was designed UTVA-56. Early testing was satisfactory, but during finalisation of the design, prior to production, it was decided to introduce a slightly more powerful engine. This, plus detail changes in design, resulted in a change of designation to UTVA-60.

Of all-metal construction, the UTVA-60 had a wing incorporating ailerons that were interlinked to droop when the trailing-edge flaps were extended. Landing gear was of conventional tailwheel type, the main units comprising cantilever steel-tube struts, with rubber-in-compression shock absorbtion. Accommodation was provided for a pilot and three passengers, but interior changes could be made easily so that the UTVA-60 could serve as an air ambulance, or for cargo-carrying.

Four other versions were available to complement the basic four-seat utility model identified as the U-60-AT1. These others comprised the U-60-AT2, intended primarily as a trainer and equipped with dual controls; the U-60-Ag agricultural version; the U-60-AM air ambulance; and the U-60H floatplane. This last differed from the others in having a strengthened fuselage structure, and in the installation of a 296-hp (221-kW) Avco Lycoming GO-480-G1H6

engine. The details which follow apply specifically to the basic U-60-AT1.

Specification
Type: four-seat general utility lightplane
Powerplant: one 270-hp (201-kW) Avco Lycoming GO-480-B1A6 flat-six piston engine
Performance: maximum cruising speed 143 mph (230 km/h); service ceiling 17,060 ft (5200 m); range 780 miles (1255 km)
Weights: empty 2,099 lb (952 kg); maximum take-off 3,571 lb (1620 kg)
Dimensions: span 37 ft 4¾ in (11.40 m); length 26 ft 11½ in

(80.22 m); height 8 ftd 11 in (2.72 wing area 194.62 sq ft (18.08 m²)

The UTVA-56 utility monoplane was built in small numbers before it was supplanted in production by the more powerful and versatile UTVA-60, which can be used for a variety of roles depending on the equipment fitted.

Varga Model 2150A Kachina

History and Notes
Not long after World War II William J. Morrisey, who had been a test pilot of the Douglas Aircraft Company, formed Morrisey Aviation Inc. to build and market an attractive two-seat lightplane of wood structure

known then as the Morrisey Nifty. The introduction of all-metal construction and powerplant changes led to the Morrisey 2150, built from 1958. Ten were produced before construction rights were acquired by Shinn Engineering Inc. This company

during the early 1960s built about 50 examples of an improved Shinn Model 2150A, before selling the manufacturing rights to the Varga Aircraft Corporation in 1965.

Varga continues to build this aircraft as the Model 2150A Kachina, which

differs primarily from its immediate predecessor by the installation of a more powerful engine. The Kachina is a cantilever low-wing monoplane, and its wing incorporates plain ailerons and two-position trailing-edge flaps. The tail unit is conventional, and the

Varga Model 2150A Kachina

landing gear of non-retractable tricycle type. Accommodation is provided for two people, and with dual controls as standard equipment the Kachina can be used for both sporting and training purposes.

Specification
Type: two-seat lightweight sport/training aircraft
Powerplant: one 150-hp (112-kW) Avco Lycoming O-320-A2C flat-four piston engine
Performance: maximum level speed 148 mph (238 km/h) at sea level; maximum cruising speed 135 mph (217 km/h); economic cruising speed 127 mph (204 km/h); service ceiling 22,000 ft (6705 m); range with maximum fuel 525 miles (845 km)
Weights: empty 1,125 lb (510 kg) maximum take-off 1,817 lb (924 kg)
Dimensions: span 30 ft 0 in (9.14 m); length 21 ft 2 in (6.45 m); height 7 ft 0 in (2.13 m); wing area 144 sq ft (13.38 m²)

The Varga Kachina is the latest version of a design that first appeared in 1957 as the Morrisey Nifty. Between the Morrisey and Varga models there was also the Model 2150-A version produced by Shinn Engineering.

Vickers Vanguard

History and Notes
Successful operations with the Vickers Viscount encouraged BEA to look for a larger-capacity replacement in the 100-seat class. Vickers had then been considering a further 'stretch' of the Viscount, but the need to provide standard seating for 100 passengers could not be met in this way, so the evolution of a completely new aircraft was begun under the Vickers company designation Type 870. The design of an airframe of this capacity represented no serious problems, once that agreement was reached between the company and BEA regarding the full operational requirements, but matters had been complicated by the fact that Trans-Canada Air Lines (now Air Canada) was also looking for a commercial transport in much the same category, but had differing views on configuration. BEA was opting for a high-wing layout, one that was most appealing to passengers but TCA demanded the far more practical low-wing configuration, and finally got its way. The ultimate design had strayed considerably from the original Type 870 concept, becoming the Type 950, with the name Vanguard, by the time that construction of 20 aircraft for BEA began in 1956. TCA, requiring longer range, ordered a generally similar aircraft, but in this version there was some strengthening of the airframe to permit operation at a higher gross weight.

Perhaps the Vanguard might have enjoyed a similar success to the Viscount, but the selection of turboprop powerplant was to spell failure for what was, in other respects, a well designed aircraft. The installation of turbojets, then less economic in operation, especially over short ranges, might have made all the difference. As it was, the Vanguard attracted only the original two buyers, despite having a maximum high-density seating capacity for 139 passengers. Other airlines looked instead for turbojet-powered aircraft, with engines that were soon developed to provide these transports with performance capabilities that were far more attractive to the fare-paying passengers. Of the total of 43 Vanguards built, one of TCA's was converted for all cargo operation. The details below apply to this type.

Specification
Type: short/medium-range transport
Powerplant: four 5,545-ehp (4135-ekW) Rolls-Royce Tyne RTy.11 Mk 512 turboprops
Performance: maximum cruising speed 425 mph (684 km/h) at 20,000 ft (6100 m); economic cruising speed 420 mph (676 km/h) at 25,000 ft (7620 m); service ceiling 30,000 ft (9145 m); range with maximum payload, no reserves 1,830 miles (2945 km); range with maximum fuel 3,100 miles (4989 km)

Vickers Vanguard

The Vickers Vanguard, like the Lockheed Electra, fell foul of customer preference for turbojet-powered airliners, but has soldiered on in limited numbers as the Merchantman freighter with operators such as Air-Bridge Carriers, which has three.

Vickers Vanguard

Weights: empty equipped 82,500 lb (37421 kg); maximum take-off 146,500 lb (66451 kg)
Dimensions: span 118 ft 7 in (36.14 m); length 122 ft 10½ in (37.45 m); height 34 ft 11 in (10.64 m); wing area 1,529.0 sq ft (142.04 m²)
Operators include: Air Bridge Carriers, British Airways, Europe Aero Service, and PT Merpati Nusantara Airlines

Vickers Vanguard of Europe Aero Service, France.

Vickers Viscount

History and Notes

The aircraft which was named originally as Viceroy, but renamed Viscount after India became an independent state within the British Commonwealth, originated from proposals of the wartime Brabazon Committee. Under the chairmanship of Lord Brabazon, this had been formed in late 1942 and charged with the task of steering British civil aviation development in the immediate years after World War II. One of the committee's recommendations was for a 24-seat short/medium-range transport for services to and within Europe, this being identified as the Brabazon IIA with piston engines, or IIB with new powerplants known as propeller-turbines (now turboprops) which were then under development.

To meet this requirement, Vickers Aircraft was requested in April 1945 to submit proposals for the turboprop-powered IIB version. The result was the company's VC2 design, which emerged in original prototype form as the Type 630. Powered by four 1,380-ehp (1029-ekW) Rolls-Royce Dart RDa.I Mark 502 engines, this flew for the first time on 16 July 1948. Although its performance was impressive, the turbine powerplant providing new standards of smooth operation, it failed to attract any real interest from the airlines because its 32-seat capacity was considered to be inadequate. Fortunately, an uprated version of the Dart turboprop became available from Rolls-Royce, and this made it possible to increase the gross weight of the Type 630 by some 16 per cent to 45,000 lb (20412 kg), which meant that the fuselage could be 'stretched' to accommodate a maximum of 43 passengers in high density seating. Discussions between Vickers and British European Airways (BEA) finalised the specification of an acceptable Type 700 Viscount, a prototype of which was ordered on 24 February 1949. This (G-AMAV) flew for the first time on 28 August 1950. Before that date, however, the original Type 630, operating under a special certificate of airworthiness, began the world's first scheduled commercial passenger service with a turbine-powered aircraft: a short-term special BEA service, between London and Paris, flown first on 29 July 1950 and lasting for two weeks. This was followed by a nine-day London-Edinburgh service, beginning on 15 August 1950, and in these two trial operating periods more than 1,800 passengers had been carried. BEA had gained valuable experience, and had been able to discover the delighted reaction of those passengers to the new age of smooth, high-speed travel.

The first production Viscount for BEA flew on 20 August 1952, this being certificated on 17 April 1953 before being used to inaugurate Viscount services between London and Cyprus on the following day. The success in service of these early Viscounts, and the favourable customer reaction to their comfort and performance, resulted in a mass of orders. When significant numbers were sold into the highly competitive North American market, it seemed that at long last the British aircraft industry had broken the USA's hold on what, since the mid-1930s, had become very much that country's field of manufacture. Later events were to prove these hopes to be premature, but the Viscount retains the record of being Britain's most extensively built airliner.

Of conventional low-wing configuration, with a circular-section pressurised fuselage, and retractable tricycle type landing gear, the Type 700 was powered by 1,400-shp (1044-kW) Dart Mk 506, or 1,600-shp

Despite its obsolescence, the Vickers Viscount is still in service, with some 100 scattered in various parts of the world. PT Merpati Nusantara Airlines of Indonesia currently deploys six Viscount 800s.

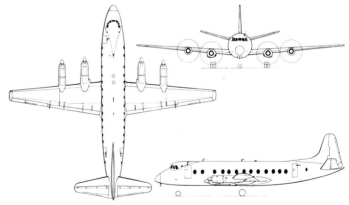

(1193-kW) Dart Mk 510 turboprops in the 700D, with accommodation for 40 to 59 passengers according to seat pitch. Dart Mk 510 turboprops also powered the lengthened-fuselage (by 3 ft 10 in: 1.17 m) Type

800, which by relocation of the cabin rear bulkhead was extended sufficiently to seat from 65 to 71 passengers. The final version was the Type 810, with Dart Mk 525 engines and structural strengthen-

Vicker Viscount 800 of British Midland Airways.

ing to allow operation at a higher gross weight. When the last examples of this version were delivered in 1964, production of all Viscounts had totalled 444. The details below apply to the Type 810.

Specification
Type: short/medium-range transport
Powerplant: four 2,100-ehp (1566-ekW) Rolls-Royce Dart RDa.7/1 Mk 525 turboprops
Performance: maximum cruising speed 350 mph (563 km/h) at 20,000 ft (6100 m); service ceiling 25,000 ft (7620 m); range with maximum payload, no reserves 1,725 miles (2776 km); range with maximum fuel, no reserves 1,760 miles (2832 km)
Weights: empty operating 41,565 lb (18854 kg); maximum take-off 72,500 lb (32885 kg)
Dimensions: span 93 ft 8½ in (28.56 m); length 85 ft 8 in (26.11 m); height 26 ft 9 in (8.15 m); wing area 963.0 sq ft (89.46 m²)
Operators include: Aeropesca Colombia, Aerovias del Cesar, Air Botswana, Air Malawi, Air Zimbabwe, Alidair, British

Airways, British Midland Airways, CAAC, Far Eastern Air Transport, Gibraltar Airways, Guernsey Airlines, Huns Air, Jersey European Airways, Kanif-Arkia

Airlines, Lao Aviation, PT Merpati Nusantara Airlines, Pluna, Protea Airways, SAN, Southern International Air Transport, Zaïre Aero Service

Another significant operator of the Vickers Viscount was British Air Ferries, but from October 1978 the company transferred its scheduled services, operated by Viscount, to Air UK.

Victa Airtourer

History and Notes
Victa Ltd, which had been a manufacturer of light two-stroke petrol engines, established an avaiation department in 1959 to initiate production of a two-seat lightplane. The brainchild of Henry Millicer, chief aerodynamicist of Australia's Government Aircraft Factories, this aircraft was designed as an entry in a light aeroplane competition sponsored by the British Royal Aero Club in 1953, and for which no fewer than 103 entries were received. Millicer's design proved to be the winner, but it was not until 31 March 1959 that the prototype flew for the first time, having been built by the Air Tourer group of the Australian Ultra Light Aircraft Association.

The first production Airtourers, built by Victa, were delivered in mid-1962, initially the Airtourer 100 with a 100-hp (75-kW) Continental O-200-A piston engine. The prototype of a generally similar Airtourer 115 with a 115-hp (86-kW) Avco Lycoming O-235-C2 engine flew for the first time on 17 September 1962, with deliveries of production aircraft beginning after the attainment of certification on 6 July 1963. A total of 170 Airtourers was built by Victa before production ended in late 1966.

However, manufacture of Air-

tourers was to continue in New Zealand, where Aero Engine Services Ltd (AESL) acquired the production rights. AESL did not resume construction of the Airtourer 100, concentrating initially oin the Airtourer 115, but flying in September 1968 the prototype of a generally similar Airtourer 150 with the 150-hp (112-kW) Avco Lycoming O-320-E2A, and in November 1968 a Super Airtourer 150, which differed by the addition of a constant-speed propeller. But production came to an end in 1973, when AESL merged with Air Parts (NZ) Ltd to form New Zealand Aerospace Industries Ltd, and the standard Airtourer was dropped in favour of a four-seat development known as the Aerospace Airtrainer.

Apart from powerplant changes, all Airtourers were generally similar, being of cantilever low-wing monoplane configuration, with a fixed tricycle landing gear. Advanced features of this small tourer, that had undoubtedly led to its success in the 1953 competition, included interconnected ailerons and flaps, so that both functioned simultaneously as ailerons and flaps; a steerable nosewheel; and enclosed accommodation in a cabin that included as standard dual controls, heating and ventilation, good soundproofing, and space for

100 lb (45 kg) of luggage.

Specification
Type: two-seat sport/trainer aircraft
Powerplant (Airtourer 115); one 115-hp (86-kW) Avco Lycoming O-235-C2 flat-four piston engine
Performance: maximum level speed at sea level 142 mph (229 km/h); maximum cruising speed 131 mph (211 km/h) at 4,000 ft (1220 m); economic cruising speed 110 mph (177 km/h) at 5,000 ft (1525 m); service ceiling

The Victa Airtourer is a highly compact two-seat touring aircraft of Australian design. The rights to the aircraft were bought in the 1960s by Aero Engine Services Ltd (AESL), now New Zealand Aerospace Industries.

14,000 ft (4265 m); range with maximum fuel 710 miles (1143 km)
Weights: empty 1,080 lb (490 kg); maximum take-off 1,650 lb (748 kg)
Dimensions: span 26 ft 0 in (7.92 m); length 21 ft 6 in (6.55 m); height 7 ft 0 in (2.13 m); wing area 120 sq ft (11.15 m²)

Wassmer WA.40 and 41/Cerva CE.43 Series

History and Notes
Wassmer Aviation was one of France's oldest aircraft companies, initially a repair and overhaul organisation founded in 1905 as Société Wassmer.

After World War II some aircraft were licence-built, but in 1955 the company started a design department. The first type to enter production was a variant of the famous Jodel series, the D.120 Paris-Nice. Production of Jodels and sailplanes formed the backbone of the company's manufacturing business well into the 1960s, but in June 1959 the prototype of a new four/five-seat touring monoplane was flown. Designated WA.40, this had a retractable tricycle landing gear and a 180-hp (134-kW) Avco Lycoming O-360-

A1A engine. The new aircraft went into production and by the middle of 1961, when 25 had been delivered, the construction rate was three a month. Three versions were available. All were WA.40 Super IVs, so the individual models were distinguished by name: the Pariou was the basic version, the Baladou was a deluxe model, and the Sancy was an up-market Baladou with equipment for IFR flying. Improvements intro-

The Wassmer WA.40 series was developed in three basic models: the WA.40 and WA.40A original variants, the latter having swept vertical surfaces; the WA.4/21 with an extra 70 hp (52 kW) of power; and the WA.41 which had fixed landing gear.

duced from the 53rd production aircraft included a swept fin and rudder, and the type was designated WA.40A, the first flying in January 1963 and receiving French certification in March. By the following January deliveries had reached 23, and the three variants had received new names: Super IV Directeur, Commandant du Bord and Président.

In 1965 a version with fixed landing gear was flown, the WA.41, and the name Baladou was revived for it. A newcomer appeared in March 1967, known as the Super 4/21 Prestige, powered by a 235-hp (175-kW) Avco Lycoming O-540 engine, and having a McCauley variable-pitch propeller, and other refinements including autopilot, blind-flying instruments, and electric flaps.

By the beginning of 1970, 25 Prestiges had been completed plus 60 Baladous and 180 Super IVs; production of the Super IV ended in 1971, but deliveries of the Prestige continued at a slow pace, perhaps being affected by the announcement of a new all-metal derivative, the CE-43 Guépard (Cheetah) to be produced by Cerva, a company formed jointly by Wassmer and Siren SA.

The Guépard had the same engine as the Prestige (by then a 250-hp: 186-kW) Avco Lycoming IO-540) and flew in May 1971; by January 1977 deliveries numbered 43 Guépards, and the Prestige was out of production. Wassmer was in financial difficulties and went into liquidation in September 1977. The Guépard then offered an optional sixth seat, and two new variants were proposed: the CE.44 Cougar and CE.45 Léopard. But on Wassmer's liquidation these were not developed, and production of the Guépard was terminated. The specification applies to the WA.41.

Specification
Type: four/five-seat light monoplane
Powerplant: one 180-hp (134-kW) Avco Lycoming O-360-A2A flat-four piston engine
Performance: maximum speed 158 mph (255 km/h) at sea level; cruising speed 149 mph (240 km/h) at 6,000 ft (1830 m); service ceiling 16,400 ft (5000 m); range 1,056 miles (1700 km)
Weights: empty 1,565 lb (710 kg); maximum take-off 2,645 lb (1200 kg)
Dimensions: span 32 ft 9½ in (10.00 m); length 26 ft 6½ in (8.09 m); height 9 ft 5 in (2.87 m); wing area 172.23 sq ft (16.00 m²)

Wassmer WA.51, 52 and 54 Series

History and Notes
Like several other manufacturers, before and since, Wassmer was intrigued with the possibilities offered by an all-plastics aircraft, and in March 1966 flew their prototype WA.50, a four-seat monoplane similar in general layout to the WA.40 series. Powerplant was a 150-hp (112-kW) Avco Lycoming O-320.

From the WA.50 came the first of a series of all-plastics production models, the WA.51 Pacific, flown on 17 May 1969, and bearing more resemblance to the WA.40 series than to the WA.50 prototype. The Pacific had fixed tricycle landing gear and a 150-hp 9112-kW) Avco Lycoming O-320 engine; deliveries began in 1970 and production ended in 1973. A generally similar WA.52 Europa was powered by a 160-hp (119-kW) engine driving a variable-pitch propeller.

A third model, the WA.54 Atlantic, flew in February 1973 and entered production four months later. It was the most powerful of the trio, with a 180-hp (134-kW) Avco Lycoming O-360-A, and while generally similar to the Europa had more baggage space, revised landing gear and air intake, and other improvements.

By January 1977, 190 WA.51, 52 and 54s had been sold, but in September of that year Wassmer went into liquidation. The following January a new company, Issoire-Aviation, was formed at the same address, taking over Wassmer's industrial assets. By that time the only aircraft in production was the WA.80 Piranha, a two-seater developed by Wassmer and flown in 1975. Orders for 20 had been received and 10 had been built

by the time that Issoire took over, and production continues of this aircraft, now redesignated IA.80. Powerplant was a 100-hp (75-kW) Rolls-Royce Continental O-200-A. The specification applies to the WA.54.

Specification
Type: four-seat light monoplane
Powerplant: one 180-hp (134-kW) Lycoming O-360-A flat-four piston engine
Performance: maximum speed 174 mph (280 km/h) at sea level; cruising speed 162 mph (260 km/h) at 5,500 ft (1675 m); service ceiling 14,760 ft (4500 m); range 839 miles (1340 km)
Weights: empty 1,367 lb (620 kg); maximum take-off 2,491 lb (1130 kg)

The Wassmer WA.51 Pacific is an attractive four-seater, developed in association with the Société du Verre Textile. The WA.52 and WA.54 are powered by uprated engines.

Dimensions: span 30 ft 10 in (9.40 m); length 24 ft 7¼ in (7.50 m); height 7 ft 5 in (2.26 m); wing area 133-48 sq ft (12.40 m²)

WSK-Swidnik Mi-2 Hoplite

History and Notes
The Mi-2 'Hoplite' was developed in the early 1960s by the Mil bureau as a straightforward turbine-powered version of the Mi-1, the availability of the shaft-turbine engine having revolutionised the design of the helicopter. The twin turbines develop 40% more power than the Mi-1's piston engine for barely half the dry weight, more than doubling the payload. The fuselage of the Mi-2 is completely different from that of its progenitor, carrying the engines above the cabin. Although some of the points of commonality between the Mi-1 and the Mi-2 were eliminated during development, the overall dimensions of the two types remain closely similar.

The Mi-2 was flown in 1962, but never put into production in the Soviet Union. Instead responsibility for the type was assigned to WSK-Swidnik (now PZL) in Poland as part of a Comecon rationalization programme, becoming the only Soviet-designed helicopter to be built solely outside the Soviet Union. Production in Poland started in 1965, and continues.

PZL has developed a slightly enlarged version of the Mi-2, designated Mi-2M, but this 10-seat aircraft appears to be aimed mainly at the civil market. A reported version with a lighter skid landing gear (the only use of such a feature on a recent Warsaw Pact helicopter) has not been proceeded with, but efforts have been made to sell a US-engined version of the Mi-2 in the United States.

Specification
Type: eight-passenger utility helicopter
Powerplant: two 400-shp (298-kW) Istov GTD-350 turboshafts
Performance: maximum speed at sea level 130 mph (210 km/h); cruising speed 125 mph (205 km/h);

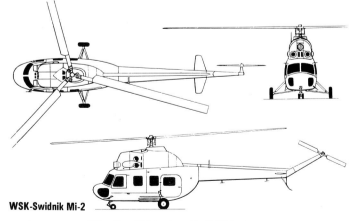

WSK-Swidnik Mi-2

maximum range 370 miles (590 km); range with eight passengers 150 miles (240 km); service ceiling 13,100 ft (4000 m)
Weights: empty 5,255 lb (234 kg); maximum slung load 1,750 lb (800 kg); maximum take-off 8,160 lb (3700 kg)
Dimensions: main rotor diameter 47 ft 7 in (14.5 m); fuselage length 39 ft 2 in (11.94 m); height 12 ft 3½ in (3.75 m); main rotor disc area 1,727 sq ft (160.5 m²)

Yakovlev Yak-18 Series

History and Notes
The Yakovlev Yak-18 'Max' basic trainer has shown extraordinary longevity; itself a development of a pre-war design, the UT-2, it remained under active development into the 1970s and its probable replacement, the Yak-52, bears a close resemblance to its predecessor. The original Yak-18 flew in 1946, with the tailwheel undercarriage of its predecessor, and the same 'helmet-type' cowling over the five-cylinder M-11FR radial engine. The tricycle undercarriage of later versions was introduced on the Yak-18U of 1954, but the main production version was the Yak-18A, introduced in 1957, which added a more aerodynamically efficient NACA-type cowling and the much more powerful AI-14 engine. The aircraft is of metal construction with fabric covering, in typical Yakovlev style.

The first single-seater version of the Yak-18 was an unsuccessful prototype of 1946, but the concept was revived in 1959 with the first Yak-18P aerobatic aircraft. The prototype Yak-18P had the single cockpit in the aft position, while the initial production aircraft had a forward-set cockpit. The pilot was moved aft of the wing again in the Yak-18PM of 1965, which was strengthened to accept aerodynamic loadings of plus 9g to minus 6g, and it was this aircraft which started the run of Soviet success in international aerobatics. The Yak-18PS of 1970 reverted to the tailwheel landing gear undercarriage of the first aircraft, to save weight, and led to the development of the Yak-50.

The latest version of the Yak-18 is the four-seat Yak-18T, first seen in 1967 and recently reported to be entering service with the Soviet Union's state flying clubs. The wing span is increased by the installation of a wider centre-section, and a new cabin-type fuselage is fitted. The inwards-retracting loading gear is basically similar to that of the Yak-18PM. About 6,700 Yak-18 trainers have been built, and the Yak-18T is still in production. The specification applies to the Yak-18A.

Specification
Type: (Yak-18A) two-seat basic trainer; (Yak-18PM) single-seat aerobatic aircraft; (Yak-18T) four-seat liaison and training aircraft
Powerplant: one 260-hp (194-kW) Ivchenko AI-14R nine-cylinder radial piston engine
Performance: maximum speed at sea level 163 mph (263 km/h); ceiling 16,600 ft (5060 m); range 440 miles (710 km)
Weights: empty 2,238 lb (1025 kg); normal take-off 2,900 lb (1316 kg)
Dimensions: span 34 ft 9½ in (10.6 m); length 27 ft 5 in (8.354 m); wing area 182.9 sq ft (17 m²)

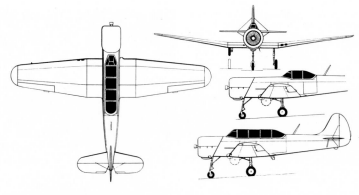

Yakovlev Yak-18A (upper side view: Yak-18P)

The Yakovlev Yak-18PM is an aerobatic variant of the basic Yak-18, differing from its progenitor in engine power, in having only a single seat, and in having retractable tricycle landing gear.

Yakovlev Yak-40

History and Notes
Alexander Yakovlev began his long association with the Soviet Union's aviation industry in 1935, initially as a designer and builder of lightweight sporting and training aircraft. During World War II he was responsible for a variety of bomber, fighter, trainer and transport aircraft. Postwar his range widened as turbojet-powered fighters and bombers were designed and developed by his design bureau, and even included a brief excursion into the design and construction of single-, twin- and tandem-rotor helicopters. In the early 1960s, yet another project was to lead to construction of a turbofan-engined feeder-liner which was the world's first aircraft in this particular category to enter commercial service.

Designed as yet another of the world's potential DC-3 (Lisunov Li-2 in the case of the Soviet Union) replacements, the Yak-40 was destined from the outset for large-scale production if it met successfully the requirements of Aeroflot. This is not surprising when it is appreciated that about half of the airline's vast passenger traffic is carried on the local services for which this feeder-liner was required. And to be able to fulfil this role, it was essential that the Yak-40 be able to operate from and to semi-prepared or grass airfields, which thus demanded good short take-off and landing characteristics. This latter requirement resulted in unswept lightly loaded wings with an aerofoil section that produced maximum lift, plus the added safety factor of a three-rather than two-engine powerplant. The first prototype Yak-40 made its

Yakovlev Yak-40 of Balkan Bulgarian Airlines.

maiden flight on 21 October 1966, with four pre-production aircraft soon following to speed the development programme. Aeroflot was therefore able to operate its first revenue service with the type on 30 September 1968. Between then and 1979-80, when production ended in the Soviet Union, it is believed that about 1,000 examples were built for service with Aeroflot and for export.

In its developed production form the Yak-40 is of low-wing configuration, the wings incorporating plain ailerons and trailing-edge flaps. The fuselage is of conventional circular-section fail-safe structure to allow for cabin pressurisation, and the tail unit is of T-tail layout. The landing gear is of retractable tricycle type, and because grass-field operation is necessary, each unit has long-stroke shock-absorbers and carries a single wheel with a low-pressure tyre. The powerplant comprises three Ivchenko AI-25 turbofans in typical rear-engine layout, the centre (rear) engine being provided with a clamshell type thrust reverser. Accommodation on the flight deck allows for a crew of two

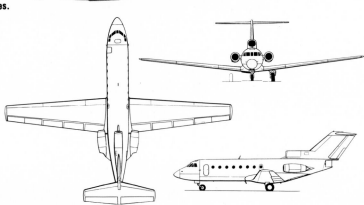

Yakovlev Yak-40

or three, and a variety of cabin arrangements caters for a maximum of 32 passengers, but includes also 27 in standard and 16 in mixed-class configurations. To ensure that the Yak-40 can be operated from airfields with minimum facilities, a hydraulically actuated ventral door with airstair is installed at the rear of the cabin; and an APU mounted within the fin fairing, just aft of the air intake to the rear engine, makes the aircraft completely independent of ground facilities for starting and the maintenance of air-conditioning/heating.

Although production of the Yak-40 has ended in the Soviet Union, a US company named ICX Aviation has negotiated sole rights to build

Yakovlev Yak-40

and market a developed version of this aircraft. To be known as the X-Avia LC-3, it is intended to be powered by three 3,700-lb (1678-kg) thrust Garrett-AiResearch TFE731-3 turbofans, and the first flight of a prototype was planned during 1981. The details below apply to the Yak-40.

Specification
Type: short-range transport
Powerplant: three 3,307-lb (1500-kg) thrust Ivchenko AI-25 turbofans
Performance: maximum cruising speed 342 mph (550 km/h) at 22,965 ft (7000 m); economic cruising speed 292 mph (470 km/h) at 26,245 ft (8000 m); range with maximum fuel, no reserves 1,118 miles (1800 km)
Weights: empty 20,723 lb (9400 kg); maximum take-off 35,274 lb (16000 kg)
Dimensions: span 82 ft 0¼ in (25.00 m); length 66 ft 9½ in (20.36 m); height 21 ft 4 in

(6.50 m); wing area 753.50 sq ft (70.00 m²)
Operators include: Aeroflot, Air Guinée, Avio Ligure, Bakhtar

Afghan Airlines, Balkan Bulgarian Airlines, Ceskoslovenske Aerolinie, Cubana, Hang Khong Vietnam, and TAAG-Angola Airlines

The Russians have built about 1,000 Yakovlev Yak-40 feeder-liners, of which Ceskoslovenske Aerolinie deploys 17, compared with Aeroflot's 750 or more.

Yakovlev Yak-42

History and Notes
Following the extensive experience of operations with the Yak-40, the Yakovlev design bureau retained this same overall configuration when Aeroflot was seeking a larger-capacity medium-range transport to replace the Antonov An-24 on local services, and the Ilyushin Il-18 and Tupolev Tu-134 on shorter-range trunk routes. Three prototype Yak-42s were ordered; the first of these, having a wing swept back 11°, made its maiden flight on 7 March 1975. The second and third prototypes had wing sweep of 23°, and this variation from the first aircraft was intended to allow a comprehensive flight evaluation of the two differing degrees of wing sweep in relation to low-speed handling and the economics of high-speed cruising flight. The result of this investigation has resulted in the selection of the 23° swept wing for production aircraft.

Considerably larger than its predecessor, the Yak-42 is also of low-wing configuration, but for good low-speed handling characteristics each of the swept wings incorporates two-section powered ailerons, single-slotted trailing-edge flaps, and upper-surface spoilers mounted forward of the flaps. The fuselage is generally similar to that of the Yak-40, but the T-tail unit has all swept surfaces. The landing gear is also similar, but in this case has twin wheels on each unit. Accommodation is provided for a crew of two on the flight deck, and 100 to 120 passengers can be seated in the cabin which is not, as in the case of the Yak-40, separated into two sections. The main ventral airstair door is retained at the rear of the cabin, to make it possible for the Yak-42 to operate from and to airfields with very limited ground facilities, and for the same reason this aircraft is also equipped with an APU. However, in view of the greater cabin capacity, a door with integral airstair is also provided at the forward end of the fuselage, with adequate wardrobe space between this door and the cabin. It is intended to produce convertible passenger/cargo versions and these will, of course, include a suitable cargo-loading door.

The powerplant comprises three Lotarev D-36 turbofans, mounted in what is now regarded as a conventional three-engine layout. Of fairly recent development, this engine is

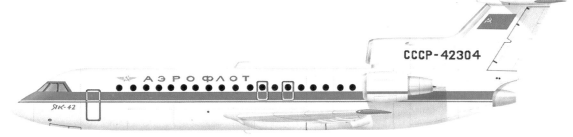

Yakovlev Yak-42 of Aeroflot, USSR.

claimed to have a very low specific fuel consumption: it is, in fact, the first true turbofan, rather than by-pass turbojet, to be developed in the Soviet Union.

Little is yet known of installed avionics, but as the Yak-42 is intended for all-weather day and night service, it can be assumed that these are of advanced specification. An initial batch of 200 aircraft is reported to be under construction, and with Aeroflot needing some 2,000 aircraft in this category a successful entry into service of the Yak-42 should assure a long production run.

Specification
Type: medium-range transport
Powerplant: three 14,330-lb (6500-kg) thrust Lotarev D-36 turbofans
Performance: cruising speed 510 mph (820 km/h) at 25,000 ft (7620 m); range with maximum payload 621 miles (1000 km); range with maximum fuel 1,864 miles (3000 km)
Weights: empty 63,846 lb (28960 kg); maximum take-off

114,640 lb (52000 kg)
Dimensions: span 112 ft 2½ in (34.20 m); length 119 ft 4¼ in (36.38 m); height 32 ft 1¾ in (9.80 m); wing area 1,614.64 sq ft (150.00 m²)
Operator: entering service with Aeroflot

The Yakovlev Yak-42 was conceived as the larger brother of the Yak-40 on Aeroflot's feeder routes, but like the Ilyushin Il-86, it had not entered full-scale service by the beginning of 1981.

Zlin Z 42/43

History and Notes
Following its success with the Z.26 series, in which the two occupants were seated in tandem, Zlin designed and built a side-by-side trainer, the Z.42, the prototype flying on 17 October, 1967. It was put into production in 1971 with the 180-hp (134-kW) Avia M137 engine as the Z.42M. A number, said to be several dozen, were supplied to East Germany. A later version has a revised fin and constant-speed propeller, production of this variant beginning in 1974. Total production to date amounts to around 180 aircraft, and other known military customers are Czechoslovakia and Hungary.

Specification
Type: two-seat training and touring monoplane
Powerplant: one 180-hp (134-kW) Avia M137 AZ piston engine
Performance: maximum speed at sea level 140 mph (226 km/h); cruising speed at 1,975 ft (600 m) 134 mph (215 km/h); rate of climb at sea level 1,025 ft (312 m) per minute; service ceiling 13,950 ft (4250 m); range 329 miles (530 km) miles (530 km)
Weights: empty 1,422 lb (645 kg); normal maximum take-off 2,138 lb (970 kg) or for aerobatics 2,028 lb (920 kg)
Dimensions: span 29 ft 11 in (9.11 m); length 23 ft 2 in (7.07 m); height 8 ft 10 in (2.69 m); wing area 141.5 sq ft (13.15 m²).

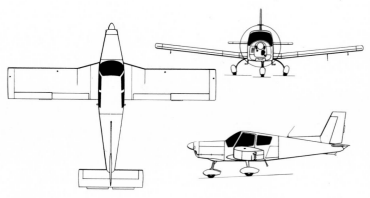

Zlin Z 43

Zlin Z 50 L

History and Notes
Early successes in world and international aerobatic contests augurs well for Zlin's Z 50 L single-seat aircraft, which has been designed to contend in this exacting and highly specialised field of aviation. Design was originated in 1973, but it was not until 18 July 1975 that the prototype flew for the first time.

Of cantilever low-wing monoplane configuration, the Z 50 L has a wing of metal construction and without trailing-edge flaps. Instead, two-section ailerons extend over almost the whole of the trailing-edge, providing a very high roll rate, which is reflected in structural stressing to +9g and -6g. The fuselage is an all-metal structure, and the tail unit is conventional but provided with a braced tailplane. Automatic trim tabs are provided for the inboard ailerons, one elevator, and the fabric-covered rudder; the port outer aileron has a ground-adjustable trim tab, and one elevator has a tab that can be adjusted mechanically in flight. This degree of control sophistication is necessary if the aircraft is to be capable of highly accurate and complex aerobatic manoeuvres. The landing gear is of non-retractable tailwheel type, and the powerplant consists of a flat-six engine driving a three-blade constant-speed and variable-pitch propeller. The standard fuel can be supplemented by wingtip auxiliary tanks for cross-country flights. The pilot is accommodated beneath a full view bubble canopy, which can be jettisoned in emergency, and his seat is designed for use with a back-pack parachute.

Specification
Type: single-seat aerobatic monoplane
Powerplant: one 260-hp (194-kw) Avco Lycoming AEIO-540-D4B5 flat-six piston engine
Performance: maximum level speed 180 mph (290 km/h) at sea level; maximum cruising speed 169 mph (272 km/h) at 3,280 ft (1000 m); economic cruising speed

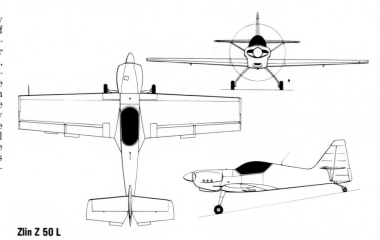

Zlin Z 50 L

154 mph (248 km/h) at 3,280 ft (1000 m); service ceiling 22,965 ft (7000 m); range with maximum standard and auxiliary fuel 397 miles (640 km)
Weights: empty 1,257 lb (570 kg);

maximum take-off 1,587 lb (720 kg)
Dimensions: span 28 ft 1¾ in (8.58 m); length 21 ft 8¾ in (6.62 m); height 6 ft 6¼ in (1.99 m); wing area 134.55 sq ft (12.50 m²)

Zlin Z 726 Universal

History and Notes
Under the original name Zlinská Letecká Akciová Spolecnost this company, more usually called quite simply Zlin, was established in Czechoslovakia in 1935. Over a period of 30 years from 1947, a long series of basic and aerobatic trainers was built, and when production of the last member of the family ended in 1977, over 1,400 had been constructed. Founder member of the series was the Z 26 of 1947, the remainder embracing the Z 126, 226, 326, 526 and 726. Benefitting from this long period of development and improvement, it is not surprising that these aircrft have achieved remarkable success in aerobatic contests, having taken first place in more than a dozen championships at world and international level.

Last of the line was the Z 726 Universal, stressed to +6g and −3g for aerobatic use. The structure was almost entirely of metal, the largest non-metal area being the fabric-covered aft fuselage. Of cantilever low-wing monoplane configuration, the Z 726 had a wing incorporating wide-span trailing-edge flaps. Landing gear was of tailwheel type, but the main units were electrically retractable. Accommodation was for two in tandem, beneath a long transparent canopy which could be jettisoned in emergency, with the seats designed to take seat-type parachutes. Dual controls were standard, with both positions fully instrumented so that the Universal could be flown solo from either seat. Two versions were available, the Z 726 being the basic model for *ab initio*, advanced, and aerobatic training, and usable also as a glider tug; the Z 726 K had a more powerful and supercharged engine, the 210-hp (157-kW) Avia M 337 AK with a variable-pitch propeller. The description that follows applies to the basic Z 726.

Specification
Type: two-seat trainer
Powerplant: one 180-hp (134-kW) Avia M 137 AZ inverted six-cylinder piston engine
Performance: maximum level speed 147 mph (237 km/h) at sea level; cruising speed 134 mph (216 km/h) at sea level; service ceiling 14,765 ft (4500 m); maximum range with standard fuel 273 miles (440 km)
Weights: empty, standard 1,543 lb (700 kg), aerobatic 1,521 lb (690 kg); maximum take-off, standard 2,205 lb (1000 kg), aerobatic 2,072 lb (940 kg)
Dimensions: span 32 ft 4¾ in (9.87 m); length 26 ft 2 in (7.98 m); height 6 ft 9 in (2.06 m); wing area 160.28 sq ft (14.89 m²)

The Zlin Z 726 Universal is identical with the Z 526 Trener apart from metal-covered tail control surfaces, shorter-span wings and a different engine.

INDEX

PICTURE CREDITS

We are grateful to the following organisations for their help in providing photographs for this book.

Pictures have been credited by page number, from left to right and from top to bottom.

9: Pilot Press Ltd/Michael Taylor. **10:** Aviation Letter Photo Service (ALPS)/Société Nationale Industrielle Aérospatiale. **11:** Tyrolean Airways. **12:** Aérospatiale. **13:** Asahi Helicopter. **14:** Aérospatiale. **15:** Asahi Helicopter. **16:** Lignes Aériennes Interieures. **17:** Aérospatiale. **22:** British Airways. **23:** Austin Brown Associates. **25:** Lineas Aereas de España (Iberia)/Iberia/Eastern Air Lines. **27:** Trans-Australia Airlines. **30:** Airbus Industrie. **32:** ALPS. **33:** ALPS/Pilot Press Ltd. **34:** Pilot Press Ltd. **35:** Pilot Press Ltd. **36:** Pilot Press Ltd/Michael J. Hooks. **37:** IPEC Aviation. **38:** Pilot Press Ltd/ALPS. **39:** Pilot Press Ltd/Pilot Press Ltd. **40:** Austin Brown Associates. **41:** Pilgrim Airlines. **42:** Beech Aircraft Corporation/Beech Aircraft Corporation. **43:** Michael J. Hooks/Beech. **44:** Beech/Austin Brown Associates. **45:** Beech/Beech. **47:** Asahi Helicopter. **49:** Bristow Helicopter Group/Bell Helicopter Textron. **50:** Bell Helicopter Textron. **52:** Aerovias Nacionales de Colombia (Avianca). **53:** Olympic Airways/German Cargo Services. **54:** Cathay Pacific Airways. **56:** Air Malta. **57:** Alaska Airlines. **59:** Trans World Airlines. **60:** Transbrasil S/A Linhas Aereas. **62:** Delta Air Lines/Wren Air Alaska. **63:** Iberia. **64:** Royal Brunei Airlines. **65:** Air Europe. **66:** Aloha Airlines. **68:** Swissair. **69:** Wardair Canada. **70:** CP Air/Cargolux Airlines International. **71:** Flying Tiger Line. **74:** Trans World Airlines. **76:** Qantas Airways. **77:** Boeing Commercial Airplane Company. **80:** Boeing Vertol Company. **82:** Austin Brown Associates. **83:** Zambia Airways Corporation. **84:** British Aerospace/British Aerospace. **85:** British Aerospace. **86:** British Aerospace. **88:** British Aerospace. **89:** British Aerospace. **90:** Philippine Airlines. **94:** British Airways. **95:** Britten-Norman (Bembridge) Ltd. **97:** Britten-Norman. **98:** Flying Tiger Line. **99:** Canadair Ltd. **100:** Canadair Ltd. **102:** Construcciones Aeronauticas SA (CASA). **103:** Cessna Aircraft Company/Cessna Aircraft Company. **104:** Michael J. Hooks. **105:** Michael J. Hooks. **106:** Cessna/Cessna. **107:** Pilot Press Ltd/Cessna. **108:** Cessna. **109:** Cessna/Cessna. **110:** Cessna. **111:** Cessna. **112:** ALPS. **113:** Aspen Airways. **114:** Spantax Transportes Aereos. **115:** Austin Brown Associates. **116:** Air Inter. **117:** Federal Express. **118** Avions Marcel Dassault-Breguet Aviation. **119:** Austin Brown Associates. **120:** ALPS/ALPS. **121:** ALPS. **122:** Air Portugal-TAP. **127:** Tyrolean Airways. **131:** Dornier GmbH/Dornier GmbH. **132:** ALPS. **133:** Karair. **134:** ALPS/ALPS. **135:** ALPS. **136:** Union de Transportes Aériens. **137:** Cargolux Airlines International/Air New Zealand. **138:** Delta Air Lines. **139:** Swissair. **140:** Austrian Airlines. **141:** McDonnell Douglas Corporation/Swissair. **142:** McDonnell Douglas Corporation. **144:** McDonnel Douglas Corporation. **146:** Federal Express. **147:** Western Air Lines/Scandinavian Airlines System. **148:** Swissair. **150:** CP Air. **151:** American Airlines. **154:** Empresa Brasileira de Aeronáutica SA (EMBRAER). **155:** EMBRAER/EMBRAER. **156:** ALPS. **157:** Fokker-VFW BV. **158:** Pilgrim Airlines. **160:** Société Luxembourgeoise de Navigation Aerienne SA (Luxair). **161:** Koninklijke Luchtvaart Maatschappij NV (KLM). **162:** Türk Hava Yollari Anonim Sirketi (THY Turkish Airlines). **165:** Government Aircraft Factories (GAF)/Gates Learjet Corporation. **167:** Gates Learjet Corporation/Gates Learjet Corporation. **170:** Austin Brown Associates. **171:** ALPS/ALPS. **172:** Grumman American Aviation Corporation/Grumman American Aviation Corporation/Pilot Press Ltd. **173:** Pilot Press Ltd/ALPS. **174:** ALPS. **175:** British Air Ferries. **176:** Michael J. Hooks. **177:** Pilot Press Ltd. **178:** ALPS. **179:** ALPS. **180:** ALPS. **181:** ALPS/ALPS. **183:** Israel Aircraft Industries Ltd. **184:** Boeing Vertol Company. **185:** Lake Aircraft Division of Consolidated Aeronautics Inc. **186:** ALPS. **187:** Lockheed Aircraft Corporation. **188:** Lockheed Aircraft Corporation. **189:** ALPS. **190:** Cathay Pacific Airways. **191:** Lockheed Aircraft Corporation/Lockheed Aircraft Corporation. **192:** Lockheed Aircraft Corporation. **196:** ALPS/Michael J. Hooks. **197:** Michael J. Hooks/Messerschmitt-Bölkow-Blohm GmbH (MBB). **198:** MBB/MBB. **199:** Klaus Niska/Pilot Press Ltd. **200:** Asahi Helicopter. **201:** Pilot Press Ltd. **202:** Mitsubishi Heavy Industries Ltd. **204:** All Nippon Airways. **205:** Sociedade Construtora Aeronáutica Neiva Ltda/Pilot Press Ltd. **206:** Pilot Press Ltd/Pilot Press Ltd. **207:** ALPS/Pilatus Flugzeugwerke AG. **208:** Pilatus/Pilot Press Ltd. **209:** Lease Air. **210:** Michael J. Hooks/Piper Aircraft Corporation. **211:** Piper/Piper. **212:** Austin Brown Associates. **213:** Piper. **214:** Piper. **215:** Piper/Piper. **216:** Piper/Piper. **218:** Pitts Aerobatics. **219:** Avions Pierre Robin/Avions Pierre Robin/Avions Pierre Robin. **220:** Austin Brown Associates/Austin Brown Associates. **221:** Michael J. Hooks. **222:** Rockwell International Corporation. **224:** Saab-Scania Aktiebolag/Saab-Scania Aktiebolag. **225:** Olympic Airways. **227:** Loganair. **228:** HeavyLift Cargo Airlines. **229:** Court Helicopters. **230:** Sikorsky Aircraft Division of United Technologies Corporation (Sikorsky). **231:** Sikorsky. **232:** Michael J. Hooks/Austin Brown Associates. **233:** Swearingen Aviation Corporation. **234:** Pilot Press Ltd. **235:** ALPS. **236:** Austin Brown Associates. **237:** Michael Taylor. **238:** ALPS. **239:** ALPS. **240:** Pilot Press Ltd. **241:** Transporturile Aeriene Romane (Tarom)/Pilot Press Ltd. **242:** Michael J. Hooks/Air Bridge. **243:** Nusatara. **244:** British Air Ferries/Austin Brown Associates/Pilot Press Ltd. **245:** Michael J. Hooks. **246:** ALPS. **247:** ALPS/ALPS. **248:** Zlin Aircraft Moravan National Corporation.